DICTIONARY OF
LAW

Visit our website for full details of all our books: **www.acblack.com**

DICTIONARY OF
LAW

fifth edition

A & C Black • London

Originally published by Peter Collin Publishing
as *English Law Dictionary*

First published 1986
Second edition published 1992
Third edition published 2000, 2001
Fourth edition published 2004 by
Bloomsbury Publishing Plc.

This fifth edition published 2007 by
A&C Black Publishers Ltd
38 Soho Square, London W1D 3HB

A CIP record for this book is available from the British Library

ISBN: 978 0 7136 8318 9

Consultant Editor
Ned Beale

Text Production and Proofreading
Heather Bateman, Katy McAdam

This book is produced using paper that is made from wood grown in
managed, sustainable forests. It is natural, renewable and recyclable. The
logging and manufacturing processes conform to the environmental
regulations of the country of origin.

Text processed and typeset by A&C Black
Printed in Spain by GraphyCems

Introduction to the 5th Edition

The A&C Black Dictionary of Law is designed for anyone who needs to check the meaning or pronunciation of words used in the legal context, and especially for anyone who is not a legal professional or for whom English is an additional language.

This 5th edition of the dictionary has been comprehensively updated to reflect legal developments since publication of the previous edition.

Many of these developments relate to the reorganisation of the UK civil service, notably the formation of the Ministry of Justice and HM Revenue & Customs. Similarly, the government has established new regulators for many industries, for example the FSA for financial services, Ofcom for the communications industry and the Solicitors Regulation Authority, which has taken over the Law Society's responsibilities for regulating solicitors. National security has also been a key driver of the government's legislative programme, and this new edition includes up-to-date terms relating to anti-terrorism measures.

In the social sphere, issues relating to juvenile crime, human rights and immigration have become of increasing importance and generated novel terms. Other developments include the relaxation of England and Wales' licensing laws in 2003 and the introduction of same-sex civil partnerships 2005. Meanwhile, 2007 sees the ban on smoking in enclosed public places already in effect in Scotland and Wales extended to England, and Home Information Packs and Energy Performance Certificates becoming compulsory for every home sold in the UK.

Finally, in the business context, the dictionary has been updated to take into account recent developments in commercial, corporate and financial law, the Enterprise Act 2002 which overhauled the law of insolvency, the increasing use of arbitration, mediation and other alternatives to court-based litigation, and the growing significance of European and international legal concepts.

Ned Beale
London
June 2007

Ned Beale is an Associate at Olswang and an Honorary Legal Adviser at Kentish Town Citizens Advice Bureau.

Pronunciation

The following symbols have been used to show the pronunciation of the main words in the dictionary.

Stress is indicated by a main stress mark (') and a secondary stress mark (,). Note that these are only guides, as the stress of the word changes according to its position in the sentence.

Vowels		*Consonants*	
æ	back	b	buck
ɑː	harm	d	dead
ɒ	stop	ð	other
aɪ	type	dʒ	jump
aʊ	how	f	fare
aɪə	hire	g	gold
aʊə	hour	h	head
ɔː	course	j	yellow
ɔɪ	annoy	k	cab
e	head	l	leave
eə	fair	m	mix
eɪ	make	n	nil
eʊ	go	ŋ	sing
ɜː	word	p	print
iː	keep	r	rest
i	happy	s	save
ə	about	ʃ	shop
ɪ	fit	t	take
ɪə	near	tʃ	change
u	annual	θ	theft
uː	pool	v	value
ʊ	book	w	work
ʊə	tour	x	loch
ʌ	shut	ʒ	measure
		z	zone

A

A.B.A. *abbreviation US* American Bar Association

abandon /ə'bændən/ *verb* **1.** to stop doing something ○ *The company has decided to abandon the project.* ○ *We have abandoned the idea of taking the family to court.* □ **to abandon an action** to stop pursuing a legal action □ **to abandon a legal right *or* claim** to accept that a right or claim cannot be legally enforced **2.** to leave someone or something without help ○ *He abandoned his family and went abroad.* ○ *The crew had to abandon the sinking ship.*

abandonment /ə'bændənmənt/ *noun* **1.** the act of giving something up voluntarily such as the right to a property **2.** the act of giving up either the whole or part of a claim put forward during civil litigation **3.** the act of a parent or guardian leaving a child on their own in circumstances covered by the Children and Young Persons Act 1933

abate /ə'beɪt/ *verb* **1.** to remove or stop a nuisance ○ *The neighbour was given 3 weeks notice to abate the noise nuisance.* **2.** to reduce a legacy **3.** to be reduced **4.** (*of a legacy*) to be reduced because there is not enough money in the estate to pay it in full

abatement /ə'beɪtmənt/ *noun* **1.** the legal right to remove or stop a nuisance once a reasonable period of notice has been given to the wrongdoer **2.** the reduction of a legacy when the deceased person has not left enough money to pay it in full **3.** the reduction or removal of a debt when a person has failed to leave enough money to cover a legacy in full. ◊ **tax abatement**

Abatement Notice /ə'beɪtmənt ˌnəʊtɪs/ *noun* a legal order to stop doing something which is creating a statutory nuisance, such as smoke or noise pollution, served under the 1990 Environmental Protection Act

ABC /ˌeɪ biː 'siː/ *abbreviation* Acceptable Behaviour Contract

abduct /æb'dʌkt/ *verb* to take someone away against their will, usually by force ○ *The bank manager was abducted at gunpoint.* ○ *The robbers abducted the heiress and held her to ransom.*

abduction /æb'dʌkʃən/ *noun* the notifiable offence of taking someone away against their will, usually by force

COMMENT: The Child Abduction Act 1984 provides for specific offences to cover the abduction of a child either by a person connected with the child or by other persons. Abduction of an adult may result in prosecutions for kidnapping and/or false imprisonment.

abductor /æb'dʌktə/ *noun* a person who takes someone away against their will

abeyance /ə'beɪəns/ *noun* **1.** □ **in abeyance** not being used or enforced at present ○ *This law is in abeyance.* □ **to fall into abeyance** to stop being used or enforced ○ *The practice was common but has fallen into abeyance.* **2.** a condition in which legal ownership of an estate has not been established

ABH *abbreviation* actual bodily harm

abide by /ə'baɪd baɪ/ *verb* to accept a rule or follow a custom ○ *He promised to abide by the decision of the court.* ○ *She did not abide by the terms of the agreement.* □ **to abide by a promise** to carry out a promise that has been made

ab initio /ˌæb ɪ'nɪʃiəʊ/ *phrase* a Latin phrase meaning 'from the beginning': used to indicate that the cancellation of an agreement or right applies retrospectively

abjuration /ˌæbdʒʊə'reɪʃ(ə)n/ *noun* the act of taking back a statement made on oath

abjure /əb'dʒʊə/ *verb* **1.** to make a public promise not to do something **2.** *US* to swear not to bear allegiance to another country

abode /ə'bəʊd/ *noun* the place where someone lives. ◊ **right of abode** □ **of no fixed abode** with no permanent address

abolish /ə'bɒlɪʃ/ *verb* to cancel or remove something such as a law or rule ○ *The Chancellor of the Exchequer refused to ask Parliament to abolish the tax on alcohol.* ○ *The Senate voted to abolish the death penalty.*

abolition /ˌæbə'lɪʃ(ə)n/ *noun* the act of abolishing something ○ *campaigning for the abolition of the death penalty*

abortion /ə'bɔːʃ(ə)n/ *noun* the ending of a pregnancy before its natural term

COMMENT: The legal limit for abortion in the UK is currently 24 weeks. The procedure may also legally be performed up to 28 weeks if there is evidence of severe foetal abnormality or if it is necessary to save the life of the mother, although in practice this is rare. After this time the foetus is considered **viable** and may not be destroyed.

abrogate /'æbrəgeɪt/ *verb* to end something such as a law or treaty

abrogation /ˌæbrə'geɪʃ(ə)n/ *noun* an act of ending something such as a law or treaty

abscond /əb'skɒnd/ *verb* **1.** to leave somewhere suddenly and without permission ○ *He was charged with absconding from lawful custody.* **2.** not to return to the court after being released on bail **3.** to escape from prison

absent /'æbsənt/ *adjective* not present when you are expected to be at something such as a meeting or hearing, or your place of work

absentee /ˌæbsən'tiː/ *noun* a person who is not present at something such as court proceedings even though they are expected to be there

absolute discharge /ˌæbsəluːt 'dɪstʃɑːdʒ/ *noun* the release of a convicted person without any punishment

absolute divorce /ˌæbsəluːt dɪ'vɔːs/ *noun* same as **divorce a vinculo matrimonii**

absolute majority /ˌæbsəluːt mə'dʒɒrɪti/ *noun* a majority over all the others counted together

absolute monopoly /ˌæbsəluːt mə'nɒpəli/ *noun* a situation where only one producer or supplier produces or supplies something

absolute privilege /ˌæbsəluːt 'prɪvɪlɪdʒ/ *noun* a rule which protects a person from being sued for defamation in specific circumstances such as when a judge or lawyer makes a statement during judicial proceedings, or when an MP speaks in the House of Commons

absolute right /ˌæbsəluːt 'raɪt/ *noun* in the European Convention on Human Rights, a right that under no circumstances may legally be interfered with (NOTE: Examples are the freedoms of thought, conscience, and religion and the prohibitions on torture.)

absolute title /ˌæbsəluːt 'taɪt(ə)l/ *noun* land registered with the Land Registry, where the owner has a guaranteed title to the land (NOTE: Absolute title also exists to leasehold land, giving the proprietor a guaranteed valid lease.)

absolutism /'æbsəluːˌtɪz(ə)m/ *noun* the political theory that any legitimate government should have absolute power

absolutist /ˌæbsə'luːtɪst/ *adjective* **1.** believing in absolutism **2.** referring to a political system where the government has absolute power ■ *noun* a person who believes in absolutism

abstain /əb'steɪn/ *verb* to refrain from doing something, especially voting

abstainee /ˌæbsteɪ'niː/ *noun* a person who voluntarily refrains from doing something, especially voting

abstention /əb'stenʃən/ *noun* **1.** the act of refraining from doing something, especially voting ○ *The motion was carried by 200 votes to 150, with 60 abstentions.* **2.** US a situation where a federal court may refuse to hear a case and passes it to a state court which then becomes competent to decide on the federal constitutional issues raised

abstract *noun* /'æbstrækt/ a short summary of a report or document ○ *to make an abstract of the deeds of a property* ■ *verb* /æb'strækt/ to make a summary

abstract of title /æbˌstrækt əv 'taɪt(ə)l/ *noun* a summary of the details of the ownership of a property which has not been registered

abuse *noun* /ə'bjuːs/ **1.** the use of something in a way in which it was not intended to be used **2.** rude or insulting language ○ *The prisoner shouted abuse at the judge.* **3.** very bad treatment of a person, usually physical or sexual ○ *child abuse* ○ *sexual abuse* **4.** a harmful or illegal practice ■ *verb* /ə'bjuːz/ **1.** to use something wrongly □ **to abuse one's authority** to use authority in an illegal or harmful way **2.** to say rude words about someone ○ *He abused the police before being taken to the cells.* **3.** to treat someone very badly, usually physically or sexually ○ *She claimed that he had abused her during their marriage.*

abuse of power /əˌbjuːs əv ˈpaʊə/ *noun* the use of legal powers in an illegal or harmful way

abuse of process /əˌbjuːz əv prəʊˈsesɪz/ *noun* the use of a legal process without proper justification or for malicious reasons

abut /əˈbʌt/, **abut on** /əˈbʌt ɒn/ *verb* (*of a piece of land*) to touch another property (NOTE: **abutting – abutted**)

abuttal /əˈbʌt(ə)l/ *noun* the boundaries of a piece of land in relation to land that is adjoining

ACAS /ˈeɪkæs/ *abbreviation* Advisory Conciliation and Arbitration Service

ACC *abbreviation* Assistant Chief Constable

accelerated possession procedure /əkˌseləreɪtɪd pəˈzeʃ(ə)n prəˌsiːdʒə/ *noun* a legal procedure that allows a landlord's claim to repossess a property at the end of a tenancy to be decided by a court purely on the basis of written representations

acceptable /əkˈseptəb(ə)l/ *adjective* good enough to be accepted, although not particularly good ○ *The offer is not acceptable to both parties.*

Acceptable Behaviour Contract /əkˌseptəb(ə)l bɪˈheɪvjə ˌkɒntrækt/ *noun* a formal written agreement, made between an individual and either a parent or guardian or another party, stating that the individual will not act in an antisocial manner in future. Abbreviation **ABC**. ◊ **Antisocial Behaviour Order** (NOTE: Acceptable Behaviour Contracts normally last for a period of 6 months.)

acceptance /əkˈseptəns/ *noun* **1.** one of the main conditions of a contract, where one party agrees to what is proposed by the other party □ **acceptance of an offer** an agreement to accept an offer and therefore to enter into a contract **2.** the act of signing a bill of exchange to show that you agree to pay it

acceptor /əkˈseptə/, **accepter** *noun* somebody who accepts an offer

access /ˈækses/ *noun* **1.** the right of the owner of a piece of land to be able to get to it easily by means of a road ○ *He complained that he was being denied access by his neighbour.* **2.** □ **to have access to something** to be able to obtain or reach something □ **to gain access to something** to reach or to get hold of something ○ *Access to the courts should be open to all citizens.* ○ *The burglar gained access through the*

window. **3.** the right of a child to see a parent regularly, or of a parent or grandparent to see a child regularly, where the child is in the care of someone else **4.** □ **right of access to a solicitor** in the EU, the right of anyone who is in police custody to see a solicitor in private to ask advice

accession /əkˈseʃ(ə)n/ *noun* **1.** the act of becoming a member of something by signing a formal agreement **2.** the act of taking up an official position □ **accession to the throne** becoming King or Queen

access order /ˌækses ˈɔːdə/ *noun* formerly, a court order allowing a parent to see a child where the child is in the care of someone else, such as the other parent in the case of a divorced couple (NOTE: Access orders have been replaced by **contact orders**.)

accessory /əkˈsesəri/ *noun* a person who helps or advises someone who commits a crime □ **accessory after the fact** a person who helps a criminal after a crime had been committed □ **accessory before the fact** a person who helps a criminal before a crime is committed

accident /ˈæksɪd(ə)nt/ *noun* something unpleasant which happens suddenly, often as the result of a mistake, sometimes resulting in damage to property, injury or death

accidental /ˌæksɪˈdent(ə)l/ *adjective* happening as an accident, or without being planned

accidental death /ˌæksɪdent(ə)l ˈdeθ/ *noun* death caused by an accident, for which there is no legal culpability. Compare **non-accidental death**

accident insurance /ˌæksɪd(ə)nt ɪn ˈʃʊərəns/ *noun* insurance which pays money if an accident takes place

accident policy /ˌæksɪd(ə)nt ˈpɒlɪsi/ *noun* an insurance policy which pays money if an accident takes place

accommodation /əˌkɒməˈdeɪʃ(ə)n/ *noun* a place to live or somewhere to stay for a short time (NOTE: In British English, **accommodation** has no plural.)

accommodation address /əˌkɒmə ˈdeɪʃ(ə)n əˌdres/ *noun* an address used for receiving messages that is not the address of the company's offices

accomplice /əˈkʌmplɪs/ *noun* somebody who helps another to commit a crime or who commits a crime with another person

accordance /əˈkɔːd(ə)ns/ *noun* □ **in accordance with** in a way that agrees with something that has been suggested or decided ○ *In accordance with your instructions we have deposited the money in your current account.* ○ *I am submitting the claim for damages in accordance with the advice of our legal advisers.*

accord and satisfaction /əˌkɔːd ən sætɪsˈfækʃən/ *noun* **1.** the payment by a debtor of a debt or part of a debt **2.** the performing by a debtor of some act or service which is accepted by the creditor in full settlement, so that the debtor is no longer liable under the contract

accordingly /əˈkɔːdɪŋli/ *adverb* in agreement with what has been decided ○ *We have received your letter and have altered the contract accordingly.*

according to /əˈkɔːdɪŋ tuː/ *preposition* **1.** as someone says or writes ○ *According to the witness, the accused carried the body on the back seat of his car.* ○ *The payments were made according to the maintenance order.* **2.** in agreement with a rule or system ○ *The papers are filed according to their date order.* **3.** in relation to

account /əˈkaʊnt/ *noun* **1.** a record of money paid or owed ○ *please send me your account* or *a detailed* or *an itemised account* □ **action for an account** a court action to establish how much money is owed by one party to another **2.** an arrangement which a customer has with a shop or supplier to buy goods and pay for them at a later date, usually the end of the month **3.** a customer who does a large amount of business with a firm and has a credit account with that firm **4.** □ **to take account of something, to take something into account** to allow for or bear in mind a particular factor or circumstance when making a decision ○ *The judge took the defendant's young age into account when passing sentence.* ■ *plural noun* **accounts** detailed records of a company's financial affairs ■ *verb* □ **to account for** to explain and record something ○ *to account for a loss* or *a discrepancy*

accountability /əˌkaʊntəˈbɪlɪti/ *noun* the fact of being responsible for something

accountable /əˈkaʊntəb(ə)l/ *adjective* being responsible for what takes place and needing to be able to explain why it has happened ○ *If money is lost, the person at the cash desk is held accountable.* ○ *The group leader will be held accountable for the actions of the group.*

account of profit /əˌkaʊnt əv ˈprɒfɪt/ *noun* in copyright law, an assessment showing how much profit has been made on the

sales of goods which infringe a copyright or patent, because the plaintiff claims the profit made by the defendant

accounts payable /əˌkaʊnts ˈpeɪəb(ə)l/ *noun* money owed to creditors

accounts receivable /əˌkaʊnts rɪˈsiːvəb(ə)l/ *noun* money owed by debtors

accredited /əˈkredɪtɪd/ *adjective* (*of an agent*) appointed by a company to act on its behalf (NOTE: A person is accredited **to** an organisation.)

accusation /ˌækjuːˈzeɪʃ(ə)n/ *noun* the act of saying that someone has committed a crime

accusatorial procedure /əˌkjuːzətɔːriəl prəˈsiːdʒə/ *noun* a procedure in countries using common law procedures, where the parties to a case have to find the evidence themselves. Compare **inquisitorial procedure.** ◊ **burden of proof**

accuse /əˈkjuːz/ *verb* **1.** to say that someone has committed a crime ○ *She was accused of stealing £25 from her boss.* ○ *He was accused of murder.* ○ *Of what has she been accused?* or *What has she been accused of?* (NOTE: You accuse someone **of** a crime.) **2.** to charge someone with a crime

accused /əˈkjuːzd/ *noun* □ **the accused** the person or persons charged with a crime ○ *All the accused pleaded not guilty.* ○ *The police brought the accused, a young man, into the court.*

acknowledge /əkˈnɒlɪdʒ/ *verb* **1.** to accept that something is true **2.** to admit that a debt is owing **3.** to confirm that a letter has been received □ **to acknowledge service** to confirm that a legal document such as a claim form has been received

acknowledged and agreed /əkˌnɒlɪdʒd ən əˈɡriːd/ *phrase* words written on an agreement to show that it has been read and approved

acknowledgement of service /əkˌnɒlɪdʒmənt əv ˈsɜːvɪs/ *noun* a document whereby a defendant confirms that a claim form or other legal document has been received

acquiescence /ˌækwiˈes(ə)ns/ *noun* consent which is either given directly or is implied (NOTE: There is a distinction between mere knowledge of a situation and positive consent to it. The latter is required in order to constitute acquiescence.)

acquired gender /əˌkwaɪəd ˈdʒendə/ *noun* the gender as which a transsexual person wishes to be identified and accepted

COMMENT: Persons undergoing gender reassignment have the right to apply for legal recognition of their acquired gender under the Gender Recognition Act of 2004.

acquis communautaire /æ,ki: kə,mju:nəʊ'teə/ *noun* the body of EU legislation which any country wishing to become an EU member state must adopt

acquisition /,ækwɪ'zɪʃ(ə)n/ *noun* the act of obtaining ownership of something ○ *The acquisition of his company was completed last summer.*

acquisitive crime /ə,kwɪzɪtɪv 'kraɪm/ *noun* crime committed in order to gain money or possessions, e.g. shoplifting, fraud, theft or drug trafficking

acquit /ə'kwɪt/ *verb* to set a person free because he or she has been found not guilty ○ *He was acquitted of the crime.* ○ *The court acquitted two of the accused.* (NOTE: **acquitting – acquitted**. Note also that you acquit someone **of** a crime.)

acquittal /ə'kwɪt(ə)l/ *noun* the act of acquitting someone of a crime ○ *After his acquittal he left the court smiling.*

COMMENT: There is no appeal against an acquittal, and a person who has been acquitted of a crime cannot usually be charged with the same crime again (the state of **double jeopardy**).

act /ækt/ *noun* **1.** something which somebody does **2. Act** ♦ **Act of Parliament**

acte clair /,ækt 'kleə/ *noun* (*in the EU*) a French legal term meaning that a legal question is clear and there can be no doubt about it

action /'ækʃən/ *noun* **1.** a proceeding heard in the civil court allowing an individual to pursue a legal right □ **action in personam** a court case in which one party claims that the other should do some act or should pay damages □ **action in rem** a court case in which one party claims property or goods in the possession of the other □ **action in tort** a court case brought by a claimant who alleges he or she has suffered damage or harm caused by the defendant □ **to take legal action** to begin a legal case, e.g. to instruct a solicitor or to sue someone **2.** something that is done, or the doing of something ○ *action to prevent the information becoming public* □ **to take action** to do something ○ *They should have taken immediate action to prevent a similar accident happening.*

actionable /'ækʃənəb(ə)l/ *adjective* referring to writing, speech or an act which

could provide the grounds for bringing a legal case against someone

actionable per se /,ækʃənəb(ə)l pɜː 'saɪ/ *adjective* being in itself sufficient grounds for bringing an action □ **torts which are actionable per se** torts which are in themselves sufficient grounds for bringing an action without the need to prove that damage has been suffered

active partner /,æktɪv 'pɑːtnə/ *noun* a partner who works in a partnership

activist /'æktɪvɪst/ *noun* a person who works actively for a political party, usually a person who is in disagreement with the main policies of the party or whose views are more extreme than those of the mainstream of the party ○ *The meeting was disrupted by an argument between the chairman and left-wing activists.* ○ *Party activists have urged the central committee to adopt a more radical approach to the problems of unemployment.*

act of God /,ækt əv 'gɒd/ *noun* a natural disaster which you do not expect to happen, and which cannot be avoided, e.g. a storm or a flood. ◊ **force majeure** (NOTE: Acts of God are usually not covered by an insurance policy.)

Act of Parliament /,ækt əv 'pɑːləmənt/ *noun* a statute which has been approved by a law-making body (NOTE: Before an Act becomes law, it is presented to Parliament in the form of a Bill. See Supplement for a description of the legislative process.)

act preparatory to terrorism /,ækt prɪ ,pærət(ə)ri tə 'terərɪz(ə)m/ *noun* the offence of making preparations to commit a terrorist act

actual bodily harm /,æktʃuəl 'bɒdɪli hɑːm/ *noun* the offence of causing injury to an individual by attacking them. Abbreviation **ABH** (NOTE: The injury does not have to be serious or permanent but it must be more than just a scratch.)

actual loss /,æktʃuəl 'lɒs/ *noun* real loss or damage which can be shown to have been suffered

actual notice /,æktʃuəl 'nəʊtɪs/ *noun* real knowledge which someone has of something

actual possession /,æktʃuəl pə 'zeʃ(ə)n/ *noun* the fact of occupying and controlling land and buildings

actual total loss /,æktʃuəl 'təʊt(ə)l lɒs/ *noun* a loss where the item insured has been destroyed or damaged beyond repair and can no longer be used for its intended purpose

actual value /ˌæktʃuəl ˈvæljuː/ *noun* the real value of something if sold on the open market

actuarial /ˌæktʃuˈeəriəl/ *adjective* calculated by an actuary ○ *The premiums are worked out according to actuarial calculations.*

actuary /ˈæktʃuəri/ *noun* a person employed by an insurance company to calculate premiums

actus reus /ˌæktəs ˈreɪəs/ *phrase* a Latin phrase meaning 'guilty act': an act which is forbidden by criminal law, one of the two elements of a crime. Compare **mens rea**. ◊ **crime**

addendum /əˈdendəm/ *noun* something that is or has been added, e.g. to a contract

address /əˈdres/ *noun* **1.** the details of number, street and town where an office is or where a person lives □ **address for service** an address where court documents such as pleadings can be sent to a party in a case **2.** a formal speech ○ *In his address to the meeting, the mayor spoke of the problems facing the town.* ■ *verb* **1.** to write the details of an address on an envelope ○ *an incorrectly addressed package* **2.** to speak to someone ○ *The defendant asked permission to address the court.* ○ *The chairman addressed the meeting.* **3.** to speak about a particular issue ○ *He then addressed the question of the late arrival of notification.* □ **to address oneself to a problem** to deal with a particular problem ○ *The government will have to address itself to problems of international trade.*

adduce /əˈdjuːs/ *verb* to offer something as a reason or proof □ **to adduce evidence** to bring evidence before a court

adeem /əˈdiːm/ *verb* to remove a legacy from a will because the item mentioned no longer exists, e.g. in the case when the person who made the will sold the item before they died

ademption /əˈdempʃ(ə)n/ *noun* the act of removing a legacy from a will, because the item concerned no longer exists

ad hoc /ˌæd ˈhɒk/ *phrase* a Latin phrase meaning 'for this particular purpose' □ **an ad hoc committee** a committee set up to study a particular problem. ◊ **standing**

ad idem /ˌæd ˈaɪdem/ *phrase* a Latin phrase meaning 'in agreement' ○ *The two parties are ad idem on this point.*

adjective law /ˈædʒɪktɪv lɔː/ *noun* an area of law which deals with practices and procedures in the courts

adjoin /əˈdʒɔɪn/ *verb* (*of a property*) to touch another property ○ *The property that adjoins ours is structurally unsound.*

adjoining /əˈdʒɔɪnɪŋ/ *adjective* next to and touching something else ○ *The developers acquired the old post office and two adjoining properties.* ○ *The fire spread to the adjoining property.*

adjourn /əˈdʒɜːn/ *verb* **1.** to stop a meeting for a period ○ *to adjourn a meeting* ○ *The meeting adjourned at midday.* □ **to adjourn sine die** to adjourn without saying when the next meeting will be ○ *The hearing was adjourned sine die.* **2.** to put off a legal hearing to a later date ○ *The chairman adjourned the tribunal until three o'clock.* ○ *The appeal was adjourned for affidavits to be obtained.*

adjournment /əˈdʒɜːnmənt/ *noun* **1.** an act of adjourning ○ *The adjournment lasted two hours.* ○ *The defendant has applied for an adjournment.* **2.** the period during which a meeting has been adjourned

adjournment sine die /əˌdʒɜːnmənt ˌsiːni ˈdiːeɪ/ **1.** the adjournment of a meeting without fixing a date for the next meeting **2.** the adjournment of a legal hearing without fixing a date for the next meeting

COMMENT: Adjournment sine die in a non-legal context usually carries the implication of permanence, e.g. of the board of directors of a company that is being liquidated. When referring to a legal hearing, the implication is the opposite – a date is expected to be set.

adjudicate /əˈdʒuːdɪkeɪt/ *verb* to give a judgment between two parties in law ○ *to adjudicate a claim* ○ *to adjudicate in a dispute* ○ *Magistrates may be paid expenses when adjudicating.* □ **to be adjudicated bankrupt** to be declared legally bankrupt

adjudication /əˌdʒuːdɪˈkeɪʃ(ə)n/ *noun* the act of giving a judgment or of deciding a legal problem

adjudication tribunal /əˌdʒuːdɪˈkeɪʃ(ə)n traɪˌbjuːn(ə)l/ *noun* a group which adjudicates in industrial disputes

adjudicator /əˈdʒuːdɪkeɪtə/ *noun* somebody who gives a decision on a problem ○ *an adjudicator in an industrial dispute*

adjust /əˈdʒʌst/ *verb* to change something to fit new conditions, especially to calculate and settle an insurance claim

adjuster /ə'dʒʌstə/, **adjustor** /ə'dʒʌstə/ *noun* somebody who calculates losses for an insurance company

adjustment /ə'dʒʌstmənt/ *noun* **1.** an act of adjusting **2.** a slight change

adjustor /ə'dʒʌstə/ *noun* same as **adjuster**

ad litem /ˌæd 'liːtəm/ *phrase* a Latin phrase meaning 'referring to the case at law': used to indicate that a person is acting as the representative of another for the purposes of a trial

administer /əd'mɪnɪstə/ *verb* **1.** to be responsible for providing, organising or managing something □ **to administer justice** to provide justice □ **to administer an oath** to make someone swear an oath **2.** to give someone a medicine, drug or medical treatment ○ *She was accused of administering a poison to the old lady.*

administration /ədˌmɪnɪ'streɪʃ(ə)n/ *noun* **1.** the organisation, control or management of something such as of the affairs of someone who has died, e.g. payment of liabilities, collection of assets or distributing property to the rightful people shown in the will □ **the administration of justice** the provision of justice through the legal system **2.** the appointment of an insolvency practitioner to a company which is in financial trouble, in order to rescue the company as a going concern, or if that is not possible, to obtain a better return for the creditors than if the company was wound up ○ *The company has gone into administration.*

administration bond /ədˌmɪnɪ'streɪʃ(ə)n bɒnd/ *noun* an oath sworn by an administrator that he or she will pay the state twice the value of the estate being administered, if it is not administered in accordance with the law

administration order /ədˌmɪnɪ'streɪʃ(ə)n ˌɔːdə/ *noun* **1.** an order by a court, appointing someone to administer the estate of someone who is not able to meet the obligations of a court order **2.** a court order putting a company into administration by placing it under the control of an administrator

administration receiver /ədˌmɪnɪ'streɪʃ(ə)n rɪˌsiːvə/ *noun* an insolvency practitioner appointed to oversee an administrative receivership

administrative /əd'mɪnɪstrətɪv/ *adjective* referring to administration

administrative law /əd'mɪnɪstrətɪv lɔː/ *noun* law relating to how government

organisations affect the lives and property of individuals

administrative receiver /əd ˌmɪnɪstrətɪv rɪ'siːvə/ *noun* a person appointed by a court to administer the affairs of a company

administrative receivership /əd ˌmɪnɪstrətɪv rɪ'siːvəʃɪp/ *noun* the appointment of an insolvency practitioner to a company in financial trouble by the company's secured creditor, in order to get back the money owed to that secured creditor

administrative tribunal /əd ˌmɪnɪstrətɪv traɪ'bjuːn(ə)l/ *noun* a tribunal which adjudicates in cases where government regulations affect and harm the lives and property of individuals

administrator /əd'mɪnɪstreɪtə/ *noun* **1.** a person appointed by a court to represent a person who has died without making a will or without naming executors, and who is recognised in law as able to manage the estate **2.** an insolvency practitioner appointed to oversee the administration of a company **3.** somebody who arranges the work of other employees in a business so that the business functions well

Admiralty /'ædm(ə)rəlti/ *noun* the British government office which is in charge of the Navy

Admiralty Court /'ædm(ə)rəlti kɔːt/ *noun* a court, part of the Queen's Bench Division, which decides in disputes involving ships

Admiralty law /'ædm(ə)rəlti lɔːw/ *noun* law relating to ships and sailors, and actions at sea

admissibility /ədˌmɪsə'bɪlɪti/ *noun* the fact of being admissible ○ *The court will decide on the admissibility of the evidence.*

admissible /əd'mɪsəb(ə)l/ *adjective* referring to evidence which a court will allow to be used ○ *The documents were not considered relevant to the case and were therefore not admissible.*

admission /əd'mɪʃ(ə)n/ *noun* **1.** permission for someone to go in ○ *free admission on Sundays* ○ *There is a £1 admission charge.* ○ *Admission is free on presentation of this card.* **2.** making a statement that you agree that some facts are correct, saying that something really happened **3.** (*in civil cases*) a statement by a defendant that a claim or part of a claim by the claimant is true ○ *When a party has made an admission* *in writing, the other party can apply for judgment on that admission.*

admit /əd'mɪt/ *verb* **1.** to allow someone to go in ○ *Children are not admitted to the bank.* ○ *Old age pensioners are admitted at half price.* **2.** to allow someone to practise as a solicitor ○ *She was admitted in 1989.* **3.** to allow evidence to be used in court ○ *The court agreed to admit the photographs as evidence.* **4.** to agree that an allegation is correct ○ *She admitted having stolen the car.* ○ *He admitted to being in the house when the murder took place.* (NOTE: **admitted – admitting**. Note also that you admit **to** something, or admit **having done** something.) **5.** to say that something is true or really happened ○ *He admitted his mistake or his liability.*

adopt /ə'dɒpt/ *verb* **1.** to become the legal parent of a child who was born to other parents **2.** to accept something so that it becomes law ○ *to adopt a resolution* ○ *The proposals were adopted unanimously.*

adoption /ə'dɒpʃən/ *noun* **1.** the act of becoming the legal parent of a child which is not your own **2.** the act of agreeing to something so that it becomes legal ○ *He moved the adoption of the resolution.*

adoption order /ə,dɒpʃən 'ɔːdə/ *noun* an order by a court which legally transfers the rights of the natural parents to the adoptive parents

adoption proceedings /ə,dɒpʃən prə'siːdɪŋz/ *plural noun* court action taken to legally adopt someone

adoptive /ə'dɒptɪv/ *adjective* resulting from the process of adoption, or from choice ○ *his adoptive country*

adoptive child /ə'dɒptɪv tʃaɪld/ *noun* a child who has been adopted

adoptive parent /ə,dɒptɪv 'peərənt/ *noun* a person who has adopted a child. Compare **biological parent** (NOTE: If a child's parents divorce, or if one parent dies, the child may be adopted by a step-father or step-mother.)

ADR *abbreviation* alternative dispute resolution

adult /'ædʌlt/ *noun* a person who is eighteen years old or older

adulteration /ə,dʌltə'reɪʃ(ə)n/ *noun* the contamination of food for sale, which makes it dangerous to eat or drink

adulterous /ə'dʌlt(ə)rəs/ *adjective* referring to adultery ○ *He had an adulterous relationship with Miss X.*

adultery /ə'dʌlt(ə)ri/ *noun* sexual intercourse by consent between a married person and someone of the opposite sex who is not that person's spouse ○ *His wife accused him of committing adultery with Miss X.*

COMMENT: Adultery is sufficient grounds for divorce in most fault-based legal systems, and is also punishable by law in countries including Korea and Taiwan.

ad valorem /,æd və'lɔːrəm/ *phrase* a Latin phrase meaning 'according to value' ○ *When importing goods into the US, duty often has to be paid ad valorem.*

ad valorem tax /,æd və'lɔːrəm ,djuːti/ *noun* a tax calculated according to the value of the goods taxed

advance /əd'vɑːns/ *adjective* early, beforehand ○ *advance booking* ○ *advance payment* □ **advance notice** early warning that something is going to happen ○ *You must give seven days' advance warning of withdrawals from the account.* ■ *noun* **1.** money paid as a loan or as a part of a payment which is to be completed later ○ *to receive an advance on your wages* **2.** □ **in advance** before something happens ○ *to pay in advance* ○ *freight payable in advance*

advancement /əd'vɑːnsmənt/ *noun* money or goods given by a parent to a child which the child would inherit in any case if the parent died

advantage /əd'vɑːntɪdʒ/ *noun* something useful which may help you to be successful □ **to learn something to your advantage** to hear news which is helpful to you, especially to hear that you have been left a legacy □ **obtaining a pecuniary advantage by deception** the offence of deceiving someone so as to derive a financial benefit

adversarial /,ædvɜː'seəriəl/ *adjective* based on people opposing each other

adversarial procedure /,ædvɜː,seəriəl 'prɒlɪtɪks/ *noun* same as **accusatorial procedure**

adversary /'ædvəs(ə)ri/ *noun* an opponent in a court case

adverse /'ædvɜːs/ *adjective* **1.** disadvantageous ○ *adverse conditions* **2.** opposing, which goes against one party

adverse outcome /,ædvɜːs 'aʊtkʌm/ *noun* a result which was unexpected and unwanted

adverse party /,ædvɜːs 'pɑːti/ *noun* the opponent in a court case

adverse possession /,ædvɜːs pə'zeʃ(ə)n/ *noun* an occupation of property by squatters or others that is contrary to the rights of the real owner

adverse witness /ˌædvɜːs ˈwɪtnəs/ *noun* a witness called by one party in a court case whose evidence goes unexpectedly against that party (NOTE: Such a witness can then be cross-examined as if the evidence were being given for the other party in the case.)

advert /ˈædvɜːt/ *verb* to refer to ○ *This case was not adverted to in Smith v. Jones Machines Ltd.*

Advertising Standards Authority /ˌædvətaɪzɪŋ ˈstændədz ɔːˌθɒrəti/ *noun* the body which regulates marketing and advertising in non-broadcast media (NOTE: Their job is to make sure that advertising is 'legal, decent, honest and truthful'.)

advice /ədˈvaɪs/ *noun* an opinion as to what action should be taken □ **as per advice** according to what is written on an advice note □ **to take legal advice** to ask a lawyer to advise about a problem in law

advice note /ədˈvaɪs nəʊt/ *noun* a written notice to a customer giving details of goods ordered and shipped but not yet delivered

advice of counsel /ədˌvaɪs əv ˈkaʊns(ə)l/ *noun* the opinion of a barrister or solicitor about a legal issue or case ○ *She dropped her claim for damages on advice of counsel.*

advise /ədˈvaɪz/ *verb* **1.** to give a professional legal opinion on something such as the strengths and weaknesses of a case **2.** to suggest to someone what should be done ○ *We are advised to take the shipping company to court.* ○ *The solicitor advised us to send the documents to the police.* □ **to advise against something** to suggest that something should not be done ○ *The bank manager advised against closing the account.* ○ *Our lawyers have advised against suing the landlord.*

advisement /ədˈvaɪzmənt/ *noun* □ **to take something under advisement** to consider something in order to make a judgment

adviser /ədˈvaɪzə/, **advisor** *noun* somebody who suggests what should be done ○ *He is consulting the company's legal adviser.*

advisory /ədˈvaɪz(ə)ri/ *adjective* as an adviser ○ *She is acting in an advisory capacity.*

advisory board /ədˈvaɪz(ə)ri ˌbɔːd/ *noun* a group of advisers

Advisory Conciliation and Arbitration Service /ədˌvaɪz(ə)ri kənˌsɪliˌeɪʃ(ə)n ən ˌɑːbɪˌtreɪʃ(ə)n ˈsɜːvɪs/ *noun* a government body which assists in furthering industrial relations and settling industrial and employment disputes. Abbreviation **ACAS**

advocacy /ˈædvəkəsi/ *noun* **1.** the skill of pleading a case orally before a court **2.** support for a cause

advocate *noun* /əˈbjuːs/ **1.** a person, usually a barrister or solicitor, with right of audience (i.e. the right to speak in open court) as the representative of a party in a case ○ *Fast track trial costs include the cost of a party's advocate in preparing the case and appearing in court.* (NOTE: Solicitors who take additional exams may qualify as solicitor-advocates and have the same rights of audience as barristers.) **2.** *US* a legal practitioner ■ *verb* /ˈædvəkeɪt/ to recommend a course of action ○ *Her solicitor advocated that she enter a guilty plea.*

Advocate General /ˌædvəkət ˈdʒen(ə)rəl/ *noun* **1.** one of the two Law Officers for Scotland **2.** one of eight independent members forming part of the European Court of Justice together with 15 judges, who summarises and presents a case to the judges to assist them in coming to a decision (NOTE: The plural is **Advocates General**.)

COMMENT: The position of the Advocates General is equal to that of the fifteen judges in the European Court of Justice; their role is to give careful advice on legal matters.

Advocate General for Scotland /ˌædvəkət ˌdʒen(ə)rəl fə ˈskɒtlənd/ *noun* the principal legal adviser on Scots law to the Scottish Executive and the UK government

affair /əˈfeə/ *noun* **1.** something which is relevant to one person or group of people only ○ *Are you involved in the copyright affair?* ○ *It's an affair for the police.* **2.** a sexual relationship where one party or both parties are married to someone else □ **to have an affair with someone** to commit adultery ■ *plural noun* **affairs** situations or activities relating to public or private life ○ *His affairs were so difficult to understand that the lawyers had to ask accountants for advice.*

affidavit /ˌæfɪˈdeɪvɪt/ *noun* a written statement which is signed and sworn before a solicitor, judge, JP, commissioner for oaths or other official and which can then be used as evidence in court hearings

affiliation order /əˌfɪliˈeɪʃ(ə)n ˌɔːdə/ *noun* formerly, a court order which made the father of an illegitimate child contribute towards the cost of the child's upbringing (NOTE: It is now replaced by a **maintenance order.**)

affirm /əˈfɜːm/ *verb* **1.** to state that you will tell the truth, though without swearing an oath **2.** to confirm that something is correct

affirmation /ˌæfəˈmeɪʃ(ə)n/ *noun* a statement in court that you will tell the truth, though without swearing an oath ∎ the act of accepting goods even though you are aware that they are faulty (NOTE: Failure to reject goods that you know are defective, or to complain about this in good time, means that you lose the right to claim compensation for the fault.) ∎ *noun* a written statement which is affirmed as true by the person making it

affirmative action /əˌfɜːmətɪv ˈækʃən/ *noun* US a policy of positive discrimination to help groups in society who have a disadvantage (NOTE: The British equivalent is **equal opportunity.**)

affirmative easement /əˌfɜːmətɪv ˈiːzmənt/ *noun* US an easement where the servient owner allows the dominant owner to do something

affix /əˈfɪks/ *verb* to attach something such as a signature to a document

affray /əˈfreɪ/ *noun* the offence of intentionally acting in a threatening way towards someone in public

COMMENT: A person is guilty of affray if he or she uses or threatens violence towards another, in a way that might make a reasonable person who happened to be present fear for his or her safety.

AFO *abbreviation* assault on a federal officer

aforethought /əˈfɔːθɔːt/ *adjective* □ **with malice aforethought** with the intention of committing a crime, especially murder

a fortiori /ˌeɪ ˌfɔːtiˈɔːraɪ/ *phrase* a Latin phrase meaning 'for a stronger reason': used to express the sentiment that if one fact is true, another related fact must also be true ○ *If the witness was present at the scene of the crime, then a fortiori he must have heard the shot.*

after the event /ˌɑːftə ðə ɪˈvent/ *adjective* □ **after the event insurance policy** a policy to cover the recovery of costs in case of failure in a case where a conditional fee arrangement is applied

age /eɪdʒ/ *noun* the number of years someone has lived. ◊ **age of consent**, **age of criminal responsibility**

age discrimination /ˈeɪdʒ dɪskrɪmɪˌneɪʃ(ə)n/ *noun* the unfair treatment of people because of their age

COMMENT: It is illegal in the UK to discriminate on grounds of age when hiring for a job.

age limit /ˈeɪdʒ ˌlɪmɪt/ *noun* the age beyond which you are no longer permitted to do something

agency /ˈeɪdʒənsi/ *noun* **1.** an arrangement where one person or company acts on behalf of another person in contractual matters ○ *They signed an agency agreement* or *an agency contract.* **2.** the office or job of representing another company in an area **3.** a branch of government ○ *the Environment Agency* ○ *the Food Standards Agency*

agent /ˈeɪdʒənt/ *noun* **1.** somebody who represents a company or another person in matters relating to contracts **2.** the person in charge of an agency ○ *advertising agent* ○ *estate agent* ○ *travel agent* **3.** somebody who works for a government agency, especially in secret

agent provocateur /ˌæʒɒn prəˌvɒkə ˈtɜːr/ *noun* a person who provokes others to commit a crime, often by taking part in it personally, in order to find out who is not reliable or in order to have his or her victim arrested

age of consent /ˌeɪdʒ əv kənˈsent/ *noun* the age at which a person is considered to be capable of consenting to sexual intercourse

COMMENT: The age of consent for both heterosexual and homosexual intercourse is currently 16 in England, Wales and Scotland and 17 in Northern Ireland.

age of criminal responsibility /ˌeɪdʒ əv ˌkrɪmɪn(ə)l rɪˌspɒnsɪˈbɪlɪti/ *noun* the age at which a person is considered to be capable of committing a crime

age of majority /ˌeɪdʒ əv məˈdʒɒrɪti/ *noun* the age at which someone becomes legally responsible for his or her actions

aggravated /ˈæɡrəveɪtɪd/ *adjective* made worse

aggravated assault /ˌæɡrəveɪtɪd əˈsɒlt/ *noun* assault causing serious injury or carried out in connection with another serious crime

aggravated burglary /ˌægrəveɪtɪd ˈbɜːgləri/ *noun* burglary where guns or other offensive weapons are carried or used

aggravated damages /ˌægrəveɪtɪd ˈdæmɪdʒɪz/ *plural noun* damages awarded by a court against a defendant who has behaved maliciously or wilfully

aggravating circumstances /ˌægrəveɪtɪŋ ˈsɜːkəmstænsɪz/ *noun* circumstances which make a crime worse

aggravation /ˌægrəˈveɪʃ(ə)n/ *noun* an action, especially the carrying of a weapon, which makes a crime more serious

aggrieved /əˈɡriːvd/ *adjective* injured or harmed by the actions of a defendant ○ *the aggrieved party*

agree /əˈɡriː/ *verb* **1.** to approve or accept something ○ *The figures were agreed between the two parties.* ○ *Terms of the contract are still to be agreed.* **2.** □ **to agree to do something** to say that you will do something □ **to agree with someone** to say that your opinions are the same as someone else's □ **to agree with something** to be the same as something else ○ *The accused's statement does not agree with that of the witness.*

agreed /əˈɡriːd/ *adjective* having been accepted by everyone ○ *an agreed amount* ○ *on agreed terms* or *on terms which have been agreed upon*

agreed price /əˌɡriːd ˈpraɪs/ *noun* the price which has been accepted by both the buyer and seller

agreement /əˈɡriːmənt/ *noun* **1.** a contract between two people or groups where one party makes an offer, and the other party accepts it ○ *written agreement* ○ *unwritten* or *oral agreement* ○ *to break an agreement* ○ *to reach an agreement* or *to come to an agreement on prices* or *salaries* ○ *a marketing agreement* ◊ **gentleman's agreement** □ **agreement in principle** agreement with the basic conditions of a proposal **2.** a document setting out the contractual terms agreed between two parties, ○ *to draw up* or *to draft an agreement* ○ *Both companies signed the agreement.*

aid /eɪd/ *noun* help □ **to pray in aid** to rely on something when pleading a case ○ *I pray in aid the Statute of Frauds in support of the defendant's case.* ■ *verb* to help □ **to aid and abet** to help and encourage someone to commit a crime

aiding and abetting /ˌeɪdɪŋ ənd əˈbetɪŋ/ *noun* the act of helping and encouraging someone to commit a crime such as

driving a car to help a criminal escape from the scene of a crime or keeping watch while a crime is committed. ◊ **accessory**

AIM *abbreviation* Alternative Investment Market

air rage /ˈeə reɪdʒ/ *noun* a violent attack by a passenger on a member of the crew of an aircraft, caused by drink, tiredness or annoyance at something

a. k. a. *abbreviation* also known as

al. ♦ et al.

aleatory /ˌæliˈeɪtəri/ *adjective* **1.** not certain **2.** carrying a risk

aleatory contract /ˌæliettəri ˈkɒntrækt/ *noun* an agreement such as a wager in which what is done by one party depends on something happening which is not certain to happen

alia ♦ et al., inter alia

alias /ˈeɪliəs/ *noun* a name which you use to hide your real name ○ *The confidence trickster used several aliases.* ■ *adverb* using the name of ○ *John Smith, alias Reginald Jones*

alibi /ˈælɪbaɪ/ *noun* a plea that a person charged with a crime was somewhere else when the crime was committed

alien /ˈeɪliən/ *noun* a person who is not a citizen of a country (NOTE: In the UK, an alien is a person who is not a UK citizen, not a citizen of a Commonwealth country and not a citizen of the Republic of Ireland.)

alien absconder /ˌeɪliən əbˈskɒndə/ *noun* an illegal foreign visitor to the United States who has been told to leave the country but has not done so

alienation /ˌeɪliəˈneɪʃ(ə)n/ *noun* the transfer of property, usually land, to someone else

alienation of affection /ˌeɪliəneɪʃ(ə)n əv əˈfekʃən/ *noun* US the loss of affection by one of the partners in a marriage for the other

alieni juris /eɪliˌenaɪ ˈdʒuːrɪs/ *phrase* a Latin phrase meaning 'of another's right': a person such as a minor who has a right under the authority of a guardian. Compare **sui generis**

alimony /ˈælɪməni/ *noun* the money that a court orders a husband to pay regularly to his separated or divorced wife (NOTE: It can occasionally be applied to a wife who is ordered to support her divorced husband.) □ **alimony pending suit**, **alimony pendente lite** money paid by a husband to his wife while their divorce case is being prepared. ◊ **palimony**

allegation /ˌælə'geɪʃ(ə)n/ *noun* a statement, usually given in evidence, that something has happened or is true

allege /ə'ledʒ/ *verb* to state, usually in giving evidence, that something has happened or is true ○ *The prosecution alleged that the accused was in the house when the crime was committed.*

allegiance /ə'li:dʒ(ə)ns/ *noun* loyalty to the State or the Crown. ◊ **oath of allegiance**

All England Law Reports /ˌɔːl ˌɪŋlənd 'lɔː rɪˌpɔːts/ *plural noun* reports of cases in the higher courts. Abbreviation **All E.R.**

allocate /'æləkeɪt/ *verb* to share something between several people, or decide officially how something is to be divided between different possibilities □ **to allocate a case to a track** (*of a court*) to decide which track a case should follow ○ *The court may allocate a case to a track of a higher financial value.*

allocation /ˌælə'keɪʃ(ə)n/ *noun* **1.** the division of a sum of money in various ways ○ *allocation of funds to research into crime* **2.** the act of deciding which of three systems of processing (small claims, fast track or multi-track) a case should follow, depending on the monetary value of the claim (NOTE: The allocation of a case to a particular track has implications for the speed with which the case will be processed.)

allocation hearing /ˌælə'keɪʃ(ə)n ˌhɪərɪŋ/ *noun* a court hearing to consider statements from the parties to a case and decide which system of processing (small claims, fast track or multi-track) a case should follow when an allocation questionnaire has not been submitted

allocation questionnaire /ˌælə 'keɪʃ(ə)n ˌkwestʃəneə/ *noun* a form to be filled in by each party to a claim, to give the court enough information to allow it to allocate the case to one of three systems of processing (small claims, fast track or multi-track)

allocatur /ˌælɒkeɪ'tuːə/ *phrase* a Latin word meaning 'it is allowed': a court document confirming the amount of costs to be paid by one party to another after a court action

allocution /ˌælə'kjuːʃ(ə)n/ *noun US* a request by the judge to a person who has been found guilty, asking if they want to say anything on their own behalf before sentence is passed

allow /ə'laʊ/ *verb* **1.** to say that someone can do something ○ *The law does not allow you to drive on the wrong side of the road.* ○ *Begging is not allowed in the station.* ○ *Visitors are not allowed into the prisoners' cells.* **2.** to give someone time or a privilege ○ *The court adjourned to allow the prosecution to find the missing witness.* ○ *You are allowed thirty days to pay the fine.* **3.** to approve or accept something legally ○ *to allow a claim* or *an appeal* **4.** □ **allow for** to consider something when making a decision about something else ○ *In coming to our conclusion, we allowed for his poor knowledge of the language.*

allowable /ə'laʊəb(ə)l/ *adjective* legally accepted

allowable expenses /əˌlaʊəb(ə)l ɪk 'spensɪz/ *plural noun* expenses which can be claimed against tax

all-points bulletin /ˌɔːl 'pɔːints ˌbʊlətɪn/ *noun* an urgent message broadcast to all police in an area

all rise /ˌɔːl 'raɪz/ *phrase* an instruction from the judge for everybody in a courtroom to stand up

alteram /'ɔːltərəm/ ♦ **audi alteram partem**

alteration /ˌɔːltə'reɪʃ(ə)n/ *noun* a change made to a legal document such as a will, which usually has the effect of making it invalid

alternative /ɔːl't3:nətɪv/ *noun* something which takes the place of something else ○ *They argued that they had offered a similar car as an alternative.* □ **pleading in the alternative, alternative pleading** *US* the practice of making two or more pleadings which are mutually exclusive. ◊ **service by an alternative method** ■ *adjective* similar, able to be a substitute for something else ○ *an alternative solution to the problem*

alternative dispute resolution /ɔːl ˌt3:nətɪv dɪ'spjuːt ˌrezəluːʃ(ə)n/ *noun* any of various methods which can be used to settle a dispute without going to court. Abbreviation **ADR**

Alternative Investment Market /ɔːl ˌl3:nətɪv ɪn'vestmənt ˌmaːkɪt/ *noun* the London Stock Exchange's international market for smaller growing companies. Abbreviation **AIM**

ambassador /æm'bæsədə/ *noun* somebody who is the highest level of diplomat representing his or her country in another country ○ *our ambassador in France* ○ *The* *government has recalled its ambassador for consultations.*

ambassadorial /ˌæmbæsə'dɔːriəl/ *adjective* referring to an ambassador

Amber alert /ˌæmbə ə'lɜːt/ *noun* a system of bulletins issued by police to the media, and in the USA sometimes also on electronic road signs, seeking information leading to the rapid return of a kidnapped child

ambiguity /ˌæmbɪ'ɡjuːɪti/ *noun* **1.** the fact of something being unclear because it can be understood in different ways **2.** something which is unclear because it can be understood in different ways. ◊ **latent ambiguity**

ambiguous /æm'bɪɡjuəs/ *adjective* meaning two or more things and therefore possibly misleading ○ *The wording of the clause is ambiguous and needs clarification.*

ambulance chaser /'æmbjʊləns ˌtʃeɪsə/ *noun* a lawyer or law firm which aggressively seeks to represent claimants in personal injury or medical negligence cases (*slang*)

ambulatory /ˌæmbju'leɪt(ə)ri/ *adjective* (*of a will*) only taking effect after the death of the person who made it

amend /ə'mend/ *verb* to change something ○ *Please amend your copy of the contract accordingly.*

amendment /ə'mendmənt/ *noun* **1.** a change made in a document ○ *to propose an amendment to the draft agreement* ○ *to make amendments to a contract* **2.** a change made to a statement of case, which in civil law can be done before the details of a claim are served **3.** a change proposed to a Bill which is being discussed in Parliament

amends /ə'mendz/ *plural noun* □ **to make amends** to do something to compensate for damage or harm done □ **offer of amends** an offer by a libeller to publish an apology

American Bar Association /ə ˌmerɪkən 'bɑː əˌsəʊsieɪʃ(ə)n/ *noun US* an association of lawyers practising in the USA. Abbreviation **ABA**

amicus curiae /əˌmaɪkəs 'kjʊəriaɪ/ *phrase* a Latin phrase meaning 'friend of the court': a lawyer who does not represent a party in a case but who is called upon to address the court to help clear up a difficult legal point or to explain something which is in the public interest

AML *abbreviation* anti-money laundering

amnesty /'æmnəsti/ *noun* a pardon, often for political crimes, given to several people at the same time ○ *The Home Office announced there were no plans for an amnesty on illegal immigrants.* ■ *verb* to grant convicted persons a pardon

anarchic /ə'nɑːkɪk/, **anarchical** /ə 'nɑːkɪkl/ *adjective* with no law or order ○ *the anarchic state of the country districts after the coup*

anarchism /'ænəkɪz(ə)m/ *noun* the belief that there should be no government or control of people by the state

> COMMENT: Anarchism flourished in the latter part of the 19th and early part of the 20th century. Anarchists believe that there should be no government, no army, no civil service, no courts, no laws, and that people should be free to live without anyone to rule them.

anarchist /'ænəkɪst/ *noun* somebody who believes in anarchism

anarchy /'ænəki/ *noun* absence of law and order, because a government has lost control or because there is no government ○ *When the president was assassinated, the country fell into anarchy.*

ancestor /'ænsestə/ *noun* a person living many years ago from whom someone is descended □ **common ancestor** a person from whom two or more people are descended ○ *Mr Smith and the Queen have a common ancestor in King Charles II*

ancient lights /ˌeɪnʃənt 'laɪts/ *plural noun* same as **right to light**

ancillary /æn'sɪləri/ *adjective* giving help or support

ancillary relief /ænˌsɪləri rɪ'liːf/ *noun* financial provision or adjustment of property rights ordered by a court for a spouse or child in divorce proceedings

animal cruelty /ˌænɪm(ə)l 'kruːəlti/ *noun* abuse towards pets or wild animals

Animal Welfare Act /ˌænɪm(ə)l 'welfeər ˌækt/ *noun* a law which imposes a duty on pet owners to look after their pet's health and welfare, and increases penalties for animal cruelty

animus /'ænɪməs/ *noun* intention

animus cancellandi /ˌænɪməs ˌkænsəl 'ændaɪ/ *phrase* a Latin phrase meaning 'the intention to cancel'

animus furandi /ˌænɪməs ˌfjʊə'rændaɪ/ *phrase* a Latin phrase meaning 'the intention to steal'

animus manendi /ˌænɪməs mæn
'nendaɪ/ *phrase* a Latin phrase meaning
'the intention to stay in a place'

animus revocandi /ˌænɪməs ˌrevə
'kændaɪ/ *phrase* a Latin phrase meaning
'the intention to revoke a will'

COMMENT: With all these terms, when the
phrase is 'with the intention of', **animo** is
used: e.g. *animo revocandi* 'with the intention of revoking a will'.

annexation /ˌænek'seɪʃ(ə)n/ *noun* the
act of annexing a territory

annexe, annex *noun* /'æneks/ a document added or attached to a contract ■ *verb*
/ə'neks/ **1.** to attach a document to something **2.** to take possession of a territory
which belongs to another state and attach it
to your country, so taking full sovereignty
over the territory ○ *The island was annexed
by the neighbouring republic.* ○ *The war
was caused by a dispute over the annexing
of a strip of land.*

annual /'ænjuəl/ *adjective* for one year □
on an annual basis each year

annually /'ænjuəli/ *adverb* each year ○
The figures are revised annually.

annual return /ˌænjuəl rɪ'tɜːn/ *noun* a
form to be completed by each company
once a year, giving details of the directors
and the financial state of the company

annuitant /ə'njuːɪtənt/ *noun* somebody
who receives an annuity

annuity /ə'njuːɪti/ *noun* money paid each
year to a person, usually as the result of an
investment ○ *to buy* or *to take out an annuity*
○ *He has a government annuity* or *an annuity from the government.*

annul /ə'nʌl/ *verb* **1.** to stop something
having any legal effect ○ *The contract was
annulled by the court.* **2.** to declare that
something never existed or that something
never had legal effect ○ *Their marriage has
been annulled.* (NOTE: [all senses] **annulling – annulled**)

annullable /ə'nʌləb(ə)l/ *adjective* able to
be cancelled

annulling /ə'nʌlɪŋ/ *adjective* cancelling ○
annulling clause ■ *noun* the act of cancelling ○ *the annulling of a contract*

annulment /ə'nʌlmənt/ *noun* the act of
cancelling

annulment of adjudication /ə
ˌnʌlmənt əv əˌdʒuːdɪ'keɪʃ(ə)n/ *noun* the
cancelling of an order making someone
bankrupt

annulment of marriage /əˌnʌlmənt əv
'mærɪdʒ/ *noun* the act of ending a marriage
by saying that it was never valid

annum /'ænəm/ ♦ **per annum**

answer /'ɑːnsə/ *noun* **1.** a spoken or written reply ○ *I am writing in answer to your
letter of October 6th.* ○ *I tried to phone his
office but there was no answer.* **2.** a formal
reply to an allegation made in court, especially a defence made by a respondent to a
divorce petition ■ *verb* **1.** to speak or write
after someone has spoken or written to you
□ **to answer a letter** to write a letter in reply
to a letter which you have received **2.** to
reply formally to an allegation made in
court □ **to answer charges** to plead guilty or
not guilty to a charge □ **the judge ruled
there was no case to answer** the judge
ruled that the prosecution or the claimant
had not shown that the accused or the
defendant had done anything wrong

answerable /'ɑːns(ə)rəb(ə)l/ *adjective*
being responsible for one's actions and having to explain why actions have been taken
○ *He is answerable to the Police Commissioner for the conduct of the officers in his
force.* ○ *She refused to be held answerable
for the consequences of the committee's
decision.* (NOTE: You are answerable **to**
someone **for** an action.)

ante /'ænti/ *Latin adverb meaning* 'which
has taken place earlier' or 'before'

antecedents /ˌæntɪ'siːd(ə)nts/ *plural
noun* details of the background of a convicted person given to a court before sentence is passed

antedate /ˌæntɪ'deɪt/ *verb* to put an earlier date on a document ○ *The invoice was
antedated to January 1st.*

anti- /ænti/ *prefix* against ○ *an anti-drug
campaign* ○ *the anti-terrorist squad*

anticipatory /æn'tɪsɪpət(ə)ri/ *adjective*
(*of an action*) performed before the
expected or due date

anticipatory breach /ænˌtɪsɪpət(ə)ri
'briːtʃ/ *noun* a refusal by a party to a contract to perform his or her obligations under
the contract at a time before they were due
to be performed

anti-money laundering /ˌænti 'mʌni
ˌlɔːnd(ə)rɪŋ/ *adjective* designed to combat
the laundering of money obtained by illegal
means. Abbreviation **AML**

antisocial behaviour /ˌæntisəʊʃ(ə)l bɪ
'heɪvjə/ *noun* bad or unpleasant behaviour
in public

Antisocial Behaviour Order /ˌæntisəʊˈʃ(ə)l bɪˈheɪvjə ˌɔːdə/ *noun* an order that can be applied for by the police against any individual over the age of 10 years old who is causing someone distress, harm or harassment, in order to restrict their behaviour. Abbreviation **ASBO**. ◊ **Acceptable Behaviour Contract** (NOTE: ASBOs are a provision of the Crime and Disorder Act 1998.)

anti-suit injunction /ˌænti ˈsuːt ɪnˌdʒʌŋkʃ(ə)n/ *noun* a court or arbitral order ordering a party not to commence, or to withdraw, other court or arbitration proceedings

anti-terrorism legislation /ˌænti ˈterərɪz(ə)m ˌledʒɪsleɪʃ(ə)n/ *noun* laws enacted to combat the threat of terrorism, including the Anti-Terrorism, Crime and Security Act 2001, the Prevention of Terrorism Act 2005 and the Terrorism Act 2006

anti-trust /ˌænti ˈtrʌst/ *adjective* attacking monopolies and encouraging competition ○ *anti-trust laws* or *legislation*

anti-trust laws /ˌænti ˈtrʌst ˌlɔːz/ *plural noun* legislation designed to prevent large corporations forming a monopoly to the detriment of smaller enterprises, e.g. by price-fixing (NOTE: Companies found guilty of this practice can be fined up to 10% of their annual sales under EU law.)

Anton Piller order /ˌæntɒn ˈpɪlər ˌɔːdə/ *noun* formerly, an order by a court allowing a party to inspect and remove a defendant's documents, especially where the defendant might destroy evidence (NOTE: So called after the case of *Anton Piller K.G. v. Manufacturing Processes Ltd*. Since the introduction of the Civil Procedure Rules, this term has been replaced by **search order**.)

any other business /ˌeni ˌʌðə ˈbɪznɪs/ *noun* an item at the end of an agenda, where any matter not already on the agenda can be raised. Abbreviation **AOB**

apology /əˈpɒlədʒi/ *noun* a defence made to an action of defamation where the defendant argues that the offending statement was either made innocently or unintentionally (NOTE: Even if an apology is not accepted, the offer in itself will always be capable of reducing the amount of compensation awarded to the plaintiff.)

a posteriori /ˌeɪ pɒsteriˈɔːri/ *phrase* a Latin phrase meaning 'from what has been concluded afterwards' □ **a posteriori argument** an argument based on observation

apparent /əˈpærənt/ *adjective* easily visible, or obvious □ **apparent defect** a defect which can be easily seen

appeal /əˈpiːl/ *noun* **1.** the act of asking a higher court to change a decision of a lower court ○ *The appeal against the planning decision will be heard next month.* ○ *He lost his appeal for damages against the company.* □ **to win a case on appeal** to lose a case in the first court, but to have the decision changed by an appeal court □ **appeal against conviction** the act of asking a higher court to change the decision of a lower court that a person is guilty □ **appeal against sentence** the act of asking a higher court to reduce a sentence imposed by a lower court **2.** the act of asking a government department to change a decision ■ *verb* to ask a government department to change its decision or a high law court to change a sentence ○ *The company appealed against the decision of the planning officers.* ○ *He has appealed to the Supreme Court.* (NOTE: You appeal **to** a court or **against** a decision, an appeal is **heard** and either **allowed** or **dismissed**.)

Appeal Court /əˈpiːl kɔːt/ *noun* ♦ **Court of Appeal**

appear /əˈpɪə/ *verb* **1.** to seem ○ *The witness appeared to have difficulty in remembering what had happened.* **2.** (*of a party in a case*) to come to court **3.** (*of a barrister or solicitor*) to come to court to represent a client ○ *Mr A. Clark QC is appearing on behalf of the defendant.*

appearance /əˈpɪərəns/ *noun* the act of coming to court to defend or prosecute a case □ **to enter an appearance** to register with a court that a defendant intends to defend an action

appellant /əˈpelənt/ *noun* a person who goes to a higher court to ask it to change a decision or a sentence imposed by a lower court

appellate /əˈpelət/ *adjective* referring to appeal

appellate committee /əˈpelət kəˌmɪti/ *noun* the upper house of the British Parliament, which is responsible for analysing legislation and hearing cases which have been referred to it by lower courts

appellate court /əˈpelət kɔːt/ *noun* ♦ **Court of Appeal**

appellate jurisdiction /əˌpelət ˌdʒʊərɪsˈdɪkʃ(ə)n/ *noun* the power of a judge to hear appeals from a previous decision made by a lower court (NOTE: If the

ECJ tries to decide if a national court's decision to refer a case to it is correct, then the ECJ is exercising a form of appellate jurisdiction.)

appendix /əˈpendɪks/ *noun* an additional piece of text at the end of a document ○ *The markets covered by the agency agreement are listed in the Appendix.* ○ *See Appendix B for the clear-up rates of notifiable offences.* (NOTE: The plural is **appendices**.)

applicant /ˈæplɪkənt/ *noun* **1.** somebody who applies for something ○ *an applicant for a job* or *a job applicant* ○ *There were thousands of applicants for shares in the new company.* **2.** somebody who applies for a court order

application /ˌæplɪˈkeɪʃ(ə)n/ *noun* **1.** the act or process of asking for something, usually in writing ○ *job application* **2.** the act of asking the Court to make an order ○ *His application for an injunction was refused.* ○ *Solicitors acting for the wife made an application for a maintenance order.*

COMMENT: Order applications can now be dealt with by telephone (a **telephone hearing**); urgent applications can be made without making an application notice.

application notice /ˌæplɪˈkeɪʃ(ə)n ˌnəʊtɪs/ *noun* a document by which an applicant applies for a court order (NOTE: The notice must state what type of order is being sought and the reasons for seeking it.)

apply /əˈplaɪ/ *verb* **1.** to ask for something, usually in writing ○ *to apply for a job* ○ *to apply in person* ○ *My client wishes to apply for Legal Aid.* ○ *He applied for judicial review* or *for compensation* or *for an adjournment.* □ **to apply to the Court** to ask the court to make an order ○ *he applied to the Court for an injunction* **2.** to affect or be relevant to something or someone ○ *This clause applies only to deals outside the EU.* ○ *The legal precedent applies to cases where the parents of the child are divorced.*

appoint /əˈpɔɪnt/ *verb* to choose someone for a job ○ *to appoint James Smith to the post of manager* ○ *The government has appointed a QC to head the inquiry.* ○ *The court appointed a receiver.* (NOTE: You appoint a person **to** a job or **to do** a job.)

appointee /əpɔɪnˈtiː/ *noun* somebody who is appointed to a job

appointment /əˈpɔɪntmənt/ *noun* **1.** an arrangement to meet someone ○ *to make an appointment with someone for two o'clock* ○ *He was late for his appointment.* ○ *She*

had to cancel her appointment. **2.** the act of appointing someone or being appointed to a job **3.** a job □ **legal appointments vacant** a list of legal jobs which are vacant

apportion /əˈpɔːʃ(ə)n/ *verb* to share out something such as property, rights or liabilities in appropriate proportions ○ *Costs are apportioned according to planned revenue.*

apportionment /əˈpɔːʃ(ə)nmənt/ *noun* the act of sharing out such as property, rights or liabilities in appropriate proportions

appraise /əˈpreɪz/ *verb* to make an estimate of the value of something

appraiser /əˈpreɪzə/ *noun* somebody who appraises something

apprehend /ˌæprɪˈhend/ *verb* (*formal*) **1.** to understand ○ *I apprehend that you say your client has a reference.* **2.** to arrest and take into police custody ○ *The suspect was apprehended at the scene of the crime.*

apprehension /ˌæprɪˈhenʃ(ə)n/ *noun* the act of arresting someone (*formal*)

appropriate *adjective* /əˈprəʊprɪət/ suitable for a particular purpose ○ *Is a fine an appropriate punishment for sex offences?* ■ *verb* /əˈprəʊprɪeɪt/ **1.** to take control of something illegally **2.** to take something for a particular use, e.g. taking funds from an estate to pay legacies to beneficiaries

appropriation /əˌprəʊprɪˈeɪʃ(ə)n/ *noun* the allocation of money for a particular purpose such as distributing parts of an estate to beneficiaries

approval /əˈpruːv(ə)l/ *noun* **1.** permission to do something given by someone with authority ○ *to submit a budget for approval* **2.** □ **on approval** a sale where the buyer pays for goods only if they are satisfactory

approve /əˈpruːv/ *verb* to agree to something officially ○ *to approve the terms of a contract* ○ *The proposal was approved by the board.* ○ *The motion was approved by the committee.* □ **to approve of** to think something is good

approved school /əˈpruːvd skuːl/ *noun* formerly, a school for young delinquents

appurtenances /əˈpɜːrtɪnənsɪz/ *plural noun* land or buildings attached to or belonging to a property

appurtenant /əˈpɜːrtɪnənt/ *adjective* relevant to

a priori /ˌeɪ praɪˈɔːri/ *phrase* a Latin phrase meaning 'from the first': using logic and reason to draw conclusions from what is already known □ **a priori argument** reasoning based on ideas or assumptions, not on real examples

ARA *abbreviation* Assets Recovery Agency

arbitrate /'ɑːbɪtreɪt/ *verb* (*usually used in building, shipping or employment disputes*) to settle a dispute between parties by referring it to an arbitrator instead of going to court ○ *to arbitrate in a dispute*

arbitration /ˌɑːbɪ'treɪʃ(ə)n/ *noun* the settling of a dispute by an outside person or persons agreed on by both sides ○ *to submit a dispute to arbitration* ○ *to refer a question to arbitration*

arbitration agreement /ˌɑːbɪ'treɪʃ(ə)n əˌɡriːmənt/ *noun* an agreement by two parties to submit a dispute to arbitration

arbitration award /ˌɑːbɪ'treɪʃ(ə)n əˌwɔːd/ *noun* a ruling given by an arbitrator

arbitration clause /ˌɑːbɪ'treɪʃ(ə)n klɔːz/ *noun* a written term in a contract, usually a commercial contract, requiring anyone who is party to the contract to agree to refer any contractual disputes to arbitration

arbitrator /'ɑːbɪtreɪtə/ *noun* a person not concerned with a dispute who is chosen by both sides to try to settle it ○ *an industrial arbitrator* ○ *to accept* or *to reject the arbitrator's ruling*

argue /'ɑːɡjuː/ *verb* **1.** to discuss something about which there is disagreement ○ *They argued over* or *about the price.* ○ *Counsel spent hours arguing about the precise meaning of the clause.* **2.** to give reasons for something ○ *Prosecuting counsel argued that the accused should be given exemplary sentences.* ○ *The police solicitor argued against granting bail.* (NOTE: You argue **with** someone **about** or **over** something.)

arguendo /ˌɑːɡjuː'endəʊ/ *adverb* a Latin word meaning 'for the purposes of argument': ○ *Assuming arguendo that the suspect's alibi is reliable, that still doesn't explain why his watch was found at the scene.*

argument /'ɑːɡjʊmənt/ *noun* **1.** the discussion of something without agreement ○ *They got into an argument with the judge over the relevance of the documents to the case.* ○ *He sacked his solicitor after an argument over costs.* **2.** a speech giving reasons for something ○ *The judge found the defence arguments difficult to follow.* ○ *Counsel presented the argument for the prosecution.* ○ *The Court of Appeal was*

concerned that the judge at first instance had delivered judgment without proper argument.

arise /ə'raɪz/ *verb* to happen as a result of something ○ *The situation has arisen because neither party is capable of paying the costs of the case.* ○ *The problem arises from the difficulty in understanding the regulations.*

armed neutrality /ˌɑːmd njuː'trælɪti/ *noun* the condition of a country which is neutral during a war, but maintains armed forces to defend itself

armourer /'ɑːmərə/ *noun* a criminal who supplies guns to other criminals (*slang*)

arraign /ə'reɪn/ *verb* to make an accused person appear in the court and read the indictment to him or her

arraignment /ə'reɪnmənt/ *noun* the act of reading of an indictment to the accused and hearing his or her plea

arrangement /ə'reɪndʒmənt/ *noun* **1.** a way in which something is organised ○ *The company secretary is making all the arrangements for the AGM.* **2.** the settling of a financial dispute, especially by proposing a plan for repaying creditors ○ *to come to an arrangement with the creditors*

arrears /ə'rɪəz/ *plural noun* money which has not been paid at the time when it was due ○ *to allow the payments to fall into arrears* □ **in arrears** owing money which should have been paid earlier ○ *The payments are six months in arrears.* ○ *He is six weeks in arrears with his rent.*

arrest /ə'rest/ *noun* an act of taking and keeping someone in custody legally, so that he or she can be questioned and perhaps charged with a crime □ **a warrant is out for his *or* her arrest** a magistrate has signed a warrant, giving the police the power to arrest someone for a crime □ **under arrest** kept and held by the police ○ *Six of the gang are in the police station under arrest.* ■ *verb* **1.** to hold someone legally so as to keep him or her in custody and charge them with a crime ○ *Two of the strikers were arrested.* ○ *The constable stopped the car and arrested the driver.* **2.** to seize a ship or its cargo **3.** to stop something from continuing

COMMENT: Any citizen may arrest a person who is committing a serious offence, though members of the police force have wider powers, in particular the power to arrest persons on suspicion of a serious crime or in cases where an arrest warrant has been granted. Generally a police officer is not entitled to arrest someone without a warrant if the person does not know or is not told the reason for their arrest.

arrestable offence /əˌrestəb(ə)l ə ˈfens/ *noun* a crime for which someone can be arrested without a warrant, usually an offence which carries a penalty of at least five years' imprisonment

arrest of judgment /əˌrest əv ˈdʒʌdʒmənt/ *noun* a situation where a judgment is held back because there appears to be an error in the documentation

arrest warrant /əˌrest ˈwɒrənt/ *noun* a warrant signed by a magistrate which gives the police the power to arrest someone for a crime

arson /ˈɑːs(ə)n/ *noun* the notifiable offence of setting fire to a building ○ *He was charged with arson.* ○ *During the riot there were ten cases of looting and two of arson.* ○ *The police who are investigating the fire suspect arson.* □ **an arson attack** an occasion of somebody deliberately setting fire to a building

arsonist /ˈɑːs(ə)nɪst/ *noun* somebody who commits arson

article /ˈɑːtɪk(ə)l/ *noun* **1.** a product or thing for sale ○ *a black market in imported articles of clothing* **2.** a section of a legal agreement ○ *See article 8 of the contract.* **3.** same as **articles of association**

Article 12 /ˌɑːtɪk(ə)l ˈtwelv/ *noun* a clause in the European Convention for Human Rights which protects the right to marry

Article 19 /ˌɑːtɪk(ə)l naɪnˈtiːn/ *noun* a clause in the European Convention for Human Rights which protects the right to freedom of opinion and expression

COMMENT: Article 19 defends both the right to freedom of expression and the need for legal conditions and restrictions to be placed upon expression in order to protect other rights such as the right to privacy.

Article 81 /ˌɑːtɪk(ə)l ˌeɪti ˈwʌn/ *noun* a provision contained in the Treaty of Rome designed to prevent agreements that aim to or effectively restrict, prevent or manipulate competition in the European Union (NOTE: Formerly known as Article 85.)

Article 82 /ˌɑːtɪk(ə)l ˌeɪti ˈtuː/ *noun* a provision contained in the Treaty of Rome designed to prevent businesses abusing their position of dominance within the European Union

articled clerk /ˌɑːtɪk(ə)ld ˈklɑːk/ *noun* former name for **trainee solicitor**

articles /ˈɑːtɪk(ə)lz/ *noun* formerly, the period during which someone is working in a solicitor's office to learn the law (NOTE: Now called **traineeship**.)

articles of association /ˌɑːtɪk(ə)lz əv əˌsəʊsiˈeɪʃ(ə)n/ *noun* a document which regulates the way in which a company's affairs such as the appointment of directors or rights of shareholders are managed. Also called **articles of incorporation**

articles of impeachment /ˌɑːtɪk(ə)lz əv ɪmˈpiːtʃmənt/ *noun US* a statement of the grounds on which a public official is to be impeached

articles of incorporation /ˌɑːtɪk(ə)lz əv ɪnˌkɔːpəˈreɪʃ(ə)n/ *noun* same as **articles of association**

articles of partnership /ˌɑːtɪk(ə)lz əv ˈpɑːtnəʃɪp/ *noun* a document which sets up the legal conditions of a partnership ○ *She is a director appointed under the articles of the company.* ○ *This procedure is not allowed under the articles of association of the company.*

artificial person /ˌɑːtɪfɪʃ(ə)l ˈpɜːs(ə)n/ *noun* a body such as a company which is regarded as a person in law

ASBO *abbreviation* Antisocial Behaviour Order

ascendant /əˈsendənt/ *noun* the parent or grandparent of a person (NOTE: The opposite, the children or grandchildren of a person, are **descendants**.)

ask /ɑːsk/ *verb* **1.** to put a question to someone ○ *Prosecuting counsel asked the accused to explain why the can of petrol was in his car.* **2.** to tell someone to do something ○ *The police officers asked the marchers to go home.* ○ *She asked her assistant to fetch a file from the managing director's office.* ○ *The customs officials asked him to open his case.* ○ *The judge asked the witness to write the name on a piece of paper.* **3.** □ **to ask for something** to say that you want or need something ○ *He asked for the file on 1992 debtors.* ○ *Counsel asked for more time to consult with his colleagues.* ○ *There is a man on the phone asking for Mr Smith.* □ **to ask for bail to be granted** to ask a court to allow a prisoner to be remanded on bail

assassin /əˈsæsɪn/ *noun* someone who murders a well-known person

assassinate /əˈsæsɪneɪt/ *verb* to murder a well-known person

assassination /əˌsæsɪˈneɪʃ(ə)n/ *noun* the murder of a well-known person

assault /ə'sɔːlt/ *verb* the crime or tort of acting in such a way that someone is afraid he or she will be attacked and hurt ○ *She was assaulted by two muggers.* ■ *noun* the offence of acting intentionally to make someone afraid that they will be attacked and hurt ○ *He was sent to prison for assault.* ○ *The number of cases of assault* or *the number of assaults on policemen is increasing.* (NOTE: As a crime or tort, assault has no plural. When it has a plural it means 'cases of assault'.)

COMMENT: Assault should be distinguished from battery, in that assault is the threat of violence, whereas battery is actual violence. However, because the two are so closely connected, the term 'assault' is frequently used as a general term for violence to a person. 'Aggravated assault' is assault causing serious injury or carried out in connection with another serious crime. The term 'common assault' is frequently used for any assault which is not an aggravated assault.

assaulter /ə'sɔːltə/ *noun* **1.** a member of a police hostage rescue team **2.** someone who attacks another person physically or verbally in a violent way

assemble /ə'semb(ə)l/ *verb* **1.** to come together or to gather ○ *The crowd assembled in front of the police station.* **2.** to put something together from various parts ○ *The police are still assembling all the evidence.*

assembly /ə'sembli/ *noun* the action of people meeting together in a group. ◊ **freedom of assembly, unlawful assembly**

assemblyman /ə'semblimən/ *noun* a member of an assembly

Assembly of the European Community /ə,sembli əv θə ,juərəpiən kə'mjuːnɪti/ *noun* the European Parliament

assent /ə'sent/ *noun* **1.** agreement to or approval of something **2.** notification by a personal representative that part of an estate is not needed for the administration of the estate and can be passed to the beneficiary named in the will (NOTE: The assent can be given verbally or in writing and applies to personal property and real estate.) ■ *verb* to agree to something

assent procedure /ə,sent prə'siːdʒə/ *noun* a procedure by which the approval of the European Parliament is necessary before legislation can be put into law

assess /ə'ses/ *verb* to calculate the value of something, especially for tax or insurance purposes ○ *to assess damages at £1,000* ○ *to assess a property for the purposes of insurance*

assessment /ə'sesmənt/ *noun* a calculation of value ○ *assessment of damages* ○ *assessment of property* ○ *tax assessment*

assessment of costs /ə,sesmənt əv 'kɒsts/ *noun* an assessment of the costs of a legal action by the costs judge (NOTE: Since the introduction of the Civil Procedure Rules, this term has replaced **taxation of costs**.)

assessor /ə'sesə/ *noun* an expert who helps the court when a case requires specialised technical knowledge

asset /'æset/ *noun* something which belongs to a company or person and which has a specific value ○ *He has an excess of assets over liabilities.* ○ *Her assets are only £640 as against liabilities of £24,000.*

Assets Recovery Agency /,æsets rɪ'kʌv(ə)ri ,eɪdʒənsi/ *noun* an organisation which seizes profits made from criminal activity. Abbreviation **ARA**

asset value /'æset ,væljuː/ *noun* the value of a company calculated by adding together all its assets

assign /ə'saɪn/ *verb* **1.** to give or transfer something ○ *to assign a right to someone* ○ *to assign shares to someone* ○ *to assign a debt to someone* **2.** to give someone a piece of work to do ○ *He was assigned the job of checking the numbers of stolen cars.* ○ *Three detectives have been assigned to the case.* ■ *noun* same as **assignee**

assignee /,æsaɪ'niː/ *noun* somebody who receives something which has been assigned

assignment /ə'saɪnmənt/ *noun* **1.** the legal transfer of a property or of a right ○ *assignment of a patent* or *of a copyright* ○ *assignment of a lease* **2.** a document by which something is assigned **3.** a particular task to be completed ○ *We have put six constables on that particular assignment.* **4.** in Scotland, a document such as a deed that effects a legal transfer of rights

assignor /,æsaɪ'nɔː/ *noun* somebody who assigns something to someone

assigns /ə'saɪnz/ *plural noun* people to whom property has been assigned

assist /ə'sɪst/ *verb* to help ○ *The accused had to be assisted into the dock.* ○ *She has been assisting us with our inquiries.*

Assistant Chief Constable /ə,sɪst(ə)nt tʃiːf 'kʌnstəb(ə)l/ *noun* a rank in the police force below Chief Constable

assisted person /ə,sɪstɪd 'pɜːs(ə)n/ *noun* somebody who is receiving Legal Aid

assisted suicide /əˌsɪstɪd ˈsuːɪsaɪd/ *noun* same as **euthanasia**

Assizes, Assize Courts *plural noun* formerly, the Crown Court

associate /əˈsəʊsieɪt/ *adjective* joined together with something ■ *noun* somebody who works in the same business as someone ○ *In his testimony he named six associates.* ■ *verb* to mix with or to meet people □ **to associate with criminals** to be frequently in the company of criminals

associate company /əˌsəʊsiət ˈkʌmp(ə)ni/ *noun* a company which is partly owned or controlled by another

associated /əˈsəʊsieɪtɪd/ *adjective* joined to or controlled by ○ *Smith Ltd and its associated company, Jones Brothers.*

associate director /əˌsəʊsiət daɪˈrektə/ *noun* a director who attends board meetings, but does not have the full powers of a director

associated persons /əˌsəʊsieɪtɪd ˈpɜːs(ə)n/ *plural noun* a category of personal relationships which allow one party the right to apply for a protection order against the other party. ◊ **non-molestation order, occupation order**

COMMENT: The category includes, but is not limited to, current, estranged and ex-spouses, cohabitees and ex-cohabitees, family members and co-parents.

Associate Justice /əˌsəʊsiət ˈdʒʌstɪs/ *noun* US a member of the Supreme Court who is not the Chief Justice

associate of the Crown Office /əˌsəʊsieɪt əv ðɪ kraʊn ˈɒfɪs/ *noun* an official who is responsible for the clerical and administrative work of a court

association /əˌsəʊsiˈeɪʃ(ə)n/ *noun* **1.** a group of people or of companies with the same interest ○ *trade association* ○ *employers' association* **2.** (*in prison*) the time when prisoners can leave their cells and socialise with other prisoners

assurance /əˈʃʊərəns/ *noun* an insurance agreement that in return for regular payments, one party will pay another party compensation for injury or loss of life

assure /əˈʃʊə/ *verb* to have an agreement with an insurance company that in return for regular payment, the company will pay compensation for injury or loss of life □ **the assured** the person whose interests are assured, who is entitled to the benefit in an insurance policy

COMMENT: **assure** and **assurance** are used in Britain for insurance policies relating to something which will certainly happen (such as death or the end of a given period of time); for other types of policy use **insure** and **insurance**.

assured shorthold tenancy /əˌʃʊəd ˌʃɔːthəʊld ˈtenənsi/ *noun* a tenancy allowing a landlord to bypass the usual grounds for regaining possession of an assured tenancy

COMMENT: The Housing Act states that all tenancies will automatically be classified as assured shorthold tenancies unless otherwise specified in the contract.

assured tenancy /əˌʃʊəd ˈtenənsi/ *noun* in England and Wales, a lease under the Housing Act 1988 that gives a tenant limited security of tenure and allows a landlord a specific means of terminating a lease

assurer /əˈʃʊərə/, **assuror** *noun* a company which provides insurance

asylum /əˈsaɪləm/ *noun* refuge in a country granted to a person who is subject to extradition by a foreign government

asylum seeker /əˈsaɪləm ˌsiːkə/ *noun* a person who asks to be allowed to remain in a foreign country because they would be in danger if they were to return to the home country

at issue /ət ˈɪʃuː/ ♦ **issue**

at large /ət ˈlɑːdʒ/ *adjective* not in prison ○ *Three prisoners escaped – two were recaptured, but one is still at large.*

at-risk /ət ˈrɪsk/ *adjective* vulnerable to harm ○ *We're installing more street lights in at-risk areas.* ○ *The elderly are a particularly at-risk group.*

attach /əˈtætʃ/ *verb* **1.** to include something with something else ○ *I am attaching a copy of our correspondence so far.* ○ *Please send an e-mail with your cover letter and CV attached.* **2.** to arrest a person or take property

attaché /əˈtæʃeɪ/ *noun* a person who does specialised work in an embassy abroad ○ *a military attaché* ○ *The government ordered the commercial attaché to return home.*

attachment /əˈtætʃmənt/ *noun* a court order preventing a debtor's property from being sold until debts are paid

attachment of earnings /əˌtætʃmənt əv ˈɜːnɪŋz/ *noun* a legal power to take money from a person's salary to pay money which is owed to the courts

attachment of earnings order /əˌtætʃmənt əv ˈɜːnɪŋ ˌɔːdə/ *noun* a court order to make an employer pay part of an employee's salary to the court to pay off debts

attack /ə'tæk/ *verb* **1.** to try to hurt or harm someone ○ *The security guard was attacked by three men carrying guns.* **2.** to criticise ○ *The newspaper attacked the government for not spending enough money on the police.* ■ *noun* **1.** the act of trying to hurt or harm someone ○ *There has been an increase in attacks on police* or *in terrorist attacks on planes.* **2.** criticism ○ *The newspaper published an attack on the government.* (NOTE: You attack someone, or make an attack **on** someone.)

attacker /ə'tækə/ *noun* somebody who attacks ○ *She recognised her attacker and gave his description to the police.*

attempt /ə'tempt/ *noun* **1.** an act of trying to do something ○ *The company made an attempt to break into the American market.* ○ *The takeover attempt was turned down by the board.* ○ *All his attempts to get a job have failed.* **2.** an act of trying to do something illegal (NOTE: Attempt is a crime even if the attempted offence has not been committed.)

attempted murder /ə,temptɪd 'mɜːdə/ *noun* the notifiable offence of trying to murder someone

attend /ə'tend/ *verb* to be present at ○ *The witnesses were summoned to attend the trial.*

attendance /ə'tendəns/ *noun* the fact of being present

Attendance Allowance /ə'tendəns ə,laʊəns/ *noun* financial help given by the Government to someone over the age of 65 who needs home care because of a physical or mental disability

attendance centre /ə,tendəns 'sentə/ *noun* a place where a young person may be sent by a court to take part in various activities or do hard work as a punishment (NOTE: This applies to people between the ages of 17 and 21 and is on the condition that they have not had a custodial sentence before.)

attest /ə'test/ *verb* to sign a document such as a will in the presence of a witness who also signs the document to confirm that the signature is genuine

attestation /,æte'steɪʃ(ə)n/ *noun* the act of signing a document such as a will in the presence of a witness to show that the signature is genuine

attestation clause /,æte'steɪʃ(ə)n klɔːz/ *noun* a clause showing that the signature of the person signing a legal document

has been witnessed (NOTE: The attestation clause is usually written: 'signed sealed and delivered by … in the presence of …'.)

attorn /ə'tɔːn/ *verb* to transfer

attorney /ə'tɜːni/ *noun* **1.** somebody who is legally allowed to act on behalf of someone else **2.** *US* a lawyer

attorney-at-law /ə,tɜːni ət 'lɔː/ *noun* formerly, a barrister

Attorney-General /ə,tɜːni 'dʒen(ə)rəl/ *noun* **1.** in the UK, one of the Law Officers, a Member of Parliament, who prosecutes for the Crown in some court cases, advises government departments on legal problems and decides if major criminal offences should be tried **2.** in a US state or in the federal government, the head of legal affairs (NOTE: In the US Federal Government, the Attorney-General is in charge of the Justice Department.)

attributable /ə'trɪbjʊtəb(ə)l/ *adjective* possible to attribute to someone or something

attribute /ə'trɪbjuːt/ *verb* to suggest that something came from a source ○ *remarks attributed to the Chief Constable*

audi alteram partem /,aʊdi ,ælterəm 'pɑːtəm/ *phrase* a Latin phrase meaning 'hear the other side': a rule in natural justice that everyone has the right to speak in his or her own defence and to have the case against them explained clearly

audit /'ɔːdɪt/ *noun* **1.** an examination of the books and accounts of a company ○ *to carry out an annual audit* **2.** a careful review of the effectiveness of something ○ *an audit of safety procedures* ■ *verb* **1.** to examine the books and accounts of a company ○ *to audit the accounts* ○ *The books have not yet been audited.* **2.** to review something carefully

Audit Commission /'ɔːdɪt kə,mɪʃ(ə)n/ *noun* an independent body which examines the accounts of local authorities, ensures that money is spent legally and wisely, and checks for possible fraud and corruption

auditor /'ɔːdɪtə/ *noun* somebody who audits ○ *The AGM appoints the company's auditors.*

audit trail /'ɔːdɪt treɪl/ *noun* a record in the form of computer or printed documents that shows how something happened

autarchy /'ɔːtɑːki/ *noun* a situation where a state rules itself without outside interference and has full power over its own affairs

authenticate /ɔː'θentɪkeɪt/ *verb* to show that something is true

authentication /ɔː,θentɪ'keɪʃ(ə)n/ *noun* the act of verifying that something is true or correct

authenticity /,ɔːθen'tɪsɪti/ *noun* the state of being genuine ○ *The police are checking the authenticity of the letter.* ○ *An electronic signature confirms the authenticity of the text.*

author /'ɔːθə/ *noun* the creator and owner of a piece of copyrighted work

authorisation /,ɔːθəraɪ'zeɪʃ(ə)n/, **authorization** *noun* **1.** official permission or power to do something ○ *Do you have authorisation for this expenditure?* ○ *He has no authorisation to act on our behalf.* **2.** a document showing that someone has official permission to do something ○ *He showed the bank his authorisation to inspect the contents of the safe.*

authorise /'ɔːθəraɪz/, **authorize** *verb* **1.** to give official permission for something to be done ○ *to authorise payment of £10,000* **2.** to give someone the authority to do something ○ *to authorise someone to act on your behalf*

authorised /'ɔːθəraɪzd/, **authorized** *adjective* permitted

authorised capital /,ɔːθəraɪzd 'kæpɪt(ə)l/ *noun* the amount of capital which a company is allowed to have, according to its memorandum of association

authorised dealer /,ɔːθəraɪzd 'diːlə/ *noun* a person or company such as a bank which is allowed to buy and sell foreign currency

authoritarian /ɔː,θɒrɪ'teərɪən/ *adjective* acting because of having power

authoritarianism /ɔː,θɒrɪ'teərɪən[[ðɪʃç],ɪz(ə)m/ *noun* a theory that a regime must rule its people strictly in order to be efficient

authoritarian regime /ɔː,θɒrɪteərɪən reɪ'ʒiːm/ *noun* a government which rules its people strictly and does not allow anyone to oppose its decisions

authoritative /ɔː'θɒrɪtətɪv/ *adjective* **1.** having the force of law ○ *Courts in Member States cannot give authoritative rulings on how EU law should be interpreted.* **2.** based on the best reliable information ○ *an authoritative opinion on likely trends*

authority /ɔː'θɒrɪti/ *noun* **1.** official power given to someone to do something ○

He has no authority to act on our behalf. ○ *She was acting on the authority of the court.* ○ *On whose authority was the charge brought?* **2.** □ **the authorities** the government, police or official organisations with legal powers to control things

automatism /ɔː'tɒmətɪz(ə)m/ *noun* a defence to a criminal charge whereby the accused states he or she acted involuntarily

autonomous /ɔː'tɒnəməs/ *adjective* governing itself ○ *an autonomous regional government*

autonomy /ɔː'tɒnəmi/ *noun* self-government, or freedom from outside control ○ *The separatists are demanding full autonomy for their state.* ○ *The government has granted the region a limited autonomy.*

autopsy /'ɔːtɒpsi/ *noun* an examination of a dead person to see what was the cause of death

autrefois acquit /,əʊtrəfwæ ə'kiː/ *phrase* a French phrase meaning 'previously acquitted': a plea that an accused person has already been acquitted of the crime with which he or she is charged

autrefois convict /,əʊtrəfwæ kɒn'vɪkt/ *phrase* a French phrase meaning 'previously convicted': a plea that an accused person has already been convicted of the crime with which he or she is now charged

available /ə'veɪləb(ə)l/ *adjective* able to be used ○ *The right of self-defence is only available against unlawful attack.*

aver /ə'vɜː/ *verb* to make a statement or an allegation in pleadings (NOTE: **averring – averred**)

average adjuster /,æv(ə)rɪdʒ ə'dʒʌstə/ *noun* somebody who calculates how much is due to the insured when he or she suffers the loss of or damage to a ship

average adjustment /,æv(ə)rɪdʒ ə'dʒʌstmənt/ *noun* a calculation of the share of cost of damage or loss of a ship

average income per capita /,æv(ə)rɪdʒ ,ɪnkʌm pə 'kæpɪtə/ *noun* the average income of one person

averment /ə'vɜːmənt/ *noun* a statement or allegation made in pleadings

avoid /ə'vɔɪd/ *verb* **1.** to try not to do something ○ *The company is trying to avoid bankruptcy.* ○ *My aim is to avoid paying too much tax.* ○ *We want to avoid direct competition with Smith Ltd.* □ **to avoid creditors** to make sure that creditors cannot find you so as not to pay them **2.** to make something void ○ *to avoid a contract* **3.** to quash a sentence

avoidance /ə'vɔɪd(ə)ns/ *noun* **1.** a plan or deliberate policy to avoid something or someone ○ *avoidance of an agreement* or *of a contract* ○ *tax avoidance* **2.** a confession to a charge, but suggesting it should be cancelled

award /ə'wɔːd/ *noun* a decision which settles a dispute ○ *an award made by an indus-trial tribunal* ○ *The arbitrator's award was set aside on appeal.* ■ *verb* to decide the amount of money to be given to someone ○ *to award someone a salary increase* ○ *to award damages* ○ *The judge awarded costs to the defendant.* □ **to award a contract to a company** to decide that a company will have the contract to do work for you

AWOL /'eɪwɒl/ *abbreviation* absent without leave

B

backdate /ˌbæk'deɪt/ *verb* to put an earlier date on a cheque or an invoice ○ *Backdate your invoice to April 1st.* ○ *The pay increase is backdated to January 1st.*

background /'bækɡraʊnd/ *noun* **1.** the previous experience, cultural background or family connections that someone has ○ *The accused is from a good background.* ○ *Can you tell us something of the girl's family background?* **2.** general facts about a situation including relevant information about what happened in the past ○ *He explained the background to the claim.* ○ *The court asked for details of the background to the case.* ○ *I know the contractual situation as it stands now, but can you fill in the background details?*

backsheet /'bækʃiːt/ *noun* the last sheet of paper in a legal document which, when folded, becomes the outside sheet and carries the endorsement

bad debt /ˌbæd 'det/ *noun* money owed which will never be paid back

bail /beɪl/ *noun* **1.** the release of an arrested person from custody after payment has been made to a court on condition that the person will return to face trial ○ *to stand bail of £3,000 for someone* (NOTE: The US term is **pretrial release**.) **2.** payment made to a court to release an arrested person ○ *He was granted bail on his own recognizance of £1,000.* ○ *The police opposed bail on the grounds that the accused might try to leave the country.* □ **to be remanded on bail** to be released on payment of bail money □ **to jump bail** not to appear in court after having been released on bail ■ *verb* □ **to bail someone out** to pay a debt on behalf of someone ○ *She paid £3,000 to bail him out.*

bail bandit /'beɪl ˌbændɪt/ *noun* an accused person who commits a crime while on bail awaiting trial for another offence, or who fails to appear in court on the date agreed

bail bond /'beɪl bɒnd/ *noun* a signed document which is given to the court as security for payment of a judgment

bail bondsperson /ˌbeɪl 'bɒndzpɜːs(ə)n/ *noun* someone who provides bail money or acts as surety for an accused person

bailee /ˌbeɪ'liː/ *noun* somebody who receives property by way of bailment

Bailey ♦ **Old Bailey**

bailiff /'beɪlɪf/ *noun* **1.** a person employed by the court whose responsibility is to see that documents such as summonses are served and that court orders are obeyed ○ *The court ordered the bailiffs to seize his property because he had not paid his fine.* (NOTE: The US equivalent is a **marshal**.) **2.** *US* the deputy to a sheriff

bailment /'beɪlmənt/ *noun* a transfer of goods by one person (the bailor) to another (the bailee) who then holds them until they have to be returned to the bailor

bailor /ˌbeɪ'lɔː/ *noun* somebody who transfers property by way of bailment

Bakke decision /'bæki: dɪˌsɪʒ(ə)n/ *noun* a US Supreme Court ruling that made the reservation of a specific number of places for students from minority groups unlawful because it prevented applicants not from those groups from competing for the reserved places

balance /'bæləns/ *noun* □ **balance of mind** mental state

ballot-rigging /'bælət ˌrɪɡɪŋ/ *noun* an illegal attempt to manipulate the votes in an election so that a specific candidate or party wins

ban /bæn/ *noun* an order which forbids someone from doing something or which makes an activity illegal ○ *a government ban on the sale of weapons* ○ *a ban on the copying of computer software* □ **to impose a ban on smoking** to make an order which forbids smoking □ **to lift the ban on smok-**

ing to allow people to smoke ∎ *verb* to forbid something or make it illegal ○ *The government has banned the sale of alcohol.* ○ *The sale of pirated records has been banned.*

bank /bæŋk/ *noun* a business which holds money for its clients, lends money at interest, and trades generally in money ∎ *verb* to deposit money into a bank or to have an account with a bank

bankable paper /ˌbæŋkəb(ə)l 'peɪpə/ *noun* a document which a bank will accept as security for a loan

bank account /'bæŋk əˌkaʊnt/ *noun* an arrangement which you make with a bank to keep your money safely until you want it

bank borrowings /'bæŋk ˌbɒrəʊɪŋz/ *plural noun* loans made by banks

bank charter /ˌbæŋk 'tʃɑːtə/ *noun* an official government document allowing the establishment of a bank

bank draft /'bæŋk drɑːft/ *noun* a cheque payable by a bank

banker's order /'bæŋkəz ˌɔːdə/ *noun* an order written by a customer asking a bank to make a regular payment to someone else

bank loan /'bæŋk ləʊn/ *noun* money lent by a bank

bank mandate /'bæŋk ˌmændeɪt/ *noun* a written order allowing someone to sign cheques on behalf of a company

bank note /'bæŋk nəʊt/, **banknote** /'bæŋknəʊt/ *noun* a piece of printed paper money (NOTE: The US term is **bill**.)

bank reserves /'bæŋk rɪˌzɜːvz/ *plural noun* cash and securities held by a bank to cover deposits

bankrupt /'bæŋkrʌpt/ *adjective* declared by a court not capable of paying debts ○ *He was declared bankrupt.* ○ *He went bankrupt after two years in business.* ∎ *noun* someone who has been declared by a court to be not capable of paying debts and whose affairs have been put into the hands of a trustee ∎ *verb* to make someone become bankrupt ○ *The recession bankrupted my father.*

bankruptcy /'bæŋkrʌptsi/ *noun* the state of being bankrupt ○ *The recession has caused thousands of bankruptcies.* (NOTE: The term bankruptcy is applied to individuals or partners, but for companies the term to use is **insolvency**.) ◇ **to file a petition in bankruptcy 1.** to apply to the Court to be made bankrupt **2.** to ask for someone else to be made bankrupt

COMMENT: Bankruptcy is considered a last-resort option for people unable to pay off their debts, and an **individual voluntary arrangement** will usually be reached first. If this fails and you are declared bankrupt, any personal assets (apart from those necessary to reasonably support yourself or your family) will be taken to pay off your debts. After a period of time, usually one year, any outstanding debts will be written off. A person's ability to get credit will be severely restricted both during and after the period of bankruptcy.

Bankruptcy Court /'bæŋkrʌptsi kɔːt/ *noun* a court which deals with bankruptcies

bankruptcy notice /ˌbæŋkrʌptsi 'nəʊtɪs/ *noun* a notice warning someone that they face bankruptcy if they fail to pay money which they owe

bankruptcy order /'bæŋkrʌptsi ˌɔːdə/ *noun* a legal order making someone bankrupt

bankruptcy petition /'bæŋkrʌptsi pəˌtɪʃ(ə)n/ *noun* an application to a court asking for an order making someone bankrupt

bankruptcy proceedings /'bæŋkrʌptsi prəˌsiːdɪŋz/ *plural noun* a court case to make someone bankrupt

bankruptcy restriction order /ˌbæŋkrʌptsi rɪ'strɪksən ˌɔːdə/ *noun* a court order imposing restrictions on a bankrupt granted at the request of the Official Receiver when the bankrupt has been dishonest or blameworthy

bank transfer /'bæŋk ˌtrænsfɜː/ *noun* the movement of money from a bank account to an account in another country

banning order /'bænɪŋ ˌɔːdə/ *noun* ♦ **drinking banning order, football banning order**

banns /bænz/ *plural noun* a declaration in church that a couple intend to get married ○ *to publish the banns of marriage between Anne Smith and John Jones*

bar /bɑː/ *noun* the set of rails in a court behind which the lawyers and public stand or sit □ **to be called to the bar** to pass examinations and fulfil specific requirements to become a barrister □ **prisoner at the bar** a prisoner being tried in court ∎ *verb* to forbid something, or make something illegal ○ *He was barred from attending the meeting.* ○ *The police commissioner barred the use of firearms.* ◇ **the Bar 1.** the profession of barrister **2.** all barristers or lawyers

Bar Council /'bɑː ˌkaʊns(ə)l/ *noun* the ruling body for English and Welsh barristers

bareboat charter /ˈbeəbəʊt ˌtʃɑːtə/ noun a charter of a ship in which the owner provides only the ship and not the crew, fuel or insurance

bargain /ˈbɑːgɪn/ noun **1.** something which is cheaper than usual **2.** an agreement between two people or groups to do something ■ verb to discuss something with someone in order to make an improvement for yourself

bargaining /ˈbɑːgɪnɪŋ/ noun the act of discussing something in order too reach an agreement that everyone is happy with. ◊ plea bargaining

bargaining position /ˈbɑːgɪnɪŋ pə ˌzɪʃ(ə)n/ noun a statement of position by one group during negotiations

bargaining power /ˈbɑːgɪnɪŋ ˌpaʊə/ noun the relative strength of one person or group when several people or groups are discussing prices, wages or contracts

baron /ˈbærən/ noun a prisoner who has power over other prisoners because he or she runs various rackets in a prison (slang)

barratry /ˈbærətri/ noun **1.** a criminal offence by which the master or crew of a ship damage the ship **2.** US an offence of starting a lawsuit with no grounds for doing so

barrister /ˈbærɪstə/ noun especially in England and Wales, a lawyer who can plead or argue a case in one of the higher courts

COMMENT: In England and Wales, a barrister is a member of one of the Inns of Court; he or she has passed examinations and spent one year in pupillage before being called to the Bar. Barristers have right of audience in all courts in England and Wales, that is to say they have the right to speak in court, but they do not have that right exclusively. Note also that barristers were formerly instructed only by solicitors and never by members of the public; now they can take instruction from professional people such as accountants. Barristers are now allowed to advertise their services. A barrister or a group of barristers is referred to as 'counsel'.

base /beɪs/ noun **1.** the lowest or first position **2.** the place where a company has its main office or factory, or the place where a businessperson has their office ○ The company has its base in London and branches in all European countries. ○ He has an office in Madrid which he uses as a base while he is travelling in Southern Europe. ■ verb **1.** to start to calculate or to negotiate from a position ○ We based our calculations on last year's turnover. **2.** to set up a company or a person in a place ○ a London-based sales executive ○ The European manager is based in our London office. ○ Our foreign branch is based in the Bahamas.

base costs /ˈbeɪs kɒsts/ noun the general costs of a case which apply before any percentage increase is assessed

based on /ˈbeɪst ɒn/ adjective calculating from

base year /ˈbeɪs jɪə/ noun the first year of an index, against which later years' changes are measured

basic award /ˈbeɪsɪk əˌwɔːd/ noun a minimum award, which is the first stage of assessing compensation

basic rate tax /ˈbeɪsɪk reɪt ˌtæks/ noun the lowest rate of income tax

basics /ˈbeɪsɪks/ plural noun simple and important facts □ **to get back to basics** to start discussing the basic facts again

basis /ˈbeɪsɪs/ noun **1.** a point or number from which calculations are made ○ We have calculated the turnover on the basis of a 6% price increase. **2.** the general facts on which something is based ○ We have three people working on a freelance basis. □ **on a short-term, long-term basis** for a short or long period ○ He has been appointed on a short-term basis.

bastard /ˈbɑːstəd/ noun a child who is illegitimate

BAT /bæt/ abbreviation Best Available Techniques

baton /ˈbætɒn/ noun a large stick used by the police for defence and to hit people with ○ The crowd was stopped by a row of policemen carrying batons.

baton charge /ˈbætɒn tʃɑːdʒ/ noun a charge by police using batons against a mob

baton round /ˈbætɒn raʊnd/ noun a thick bullet made of plastic fired from a special gun, used by the police only in self-defence. Also called **plastic bullet**

batter /ˈbætə/ verb to hit someone or something hard ○ The dead man had been battered to death with a hammer. ○ Police were battering on the door of the flat.

battered /ˈbætəd/ adjective frequently beaten as a punishment or act of cruelty □ **battered child**, **battered wife** a child who is frequently beaten by one of its parents, or a wife who is frequently beaten by her husband

battered wife syndrome, **battered woman syndrome** noun a situation in which a woman is subjected to regular and severe abuse by their partner, causing a mental condition similar to post-traumatic stress disorder

COMMENT: Battered wife syndrome may be used as a defence to an act of violence or murder towards the abusive partner.

battery /'bæt(ə)ri/ *noun* the crime or tort of using force against another person. Compare **assault**

beak /biːk/ *noun* a magistrate (*slang*)

bear /beə/ *verb* **1.** (*of costs*) to pay ○ *The company bore the legal costs of both parties.* **2.** □ **to bear on** to refer to or have an effect on ○ *The decision of the court bears on future cases where immigration procedures are disputed.*

bearing /'beərɪŋ/ *noun* an influence or effect □ **to have a bearing on** to refer to or have an effect on ○ *The decision of the court has a bearing on future cases where immigration procedures are disputed.*

beat /biːt/ *noun* an area which a policeman patrols regularly □ **the constable on the beat** the ordinary policeman on foot patrol ■ *verb* □ **to beat a ban** to do something which is going to be forbidden by doing it rapidly before the ban is enforced

Beddoe order /'bedəʊ ˌɔːdə/ *noun* a court order allowing a trustee to bring or defend an action and to recover any resulting costs from the trust property

behalf /bɪ'hɑːf/ *noun* □ **on behalf of** acting for someone or a company ○ *solicitors acting on behalf of the American company* ○ *I am writing on behalf of the minority shareholders.* ○ *She is acting on my behalf.*

belli ♦ **casus belli**

bellman /'belmən/ *noun* a criminal who specialises in stopping burglar alarms and other security devices (*slang*)

bench /bentʃ/ *noun* a place where judges or magistrates sit in court □ **to be up before the bench** to be in a magistrates' court, accused of a crime □ **to be on the bench** to be a magistrate

Bencher /'bentʃə/ *noun* one of the senior members of an Inn of Court

bench of magistrates /bentʃ əv 'mædʒɪˌstreɪts/ *noun* a group of magistrates in an area

bench warrant /'bentʃ ˌwɒrənt/ *noun* a warrant issued by a court for the arrest of an accused person who has not appeared to answer charges

benefactor /'benɪfæktə/ *noun* somebody who gives property or money to others, especially in a will

beneficial interest /ˌbenɪfɪʃ(ə)l 'ɪntrəst/ *noun* the interest of the beneficiary of a property or trust, which allows someone to occupy or receive rent from a property, while the property is owned by a trustee

beneficial occupier /ˌbenɪfɪʃ(ə)l 'ɒkjʊpaɪə/ *noun* somebody who occupies a property but does not own it

beneficial owner /ˌbenɪfɪʃ(ə)l 'əʊnə/ *noun* the true or ultimate owner whose interest may be concealed by a nominee

beneficial use /ˌbenɪ'fɪʃ(ə)l juːs/ *noun* the right to use, occupy or receive rent from a property which is owned by a trustee

beneficiary /ˌbenɪ'fɪʃəri/ *noun* **1.** somebody who is left property in a will ○ *The main beneficiaries of the will are the deceased's family.* **2.** somebody whose property is administered by a trustee

COMMENT: In a trust, the trustee is the legal owner of the property, while the beneficiary is the equitable owner who receives the real benefit of the trust.

benefit /'benɪfɪt/ *noun* money or advantage gained from something ○ *The estate was left to the benefit of the owner's grandsons.* ■ financial help given by the state to people with particular personal circumstances ○ *unemployment benefit* ○ *child benefit* ■ *noun* an advantage given to an employee in addition to basic salary, e.g. gym membership, parking, health insurance etc. ○ *The salary isn't wonderful but there are some great benefits.* ■ *verb* □ **to benefit from** or **by something** to be improved by something, to gain more money because of something

benefit fraud /'benɪfɪt frɔːd/ *noun* the act of fraudulently claiming money from the state to which you are not entitled

benefit thief /'benɪfɪt θiːf/ *noun* someone who commits benefit fraud (*informal*)

Benjamin order /'bendʒəmɪn ˌɔːdə/ *noun* an order from a court to a personal representative, which directs how someone's estate should be distributed

bent /bent/ *adjective* corrupt, stolen or illegal (*slang*) □ **bent copper** a corrupt policeman

bequeath /bɪ'kwiːð/ *verb* to leave property, but not freehold land, to someone in a will ○ *He bequeathed his shares to his daughter.*

bequest /bɪ'kwest/ noun money or property, but not freehold land, given to someone in a will ○ *He made several bequests to his staff.*

COMMENT: Freehold land given in a will is a **devise**.

Berne Convention /'bɜːn kən ˌvenʃ(ə)n/ noun an international agreement on the regulations governing copyright, signed in Berne in 1886. ◊ **copyright**

COMMENT: Under the Berne Convention, any book which is copyrighted in a country which has signed the convention is automatically copyrighted in the other countries. Some countries (notably the USA) did not sign the Convention, and the UCC (Universal Copyright Convention) was signed in Geneva in 1952, under the auspices of the United Nations, to try to bring together all countries under a uniform copyright agreement.

Best Available Techniques /ˌbest ə ˌveɪləb(ə)l tek'niːks/ plural noun advanced methods used in industrial production which limit the emission of pollutants, introduced by the Pollution Prevention and Control system. Abbreviation **BAT**

best evidence rule /ˌbest 'evɪd(ə)ns ˌruːl/ noun the rule that the best evidence possible should be produced, so an original document is preferred to a copy

bestiality /ˌbesti'ælɪti/ noun the offence of having sexual relations with an animal

betray /bɪ'treɪ/ verb to give away a secret ○ *He betrayed the secret to the enemy.* □ **to betray your country** to give away your country's secrets to an enemy

betrayal /bɪ'treɪəl/ noun an act of betraying someone or something

betrayal of trust /bɪˌtreɪəl əv 'trʌst/ noun an act against someone who trusts you

betting duty /ˌbetɪŋ 'djuːti/ noun a tax levied on the activity of placing bets on horse and dog races, etc.

BFP abbreviation US bona fide purchaser

bi- /baɪ/ prefix twice

bias /'baɪəs/ noun unfairly different treatment of a person or group as compared with others □ **likelihood of bias** a possibility that bias will occur because of a connection between a member of the court and a party in the case

biased /'baɪəst/ adjective unfairly favouring a person or group as compared with others

bible /'baɪb(ə)l/ noun a collection of signed agreements relating to a particular transaction

bigamist /'bɪɡəmɪst/ noun somebody who is married to two people at the same time

bigamous /'bɪɡəməs/ adjective referring to bigamy ○ *They went through a bigamous marriage ceremony.*

bigamy /'bɪɡəmi/ noun the notifiable offence of going through a ceremony of marriage to someone when you are still married to someone else. Compare **monogamy, polygamy**

bilateral /baɪ'læt(ə)rəl/ adjective (of an agreement) between two parties or countries ○ *The minister signed a bilateral trade agreement.*

bilateral contract /baɪˌlæt(ə)rəl kən 'trækt/ noun a contract where the two parties each have duties to the other

bilateral discharge /ˌbaɪlæt(ə)rəl 'dɪstʃɑːdʒ/ noun an agreement by two parties to bring a contract to an end by releasing each other from their existing obligations

bilateral investment treaty /baɪ ˌlæt(ə)rəl ɪn'vestmənt ˌtriːti/ noun treaties between two countries to promote and protect private investments between those two countries. Abbreviation **BIT**

bilaterally /ˌbaɪ'læt̬ər(ə)li/ adverb between two parties or countries ○ *The agreement was reached bilaterally.*

bilking /'baɪkɪŋ/ noun the offence of removing goods without paying for them, or of refusing to pay a bill

bill /bɪl/ noun 1. a written list of charges to be paid ○ *The salesman wrote out the bill.* ○ *Does the bill include VAT?* ○ *The builder sent in his bill.* ○ *He left the country without paying his bills.* □ **to foot the bill** to pay the costs 2. a list of charges in a restaurant ○ *Can I have the bill please?* ○ *The bill comes to £20 including service.* 3. a draft of a new law to be discussed by a legislature ○ *The house is discussing the Noise Prevention Bill.* ○ *The Finance Bill had its second reading yesterday.* 4. a written paper promising to pay money 5. *US* a piece of paper money ■ verb to present a bill to someone so that it can be paid ○ *The builders billed him for the repairs to his neighbour's house.*

COMMENT: In the UK, a Bill passes through the following stages in Parliament: **First Reading, Second Reading, Committee Stage, Report Stage** and **Third Reading.** The Bill goes through these stages first in the House of Commons and then in the House of Lords. When all the stages have been passed the Bill is given the Royal Assent and becomes law as an Act of Parliament. In the USA, a Bill is introduced either in the House or in the Senate, is referred to an appropriate committee with public hearings, then to general debate in the full House. The Bill is debated section by section and after being passed by both House and Senate is engrossed and sent to the President as a **joint resolution** for signature or veto.

bill of attainder /ˌbɪl əv əˈteɪndə/ *noun* formerly, a way of punishing a person legally without a trial, by passing a law to convict and sentence him or her

bill of exchange /ˌbɪl əv ɪksˈtʃeɪndʒ/ *noun* a document ordering the person to whom it is directed to pay a person money on demand or at a specified date

bill of health /ˌbɪl əv ˈhelθ/ *noun* a document given to the master of a ship showing that the ship is free of disease

bill of indictment /ˌbɪl əv ɪnˈdaɪtmənt/ *noun US* **1.** a draft of an indictment which is examined by the court, and when signed becomes an indictment **2.** a list of charges given to a grand jury, asking them to indict the accused

bill of lading /ˌbɪl əv ˈleɪdɪŋ/ *noun* a list of goods being shipped, which the shipper gives to the person sending the goods to show that they have been loaded

Bill of Rights /ˌbɪl əv ˈraɪts/ *noun US* those sections (i.e. the first ten amendments) of the constitution of the United States which refer to the rights and privileges of an individual

bill of sale /ˌbɪl əv ˈseɪl/ *noun* **1.** a document which the seller gives to the buyer to show that the sale has taken place **2.** a document given to a lender by a borrower to show that the lender owns the property as security for the loan

bills for collection /ˌbɪlz fə kəˈlekʃən/ *noun* bills where payment is due

bills payable /ˌbɪlz ˈpeɪəb(ə)l/ *noun* bills which a debtor will have to pay

bind /baɪnd/ *verb* to make someone obliged to obey a rule or keep a promise ○ *The company is bound by its articles of association.* ○ *He does not consider himself bound by the agreement which was signed by his predecessor.* ○ *High Court judges are bound by the decisions of the House of Lords.*

binder /ˈbaɪndə/ *noun US* a temporary acknowledgement of a contract of insurance sent before the insurance policy is issued (NOTE: The British English term is **cover note**.)

binding /ˈbaɪndɪŋ/ *adjective* having the ability to force someone to do something ○ *This document is legally binding* or *it is a legally binding document.* □ **the agreement is binding on all parties** all parties signing the agreement must do what is agreed

binding precedent /ˌbaɪndɪŋ ˈpresɪd(ə)nt/ *noun* a decision of a higher court which has to be followed by a judge in a lower court. Compare **persuasive precedent**

bind over /ˌbaɪnd ˈəʊvə/ *verb* **1.** to make someone promise to behave well and not commit another offence, or to return to court at a later date to face charges ○ *He was bound over (to keep the peace* or *to be of good behaviour) for six months.* **2.** *US* to order a defendant to be kept in custody while a criminal case is being prepared

bind-over order /ˌbaɪnd ˈəʊvə ˌɔːdə/ *noun* a court order which binds someone over ○ *The applicant sought judicial review to quash the bind-over order.*

biological parent /ˌbaɪəˌlɒdʒɪk(ə)l ˈpeərənt/ *noun* the mother or father to whom a child is born. Compare **adoptive parent, stepparent, foster parent**

biometric /ˌbaɪəʊˈmetrɪk/ *adjective* relating to physical or behavioural characteristics

biometric passport /ˌbaɪəʊmetrɪk ˈpɑːspɔːt/ *noun* a passport with a computer chip containing the holder's biometric information, launched in the UK in 2006

biometrics /ˌbaɪəʊˈmetrɪks/ *noun* the study of physical or behavioural characteristics, often used for the purposes of identity authentication

birth /bɜːθ/ *noun* the occasion of being born, or the social position relating to the circumstances of it. ◊ **concealment of birth** □ **by birth** according to where or to what family someone was born ○ *He's English by birth.* □ **date and place of birth** the day of the year when someone was born and the town where he or she was born

birth certificate /ˈbɜːθ səˌtɪfɪkət/ *noun* a document giving details of a person's date and place of birth

BIT *abbreviation* bilateral investment treaty

black /blæk/ *adjective* □ **to pay black market prices** to pay high prices to get items which are not easily available

black economy /ˌblæk ɪ'kɒnəmi/ *noun* the system by which work is paid for in cash or goods and not declared to the tax authorities

black letter law /ˌblæk 'letə ˌlɔː/ *noun* emphasis on the fundamental principles of law, as opposed to discussion of possible changes to the legal system to make it more perfect (*informal*)

black list /'blæk lɪst/ *noun* a list of goods, people or companies which are excluded from consideration or from receiving a privilege or service

blacklist /'blæklɪst/ *verb* to put goods, people or a company on a black list ○ *His firm was blacklisted by the government.*

blackmail /'blækmeɪl/ *noun* the notifiable offence of getting money from someone by threatening to make public information which he or she does not want revealed or by threatening violence ○ *He was charged with blackmail.* ○ *They got £25,000 from the managing director by blackmail.* ○ *She was sent to prison for blackmail.* ■ *verb* to threaten someone that you will make public information which he or she does not want revealed or to threaten an act of violence unless he or she does what you ask ○ *He was blackmailed by his former boss.*

blackmailer /'blækmeɪlə/ *noun* somebody who blackmails someone

black market /ˌblæk 'mɑːkɪt/ *noun* the illegal buying and selling goods that are not easily available or in order to avoid taxes ○ *There is a lucrative black market in spare parts for cars.* ○ *You can buy gold coins on the black market.* ■ *adjective* **black-market** bought on the black market ○ *They lived well on black-market goods.*

black marketeer /ˌblæk ˌmɑːkə'tiːə/ *noun* somebody who sells goods on the black market

blag /blæg/ *noun* a robbery by an armed gang (*slang*)

blanche ♦ **carte blanche**

blank cheque /ˌblæŋk 'tʃek/ *noun* a cheque with the amount of money and the payee left blank, but signed by the drawer

blanket agreement /ˌblæŋkɪt ə'griːmənt/ *noun* an agreement which covers many different items

blanket insurance policy /ˌblæŋkɪt ɪn 'ʃʊərəns ˌpɒlɪsi/ *noun* a policy covering several items

blaspheme /blæs'fiːm/ *verb* to ridicule or deny God or the Christian religion

blasphemy /'blæsfəmi/ *noun* formerly, the crime of ridiculing or denying God or the Christian religion in a scandalous way

block /blɒk/ *noun* **1.** a series of items grouped together ○ *He bought a block of 6,000 shares.* **2.** a series of buildings forming a square with streets on all sides **3.** a building in a prison ○ *a cell block* ○ *a hospital block* ■ *verb* to stop something taking place ○ *He used his casting vote to block the motion.* ○ *The planning committee blocked the plan to build a motorway through the middle of the town.*

blocked currency /ˌblɒkt 'kʌrənsi/ *noun* a currency which cannot be taken out of a country because of exchange controls

block exemption /ˌblɒk ɪg'zempʃ(ə)n/ *noun* an exemption granted to a large business or group of businesses exempting them from some obligations under competition law

blood relationship /ˌblʌd rɪ 'leɪʃ(ə)nʃɪp/ *noun* a relationship between people who have a common ancestor

blood sample /'blʌd ˌsɑːmpəl/ *noun* a small amount of blood taken from someone for a blood test

blood test /'blʌd test/ *noun* a test carried out on a blood sample to establish the paternity of a child, diagnose an illness or determine the alcohol content of the blood

blotter /'blɒtə/ *noun* US a book in which arrests are recorded at a police station

blue bag /'bluː bæg/ *noun* the blue bag in which a junior barrister carries his or her gown. ◊ **red bag**

Blue Book /ˌbluː 'bʊk/ *noun* an official report of a Royal Commission, bound in blue covers

blue laws /'bluː lɔːz/ *plural noun* US laws intended to uphold religious and moral standards, especially those prohibiting sale of goods on a Sunday

blue sky laws /ˌbluː 'skaɪ ˌlɔːz/ *plural noun* US state laws to protect investors against fraudulent traders in securities

board meeting /'bɔːd ˌmiːtɪŋ/ *noun* a meeting of the directors of a company

board of visitors /ˌbɔːd əv 'vɪzɪtəs/ *noun* in the UK, a group of people appointed by the Home Secretary to visit and inspect the conditions in prisons

bobby /'bɒbi/ *noun* a policeman (*informal*)

bodily /'bɒdɪli/ *adjective* affecting someone's body ○ *Fortunately no bodily harm had been caused.* ■ *adverb* **1.** in a way that has an effect on the body ○ *The police lifted the protester bodily and removed him from the street.* **2.** in person ○ *She had not been bodily present when the fight had started.*

body /'bɒdi/ *noun* **1.** the whole of a person or animal **2.** an organisation or group of people who work together ○ *Parliament is an elected body.* ○ *The governing body of the university has to approve the plan to give the President a honorary degree.* **3.** a large group or amount ○ *a body of evidence* □ **body of opinion** a group of people who have the same view about something ○ *There is a considerable body of opinion which believes that capital punishment should be reintroduced.*

bodyguard /'bɒdigɑːd/ *noun* somebody who protects someone ○ *The minister was followed by his three bodyguards.*

bogus caller /ˌbəʊgəs 'kɔːlə/ *noun* same as **distraction burglar**

boilerplate /'bɔɪləpleɪt/ *noun US* a standard form of agreement or contract with blank spaces to be filled in

bomb hoax /'bɒm həʊks/ *noun* the act of placing an imitation bomb in a public place or making a phone call to report a bomb which does not exist

bona fide purchaser /ˌbəʊnə ˌfaɪdi 'pɜːtʃəsə/ *noun* a purchaser who buys something in good faith

bona fides /ˌbəʊnə 'faɪdiːz/, **bona fide** /ˌbəʊnə 'faɪdi/ *phrase* a Latin phrase meaning 'good faith' or 'in good faith' ○ *He acted bona fide.* ○ *The respondent was not acting bona fides.* □ **a bona fide offer** an offer which is made honestly, which can be trusted

bona vacantia /ˌbəʊnə vəˈkæntiə/ *noun* property with no owner, or which does not have an obvious owner, and which usually passes to the Crown, as in the case of the estate of a person without living relatives dying without having made a will

bond /bɒnd/ *noun* **1.** a contract document promising to repay money borrowed by a company or by the government ○ *government bonds* or *treasury bonds* **2.** a contract document promising to repay money borrowed by a person **3.** a signed legal document which binds one or more parties to do or not to do something □ **goods (held) in bond** goods held by customs until duty has been paid □ **entry of goods under bond** bringing goods into a country in bond □ **to take goods out of bond** to pay duty on goods so that they can be released by customs

bonded /'bɒndɪd/ *adjective* held in bond

bonded goods /'bɒndɪd gʊdz/ *plural noun* goods which are held by customs under a bond until duty has been paid

bondholder /'bɒndˌhəʊldə/ *noun* somebody who holds government bonds

bondsman /'bɒndzmən/, **bondsperson** /'bɒndzˌpɜːs(ə)n/ *noun* somebody who has stood surety for another person

book /bʊk/ *noun* □ **to bring someone to book** to find a suspect and charge him or her with a crime □ **to throw the book at someone** to charge someone with every possible crime (*informal*) ○ *If ever we get the gang in the police station, we'll throw the book at them.* ■ *verb* **1.** to charge someone with a crime (*informal*) ○ *He was booked for driving on the wrong side of the road.* **2.** to order or to reserve something ○ *to book a room in a hotel* or *a table at a restaurant* or *a ticket on a plane* ○ *I booked a table for 7.45.* ○ *He booked a ticket through to Cairo.* □ **to book someone into a hotel**, **onto a flight** to order a room or a plane ticket for someone

book value /'bʊk ˌvæljuː/ *noun* the value of a company's assets as shown in the company accounts

boot camp /'buːt kæmp/ *noun US* a camp providing a form of treatment for young offenders where they are subjected to harsh discipline for a short period

bootleg /'buːtleg/ *adjective* (*of alcohol*) illegally produced and sold

bootlegger /'buːtlegə/ *noun* somebody who makes or supplies illicit alcohol

bootlegging /'buːtlegɪŋ/ *noun* **1.** the production of illicit alcohol **2.** the production of illegal records or tapes from live concerts

border control /'bɔːdə kənˌtrəʊl/ *noun* the monitoring and control of a country's borders, often to prevent illegal immigration

borrow /'bɒrəʊ/ *verb* **1.** to take money from someone for a time, possibly paying interest for it, and repaying it at the end of the period ○ *He borrowed £1,000 from the bank.* ○ *The company had to borrow heavily to repay its debts.* ○ *They borrowed £25,000* *against the security of the factory.* **2.** to steal (*slang*)

borrower /'bɒrəʊə/ *noun* somebody who borrows ○ *Borrowers from the bank pay 12% interest.*

borrowing /'bɒrəʊɪŋ/ *noun* the action of borrowing money ○ *The new factory was financed by bank borrowing.*

borrowing power /'bɒrəʊɪŋ ˌpaʊə/ *noun* the amount of money which an individual or group can borrow

borrowings /'bɒrəʊɪŋz/ *plural noun* money borrowed ○ *The company's borrowings have doubled.*

borstal /'bɔːst(ə)l/ *noun* formerly, a centre where a young offender was sent for training after committing a crime which would normally be punishable by a prison sentence (NOTE: Now replaced by **Young Offender Institutions.**)

boss /bɒs/ *noun* the head of a Mafia family or other criminal gang (*slang*)

bottomry /'bɒtəmri/ *noun* the mortgage of a ship or cargo

bottomry bond /'bɒtəmri bɒnd/ *noun* a bond which secures a ship or cargo against a loan

bounce /baʊns/ *verb* (*of a cheque*) to be returned unpaid to the person who has tried to cash it, because there is not enough money in the payer's account (*informal*) ○ *He paid for the car with a cheque that bounced.*

bounced cheque /ˌbaʊnst 'tʃek/ *noun* a cheque which the bank refuses to pay because the person writing it has not enough money in his or her bank account to cover it

bound /baʊnd/ ♦ **duty bound**

boundary /'baʊnd(ə)ri/, **boundary line** /'baʊnd(ə)ri laɪn/ *noun* a line marking the edge of a piece of land owned by someone ○ *The boundary dispute dragged through the courts for years.*

Boundary Commission /ˌbaʊnd(ə)ri kə'mɪʃ(ə)n/ *noun* a committee which examines the area and population of constituencies for the House of Commons and recommends changes to ensure that each Member of Parliament represents approximately the same number of people

bounty /'baʊnti/ *noun* a payment made by government to someone who has saved lives or found treasure

box /bɒks/ *noun* ♦ **witness box**

bracelets /'breɪsləts/ *plural noun* handcuffs (*slang*)

branch /brɑːntʃ/ *noun* **1.** a local office of a bank or large business ○ *The bank or the store has branches in most towns in the south of the country.* ○ *The insurance company has closed its branches in South America.* ○ *He is the manager of our local branch of Lloyds bank.* **2.** a local shop of a large chain of shops **3.** a part or separate section of a area of knowledge or study such as the law ○ *The Law of Contract and the Law of Tort are branches of civil law.* **4.** ♦ **Special Branch**

breach /briːtʃ/ *noun* **1.** failure to carry out the terms of an agreement ○ *They alleged that a breach of international obligations had been committed.* □ **in breach of** failing to do something which was agreed, not acting according to ○ *We are in breach of Community law.* ○ *The defendant is in breach of his statutory duty.* **2.** failure to obey the law ○ *The soldier was charged with a serious breach of discipline.*

breach of confidence /ˌbriːtʃ əv 'kɒnfɪd(ə)ns/ *noun* the release of confidential information without permission

breach of contract /ˌbriːtʃ əv 'kɒntrækt/ *noun* an act of breaking the terms of a contract □ **the company is in breach of contract** the company has failed to carry out what was agreed in the contract

breach of promise /ˌbriːtʃ əv 'prɒmɪs/ *noun* formerly, a complaint in court that someone had promised to marry the claimant and then had not done so

breach of the peace /ˌbriːtʃ əv ðə 'piːs/ *noun* the act of creating a disturbance which is likely to annoy or frighten people

COMMENT: A police officer can arrest someone for breach of the peace who has not yet committed the offence, as long as there is reasonable belief that they would do if allowed to continue.

breach of trust /ˌbriːtʃ əv 'trʌst/ *noun* a failure on the part of a trustee to act properly in regard to a trust

breach of warranty /ˌbriːtʃ əv 'wɒrənti/ *noun* a failure to supply goods which not meet the standards of the warranty applied to them

break /breɪk/ *noun* a short space of time when you can rest ○ *The court adjourned for a ten-minute break.* ■ *verb* **1.** □ **to break the law** to do something which is against the law ○ *If you hit a policeman you will be breaking the law.* ○ *He is breaking the law by parking on the pavement.* ○ *The company broke section 26 of the Companies Act.* **2.** ○

The company has broken the contract or the agreement. □ **to break a contract** to fail to carry out the duties of a contract ○ *The company has broken the contract or the agreement.* □ **to break an engagement to do something** not to do what has been agreed

break down /ˌbreɪk ˈdaʊn/ *verb* **1.** to stop working because of mechanical failure ○ *The two-way radio has broken down.* ○ *What do you do when your squad car breaks down?* **2.** to stop ○ *negotiations broke down after six hours* ○ *Their marriage broke down and they separated.* **3.** to show all the items in a total list ○ *We broke the crime figures down into crimes against the person and crimes against property.* ○ *Can you break down this invoice into spare parts and labour?*

breakdown /ˈbreɪkdaʊn/ *noun* **1.** an occasion of stopping work because of mechanical failure ○ *We cannot communicate with our squad car because of the breakdown of the radio link.* **2.** a situation in which something such as discussions or negotiations fail or begin to fail ○ *a breakdown in talks* **3.** □ **irretrievable breakdown of a marriage** a situation where the two spouses can no longer live together, where the marriage cannot be saved and therefore divorce proceedings can be started **4.** the process of showing details item by item ○ *Give me a breakdown of the latest clear-up figures.*

break in /ˌbreɪk ˈɪn/ *verb* to go into a building by force in order to steal ○ *Burglars broke in through a window at the back of the house.*

break-in /ˈbreɪk ɪn/ *noun* the crime of breaking into a house (*informal*) ○ *There have been three break-ins in our street in one week.*

breaking and entering /ˌbreɪkɪŋ ənd ˈentərɪŋ/ *noun* the crime of going into a building by force and stealing things ○ *He was charged with breaking and entering.* ◊ **burglary**

break into /ˌbreɪk ˈɪntʊ/ *verb* to go into a building by force to steal things ○ *Their house was broken into while they were on holiday.* ○ *Looters broke into the supermarket.*

break off /ˌbreɪk ˈɒf/ *verb* to stop ○ *We broke off the discussion at midnight.* ○ *Management broke off negotiations with the union.*

break up /ˌbreɪk ˈʌp/ *verb* **1.** to split something large into small sections ○ *The*

company was broken up and separate divisions sold off. **2.** to come to an end, or make something come to an end ○ *The meeting broke up at 12.30.* ○ *The police broke up the protest meeting.*

breathalyse /ˈbreθəlaɪz/ *verb* to test someone's breath using a breathalyser

breathalyser /ˈbreθəlaɪzə/ *noun* a device for testing the amount of alcohol a person has drunk by testing his or her breath

breath test /ˈbreθ test/ *noun* a test where a person's breath is sampled to establish the amount of alcohol he or she has drunk

bribe /braɪb/ *noun* money offered corruptly to someone to get them to do something that helps you ○ *The police sergeant was dismissed for taking bribes.* ■ *verb* to give someone a bribe ○ *He bribed the police sergeant to get the charges dropped.*

bribery /ˈbraɪb(ə)ri/ *noun* the crime of giving someone a bribe ○ *Bribery in the security warehouse is impossible to stamp out.*

brief /briːf/ *noun* **1.** details of a client's case, prepared by a solicitor and given to the barrister who is going to argue the case in court **2.** a lawyer or barrister (*slang*) ■ *verb* to explain something to someone in detail ○ *The superintendent briefed the press on the progress of the investigation.* □ **to brief a barrister** to give a barrister all the details of the case which he or she will argue in court

briefing /ˈbriːfɪŋ/ *noun* an occasion when someone is given details about something that is going to happen ○ *All the detectives on the case attended a briefing given by the commander.*

bring forward /ˌbrɪŋ ˈfɔːwəd/ *verb* to make earlier ○ *to bring forward the date of repayment* ○ *The date of the hearing has been brought forward to March.*

bring in /ˌbrɪŋ ˈɪn/ *verb* to decide a verdict ○ *The jury brought in a verdict of not guilty.*

bring up /ˌbrɪŋ ˈʌp/ *verb* to refer to something for the first time ○ *The chairman brought up the question of corruption in the police force.*

broker /ˈbrəʊkə/ *noun* someone who buys or sells something on behalf of someone else, often as an agent ○ *stockbroker* ○ *insurance broker*

brothel /ˈbrɒθ(ə)l/ *noun* a house where sexual intercourse is offered for money

Budgeting Loan /ˈbʌdʒɪtɪŋ ləʊn/ *noun* an interest-free loan made by the Government to people on income support to help with unexpected expenses, e.g. emergency repairs (NOTE: This is made out of the Government's **Social Fund**.)

bug /bʌg/ *noun* a small device which can record conversations secretly and send them to a secret radio receiver ○ *The cleaners planted a bug under the lawyer's desk.* Also called **bugging device**, **surveillance device** ■ *verb* to place a secret device in a place so that conversations can be heard and recorded secretly ○ *The agents bugged the President's office.*

buggery /'bʌgəri/ *noun* a former notifiable offence of sexual intercourse with animals, or rectal intercourse with a man (NOTE: It was repealed as an offence by the Sexual Offences Act 2003, along with **gross indecency**.)

bugging device /'bʌgɪŋ dɪ,vaɪs/ *noun* same as **bug** ○ *Police found a bugging device under the lawyer's desk.*

building permit /'bɪldɪŋ ,pɜːmɪt/ *noun* an official document which allows someone to build on a piece of land

Bullock order /'bʊlək ,ɔːdə/ *noun* in civil proceedings where the claimant has succeeded in establishing a claim against one defendant but has failed in relation to the second defendant, an order that requires the claimant to pay the successful defendant's costs but allows the money which will come from the unsuccessful defendant to be included

bumping /'bʌmpɪŋ/ *noun* **1.** a series of movements of staff between jobs which results in the final person in the chain being made redundant **2.** *US* a situation where a senior employee takes the place of a junior employee

bunco /'bʌŋkəʊ/ *noun* a dishonest act of cheating someone out of money, usually at cards (*slang*)

bundle /'bʌnd(ə)l/ *noun* ♦ **trial bundle**

burden of proof /,bɜːd(ə)n əv 'pruːf/ *noun* the duty to prove that something which has been alleged in court is true □ **to**

discharge a burden of proof to prove something which has been alleged in court □ **the burden of proof is on the prosecution** the prosecution must prove that what it alleges is true

bureau /'bjʊərəʊ/ *noun* an office which specialises in particular work

burglar /'bɜːglə/ *noun* a person who steals or tries to steal goods from property, or who enters property intending to commit a crime

burglar alarm /'bɜːglər ə,lɑːm/ *noun* a bell which is set to ring when someone tries to break into a house or shop ○ *As he put his hand through the window he set off the burglar alarm.*

burglarize *verb* *US* to steal goods from property (*informal*)

burglary /'bɜːgləri/ *noun* the crime of going into a building at night, usually by force, and stealing things ○ *He was charged with burglary.* ○ *There has been a series of burglaries in our street.*

burgle /'bɜːg(ə)l/ *verb* to steal goods from property ○ *The school was burgled when the caretaker was on holiday.*

business name /'bɪznɪs neɪm/ *noun* the name under which a firm or company trades

business premises /'bɪznɪs ,premɪsɪz/ *plural noun* a building or set of buildings and land used for the purpose of carrying out a business activity

bust /bʌst/ *verb* to catch and punish someone for doing something that is illegal

bylaw /'baɪlɔː/, **byelaw, by-law** /baɪ lɔː/, **bye-law** *noun* **1.** a rule governing an aspect of the internal running of a corporation, club or association such as number of meetings or election of officers **2.** a rule or law made by a local authority or public body and not by central government ○ *The bylaws forbid playing ball in the public gardens.* ○ *According to the local bylaws, noise must be limited in the town centre.*

COMMENT: Bylaws must be made by bodies which have been authorised by Parliament before they can become legally effective.

C

© the copyright symbol

COMMENT: The symbol was adopted by the Universal Copyright Convention in Geneva in 1952. Publications bearing the symbol are automatically covered by the convention. The copyright line in a book should give the © followed by the name of the copyright holder and the date.

CAB /ˌsi: eɪ ˈbi:, kæb/ *abbreviation* Citizens' Advice Bureaux

cadaver /kəˈdævə/ *noun US* a dead human body (NOTE: The British term is **corpse**.)

cadet /kəˈdet/ *noun* a trainee police officer ○ *He has entered the police cadet college.* ○ *She joined the police force as a cadet.*

Calderbank Letter /ˈkɔːldəbæŋk ˌletə/ *noun* an offer or payment made during divorce proceedings by a defendant to a claimant to settle all or part of a claim (NOTE: This is equivalent to a **Part 36 offer**, but is specific to divorce proceedings.)

calendar /ˈkælɪndə/ *noun* a book or set of sheets of paper showing all the days and months in a year ○ *a desk calendar*

calendar month /ˈkælɪndə mʌnθ/ *noun* a whole month as on a calendar, from the 1st to the 28th, 30th or 31st

calendar year /ˌkælɪndə ˈjɪə/ *noun* one year from the 1st January to 31st December

call /kɔːl/ *noun* **1.** a conversation on the telephone **2.** a demand for repayment of a loan by a lender **3.** the admission of a barrister to the bar **4.** a particular number of years a barrister has practised at the bar □ **to be ten years' call** to have been practising for ten years **5.** a visit ○ *The doctor makes six calls a day.* ■ *verb* **1.** to telephone to someone ○ *I shall call you at your office tomorrow.* **2.** to admit someone to the bar to practise as a barrister ○ *He was called (to the bar) in 2005.*

call in /ˌkɔːl ˈɪn/ *verb* **1.** to ask someone to come to help ○ *The local police decided to call in the CID to help in the murder hunt.* **2.** to ask for plans to be sent to the ministry for examination ○ *The minister has called in the plans for the new supermarket.*

camera /ˈkæm(ə)rə/ ♦ **in camera**

campaign /kæmˈpeɪn/ *noun* a planned method of working ○ *The government has launched a campaign against drunken drivers.* ■ *verb* to try to change something by writing about it, organising protest meetings or lobbying Members of Parliament ○ *They are campaigning for the abolition of the death penalty* or *they are campaigning against the death penalty.* ○ *He is campaigning for a revision of the Official Secrets Act.*

campaigner /kæmˈpeɪnə/ *noun* a person who is working actively to support an issue or organisation ○ *He is an experienced political campaigner.* ○ *She is a campaigner for women's rights.*

cancel /ˈkæns(ə)l/ *verb* **1.** to stop something which has been agreed or planned ○ *to cancel an appointment* or *a meeting* ○ *to cancel a contract* **2.** □ **to cancel a cheque** to stop payment of a cheque which you have signed

cancellandi ♦ **animus cancellandi**

cancellation /ˌkænsəˈleɪʃ(ə)n/ *noun* the act of stopping something which has been agreed or planned ○ *cancellation of an appointment* ○ *cancellation of an agreement*

cancellation clause /ˌkænsəˈleɪʃ(ə)n klɔːz/ *noun* a clause in a contract which states the terms on which the contract may be cancelled

candidacy /ˈkændɪdəsi/, **candidature** /ˈkændɪdətʃə/ *noun* the state of being a candidate ○ *The Senator has announced his candidacy for the Presidential election.*

candidate /ˈkændɪdeɪt/ *noun* **1.** somebody who applies for a job ○ *There are six candidates for the post of security guard.* ○ *We interviewed ten candidates for the job.* **2.** somebody who puts themselves forward for election ○ *Which candidate are you voting for?*

canon law /ˌkænən ˈlɔː/ *noun* law applied by the Anglican and Roman Catholic churches to priests (NOTE: Formerly it was also applied to other members of the church in cases of marriage, legitimacy and personal property.)

capacity /kəˈpæsɪti/ *noun* **1.** the amount of something which can be produced or contained **2.** ability ○ *He has a particular capacity for hard work.* **3.** the ability to enter into a legally binding agreement, which is one of the essential elements of a contract □ **person of full age and capacity** person who is over eighteen years of age and of sound mind, and therefore able to enter into a contract **4.** a role or job □ **in his capacity as chairman** acting as chairman □ **speaking in an official capacity** speaking officially

capax ♦ **doli capax**

capias /ˈkæpiæs/ *phrase* a Latin word meaning 'that you take': used in phrases to indicate that several writs have been issued together

capias ad respondendum /ˌkæpiæs æd ˌrespɒnˈdendəm/ *phrase* a Latin phrase meaning 'that you take to hear the judgment': an order summoning a defendant who has not attended their hearing to come and hear the judgment

capita /ˈkæpɪtə/ ♦ **per capita**

capital /ˈkæpɪt(ə)l/ *noun* **1.** the money, property and assets used in a business □ **to make political capital out of something** to use something to give you an advantage in politics ○ *The Opposition made a lot of capital out of the Minister's mistake on TV.* ◊ **expenditure 2.** a town or city where the government of a province or country is situated

capital allowance /ˌkæpɪt(əl əˈlaʊəns/ *noun* a variable tax reduction resulting from the expenditure on items such as machinery used in connection with the business

capital assets /ˌkæpɪt(ə)l ˈæsets/ *plural noun* property or machinery which a company owns and uses in its business

capital crime /ˌkæpɪt(ə)l ˈkraɪm/ *noun* a crime for which the punishment is death

COMMENT: Under the 13th Protocol of the European Convention of Human Rights, the death penalty is prohibited under all circumstances. The UK acceded to this in 2003.

capital expenditure /ˌkæpɪt(ə)l ɪk ˈspendɪtʃə/ *noun* **1.** money spent on assets such as property or machinery **2.** the major costs of a council or central government, such as schools, roads, hospitals, etc.

capital gains /ˌkæpɪt(ə)l ˈɡeɪnz/ *plural noun* money made by selling a fixed asset or by selling shares at a profit

capital gains tax /ˌkæpɪt(ə)l ˈɡeɪnz ˌtæks/ *noun* the tax payable where an asset has increased in value during the period of ownership. Abbreviation **CGT**

capital goods /ˈkæpɪt(ə)l ɡʊdz/ *plural noun* machinery, buildings and raw materials which are used in the production of goods

capital levy /ˌkæpɪt(ə)l ˈlevi/ *noun* a tax on the value of a person's property and possessions

capital loss /ˌkæpɪt(ə)l ˈlɒs/ *noun* a loss made by selling assets

capital punishment /ˌkæpɪt(ə)l ˈpʌnɪʃmənt/ *noun* punishment of a criminal by execution

COMMENT: Capital punishment has been abolished in many countries including the majority of Europe, Australasia and South America. North America, the Caribbean, Japan and India are among the countries which can still award the death penalty, usually for murder and treason and sometimes for large-scale drugs offences. Methods of execution include the electric chair, lethal injection and hanging.

capital transfer tax /ˌkæpɪt(ə)l ˈtrænsfɜː ˌtæks/ *noun* a tax paid on the transfer of capital or assets from one person to another. Abbreviation **CTT**

caption /ˈkæpʃən/ *noun* a formal heading for an indictment, affidavit or other court document, giving details such as the names of the parties, the court which is hearing the case, and relevant reference numbers

carbon permit /ˈkɑːbən ˌpɜːmɪt/ *noun* government-issued licence under the Kyoto Agreement, allowing a company to emit a limited amount of industrial greenhouse gases (NOTE: The production of greenhouse gases without a licence is punishable by a fine or other sanction.)

carbon trading /ˈkɑːbən ˌtreɪdɪŋ/ *noun* same as **emissions trading**

card not present fraud /ˌkɑːd nɒt ˈprezənt ˌfrɔːd/ *noun* the fraudulent use of credit or debit card details for transactions where the card itself does not need to be present, such as via the internet or mail order

care /keə/ *noun* **1.** the act of looking after someone ○ *The children were put in the care of the social services department.* **2.** the activity of making sure that someone is not harmed

care and control /ˌkeə ən kən'trəʊl/ *noun* responsibility for day-to-day decisions relating to the welfare of a child

caregiver /'keə,gɪvə/ *noun* same as **carer**

careless /'keələs/ *adjective* without paying attention to other people

careless driving /ˌkeələs 'draɪvɪŋ/ *noun* driving without due care and attention □ **causing death by careless driving** the offence committed by an individual who drives despite being unfit to do so as a result of drink or drugs, causing the death of another person

care order /'keə ,ɔːdə/ *noun* a court order placing a child under the care of a local authority, granted when the child is suffering or likely to suffer significant harm if it continues to remain under its parents care

care proceedings /'keə prə,siːdɪŋz/ *plural noun* court proceedings to determine whether a child should be made the subject of a care order. ◊ **care order**

carer /'keərə/ *noun* someone who looks after an adult with special mental or physical needs, often a spouse or family member

carer's allowance /'keərəz ə,laʊəns/ *noun* a payment given by the Government to someone over the age of 16 who spends more than 35 hours a week caring for an adult with special mental or physical needs

car insurance /'kɑːr ɪn,ʃʊərəns/ *noun* a policy insuring a car, the driver and passengers in case of accident

carjacking /'kɑːdʒækɪŋ/ *noun US* the crime of stealing a vehicle while it is occupied, typically by forcing entry and physically ejecting the driver

carriageway /'kærɪdʒweɪ/ *noun* a public way where people have a right to go in vehicles

carrier /'kæriə/ *noun* a person or company which takes goods from one place to another

carrier's lien /ˌkæriəz 'liːən/ *noun* the right of a carrier to hold goods until he or she has been paid for carrying them

carry /'kæri/ *verb* **1.** to take from one place to another ○ *The train was carrying a consignment of cars.* □ **carrying offensive weapons** the offence of holding a weapon or something such as a bottle which could

be used as a weapon **2.** to be punishable by ○ *The offence carries a maximum sentence of two years' imprisonment.* **3.** to vote to approve □ **to carry a motion** to accept a motion following a vote

carte blanche /ˌkɑːt 'blɑːntʃ/ *phrase* permission given by someone to another person, allowing him or her to act in any way necessary to achieve something ○ *He has carte blanche to act on behalf of the company* or *the company has given him carte blanche to act on its behalf.*

cartel /kɑː'tel/ *noun* a group of companies who illegally and secretly agree to fix the price of their products in order to destroy the competition

case /keɪs/ *noun* **1.** a possible crime and its investigation by the police ○ *We have three detectives working on the case.* ○ *The police are treating the case as murder* or *are treating it as a murder case.* ○ *We had six cases of looting during the night.* **2.** a set of arguments or facts put forward by one side in legal proceedings ○ *Defence counsel put his case.* ○ *There is a strong case against the accused.* □ **the case rests** all the arguments for one side have been put forward □ **no case to answer** a submission by the defence (after the prosecution has put its case) that the case should be dismissed ■ *verb* □ **to case a joint** to look at a building carefully before deciding how to break into it (*slang*)

COMMENT: A case is referred to by the names of the parties, the date and the reference source where details of it can be found: *Smith v. Jones 2007 2 W.L.R. 250* This shows that the case involved Smith as plaintiff and Jones as defendant, it was heard in 2007, and is reported in the second volume of the Weekly Law Reports for that year on page 250.

case law /'keɪs lɔː/ *noun* law established by precedents, that is by the decisions of courts in earlier similar cases

case management conference /keɪs ˌmænɪdʒmənt 'kɒnf(ə)rəns/ *noun* a court hearing fixed when a case is allocated, when the parties involved and their legal representatives are asked about their preparations for the case and the court decides on matters such as the disclosure of documents and expert evidence

case stated /ˌkeɪs 'steɪtɪd/ *noun* a statement of the facts of a case which has been heard in a lower court such as a Magistrates' Court, drawn up so that a higher court such as the High Court can decide on an appeal

case summary /ˌkeɪs 'sʌməri/ *noun* a short document of not more than 500 words prepared by a claimant to help the court understand what the case is about

cash settlement /ˌkæʃ 'set(ə)lmənt/ *noun* the payment of an invoice in cash, not by cheque

cash terms /'kæʃ tɜːmz/ *plural noun* lower terms which apply if the customer pays cash

cast /kɑːst/ *verb* □ **to cast a vote** to vote ○ *The number of votes cast in the election was 125,458.*

casting vote /ˌkɑːstɪŋ 'vəʊt/ *noun* a vote used by the chair in a case where the votes for and against a proposal are equal ○ *The chairman has a casting vote.* ○ *He used his casting vote to block the motion.* (NOTE: **casting – cast – has cast**)

casual /'kæʒuəl/ *adjective* not permanent or not regular ○ *a casual employee*

casual labour /ˌkæʒuəl 'leɪbə/ *noun* people who are hired to work for a short period

casual work /'kæʒuəl wɜːk/ *noun* work where people are hired for a short period

casus belli /ˌkɑːzəs 'beliː/ *phrase* a Latin phrase meaning 'case for war': a reason which is used to justify a declaration of war

category /'kætɪg(ə)ri/ *noun* a type of item ○ *The theft comes into the category of petty crime.*

category A prisoner /ˌkætɪg(ə)ri eɪ 'prɪz(ə)nə/ *noun* a prisoner who is regarded as a danger to the public and must be closely guarded to prevent escape

category B prisoner /ˌkætɪg(ə)ri biː 'prɪz(ə)nə/ *noun* a prisoner who is less dangerous than a category A prisoner but who still has to be guarded carefully to prevent escape

category C prisoner /ˌkætɪg(ə)ri siː 'prɪz(ə)nə/ *noun* a prisoner who is not likely to try to escape, but who cannot be kept in an open prison

category D prisoner /ˌkætɪg(ə)ri diː 'prɪz(ə)nə/ *noun* a reliable prisoner who can be kept in an open prison

causa ♦ **donatio mortis causa**

cause /kɔːz/ *noun* **1.** something which makes something happen □ **to show cause** to appear before a court to show why an order nisi should not be made absolute ○ *The judgment debtor was given fourteen*

days in which to show cause why the charging order should not be made absolute. **2.** legal proceedings ■ *verb* to make something happen ○ *The recession caused hundreds of bankruptcies.*

cause list /'kɔːz lɪst/ *noun* a list of cases which are to be heard by a court

cause of action /ˌkɔːz əv 'ækʃən/ *noun* the reasons that entitle someone to start legal proceedings

caution /'kɔːʃ(ə)n/ *noun* **1.** a warning from a police officer, telling someone not to repeat a minor crime ○ *The boys were let off with a caution.* **2.** a warning by a police officer to someone who is to be charged with a crime that what he or she says may be used as evidence in a trial ○ *He was arrested under caution.* **3.** a document lodged at the Land Registry to prevent land or property being sold without notice to the cautioner (NOTE: In senses 2 and 3 **caution** can be used without **the** or **a**: *to lodge caution*.) ■ *verb* **1.** to warn someone that what he or she has done is wrong and should not be repeated ○ *The boys were cautioned after they were caught stealing sweets.* **2.** to warn someone who is to be charged with a crime that what he or she says may be used as evidence in a trial ○ *The accused was arrested by the detectives and cautioned.*

cautioner /'kɔːʃ(ə)nə/ *noun* somebody who lodges caution at the Land Registry

caveat /'kæviæt/ *noun* a warning □ **to enter a caveat** to warn legally that you have an interest in a case or a grant of probate, and that no steps can be taken without notice to you

caveat emptor /ˌkæviæt 'emptɔː/ *phrase* a Latin phrase meaning 'let the buyer beware': used to show that the buyer is personally responsible for checking that what he or she buys is in good order

caveator /'kæviætə/ *noun* somebody who warns the court not to give probate without asking his or her consent

CB *abbreviation* confined to barracks

CC /ˌsiː 'siː/ *abbreviation* Chief Constable

CCJ *abbreviation* county court judgment

CCR *abbreviation* County Court Rules

CCRC *abbreviation* Criminal Cases Review Commission

CD /ˌsiː 'diː/ *abbreviation* certificate of deposit

CDS *abbreviation* Criminal Defence Service

cease and desist order /ˌsiːs ən dɪ ˈzɪst ˌɔːdə/ *noun US* a court order telling someone to stop doing something

CEDR *abbreviation* Centre for Effective Dispute Resolution

cell /sel/ *noun* a small room in a prison or police station where a criminal can be kept locked up ○ *She was put in a small cell for the night.* ○ *He shares a cell with two other prisoners.*

cellmate /ˈselmeɪt/ *noun* somebody who shares a prison cell with someone else

censor /ˈsensə/ *noun* an official whose job is to say whether books, films or TV programmes, etc., are acceptable and can be published or shown to the public ○ *The film was cut* or *was banned* or *was passed by the censor.* ■ *verb* to say that a book, film or TV programme, etc., cannot be shown or published, e.g. because it is potentially offensive ○ *All press reports are censored by the government.* ○ *The TV report has been censored and only parts of it can be shown.*

censorship /ˈsensəʃɪp/ *noun* the act of restricting or editing material that is published, e.g. because it is potentially offensive ○ *TV reporters complained of government censorship.* ○ *The government has imposed strict press censorship* or *censorship of the press.*

censure /ˈsenʃə/ *noun* a criticism ■ *verb* to criticise

Central Criminal Court /ˌsentrəl ˈkrɪmɪn(ə)l kɔːt/ *noun* the Crown Court in central London. Also called **Old Bailey**

central government /ˌsentrəl ˈɡʌv(ə)nmənt/ *noun* the main organisation dealing with the affairs of an entire country

central office /ˌsentrəl ˈɒfɪs/ *noun* the main office which controls all smaller offices

centre /ˈsentə/ *noun* an office or building where people can go for information and advice. ◊ **Legal Aid Centre**

Centre for Effective Dispute Resolution /ˌsentə fər ɪˌfektɪv dɪsˈpjuːt ˌrezəluːʃ(ə)n/ *noun* an institution providing alternative dispute resolution services such as mediation. Abbreviation **CEDR**

CEOP *abbreviation* Child Exploitation and Online Protection Centre

certificate /səˈtɪfɪkət/ *noun* an official document which confirms a fact ○ *birth certificate*

certificated bankrupt /səˌtɪfɪkeɪtɪd ˈbæŋkrʌpt/ *noun* a bankrupt who has been

discharged from bankruptcy with a certificate to show that he or she was not at fault

certificate of approval /səˌtɪfɪkət əv ə ˈpruːv(ə)l/ *noun* a document showing that an item has been officially approved

certificate of deposit /səˌtɪfɪkət əv dɪ ˈpɒzɪt/ *noun* a document from a bank showing that money has been deposited. Abbreviation **CD**

certificate of incorporation /səˌtɪfɪkət əv ɪnˌkɔːpəˈreɪʃ(ə)n/ *noun* a certificate issued by the Registrar of Companies showing that a company has been officially incorporated and the date at which it came into existence

certificate of judgment /səˌtɪfɪkət əv ˈdʒʌdʒmənt/ *noun* an official document showing the decision of a court

certificate of origin /səˌtɪfɪkət əv ˈɒrɪdʒɪn/ *noun* a document showing where goods were made or produced

certificate of registration /səˌtɪfɪkət əv ˌredʒɪˈstreɪʃ(ə)n/ *noun* a document showing that an item has been registered

certificate of registry /səˌtɪfɪkət əv ˈredʒɪstri/ *noun* a document showing that a ship has been officially registered

certificate of service /səˌtɪfɪkət əv ˈsɜːvɪs/ *noun* a certificate by which a court proves that a document was sent and is deemed to have been served

certified accountant /ˌsɜːtɪfaɪd ə ˈkaʊntənt/ *noun* an accountant who has passed the professional examinations and is a member of the Chartered Association of Certified Accountants

certified cheque /ˌsɜːtɪfaɪd ˈtʃek/ *noun* a cheque which a bank says is good and will be paid out of money put aside from the bank account

certified copy /ˌsɜːtɪfaɪd ˈkɒpi/ *noun* a document which is certified as being exactly the same in content as the original

certify /ˈsɜːtɪfaɪ/ *verb* to make an official declaration in writing ○ *I certify that this is a true copy.* ○ *The document is certified as a true copy.*

certiorari /ˌsɜːtiəˈrɑːri/ *phrase* a Latin word meaning 'to be informed' □ **order of certiorari** formerly, an order made by a superior court to an inferior one ordering that a case be referred to the superior court for review

cessate grant /ˈseseɪt ˌɡrɑːnt/ *noun* a special grant of probate made because of the incapacity of an executor, or a grant made to renew a grant which has expired

cesser /'sesə/ *noun* (*of a mortgage, charter, etc.*) the ending

cession /'seʃ(ə)n/ *noun* the act of giving up property to someone, especially a creditor

CFI *abbreviation* Court of First Instance

CFR *abbreviation* common frame of reference

CGT *abbreviation* capital gains tax

chair /tʃeə/ *noun* the role of chairperson presiding over a meeting ○ *to be in the chair* ○ *She is Chair of the Finance Committee.* ○ *This can be done by Chair's action and confirmed later.* □ **Mr Jones took the chair** Mr Jones presided over the meeting □ **to address the chair** in a meeting, to speak to the chairman and not directly to the rest of the people at the meeting □ **to ask a question through the chair** to ask someone a question directly, by speaking to him or her through the chairman ○ *May I ask the councillor through the chair why he did not declare his interest in the matter?* ■ *verb* to preside over a meeting ○ *The meeting was chaired by Mrs Smith.*

chairman /'tʃeəmən/ *noun* **1.** a person who is in charge of a meeting and holds the casting vote ○ *chairman of the magistrates* or *of the bench* ○ *Mr Howard was chairman* or *acted as chairman.* □ **Mr Chairman, Madam Chairman** the proper way of addressing the chairman **2.** a person who presides over meetings of a Committee of the House of Commons or of a local council **3.** somebody who presides over the board meetings of a company ○ *the chairman of the board* or *the company chairman*

chairman and managing director /ˌtʃeəmən ən ˌmænɪdʒɪŋ daɪ'rektə/ *noun* a managing director who is also chairman of the board of directors

chairman of the justices /ˌtʃeəmən əv ðɪ 'dʒʌstɪsɪz/ *noun* the chief magistrate in a magistrates' court

chairmanship /'tʃeəmənʃɪp/ *noun* the role of being a chairman □ **the committee met under the chairmanship of Mr Jones** Mr Jones chaired the meeting of the committee

chairperson /'tʃeəpɜːs(ə)n/ *noun* a person who is in charge of a meeting and holds the casting vote

chairwoman /'tʃeəwʊmən/ *noun* a woman who is in charge of a meeting and holds the casting vote

challenge /'tʃælɪndʒ/ *noun* the act of objecting to a decision and asking for it to be set aside ■ *verb* to refuse to accept a juror or piece of evidence ○ *to challenge a sentence by appeal to a higher court*

challenge for cause /ˌtʃælɪndʒ fə 'kɔːz/ *noun US* an objection to a proposed juror, stating the reasons for the objection

challenge without cause /ˌtʃælɪndʒ wɪ'ðaʊt kɔːz/ *noun US* an objection to a proposed juror, not stating the reasons for the objection

chamber /'tʃeɪmbə/ *noun* a room where a committee or legislature meets ○ *The meeting will be held in the council chamber.*

chambers /'tʃeɪmbəz/ *plural noun* **1.** the offices of a group of barristers who work together and share the same staff (NOTE: actually called 'a set of chambers') **2.** the office of a judge □ **to hear a case in chambers** to hear a case in private rooms, without the public being present and not in open court

champerty /'tʃæmpəti/ *noun* formerly, financial help given to a person starting a proceedings against a party, where the person giving help has a share in the damages to be recovered

Chancellor /'tʃɑːns(ə)lə/ *noun* **1.** ♦ **Lord Chancellor 2.** *US* a judge who presides over a court of equity

Chancellor of the Duchy of Lancaster /ˌtʃɑːnsələ əv ðiː 'dʌtʃi/ *noun* a member of the British government with no specific responsibilities

Chancellor of the Exchequer /ˌtʃɑːnsələr əv ðiː ɪks'tʃekə/ *noun* the chief finance minister in the British government

Chancery Bar /'tʃɑːnsəri bɑː/ *noun* the group of barristers who specialise in the Chancery Division

Chancery business /ˌtʃɑːnsəri 'bɪznɪs/ *noun* the range of legal cases relating to the sale of land, mortgages, trusts, estates, bankruptcies, partnerships, patents and copyrights, probate, and cases involving companies

Chancery Court /'tʃɑːnsəri kɔːt/ *noun* formerly, the court presided over by the Lord Chancellor, which established case law or equity

Chancery Division /ˌtʃɑːnsəri dɪ'vɪʒ(ə)n/ *noun* one of the three divisions of the High Court, dealing with matters such as wills, partnerships and companies, taxation and bankruptcies

change of use /ˌtʃeɪndʒ əv ˈjuːs/ *noun* an order allowing a property to be used in a different way, e.g. a house to be used as a business office, or a shop to be used as a factory

channel /ˈtʃæn(ə)l/ *noun* the way in which information or goods are passed from one place to another □ **to go through the official channels** to deal with government officials, especially when making a request □ **to open up new channels of communication** to find new ways of communicating with someone

chapter /ˈtʃæptə/ *noun* **1.** an official term for an Act of Parliament **2.** *US* a section of an Act of Congress

Chapter 7 /ˌtʃæptə ˈsevən/ *noun US* a section of the US Bankruptcy Reform Act 1978 which sets out the rules for the liquidation of an incorporated company

Chapter 11 /ˌtʃæptə ˈten/ *noun US* a section of the US Bankruptcy Reform Act 1978, which allows a corporation to be protected from demands made by its creditors for a period of time, while it is reorganised with a view to paying its debts (NOTE: The officers of the corporation will negotiate with its creditors as to the best way of reorganising the business.)

Chapter 13 /ˌtʃæptə ˈθɜːrˈtiːn/ *noun US* a section of the Bankruptcy Reform Act 1978 which allows a business to continue trading and to pay off its creditors by regular monthly payments over a period of time

character /ˈkærɪktə/ *noun* the general qualities of a person which make him or her different from others □ **of good character** honest, hard-working or decent □ **to give someone a character reference** to say that someone has good qualities □ **to introduce character evidence** to produce witnesses to say that a person is of good or bad character

charge /tʃɑːdʒ/ *noun* **1.** money which must be paid as the price of a service ○ *to make no charge for delivery* ○ *to make a small charge for rental* ○ *There is no charge for service* or *no charge is made for service.* **2.** □ **charge on land**, **charge over property** a mortgage or liability on a property which has been used as security for a loan □ **charge by way of legal mortgage** a way of borrowing money on the security of a property, where the mortgagor signs a deed which gives the mortgagee an interest in the property **3.** an official statement in a court

accusing someone of having committed a crime ○ *He appeared in court on a charge of embezzling* or *on an embezzlement charge.* ○ *The clerk of the court read out the charges.* □ **to answer charges** to plead guilty or not guilty to a charge □ **to have the charges against you withdrawn** or **dropped** to be let off and have your trial discontinued □ **to press charges against someone** to say formally that someone has committed a crime ○ *He was very angry when his neighbour's son set fire to his car, but decided not to press charges.* **4.** a set of instructions given by a judge to a jury, summing up the evidence and giving advice on the points of law which have to be considered ■ *verb* **1.** to ask someone to pay for services ○ *to charge £5 for delivery* ○ *How much does he charge?* □ **to charge £20 an hour** to ask to be paid £20 for an hour's work **2.** (*in a court*) to accuse someone formally of having committed a crime ○ *He was charged with embezzling his clients' money.* ○ *They were charged with murder.* (NOTE: You charge someone **with** a crime.)

chargeable /ˈtʃɑːdʒəb(ə)l/ *adjective* possible to charge to somebody

chargee /tʃɑːˈdʒiː/ *noun* somebody who holds a charge over a property

charge sheet /ˈtʃɑːdʒ ʃiːt/ *noun* a document listing the charges which a magistrate will hear, listing the charges against the accused together with details of the crime committed

charging order /ˈtʃɑːdʒɪŋ ˌɔːdə/ *noun* a court order made in favour of a judgment creditor granting them a charge over a debtor's property

charitable trust /ˈtʃærɪtəb(ə)l trʌst/, **charitable corporation** *US* /ˌtʃærɪtəb(ə)l ˌkɔːpəˈreɪʃ(ə)n/ *noun* a trust which benefits the public as a whole, by promoting education or religion, helping the poor or doing other useful work

Charity Commissioners /ˈtʃærɪti kə ˌmɪʃ(ə)nəz/ *plural noun* a UK body which governs charities and sees that they follow the law and use their funds for the purposes intended

charter /ˈtʃɑːtə/ *noun* **1.** a document from the Crown establishing a town, a corporation, a university or a company **2.** the hire of transport for a special purpose

chartered /ˈtʃɑːtəd/ *adjective* **1.** (*of a company*) set up by royal charter and not registered as a company **2.** □ **chartered**

ship, **bus**, **plane** ship or bus or plane which has been hired for a special purpose

Chartered Accountant /ˌtʃɑːtəd ə 'kaʊntənt/ *noun* an accountant who has passed the professional examinations and is a member of the Institute of Chartered Accountants

charterparty /'tʃɑːtəpɑːti/ *noun* a contract where the owner of a ship charters it to someone for carrying goods

chattel mortgage /'tʃæt(ə)l ˌmɔːɡɪdʒ/ *noun US* a mortgage using personal property as security

chattels personal /ˌtʃæt(ə)lz 'pɜːs(ə)n(ə)l/ *noun* any property that is not real property

chattels real /ˌtʃæt(ə)lz 'rɪəl/ *noun* leaseholds

check /tʃek/ *noun* **1.** a sudden stop □ **to put a check on the sale of firearms** to stop some firearms being sold **2.** an investigation or examination ○ *A routine check of the fire equipment* ○ *The auditors carried out checks on the petty cash book.* ■ *verb* **1.** to stop or delay something ○ *to check the entry of contraband into the country* **2.** to examine or to investigate ○ *to check that an invoice is correct* ○ *to check and sign for goods*

check sample /'tʃek ˌsɑːmp(ə)l/ *noun* a sample to be used to see if a consignment is acceptable

cheque /tʃek/, **check** *US* /tʃek/ *noun* **1.** an order to a bank to pay money from your account to the person whose name is written on it **2.** □ **to endorse a cheque** to sign a cheque on the back to make it payable to someone else □ **to make out a cheque to someone** to write out a cheque to someone □ **to pay by cheque** to pay by writing a cheque, and not by using cash or a credit card □ **to pay a cheque into your account** to deposit a cheque □ **to bounce a cheque** to refuse to pay a cheque because there is not enough money in the account to pay it (*informal*) □ **the bank referred the cheque to drawer** the bank returned the cheque to person who wrote it because there was not enough money in the account to pay it □ **to sign a cheque** to sign on the front of a cheque to show that you authorise the bank to pay the money from your account □ **to stop a cheque** to ask a bank not to pay a cheque which you have written

cheque account /'tʃek əˌkaʊnt/ *noun* a bank account which allows the customer to write cheques

chief /tʃiːf/ *adjective* □ **in chief** in person

Chief Constable /ˌtʃiːf 'kʌnstəb(ə)l/ *noun* the person in charge of a police force

Chief Inspector /ˌtʃiːf ɪn'spektə/ *noun* a rank in the police force above Inspector or Superintendent

Chief Inspector of Prisons /ˌtʃiːf ɪn ˌspektə əv 'prɪzənz/ *noun* a government official who is the head of the Inspectorate of Prisons, and whose job is to inspect prisons to see that they are being run correctly and efficiently

Chief Justice /ˌtʃiːf 'dʒʌstɪs/ *noun* **1.** *US* a senior judge in a court **2.** the presiding justice of the US Supreme Court

child /tʃaɪld/ *noun* a person under the age of 18

COMMENT: In Great Britain a child does not have full legal status until the age of eighteen. A contract is not binding on a child, and a child cannot own land, make a will or vote. A child cannot marry before the age of sixteen, and can only marry between the ages of 16 and 18 with written permission of his or her parents. A child who is less than ten years old is not considered capable of committing a crime; a child between ten and fourteen years of age may be considered capable of committing a crime if there is evidence of malice or knowledge, and so children of these ages can in certain circumstances be convicted. In criminal law the term 'child' is used for children between the ages of 10 and 14; for children between 14 and 17, the term 'young person' is used; all children are termed 'juveniles'.

child benefit /ˌtʃaɪld 'benɪfɪt/ *noun* money paid by the state to a person responsible for a child under 16 years of age, or between 16–18 and in full-time education

childcare /'tʃaɪldkeə/ *noun* the fact of having somebody to look after your children while you are at work or in education

child destruction /ˌtʃaɪld dɪ'strʌkʃən/ *noun* the notifiable offence of killing an unborn child capable of being born alive

Child Exploitation and Online Protection Centre /ˌtʃaɪld ˌeksplɔɪteɪʃ(ə)n ənd ˌɒnlaɪn prə'tekʃ(ə)n ˌsentə/ *noun* a Government agency which investigates and seeks to bring a halt to child sex abuse on the Internet. Abbreviation **CEOP**

child in care /ˌtʃaɪld ɪn 'keə/ *noun* a child who is the subject of a care order and is therefore in the care of the local social services department

child stealing /'tʃaɪld ˌstiːlɪŋ/ *noun US* the notifiable offence of taking away a child from its parents or guardian

child support /'tʃaɪld sə,pɔːt/ *noun US* money paid as part of a divorce settlement, to help maintain a child of divorced parents

Child Support Agency /,tʃaɪld sə'pɔːt ,eɪdʒənsi/ *noun* an agency of the Department for Work and Pensions, created by the Child Support Act 1991, which has responsibility for the assessment, review, collection and enforcement of maintenance for children, which was previously supervised by the courts. Abbreviation **CSA**

Child Tax Credit /,tʃaɪld 'tæks ,kredɪt/ *noun* a tax credit given to a person responsible for a child under 16 years of age, or between 16–18 and in full-time education, calculated according to their salary

chose /tʃəʊz/ *noun* a French word meaning 'item' or 'thing' □ **chose in action** a personal right which can be enforced or claimed as if it were property (such as a patent, copyright, debt or cheque) □ **chose in possession** a physical thing which can be owned such as a piece of furniture

Christmas Day /,krɪsməs 'deɪ/ *noun* 25th December, one of the four quarter days when rent is payable on land

chronology /krə'nɒlədʒi/ *noun* a description of events in the order in which they occurred, often used in legal proceedings

CID /siːaɪ'diː/ *abbreviation* Criminal Investigation department

circuit /'sɜːkɪt/ *noun* one of six divisions of England and Wales for legal purposes ○ *He is a judge on the Welsh Circuit.*

COMMENT: The six circuits are: Northern, North-Eastern, Midland, Wales and Chester, South-Eastern, and Western.

circuit judge /'sɜːkɪt dʒʌdʒ/ *noun* a judge in the Crown Court or a County Court

circulation /,sɜːkjʊ'leɪʃ(ə)n/ *noun* □ **to put money into circulation** to issue new notes to business and the public

circumstances /'sɜːkəmstænsɪz/ *plural noun* the situation as it is when something happens ○ *The police inspector described the circumstances leading to the riot.* ◊ **extenuating circumstances**

circumstantial /,sɜːkəm'stænʃ(ə)l/ *adjective* allowing someone to infer facts

circumstantial evidence /,sɜːkəmstænʃ(ə)l 'evɪd(ə)ns/ *noun* evidence which suggests that something must

have happened, but does not give firm proof of it

citation /saɪ'teɪʃ(ə)n/ *noun* **1.** an official request asking someone to appear in court (NOTE: used mainly in the Scottish and American courts) **2.** the quoting of a legal case, authority or precedent **3.** a set of words used in giving someone an award or honour, explaining why the award is being made

citation clause /saɪ'teɪʃ(ə)n klɔːz/ *noun* a clause in a Bill which gives the short title by which it should be known when it becomes an Act

cite /saɪt/ *verb* **1.** to summon someone to appear in court **2.** to refer to something ○ *The judge cited several previous cases in his summing up.* **3.** to refer to an Act of Parliament using the short title ○ *This Act may be cited as the Electronic Communications Act 1999.*

citizen /'sɪtɪz(ə)n/ *noun* **1.** somebody who lives in a city **2.** somebody who has the nationality of a specific country ○ *He is a French citizen by birth.*

Citizens' Advice Bureaux /,sɪtɪzənz əd'vaɪs ,bjʊərəʊ/ *plural noun* a network of local offices established to help people resolve their legal, financial and other problems by providing free information and advice. Abbreviation **CAB**

citizen's arrest /,sɪtɪz(ə)nz ə'rest/ *noun* the right of a private person to arrest someone suspected of committing a crime without a warrant

Citizen's Charter /,sɪtɪzənz 'tʃɑːtə/ *noun* a promise by the government that people must be fairly dealt with, in particular by government departments and state-controlled bodies

citizenship /'sɪtɪz(ə)nʃɪp/ *noun* the right of being a citizen of a country ○ *The Treaty has established European citizenship for everyone who is a citizen of the Member State of the EU.*

COMMENT: A person may acquire British citizenship by being born to (or adopted by) a British citizen parent in the UK, by descent from a British citizen parent, or by naturalisation. Citizenship by naturalisation is granted to a foreign national of 'good character' who has lived legally in the UK for 5 years, or has married a British citizen and lived legally in the UK for 3 years.

civic /'sɪvɪk/ *adjective* referring to a city or the official business of running a city ○ *Their civic pride showed in the beautiful gardens to be found everywhere in the city.*

civic centre /ˌsɪvɪk 'sentə/ *noun* the main offices of a city council

civic dignitaries /ˌsɪvɪk 'dɪgnɪt(ə)riz/ *plural noun* the mayor and other senior officials of a city or town

civil /'sɪv(ə)l/ *adjective* **1.** referring to the rights and duties of private persons or corporate bodies, as opposed to criminal, military or ecclesiastical bodies **2.** referring to the public in general

civil action /ˌsɪv(ə)l 'ækʃən/ *noun* a court case brought by a person or a company (the claimant) against someone who is alleged to have done them wrong (the defendant)

civil court /ˌsɪv(ə)l 'kɔːt/ *noun* a court where civil actions are heard

civil disobedience /ˌsɪv(ə)l dɪsə 'biːdiəns/ *noun* the activity of disobeying the orders of the civil authorities such as the police as an act of protest ○ *The group planned a campaign of civil disobedience as a protest against restrictions on immigrants.*

civil disorder /ˌsɪv(ə)l dɪs'ɔːdə/ *noun US* riots or fighting in public places

civilian /sə'vɪliən/ *adjective* referring to people who are not in the armed forces ○ *Civilian rule was restored after several years of military dictatorship.* ○ *The military leaders called general elections and gave way to a democratically elected civilian government.* ■ *noun* someone who is not a member of the armed forces ○ *The head of the military junta has appointed several civilians to the Cabinet.*

civil law /ˌsɪv(ə)l 'lɔː/ *noun* **1.** laws relating to people's rights and to agreements between individuals. Compare **criminal law 2.** legal systems based upon Roman law, such as those of continental Europe

civil liberties /ˌsɪv(ə)l 'lɪbətiz/ *plural noun* the freedom for people to work or write or speak as they want, providing they keep within the law

Civil List /ˌsɪv(ə)l 'lɪst/ *noun* money appropriated from the Consolidated Fund for paying the Royal Family and their expenses

civil partner /ˌsɪv(ə)l 'pɑːtnə/ *noun* a member of a civil partnership

civil partnership /ˌsɪv(ə)l 'pɑːtnəʃɪp/ *noun* a civil union of two people of the same sex registered with the UK General Register Office, conferring many of the same rights enjoyed by married couples

Civil Procedure Rules /ˌsɪv(ə)l prə 'siːdʒə ˌruːlz/ *plural noun* official rules setting out how civil cases are to be brought to court and heard. Abbreviation **CPR**

civil rights /ˌsɪv(ə)l 'raɪts/ *plural noun* rights and privileges of each individual according to the law

civil strife /ˌsɪv(ə)l 'straɪf/ *noun* trouble occurring when groups of people fight each other, usually over matters of principle

Civil Trial Centre /ˌsɪv(ə)l 'traɪəl ˌsentə/ *noun* a court which deals with multi-track claims

civil union /ˌsɪv(ə)l 'juːnjən/ *noun* in some US states, a civil partnership registered between a same-sex couple

CJ *abbreviation* Chief Justice

claim /kleɪm/ *noun* **1.** an assertion of a legal right **2.** a document used in the County Court to start a legal action □ **claim for personal injuries** a claim where the claimant claims damages for physical or mental impairment caused by somebody else's actions **3.** a statement that someone has a right to property held by another person **4.** a request for money that you believe you should have ○ *an insurance claim* ○ *a wage claim* **5.** □ **no claims bonus** reduction of premiums to be paid because no claims have been made against the insurance policy □ **to put in a claim** to ask the insurance company officially to pay for damage or loss ○ *She put in a claim for repairs to the car.* □ **to settle a claim** to agree to pay what is asked for ■ *verb* **1.** to state a grievance in court **2.** to ask for money ○ *He claimed £100,000 damages against the cleaning firm.* ○ *She claimed for repairs to the car against her insurance.* **3.** to say that you have a right to property held by someone else ○ *He is claiming possession of the house.* ○ *No one claimed the umbrella found in my office.* **4.** to state that something is a fact ○ *He claims he never received the goods.* ○ *She claims that the shares are her property.* **5.** to attack someone in prison (*slang*) **6.** to arrest someone (*slang*)

claimant /'kleɪmənt/ *noun* **1.** someone who claims something such as state benefits or an inheritance **2.** someone who brings a lawsuit in a civil court against a person or organisation. Compare **defendant** (NOTE: Since the introduction of the Civil Procedure Rules, this term has replaced **plaintiff.**)

claim back /ˌkleɪm 'bæk/ *verb* to ask for money to be paid back ○ *She paid for the* *emergency repairs herself and claimed the money back from the landlord.*

claim form /'kleɪm fɔːm/ *noun* **1. Claim Form** a form used by a claimant to begin court proceedings ○ *He issued the Claim Form on Friday and served it on the defendant on Monday.* (NOTE: Since the introduction of the Civil Procedure Rules, this term has replaced **writ of summons**.) **2.** a form used to make an insurance claim ○ *He filled in the claim form and sent it to the insurance company.*

> COMMENT: The Claim Form must be served on the defendant within four months of being issued. If a Claim Form has been issued but not served, the defendant can ask for it to be served, and if the claimant does not do so, the claim may be dismissed.

Claim Production Centre /prə ˌdʌkʃ(ə)n 'sentə/ *noun* a central office which issues Claim Forms. Abbreviation **CPC**

class action /ˌklɑːs 'ækʃən/ *noun US* a legal action brought on behalf of a group of people

Class A drug /ˌklɑːs eɪ 'drʌg/ *noun* a strong and dangerous drug such as cocaine, heroin, crack, or LSD

Class B drug /ˌklɑːs biː 'drʌg/ *noun* a drug such as amphetamine, cannabis or codeine

Class C drug /ˌklɑːs siː 'drʌg/ *noun* a drug which is related to amphetamine, e.g. benzphetamine

Class F charge /ˌklɑːs 'ef ˌtʃɑːdʒ/ *noun* a charge on a property registered by a spouse who is not the owner, claiming a right to live in the property

class gift /'klɑːs gɪft/ *noun US* a gift to a defined group of people

classified information /ˌklæsɪfaɪd ˌɪnfə'meɪʃ(ə)n/ *noun* information which is secret and can be told only to specified people

classify /'klæsɪfaɪ/ *verb* **1.** to put into groups or categories **2.** to make information secret

clause /klɔːz/ *noun* a distinct section of a document, especially a legal document, that is usually separately numbered ○ *There are ten clauses in the contract.* ○ *According to clause six, payment will not be due until next year.*

claw back /ˌklɔː 'bæk/ *verb* **1.** to take back money which has been allocated ○ *Income tax claws back 25% of pensions paid out by the government.* **2.** (*of HM Rev-*

enue and Customs) to take back tax relief which was previously granted ○ *Of the £1m allocated to the development of the system, the government clawed back £100,000 in taxes.*

clawback /'klɔːbæk/ *noun* **1.** money taken back **2.** the loss of tax relief previously granted

clean hands /ˌkliːn 'hændz/ *plural noun* the principle that a claimant cannot claim successfully if his or her motives or actions are dishonest, or if his or her own obligations to the defendant have not been discharged (NOTE: From the maxim: 'he who comes to equity must come with clean hands'.)

clear /klɪə/ *adjective* **1.** easily understood ○ *He made it clear that he wanted the manager to resign.* ○ *There was no clear evidence or clear proof that he was in the house at the time of the murder.* **2.** □ **to have a clear title to something** to have a right to something with no limitations or charges **3.** □ **three clear days** a period of time, calculated without including the first day when the period starts and the last day when it finishes, that includes three full days ○ *Allow three clear days for the cheque to be paid into your account.* ■ *noun* □ **in the clear** found not guilty ■ *verb* **1.** □ **to clear someone of charges** to find that someone is not guilty of the charges against him or her ○ *He was cleared of all charges* or *he was cleared on all counts.* **2.** □ **to clear a debt** to pay all of a debt **3.** □ **to clear goods through customs** to have all documentation passed by customs so that goods can leave the country **4.** □ **to clear a cheque** to pass a cheque through the banking system, so that the money is transferred from the payer's account to another account ○ *The cheque took ten days to clear* or *the bank took ten days to clear the cheque.*

clearing /'klɪərɪŋ/ *noun* **1.** □ **clearing of goods through customs** the passing of goods through customs **2.** □ **clearing of a debt** the payment of all of a debt

clearing bank /'klɪərɪŋ bæŋk/ *noun* a bank which clears cheques by transferring money from the payer's account to another account

clearing house /'klɪərɪŋ haʊs/ *noun* a central office where clearing banks exchange cheques

clear up /ˌklɪər 'ʌp/ *verb* to discover who has committed a crime and arrest them ○

Half the crimes committed are never cleared up.

clear-up /ˈklɪə ʌp ˌreɪt/ *noun* an incident of a crime being solved □ **clear-up rate** the number of crimes solved, as a percentage of all crimes committed

COMMENT: Clear-ups can be divided into two categories: **primary clear-up**, when a crime is solved by arresting the suspect, and **secondary clear-up**, where a person charged with one crime then confesses to another which had not previously been solved.

clemency /ˈklemənsi/ *noun* pardon or mercy ○ *As an act of clemency, the president granted an amnesty to all political prisoners.*

clerk *US* /klɑːk/ *noun* somebody who works in an office or does clerical work ○ *accounts clerk* ○ *sales clerk*

clerkship /ˈklɜːkʃɪp/ *noun US* the time when a student lawyer is working in the office of a lawyer before being admitted to the bar (NOTE: The British term is **traineeship**.)

click-wrap agreement /ˈklɪk ræp ə ˌɡriːmənt/ *noun* a contract entered into when purchasing an item on the Internet, where no paper documentation exists and the agreement to purchase is made by clicking on the appropriate button

client /ˈklaɪənt/ *noun* **1.** a person who pays for a service carried out by a professional person such as an accountant or a solicitor **2.** somebody who is represented by a lawyer ○ *The solicitor paid the fine on behalf of his client.*

cloning /ˈkləʊnɪŋ/ *noun* the act of making a copy of a debit or credit card to illegally withdraw funds from the cardholder's account

close *adjective* □ **close to** very near, almost ○ *The company was close to bankruptcy.* ○ *We are close to solving the crime.* ■ *verb* □ **to close the accounts** to come to the end of an accounting period and make up the profit and loss account ◇ **to close an account 1.** to stop supplying a customer on credit **2.** to take all the money out of a bank account and stop the account

close down /ˌkləʊz ˈdaʊn/ *verb* to shut a shop or factory for a long period or for ever ○ *The company is closing down its London office.*

closed session /ˌkləʊzd ˈseʃ(ə)n/ *noun* a meeting which is not open to the public or to journalists ○ *The town council met in*

closed session to discuss staff problems in the Education Department. ○ *The public gallery was cleared when the meeting went into closed session.*

close protection officer /ˌkləʊs prə ˈtekʃ(ə)n ˌɒfɪsə/ *noun* someone who is employed to protect a celebrity or public figure from attack

closing /ˈkləʊzɪŋ/ *adjective* coming at the end of something

closing speeches /ˌkləʊsɪŋ ˈspiːtʃəz/ *plural noun* final speeches for and against a motion in a debate, or for prosecution and defence at the end of a trial

closing stock /ˌkləʊzɪŋ ˈstɒk/ *noun* the value of stock at the end of an accounting period

closing time /ˈkləʊzɪŋ taɪm/ *noun* the time when a public house stops serving customers

closure /ˈkləʊʒə/ *noun* **1.** the act of closing **2.** (*in the House of Commons*) the ending of a debate

closure motion /ˌkləʊʒə ˈməʊʃ(ə)n/ *noun* a proposal to end a debate

CLS /ˌsiː el ˈes/ *abbreviation* Community Legal Service

clue /kluː/ *noun* something which helps someone solve a crime ○ *The police have searched the room for clues.* ○ *The police have several clues to the identity of the murdered.*

Co *abbreviation* company ○ *J. Smith & Co Ltd*

co- /kəʊ/ *prefix* working or acting together

c/o *abbreviation* care of

co-creditor /ˌkəʊ ˈkredɪtə/ *noun* somebody who is a creditor of the same company as another person

code /kəʊd/ *noun* **1.** an official set of laws or regulations. ◊ **Highway Code, penal code 2.** the set of laws of a country □ **the Louisiana Code** *US* the laws of the state of Louisiana **3.** a set of semi-official rules **4.** a system of signs, numbers or letters which mean something ○ *The spy sent his message in code.* ■ *verb* to write a message using secret signs ○ *We received coded instructions from our agent in New York.*

co-decision procedure /ˌkəʊ dɪ ˈsɪʒ(ə)n prəˌsiːdʒə/ *noun* (*in the EU*) a procedure by which the Commission sends proposed legislation to both the Council of the European Union and the European Parliament for approval

co-defendant /ˌkəʊ dɪˈfendənt/ *noun* somebody who appears in a case with another defendant

Code Napoleon /ˌkəʊd nəˈpəʊliən/ *noun* ♦ **Napoleonic Code**

code of conduct /ˌkəʊd əv ˈkɒndʌkt/ *noun* a set of rules of behaviour by which a group of people work

code of practice /ˌkəʊd əv ˈpræktɪs/ *noun* **1.** a set of rules to be followed when applying a law **2.** a set of rules drawn up by a trade association, which its members must adhere to in their work

codicil /ˈkəʊdɪsɪl/ *noun* a document executed in the same way as a will, making additions or changes to an existing will

codification /ˌkəʊdɪfɪˈkeɪʃ(ə)n/ *noun* **1.** the act of bringing together all statutes and case law relating to a specific issue to make a single Act of Parliament. ◊ **consolidation 2.** the act of bringing all laws together into a formal legal code

codify /ˈkəʊdɪfaɪ/ *verb* to consolidate statutes and case law into a single Act of Parliament

coding /ˈkəʊdɪŋ/ *noun* the act of putting a code on something to identify or classify it ○ *the coding of invoices*

co-director /ˈkəʊ daɪˌrektə/ *noun* a person who is a director of the same company as another person

coercion /kəʊˈɜːʃ(ə)n/ *noun* the use of force to make someone commit a crime or do some act

cohabit /kəʊˈhæbɪt/ *verb* (*of a man and a woman*) to live together as husband and wife

cohabitant /kəʊˈhæbɪtənt/ *noun* same as **cohabiter**

cohabitation /kəʊˌhæbɪˈteɪʃ(ə)n/ *noun* the practice of living together as husband and wife, whether legally married or not

cohabiter /kəʊˈhæbɪtə/, **cohabitee** /kəʊˌhæbɪˈtiː/ *noun* a person who lives with another as husband or wife but is not legally married

co-heir /kəʊ ˈeə/ *noun* somebody who is an heir with others

co-insurance /ˌkəʊ ɪnˈʃʊərəns/ *noun* insurance where the risk is shared among several insurers

cold case /ˈkəʊld keɪs/ *noun* a criminal case which remains unsolved despite investigation, and is left open indefinitely (NOTE: This is a mainly US term.)

cold weather payment /ˌkəʊld ˈweðə ˌpeɪmənt/ *noun* a one-off payment made by the Government to someone who is over 60 years old when the weather is particularly cold (NOTE: This is made out of the Government's **Social Fund**.)

collaborative divorce /kəˌlæb(ə)rətɪv dɪˈvɔːs/ *noun* a divorce of which the terms are agreed by both spouses and their solicitors before presenting the final agreement to a judge without a trial

collateral /kəˈlæt(ə)rəl/ *noun* security used to provide a guarantee for a loan ■ *adjective* providing security for a loan

collateral contract /kəˌlæt(ə)rəl ˈkɒntrækt/ *noun* a contract which induces a person to enter into a more important contract

collateral issue /kəˌlæt(ə)rəl ˈɪʃuː/ *noun* an issue which arises from a plea in a criminal court

collation /kəˈleɪʃ(ə)n/ *noun* **1.** the comparison of a copy with the original to see if it is perfect **2.** the arrangement of documents in the proper sequence

collect /kəˈlekt/ *verb* **1.** to make someone pay money which is owed □ **to collect a debt** to go and make someone pay a debt **2.** to take goods away from a place ○ *We have to collect the stock from the warehouse.*

collection /kəˈlekʃən/ *noun* **1.** the activity of making someone pay money which is owed **2.** the act of fetching goods ○ *The stock is in the warehouse awaiting collection.* □ **to hand something in for collection** to leave something for someone to come and collect **3.** the taking of letters from a letter box or mail room to the post office to be sent off ○ *There are six collections a day from the letter box.*

collection charges /kəˈlekʃən ˌtʃɑːdʒɪz/ *plural noun* charges which have to be paid for collecting something

collection-proof /kəˈlekʃən pruːf/ *adjective US* same as **judgment-proof**

collective /kəˈlektɪv/ *adjective* working together

collective ownership /kəˌlektɪv ˈəʊnəʃɪp/ *noun* ownership of a business by the employees who work in it

collective responsibility /kəˌlektɪv rɪ ˌspɒnsɪˈbɪlɪti/ *noun* a doctrine that all members of a group are responsible together for the actions of that group

collector /kəˈlektə/ *noun* somebody who makes people pay money which is owed ○

collector of taxes or *tax collector* ○ *debt collector*

collusion /kə'luːʒ(ə)n/ *noun* illicit co-operation between people in order to cheat another party or to defraud another party of a right ○ *He was suspected of collusion with the owner of the property.* □ **to act in collusion with** to co-operate with someone in a way that is not allowed in order to cheat or defraud another party ○ *They had acted in collusion with a former employee.*

collusive action /kə,luːsɪv 'ækʃən/ *noun* an action which is taken in collusion with another party

comity /'kɒmɪti/ *noun US* the custom by which courts in one state defer to the jurisdiction of courts in other states or to federal courts

comity of nations /,kɒmɪti əv 'neɪʃ(ə)nz/ *noun* the custom whereby the courts of one country acknowledge and apply the laws of another country

command /kə'mɑːnd/ *noun* an order □ **by Royal Command** by order of the Queen or King

commander /kə'mɑːndə/ *noun* a high rank in the Metropolitan Police force, equivalent to Assistant Chief Constable

commencement /kə'mensmənt/ *noun* the beginning □ **commencement of proceedings** the start of proceedings in a County Court □ **date of commencement** the date when an Act of Parliament takes effect

comment /'kɒment/ *noun* a remark giving a spoken or written opinion ○ *The judge made a comment on the evidence presented by the defence.* ○ *The newspaper has some short comments about the trial.*

commentary /'kɒmənt(ə)ri/ *noun* **1.** a textbook which comments on the law **2.** brief notes which comment on the main points of a judgment

Commercial Court /kə'mɜːʃ(ə)l kɔːt/ *noun* a court in the Queen's Bench Division which hears cases relating to business disputes

commercial e-mail /kə,mɜːʃ(ə)l 'iːmeɪl/ *noun* an e-mail which is offering something for sale, often unsolicited

commercial law /kə,mɜːʃ(ə)l 'lɔː/ *noun* law regarding the conduct of businesses

commercial lawyer /kə,mɜːʃ(ə)l 'lɔːjə/ *noun US* someone who specialises in company law or who advises companies on legal problems

commercial premises /kə,mɜːʃ(ə)l 'premɪsɪz/ *plural noun* same as **business premises**

commission /kə'mɪʃ(ə)n/ *noun* **1.** a group of people officially appointed to examine or be in charge of something ○ *The government has appointed a commission of inquiry to look into the problems of prison overcrowding.* ○ *He is the chairman of the government commission on football violence.* ◊ **Law Commission, Royal Commission 2.** a request to someone such as an artist or architect to do a piece of work for which they will be paid **3.** a payment, usually a percentage of turnover, made to an agent ○ *She has an agent's commission of 15% of sales.* **4.** an official position of being an officer in the army **5.** the act of committing a crime

commission agent /kə'mɪʃ(ə)n ,eɪdʒənt/ *noun* an agent who is paid by commission, not by fee

commissioner /kə'mɪʃ(ə)nə/ *noun* a person who has an official commission

commissioner for oaths /kə,mɪʃ(ə)nə fər 'əʊðs/ *noun* a solicitor appointed by the Lord Chancellor to administer affidavits which may be used in court

commissioner of police /kə ,mɪʃ(ə)nər əv pə'liːs/ *noun* the highest rank in a police force

Commission for Racial Equality /kə ,mɪʃ(ə)n fə ,reɪʃ(ə)l ɪ'kwɒlɪti/ *noun* in the UK, an official committee set up to deal with issues relating to equal treatment of ethnic groups. Abbreviation **CRE**

commit /kə'mɪt/ *verb* **1.** to send someone to prison or to a court ○ *He was committed for trial in the Central Criminal Court.* ○ *The magistrates committed her for trial at the Crown Court.* **2.** to carry out a crime ○ *The gang committed six robberies before they were caught.* (NOTE: **committing – committed**)

commitment /kə'mɪtmənt/ *noun* an order for sending someone to prison

commitments /kə'mɪtmənts/ *plural noun* things which have to be done □ **financial commitments** debts which have to be paid □ **to honour your commitments** to do what you are obliged to do

committal /kə'mɪt(ə)l/ *noun* the act of sending someone to a court or to prison □ **committal for trial** the act of sending someone to be tried in a higher court following committal proceedings in a magistrates' court □ **committal for sentence** the act of sending someone who has been convicted in a magistrates court to be sentenced in a higher court

committal order /kə,mɪt(ə)l 'ɔːdə/ noun an order sending someone to prison for a contempt of court offence such as perjury

committal proceedings /kə,mɪt(ə)l prə'siːdɪŋz/ plural noun the preliminary hearing of a case in a magistrates' court, to decide if it is serious enough to be tried before a jury in a higher court

committal warrant /kə,mɪt(ə)l 'wɒrənt/ noun an order sending someone to serve a prison sentence

committee /kə'mɪti/ noun **1.** an official group of people who organise or plan for a larger group ○ to be a member of a committee or to sit on a committee ○ The new plans have to be approved by the committee members. ○ She is the secretary of the Housing Committee. □ to chair a committee to be the chairperson of a committee **2.** a section of a legislature which considers bills passed to it by the main chamber **3.** a person to whom something such as the charge of someone who is incapable of looking after himself or herself is officially given

Committee of Privileges /kə,mɪti əv 'prɪvɪlɪdʒɪz/ noun a special committee of the House of Commons which examines cases of breach of privilege

Committee of the Parliamentary Commission /kə,mɪti əv ðə ,pɑːlə'ment(ə)ri kə,mɪʃ(ə)n/ noun a committee which examines reports by the Ombudsman

Committee of Ways and Means /kə ,mɪti əv ,weɪz ən 'miːnz/ noun a committee of the whole House of Commons which examines a Supply Bill

Committee Stage /kə'mɪti steɪdʒ/ noun one of the stages in the discussion of a Bill, where each clause is examined in detail ○ The Bill is at Committee Stage and will not become law for several months.

commodities /kə'mɒdɪtiz/ plural noun physical items which can be traded, e.g. oil, diamonds, sugar

common /'kɒmən/ adjective **1.** which happens very often ○ Putting the headed paper into the photocopier upside down is a common mistake. **2.** referring to or belonging to several different people or to everyone **3.** □ in common together or jointly. ◊ tenancy in common

common ancestor /,kɒmən 'ænsestə/ noun a person from whom two or more people are descended

common assault /,kɒmən ə'sɔːlt/ noun a charge which is available to police if a person has committed an assault or battery resulting in a minor injury (a scratch, bruise or graze)

common carrier /,kɒmən 'kæriə/ noun a firm which carries goods or passengers, which cannot usually refuse to do so, and which can be used by anyone

common frame of reference /,kɒmən freɪm əv 'ref(ə)rəns/ noun a set of rules and defined vocabulary intended to increase the coherence and harmonisation of the consumer and contract laws of the different states of the EU. Abbreviation **CFR**

common land /,kɒmən 'lænd/ noun an area of land registered as common under the Commons Act 2006, to which the public has right of access

common law /,kɒmən 'lɔː/ noun **1.** a law established on the basis of decisions by the courts, rather than by statute **2.** a general system of laws which formerly were the only laws existing in England, but which in some cases have been superseded by statute (NOTE: You say **at common law** when referring to something happening according to the principles of common law.) **3.** legal systems based upon the English model, such as that of Australia and most US states

common-law /'kɒmən lɔː/ adjective according to the old unwritten system of law □ **common-law marriage** a situation where two people live together as husband and wife without being married □ **common-law spouse** somebody who has lived or is living with another as husband or wife, although they have not been legally married

COMMENT: In the UK common-law spouses do not have the same legal rights as married couples.

common mistake /,kɒmən mɪ'steɪk/ noun a situation in which the legality of a contract is challenged, on the grounds that both parties misunderstood the other's situation or intentions at the time of signing

common ownership /,kɒmən 'əʊnəʃɪp/ noun ownership of a company or of a property by a group of people who each own a part

common position /,kɒmən pə'zɪʃ(ə)n/ noun a position taken by the Council of the European Union on proposed legislation, which is then passed to the European Parliament for approval (NOTE: It can be adopted or rejected by the Parliament, and the Parliament may propose changes to the proposed common position.)

Commons /'kɒmənz/ *plural noun* same as **House of Commons** ○ *The Commons voted against the Bill.* ○ *The majority of the Commons are in favour of law reform.*

common seal /ˌkɒmən 'siːl/ *noun* a metal stamp which every company must possess, used to stamp documents with the name of the company to show they have been approved officially

Common Serjeant /ˌkɒmən 'sɑːdʒənt/ *noun* a senior barrister who sits as a judge in the City of London and acts as adviser to the City of London Corporation

Commonwealth /'kɒmənwelθ/ *noun* □ **the Commonwealth** an association of independent states, nearly all of which were once British territories

commorientes /kəʊˌmɒri'entiːz/ *plural noun* people who die at the same time, e.g. a husband and wife who both die in the same accident

COMMENT: In such cases, the law assumes that the younger person has died after the older one; this rule also applies to testators and beneficiaries who die at the same time.

community /kə'mjuːnɪti/ *noun* **1.** a group of people living or working in the same place □ **the local business community** the business people living and working in the area **2.** same as **European Community**

Community act /kə'mjuːnɪti ækt/ *noun* a legal act of the European Union which has the force of law

community care /kəˌmjuːnɪti 'keə/ *noun* the principle that vulnerable people should be cared for in the community rather than in institutions, enshrined in the NHS and Community Care Act 1990

community care grant /kəˌmjuːnɪti 'keə ˌgrɑːnt/ *noun* a one-off payment made by the Government to someone who is on a low income and is receiving treatment for mental illness (NOTE: This is made out of the Government's **Social Fund.**)

community charge /kə'mjuːnɪti tʃɑːdʒ/ *noun* a local tax levied on each eligible taxpayer. Also known as **poll tax**

community home /kə'mjuːnɪti həʊm/ *noun* a house which belongs to a local authority, where children in care can live

Community Legal Service /kə ˌmjuːnɪti ˌliːg(ə)l 'sɜːvɪs/ *noun* a network

of organisations which provide free civil legal advice and representation. Abbreviation **CLS**

COMMENT: It is administered by the Legal Services Commission who ensure that public funds are made available to those individuals in need of it most. Legal assistance is broken down into six differing levels of assistance: (1) legal help (2) help at court; (3) investigative help; (4) full representation (5) support funding; (6) specific directions.

Community legislation /kəˌmjuːnɪti ledʒɪ'sleɪʃ(ə)n/, **Community law** *noun* **1.** regulations or directives issued by the EC Council of Ministers or the EC Commission **2.** laws created by the European Community which are binding on Member States and their citizens

community policing /kəˌmjuːnɪti pə 'liːsɪŋ/ *noun* a way of policing a section of a town, where the members of the local community and the local police force act together to prevent crime and disorder, with policemen on foot patrol rather than in patrol cars

community property /kəˌmjuːnɪti 'prɒpəti/ *noun* in the USA, Canada, France and many other countries, a situation where a husband and wife jointly own any property which they acquire during the course of their marriage. Compare **separate property**

Community Punishment and Rehabilitation Order /kəˌmjuːnɪti ˌpʌnɪʃmənt ən ˌriːəbɪlɪ'teɪʃ(ə)n ˌɔːdə/ *noun* a community order which requires the offender to do unpaid work in the community under the supervision of a probation officer. Abbreviation **CRPO**

Community Punishment Order /kə ˌmjuːnɪti 'pʌnɪʃmənt ˌɔːdə/ *noun* a community order which requires the offender to do unpaid work in the community, from 40 to 240 hours. Abbreviation **CPO**

community safety /kəˌmjuːnɪti 'seɪfti/ *noun* the fact of a community being protected from the risk of crime ○ *We're working to improve community safety by increasing the number of street lights in at-risk areas.*

community service /kəˌmjuːnɪti 'sɜːvɪs/ *noun* work that someone has to do in their spare time as punishment for some offences instead of going to prison

community service order /kə ˌmjuːnɪti 'sɜːvɪs ˌɔːdə/ *noun* a punishment where a convicted person is sentenced to do unpaid work in the local community. Abbreviation **CSO**

community support officer /kə ˌmjuːnɪti səˈpɔːt ˌɒfɪsə/ *noun* ♦ **Police Community Support Officer**

commutation /ˌkɒmjʊˈteɪʃ(ə)n/ *noun* the reduction of a punishment to one that is less severe

commute /kəˈmjuːt/ *verb* **1.** to travel to work from home each day ○ *He commutes from the country to his office in the centre of town.* **2.** to change a right into cash **3.** to reduce a harsh sentence to a lesser one ○ *The death sentence was commuted to life imprisonment.*

compact /ˈkɒmpækt/ *noun* an agreement

Companies Act /ˈkʌmp(ə)niz ækt/ *noun* in the UK, an Act which states the legal limits within which a company may do business

Companies House /ˌkʌmpəniz ˈhaʊs/ *noun* in the UK, an office which keeps details of incorporated companies

companies' register /ˌkʌmpəniz ˈredʒɪstə/ *noun* a list of companies showing their directors and registered addresses, and statutory information kept at Companies House for public inspection

company /ˈkʌmp(ə)ni/ *noun* **1.** a group of people organised to buy, sell or provide a service **2.** a group of people organised to buy or sell or provide a service which has been legally incorporated, and so is a legal entity separate from its individual members □ **a company of good standing** a very reputable company □ **to put a company into liquidation** to close a company by selling its assets to pay its creditors □ **to set up a company** to start a company legally **3.** an organisation in the City of London which does mainly charitable work and is derived from one of the former trade associations ○ *the Drapers' Company* ○ *the Grocers' Company*

company law /ˌkʌmp(ə)ni ˈlɔː/ *noun* law relating to the way companies may operate

company limited by guarantee /ˌkʌmp(ə)ni ˌlɪmɪtɪd baɪ ˌgærənˈtiː/ *noun* a type of incorporation used primarily for charity organisations, in which the members are guarantors rather than shareholders and do not receive profits

company promoter /ˌkʌmp(ə)ni prə ˈməʊtə/ *noun* a person who organises the setting up of a new company

company secretary /ˌkʌmp(ə)ni ˈsekrɪt(ə)ri/ *noun* somebody who is responsible for a company's legal and financial affairs

company voluntary arrangement /ˌkʌmp(ə)ni ˌvɒlənt(ə)ri əˈreɪndʒmənt/ *noun* an arrangement proposed by a company and approved by its shareholders and creditors for the reorganisation or compromise of its debts. Abbreviation **CVA**

comparative law /kəmˈpærətɪv lɔː/ *noun* a study which compares the legal systems of different countries

compel /kəmˈpel/ *verb* to force someone to do something ○ *The Act compels all drivers to have adequate insurance.* (NOTE: **compelling – compelled**)

compellability /kəmˌpeləˈbɪlɪti/ *noun* the fact of being compellable

compellable /kəmˈpeləb(ə)l/ *adjective* able to be forced to do something ○ *a compellable witness*

compensate /ˈkɒmpənseɪt/ *verb* to pay for damage done ○ *He was compensated for loss of earnings following the injury.*

compensation /ˌkɒmpənˈseɪʃ(ə)n/ *noun* **1.** payment made by someone to cover the cost of damage or hardship which he or she has caused ○ *Unlimited compensation may be awarded in the Crown Court.* □ **compensation for damage** a payment made for damage done □ **compensation for loss of office** a payment made to a director who is asked to leave a company before his or her contract ends □ **compensation for loss of earnings** a payment made to someone who has stopped earning money or who is not able to earn money **2.** *US* a payment made to someone for work which has been done

compensation fund /ˌkɒmpən ˈseɪʃ(ə)n fʌnd/ *noun* a special fund set up by the Law Society to compensate clients for loss suffered because of the actions of solicitors

compensation order /ˌkɒmpən ˈseɪʃ(ə)n ˌɔːdə/ *noun* an order made by a criminal court which forces a criminal to pay compensation to his or her victim

compensation package /ˌkɒmpən ˈseɪʃ(ə)n ˌpækɪdʒ/ *noun* the salary, pension and other benefits offered with a job

compensatory damages /ˌkɒmpənseɪt(ə)ri ˈdæmɪdʒɪz/ *plural noun* damages which compensate for loss or harm suffered

compete /kəmˈpiːt/ *verb* □ **to compete with someone or with a company** to try to do better than another person or another company

competence /ˈkɒmpɪt(ə)ns/, **competency** /ˈkɒmpɪt(ə)nsi/ *noun* **1.** the ability to do something effectively **2.** the fact of being able to give evidence (NOTE: Anyone is able to give evidence, except the sovereign, persons who are mentally ill, and spouses when the other spouse is being prosecuted.) **3.** legal jurisdiction □ **the case falls within the competence of the court** the court is legally able to deal with the case

competent /ˈkɒmpɪt(ə)nt/ *adjective* **1.** able to do something ○ *She is a competent manager.* **2.** efficient **3.** legally able to do something ○ *Most people are competent to give evidence.* □ **the court is not competent to deal with this case** the court is not legally able to deal with the case

competition /ˌkɒmpəˈtɪʃ(ə)n/ *noun* the process of attempting to do better and be more successful than another company

competitor /kəmˈpetɪtə/ *noun* a person or company which competes ○ *Two German firms are our main competitors.* ○ *The contract of employment forbids members of staff from leaving to go to work for competitors.*

complainant /kəmˈpleɪnənt/ *noun* somebody who makes a complaint or who starts proceedings against someone

complaint /kəmˈpleɪnt/ *noun* **1.** a statement that you feel something is wrong ○ *When making a complaint, always quote the reference number.* ○ *She sent her letter of complaint to the managing director.* □ **to make** or **lodge a complaint against someone** to write and send an official complaint to someone's superior **2.** a document signed to start proceedings in a Magistrates' Court **3.** a statement of the case made by the claimant at the beginning of a civil action

complaints procedure /kəmˈpleɪnts prəˌsiːdʒə/ *noun* an agreed way of presenting complaints formally, e.g. from an employee to the management of a company

complete /kəmˈpliːt/ *adjective* whole, with nothing missing ○ *The order is complete and ready for sending.* ○ *The order should be delivered only if it is complete.* ■ *verb* **1.** to finish ○ *The factory completed the order in two weeks.* ○ *How long will it take you to complete the job?* **2.** □ **to complete a conveyance** to convey a property to a purchaser, when the purchaser pays the purchase price and the vendor hands over the

signed conveyance and the deeds of the property

completion /kəmˈpliːʃ(ə)n/ *noun* **1.** the act of finishing something **2.** the last stage in the sale of a property when the solicitors for the two parties meet, when the purchaser pays and the vendor passes the conveyance and the deeds to the purchaser

completion date /kəmˈpliːʃ(ə)n deɪt/ *noun* **1.** the date when something will be finished **2.** the date on which completion on a house sale takes place, or is due to take place

completion statement /kəmˌpliːʃ(ə)n ˈsteɪtmənt/ *noun* a statement of account from a solicitor to a client showing all the costs of the sale or purchase of a property

compliance /kəmˈplaɪəns/ *noun* the fact that someone's work or behaviour complies with instructions, regulations or laws ○ *The documents have been drawn up in compliance with the provisions of the Act.*

compliant /kəmˈplaɪənt/ *adjective* made or done in accordance with instructions, regulations or laws □ **not compliant with** not in agreement with ○ *The settlement is not compliant with the earlier order of the court.*

comply /kəmˈplaɪ/ *verb* □ **to comply with** to obey ○ *The company has complied with the court order.* ○ *She refused to comply with the injunction.*

composition /ˌkɒmpəˈzɪʃ(ə)n/ *noun* an agreement between a debtor and creditors to settle a debt immediately by repaying only part of it

compos mentis /ˌkɒmpɒs ˈmentɪs/ *phrase* a Latin phrase meaning 'of sound mind' or 'sane'

compound /kəmˈpaʊnd/ *verb* **1.** to agree with creditors to settle a debt by paying part of what is owed **2.** □ **to compound an offence** to agree (in return for payment) not to prosecute someone who has committed an offence

comprehensive /ˌkɒmprɪˈhensɪv/ *adjective* including everything

comprehensive insurance /ˌkɒmprɪhensɪv ɪnˈʃʊərəns/ *noun* insurance which offers coverage against a large number of possible risks

comprehensive policy /ˌkɒmprɪhensɪv ˈpɒlɪsi/ *noun* an insurance policy which covers risks of any kind, with no exclusions

compromise /'kɒmprəmaɪz/ *noun* an agreement between two sides, where each side gives way a little in order to reach a settlement ○ *After some discussion a compromise solution was reached.* ■ *verb* **1.** to reach an agreement by giving way a little ○ *He asked £15 for it, I offered £7 and we compromised on £10.* **2.** to involve someone in something which makes his or her reputation less good ○ *The minister was compromised in the bribery case.*

comptroller /kən'trəʊlə/ *noun* the person in charge, especially referring to accounts

Comptroller and Auditor-General /kən,trəʊlə ənd ,ɔːdɪtə 'dʒen(ə)rəl/ *noun* an official whose duty is to examine the accounts of ministries and government departments and who heads the National Audit Office

compulsory /kəm'pʌlsəri/ *adjective* being forced or ordered

compulsory liquidation /kəm,pʌlsəri ,lɪkwɪ'deɪʃ(ə)n/ *noun* liquidation which is ordered by a court

compulsory purchase /kəm,pʌlsəri 'pɜːtʃɪs/ *noun* the buying of a property by the local council or the government even if the owner does not want to sell

compulsory purchase order /kəm ,pʌlsəri 'pɜːtʃɪs ,ɔːdə/ *noun* an official order from a local authority or from the government ordering an owner to sell his or her property to them

compulsory winding up order /kəm ,pʌlsəri ,waɪndɪŋ 'ʌp ,ɔːdə/ *noun* an order from a court saying that a company must stop trading

computer crime /kəm'pjuːtə kraɪm/ *noun* illegal activities carried out on or by means of a computer

COMMENT: Computer crime includes criminal trespass into another computer system, theft of computerised data and the use of an online system to commit or aid in the commission of fraud.

computer fraud /kəm'pjuːtə frɔːd/ *noun* fraud committed by using data stored on a computer

con /kɒn/ *noun* **1.** a trick done to try to get money from someone (*informal*) ○ *Claiming back all those inflated expenses from the company was just a con.* **2.** same as **convict** (*slang*) **3.** same as **conviction** (*slang*) ■ *verb* to trick someone to try to get money (*informal*) ○ *They conned the bank into lending them £25,000 with no security.* ○ *He*

conned the finance company out of £100,000. (NOTE: **conning – conned**. Note also you con someone **into** doing something.)

conceal /kən'siːl/ *verb* to hide ○ *She was accused of concealing information.* ○ *The accused had a gun concealed under his coat.*

concealment /kən'siːlmənt/ *noun* the act hiding something for criminal purposes □ **concealment of assets** the act of hiding assets so that creditors do not know they exist □ **concealment of birth** a notifiable offence of hiding the fact that a child has been born

concede /kən'siːd/ *verb* to admit that an opposing party is right ○ *Counsel conceded that his client owed the money.* ○ *The witness conceded under questioning that he had never been near the house.* □ **to concede defeat** to admit that you have lost

concern /kən'sɜːn/ *noun* a business or company □ **a going concern** a business which is working and making a profit □ **sold as a going concern** sold as an actively trading company ■ *verb* to deal with, to be connected with ○ *The court is not concerned with the value of the items stolen.* ○ *The report does not concern itself with the impartiality of the judge.* ○ *He has been asked to give evidence to the commission of inquiry concerning the breakdown of law and order.* ○ *The contract was drawn up with the agreement of all parties concerned.*

concert party /'kɒnsət ,pɑːti/ *noun* an arrangement by which several people or companies act together in secret to take over a company

concession /kən'seʃ(ə)n/ *noun* **1.** the right to use someone else's property for business purposes **2.** the right to be the only seller of a product in a place ○ *She runs a jewellery concession in a department store.* **3.** an allowance **4.** an act of accepting defeat

concessionaire /kən,seʃə'neə/ *noun* somebody who has the right to be the only seller of a product in a place

conciliation /kən,sɪli'eɪʃ(ə)n/ *noun* the act of bringing together the parties in a dispute so that the dispute can be settled

Conciliation Service /kən,sɪli'eɪʃ(ə)n ,sɜːvɪs/ *noun* same as **Advisory Conciliation and Arbitration Service**

conclude /kən'kluːd/ *verb* **1.** to complete successfully ○ *to conclude an agreement with someone* **2.** to believe from evidence ○

The police concluded that the thief had got into the building through the main entrance.

conclusion /kən'kluːʒ(ə)n/ *noun* **1.** an opinion which is reached after careful thought and examination of the evidence ○ *The police have come to the conclusion or have reached the conclusion that the bomb was set off by radio control.* **2.** □ **conclusion of fact** *US* a statement of a decision by a judge, based on facts □ **conclusion of law** a statement of a decision by a judge, based on rules of law **3.** the final completion ○ *the conclusion of the defence counsel's address* □ **in conclusion** finally, at the end ○ *In conclusion, the judge thanked the jury for their long and patient service.*

conclusive /kən'kluːsɪv/ *adjective* proving something ○ *The fingerprints on the gun were conclusive evidence of the accused's guilt.*

conclusively /kən'kluːsɪvli/ *adverb* in a way which proves a fact ○ *The evidence of the eye witness proved conclusively that the accused was in the town at the time the robbery was committed.*

concordat /kən'kɔːdæt/ *noun* an agreement between the Roman Catholic Church and a government, which allows the Church specific rights and privileges

concur /kən'kɜː/ *verb* to agree ○ *Smith LJ dismissed the appeal, Jones and White LJJ concurring.*

concurrence /kən'kʌrəns/ *noun* agreement between different people ○ *In concurrence with the other judges, Smith LJ dismissed the appeal.*

concurrent /kən'kʌrənt/ *adjective* taking place at the same time. ◊ **consecutive**

concurrently /kən'kʌrəntli/ *adverb* taking place at the same time ○ *He was sentenced to two periods of two years in prison, the sentences to run concurrently.* ◊ **consecutively**

concurrent power /kən,kʌrənt 'pauə/ *noun* a power which is held concurrently by a Member State and by the community, where the Member State can exercise the power up to the point at which the community exercises its rights (NOTE: If the community acts, the power becomes exclusive to the community and the Member State can no longer act.)

concurrent sentence /kən,kʌrənt 'sentəns/ *noun* a sentence which takes place at the same time as another ○ *He was given two concurrent jail sentences of six months.*

condemn /kən'dem/ *verb* **1.** to sentence someone to be punished ○ *The prisoners were condemned to death.* **2.** to say that a dwelling is not fit for people to live in

condemnation /,kɒndem'neɪʃ(ə)n/ *noun* **1.** the act of sentencing of someone to a particular severe punishment **2.** the forfeit of a piece of property when it has been legally seized

condemned cell /kən'demd sel/ *noun* *US* a cell where a prisoner is kept who has been sentenced to death

condition /kən'dɪʃ(ə)n/ *noun* **1.** a term of a contract or duty which has to be carried out as part of a contract, or something which has to be agreed before a contract becomes valid □ **on condition that** provided that ○ *They were granted the lease on condition that they paid the legal costs.* **2.** a general state ○ *item sold in good condition* ○ *What was the condition of the car when it was sold?*

conditional /kən'dɪʃ(ə)n(ə)l/ *adjective* only able to happen if something else happens first □ **to give a conditional acceptance** to accept, provided that specific things happen or terms apply □ **to make a conditional offer** to offer to buy something, provided that specific terms apply ■ **conditional on** □ **the offer is conditional on the board's acceptance** the offer will only go through if the board accepts it

conditional contract /kən,dɪʃ(ə)n(ə)l 'kɒntrækt/ *noun* a contract to transfer ownership of property that places certain conditions on one or both parties

conditional discharge /kən ,dɪʃ(ə)n(ə)l 'dɪstʃɑːdʒ/ *noun* an act of allowing an offender to be set free without any immediate punishment on condition that he or she does not commit an offence during the following period

conditional fee /kən'dɪʃ(ə)n(ə)l fiː/ *noun* a fee which is paid only if the case is won. Also called **contingency fee**

conditional fee agreement /kən ,dɪʃ(ə)n(ə)l 'fiː ə,griːmənt/ *noun* an agreement between a client and their representation that the legal fees will only be paid if the case is successful. Also known as **no win no fee**

COMMENT: Conditional fee agreements originally covered a limited range of cases, but are now applied to insolvency, defamation, civil liberties, intellectual property, employment and many other areas of action. These agreements allow clients to agree with their lawyers that the lawyers will not receive all or part of the usual fees or expenses if the case is lost; if the case is won, on the other hand, the client agrees to pay an extra fee in addition to the normal fee. Insurance policies are available to people contemplating legal action to cover the costs of the other party and the client's own fees if the case is lost.

conditionally /kən'dɪʃ(ə)n(ə)li/ *adverb* provided some things take place □ **to accept an offer conditionally** to accept provided some conditions are fulfilled

conditional will /kən'dɪʃ(ə)n(ə)l wɪl/ *noun* a will which takes effect when the person dies, but only if specific conditions apply

condition precedent /kən,dɪʃ(ə)n 'presɪd(ə)nt/ *noun* a condition which says that a right will not be granted until something is done

conditions of employment /kən,dɪʃ(ə)nz əv ɪm'plɔɪmənt/ *plural noun* the terms of a contract of employment, which must be supplied in writing to an employee within two months of the start of employment

conditions of sale /kən,dɪʃ(ə)nz əv 'seɪl/ *plural noun* a list of the terms such as discounts and credit terms under which a sale takes place

condition subsequent /kən,dɪʃ(ə)n 'sʌbsɪkwənt/ *noun* a condition which says that a contract will be modified or annulled if something is not done

condominium /,kɒndə'mɪniəm/ *noun US* a system of ownership, where a person owns an individual apartment in a building, together with a share of the land and common parts such as stairs and roof

condonation /,kɒndə'neɪʃ(ə)n/ *noun* the forgiving by one spouse of an act, especially adultery, of the other

condone /kən'dəʊn/ *verb* to fail to criticise bad or criminal behaviour and so imply that it is acceptable ○ *The court cannot condone your treatment of your children.*

conducive /kən'djuːsɪv/ *adjective* likely to lead to or produce ○ *The threat of legal action is not conducive to an easy solution to the dispute.*

conduct /kən'dʌkt/ *noun* a way of behaving ○ *She was arrested for disorderly conduct in the street.* □ **conduct conducive to a breach of the peace** a way of behaving, using rude or threatening language in speech or writing, which seems likely to

cause a breach of the peace ■ *verb* to carry out an activity ○ *to conduct discussions* or *negotiations* ○ *The chairman conducted the proceedings very efficiently.*

confederation /kən,fedə'reɪʃ(ə)n/, **confederacy** /kən'fed(ə)rəsi/ *noun* a group of organisations working together for common aims ○ *a loose confederation of local businesses*

confer /kən'fɜː/ *verb* **1.** to give power or responsibility to someone ○ *the discretionary powers conferred on the tribunal by statute* **2.** to discuss ○ *The Chief Constable conferred with the Superintendent in charge of the case.*

conference /'kɒnf(ə)rəns/ *noun* a meeting of a group of people to discuss something ○ *The Police Federation is holding its annual conference this week.* ○ *The Labour Party Annual Conference was held in Brighton this year.* ○ *He presented a motion to the conference.* ○ *The conference passed a motion in favour of unilateral nuclear disarmament.*

conference table /,kɒnf(ə)rəns 'teɪb(ə)l/ *noun* a table around which people sit to negotiate

conference with counsel /,kɒnf(ə)rəns wɪð 'kaʊns(ə)l/ *noun* a formal meeting with a barrister

confess /kən'fes/ *verb* to admit that you have committed a crime ○ *After six hours' questioning by the police the accused man confessed.*

confession /kən'feʃ(ə)n/ *noun* **1.** a statement by a defendant that they have committed a crime ○ *She claimed that she had made her confession under duress.* **2.** a document in which you admit that you have committed a crime ○ *The police sergeant asked him to sign his confession.*

confession and avoidance /kən,feʃ(ə)n ən ə'vɔɪd(ə)ns/ *noun* an admission by a party of the allegations made against him or her, but at the same time bringing forward new pleadings which make the allegations void

confidence /'kɒnfɪd(ə)ns/ *noun* **1.** feeling sure about something or having trust in someone ○ *The sales teams do not have much confidence in their manager.* ○ *The board has total confidence in the managing director.* **2.** the ability to trust someone with a secret □ **in confidence** in secret ○ *I will show you the report in confidence.*

confidence trick /'kɒnfɪd(ə)ns ,trɪk/, **confidence game** *US* /'kɒnfɪd(ə)ns geɪm/ *noun* a business deal where someone persuades another person to trust them, and then tricks him or her

confidence trickster /'kɒnfɪd(ə)ns ˌtrɪkstə/, **confidence man** *US* /'kɒnfɪd(ə)ns mæn/ *noun* somebody who carries out confidence tricks on people

confidence vote /'kɒnfɪd(ə)ns vəʊt/ *noun* a vote to show that a person or group is or is not trusted ○ *He proposed a vote of confidence in the government.* ○ *The chairman resigned after the motion of no confidence was passed at the AGM.*

confidential /ˌkɒnfɪ'denʃəl/ *adjective* secret between two persons or a small group of people ○ *What was discussed at the board meeting is obviously confidential.*

confidential information /ˌkɒnfɪdenʃəl ˌɪnfə'meɪʃ(ə)n/ *noun* information which is secret, and which must not be passed on to other people ○ *He was accused of passing on confidential information.* ○ *The knowledge which an employee has of the working of the firm for which he works can be seen to be confidential information which he must not pass on to another firm.*

confidentiality /ˌkɒnfɪdenʃi'ælɪti/ *noun* an understanding between two or more parties that specified information remains secret

confidentiality agreement /ˌkɒnfɪdenʃi'ælɪti əˌgriːmənt/ *noun* same as **non-disclosure agreement**

confidential report /ˌkɒnfɪdenʃəl rɪ'pɔːt/ *noun* a secret document which must not be shown to other than a few named persons

confine /kən'faɪn/ *verb* to keep a criminal in a room or restricted area

confined to barracks /kənˌfaɪnd tə 'bærəks/ *adjective* (*of a soldier*) sentenced to stay in the barracks for a set period of time and not to go outside. Abbreviation **CB**

confinement /kən'faɪnmənt/ *noun* the situation of being kept in a place without being free to leave, especially as a punishment

confirm /kən'fɜːm/ *verb* to say that something is certain or is correct ○ *The Court of Appeal has confirmed the judge's decision.* ○ *Her PA phoned to confirm the hotel room booking.* □ **to confirm someone in a job** to say that someone is now permanently in a particular job

confiscate /'kɒnfɪskeɪt/ *verb* to take away private property into the possession of the state ○ *The court ordered the drugs to be confiscated.*

confiscation /ˌkɒnfɪs'keɪʃ(ə)n/ *noun* the act of confiscating

conflict *noun* /'kɒnflɪkt/ disagreement □ **to be in** *or* **come into conflict with** to disagree with someone over something ■ *verb* /kən'flɪkt/ not to agree ○ *The evidence of the wife conflicts with that of her husband.* ○ *The UK legislation conflicts with the directives of the EU.*

conflicting evidence /ˌkɒnflɪktɪŋ 'evɪd(ə)ns/ *noun* evidence from different witnesses which does not agree ○ *The jury has to decide who to believe among a mass of conflicting evidence.*

conflict of interest /ˌkɒnflɪkt əv 'ɪntrəst/, **conflict of interests** /ˌkɒnflɪkt əv 'ɪntrəsts/ *noun* a situation in which a person may profit personally from decisions which he or she takes in their official capacity, or may not be able to act independently because of connections with other people or organisations

conflict of laws /ˌkɒnflɪkt əv 'lɔːz/ *noun* a section in a country's statutes which deals with disputes between that country's laws and those of another country

conform /kən'fɔːm/ *verb* to act in accordance with something ○ *The proposed Bill conforms to the recommendations of the Royal Commission.*

conformance /kən'fɔːməns/ *noun* behaviour in accordance with a rule ○ *in conformance with the directives of the Commission* ○ *He was criticised for non-conformance with the regulations.*

conformity /kən'fɔːmɪti/ *noun* □ **in conformity with** agreeing with ○ *He has acted in conformity with the regulations.*

congestion charge /kən'dʒestʃən tʃɑːdʒ/ *noun* a charge levied by local government for driving in a particular area

Congress /'kɒŋgres/ *noun US* the elected federal legislative body in many countries, especially in the USA where it is formed of the House of Representatives and the Senate ○ *He was first elected to Congress in 2004.* ○ *At a joint session of Congress, the President called for support for his plan.* (NOTE: often used without **the** except when referring to a particular legislature: *The US Congress met in emergency session*; *The Republicans had a majority in both houses of the 1974 Congress.*)

Congressional /kənˈɡreʃ(ə)n(ə)l/ adjective US referring to Congress ○ a Congressional subcommittee

conjugal /ˈkɒndʒʊɡ(ə)l/ adjective referring to marriage

conjugal rights /ˌkɒndʒʊɡ(ə)l ˈraɪts/ plural noun the rights of a husband and wife in relation to each other, especially with regard to sexual intimacy

conjugal visit /ˌkɒndʒʊɡ(ə)l ˈvɪzɪt/ noun in some countries, a private visit allowed by a prisoner's spouse in order to have sexual intercourse

conman /ˈkɒnmæn/ noun same as **confidence trickster** (informal)

connected persons /kəˌnektɪd ˈpɜːs(ə)nz/ plural noun people who are closely related to, or have a close business association with, a company director

connection /kəˈnekʃən/ noun something which joins one person or thing to another ○ Is there a connection between the loss of the documents and the death of the lawyer? □ **in connection with** referring to ○ The police want to interview the man in connection with burglaries committed last November.

connivance /kəˈnaɪvəns/ noun the act of not reporting a crime that you know is being or is about to be committed ○ With the connivance of the customs officers, he managed to bring the goods into the country.

connive /kəˈnaɪv/ verb □ **to connive at something** to shut one's eyes to wrongdoing, to know that a crime is being committed, but not to report it

conscience clause /ˈkɒnʃəns klɔːz/ noun a clause in the Gender Recognition Act which excuses members of the clergy from performing marriage ceremonies involving transgender persons, if they do not wish to

consecutive /kənˈsekjʊtɪv/ adjective following. ◊ **concurrent** □ **consecutive sentences** two or more sentences which follow one after the other

consecutively /kəˈsekjʊtɪvli/ adverb following ○ He was sentenced to two periods of two years in jail, the sentences to run consecutively. ◊ **concurrently**

consensual /kənˈsensjʊəl/ adjective happening by agreement

consensual acts /kənˌsensjʊəl ˈækts/ plural noun sexual acts which both parties agree should take place

consensus /kənˈsensəs/ noun general agreement ○ There was a consensus between all parties as to the next steps to be taken. ○ In the absence of a consensus, no decisions could be reached.

consensus ad idem /kənˌsensəs æd ˈaɪdem/ phrase a Latin phrase meaning 'agreement to this same thing': a real agreement to a contract by both parties

consent /kənˈsent/ noun agreement or permission that something should happen ○ He borrowed the car without the owner's consent. ◊ **age of consent** ■ verb to agree that something should be done ○ The judge consented to the request of the prosecution counsel.

consent judgment /kənˌsent ˈdʒʌdʒmənt/ noun an agreement of the parties in a lawsuit to a judgment which then becomes the settlement

consent order /kənˌsent ˈɔːdə/ noun a court order that someone must not do something without the agreement of another party

consequential /ˌkɒnsɪˈkwenʃəl/ adjective following as a result of

consequential damages /ˌkɒnsɪkwenʃəl ˈdæmɪdʒɪz/ plural noun damages suffered as a consequence of using a piece of equipment, software, etc., e.g. the stoppage of business activities because of computer or software failure

consequent on /ˈkɒnsɪkwənt ɒn/, **upon** /ʌˈpɒn/ adjective following as a result of ○ The manufacturer is not liable for injuries consequent on the use of this apparatus.

conservation area /ˌkɒnsəˈveɪʃ(ə)n ˌeəriə/ noun an area of special environmental or historical importance that is protected by law from changes that have not received official permission

consider /kənˈsɪdə/ verb **1.** to think seriously about something □ **to consider the terms of a contract** to examine and discuss if the terms are acceptable □ **to consider a verdict** (of a jury) to discuss the evidence they have heard and decide if the accused was guilty or not **2.** to believe ○ He is considered to be one of the leading divorce lawyers. ○ The law on libel is considered too lenient.

consideration /kənˌsɪdəˈreɪʃ(ə)n/ noun **1.** serious thought ○ We are giving consideration to moving the head office to Scotland. □ **to take something into consideration** to think about something when deciding what to do ○ Having taken the age of the accused into consideration, the court has decided to give him a suspended sentence. □ **to ask for**

other offences to be taken into consideration to confess to other offences after being accused or convicted of one offence, so that the sentence can cover all of them ○ *The accused admitted six other offences, and asked for them to be taken into consideration.* **2.** the price, in money, goods, or some other reward, paid by one person in exchange for another person promising to do something, which is an essential element in the formation of a contract □ **for a small consideration** for a small fee or payment

consign /kənˈsaɪn/ *verb* □ **to consign goods to someone** to hand over goods to someone for him or her to sell for you

consignation /ˌkɒnsaɪˈneɪʃ(ə)n/ *noun* the act of consigning

consignee /ˌkɒnsaɪˈniː/ *noun* somebody who receives goods from someone for his or her own use or to sell for the person who sends them

consignment /kənˈsaɪnmənt/ *noun* the sending of goods to someone who will hold them for you and sell them on your behalf □ **goods on consignment** goods kept for another company to be sold on their behalf for a commission

consignment note /kənˈsaɪnmənt nəʊt/ *noun* a note saying that goods have been sent

consignor /kənˈsaɪnə/ *noun* somebody who consigns goods to someone

COMMENT: The goods remain the legal property of the consignor until the consignee sells them.

consistent /kənˈsɪstənt/ *adjective* agreeing with and not contradicting something ○ *The sentence is consistent with government policy on the treatment of young offenders.*

consolidate /kənˈsɒlɪdeɪt/ *verb* **1.** to bring several Acts of Parliament together into one act **2.** to hear several sets of proceedings together ○ *The judge ordered the actions to be consolidated.*

Consolidated Fund /kənˌsɒlɪdeɪtɪd ˈfʌnd/ *noun* a fund of money formed of all taxes and other government revenues. ◊ **Exchequer**

consolidated shipment /kənˌsɒlɪdeɪtɪd ˈʃɪpmənt/ *noun* goods from different companies grouped together into a single shipment

Consolidating Act /kənˈsɒlɪdeɪtɪŋ ˌækt/ *noun* an Act of Parliament which brings together several previous Acts which relate to the same subject. ◊ **codification**

consolidation /kənˌsɒlɪˈdeɪʃ(ə)n/ *noun* **1.** the act of bringing together various Acts of Parliament which deal with one subject into one single Act **2.** a procedure whereby several sets of proceedings are heard together by the court

consortium /kənˈsɔːtiəm/ *noun* **1.** a group of different companies which work together on one project **2.** the right of a husband and wife to the love and support of the other

conspiracy /kənˈspɪrəsi/ *noun* a plan made with another person or other people to commit a crime or tort (NOTE: Conspiracy to commit a crime is itself a crime.)

conspire /kənˈspaɪə/ *verb* to agree with another person or other people to commit a crime or tort

constitute /ˈkɒnstɪtjuːt/ *verb* to make or to form ○ *The documents constitute primary evidence.* ○ *This Act constitutes a major change in government policy.* ○ *Conduct tending to interfere with the course of justice constitutes contempt of court.*

constitution /ˌkɒnstɪˈtjuːʃ(ə)n/ *noun* **1.** the set of laws, usually written down, under which a country is ruled ○ *The freedom of the individual is guaranteed by the country's constitution.* ○ *The new president asked the assembly to draft a new constitution.* **2.** the written rules of a society, association or club ○ *Under the society's constitution, the chairman is elected for a two-year period.* ○ *Payments to officers of the association are not allowed by the constitution.*

COMMENT: Most countries have written constitutions, usually drafted by lawyers, which can be amended by an Act of the country's legislative body. The United States constitution was drawn up by Thomas Jefferson after the country became independent, and has numerous amendments (the first ten amendments being the Bill of Rights). Great Britain is unusual in that it has no written constitution, and relies on precedent and the body of laws passed over the years to act as a safeguard of the rights of the citizens and the legality of government.

constitutional /ˌkɒnstɪˈtjuːʃ(ə)nəl/ *adjective* **1.** referring to a country's constitution ○ *Censorship of the press is not constitutional.* **2.** according to a constitution ○ *The re-election of the chairman for a second term is not constitutional.* ◊ **unconstitutional**

constitutional law /ˌkɒnstɪˈtjuːʃ(ə)nəl lɔː/ *noun* the set of laws relating to government and its function under which a country is ruled

constitutional lawyer
/ˌkɒnstɪtjuːʃ(ə)nəl ˈlɔːjə/ noun a lawyer who specialises in drafting or interpreting constitutions

constitutional reform
/ˌkɒnstɪtjuːʃ(ə)nəl rɪˈfɔːm/ noun the act of modernising the way a country is run

COMMENT: The Constitutional Reform Act of 2005 in the UK made changes to the office of **Lord Chancellor** and made provisions for a Supreme Court to be set up in the UK to replace the judicial function of the House of Lords.

constitutional right /ˌkɒnstɪ ˈtjuːʃ(ə)nəl raɪt/ noun a right which is guaranteed by the constitution of a country

construction /kənˈstrʌkʃən/ noun an interpretation of the meaning of words □ **to put a construction on words** to suggest a meaning for words which is not immediately obvious

construction company /kənˈstrʌkʃən ˌkʌmp(ə)ni/ noun a company which specialises in building

constructive /kənˈstrʌktɪv/ adjective useful, helping to improve something ○ She made some constructive suggestions for improving employer-employee relations.

constructive dismissal /kənˌstrʌktɪv dɪsˈmɪs(ə)l/ noun a situation when a worker leaves his or her job voluntarily, but because of unreasonable pressure from the management

constructive knowledge /kən ˌstrʌktɪv ˈnɒlɪdʒ/, **constructive notice** /kənˌstrʌktɪv ˈnəʊtɪs/ noun knowledge of a fact or matter which the law says a person has available to them, whether or not that person actually has it

constructive total loss /kənˌstrʌktɪv ˈtəʊt(ə)l lɒs/ noun a loss where the item insured has been thrown away as it is likely to be irreplaceable

constructive trust /kənˈstrʌktɪv trʌst/ noun trust arising by reason of a person's behaviour

construe /kənˈstruː/ verb to interpret the meaning of words or of a document ○ The court construed the words to mean that there was a contract between the parties. ○ Written opinion is not admissible as evidence for the purposes of construing a deed of settlement.

consult /kənˈsʌlt/ verb to ask an expert for advice ○ He consulted his solicitor about the letter.

consultancy /kənˈsʌltənsi/ noun the act of giving specialist advice ○ a consultancy firm ○ He offers a consultancy service.

consultant /kənˈsʌltənt/ noun a specialist who gives advice ○ engineering consultant ○ management consultant ○ tax consultant

consultation /ˌkɒnsəlˈteɪʃ(ə)n/ noun **1.** a meeting with someone who can give specialist advice **2.** a meeting between a client and a professional adviser such as a solicitor or QC

consultation document /ˌkɒnsəl ˈteɪʃ(ə)n ˌdɒkjʊmənt/ noun a paper which is issued by a government department to people who are asked to comment and make suggestions for improvement

consultative /kənˈsʌltətɪv/ adjective being asked to give advice ○ the report of a consultative body ○ She is acting in a consultative capacity.

consultative document /kənˌsʌltətɪv ˈdɒkjʊmənt/ noun same as **consultation document**

consulting /kənˈsʌltɪŋ/ adjective able to give specialist advice ○ consulting engineer

consumer /kənˈsjuːmə/ noun a person or company which buys and uses goods and services ○ Gas consumers are protesting at the increase in prices. ○ The factory is a heavy consumer of water.

consumer contract /kənˌsjuːmə ˈkɒntrækt/ noun the contract made between a trader who is selling something and a customer who is buying it (NOTE: Consumer contracts are subject to the Sale Of Goods Act.)

consumer council /kənˌsjuːmə ˈkaʊns(ə)l/ noun a group representing the interests of consumers

consumer credit /kənˌsjuːmə ˈkredɪt/ noun the provision of loans by finance companies to help people buy goods

consumer goods /kənˌsjuːmə ˈɡʊdz/ plural noun goods bought by the general public and not by businesses

consumer legislation /kənˌsjuːmə ˌledʒɪˈsleɪʃ(ə)n/ noun laws which give rights to people who buy goods or who pay for services

consumer protection /kənˌsjuːmə prə ˈtekʃən/ noun the activity of protecting consumers from unfair or illegal business practices

consumer rights /kənˌsjuːmə ˈraɪts/ *plural noun* same as **statutory rights**

consummation /ˌkɒnsəˈmeɪʃ(ə)n/ *noun* the act of having sexual intercourse for the first time after the marriage ceremony

COMMENT: Failure or lack of intention to consummate a marriage may be valid grounds for annulment.

contact /ˈkɒntækt/ *noun* **1.** a person you know who can give you help such as finding work or advice and information ○ *He has many contacts in the city.* ○ *Who is your contact in the Ministry?* **2.** the act of getting in touch with someone □ **I have lost contact with them** I do not communicate with them any longer □ **he put me in contact with a good lawyer** he told me how to get in touch with a good lawyer

contact order /ˈkɒntækt ˌɔːdə/ *noun* a court order allowing a parent to see a child where the child is in the care of someone else, such as the other parent in the case of a divorced couple. Former name **access order**

contemnor /kənˈtemnə/ *noun* somebody who commits a contempt of court

contempt /kənˈtempt/ *noun* the act of showing a lack of respect to a court or Parliament □ **to be in contempt** to have shown disrespect to a court, especially by disobeying a court order □ **to purge one's contempt** to apologise, to do something to show that you are sorry for the lack of respect shown

contempt of court /kənˌtempt əv ˈkɔːt/ *noun* the act of showing a lack of respect to a court, by bad behaviour in court or by refusing to carry out a court order ○ *At common law, conduct tending to interfere with the course of justice in particular legal proceedings constitutes criminal contempt.*

contentious /kənˈtenʃəs/ *adjective, noun* (*of legal business*) where there is a dispute

contents /ˈkɒntents/ *plural noun* things contained in something ○ *The contents of the bottle poured out onto the floor.* ○ *The customs officials inspected the contents of the box.*

contest /kənˈtest/ *noun* a situation in which people or groups try to gain an advantage ■ *verb* **1.** to argue that a decision or a ruling is wrong ○ *I wish to contest the statement made by the witness.* **2.** to com-

pete to be successful in something such as an election

contested takeover /kənˌtestɪd ˈteɪkəʊvə/ *noun* a takeover where the directors of the company being bought do not recommend the bid and try to fight it

context /ˈkɒntekst/ *noun* **1.** other words which surround a word or phrase ○ *The words can only be understood in the context of the phrase in which they occur.* □ **out of context** seen without its surrounding circumstances, so as to change meaning or give a different impression **2.** the general situation in which something happens ○ *The action of the police has to be seen in the context of the riots against the government.*

contiguous zone /kənˈtɪɡjʊəs ˌzəʊn/ *noun* the part of the sea beyond territorial waters, extending up to 24 nautical miles beyond a coastline, over which the country may extend its jurisdiction for reasons of national security

contingency /kənˈtɪndʒənsi/ *noun* a possible state of emergency when decisions will have to be taken quickly

contingency fee /kənˈtɪndʒənt fiː/ *noun US* same as **conditional fee**

contingency fund /kənˈtɪndʒənsi fʌnd/ *noun* money set aside in case it is needed urgently

contingency plan /kənˈtɪndʒənsi plæn/ *noun* a plan which will be put into action if there is an emergency

contingent /kənˈtɪndʒənt/ *adjective* □ **to be contingent on** to only take place or be valid if something happens

contingent expenses /kənˌtɪndʒənt ɪkˈspensɪz/ *plural noun* expenses which will be incurred only if something happens

contingent interest /kənˌtɪndʒənt ˈɪntrəst/ *noun US* an interest in property which may or may not exist in the future

contingent policy /kənˌtɪndʒənt ˈpɒlɪsi/ *noun* a policy which pays out only if something happens, e.g. if the person named in the policy dies before the person who is to benefit from it

contingent remainder /kənˌtɪndʒənt rɪˈmeɪndə/ *noun* a remainder which is contingent upon something happening in the future

continuing professional development /kənˌtɪnjuɪŋ prəˌfeʃ(ə)n(ə)l dɪˈveləpmənt/ *noun* professional training which practicing solicitors in England and

Wales are required to undergo. Abbreviation **CPD**

contra /ˈkɒntrə/ *prefix* against, opposite, or contrasting

contract /kənˈtrækt/ *noun* **1.** a legal agreement between two or more parties ○ *to draw up a contract* ○ *to draft a contract* ○ *to sign a contract* □ **the contract is binding on both parties** both parties signing the contract must do what is agreed □ **in breach of contract** having failed to do what was agreed in the contract □ **under contract** bound by the terms of a contract ○ *The firm is under contract to deliver the goods by November.* □ **to void a contract** to make a contract invalid **2.** □ **contract for services** an agreement for the supply of a service or goods **3.** an agreement to kill someone for a payment (*slang*) □ **to take a contract out on someone** to arrange for someone to be killed ■ *verb* to agree to do something on the basis of a contract ○ *to contract to supply spare parts* or *to contract for the supply of spare parts*

COMMENT: A contract is an agreement between two or more parties to create legal obligations between them. Some contracts are made 'under seal', i.e. they are signed and sealed by the parties; most contracts are made orally or in writing. The essential elements of a contract are: (a) that an offer made by one party should be **accepted** by the other; (b) **consideration**; (c) the **intention** to create legal relations. The terms of a contract may be **express** or **implied**. A breach of contract by one party entitles the other party to sue for damages or in some cases to seek specific performance.

contracting party /kənˌtræktɪŋ ˈpɑːti/ *noun* the person or company that signs a contract

contract killer /ˌkɒntrækt ˈkɪlə/ *noun* somebody who will kill someone if paid to do so

contract law /ˈkɒntrækt lɔː/ *noun* law relating to agreements

contract of employment /ˌkɒntrækt əv ɪmˈplɔɪmənt/, **contract of service** /ˌkɒntrækt əv ˈsɜːvɪs/ *noun* a contract between an employer and an employee showing all the conditions of work

contractor /kənˈtræktə/ *noun* a person who enters into a contract, especially a person or company that does work according to a written agreement

contractual /kənˈtræktʃuəl/ *adjective* according to a contract □ **to fulfil your contractual obligations** to do what you have

agreed to do in a contract □ **to be under a contractual obligation** to have signed an agreement to do something

contractual liability /kənˌtræktʃuəl ˌlaɪəˈbɪlɪti/ *noun* a legal responsibility for something as stated in a contract

contractually /kənˈtræktʃuəli/ *adverb* according to a contract ○ *The company is contractually bound to pay his expenses.*

contract under seal /ˌkɒntrækt ˈʌndə siːl/ *noun* a contract which has been signed and legally approved with the seal of the company or the person entering into it. Compare **simple contract**

contract work /ˈkɒntrækt wɜːk/ *noun* work done according to a written agreement

contradict /ˌkɒntrəˈdɪkt/ *verb* **1.** to say exactly the opposite of something ○ *The witness contradicted himself several times.* **2.** to disagree in various details with another statement, story or report, so that both cannot be true ○ *The statement contradicts the report in the newspapers.*

contradiction /ˌkɒntrəˈdɪkʃən/ *noun* a statement which contradicts ○ *The witness' evidence was a mass of contradictions.* ○ *There is a contradiction between the Minister's statement in the House of Commons and the reports published in the newspapers.*

contradictory /ˌkɒntrəˈdɪkt(ə)ri/ *adjective* not agreeing ○ *a mass of contradictory evidence*

contra entry /ˈkɒntrə ˌentri/ *noun* an entry made in the opposite side of an account to make an earlier entry worthless, i.e. a debit against a credit

contra proferentem /ˌkɒntrə ˌprɒfə ˈrentem/ *phrase* a Latin phrase meaning 'against the one making the point': the rule that an ambiguity in a document is construed against the party who drafted it

contrary /ˈkɒntrəri/ *noun* the opposite ○ *Information suggests that the contrary is true.* □ **on the contrary** used for emphasising an opposite statement ○ *Counsel was not annoyed with the witness – on the contrary, she praised him.* □ **quite the contrary** used for emphasising an opposite statement ○ *I don't dislike his manner of working – quite the contrary, I think it's very effective.* □ **to the contrary** suggesting that the opposite is true or should happen ○ *You should continue to do it this way, unless you receive instructions to the contrary.*

contravene /ˌkɒntrəˈviːn/ *verb* to do something that is not allowed by rules or regulations ○ *The workshop has contravened the employment regulations.* ○ *The fire department can close a restaurant if it contravenes the safety regulations.*

contravention /ˌkɒntrəˈvenʃən/ *noun* the act of breaking a regulation □ **in contravention of** contravening, going against ○ *The restaurant is in contravention of the safety regulations.* ○ *The management of the cinema locked the fire exits in contravention of the fire regulations.*

contribute /kənˈtrɪbjuːt/ *verb* □ **to contribute to** to help something ○ *The public response to the request for information contributed to the capture of the gang.*

contribution /ˌkɒntrɪˈbjuːʃ(ə)n/ *noun* **1.** money paid to add to a sum **2.** (*in civil cases*) the right of someone to get money from a third party to cover the amount which he or she personally has to pay

contributory causes /kənˌtrɪbjʊt(ə)ri ˈkɔːzɪz/ *plural noun* causes which help something to take place ○ *The report listed bad community relations as one of the contributory causes to the riot.*

contributory factor /kənˌtrɪbjʊt(ə)ri ˈfæktə/ *noun* something which contributes to a result

contributory negligence /kən ˌtrɪbjʊt(ə)ri ˈneglɪdʒəns/ *noun* the fact of being partly responsible for harm or damage caused to you because of your own negligent actions

con trick /ˈkɒn trɪk/ *noun* same as **confidence trick** (*informal*)

control /kənˈtrəʊl/ *noun* the fact of keeping someone or something in order or being able to direct them ○ *The company is under the control of three shareholders.* ○ *The family lost control of its business.* ■ *verb* **1.** to have the power to decide what should happen to someone or something **2.** to make sure that something is restricted or kept at the correct level ○ *The government is fighting to control inflation* or *to control the rise in the cost of living.*

controlled /kənˈtrəʊld/ *adjective* **1.** limited by law ○ *controlled chemicals* **2.** carried out in a way that will give accurate results and information ○ *controlled trials* **3.** able to show no emotion when you are angry or upset ○ *There were tears in her eyes as she replied but her voice was controlled.*

controlled drug /kənˌtrəʊld ˈdrʌg/, **controlled substance** /kənˌtrəʊld ˈsʌbstəns/ *noun* a drug or other substance which is restricted by law and of which possession may be an offence

control order /kənˈtrəʊl ˌɔːdə/ *noun* an order under anti-terrorism legislation curtailing an individual's freedom

control systems /kənˈtrəʊl ˌsɪstəmz/ *plural noun* systems used to check that a computer system is working correctly

control test /kənˈtrəʊl test/ *noun* a test to decide if someone is an employee or is self-employed, used for purposes of tax assessment

convene /kənˈviːn/ *verb* to ask people to come together ○ *to convene a meeting of shareholders*

convenience /kənˈviːniəns/ *noun* □ **at your earliest convenience** as soon as you find it possible □ **ship sailing under a flag of convenience** a ship flying the flag of a country which may have no ships of its own but allows ships of other countries to be registered in its ports

convenor /kənˈviːnə/ *noun* a person who calls other people together for a meeting

convention /kənˈvenʃən/ *noun* **1.** the way in which something is usually done, accepted as the normal way to do it ○ *It is the convention for American lawyers to designate themselves 'Esquire'.* **2.** a meeting or series of meetings held to discuss and decide important matters **3.** an international treaty ○ *the Geneva Convention on Human Rights* ○ *The three countries are all signatories of the convention.*

conversion /kənˈvɜːʃ(ə)n/ *noun* the tort of dealing with a person's property in a way which is not consistent with that person's rights over it

conversion of funds /kənˌvɜːʃ(ə)n əv ˈfʌndz/ *noun* the use of money which does not belong to you for a purpose for which it is not supposed to be used

convert /kənˈvɜːt/ *verb* **1.** to change property into another form such as cash **2.** □ **to convert funds to one's own use** to use someone else's money for yourself

convey /kənˈveɪ/ *verb* **1.** to carry goods from one place to another **2.** □ **to convey a property to a purchaser** to pass the ownership of the property to the purchaser

conveyance /kənˈveɪəns/ *noun* **1.** the act of transferring the ownership of land from one person to another **2.** a legal document which transfers the ownership of land from the seller to the buyer

conveyancer /kən'veɪənsə/ *noun* somebody who draws up a conveyance

conveyancing /kən'veɪənsɪŋ/ *noun* **1.** the act of drawing up the document which legally transfers a property from a seller to a buyer **2.** law and procedure relating to the purchase and sale of property

convict /kən'vɪkt/ *noun* somebody who is kept in prison as a punishment for a crime ■ *verb* □ **to convict someone of a crime** to find that someone is guilty of a crime ○ *He was convicted of manslaughter and sentenced to 6 years in prison.*

convicted criminal /kən,vɪktɪd 'krɪmɪn(ə)l/ *noun* a criminal who has been found guilty and sentenced

conviction /kən'vɪkʃən/ *noun* **1.** the feeling of being sure that something is true ○ *It is his conviction that the claimant has brought the case maliciously.* **2.** a decision that a person accused of a crime is guilty ○ *He has had ten convictions for burglary.* ◊ **spent conviction**. Compare **sentence**

convict settlement /kən,vɪkt 'set(ə)lmənt/ *noun US* a prison camp where convicts are sent

cooling off period /,kuːlɪŋ 'ɒf ,pɪəriəd/, **cooling time** *US* /'kuːlɪŋ taɪm/ *noun* **1.** during an industrial dispute, a period when negotiations have to be carried on and no action can be taken by either side **2.** a period of reflection allowed before making a legally-binding commitment, e.g. before formally accepting an insurance policy

co-operation procedure /kəʊ ,ɒpə 'reɪʃ(ə)n prə,siːdʒə/ *noun* (*in the EU*) a procedure introduced by the Single European Act which gives the European Parliament a more important role than before in considering European legislation. ◊ **common position**

COMMENT: Originally the co-operation procedure was restricted to measures concerning the internal market (free movement of people within the union, no discrimination on grounds of nationality, harmonisation of health and safety in the workplace, etc.). It is now also used in connection with European transport policy, training, environmental issues, etc. The co-operation procedure implies that at the end of a discussion period the Council will adopt a **common position** which must then be approved by the European Parliament.

co-operative /kəʊ 'ɒp(ə)rətɪv/ *noun* a business run by a group of workers who are the owners and who share the profits ○ *an industrial co-operative* ○ *to set up a workers' co-operative*

co-opt /,kəʊ 'ɒpt/ *verb* □ **to co-opt someone onto a committee** to ask someone to join a committee without being elected

co-owner /,kəʊ 'əʊnə/ *noun* somebody who owns something jointly with another person or persons ○ *The two sisters are co-owners of the property.*

co-ownership /,kəʊ 'əʊnəʃɪp/ *noun* **1.** an arrangement where two or more persons own a property **2.** an arrangement where partners or employees have shares in a company

cop /kɒp/ *noun* **1.** a policeman (*informal*) **2.** an arrest (*informal*) □ **it's a fair cop** you have caught me ■ *verb* **1.** to catch or arrest someone (*slang*) **2.** to get or to receive something (*slang*) □ **to cop a plea** to plead guilty to a lesser charge and so hope the court will give a shorter sentence to save the time of a full trial

co-partner /kəʊ 'pɑːtnə/ *noun* somebody who is a partner in a business with another person

co-partnership /kəʊ 'pɑːtnəʃɪp/ *noun* an arrangement where partners or employees have shares in the company

COPFS *abbreviation* Crown Office and Procurator Fiscal Service

copper /'kɒpə/ *noun* a policeman (*informal*)

copper-bottomed /,kɒpə 'bɒtəmd/ *adjective* (*of a guarantee or promise*) able to be completely trusted

co-property /kəʊ 'prɒpəti/ *noun* ownership of property by two or more people together

co-proprietor /,kəʊ prə'praɪətə/ *noun* somebody who owns a property with another person or several other people

cop shop /'kɒp ʃɒp/ *noun* a police station (*slang*)

copy /'kɒpi/ *noun* **1.** a document which looks the same as another **2.** anything which copies information in a document, by whatever means, including electronic copies, recordings, etc. ○ *an illegal copy* **3.** any document ■ *verb* **1.** to make a second item which is like the first ○ *He copied the company report at night and took it home.* **2.** to make something which is similar to something else ○ *She simply copied the design from another fashion designer.* ○ *He is successful because he copies good ideas from other businesses.*

copyleft /ˈkɒpileft/ *noun* a type of copyright licence which gives the user the freedom to copy, alter and distribute the work freely for non-commercial purposes

COMMENT: Copyleft licences are typically applied to software and carry few restrictions, other than that the author(s) should be acknowledged whenever the work is passed on. The concept is distinct from putting the work into the **public domain**, where there would be no restrictions at all.

copyright /ˈkɒpiraɪt/ *noun* an author's legal right to publish his or her own work and not to have it copied, which lasts 50 years after the author's death under the Berne Convention, or a similar right of an artist, film maker or musician □ **work which is out of copyright** work by a writer, etc., who has been dead for fifty years, and which anyone can publish □ **work still in copyright** work by a living writer, or by a writer who has not been dead for fifty years ■ *verb* to confirm the copyright of a written work by printing a copyright notice and publishing the work ■ *adjective* covered by the laws of copyright ○ *It is illegal to take copies of a copyright work.*

COMMENT: Copyright exists in original written works, in works of art and works of music; it covers films, broadcasts, recordings, etc.; it also covers the layout of books, newspapers and magazines. Copyright only exists if the work is created by a person who is qualified to hold a copyright, and is published in a country which is qualified to hold a copyright. There is no copyright in ideas, items of news, historical events, items of information, or in titles of artistic works. When a copyright is established, the owner of the copyright can make personal copies of the work, sell copies of it to the public, perform it or exhibit it in public, broadcast it, or adapt it in some way. No other person has the right to do any of these things. Copyright lasts for 50 years after the author's death according to the Berne Convention, and for 25 years according to the Universal Copyright Convention. In the USA, copyright is for 50 years after the death of an author for books published after January 1st, 1978. For books published before that date, the original copyright was for 28 years after the death of the author, and this can be extended for a further 28 year period up to a maximum of 75 years. In 1995, the European Union adopted a copyright term of 70 years after the death of the author. The copyright holder has the right to refuse or to grant permission to copy copyright material, though under the Paris agreement of 1971, the original publishers (representing the author or copyright holder) must, under certain circumstances, grant licences to reprint copyright material. The copyright notice has to include the symbol ©, the name of the copyright holder and the date of the copyright (which is usually the date of first publication). The notice must be printed in the book and usually appears on the reverse of the title page. A copyright notice is also printed on other forms of printed material such as posters.

Copyright Act /ˈkɒpiraɪt ækt/ *noun* an Act of Parliament such as the Copyright Acts 1911, 1956 or 1988 making copyright legal and controlling the copying of copyright material

copyright deposit /ˌkɒpiraɪt dɪˈpɒzɪt/ *noun* the act of placing a copy of a published work in a copyright library, usually the main national library, which is part of the formal process of copyrighting printed material

copyrighted /ˈkɒpiraɪtɪd/ *adjective* protected by a valid copyright

copyright holder /ˈkɒpiraɪt ˌhəʊldə/ *noun* somebody who owns the copyright in a work

copyright law /ˈkɒpiraɪt lɔː/ *noun* law dealing with the protection of copyright

copyright licence /ˈkɒpiraɪt ˌlaɪs(ə)ns/ *noun* official permission to produce, copy and sell works that are protected by copyright law

copyright notice /ˈkɒpiraɪt ˌnəʊtɪs/ *noun* a note in a book showing who owns the copyright and the date of ownership

cordon /ˈkɔːd(ə)n/ *noun* □ **a police cordon** police officers stationed round an area with barriers, to prevent anyone getting near it ■ *verb* □ **to cordon off** to station police officers round (an area) with barriers so that no one can get near it ○ *The street was cordoned off after the bomb was discovered.*

co-respondent /ˌkəʊ rɪˈspɒndənt/ *noun* a party to divorce proceedings who has committed adultery with another person (NOTE: Do not confuse with **correspondent**.)

coroner /ˈkɒrənə/ *noun* a public official, either a doctor or a lawyer, who investigates suspicious deaths

COMMENT: Coroners investigate deaths which are violent or unexpected, deaths which may be murder or manslaughter, deaths of prisoners and deaths involving the police.

coroner's court /ˈkɒrənəz kɔːt/ *noun* a court presided over by a coroner

coroner's inquest /ˌkɒrənəz ˈɪnkwest/ *noun* an inquest carried out by a coroner into a death, or into a case of treasure trove

corporal punishment /ˌkɔːp(ə)rəl ˈpʌnɪʃmənt/ *noun* the physical punishment of someone by beating him or her

corporate /ˈkɔːp(ə)rət/ *adjective* referring to a company

corporate homicide /ˌkɔːp(ə)rət ˈhɒmɪsaɪd/ *noun* same as **corporate manslaughter**

corporate killing /ˌkɔːp(ə)rət ˈkɪlɪŋ/ *noun* a proposed criminal offence under which companies and similar organisations would be held responsible for any deaths occurring as a result of the company's negligence

corporate manslaughter /ˌkɔːp(ə)rət ˈmænslɔːtə/ *noun* a situation in which a limited company is charged with manslaughter, usually by means of gross negligence, as a legally-culpable entity

corporate name /ˌkɔːp(ə)rət ˈneɪm/ *noun* the name of a large corporation

corporate personality /ˌkɔːp(ə)rət ˌpɜːsəˈnælɪti/ *noun* the legal status of a company, so that it can be treated as a person

corporate profits /ˌkɔːp(ə)rət ˈprɒfɪts/ *noun* the profits of a corporation

corporate recovery /ˌkɔːp(ə)rət rɪ ˈkʌvəri/ *noun* a situation in which a company is saved from insolvency by means of restructuring, debt management or external investment

corporation /ˌkɔːpəˈreɪʃ(ə)n/ *noun* **1.** a legal body such as a limited company or town council which has been incorporated **2.** *US* a company which is incorporated in the United States **3.** any large company

corporeal /kɔːˈpɔːriəl/ *adjective* having physical form which you can see or touch

corporeal hereditament /kɔːˌpɔːriəl herɪˈdɪtəmənts/ *plural noun* a hereditament which physically exists, such as a house or piece of jewellery

corpse /kɔːps/ *noun* the body of a dead person (NOTE: The US term is **cadaver**.)

corpus /ˈkɔːpəs/ *noun* a body of laws. ◊ **habeas corpus** (NOTE: The plural is **corpora**.)

corpus delicti /ˌkɔːpəs dɪˈlɪktaɪ/ *phrase* a Latin phrase meaning 'the body of the crime': the real proof that a crime has been committed

corpus legis /ˌkɔːpəs ˈledʒɪs/ *phrase* a Latin phrase meaning 'body of laws': books containing Roman civil law

correctional institution /kəˌrekʃn(ə)l ˌɪnstɪˈtjuːʃ(ə)n/ *noun US* a prison

corrective /kəˈrektɪv/ *adjective* treating someone in such a way that he or she improves their behaviour or attitude ○ *He was sent to the detention centre for corrective training.*

corrective training /kəˌrektɪv ˈtreɪnɪŋ/ *noun* education or training intended to make a person improve their behaviour or attitude

correspond /ˌkɒrɪˈspɒnd/ *verb* to fit the description given (NOTE: Items sold under a consumer contract must correspond with their sales description, according to the Sales of Goods Act.)

correspondent /ˌkɒrɪˈspɒndənt/ *noun* **1.** somebody who writes letters **2.** a journalist who writes articles for a newspaper on specialist subjects ○ *The Times' legal correspondent* □ **court correspondent** a journalist who reports on the activities of a king or queen and the royal family □ **lobby correspondent** a journalist from a newspaper who is part of the lobby which gets private briefings from government ministers

corrigendum /ˌkɒrɪˈgendəm/ *noun* an item which has been corrected (NOTE: The plural is **corrigenda**.)

corroborate /kəˈrɒbəreɪt/ *verb* to prove evidence which has already been given ○ *The witness corroborated the accused's alibi, saying that at the time of the murder she had seen him in Brighton.*

corroboration /kəˌrɒbəˈreɪʃ(ə)n/ *noun* evidence which confirms and supports other evidence ○ *The witness was unable to provide corroboration of what he had told the police.*

corroborative /kəˈrɒbərətɪv/ *adjective* adding support to something such as a statement or evidence ○ *The letter provides corroborative evidence, showing that the accused did know that the victim lived alone.*

corrupt /kəˈrʌpt/ *adjective* willing to take bribes ■ *verb* □ **to corrupt someone's morals** to make someone behave in a way which goes against the normal standard of behaviour

corruption /kəˈrʌpʃən/ *noun* dishonest behaviour such as paying or accepting money or giving a favour to make sure that something is done ○ *The government is keen to stamp out corruption in the police force.*

○ *Bribery and corruption are difficult to control.*

corruptly /kəˈrʌptli/ *adverb* in a corrupt way ○ *He corruptly offered the officer money to get the charges dropped.*

cosponsor /ˌkəʊˈspɒnsə/ *noun* somebody who sponsors something with someone else ○ *the three cosponsors of the bill*

cost /kɒst/ *noun* **1.** the amount of money which has to be paid for something ○ *Computer costs are falling each year.* ○ *We cannot afford the cost of two telephone lines.* □ **to cover costs** to produce enough money in sales to pay for the costs of production **2.** □ **to pay costs** to pay the costs of a court case ■ *verb* **1.** to have a price ○ *How much does the machine cost?* ○ *Rent of the room will cost £50 a day.* **2.** □ **to cost something** to calculate how much money will be needed to make or do something

cost of living /ˌkɒst əv ˈlɪvɪŋ/ *noun* money which has to be paid for essential items such as food, accommodation or heating

cost-of-living increase /ˌkɒst əv ˈlɪvɪŋ ˌɪnkriːs/ *noun* an increase in salary to allow it to keep up with the increased cost of living

cost-of-living index /ˌkɒst əv ˈlɪvɪŋ ˌɪndeks/ *noun* a way of measuring the cost of living which is shown as a percentage increase on the figure for the previous year

cost-plus contract /ˌkɒst ˈplʌs ˌkɒntrækt/ *noun* a contract for work done in which the contractor will receive a fee reflecting the full cost of labour and materials, plus profit. Compare **fixed-price contract**

costs /kɒsts/ *plural noun* the expenses involved in a court case, including the fees, expenses and charges levied by the court itself, which can be awarded by the judge to the party which wins, so that the losing side pays the expenses of both sides ○ *The judge awarded costs to the defendant.* ○ *Costs of the case will be borne by the prosecution.* ○ *The court awarded the claimant £2,000 in damages, with costs.*

costs draftsman /ˈkɒsts ˌdrɑːftsmən/ *noun* someone who draws up a bill of costs for assessment by the costs judge

costs judge /ˈkɒsts dʒʌdʒ/ *noun* an official of the Supreme Court who assesses the costs of a court action (NOTE: Since the introduction of the Civil Procedure Rules, this term has in some cases replaced **Taxing Master**.)

costs order /ˈkɒsts ˌɔːdə/ *noun* a court order requiring someone to pay costs

coterminous /kəʊˈtɜːmɪnəs/ *adjective* referring to two things which end at the same time ○ *The leases are coterminous.*

council /ˈkaʊnsəl/ *noun* **1.** an official group chosen to run something or to advise on a problem **2.** same as **Privy Council**

Council of Ministers /ˌkaʊnsəl əv ˈmɪnɪstəz/ *noun* ◆ **Council of the European Union**

Council of the European Union /ˌkaʊnsəl əv ðə ˌjʊərəpiən ˈjuːnjən/ *noun* the legislative arm of the European Union (NOTE: not to be confused with the **European Council**. Formerly the Council of the European Union was called the **Council of Ministers** and it is still sometimes called this.)

COMMENT: The Council does not have fixed members, but the Member States are each represented by the relevant government minister. The Council is headed by a President, and the Presidency rotates among the Member States in alphabetical order, each serving for a six-month period. In practice this means that each Member State can control the agenda of the Council, and therefore that of the European Union, for a period of six months, and can try to get as many of its proposals put into legislation as it can during that period. When meeting to discuss general matters the Council is formed of the foreign ministers of the Member States, but when it discusses specialised problems it is formed of the relevant government ministers: so when discussing agriculture, for example, it is formed of the Agriculture Ministers of the Member States.

Council of the Notariats of the European Union /ˌkaʊnsəl əv ðə nəʊ ˌteəriəts əv ðə ˌjʊərəpiən ˈjuːnjən/ *noun* an organisation that represents the notarial profession in European institutions, handling negotiation and decision-making for all civil law notaries in the European Union

Council on Tribunals /ˌkaʊnsəl ɒn traɪ ˈbjuːnəlz/ *noun* a standing body which reviews the constitution and working of tribunals and inquiries in Great Britain to ensure they are open, fair and impartial

counsel /ˈkaʊnsəl/ *noun* a barrister or barristers acting for one of the parties in a legal action ○ *defence counsel* ○ *prosecution counsel* ○ *The claimant appeared in court with his solicitor and two counsel.* (NOTE: There is no plural for **counsel** which is always used in the singular whether it refers to one barrister or several, and it is never used with the articles **the** or **a**.)

counsellor /'kaʊnsələ/ *noun* **1.** a trained person who gives advice or help ○ *They went to see a marriage guidance counsellor.* **2.** *US* a legal practitioner who advises a person in a case

counsel's advice /ˌkaʊnsəlz əd'vaɪs/, **counsel's opinion** /ˌkaʊnsəlz ə'pɪnjən/ *noun* same as **advice of counsel**

count /kaʊnt/ *noun* a separate charge against an accused person read out in court in the indictment ○ *He was found guilty on all four counts.*

counter /'kaʊntə/ *noun* a long flat surface in a shop for displaying and selling goods □ **over the counter** legally □ **goods sold over the counter** retail sales of goods in shops □ **under the counter** illegally □ **under-the-counter sales** black market sales ■ *adjective, adverb* opposite, or with an opposite effect

counter- /kaʊntə/ *prefix* opposing

counterclaim /'kaʊntəklaɪm/ *noun* **1.** in a court, a claim by a defendant against whom a claimant is bringing a claim. Also called **Part 20 claim** (NOTE: The counterclaim is included in the same proceedings and statement of case as the original claim.) **2.** a claim for damages made in reply to a previous claim ○ *Jones claimed £25,000 in damages against Smith, and Smith entered a counterclaim of £50,000 for loss of office.* ■ *verb* to put in a counterclaim

counterfeit /'kaʊntəfɪt/ *adjective* (*especially of money or objects of value*) false or imitation ○ *He was charged with passing counterfeit notes in shops.* ○ *She was selling counterfeit Rolex watches.* ■ *verb* to make imitation money or other objects of value

counterfeiting /'kaʊntə,fɪtɪŋ/ *noun* the crime of making imitation money or other objects of value

counter-intelligence /ˌkaʊntər ɪn'telɪdʒəns/ *noun* an organisation of secret agents whose job is to work against the secret agents of another country ○ *The offices were bugged by counter-intelligence agents.*

countermand /ˌkaʊntə'mɑːnd/ *verb* □ **to countermand an order** to say that an order must not be carried out

counteroffer /'kaʊntər,ɒfə/ *noun* an offer made in reply to another offer

counterpart /'kaʊntəpɑːt/ *noun* a copy of a legal document such as a contract ■ **in counterparts** □ **to be signed in counter-**

parts of a contract, to have the signatures of the parties appear on separate copies ■ *noun* somebody who has a similar job in another company

counter-promise /ˌkaʊntə 'prɒmɪs/ *noun* a promise made in reply to a promise

countersign /'kaʊntəsaɪn/ *verb* to sign a document which has already been signed by someone else ○ *The payment has to be countersigned by the mortgagor.*

counter to /'kaʊntə tə/ *noun* against, opposite ○ *The decision of the court runs counter to the advice of the clerk to the justices.*

country of origin /ˌkʌntri əv 'ɒrɪdʒɪn/ *noun* a country where someone was born or from where someone has come, or where goods were produced ○ *There is a space on the form for 'country of origin'.*

County Court /ˌkaʊnti 'kɔːt/ *noun* one of the types of court in England and Wales which hears local civil cases

COMMENT: There are about 270 County Courts in England and Wales. County Courts are presided over by either district judges or circuit judges. They deal mainly with claims regarding money, but also deal with family matters, bankruptcies and claims concerning land. A district judge will hear most civil cases up to a value of £50,000, and a circuit judge will deal with more serious cases.

county court judgment /ˌkaʊnti 'kɔːt ˌdʒʌdʒmənt/ *noun* a judgment against a person who has failed to keep up the terms of a credit agreement. Abbreviation **CCJ**

COMMENT: A county court judgment will appear on a person's credit record and may affect future applications for credit.

County Court Rules /ˌkaʊnti kɔːt 'ruːlz/ *noun* a book of procedural rules for County Courts. Abbreviation **CCR**

coup /kuː/, **coup d'état** /ˌkuː deɪ'tæ/ *noun* a rapid change of government which removes one government by force and replaces it by another ○ *After the coup, groups of students attacked the police stations.*

COMMENT: A coup is usually carried out by a small number of people, who already have some power (such as army officers), while a revolution is a general uprising of a large number of ordinary people. A coup changes the members of a government, but a revolution changes the whole social system.

court /kɔːt/ *noun* **1.** a place where a trial is held □ **to take someone to court** to start legal proceedings against someone □ **in**

court present during a trial ○ *The defendant was in court for three hours.* □ **in open court** in a courtroom with members of the public present □ **to settle out of court, to reach an out-of-court settlement** to settle a dispute between two parties privately without continuing the court case **2.** □ **Criminal Court, Civil Court** a court where criminal or civil cases are heard **3.** the judges or magistrates in a court ○ *The court will retire for thirty minutes.*

COMMENT: See Supplement for descriptions of the court systems of England and Wales, Scotland, Northern Ireland and the US

court action /'kɔːt ˌækʃən/ *noun* a civil case in a law court where a person files a claim against another person (NOTE: In general, **action** has now been replaced by **claim**.)

court case /'kɔːt keɪs/ *noun* same as **court action**

court clerk /ˌkɔːt 'klɑːk/ *noun* an officer of the court whose job it is to maintain court records

courthouse /'kɔːthaʊs/ *noun especially US* a building in which trials take place ○ *There was police cordon round the courthouse.*

court-martial /ˌkɔːt 'mɑːʃ(ə)l/ *noun* **1.** a court which tries someone serving in the armed forces for offences against military discipline ○ *He was found guilty by the court-martial and sentenced to imprisonment.* **2.** the trial of someone serving in the armed forces by the armed forces authorities ○ *The court-martial was held in the army headquarters.* (NOTE: The plural is **courts-martial**.) ■ *verb* to try someone who is serving in the armed forces (NOTE: **court-martialled**)

Court of Appeal /ˌkɔːt əv ə'piːl/, **Court of Appeals** /ˌkɔːt əv ə'piːlz/ *noun* a civil or criminal court to which a person may go to ask for an award or a sentence to be changed. Also called **Appeal Court**

COMMENT: In the majority of cases in English law, decisions of lower courts and of the High Court can be appealed to the Court of Appeal. The Court of Appeal is divided into the Civil Division and the Criminal Division. The Civil Division hears appeals from the County Court and the High Court; the Criminal Division hears appeals from the Crown Court. From the Court of Appeal, appeal lies to the House of Lords. When the remedies available under English law are exhausted, it is in some cases possible to appeal to the European Court of Justice. For many countries, especially Commonwealth countries,

appeals from the highest court of these countries may be heard by the Privy Council.

court officer /ˌkɔːt 'ɒfɪsə/ *noun* same as **officer of the court**

court of first instance /ˌkɔːt əv fɜːst 'ɪnstəns/ *noun* **1.** a court where a case is heard first **2. Court of First Instance** a court set up under the Single European Act, formed of 15 judges, whose judgments can be appealed to the European Court of Justice. Abbreviation **CFI**

Court of Justice of the European Communities /ˌkɔːt əv ˌdʒʌstɪs əv ðə ˌjʊərəpiən kə'mjuːnɪtiz/ *noun* ♦ **European Court of Justice**

court of last resort /ˌkɔːt əv lɑːst rɪ'zɔːt/ *noun US* the highest court from which no appeals can be made

court of law /ˌkɔːt əv 'lɔː/ *noun* same as **court** ○ *Verbal agreements may not be enforceable in a court of law.*

Court of Protection /ˌkɔːt əv prə'tekʃ(ə)n/ *noun* a court appointed to protect the interests of people who are incapable of dealing with their own affairs, such as patients who are mentally ill

Court of Session /ˌkɔːt əv 'seʃ(ə)n/ *noun* the highest civil court in Scotland

court order /'kɔːt ˌɔːdə/ *noun* a legal order made by a court, telling someone to do or not to do something ○ *He refused to obey the court order and was sent to prison for contempt.*

court or tribunal /ˌkɔːt ɔː traɪ'bjuːn(ə)l/ *noun* any body which has official status and which has the power to give binding rulings on legal rights and obligation, although it may not have the actual title of 'court' (NOTE: The Deputy High Bailiff's Court in the Isle of Man and the Dutch Appeals Committee for General Medicine have each been held to be a 'court or tribunal' according to European Union law.)

courtroom /'kɔːtruːm/ *noun* a room where a judge presides over a trial

covenant /'kʌvənənt/ *noun* **1.** a solemn agreement that is binding on all parties **2.** a formal and legally binding agreement or contract, e.g. a lease, or a clause in an agreement of this kind ○ *He signed a covenant against underletting the premises.* **3.** a lawsuit for damages that is brought because of the breaking of a legal covenant ■ *verb* to enter into a covenant

COMMENT: There is a tax advantage to the recipient of covenanted money; a charity pays no tax, so it can reclaim tax at the standard rate on the money covenanted to it.

covenant marriage /ˈkʌvənənt ˌmærɪdʒ/ *noun* in the US, a form of marriage contract which imposes stricter than usual conditions on the couple, including mandatory pre-marriage counselling and a two-year separation before a divorce

covenant to repair /ˌkʌvənənt tə rɪˈpeə/ *noun* an agreement by a landlord or tenant to keep a rented property in good repair

cover /ˈkʌvə/ *noun* 1. insurance □ **to operate without adequate cover** without being protected by insurance □ **to ask for additional cover** to ask the insurance company to increase the amount for which you are insured 2. □ **to send something under separate cover** in a separate envelope □ **to send a document under plain cover** in an ordinary envelope with no company name printed on it ■ *verb* 1. to include and deal with something ○ *The agreement covers all agencies.* ○ *The newspapers have covered the murder trial.* ○ *The fraud case has been covered by the consumer protection legislation.* 2. □ **to cover a risk** to be protected by insurance against a risk □ **to be fully covered** to have insurance against all risks 3. *US* to purchase goods from another supplier to replace those which have not been delivered according to contract 4. to have enough money to pay □ **to be covered by insurance** to be able to claim on an insurance policy □ **to cover a position** to have enough money to pay for a forward purchase 5. to ask for security against a loan which you are making 6. to earn enough money to pay for costs, expenses, etc. ○ *We do not make enough sales to cover the expense of running the shop.* ○ *We hope to reach the point soon when sales will cover all costs.*

coverage /ˈkʌv(ə)rɪdʒ/ *noun* 1. ♦ **press coverage** 2. *US* protection guaranteed by insurance ○ *Do you have coverage against fire damage?*

cover note /ˈkʌvə nəʊt/ *noun* a letter from an insurance company giving basic details of an insurance policy and confirming that the policy exists

covert /ˈkəʊvət, ˈkʌvət/ *adjective* secret

covert action /ˌkəʊvət ˈækʃən/ *noun* an action which is carried out secretly

coverture /ˈkʌvətʃʊə/ *noun* formerly, the concept that a woman had no separate legal existence or rights after marriage

CPC *abbreviation* Claim Production Centre

CPD /ˌsiː piː diː/ *abbreviation* continuing professional development

CPO *abbreviation* Community Punishment Order

CPR *abbreviation* Civil Procedure Rules

CPS *abbreviation* Crown Prosecution Service

cracksman /ˈkræksmən/ *noun* a criminal who specialises in breaking safes (*slang*)

credere /ˈkreɪdəri/ ♦ **del credere agent**

credit /ˈkredɪt/ *noun* money borrowed by a person or company, usually under a contractual agreement stating how and by when it must be repaid ○ *He found it difficult to get credit as a discharged bankrupt.* □ **to buy something on credit** to buy something without paying immediately ■ *verb* to note money received in an account ○ *The money will be credited to your account after 3 working days.*

credit card /ˈkredɪt kɑːd/ *noun* a bank card which allows the holder to buy goods on credit

credit limit /ˈkredɪt ˌlɪmɪt/ *noun* a fixed amount of money which is the most a client can owe

credit note /ˈkredɪt nəʊt/ *noun* an instrument which gives a consumer the right to purchase goods to a specific value from a vendor at some future date (NOTE: Usually given instead of a cash refund for returned goods, when the return is not covered by the Sale of Goods Act.)

creditor /ˈkredɪtə/ *noun* somebody who is owed money. ◊ **secured creditor, unsecured creditor**

creditors' meeting /ˈkredɪtəz ˌmiːtɪŋ/ *noun* a meeting of all persons to whom a company in receivership owes money

creditors' voluntary liquidation /ˌkredɪtəz ˌvɒlənt(ə)ri ˌlɪkwɪˈdeɪʃ(ə)n/ *noun* the liquidation of a company by the decision of its creditors, conducted by an insolvency practitioner

credit rating /ˈkredɪt ˌreɪtɪŋ/ *noun* a statistical analysis of a person's history of borrowing and repaying debts

COMMENT: A person's credit rating is usually checked when they apply for a new credit card, loan or mortgage. A poor credit rating can lead to the application being rejected.

credit record /ˈkredɪt ˌrekɔːd/ *noun* a person's history of borrowing and repaying debts

credit reference agency /'kredɪt ˌref(ə)rəns ˌeɪdʒənsi/ *noun* an organisation which reports a person's credit rating to potential creditors

credit score /'kredɪt skɔː/ *noun* same as **credit rating**

credit transfer /'kredɪt ˌtrænsfɜː/ *noun* the movement of money from one account to another

crime /kraɪm/ *noun* **1.** an act which is against the law and which is punishable by law ○ *There has been a 50% increase in crimes of violence.* **2.** illegal acts in general ○ *crime is on the increase* ○ *There has been an increase in violent crime.*

COMMENT: A crime is an illegal act which may result in prosecution and punishment by the state if the accused is convicted. Generally, in order to be convicted of a crime, the accused must be shown to have committed an unlawful act (**actus reus**) with a criminal state of mind (**mens rea**). The main types of crime are: **1. crimes against the person**: murder; manslaughter; assault, battery, wounding; grievous bodily harm; abduction; **2. crimes against property**: theft; robbery; burglary; obtaining property or services or pecuniary advantage by deception; blackmail; handling stolen goods; going equipped to steal; criminal damage; possessing something with intent to damage or destroy property; forgery; **3. sexual offences**: rape; buggery; bigamy; indecency; **4. political offences**: treason; terrorism; sedition; breach of the Official Secrets Act; **5. offences against justice**: assisting an offender; conspiracy; perjury; contempt of court; perverting the course of justice; **6. public order offences**: obstruction of the police; unlawful assembly; obscenity; possessing weapons; misuse of drugs; breach of the peace; **7. road traffic offences**: careless or reckless driving; drunken driving; driving without a licence or insurance.

crime number /'kraɪm ˌnʌmbə/ *noun* a reference number given to you by the police when you report a crime such as burglary or petty theft (NOTE: Many insurance companies require you to give a crime number when claiming for losses caused by crime.)

crime rate /'kraɪm reɪt/ *noun* the number of crimes committed in a specific period, shown as a percentage of the total population

crime scene /'kraɪm siːn/ *noun* the place where a crime has been committed

crime scene investigator /'kraɪm siːn ɪnˌvestɪgeɪtə/ *noun* a person who works with police to gather forensic evidence from crime scenes

crime scene tape /'kraɪm siːn ˌteɪp/ *noun* US tape that is used to cordon off an area and warn people of a crime scene (NOTE: The UK term is **incident tape**.)

Crimestoppers /'kraɪmˌstɒpəz/ *noun* a UK charity providing an anonymous, untraceable phone service, which can be used by members of the public to give information that may help the police

crime wave /'kraɪm weɪv/ *noun* a sudden increase in crime

criminal /'krɪmɪn(ə)l/ *adjective* **1.** illegal ○ *Misappropriation of funds is a criminal act.* **2.** referring to crime □ **the criminal population** all people who have committed crimes ■ *noun* a person who has committed a crime or who often commits crimes ○ *The police have contacted known criminals to get leads on the gangland murder.* □ **a hardened criminal** a person who has committed many crimes

criminal action /ˌkrɪmɪn(ə)l 'ækʃən/ *noun* a case brought usually by the state against someone who is charged with a crime

criminal bankruptcy /ˌkrɪmɪn(ə)l 'bæŋkrʌptsi/ *noun* bankruptcy of a criminal in the Crown Court as a result of crimes of which he or she has been convicted

criminal bankruptcy order /ˌkrɪmɪn(ə)l 'bæŋkrʌptsi ˌɔːdə/ *noun* an order made against someone who has been convicted in the Crown Court of an offence which has resulted in damage above a specific sum to other identified parties

Criminal Cases Review Commission /ˌkrɪmɪn(ə)l ˌkeɪsɪz rɪ'vjuː kəˌmɪʃ(ə)n/ *noun* an independent body in the UK which assesses whether criminal convictions should be sent to appeal. Abbreviation **CCRC**

criminal court /'krɪmɪn(ə)l kɔːt/ *noun* a court such as a Crown Court which deals with criminal cases

criminal damage /ˌkrɪmɪn(ə)l 'dæmɪdʒ/ *noun* the notifiable offence of causing serious damage to property

Criminal Defence Service /ˌkrɪmɪn(ə)l dɪ'fens ˌsɜːvɪs/ *noun* a British government service which provides legal advice and assistance to people with very little money who are suspected of criminal offences or are facing criminal proceedings. Abbreviation **CDS**

COMMENT: The service replaces part of the Legal Aid scheme (the Community Legal Service deals with civil and family cases).

criminal fraternity /ˌkrɪmɪn(ə)l frəˈtɜːnɪti/ noun a community of criminals who protect each other and do not co-operate with the police

Criminal Injuries Compensation Board /ˌkrɪmɪn(ə)l ˌɪndʒəriz ˌkɒmpənˈseɪʃ(ə)n ˌbɔːd/ noun a committee which administers the awarding of compensation to victims of crime

Criminal Investigation department /ˌkrɪmɪn(ə)l ɪnˌvestɪˈgeɪʃ(ə)n dɪˌpɑːtmənt/ noun a section of the British police which investigates serious crimes. Abbreviation **CID**

criminal law /ˌkrɪmɪn(ə)l ˈlɔː/ noun law relating to acts committed against the laws of the land and which are punishable by the state

criminal libel /ˌkrɪmɪn(ə)l ˈlaɪb(ə)l/ noun a serious libel which might cause a breach of the peace

criminal negligence /ˌkrɪmɪn(ə)l ˈneglɪdʒəns/ noun the offence of acting recklessly with the result that harm is done to other people

criminal offence /ˌkrɪmɪn(ə)l əˈfens/ noun an action which is against the law

criminal record /ˌkrɪmɪn(ə)l ˈrekɔːd/ noun a note of previous crimes for which someone has been convicted ○ The accused had no criminal record. ○ He has a criminal record going back to the time when he was still at school.

criminal responsibility /ˌkrɪmɪn(ə)l rɪˌspɒnsɪˈbɪlɪti/ noun the fact of being responsible for a crime that has been committed (NOTE: The age of criminal responsibility in the UK is ten years. Children under ten years old cannot be charged with a crime.)

criminology /ˌkrɪmɪˈnɒlədʒi/ noun the academic study of crime

Crisis Loan /ˈkraɪsɪs ləʊn/ noun a repayable loan given by the Government to someone in an emergency situation who cannot meet their basic costs (such as rent), which jeopardises their family's safety (NOTE: This is made out of the Government's **Social Fund**.)

criticise /ˈkrɪtɪsaɪz/ verb to say that someone or something is bad or wrong ○ The procedures were severely criticised as being discriminatory. (NOTE: **criticised – criticising**)

criticism /ˈkrɪtɪsɪz(ə)m/ noun **1.** a comment ○ If you have any constructive criticisms to make, I shall be glad to hear them. **2.** an unfavourable comment or series of comments ○ There was a lot of criticism of the proposed changes. ○ My detailed criticisms relate to section 3 of the report.

crook /krʊk/ noun a person who has committed a crime, especially a crime involving deceit (slang)

crossed cheque /ˌkrɒst ˈtʃek/ noun a cheque with two lines across it showing that it can only be deposited at a bank and not exchanged for cash

cross-examination /ˌkrɒs ɪgzæmɪˈneɪʃ(ə)n/ noun the questioning of a witness called by the opposing side in a case. Opposite **evidence in chief** (NOTE: The opposite is **evidence in chief**.)

cross-examine /ˌkrɒs ɪgˈzæmɪn/ verb to question witnesses called by the other side in a case, in the hope that you can discredit or weaken their evidence

cross holdings /ˈkrɒs ˌhəʊldɪŋz/ plural noun a situation where two companies own shares in each other in order to stop each from being taken over ○ The two companies have protected themselves from takeover by a system of cross holdings.

crowd control /ˈkraʊd kənˌtrəʊl/ noun methods used by police for controlling large groups of people, such as at sports matches

Crown /kraʊn/ noun □ **the Crown** the state as a legal authority, as represented by the ruling king of queen ○ Mr Smith is appearing for the Crown. ○ The Crown submitted that the maximum sentence should be applied in this case. ○ The Crown case or the case for the Crown was that the defendants were guilty of espionage.

Crown copyright /ˌkraʊn ˈkɒpiraɪt/ noun copyright in government publications

Crown Court /ˌkraʊn ˈkɔːt/ noun a court, above the level of the magistrates' courts, which is based on the six circuits in England and Wales and which hears criminal cases

COMMENT: A Crown Court is formed of a circuit judge and jury, and hears major criminal cases.

Crown Lands /ˌkraʊn ˈlɑːndz/ plural noun land or property belonging to the King or Queen

Crown privilege /ˌkraʊn ˈprɪvɪlɪdʒ/ noun the right of the Crown or the government not to have to produce documents to a court by reason of the interest of the state

Crown Prosecution Service /ˌkraʊn ˌprɒsɪˈkjuːʃ(ə)n ˌsɜːvɪs/ *noun* a government department, headed by the Director of Public Prosecutions, which is responsible for the conduct of all criminal cases instituted by the police in England and Wales, except for those prosecuted by the Serious Fraud Office. Abbreviation **CPS**

Crown prosecutor /ˌkraʊn ˈprɒsɪkjuːtə/ *noun* an official of the Crown Prosecution Service who is responsible for prosecuting criminals in one of 13 areas in England Wales

CRPO *abbreviation* Community Punishment and Rehabilitation Order

cruelty /ˈkruːəlti/ *noun* **1.** behaviour which causes pain or injury to a person or animal **2.** cruel behaviour towards a spouse

crystallisation /ˌkrɪstəlaɪˈzeɪʃ(ə)n/ *noun* a situation in which a floating charge is converted to a fixed charge over the assets that it covers at that time

CS gas /ˌsiː es ˈɡæs/ *noun* gas given off by solid crystals of $C_6H_4(Cl)CH$, used by police as a method of crowd control

CSO *abbreviation* community service order

CTT *abbreviation* capital transfer tax

culpability /ˌkʌlpəˈbɪlɪti/ *noun* the fact of being culpable

culpable /ˈkʌlpəb(ə)l/ *adjective* answerable or responsible, attracting blame

culpable homicide /ˌkʌlpəb(ə)l ˈhɒmɪsaɪd/ *noun US* murder or manslaughter

culpable negligence /ˌkʌlpəb(ə)l ˈneɡlɪdʒəns/ *noun US* negligence which is so bad that it amounts to an offence

culprit /ˈkʌlprɪt/ *noun* somebody who is responsible for a crime or for something which has gone wrong

curfew /ˈkɜːfjuː/ *noun* a prohibition on being in public or leaving home during particular times

curiam ♦ per curiam

currency /ˈkʌrənsi/ *noun* money in coins and notes which is used in a particular country

current account /ˈkʌrənt əˌkaʊnt/ *noun* an ordinary account in a bank into which money can be deposited and on which cheques can be drawn

current assets /ˌkʌrənt ˈæsets/ *plural noun* assets used by a company in its ordinary work, e.g. materials, finished goods, cash

current liabilities /ˌkʌrənt ˌlaɪəˈbɪlɪtiz/ *plural noun* debts which a company has to pay within the next accounting period

curriculum vitae /kəˌrɪkjʊləm ˈviːtaɪ/ *noun* a summary of a person's life story showing details of education and work experience ○ *Candidates should send a letter of application with a curriculum vitae to the administrative office.* Abbreviation **CV** (NOTE: The US term is **résumé**.)

curtilage /ˈkɜːtɪlɪdʒ/ *noun* land round a house

custodial establishment /kʌˌstəʊdiəl ɪˈstæblɪʃmənt/ *noun* a prison or other institution where criminals are kept

custodial sentence /kʌˌstəʊdiəl ˈsentəns/ *noun* a sentence which involves sending someone to prison

custodian /kʌˈstəʊdiən/ *noun* somebody who protects, guards or looks after something or someone

custody /ˈkʌstədi/ *noun* **1.** the condition of being kept in prison or in a cell □ **in police custody** held by the police, but not actually arrested, while helping the police with their inquiries ○ *The young men were kept in police custody overnight.* **2.** the legal right of a parent to keep and bring up a child after a divorce ○ *Custody of the children was awarded to the mother.* ○ *The court granted the mother custody of both children.* **3.** the control and care of something by someone ○ *The files are in the custody of my lawyer or in my lawyer's custody.*

custom /ˈkʌstəm/ *noun* **1.** unwritten rules which lay down how things are usually done and have been done for a long time ○ *It is the custom that everyone stands up when the magistrates enter the courtroom.* □ **the customs of the trade** the general way of working in a trade **2.** the use of a shop by regular shoppers □ **to lose someone's custom** to do something which makes a regular customer go to another shop

customer /ˈkʌstəmə/ *noun* a person who buys a product or uses a service, especially regularly

customs /ˈkʌstəmz/ *plural noun* **1.** same as **Her Majesty's Revenue & Customs** □ **to go through customs** to pass through the area of a port or airport where customs officials examine goods **2.** an office of this department at a port or airport

Customs and Excise /ˌkʌstəmz ən ˈeksaɪz/ *noun* a former government department which dealt with VAT and import taxes, now part of HM Revenue and Customs

customs barrier /'kʌstəmz ˌbæriə/ *noun* the existence of customs duty intended to prevent imports

customs clearance /'kʌstəmz ˌklɪərəns/ *noun* the act of clearing goods through customs

customs declaration /'kʌstəmz deklə ˌreɪʃ(ə)n/ *noun* a statement declaring goods brought into a country on which customs duty may be paid

customs duty /'kʌstəmz ˌdjuːti/ *noun* a tax on goods imported into a country

customs examination /'kʌstəmz ɪg ˌzæmɪneɪʃ(ə)n/ *noun* the examination of goods or baggage by customs officials

customs formalities /'kʌstəmz fɔː ˌmælɪtiz/ *plural noun* the declaration of goods by the shipper and examination of them by customs

customs officer /'kʌstəmz ˌɒfɪsə/, **customs official** /'kʌstəmz əˌfɪʃ(ə)l/ *noun* somebody working for HM Revenue and Customs

customs seal /'kʌstəmz siːl/ *noun* a seal attached by customs officers to a box to show that the contents have passed through customs

customs tariffs /ˌkʌstəmz 'tærɪfs/ *plural noun* tax to be paid for importing or exporting goods

customs union /'kʌstəmz ˌjuːnjən/ *noun* an agreement between several countries that goods can travel between them without paying duty, while goods from other countries have to pay special duties

cut in on /ˌkʌt 'ɪn ˌɒn/ *verb* □ **to cut someone in on** to offer someone part of the profits of a deal

CV /ˌsiː 'viː/ *abbreviation* curriculum vitae ○ *Please apply in writing, enclosing a current CV.*

CVA *abbreviation* company voluntary arrangement

cybercrime /'saɪbəkraɪm/ *noun* the use of a computer network, especially the internet, for crime such as fraud or data theft

cyberlaw /'saɪbəlɔː/ *noun* law dealing with use of the Internet, especially commercial law relating to commercial transactions, copyright law on information, or defamation law regarding statements made public

cy-près /ˌsiː 'preɪ/ *adjective, adverb* as near as possible

cy-près doctrine /ˌsiː 'preɪ ˌdɒktrɪn/ *noun* a rule that if a charity cannot apply its funds to the purposes for which they were intended, a court can apply the funds to a purpose which is as close as possible to the original intention

D

DA *abbreviation US* district attorney

dabs /dæbz/ *plural noun* fingerprints (*slang*)

Dáil /dɔɪl/, **Dáil Éireann** *noun* the lower house of the parliament in the Republic of Ireland ○ *The Foreign Minister reported on the meeting to the Dáil.* (NOTE: The members of the Dáil are called **Teachta Dala** (TD).)

damage /ˈdæmɪdʒ/ *noun* harm done to things. ◊ **criminal damage** □ **to suffer damage** to be harmed □ **to cause damage** to harm something ■ *verb* to harm ○ *The storm damaged the cargo.* ○ *stock which has been damaged by water.* ○ *He alleged that the newspaper article was damaging to the company's reputation.*

damaged /ˈdæmɪdʒd/ *adjective* having suffered damage or which has been harmed ○ *fire-damaged* ○ *damaged goods*

damage feasant /ˌdæmɪdʒ ˈfiːzənt/ *noun* a situation where the animals of one person damage the property of another person

damages /ˈdæmɪdʒɪz/ *plural noun* **1.** money claimed by a claimant from a defendant as compensation for harm done ○ *to claim £1,000 in damages* **2.** money awarded by a court as compensation to a claimant ○ *to be liable for* or *in damages* ○ *to pay £25,000 in damages* □ **to bring an action for damages against someone** to take someone to court and claim damages

danger /ˈdeɪndʒə/ *noun* **1.** the possibility of being harmed or killed ○ *There is danger to the employees in using old machinery.* **2.** likelihood or possibility □ **in danger of** being easily able to happen ○ *He is in danger of being in contempt of court.*

dangerous /ˈdeɪndʒərəs/ *adjective* being possibly harmful □ **dangerous animals** animals, such as some breeds of dog and some wild animals, which may attack people and have to be kept under strict conditions, or for which a licence has to be held □ **danger-**

ous job a job where employees may be killed or hurt □ **dangerous weapon** a device or weapon which can hurt someone

dangerous driving /ˌdeɪndʒərəs ˈdraɪvɪŋ/ *noun* formerly, an offence of driving dangerously (NOTE: Now called **reckless driving**.) □ **causing death by dangerous driving** the offence committed by a driver causing the death of another person

dark /dɑːk/ *adjective* not being used for hearings, trials, or other proceedings

data protection /ˈdeɪtə prəˌtekʃən/ *noun* protecting information such as records of individuals stored in a computer from being copied or used wrongly (NOTE: **data** is usually singular: *the data is easily available*)

date of commencement /ˌdeɪt əv kə ˈmensmənt/ *noun* the date when an Act of Parliament takes effect

date rape /ˈdeɪt reɪp/ *noun* a sexual assault committed against somebody during or after a date

date rape drug /ˈdeɪt reɪp ˌdrʌg/ *noun* a drug given to a person without their knowledge to facilitate a sexual assault

day training centre /deɪ ˌtreɪnɪŋ ˈsentə/ *noun* a centre where young offenders attend courses as a condition of being on probation

DC *abbreviation* detective constable

DCA /ˌdiː siː ˈeɪ/ *abbreviation* Department for Constitutional Affairs

DCC /ˌdiː siː ˈsiː/ *abbreviation* Deputy Chief Constable

dead /ded/ *adjective* **1.** not alive ○ *Six people were dead as a result of the accident.* ○ *We inherited the house from my dead grandfather.* **2.** not working

dead account /ˌded əˈkaʊnt/ *noun* an account which is no longer used

dead letter /ˌded ˈletə/ *noun US* a regulation which is no longer valid ○ *This law has become a dead letter.*

dead loss /ˌded 'lɒs/ *noun* something that is so badly damaged that it loses all its value ○ *The car was written off as a dead loss.*

dealings /'diːlɪŋz/ *plural noun* □ **to have dealings with someone** to do business with someone

death /deθ/ *noun* the act of dying or the state of being dead □ **to sentence someone to death** to give a sentence that somebody should be executed □ **to put someone to death** to execute someone

death benefit /'deθ ˌbenɪfɪt/ *noun* money paid to the family of someone who dies in an accident at work

death certificate /'deθ səˌtɪfɪkət/ *noun* an official certificate signed by a doctor, stating that a person has died and giving details of the person

death grant /'deθ ɡrɑːnt/ *noun US* a government grant to the family of a person who has died, which is supposed to contribute to the funeral expenses

death in service /ˌdeθ ɪn 'sɜːvɪs/ *noun* insurance benefit or pension paid when someone dies while employed by a company

death penalty /'deθ ˌpen(ə)lti/ *noun* same as **capital punishment**

debate /dɪ'beɪt/ *noun* a discussion about a subject, especially a formal discussion leading to a vote ○ *The Bill passed its Second Reading after a short debate.* ○ *The debate continued until 3 a.m.* ■ *verb* to discuss a subject, especially in a formal way that leads to a vote

debenture /dɪ'bentʃə/ *noun* a document whereby a company acknowledges it owes a debt and gives the company's assets as security □ **debenture register, register of debentures** list of debenture holders of a company

debenture bond /dɪ'bentʃə bɒnd/ *noun* a certificate showing that a debenture has been issued

debenture capital /dɪ'bentʃə ˌkæpɪt(ə)l/ *noun* capital borrowed by a company using its fixed assets as security

debenture holder /dɪ'bentʃə ˌhəʊldə/ *noun* somebody who holds a debenture for money lent

debenture issue /dɪ'bentʃə ˌɪʃuː/ *noun* borrowing money against the security of the company's assets

debit /'debɪt/ *verb* □ **to debit an account** to charge an account with a cost ○ *His account was debited with the sum of £25.*

debit and credit /ˌdebɪt ən 'kredɪt/ *noun* the money that a company owes and which it is entitled to receive

debit balance /'debɪt ˌbæləns/ *noun* the balance in an account showing that more money is owed to or has been received by someone than is owed or has been paid by them

debit note /'debɪt nəʊt/ *noun* a note showing that a customer owes money

debt /det/ *noun* money owed for goods or services ○ *The company stopped trading with debts of over £1 million.* □ **to be in debt** to owe money □ **to get into debt** to start to borrow more money than you can pay back □ **to be out of debt** to not owe money any more □ **to pay back a debt** to pay all the money owed □ **to pay off a debt** to finish paying money owed □ **to service a debt** to pay off a debt

debt collection /'det kəˌlekʃən/ *noun* the act of collecting money which is owed

debt collection agency /'det kəˌlekʃən ˌeɪdʒənsi/ a company which buys debts from other companies at a discount and enforces them ■ *noun* a company which enforces debts for other companies for a commission

debt collector /'det kəˌlektə/ *noun* somebody who collects debts

debt consolidation /'det kənˌsɒlɪdeɪʃ(ə)n/ *noun* the act of transferring all one's debts to a single loan company, to simplify and/or reduce repayments

debt factor /'det ˌfæktə/ *noun* an individual who does the work of a debt collection agency

debt management /'det ˌmænɪdʒmənt/ *noun* the reduction of debt repayments to an affordable level, e.g. by consolidation of debts

debtor /'detə/ *noun* somebody who owes money

decease /dɪ'siːs/ *noun* death (*formal*) ○ *On his decease all his property will go to his widow.*

deceased /dɪ'siːst/ *adjective* (*of people*) recently dead ○ *The deceased left all his property to his widow.* ○ *She inherited the estate of a deceased aunt.* ■ *noun* a person who has died recently, or people who have died recently

deceit /dɪ'siːt/ *noun* dishonest behaviour intended to trick someone into paying money or doing something ○ *He built up a* *career based on lies and deceit over several years.*

decentralisation /ˌdiːsentrəlaɪˈzeɪʃ(ə)n/ *noun* the act of transferring power to govern or to make decisions from a central authority to a local authority

deception /dɪˈsepʃən/ *noun* an act of tricking someone into believing or doing something ○ *He obtained her key by deception.* □ **obtaining a pecuniary advantage by deception** the offence of deceiving someone so as to derive a financial benefit □ **obtaining property by deception** the offence of tricking someone into handing over possession of property

decide /dɪˈsaɪd/ *verb* **1.** to give a judgment in a civil case ○ *The judge decided in favour of the claimant.* □ **to decide for** to give a ruling in favour of a party □ **to decide against** to give a ruling in favour of the other party **2.** to make up your mind to do something ○ *We have decided to take our neighbours to court.* ○ *The tribunal decided against awarding any damages.*

decided case /dɪˈsaɪdɪd ˌkeɪs/ *noun* a case where a court has made a decision and that decision then becomes a precedent

decidendi ♦ **ratio decidendi**

deciding factor /dɪˌsaɪdɪŋ ˈfæktə/ *noun* the most important factor which influences a decision

decision /dɪˈsɪʒ(ə)n/ *noun* **1.** a judgment in a civil court □ **the decision of the House of Lords is final** there is no appeal against a decision of the House of Lords **2.** the process of deciding to do something ○ *to come to a decision* or *to reach a decision* **3.** □ **decisions** (*in the EU*) legally binding acts of the European Community which apply to individual Member States of the EU or to groups of people or individual citizens of those states

decision maker /dɪˈsɪʒ(ə)n ˌmeɪkə/ *noun* somebody who has to decide between various options or courses of action

decision making /dɪˌsɪʒ(ə)n ˈmeɪkɪŋ/ *noun* the act of coming to a decision □ **the decision-making processes** the ways in which decisions are reached

decisis ♦ **stare decisis**

declaration /ˌdekləˈreɪʃ(ə)n/ *noun* an official statement

declaration of association /ˌdekləreɪʃ(ə)n əv əˌsəʊsiˈeɪʃ(ə)n/ *noun* a statement in the articles of association of a company, saying that the members have

agreed to form the company and buy shares in it

declaration of compliance /ˌdekləreɪʃ(ə)n əv kəmˈplaɪəns/ *noun* a declaration made by a person forming a limited company that the requirements of the Companies' Act have been met

declaration of income /ˌdekləreɪʃ(ə)n əv ˈɪnkʌm/ *noun* a statement declaring income to the tax office

declaratory judgment /dɪˌklærət(ə)ri ˈdʒʌdʒmənt/ *noun* a judgment where a court states what the legal position of the various parties is

declare /dɪˈkleə/ *verb* to make an official statement ○ *to declare someone bankrupt* ○ *to declare a dividend of 10%* □ **to declare goods to customs** to state that you are importing goods which are liable to duty □ **to declare an interest** to state in public that you own shares in a company being investigated, that you are related to someone who can benefit from your contacts, etc.

declared /dɪˈkleəd/ *adjective* having been made public or officially stated

declared value /dɪˌkleəd ˈvæljuː/ *noun* the value of goods entered on a customs declaration

declassification /diːˌklæsɪfɪˈkeɪʃ(ə)n/ *noun* the act of making something no longer secret

declassify /diːˈklæsɪfaɪ/ *verb* to make a secret document or piece of information no longer secret ○ *The government papers relating to the war have recently been declassified.*

decontrol /diːkənˈtrəʊl/ *verb* to stop or remove controls from something □ **to decontrol the price of petrol** to stop controlling the price of petrol so that a free market price can be reached

decree /dɪˈkriː/ *noun* **1.** an order made by a head of state or government which is not approved by a parliament □ **to govern by decree** to rule a country by issuing orders without having them debated and voted in a parliament **2.** an order made by a court ■ *verb* to make an order ○ *The President decreed that June 1st (his birthday) should be a National Holiday.*

decree absolute /dɪˌkriː ˈæbsəluːt/ *noun* an order from a court which ends a marriage finally

decree nisi /dɪˌkriː ˈnaɪsaɪ/ *noun* an order from a court which ends a marriage subject to a decree absolute at a later time

decriminalise /diːˈkrɪmɪnəlaɪz/, **decriminalize** *verb* to make the possession or use of something no longer a crime ○ *There are plans to decriminalise some soft drugs.*

deducing title /dɪˈdjuːsɪŋ ˌtaɪt(ə)l/ *noun* the act of a vendor proving a valid right to the property being sold

deduction /dɪˈdʌkʃən/ *noun* **1.** a conclusion which is reached by observing something ○ *By deduction, the detective came to the conclusion that the dead person had not been murdered.* **2.** the removal of money from a total, or money removed from a total ○ *Net salary is salary after deduction of tax and National Insurance contributions.* □ **deduction from salary**, **salary deduction**, **deduction at source** money which a company removes from a salary to give to the government as tax, national insurance contributions, fines etc.

deed /diːd/ *noun* a legal document which has been signed and delivered by the person making it in the presence of two witnesses

deed of arrangement /ˌdiːd əv əˈreɪndʒmənt/ *noun* an agreement made between a debtor and his or her creditors whereby the creditors accept an agreed sum in settlement of their claim rather than make the debtor bankrupt

deed of assignment /ˌdiːd əv əˈsaɪnmənt/ *noun* an agreement which legally transfers a property from a debtor to a creditor

deed of covenant /ˌdiːd əv ˈkʌvənənt/ *noun* an officially signed agreement to do something such as to pay someone a sum of money each year

deed of easement /ˌdiːd əv ˈiːzmənt/ *noun* a legal document that sets out the terms of an easement

deed of partnership /ˌdiːd əv ˈpɑːtnəʃɪp/ *noun* an agreement which sets up a partnership

deed of transfer /ˌdiːd əv ˈtrænsfɜː/ *noun* an agreement which completes the sale of a property and transfers it to the purchaser

deed of variation /ˌdiːd əv ˌveəri ˈeɪʃ(ə)n/ *noun* a legal document that allows the beneficiaries of a will to change its terms after the death of the testator

deed poll /ˈdiːd pəʊl/ *noun* a written legal instrument to which there is only one party, e.g. the validation of a change of name □ **to change one's name by deed poll** to sign a legal document by which you change your name

deem /diːm/ *verb* to believe or to consider ○ *The judge deemed it necessary to order the court to be cleared.* ○ *If no payment is made, the party shall be deemed to have defaulted.*

deeming provision /ˌdiːmɪŋ prə ˈvɪʒ(ə)n/ *noun* a clause in a statute which deems what should be taken to be the case if the actual situation is unclear

COMMENT: A deeming provision creates a legal fiction that minimises delays. For example, it can assume that legal documents will have been received and read by their intended recipient within two days of service, even if this is not confirmed. Proceedings can then continue.

de facto /ˌdeɪ ˈfæktəʊ/ *phrase* a Latin phrase meaning 'taken as a matter of fact': accepted even though the legal status may not be certain ○ *He is the de facto owner of the property.* ○ *The de facto government has been recognised.*

de facto authority /ˌdeɪ ˌfæktəʊ ɔː ˈθɒrɪti/ *noun* the authority or rule of a country by a group because it is actually ruling

defalcation /ˌdiːfælˈkeɪʃ(ə)n/ *noun* the illegal use of money by someone who is not the owner but who has been trusted to look after it

defamation of character /ˌdefəmeɪʃ(ə)n əv ˈkærɪktə/ *noun* the act of injuring someone's reputation by maliciously saying or writing things about him or her

defamatory statement /dɪˌfæmət(ə)ri ˈsteɪtmənt/ *noun* an untrue statement which is capable of lowering the reputation of the stated individual in the eyes of right-thinking people in the community. ◊ **defamation of character**

defame /dɪˈfeɪm/ *verb* to say or write things about the character of someone so as to damage his or her reputation

default /dɪˈfɔːlt/ *noun* a failure to do something which is required by law, such as a failure to carry out the terms of a contract, especially a failure to pay back a debt □ **in default of payment** if no payment is made □ **to be in default** not to do or not to have done something which is required by law □ **by default** because no one else will act ■ *verb* to fail to carry out the terms of a contract, especially to fail to pay back a debt □ **to default on payments** not to make payments which are due under the terms of a contract

default action /dɪˌfɔːlt ˈækʃən/ *noun* a County Court action to get back money owed

defaulter /dɪˈfɔːltə/ *noun* somebody who defaults

default summons /dɪˌfɔːlt ˈsʌmənz/ *noun* a County Court summons to someone to pay what is owed

defeasance /dɪˈfiːz(ə)ns/ *noun* in a collateral deed, a clause which says that a contract, bond or recognisance will be revoked if something happens or if some act is performed

defeat /dɪˈfiːt/ *verb* to revoke or render invalid an agreement, contract or bond

defect /dɪˈfekt/ *noun* a fault ■ *verb* (*of a spy, agent or government employee*) to leave your country and go to work for an enemy country

defective /dɪˈfektɪv/ *adjective* **1.** not working properly ○ *The machine broke down because of a defective cooling system.* **2.** not legally valid ○ *His title to the property is defective.*

defence /dɪˈfens/ *noun* **1.** the party in a legal case that is being sued by the claimant **2.** the party in a criminal case that is being prosecuted **3.** the legal team representing a party being sued or prosecuted **4.** the arguments used when fighting a case ○ *His defence was that he did not know the property was stolen.* **5.** a document or statement setting out a defendant's case (NOTE: A defence must say which parts of a claim are denied or admitted, and which must be proved by the claimant.) □ **to file a defence** to state that you wish to defend a case, and outline the reasons for doing so **6.** the protection of someone or something against attack

defence before claim /dɪˌfens bɪˈfɔː kleɪm/ *noun* a defence that the defendant offered the claimant the amount of money claimed before the claimant started proceedings against him or her. Also called **tender before claim**

defence counsel /dɪˈfens ˌkaʊnsəl/ *noun* a solicitor who represents the defendant or the accused

Defence Secretary /ˌsekrət(ə)ri əv steɪt fə dɪˈfens/ *noun* same as **Secretary of State for Defence**

defence statement /dɪˈfens ˌsteɪtmənt/ *noun* a document used in crim-

inal proceedings that sets out the accused's defence before going to trial

defence witness /dɪˌfens ˈwɪtnəs/ *noun* somebody who is called to court to give evidence which helps the case of the defendant or of the accused

defend /dɪˈfend/ *verb* **1.** to fight to protect someone or something which is being attacked ○ *The company is defending itself against the takeover bid.* **2.** to speak on behalf of someone who has been charged with a crime ○ *He hired the best lawyers to defend him against the tax authorities.* □ **to defend an action** to appear in court to state your case when accused of something

defendant /dɪˈfendənt/ *noun* **1.** somebody who is sued in a civil case. Compare **claimant**, **plaintiff 2.** somebody who is accused of a crime in a criminal case (NOTE: usually called the **accused**)

defensible /dɪˈfensɪb(ə)l/ *adjective* **1.** possible to justify or defend ○ *She argued that his actions were defensible given the circumstances.* **2.** capable of being defended ○ *It is important to make borders defensible.*

defer /dɪˈfɜː/ *verb* to arrange a meeting or activity for a later date than originally planned ○ *to defer judgment* ○ *The decision has been deferred until the next meeting.* (NOTE: **deferring – deferred**)

deferment /dɪˈfɜːmənt/ *noun* the act of arranging a meeting or activity for a later date than originally planned ○ *deferment of payment* ○ *deferment of a decision*

deferment of sentence /dɪˌfɜːmənt əv ˈsentəns/ *noun* a decision to delay sentencing a convicted criminal for up to six months to assess their behaviour in that period

deferred /dɪˈfɜːd/ *adjective* delayed until a later date

deferred creditor /dɪˌfɜːd ˈkredɪtə/ *noun* somebody who is owed money by a bankrupt but who is paid only after all other creditors

deferred payment /dɪˌfɜːd ˈpeɪmənt/ *noun* payment for goods by instalments over a long period

deficiency /dɪˈfɪʃ(ə)nsi/ *noun US* the amount of tax owing by a taxpayer after he or she has submitted a tax return which is too low

deforce /diːˈfɔːs/ *verb* to take wrongfully and hold land which belongs to someone else

deforcement /diː'fɔːsmənt/ *noun* the wrongful taking and holding of another person's land

defraud /dɪ'frɔːd/ *verb* to trick someone so as to obtain money illegally ○ *He defrauded the Inland Revenue of thousands of pounds.* (NOTE: You defraud someone **of** something.)

defray /dɪ'freɪ/ *verb* to provide money to pay the cost of something ○ *The company agreed to defray the costs of the prosecution.*

degrading treatment or punishment /dɪˌɡreɪdɪŋ ˌtriːtmənt ɔː 'pʌnɪʃmənt/ *noun* an absolute right prohibiting an individual from being subjected to a feeling of fear, anguish and inferiority which has the possible effect of humiliating the victim (NOTE: It was introduced into UK law by the Human Rights Act 1998.)

degree /dɪ'ɡriː/ *noun* **1.** a level or measure of a relationship **2.** *US* a system for classifying murders

de jure /ˌdeɪ 'dʒʊəri/ *phrase* a Latin phrase meaning 'as a matter of law', where the legal title is clear ○ *He is the de jure owner of the property.* ◊ **de facto**

del credere agent /ˌdel 'kreɪdərɪ ˌeɪdʒənt/ *noun* an agent who receives a high commission because he or she guarantees payment by customers to his or her principal

delegate *noun* /'delɪɡət/ somebody who is elected by others to put their case at a meeting ○ *The company sent a delegate to the conference in Hong Kong* ■ *verb* /'deləɡeɪt/ to pass authority or responsibility to someone else

delegated legislation /ˌdeləɡeɪtɪd ˌledʒɪ'sleɪʃ(ə)n/ *noun* **1.** (*in the UK*) legislation which has the power of an Act of Parliament but which is passed by a minister to whom Parliament has delegated its authority **2.** (*in the EU*) legislation which is proposed by the Commission and implemented by the Council of Ministers

delegatus non potest delegare /ˌdeliɡɑːtəs nɒn pɒˌtest ˌdeliˈɡɑːreɪ/ *phrase* a Latin phrase meaning 'the delegate cannot delegate to someone else'

deliberate *adjective* /dɪ'lɪb(ə)rət/ done on purpose ○ *The police suggest that the letter was a deliberate attempt to encourage disorder.* ■ *verb* /dɪ'lɪbəreɪt/ to consider or to discuss a problem ○ *The committee deliberated for several hours before reaching a decision.*

deliberations /dɪˌlɪbə'reɪʃ(ə)nz/ *plural noun* discussions ○ *The result of the committee's deliberations was passed to the newspapers.*

delicti ♦ **corpus delicti**

delicto ♦ **in flagrante delicto**

delinquency /dɪ'lɪŋkwənsi/ *noun* **1.** the act of committing crime, usually minor crime **2.** the fact of a payment being seriously overdue, without yet being in default

delinquent /dɪ'lɪŋkwənt/ *adjective* **1.** *US* (*of a debt*) overdue **2.** (*of behaviour*) antisocial or criminal ■ *noun* someone, especially a young person, who has acted in an antisocial way or broken the law □ **a juvenile delinquent**, **a delinquent** *US* a young criminal who commits minor crimes, especially crimes against property

delivery /dɪ'lɪv(ə)ri/ *noun* **1.** goods being transferred from the possession of person to another **2.** the transfer of a bill of exchange **3.** a formal act whereby a deed becomes effective ○ *Deeds take effect only from the time of delivery.*

delivery up /dɪ'lɪv(ə)ri ʌp/ *noun* the action of delivering goods which have been made in infringement of a copyright or patent to the claimant, so that they can be destroyed

demanding with menaces /dɪ ˌmɑːndɪŋ wɪð 'menəss/ *noun* the offence of attempting to make someone give you something by threatening them with violence

de minimis non curat lex /ˌdeɪ ˌmɪnɪmis nɒn ˌkjʊəræt 'leks/ *phrase* a Latin phrase meaning 'the law does not deal with trivial things'

demise /dɪ'maɪz/ *noun* **1.** death ○ *On his demise the estate passed to his daughter.* **2.** the granting of property on a lease

demise charter /dɪˌmaɪz 'tʃɑːtə/ *noun* the charter of a ship without the crew

demise of the Crown /dɪˌmaɪz əv ðə 'kraʊn/ *noun* the death of a king or queen

democracy /dɪ'mɒkrəsi/ *noun* **1.** a theory or system of government by freely elected representatives of the people ○ *After the coup, democracy was replaced by a military dictatorship.* **2.** the right to fair government, free election of representatives and equality in voting **3.** a country ruled in this way ○ *The pact was welcomed by western democracies.*

democratic /ˌdemə'krætɪk/ *adjective* **1.** referring to a democracy ○ *After the coup* *the democratic processes of government were replaced by government by decree.* **2.** free and fair, reflecting the views of the majority ○ *The resolution was passed by a democratic vote of the council.* ○ *The action of the leader is against the wishes of the party as expressed in a democratic vote at the party conference.*

demonstrative legacy /dɪˌmɒnstrətɪv ˈlegəsi/ *noun* a gift in a will which is ordered to be paid out of a special account

demur /dɪˈmɜː/ *noun* an objection ○ *Counsel made no demur to the proposal.* ■ *verb* **1.** not to agree ○ *Counsel stated that there was no case to answer, but the judge demurred.* **2.** to make a formal objection that the facts as alleged are not sufficient to warrant the civil action (NOTE: **demurring – demurred**)

demurrage /dɪˈmʌrɪdʒ/ *noun* money paid to the owner of a cargo when a ship is delayed in a port

demurrer /dɪˈmɜːrə/ *noun* in a civil action, a plea that although the facts of the case are correct, they are not sufficient to warrant the action

denial /dɪˈnaɪəl/ *noun* **1.** the act of not allowing something **2.** the act of stating that you have not done something ○ *In spite of his denials he was found guilty.*

denial of human rights /dɪˌnaɪəl əv ˈhjuːmən raɪts/ *noun* the act of refusing someone a generally-accepted right

denial of justice /dɪˌnaɪəl əv ˈdʒʌstɪs/ *noun* a situation where justice appears not to have been done

denial-of-service attack /dɪˌnaɪəl əv ˈsɜːvɪs əˌtæk/ *noun* an illegal attempt to cause a computer system to crash by sending it data from many sources simultaneously

de novo /ˌdeɪ ˈnəʊvəʊ/ *phrase* a Latin phrase meaning 'starting again'

deny /dɪˈnaɪ/ *verb* **1.** not to allow something ○ *She was denied the right to see her lawyer.* **2.** to say that you have not done something ○ *He denied being in the house at the time of the murder.* (NOTE: You deny someone something *or* deny doing *or* having done something.)

deoxyribonucleic acid /diːˌɒksiraɪbəʊnjuːˌkleɪɪk ˈæsɪd/ *noun* full form of DNA

depart /dɪˈpɑːt/ *verb* □ **to depart from normal practice** to act in a different way from the normal practice

Department for Constitutional Affairs /dɪˌpɑːtmənt fə ˌkɒnstɪtjuːʃ(ə)nəl əˈfeəz/ *noun* formerly, the UK government department responsible for justice, rights and democracy. Abbreviation **DCA** (NOTE: It has now been replaced by the **Ministry of Justice**.)

Department of Justice /dɪˌpɑːtmənt əv ˈdʒʌstɪs/ *noun US* the department of the US government responsible for federal legal cases, headed by the Attorney-General

Department of Justice Canada /dɪ ˌpɑːtmənt əv ˌdʒʌstɪs ˈkænədə/ *noun* the Canadian government department that is responsible for developing policies affecting the justice system and providing legal services to the federal government

Department of State /dɪˌpɑːtmənt əv ˌseʊʃ(ə)l ˈsteɪt/ *noun* **1.** a major section of the British government headed by a Secretary of State ○ *the Department of Trade and Industry* **2.** a major section of the US government headed by a Secretary ○ *the Lord Chancellor's Department*

Department of Trade and Industry /dɪˌpɑːtmənt əv ˌtreɪd ənd ˈɪndəstri/ *noun* a UK government department that promotes UK business and protects the rights of working people and consumers. Abbreviation **DTI**

departure /dɪˈpɑːtʃə/ *noun* the act of leaving □ **a departure from the usual practice** the fact of doing something differently ○ *Any departure from the terms and conditions of the contract must be advised in writing.*

dependant /dɪˈpendənt/ *noun* **1.** somebody who is supported financially by someone else ○ *He has to provide for his family and dependants out of a very small salary.* **2.** a person who is a member of the family of someone who works in the European Union, even if not a EU citizen

COMMENT: For the purposes of EU law, dependants are classified as an EU citizen's spouse, parents, grandparents, and children and grandchildren up to the age of 21.

dependent /dɪˈpendənt/ *adjective* **1.** being supported financially by someone else ○ *Tax relief is allowed for dependent relatives.* **2.** referring to a dependant

dependent rights /dɪˈpendənt raɪts/ *plural noun* the rights of a dependant of an EU citizen to enter a EU country along with a parent or other close relative

deponent /dɪˈpəʊnənt/ noun somebody who makes a statement under oath, by affirmation or by affidavit

deport /dɪˈpɔːt/ verb to send someone away from a country permanently ○ *The illegal immigrants were deported.*

deportation /ˌdiːpɔːˈteɪʃ(ə)n/ noun the sending of someone away from a country ○ *The convicts were sentenced to deportation.*

deportation order /ˌdiːpɔːˈteɪʃ(ə)n ˌɔːdə/ noun an official order to send someone away from a country ○ *The minister signed the deportation order.*

depose /dɪˈpəʊz/ verb **1.** to state under oath **2.** to remove a monarch from the throne

deposit /dɪˈpɒzɪt/ noun **1.** money placed in a bank for safe keeping or to earn interest **2.** money given in advance so that the thing which you want to buy will not be sold to someone else ○ *to leave £10 as deposit* □ **to forfeit a deposit** to lose a deposit because you have decided not to buy the item ■ verb **1.** to put documents somewhere for safe keeping ○ *We have deposited the deeds of the house with the bank.* ○ *He deposited his will with his solicitor.* **2.** to put money into a bank account ○ *to deposit £100 in a current account*

deposit account /dɪˈpɒzɪt əˌkaʊnt/ noun a bank account which pays interest but on which notice has to be given to withdraw money

depositary /dɪˈpɒzɪtəri/ noun US a person or corporation that can place money or documents for safekeeping with a depository (NOTE: Do not confuse with **depository**.)

deposition /ˌdepəˈzɪʃ(ə)n/ noun a written statement of evidence from a witness

depositor /dɪˈpɒzɪtə/ noun somebody who deposits money in a bank

depository /dɪˈpɒzɪt(ə)ri/ noun a person or company with whom money or documents can be deposited (NOTE: Do not confuse with **depositary**.)

deprave /dɪˈpreɪv/ verb to make someone's character bad ○ *Such TV programmes which may deprave the minds of children who watch them.*

depraved /dɪˈpreɪvd/ adjective morally perverted or corrupt ○ *The defendant was accused of disseminating depraved material to minors.*

deputise /ˈdepjʊtaɪz/, **deputize** verb □ **to deputise for someone** to take the place of someone who is absent □ **to deputise someone** to appoint someone as a deputy

deputy /ˈdepjʊti/ noun **1.** somebody who takes the place of a higher official, who assists a higher official ○ *He acted as deputy for the chairman* or *he acted as the chairman's deputy.* **2.** US somebody who acts for or assists a sheriff

derelict /ˈderɪlɪkt/ adjective **1.** abandoned, fallen into disrepair ○ *The derelict house was judged unsafe to enter.* **2.** negligent ○ *He was accused of being derelict in his repayments.* ■ noun an abandoned floating boat

dereliction of duty /ˌderɪˌlɪkʃən əv ˈdjuːti/ noun failure to do what you ought to do ○ *She was found guilty of gross dereliction of duty.*

derivative /dɪˈrɪvətɪv/ noun ♦ **financial derivative**

derogate /ˈderəgeɪt/ verb □ **to derogate from something which has been agreed** to act to prevent something which has been agreed from being fully implemented

derogation /ˌderəˈgeɪʃ(ə)n/ noun **1.** the act of avoiding or destroying something **2.** (in the EU) an action by which an EC directive is not applied

COMMENT: For example, a derogation from the principle of equality of access to employment may be where the job can only be done by someone of one particular sex, such as modelling gender-specific clothes.

derogation of responsibility /ˌderəgeɪʃ(ə)n əv rɪˌspɒnsɪˈbɪlɪti/ noun the avoidance of doing something that should be done

descendant /dɪˈsendənt/ noun (in the EU) a child or grandchild of a person (NOTE: The opposite, the parents or grandparents of a person, are **ascendants**.)

descent /dɪˈsent/ noun **1.** family ties of inheritance between parents and children □ **British by descent, of British descent** having at least one British parent **2.** □ **by descent** way of inheriting property by an heir, where there is no will

described /dɪˈskraɪbd/ adjective □ **as described** of goods sold, corresponding with the sales description given

COMMENT: Under the Sale Of Goods Act, the goods sold must be as described, as well as being fit for purpose and of satisfactory quality

desegregate /diːˈsegrɪgeɪt/ verb to end a policy of segregation

desegregation /ˌdiːsegrɪˈɡeɪʃ(ə)n/ noun the ending of segregation

deselect /ˌdiːsɪˈlekt/ verb to decide that a person who had been selected by a political party as a candidate for a constituency is no longer the candidate

deselection /ˌdiːsɪˈlekʃ(ə)n/ noun the act of deselecting ○ *Some factions in the local party have proposed the deselection of the candidate.*

desert /dɪˈzɜːt/ verb **1.** to leave the armed forces without permission ○ *He deserted and went to live in South America.* **2.** to leave a family or spouse ○ *The two children have been deserted by their father.*

deserter /dɪˈzɜːtə/ noun somebody who has left the armed forces without permission

desertion /dɪˈzɜːʃ(ə)n/ noun **1.** the act of leaving the armed forces without permission **2.** the act of leaving a spouse ○ *He divorced his wife because of her desertion.*

despatch /dɪˈspætʃ/ verb to send ○ *The letters about the rates were despatched yesterday.* ○ *The Defence Minister was despatched to take charge of the operation.*

despatch box /dɪˈspætʃ bɒks/ noun **1.** a red box in which government papers are sent to ministers **2.** one of two boxes on the centre table in the House of Commons at which a Minister or member of the Opposition Front Bench stands to speak □ **to be at the despatch box** (*of a minister*) to be speaking in parliament

destruction /dɪˈstrʌkʃən/ noun the action of killing someone, or of ending the existence of something completely ○ *The destruction of the evidence in the fire at the police station made it difficult to prosecute.*

detain /dɪˈteɪn/ verb to hold a person so that he or she cannot leave ○ *The suspects were detained by the police for questioning.*

detainee /ˌdiːteɪˈniː/ noun somebody who has been detained

detainer /dɪˈteɪnə/ noun the act of holding a person

detect /dɪˈtekt/ verb to notice or discover something which is hidden or difficult to see ○ *The machine can detect explosives.*

detection /dɪˈtekʃən/ noun the process of discovering something, especially discovering who has committed a crime or how a crime has been committed

detection rate /dɪˈtekʃ(ə)n reɪt/ noun the number of crimes which are solved, as a percentage of all crimes

detective /dɪˈtektɪv/ noun somebody, usually a policeman, who tries to solve a crime

COMMENT: The ranks of detectives in the British Police Force are Detective Constable, Detective Sergeant, Detective Inspector, Detective Chief Inspector, Detective Superintendent, and Detective Chief Superintendent.

detective agency /dɪˌtektɪv ˈeɪdʒənsi/ noun an office which hires out the services of private detectives

detention /dɪˈtenʃ(ə)n/ noun **1.** the act of keeping someone so that he or she cannot escape ○ *The suspects were placed in detention.* **2.** wrongfully holding goods which belong to someone else

detention centre /dɪˈtenʃ(ə)n ˌsentə/ noun **1.** a place where young offenders aged between 14 and 21 can be kept for corrective training, instead of being sent to prison, if they are convicted of crimes which would usually carry a sentence of three months' imprisonment or more **2.** a place where foreign nationals seeking asylum must await decisions on whether they can stay or must leave the country"

detention order /dɪˌtenʃ(ə)n ˈɔːdə/ noun a court order asking for someone to be kept in detention

determine /dɪˈtɜːmɪn/ verb **1.** to control what will happen or what something will be like ○ *Their attitudes have been determined by their experiences.* **2.** to discover something ○ *We need to determine what the long-term effects of this decision might be.*

deterrence /dɪˈterəns/ noun the idea that the harsh punishment of one criminal will deter other people from committing crimes

deterrent /dɪˈterənt/ noun a punishment which is strong enough to stop people from committing a crime ○ *A long prison sentence will act as a deterrent to other possible criminals.*

deterrent sentence /dɪˌterənt ˈsentəns/ noun a harsh sentence which the judge hopes will deter other people from committing crimes

detinue /ˈdetɪnjuː/ noun the tort of wrongfully holding goods which belong to someone else □ **action in detinue** action formerly brought to regain possession of goods which were wrongfully held by someone

detriment /ˈdetrɪmənt/ noun damage or harm □ **without detriment to the claim** without harming the claim

detrimental /ˌdetrɪˈment(ə)l/ *adjective* harmful ○ *action detrimental to the maintenance of public order*

developer /dɪˈveləpə/ *noun* □ **a property developer** person who plans and builds a group of new houses or new factories

development area /dɪˈveləpmənt ˌeəriə/ *noun* an area which has been given special help from a government to encourage businesses and factories to be set up there

devil /ˈdev(ə)l/ *noun* **1.** (*in England and Wales*) a junior barrister who does legal work for a more senior barrister as part of a private arrangement **2.** (*in Scotland and Ireland*) a junior barrister undergoing a period of pupillage to a senior barrister, usually lasting one year ■ *verb* to act as a devil for a more senior barrister

devilmaster /ˈdev(ə)lˌmɑːstə/ *noun* in Scotland, a senior barrister who oversees a junior's period of pupillage

devise /dɪˈvaɪz/ *noun* a gift of freehold land to someone in a will ■ *verb* to give freehold property to someone in a will

COMMENT: Giving of other types of property is a **bequest**.

devisee /dɪvaɪˈziː/ *noun* somebody who receives freehold property in a will

devolution /ˌdiːvəˈluːʃ(ə)n/ *noun* the act of transferring power to govern or to make decisions from a central authority to a local authority

COMMENT: Devolution involves passing more power than **decentralisation**. In a devolved state, the regional authorities are almost autonomous.

devolve /dɪˈvɒlv/ *verb* to pass to someone under the terms of a will

devolved government /dɪˌvɒlvd ˈɡʌv(ə)nmənt/ *noun* a regional government which has been formed by devolution, such as the Scottish Executive, Welsh Assembly or Northern Ireland Assembly

dictum /ˈdɪktəm/ *noun* a statement made by a judge

die /daɪ/ *verb* to stop living. ◊ **death** (NOTE: **dying – died**)

digest /ˈdaɪdʒest/ *noun* a book which collects summaries of court decisions together, used for reference purposes by legal practitioners

digital rights management /ˌdɪdʒɪt(ə)l ˈraɪts ˌmænɪdʒmənt/ *noun* methods of preventing unauthorised copy-

ing of digital products such as CD and DVDs. Abbreviation **DRM**

dilapidation /dɪˌlæpɪˈdeɪʃ(ə)n/ *noun* damage arising through neglect

dilatory /ˈdɪlət(ə)ri/ *adjective* too slow ○ *She is dilatory in her work habits.*

dilatory motion /ˌdɪlət(ə)ri ˈməʊʃ(ə)n/ *noun* a motion in the House of Commons to delay the debate on a proposal

dilatory plea /ˈdɪlət(ə)ri pliː/ *noun* a plea by a defendant relating to the jurisdiction of the court, which has the effect of delaying the action

dilatory tactics /ˈdɪlət(ə)ri ˌtæktɪks/ *plural noun* attempts made by one party to postpone court proceedings, because the delay would be advantageous to him or her

diminished responsibility /dɪˌmɪnɪʃt rɪˌspɒnsɪˈbɪlɪti/ *noun* a mental state, either inherited or caused by illness or injury, which means that he or she cannot be held responsible for the crime which has been committed

DInsp *abbreviation* detective inspector

dip /dɪp/ *noun* a pickpocket (*slang*)

diplomat /ˈdɪpləmæt/ *noun* a person such as an ambassador who is an official representative of their country in another country

diplomatic agent /ˌdɪpləmætɪk ˈeɪdʒənt/ *noun* a person officially employed by the embassy of a foreign country

diplomatic channels /ˌdɪpləmætɪk ˈtʃæn(ə)lz/ *plural noun* communicating between countries through their diplomats ○ *The message was delivered by diplomatic channels.* ○ *They are working to restore diplomatic channels between the two countries.*

diplomatic corps /ˌdɪpləˈmætɪk kɔː/ *plural noun* all foreign diplomats in a city or country

diplomatic immunity /ˌdɪpləmætɪk ɪˈmjuːnɪti/ *noun* not subject to the laws of a country because of being a foreign diplomat ○ *He claimed diplomatic immunity to avoid being arrested.*

direct /daɪˈrekt/ *verb* to give an order to someone ○ *The judge directed the jury to acquit all the defendants.* ○ *The Crown Court directed the justices to rehear the case.*

direct discrimination /daɪˌrekt dɪˌskrɪmɪˈneɪʃ(ə)n/ *noun* illegal discrimination where similar cases are treated differently or where different cases are treated in the same way

direct effect /daɪˌrekt ɪˈfekt/ *noun* the effect of a legal decision of the European Union which creates rights for citizens. ◊ **supremacy**

COMMENT: Direct effect applies vertically, from the state giving a right to the citizen, and from the citizen who has an obligation to the state. It can also apply horizontally between individual citizens who have rights and obligations to each other.

direct evidence /daɪˌrekt ˈevɪd(ə)ns/ *noun* first-hand evidence such as the testimony of an eyewitness or the production of original documents

direct examination /daɪˌrekt ɪɡˌzæmɪ ˈneɪʃ(ə)n/ *noun* the questioning of a witness by his or her own lawyers in court

direction /daɪˈrekʃən/ ◊ **directions 1.** an order which explains how something should be done ○ *The court is not able to give directions to the local authority.* **2.** instructions from a judge to a jury **3.** orders given by a judge concerning the general way of proceeding with a case

directive /daɪˈrektɪv/ *noun* **1.** an order or command to someone to do something **2.** (*in the EU*) a legally binding act of the European Community which is binding on the Member States of the EU, but not on individuals until it has been made part of national law ○ *The Commission issued a directive on food prices.* Compare **regulations**

COMMENT: A directive is binding in the result which is to be achieved. Directives do not have a direct effect before any time limit for their implementation has expired, and they do not have any horizontal direct effect (i.e. an effect between citizens).

Director-General /daɪˌrektə ˈdʒen(ə)rəl/ *noun* (*in the EU*) the head of the Directorates General in the Commission (NOTE: The plural is **Directors-General**.)

Director-General of Fair Trading /daɪ ˌrektə ˌdʒen(ə)rəl əv ˌfeə ˈtreɪdɪŋ/ *noun* an official in charge of the Office of Fair Trading, dealing with consumers and the law

Director of Public Prosecutions /daɪ ˌrektər əv ˌpʌblɪk ˌprɒsɪˈkjuːʃ(ə)nz/ *noun* a government official in charge of the Crown Prosecution Service, working under the Attorney-General, who can prosecute in important cases and advises other government departments if prosecutions should be started ○ *The papers in the fraud case have been sent to the Director of Public Prosecutions.* Abbreviation **DPP**

direct payment /daɪˌrekt ˈpeɪmənt/ *noun* payment straight into a person's bank account, rather than in the form of a cheque (NOTE: Many Government benefits can be paid by this method.)

direct selling /daɪˌrekt ˈselɪŋ/ *noun* the activity of selling a product direct to the customer without going through a shop

direct sexual discrimination /daɪ ˌrekt ˌsekʃuəl dɪˌskrɪmɪˈneɪʃ(ə)n/ *noun* an instance of sexual discrimination that is overt, e.g. failure to pay one sex the same wage as the other in an equivalent job. ◊ **indirect sexual discrimination**

direct taxation /daɪˌrekt tækˈseɪʃ(ə)n/ *noun* a tax such as income tax which is paid direct to the government

disability /ˌdɪsəˈbɪlɪti/ *noun* **1.** the condition of being unable to use a part of the body properly **2.** a lack of legal capacity to act in your own right because of age or mental state □ **under a disability** not capable to taking legal action for him or herself

Disability Living Allowance /ˌdɪsəbɪlɪti ˈlɪvɪŋ əˌlaʊəns/ *noun* financial help given by the Government to someone who has a physical or mental disability and is unable to be wholly self-sufficient. Abbreviation **DLA**

Disability Rights Commission /ˌdɪsəbɪlɪti ˌraɪts kəˌmɪʃ(ə)n/ *noun* an official committee set up to deal with issues relating to discrimination against people with disabilities. Abbreviation **DRC**

disabled person /dɪsˌeɪb(ə)ld ˈpɜːs(ə)n/ *noun* a person with physical disabilities

disallow /ˌdɪsəˈlaʊ/ *verb* not to accept something ○ *The judge disallowed the defence evidence.* ○ *He claimed £2000 for fire damage, but the claim was disallowed.*

disapproval /ˌdɪsəˈpruːv(ə)l/ *noun* the act of disapproving a decision made by a lower court

disapprove /ˌdɪsəˈpruːv/ *verb* **1.** to show doubt about a decision made by a lower court, but not to reverse or overrule it ○ *The Appeal Court disapproved the County Court decision.* **2.** □ **to disapprove of something** to show that you do not approve of something, that you do not think something is good ○ *The judge openly disapproves of juries.*

disbar /dɪsˈbɑː/ *verb* to stop a barrister from practising (NOTE: **disbarring – disbarred**)

disburse /dɪsˈbɜːs/ *verb* to pay money

disbursement /dɪsˈbɜːsmənt/ *noun* an amount of money paid from a fund held for a particular purpose, or the process of making such a payment

discharge /dɪsˈtʃɑːdʒ/ *noun* /ˈdɪstʃɑːdʒ/ **1.** the ending of a contract by performing all the conditions of the contract, releasing a party from the terms of the contract, or being in breach of contract **2.** payment of debt □ **in full discharge of a debt** having paid off a debt completely **3.** release from prison or from military service **4.** □ **in discharge of one's duties** carrying out one's duties ■ *verb* **1.** to let someone go free ○ *The prisoners were discharged by the judge.* □ **to discharge a jury** to tell a jury that they are no longer needed **2.** □ **to discharge a bankrupt** to release someone from bankruptcy (as when a person has paid his or her debts) **3.** □ **to discharge a debt**, **to discharge one's liabilities** to pay a debt or one's liabilities in full **4.** to dismiss someone from a job or position ○ *to discharge an employee*

discharge by agreement /ˌdɪstʃɑːdʒ baɪ əˈɡriːmənt/ *noun* a situation where both parties agree to end a contract

discharge by performance /dɪs ˌtʃɑːdʒ baɪ pəˈfɔːməns/ *noun* a situation where the terms of a contract have been fulfilled

discharged bankrupt /dɪsˌtʃɑːdʒd ˈbæŋkrʌpt/ *noun* somebody who has been released from being bankrupt

discharge in bankruptcy /ˌdɪstʃɑːdʒ ɪn ˈbæŋkrʌptsi/ *noun* an order of a court to release someone from bankruptcy

disciplinary /ˌdɪsɪˈplɪnəri/ *adjective* □ **to take disciplinary action against someone** to punish someone

disciplinary procedure /ˌdɪsɪˈplɪnəri prəˌsiːdʒə/ *noun* a way of warning an employee officially that he or she is breaking rules or that their standard of work is unacceptable

discipline /ˈdɪsɪplɪn/ *verb* to punish someone ○ *The clerk was disciplined for leaking the report to the newspapers.*

disclaim /dɪsˈkleɪm/ *verb* **1.** to refuse to admit ○ *He disclaimed all knowledge of the bomb.* ○ *The management disclaims all responsibility for customers' property.* **2.** to refuse to accept a legacy or devise made to you under someone's will

disclaimer /dɪsˈkleɪmə/ *noun* **1.** a legal refusal to accept responsibility or to accept a right **2.** a clause in a contract where a party

disclaims responsibility for something **3.** a refusal to accept property bequeathed under someone's will

disclose /dɪsˈkləʊz/ *verb* **1.** to tell details ○ *The bank has no right to disclose details of my account to the tax office.* **2.** (*in civil cases*) to say that a document exists ○ *Parties to a case are required to disclose relevant documents.*

disclosure /dɪsˈkləʊʒə/ *noun* **1.** the act of telling details or of publishing a secret ○ *The disclosure of the takeover bid raised the price of the shares.* ○ *The defendant's case was made stronger by the disclosure that the claimant was an undischarged bankrupt.* ◊ **non-disclosure 2.** the act of stating that documents exist or have existed before a hearing starts in the civil courts, usually done by preparing a list of documents (NOTE: Parties to whom documents have been disclosed have the right to inspect them. Since the introduction of the Civil Procedure Rules, this term has replaced **discovery.**)

disclosure of documents /dɪ ˌskləʊ(ə)ri əv ˈdɒkjʊmənts/ *noun* disclosure of each party's documents to the other before a hearing starts in the civil courts (NOTE: Disclosure is known as **discovery** in the US)

discontinuance /ˌdɪskənˈtɪnjuəns/ *noun* the action of discontinuing a claim or action ○ *The claimant has served notice of discontinuance.*

discontinue /ˌdɪskənˈtɪnjuː/ *verb* to stop a claim which has been issued or an action which has started ○ *A claimant may need to seek permission of the court to discontinue a claim.*

discovery /dɪˈskʌv(ə)ri/ *noun* ♦ **disclosure**

discredit /dɪsˈkredɪt/ *verb* to show that a person is not reliable ○ *The prosecution counsel tried to discredit the defence witnesses.*

discretion /dɪˈskreʃ(ə)n/ *noun* the ability to decide correctly what should be done ○ *Magistrates have the discretion to allow an accused person to change their election if requested.* ○ *The judge refused the application, on the ground that he had a judicial discretion to examine inadmissible evidence.* □ **to exercise one's discretion** to decide which of several possible ways to act □ **to leave something to someone's discretion** to leave it for someone to decide what to do □ **at the discretion of someone** if someone decides ○ *Membership is at the discretion of the committee.* ○ *Sentencing is at the discretion of the judge.* ○ *The granting of an injunction is at the discretion of the court.*

discretionary /dɪˈskreʃ(ə)n(ə)ri/ *adjective* being possible if someone wants □ **discretionary powers** powers which somebody could use if he or she thought it suitable □ **the tribunal has wide discretionary power** the tribunal can decide on many different courses of action

discretionary life sentence /dɪsˌkreʃ(ə)n(ə)ri laɪf ˈsentəns/ *noun* a sentence imposed for those over the age of 21 as the maximum penalty for a serious offence

discretionary trust /dɪˌskreʃ(ə)n(ə)ri ˈtrʌst/ *noun* a trust where the trustees decide how to invest the income and when and how much income should be paid to the beneficiaries

discriminate /dɪˈskrɪmɪneɪt/ *verb* to note differences between things and act accordingly ○ *The planning committee finds it difficult to discriminate between applications which improve the community, and those which are purely commercial.* □ **to discriminate against someone** to treat someone unequally ○ *The council was accused of discriminating against women in its recruitment policy.* ○ *He claimed he had been discriminated against because of his colour.*

discrimination /dɪˌskrɪmɪˈneɪʃ(ə)n/ *noun* **1.** the unfair treatment of someone because of their colour, class, language, race, religion, sex or a disability ○ *Racial discrimination is against the law.* ○ *There should be no discrimination on the grounds of disability.* **2.** the ability to notice the differences between things ○ *The tests are designed to give clear discrimination between the three categories.* **3.** good judgement and decision-making ○ *The committee showed discrimination in its choice of advisers for the project.*

COMMENT: The UK has passed a range of legislation including the Employment Equality (Age) Regulations 2006, the Employment Equality (Sexual Orientation) Regulations 2003, the Sex Discrimination Act 1975 (Amendment) Regulations 2003, the Disability Discrimination Act 2005 and the Race Relations Act 1976 (Amendment) Regulations 2003, which protect against most forms of discrimination in the UK The Human Rights Act 1998 Article 14 also protects against discrimination on grounds of 'sex, race, colour, language, religion, political or other opinion, national or social origin, association with a national minority, property, birth or other status'.

disenfranchise /ˌdɪsɪnˈfræntʃaɪz/, **disfranchise** *verb* to take away someone's right to vote ○ *The company has tried to disenfranchise the ordinary shareholders.*

dishonour /dɪsˈɒnə/ *verb* to refuse to pay a cheque or bill of exchange because there is not enough money in the account to pay it ○ *The bank dishonoured his cheque.* ■ *noun* the act of dishonouring a cheque ○ *The dishonour of the cheque brought her business to a stop.*

disinherit /ˌdɪsɪnˈherɪt/ *verb* to make a will which prevents someone from inheriting ○ *He was disinherited by his father.*

dismiss /dɪsˈmɪs/ *verb* **1.** □ **to dismiss an employee** to remove an employee from a job ○ *He was dismissed for being late.* **2.** to refuse to accept ○ *The court dismissed the appeal* or *the application* or *the action.* ○ *The justices dismissed the witness' evidence out of hand.*

dismissal /dɪsˈmɪs(ə)l/ *noun* **1.** the removal of an employee from a job, especially as a result of something they have done wrong. ◊ **wrongful dismissal, unfair dismissal 2.** an unwillingness to accept that something might be true ○ *the company's public dismissal of the allegation of fraud* **3.** an order telling someone to leave a place, or to stop carrying out a role ○ *the dismissal of jurors* **4.** a judge's decision that a court case should not continue

dismissal procedure /dɪsˌmɪs(ə)l prəˈsiːdʒə/ *noun* the process of dismissing an employee, following the rules in the contract of employment

disobedience /ˌdɪsəˈbiːdiəns/ *noun* bad behaviour which ignores rules or requests to do something ○ *The prisoners were put in solitary confinement as punishment for their disobedience of the governor's orders.*

disorder /dɪsˈɔːdə/ *noun* a lack of order or of control

disorderly /dɪsˈɔːdəli/ *adjective* badly behaved ○ *She was charged with disorderly conduct.* ◊ **drunk and disorderly**

dispensation /ˌdɪspenˈseɪʃ(ə)n/ *noun* **1.** the act of giving out justice **2.** special permission to do something which is normally not allowed or is against the law

dispense /dɪˈspens/ *verb* **1.** to provide something, especially officially ○ *to dis-*

pense justice **2.** □ **to dispense with something** not to use something, to do without something ○ *The chairman of the tribunal dispensed with the formality of taking minutes.* ○ *The accused decided to dispense with the services of a lawyer.*

displaced person /dɪsˌpleɪsd 'pɜːs(ə)n/ *noun* a man or woman who has been forced to leave home and move to another country because of war

dispose /dɪ'spəʊz/ *verb* □ **to dispose of** to get rid of, to sell cheaply ○ *to dispose of excess stock* ○ *to dispose of one's business*

disposition /ˌdɪspə'zɪʃ(ə)n/ *noun* the act of passing property in the form of land or goods to another person. ◊ **testamentary disposition**

dispossess /ˌdɪspə'zes/ *verb* to deprive someone wrongfully of his or her possession of land

dispossession /ˌdɪspə'zeʃ(ə)n/ *noun* the act of wrongfully depriving someone of possession of land

dispute /dɪ'spjuːt, 'dɪspjuːt/ *noun* a disagreement or argument between parties □ **to mediate in a dispute** to try to settle a dispute between other parties ■ *verb* to argue against something □ **to dispute a claim** to argue that a claim is not correct □ **to dispute the jurisdiction of a court** to argue that a court has no jurisdiction over a case

dispute resolution /dɪ'spjuːt ˌrezəluːʃ(ə)n/ *noun* the act of resolving legal disputes

disqualification /dɪsˌkwɒlɪfɪ'keɪʃ(ə)n/ *noun* **1.** a situation in which someone is legally prevented from doing something **2.** the fact of being legally prevented from driving a car

disqualification from office /dɪs ˌkwɒlɪfɪkeɪʃ(ə)n frəm 'ɒfɪs/ *noun* a rule which forces a director to be removed from a directorship if he or she does not fulfil the conditions

disqualify /dɪs'kwɒlɪfaɪ/ *verb* to not allow someone to do something, because they have done something which is not allowed or have committed a legal offence ○ *Being a judge disqualifies him from being a Member of Parliament.* ○ *After the accident she was fined £1000 and disqualified from driving for two years.* ○ *He was convicted of driving a motor vehicle while disqualified.*

disrepute /ˌdɪsrɪ'pjuːt/ *noun* a situation where something is not regarded very highly □ **to bring something into disrepute** to give something a bad reputation ○

He was accused of bringing the club into disrepute by his bad behaviour.

disseisin /dɪs'siːzɪn/ *noun* illegally depriving someone of possession of land

dissemination /dɪˌsemɪ'neɪʃ(ə)n/ *noun* the act of passing information to other members of the public

dissent /dɪ'sent/ *noun* disagreement with the majority of other people or with the authorities ○ *The opposition showed its dissent by voting against the Bill.* ■ *verb* to disagree in writing with a majority opinion in a court judgment ○ *One of the appeal judges dissented.*

dissenting judgment /dɪˌsentɪŋ 'dʒʌdʒmənt/ *noun* the judgment of a judge, showing that he or she disagrees with other judges in a case which has been heard by several judges

dissolve /dɪ'zɒlv/ *verb* to bring to an end ○ *to dissolve a marriage* or *a partnership or a company* □ **to dissolve Parliament** to end a session of Parliament, and so force a general election

distraction burglar /dɪs'trækʃ(ə)n ˌbɜːɡlə/ *noun* a person who tricks their way into a person's home for the purposes of stealing from them, e.g. by pretending to be from a company

distrain /dɪ'streɪn/ *verb* to seize goods to pay for debts

distress /dɪ'stres/ *noun* the taking of someone's goods to pay for debts

distress sale /dɪ'stres seɪl/ *noun* the selling of someone's goods to pay his or her debts

distribution /ˌdɪstrɪ'bjuːʃ(ə)n/ *noun* sharing out property in an estate

distribution of assets /ˌdɪstrɪbjuːʃ(ə)n əv 'æsets/ *noun* sharing the assets of a company among the shareholders

district /'dɪstrɪkt/ *noun* a section of a town or of a country

district attorney /ˌdɪstrɪkt ə'tɜːni/ *noun US* **1.** a prosecuting attorney in a federal district **2.** the state prosecuting attorney ▶ **abbreviation DA**

district court /'dɪstrɪkt kɔːt/ *noun US* a court in a federal district

district registrar /ˌdɪstrɪkt ˌredʒɪ 'strɑː/ *noun* an official who registers births, marriages and deaths in a specific area

district registry /ˌdɪstrɪkt 'redʒɪstri/ *noun* an office where records of births, marriages and deaths are kept

disturb /dɪ'stɜːb/ *verb* □ **to disturb the peace** to make a noise which annoys people in the area

disturbance /dɪ'stɜːbəns/ *noun* a noise or movement of people which annoys other people ○ *Street disturbances forced the government to resign.* ○ *He was accused of making a disturbance in the public library.*

disturbed balance of mind /dɪˌstɜːbd 'bæləns əv maɪnd/ *noun US* a state of mind when someone is temporarily incapable of rational action because of depression or mental distress ○ *The verdict of the coroner's court was suicide while the balance of mind was disturbed.*

division /dɪ'vɪʒ(ə)n/ *noun* **1.** one section of something which is divided into several sections ○ *Smith's is now a division of the Brown group of companies.* **2.** a separate section of the High Court ○ *Queen's Bench Division* ○ *Family Division* ○ *Chancery Division* **3.** a separate section of the Appeal Court ○ *Civil Division* ○ *Criminal Division* **4.** the act of dividing or of being divided □ **to have a division of opinion** to disagree **5.** (*in the EU*) one of the subdivisions of a Directorate in the Commission, with a Head of Division at its head

divisional court /dɪ'vɪʒ(ə)n(ə)l kɔːt/ *noun* one of courts of the High Court

divisional judge /dɪ'vɪʒ(ə)n(ə)l dʒʌdʒ/ *noun* a judge in a division of the High Court

division of responsibility /dɪˌvɪʒ(ə)n əv rɪˌspɒnsɪ'bɪlɪti/ *noun* the act of splitting the responsibility for something between several people

divorce /dɪ'vɔːs/ *noun* the legal ending of a marriage ■ *verb* to legally end a marriage to someone ○ *They are divorcing after 15 years together.*

COMMENT: Under English law, the only basis of divorce is the irretrievable breakdown of marriage. This is proved by one of five grounds: (a) adultery; (b) unreasonable behaviour; (c) one of the parties has deserted the other for a period of two years; (d) the parties have lived apart for two years and agree to a divorce; (e) the parties have lived apart for five years. In the context of divorce proceedings the court has wide powers to make orders regarding residence and contact orders for children, and ancillary relief. Divorce proceedings are normally dealt with by the County Court, or in London at the Divorce Registry. Where divorce proceedings are defended, they are transferred to the High Court, but this is rare and most divorce cases are now conducted by what is called the 'special procedure'.

divorce a mensa y toro /dɪˌvɔːs æ ˌmensə iː 'tɔːrəʊ/ *phrase* a Latin phrase meaning 'from bed and board'. Same as **legal separation**

divorce a vinculo matrimonii /dɪˌvɔːs æ ˌvɪŋkjʊləʊ ˌmætrɪ'məʊniəʊ/ *phrase* a Latin phrase meaning 'from the bonds of matrimony': a full divorce given by a court of law. Also called **absolute divorce**

divorcee /dɪvɔː'siː/ *noun* someone who is divorced

divorce petition /dɪˌvɔːs pə'tɪʃ(ə)n/ *noun* an official request to a court to end a marriage ○ *She was granted a divorce on the grounds of unreasonable behaviour by her husband.*

Divorce Registry /dɪˌvɔːs 'redʒɪstri/ *noun* a court which deals with divorce cases in London

DLA *abbreviation* Disability Living Allowance

DMC *abbreviation* donatio mortis causa

DNA /ˌdiː en 'eɪ/ *noun* nucleic acid containing a living organism's genetic code, used as evidence in court proceedings ○ *The DNA evidence shows that Mr Smith was at the scene of the crime.* Full form **deoxyribonucleic acid**

DNA test /ˌdiː en 'eɪ ˌtest/ *noun* the forensic analysis of DNA from body tissues such as blood, saliva, or semen in order to establish somebody's identity

dock /dɒk/ *noun* the part of a court where an accused prisoner stands □ **the prisoner in the dock** the prisoner who is being tried for a crime

dock brief /'dɒk briːf/ *noun* a former system where an accused person could choose a barrister from those present in court to represent them for a small fee

dock dues /'dɒk djuːz/ *noun* the payment which a ship makes to the harbour authorities for the right to use the harbour

docket /'dɒkɪt/ *noun* **1.** a list of contents of a package which is being sent **2.** *US* a list of cases for trial

doctrine /'dɒktrɪn/ *noun* a general principle of law

doctrine of laches /ˌdɒktrɪn əv 'lætʃɪz/ *noun* the principle in equity law that a person who neglects to assert a legal right in good time forfeits that right

document /'dɒkjʊmənt/ *noun* **1.** a paper or set of papers, printed or handwritten, which contains information ○ *Deeds, contracts and wills are all legal documents.* **2.**

anything in which information is recorded, e.g. maps, designs, computer files, databases **3.** an official paper from a government department ■ *verb* to put in a published paper ○ *The cases of unparliamentary language are well documented in Hansard.*

documentary /ˌdɒkjʊ'ment(ə)ri/ *adjective* in the form of documents ○ *documentary evidence* ○ *documentary proof*

documentary **evidence** /ˌdɒkjʊment(ə)ri 'evɪd(ə)ns/ *noun* evidence in the form of documents

documentary proof /ˌdɒkjʊment(ə)ri 'pruːf/ *noun* proof in the form of a document

documentation /ˌdɒkjʊmen'teɪʃ(ə)n/ *noun* all documents referring to something ○ *Please send me the complete documentation concerning the sale.*

document exchange /ˌdɒkjʊmənt ɪks 'tʃeɪndʒ/ *noun* a bureau which receives documents for clients and holds them securely in numbered boxes. Abbreviation **DX** (NOTE: Service can be effected through a document exchange in cases where this is given as the address for service.)

Doe ♦ **John Doe**

do-it-yourself conveyancing /ˌduː ɪt jə,self kən'veɪənsɪŋ/ *noun* drawing up a legal conveyance without the help of a lawyer

dole /dəʊl/ *noun* same as **jobseeker's allowance**

doli capax, doli incapax *phrase* Latin phrases meaning 'capable of crime' or 'incapable of crime'

COMMENT: Children under ten years of age are doli incapax and cannot be prosecuted for criminal offences; children aged between 10 and 14 are presumed to be doli incapax but the presumption can be reversed if there is evidence of malice or knowledge.

Domesday Book /'duːmzdeɪ bʊk/ *noun* a record made for King William I in 1086, which recorded all the land in England and the owners and inhabitants for tax purposes

domestic /də'mestɪk/ *adjective* **1.** referring to a family **2.** referring to the market of the country where a business is situated

domestic **burglary** /də,mestɪk 'bɜːgləri/ *noun* burglary of a person's home

domestic consumption /də,mestɪk kən'sʌmpʃən/ *noun* the amount of a product that is consumed by the home market

domestic court /də'mestɪk kɔːt/ *noun US* a court which covers the district in

which a defendant lives or has his or her address for service (NOTE: The British term is **home court**.)

domestic **partnership** /də,mestɪk 'pɑːtnəʃɪp/ *noun US* in some states, a civil partnership registered between a same-sex couple

domestic **premises** /də,mestɪk 'premɪsɪz/ *plural noun* a house, flat, or other unit used for private accommodation

domestic **proceedings** /də,mestɪk prə'siːdɪŋz/ *plural noun* a court case which involves a husband and wife, or parents and children

domestic production /də,mestɪk prə 'dʌkʃən/ *noun* production of goods in the home country

domestic sales /də'mestɪk seɪlz/ *plural noun* sales in the home market

domestic **violence** /də,mestɪk 'vaɪələns/ *noun* threatening behaviour, abuse or violence between husband and wife or between family members

domicile /'dɒmɪsaɪl/ *noun* someone's true, fixed and legally recognised place of residence, especially in cases of prolonged absence that require him or her to prove a continuing and significant connection with the place ■ *verb* to live in a place officially ○ *The defendant is domiciled in Scotland.* □ **bills domiciled in the UK** bills of exchange which have to be paid in the UK

domiciled /'dɒmɪsaɪld/ *adjective* living in a particular place

domicile of choice /ˌdɒmɪsaɪl əv 'tʃɔɪs/ *noun* a country where someone has chosen to live, which is not the domicile of origin

domicile of origin /ˌdɒmɪsaɪl əv 'prɪdʒɪn/ *noun* a domicile which a person has from birth, usually the domicile of the father

dominant owner /ˌdɒmɪnənt 'əʊnə/ *noun* someone who has the right to use someone else's property. Compare **servient owner**

dominant tenement /ˌdɒmɪnənt 'tenəmənt/ *noun* land which has been granted an easement over another property. Compare **servient tenement**

dominion /də'mɪnjən/ *noun* □ **a Dominion** an independent state, part of the British Commonwealth ○ *the Dominion of Canada*

donatio mortis causa /də,nɑːtiəʊ ,mɔːtɪs 'kəʊzə/ *phrase* a Latin phrase meaning 'gift because of death': a transfer of property made when death is imminent

donee /ˌdəʊˈniː/ *noun* somebody who receives a gift from a donor

donor /ˈdəʊnə/ *noun* somebody who gives property to another

dope /dəʊp/ *noun* **1.** a drug given illegally to affect sporting performance **2.** an illegal drug, especially cannabis (*slang*) ∎ *verb* to add a drug to food or drink secretly in order to affect sporting performance

doping /ˈdəʊpɪŋ/ *noun* the use of illegal drugs, e.g. steroids, in sport

dormant account /ˌdɔːmənt əˈkaʊnt/ *noun* a bank account which is not used

double /ˈdʌb(ə)l/ *verb* to make something twice as big

double jeopardy /ˌdʌb(ə)l ˈdʒepədi/ *noun US* the possibility that a citizen may be tried twice for the same crime, prohibited in most legal systems

double taxation agreement /ˌdʌb(ə)l tækˈseɪʃ(ə)n əˌɡriːmənt/, **double taxation treaty** /ˌdʌb(ə)l tækˈseɪʃ(ə)n ˌtriːti/, **double tax treaty** /ˌdʌb(ə)l tæks ˈtriːti/ *noun* an agreement between two countries that a person living in one country shall not be taxed in both countries on the income earned in the other country

doubt /daʊt/ *noun* a feeling of not being sure that something is correct □ **beyond reasonable doubt**, **beyond a reasonable doubt** *US* to a degree of certainty that is considered acceptable in convicting a person in a criminal case □ **open to doubt** not certain and even unlikely ○ *Her ability to recognise him after so long is open to doubt.*

down payment /ˌdaʊn ˈpeɪmənt/ *noun* part of a total payment made in advance

dowry /ˈdaʊri/ *noun* money or property brought by a wife to her husband when she marries him

DPP *abbreviation* Director of Public Prosecutions

draft /drɑːft/ *noun* **1.** an order for money to be paid by a bank □ **to make a draft on a bank** to ask a bank to pay money for you **2.** the first rough plan of a document which has not been finished ○ *He drew up the draft agreement on the back of an envelope.* ○ *The first draft of the contract was corrected by the managing director.* ○ *The draft Bill is with the House of Commons lawyers.* ∎ *verb* to make a first rough plan of a document ○ *to draft a contract* or *a document* or *a bill* ○

The contract is still being drafted or *is still in the drafting stage.*

draft contract /ˈdrɑːft ˌkɒntrækt/ *noun* a contract that contains details of all provisions and liabilities but not details such as price or cost that are negotiated individually

drafter /ˈdrɑːftə/ *noun* somebody who makes a draft

drafting /ˈdrɑːftɪŋ/ *noun* the act of preparing the draft of a document ○ *The drafting of the contract took six weeks.* ○ *The drafting stage of a parliamentary Bill.*

draftsman /ˈdrɑːftsmən/ *noun* somebody who drafts documents

drawee /drɔːˈiː/ *noun* a person or bank asked to make a payment by a drawer

drawings /ˈdrɔːɪŋz/ *plural noun* money taken out of a partnership by a partner as his or her salary

draw up /ˌdrɔː ˈʌp/ *verb* to write a legal document ○ *to draw up a contract* or *an agreement* ○ *to draw up a company's articles of association*

drink-driving /ˌdrɪŋk ˈdraɪvɪŋ/ *noun* the act of driving while illegally intoxicated

COMMENT: The drink-drive limit in the UK is 0.8mg of alcohol per ml of blood. If found guilty of drink-driving, the offender will receive a mandatory 12 driving disqualification, as well as an optional fine or custodial sentence.

drinking banning order /ˌdrɪŋkɪŋ ˈbænɪŋ ˌɔːdə/ *noun* a civil order which excludes a person from a particular place because they have been disorderly or violent there while under the influence of alcohol

driving licence /ˈdraɪvɪŋ ˌlaɪs(ə)ns/ *noun* a document which shows that you have passed a driving test and can legally drive a car, truck, etc. ○ *Applicants for the police force should hold a valid driving licence.*

driving without due care and attention /ˌdraɪvɪŋ wɪˌðaʊt djuː ˌkeə ən ə ˈtenʃən/ *noun* the offence of driving a car in a careless way, so that other people are in danger

DRM *abbreviation* digital rights management

drop /drɒp/ *noun* a fall ○ *drop in sales* ○ *sales show a drop of 10%* ○ *a drop in prices* ∎ *verb* **1.** to fall ○ *Sales have dropped by 10%* or *have dropped 10%.* ○ *The pound dropped three points against the dollar.* **2.** to stop a case ○ *The prosecution dropped all charges against the accused.* ○ *The claim-*

ant decided to drop the case against his neighbour. (NOTE: **dropping – dropped**)

drop ship /ˌdrɒp ˈʃɪp/ *verb* to deliver a large order direct to a customer

drop shipment /ˈdrɒp ˌʃɪpmənt/ *noun* a delivery of a large order from the factory direct to a customer's shop or warehouse without going through an agent or wholesaler

drug /drʌg/ *noun* **1.** an illegal substance which can be harmful, especially if taken regularly **2.** a medicine given by a doctor to treat a medical problem ◾ *verb* to give a substance to someone or put it in their food or drink, especially secretly, to make them go to sleep or become unconscious

COMMENT: There are three classes of controlled drugs: **Class A drugs:** (cocaine, heroin, crack, LSD, etc.); **Class B drugs:** (amphetamines, cannabis, codeine, etc.); and **Class C drugs:** (drugs which are related to the amphetamines, such as benzphetamine). The drugs are covered by five schedules under the Misuse of Drugs Regulations: **Schedule 1:** drugs which are not used medicinally, such as cannabis and LSD, for which possession and supply are prohibited; **Schedule 2:** drugs which can be used medicinally, such as heroin, morphine, cocaine, and amphetamines: these are fully controlled as regards prescriptions by doctors, safe custody in pharmacies, registering of sales, etc.; **Schedule 3:** barbiturates, which are controlled as regards prescriptions, but need not be kept in safe custody; **Schedule 4:** benzodiazepines, which are controlled as regards registers of purchasers; **Schedule 5:** other substances for which invoices showing purchase must be kept.

drug abuse /ˈdrʌg əˌbjuːs/ *noun* the regular use of drugs for non-medical reasons

drug addict /ˈdrʌg ˌædɪkt/ *noun* somebody who is physically and mentally dependent on taking drugs regularly

drug addiction /ˈdrʌg əˌdɪkʃən/ *noun* mental and physical dependence on taking a drug regularly

drug baron /ˈdrʌg ˌbærən/ *noun* a person with an important position in an organisation that sells illegal drugs

drug czar /ˈdrʌg sɑː/ *noun* a person employed by a government to lead a campaign against the sale and use of illegal drugs

drug runner /ˈdrʌg ˌrʌnə/ *noun* a person who takes or makes someone else take drugs illegally from one country to another

Drug Squad /ˈdrʌg skwɒd/ *noun* a section of the police force which investigates crime related to drugs

drug trafficking /ˈdrʌg ˌtræfɪkɪŋ/ *noun* the activity of buying and selling drugs illegally

drunk /drʌŋk/ *adjective* incapable because of having drunk too much alcohol

drunk and disorderly /ˌdrʌŋk ən dɪsˈɔːdəli/ *adjective* incapable and behaving in a wild way because of having drunk too much alcohol

drunk and incapable /ˌdrʌŋk ən ɪnˈkeɪpəb(ə)l/ *noun* the offence of having drunk so much alcohol that you are not able to act normally

drunkard /ˈdrʌŋkəd/ *noun* somebody who is frequently drunk. ◊ **habitual**

drunken driving /ˌdrʌŋkən ˈdraɪvɪŋ/ *noun* an offence of driving a car when under the influence of alcohol. Also called **driving with alcohol concentrations above a certain limit**

DSgt *abbreviation* detective sergeant

DTI *abbreviation* Department of Trade and Industry

dud /dʌd/ *adjective, noun* (*of a coin, banknote or cheque*) worth nothing because it is false (*informal*) ○ *The £50 note was a dud.*

dud cheque /ˌdʌd ˈtʃek/ *noun* a cheque which the bank refuses to pay because the person writing it has not enough money in his or her account to pay it

due /djuː/ *adjective* **1.** owed □ **to fall due**, **to become due** to be ready for payment □ **bill due on May 1st** bill which has to be paid on May 1st □ **balance due** amount owed which should be paid **2.** expected to arrive ○ *The plane is due to arrive at 10.30* or *is due at 10.30.* **3.** according to what is expected as usual or correct □ **in due form** written in the correct legal form ○ *receipt in due form* ○ *contract drawn up in due form* □ **after due consideration of the problem** after thinking seriously about the problem

due date /ˈdjuː deɪt/ *noun* the date on which a debt has to be paid

due diligence /ˌdjuː ˈdɪlɪdʒəns/ *noun* the carrying out of your duty as efficiently as is necessary ○ *The executor acted with due diligence to pay the liabilities of the estate.*

due execution of a will /djuː ˌeksɪˈkjuːʃ(ə)n əv eɪ wɪl/ *noun* the act of making a will in the correct way

COMMENT: A will must be written (handwritten, printed, or written on a standard form, etc.), signed by the testator and witnessed by two witnesses in the presence of the testator.

due process /ˌdjuː ˈprəʊses/ *noun* a rule that the forms of law must be followed correctly □ **the due process of the law** the formal work of a fair legal action

duly /ˈdjuːli/ *adverb* **1.** properly ○ *duly authorised representative* **2.** as was expected ○ *We duly received his letter of 21st October.*

duress /djʊˈres/ *noun* an illegal threat to use force on someone to make him or her do something ○ *Duress provides no defence to a charge of murder.* □ **under duress** being forced to do something ○ *They alleged they had committed the crime under duress.* □ **to sign a confession under duress** to sign a confession because of feeling threatened

dutiable goods /ˌdjuːtiəb(ə)l ˈɡʊdz/ *plural noun* goods on which a customs or excise duty has to be paid

duty /ˈdjuːti/ *noun* **1.** work which a person has to do ○ *It is the duty of every citizen to serve on a jury if called.* ○ *The government has a duty to protect the citizens from criminals.* **2.** official work which you have to do in a job □ **to be on duty** to be doing official work **3.** a tax which has to be paid ○ *to take the duty off alcohol* ○ *to put a duty on cigarettes* □ **goods which are liable to duty**

goods on which customs or excise tax has to be paid □ **duty-paid goods** goods where the duty has been paid

duty bound /ˈdjuːti baʊnd/ *adjective* bound to do something because it is your duty ○ *Witnesses under oath are duty bound to tell the truth.*

duty-free /ˌdjuːti ˈfriː/ *adjective, adverb* sold with no duty to be paid ○ *He bought a duty-free watch at the airport* or *he bought the watch duty-free.* □ **duty-free shop** a shop at an airport or on a ship where goods can be bought without paying duty

duty of care /ˌdjuːti əv ˈkeə/ *noun* a legal obligation which imposes a duty on individuals not to act negligently

duty sergeant /ˌdjuːti ˈsɑːdʒənt/ *noun* a police sergeant who is on duty at a particular time

duty solicitor /ˌdjuːti səˈlɪsɪtə/ *noun* a solicitor who is on duty at a magistrates' court and can be contacted at any time by a party who is appearing in that court or by a party who has been taken to a police station under arrest or for questioning

dwelling /ˈdwelɪŋ/ *noun* a place where someone lives such as a house or flat ○ *The tax on dwellings has been raised.*

DWI *abbreviation US* driving while intoxicated

DX /diː eks/ *abbreviation* document exchange

E

EA *abbreviation* Environmental Agency

e. & o.e. *abbreviation* errors and omissions excepted

earn /ɜːn/ *verb* **1.** to be paid money for working ○ *to earn £150 a week* ○ *Our agent in Paris certainly does not earn his commission.* **2.** to produce interest or dividends ○ *account which earns interest at 10%* ○ *What level of dividend do these shares earn?*

earnest /'ɜːnɪst/ *noun* money paid as a down payment to show one's serious intention to proceed with a contract ○ *He deposited £1,000 with the solicitor as earnest of his intention to purchase.*

earning power /'ɜːnɪŋ ˌpaʊə/ *noun* the amount of money someone should be able to earn

earnings /'ɜːnɪŋz/ *plural noun* **1.** the salary or wages, profits and dividends or interest received by an individual **2.** the profits of a business

earnings-related pension /ˌɜːnɪŋz rɪ ˌleɪtɪd 'penʃən/ *noun* a pension which is linked to the size of the salary

easement /'iːzmənt/ *noun* a right which someone (the dominant owner) has to make use of land belonging to someone else (the servient owner) for a purpose such as a path

Easter /'iːstə/ *noun* **1.** one of the four sittings of the Law Courts **2.** one of the four law terms

EC *abbreviation* European Community ○ *EC ministers met today in Brussels.* ○ *The USA is increasing its trade with the EC.*

ECB *abbreviation* European Central Bank

ecclesiastical /ɪˌkliːziˈæstɪk(ə)l/ *adjective* referring to the church

ecclesiastical court /ɪˌkliːziˈæstɪk(ə)l kɔːt/ *noun* a court which hears matters referring to the church

ECJ *abbreviation* European Court of Justice

e-commerce /ˌiː 'kɒmɜːs/ *noun* buying and selling over the internet, regulated by the Consumer Protection (Distance Selling) Regulations 2000. Full form **electronic commerce**

economic activity /ˌiːkənɒmɪk æk ˈtɪvɪti/ *noun* work which earns money

economically /ˌiːkəˈnɒmɪkli/ *adverb* □ **economically active** (*in the EU*) being an active worker ○ *Economically active persons have the right to move freely from one EU country to another with their families.*

economic duress /ˌiːkənɒmɪk djʊˈres/ *noun* forcing someone to enter a contract by the unlawful application of commercial pressure

economic migrant /ˌiːkənɒmɪk ˈmaɪɡrənt/ *noun* someone who immigrates to a foreign country for economic reasons

economic planning /ˌiːkənɒmɪk ˈplænɪŋ/ *noun* the activity of planning the future financial state of the country for the government

economic sanctions /ˌiːkənɒmɪk ˈsæŋkʃ(ə)nz/ *plural noun* restrictions on trade with a country in order to influence its political situation or in order to make its government change its policy

e-conveyancing /ˈiː kənˌveɪənsɪŋ/ *noun* ♦ **electronic transfer**

ecoterrorist /'iːkəʊˌterərɪst/ *noun* somebody who attacks things for ecological reasons ○ *Ecoterrorists attacked several fields of crops.*

e-crime /ˈiː ˌkraɪm/ *noun* the use of the internet to commit crime such as fraud or data theft

edict /'iːdɪkt/ *noun* the public announcement of a law

e-disclosure /ˈiː dɪsˌkləʊʒə/ *noun* the disclosure of digital evidence

education welfare officer /ˌedjʊkeɪʃ(ə)n ˈwelfeə ˌɒfɪsə/ *noun* a social worker who looks after schoolchildren, and deals with attendance and family problems

EEC *abbreviation* European Economic Community

EEZ *abbreviation* Exclusive Economic Zone

effective date /ɪˈfektɪv deɪt/ *noun* the date on which a rule or a contract starts to be applied

effective date of termination /ɪ ˌfektɪv deɪt əv ˌtɜːmɪˈneɪʃ(ə)n/ *noun* the date on which a contract of employment expires

E-FIT™ /ˈiː fɪt/ a trademark for software that produces an image of the face of a police suspect on the basis of what a witness can remember

e-fraud /ˈiː frɔːd/ *noun* the use of the internet to commit an act of fraud, often by assuming a false identity

e-gaming /ˈiː ˌɡeɪmɪŋ/ *noun* gambling over the internet

eggshell skull /ˈeɡʃel skʌl/ *noun* the hypothetical state of having a pre-existing vulnerability or condition, which makes a person liable to suffer more damage during an assault then could be foreseen

eggshell skull rule /ˈeɡʃel skʌl ˌruːl/ *noun* a legal principle that a person is responsible for the damage caused by their crime, even if it was not foreseeable

eject /ɪˈdʒekt/ *verb* to make someone leave a property which he or she is occupying illegally

ejection /ɪˈdʒekʃən/ *noun* the action of making someone leave a property which he or she is occupying illegally

COMMENT: The ejection of someone who is legally occupying a property is an **ouster,** while removing a tenant is **eviction.**

ejectment /ɪˈdʒektmənt/ *noun* □ **action of ejectment** a court action to force someone to leave a property which he or she is occupying illegally

ejusdem generis /iːˌdʒʊsdem ˈdʒenərɪs/, **eiusdem generis** /eɪˌjuːsdem ˈdʒenərɪs/ *phrase* a Latin phrase meaning 'of the same kind': a rule of legal interpretation that when a word or phrase follows two or more other words or phrases, it is construed to be of the same type as the words or phrases which precede it

COMMENT: For example, in the phrase **houses, flats and other buildings,** other buildings can mean only other dwellings, and would not include, for example, a church.

elapse /ɪˈlæps/ *verb* (*of time*) to pass ○ *Six weeks elapsed before the court order was*

put into effect. ○ *We must allow sufficient time to elapse before making a complaint.*

elect /ɪˈlekt/ *verb* **1.** to choose someone by a vote ○ *a vote to elect the officers of an association* ○ *She was elected chair of the committee.* ○ *He was first elected for this constituency in 1992.* **2.** to choose to do something ○ *He elected to stand trial by jury.*

election /ɪˈlekʃən/ *noun* **1.** the act of electing a representative or representatives **2.** the fact of electing or having been elected ○ *his election as president of the society* **3.** the act of choosing a course of action ○ *The accused made his election for jury trial.* **4.** a choice by a legatee to take a benefit under a will and relinquish a claim to the estate at the same time

COMMENT: In Britain, a Parliament can only last for a maximum of five years, and a dissolution is usually called by the Prime Minister before the end of that period. The Lord Chancellor then issues a writ for the election of MPs. All British subjects (including Commonwealth and Irish citizens), are eligible to vote in British elections provided they are on the electoral register, are over 18 years of age, are sane, are not members of the House of Lords and are not serving prison sentences for serious crime. In the USA, members of the House of Representatives are elected for a two-year period. Senators are elected for six-year terms, one third of the Senate being elected every two years. The President of the USA is elected by an electoral college made up of people elected by voters in each of the states of the USA. Each state elects the same number of electors to the electoral college as it has Congressmen, plus two. This guarantees that the college is broadly representative of voters across the country. The presidential candidate with an overall majority in the college is elected president. A presidential term of office is four years, and a president can stand for re-election once.

electoral reform /ɪˌlekt(ə)rəl rɪˈfɔːm/ *noun* the activity of changing the electoral system to make it fairer

electric chair /ɪˌlektrɪk ˈtʃeə/ *noun* a chair attached to a powerful electric current, used in some states of the USA for executing criminals

electronic communication /ˌelektrɒnɪk kəˌmjuːnɪˈkeɪʃ(ə)n/ *noun* a message which is sent from one person to another by telephone or by other electronic means

electronic   conveyancing /ˌelektrɒnɪk kənˈveɪənsɪŋ/ *noun* ♦ **electronic transfer**

electronic   signature /ˌelektrɒnɪk ˈsɪɡnɪtʃə/ *noun* electronic text or symbols attached to a document sent by email which acts in a similar way to a handwritten signature, in that they prove the authenticity of the document

electronic surveillance /ˌelektrɒnɪk səˈveɪləns/ *noun* surveillance using hidden microphones, cameras, etc.

electronic   transfer /ˌelektrɒnɪk ˈtrænsfɜː/ *noun* **1.** a payment made electronically from one bank account to another ○ *She requested to be paid by electronic transfer.* **2.** the transfer of interests in land by electronic methods rather than paper documents

electroshock weapon /ɪˌlektrəʊˈʃɒk ˌwepən/ *noun* a weapon which delivers an incapacitating but non-fatal electric shock, used by some police forces as a safer alternative to firearms

COMMENT: Electroshock weapons are used by some police forces as a method of incapacitating an armed suspect quickly and without causing lasting injury. They deliver a painful shock which interrupts muscle function for a short while, allowing officers to move in. Although electroshock weapons are thought to cause no lasting damage to the victim, their use is still controversial.

eligible /ˈelɪdʒɪb(ə)l/ *adjective* qualified or able to be chosen ○ *She is eligible for re-election.*

E list /ˈiː lɪst/ *noun* a list of the names of prisoners who frequently try to escape from prison

embargo /ɪmˈbɑːɡəʊ/ *noun* a government order which stops a type of trade □ **to put an embargo on trade with a country** to say that trade with a country must not take place □ **to lift an embargo** to allow trade to start again □ **to be under an embargo** to be forbidden ■ *verb* not to allow something to take place ○ *The government has embargoed trade with the Eastern countries.* □ **to be embargoed until** to be banned from being published until a particular time ○ *The press release was embargoed until January 1st.*

embezzle /ɪmˈbez(ə)l/ *verb* to use illegally or steal money which you are responsible for as part of your work ○ *He was sent to prison for six months for embezzling his clients' money.*

embezzlement /ɪmˈbez(ə)lmənt/ *noun* the act of embezzling ○ *He was sent to prison for six months for embezzlement.*

embezzler /ɪmˈbez(ə)lə/ *noun* somebody who embezzles

emblements /ˈembləmənts/ *plural noun* vegetable products which come from farming

embracery /ɪmˈbreɪs(ə)ri/ *noun* the offence of corruptly seeking to influence jurors

emergency   powers /ɪˌmɜːdʒənsi ˈpaʊəz/ *plural noun* special powers granted by law to a government or to a minister to deal with an emergency, usually without going through the usual democratic processes

emergency protection order /ɪ ˌmɜːdʒənsi prəˈtekʃ(ə)n ˌɔːdə/ *noun* a court order, established under the Children's Act 1989, which gives a local authority or the National Society for the Prevention of Cruelty to Children (NSPCC) the right to remove a child from the care of its parents for a period of eight days, with the right to apply for a seven-day extension. ◊ **parental responsibility**

COMMENT: Such an order gives the local authority parental responsibility for the child, allowing decisions to be made in relation to its welfare. An order will only be granted if the court is satisfied that there is reasonable cause to believe that the child is suffering or likely to suffer significant harm unless the order is made.

emergency   services /ɪˈmɜːdʒənsi ˌsɜːvɪsɪz/ *plural noun* police, fire and ambulance services, which are ready for action if an emergency arises

emigrant /ˈemɪɡrənt/ *noun* somebody who emigrates. Compare **immigrant**

emigrate /ˈemɪɡreɪt/ *verb* to go to another country to live permanently. Compare **immigrate**

emigration /ˌemɪˈɡreɪʃ(ə)n/ *noun* the act of leaving a country to go to live permanently in another country. Compare **immigration**

eminent domain /ˌemɪnənt dəʊˈmeɪn/ *noun* the right of the state to appropriate private property for public use

emissions   trading /ɪˈmɪʃ(ə)nz ˌtreɪdɪŋ/ *noun* the free trade of carbon permits between groups of nations. Also called **carbon trading**

COMMENT: Emissions trading is thought to encourage the development of greener methods of industrial production, by making it possible to sell unused carbon permits at a premium.

emoluments /ɪˈmɒljʊmənts/ *plural noun* wages, salaries, fees or any monetary benefit from an employment (*formal or humorous, not technical*)

emotional welfare /ɪˌməʊʃ(ə)nəl ˈwelfeə/ *noun* the fact of being cared for properly and feeling happy and secure ○ *It is this courts intention to protect the child's emotional welfare.* ◊ **material welfare**

empanel /ɪmˈpæn(ə)l/ *verb* □ **to empanel a jury** to choose and swear in jurors

employed advocate /ɪmˌplɔɪd ˈædvəkət/ *noun* a person employed to plead in court such as a Crown Prosecutor

employee /ɪmˈplɔɪiː/ *noun* a person who is employed by someone else ○ *Employees of the firm are eligible to join a profit-sharing scheme.* ○ *Relations between management and employees have improved.* ○ *The company has decided to take on new employees.*

employee benefits /ɪmˌplɔɪiː ˈbenɪfɪts/ *plural noun* advantages given to employees in addition to basic salary, e.g. gym membership, parking, health insurance etc.

employer /ɪmˈplɔɪə/ *noun* a person or company which has employees and pays them

employer's contribution /ɪmˌplɔɪəz ˌkɒntrɪˈbjuːʃ(ə)n/ *noun* money paid by the employer towards an employee's pension

employer's liability /ɪmˌplɔɪəz laɪə ˈbɪlɪti/ *noun* the legal responsibility of an employer when employees are subject to accidents due to negligence on the part of the employer

employers' organisation /ɪmˈplɔɪəz ˌɔːgənaɪzeɪʃ(ə)n/ *noun* US a group of employers with similar interests

employment /ɪmˈplɔɪmənt/ *noun* a contractual relationship between an employer and his or her employees

Employment Appeal Tribunal /ɪm ˌplɔɪmənt əˈpiːl traɪˌbjuːn(ə)l/ *noun* a court which hears appeals from employment tribunals

employment bureau /ɪmˈplɔɪmənt ˌbjʊərəʊ/ *noun* an office which finds jobs for people

employment law /ɪmˈplɔɪmənt ˌbjʊərəʊ/ *noun* law referring to the rights and responsibilities of employers and employees

employment office /ɪmˈplɔɪmənt ˌɒfɪs/ *noun* an office which finds jobs for people

employment tribunal /ɪmˈplɔɪmənt traɪˌbjuːnəl/ *noun* a body responsible for hearing work-related complaints as specified by statute. Former name **industrial tribunal**

COMMENT: The panel hearing each case consists of a legally qualified chairperson and two independent lay people who have experience of employment issues. Decisions need to be enforced by a separate application to the court.

empower /ɪmˈpaʊə/ *verb* to give someone the power to do something ○ *The agent is empowered to sell the property.* ○ *She was empowered by the company to sign the contract.* ○ *A constable is empowered to arrest a person whom he suspects of having committed an offence.*

emptor /ˈemptə/ ♦ **caveat emptor** ■ *noun* a person who buys something

enact /ɪnˈækt/ *verb* to make a law

enacting clause /ɪnˈæktɪŋ klɔːz/ *noun* the first clause in a bill or act, starting with the words 'be it enacted that', which makes the act lawful

enactment /ɪˈnæktmənt/ *noun* **1.** the action of making a law **2.** an Act of Parliament

enclosure /ɪnˈkləʊʒə/ *noun* **1.** a document enclosed with a letter **2.** the act of removing land from common use by putting fences round it

encouragement to terrorism /ɪn ˌkʌrɪdʒmənt tə ˈterərɪz(ə)m/ *noun* the offence of encouraging or inciting people to commit terrorist acts

encroachment /ɪnˈkrəʊtʃmənt/ *noun* illegally taking over someone's property little by little

encumbrance /ɪnˈkʌmbrəns/ *noun* a liability such as a mortgage or charge which is attached usually to a property or piece of land

endanger /ɪnˈdeɪndʒə/ *verb* to put someone in danger of being killed or hurt □ **endangering life** the notifiable offence of putting human life at risk

endorse /ɪnˈdɔːs/ *verb* **1.** to agree with ○ *The court endorsed counsel's view.* **2.** to sign a bill or a cheque on the back to make it payable to someone else ○ *The writ was indorsed with details of the claimant's claim.* **3.** to make a note on a driving licence that the holder has been convicted of a traffic offence **4.** to write a summary of the contents of a legal document on the outside of the folded document

endorsee /ˌendɔːˈsiː/ *noun* a person in whose favour a bill or a cheque is endorsed

endorsement /ɪnˈdɔːsmənt/ *noun* **1.** the act of endorsing **2.** a signature on a document which endorses it **3.** a summary of a legal document noted on the outside of the folded document **4.** a note on an insurance policy which adds conditions to the policy **5.** a note on a driving licence to show that the holder has been convicted of a traffic offence. ◊ **totting up**

endorser /ɪnˈdɔːsə/ *noun* somebody who endorses a bill or cheque

endowment /ɪnˈdaʊmənt/ *noun* a gift of money to provide a regular income

endowment assurance /ɪnˈdaʊmənt ə ˌʃʊərəns/ *noun* an assurance policy where a sum of money is paid to the insured person on a specific date, or to the heirs if he or she dies

endowment mortgage /ɪnˈdaʊmənt ˌmɔːɡɪdʒ/ *noun* a mortgage backed by an endowment policy

end user /ˌend ˈjuːzə/ *noun* somebody who actually uses a product

end user licence agreement /ˌend ˌjuːzə ˈlaɪs(ə)ns əˌɡriːmənt/ *noun* a paper or electronic contract which constitutes a software licence. Abbreviation **EULA**

Energy Performance Certificate /ˌenədʒi pəˈfɔːməns səˌtɪfɪkət/ *noun* a certificate stating how energy efficient a home is required to be included in a HIP

enforce /ɪnˈfɔːs/ *verb* to make sure something is done or is obeyed ○ *to enforce the terms of a contract* □ **to enforce a debt** to make sure a debt is paid

enforceable /ɪnˈfɔːsəb(ə)l/ *adjective* being possible to enforce

enforcement /ɪnˈfɔːsmənt/ *noun* **1.** the process of making sure that something is obeyed ○ *enforcement of the terms of a contract* **2.** (*in the EU*) the power to force someone to comply with the law

enforcement notice /ɪnˈfɔːsmənt ˌnəʊtɪs/ *noun* a notice issued by a local planning authority which outlines the steps that need to be taken within a specified time to stop or repair a breach of planning control

enforcement proceedings /ɪn ˌfɔːsmənt prəˈsiːdɪŋz/ *plural noun* legal proceedings used by the Commission to

ensure that Member States fulfil their treaty obligations

enfranchisement /ɪnˈfræntʃaɪzmənt/ *noun* the action of giving someone a vote

engage /ɪnˈɡeɪdʒ/ *verb* **1.** □ **to engage someone to do something** to bind someone contractually to do something ○ *The contract engages the company to purchase minimum annual quantities of goods.* **2.** □ **to be engaged in** to be busy with ○ *He is engaged in work on computers.* ○ *The company is engaged in trade with Africa.*

English for Speakers of Other Languages /ˌɪŋɡlɪʃ fə ˌspiːkəz əv ˌʌðə ˈlæŋɡwɪdʒɪz/ *noun* a test that some immigrants are required to take in order to be naturalised as British citizens. Abbreviation **ESOL**

engross /ɪnˈɡrəʊs/ *verb* to draw up a legal document in its final form ready for signature

engrossment /ɪnˈɡrəʊsmənt/ *noun* **1.** the process of drawing up a legal document in its final form **2.** a legal document in its final form

engrossment paper /ɪnˈɡrəʊsmənt ˌpeɪpə/ *noun* a thick heavy paper on which court documents are engrossed

enjoin /ɪnˈdʒɔɪn/ *verb* to order someone to do something

enjoyment /ɪnˈdʒɔɪmənt/ *noun* □ **quiet enjoyment of land** the right of an occupier to occupy a property under a tenancy without anyone interfering with that right

enquire /ɪnˈkwaɪə/ another spelling of **inquire**

entail /ɪnˈteɪl/ *noun* an interest in land where the land is given to another person and the heirs of his or her body, but reverts to the donor when the donee and heirs have all died. ◊ **fee tail**

entente /ɒnˈtɒnt/ *noun* an agreement between two countries or groups, used especially of the 'Entente Cordiale' between Britain and France in 1904

enter /ˈentə/ ◊ **to enter into 1.** to begin to do something ○ *to enter into relations with someone* **2.** to agree to do something ○ *to enter into negotiations with a foreign government* ○ *to enter into a partnership with a friend* ○ *to enter into an agreement* or *a contract*

entering /ˈentərɪŋ/ *noun* the act of writing items in a record

entering of appearance /ˌentərɪŋ əv ə
ˈpɪərəns/ *noun* same as **entry of appearance**

entertain /ˌentəˈteɪn/ *verb* to be ready to
consider a proposal ○ *The judge will not
entertain any proposal from the prosecution
to delay the start of the hearing.*

entertainment expenses /ˌentə
ˈteɪnmənt ɪkˌspensɪz/ *plural noun* money
spent on giving meals to business visitors

entice /ɪnˈtaɪs/ *verb* to try to persuade
someone to do something by offering
money ○ *They tried to entice the managers
to join the new company.*

enticement /ɪnˈtaɪsmənt/ *noun* the act of
trying to persuade someone to do something, especially trying to persuade somebody to break a contract

entitle /ɪnˈtaɪt(ə)l/ *verb* to give someone
the right to something □ **to be entitled to
something** to have the right to have something

entitlement /ɪnˈtaɪt(ə)lmənt/ *noun*
something to which you are entitled

entity /ˈentɪti/ *noun* something which
exists in law ○ *His private company is a separate entity.*

entrapment /ɪnˈtræpmənt/ *noun* the act
of enticing someone to commit a crime so as
to be able to arrest him or her, by someone
in authority such as a police officer (NOTE: It
is not a defence in British law, but exists in
US law.)

entrenched /ɪnˈtrentʃt/ *adjective* (*of
ideas and practices*) existing in the same
way for a long time and very difficult to
change ○ *the government's entrenched position on employees' rights*

entrenched clause /ɪnˈtrentʃt klɔːz/
noun a clause in a constitution which stipulates that it cannot be amended except by an
extraordinary process

entry clearance /ˈentri ˌklɪərəns/ *noun*
the act of officially clearing a person for
entry into a particular country, usually
shown by a visa stamped into that person's
passport

entryism /ˈentriˌɪz(ə)m/ *noun* a way of
taking control of a political party or elected
body, where extremists join or are elected
and are then able to take control because
they are more numerous or more active than
other members

entryist /ˈentriɪst/ *adjective* referring to
entryism ○ *The party leader condemned
entryist techniques.*

entry of appearance /ˌentri əv ə
ˈpɪərəns/ *noun* the lodging of a document
in court by the defendant to confirm his or
her intention to defend an action

entry of judgment /ˌentri əv
ˈdʒʌdʒmənt/ *noun* the act of recording the
judgment of a court in the official records

entry permit /ˌentri pəˈmɪt/ *noun* a document allowing someone to enter a country

entry visa /ˈentri ˌviːzə/ *noun* a visa
allowing someone to enter a country

Environmental Agency /ɪnˌvaɪrə
ˈment(ə)l ˌeɪdʒənsi/ *noun* a public body
that works to protect and improve the environment in England and Wales. Abbreviation **EA**

environmental health /ɪn
ˌvaɪrənment(ə)l ˈhelθ/ *noun* the health of
the public as a whole

environmental pollution /ɪn
ˌvaɪrənment(ə)l pəˈluːʃ(ə)n/ *noun* the
polluting of the environment

ePassport /ˈiː ˌpɑːspɔːt/ *noun* same as
biometric passport

equality /ɪˈkwɒlɪti/ *noun* the principle
that all citizens are equal, have equal rights
and are treated equally by the state

equality of access /ɪˌkwɒlɪti əv
ˈækses/ *noun* a situation in which everyone
must be given the same opportunities for
education, employment and other activities

equality of opportunity /ɪˌkwɒlɪti əv
ˌɒpəˈtjuːnɪti/ *noun* a situation in which
everyone has the same opportunities to
receive education, employment, election,
etc.

equality of treatment /ɪˌkwɒlɪti əv
ˈtriːtmənt/ *noun* **1.** a situation in which
everyone receives the same fair treatment in
education, at work and in the community **2.**
a right of workers who are nationals of other
Member States of the European Union to be
treated equally to nationals of the country
where they work

Equal Opportunities Commission
/ˌiːkwəl ɒpəˈtjuːnɪtiz kəˌmɪʃ(ə)n/ *noun*
an official committee set up to make sure
that men and women have equal chances of
employment and to remove discrimination
between the sexes (NOTE: The US term is
**Equal Employment Opportunity Com-
mission.**)

equal opportunities programme
/ˌiːkwəl ɒpəˈtjuːnɪtiz ˌprəʊɡræm/ *noun* a
programme to avoid discrimination in

employment (NOTE: The US term is **affirmative action program**.)

equal pay /ˌiːkwəl ˈpeɪ/ *noun* the situation in which the same salary is paid for the same type of work regardless of whether it is done by, e.g., men or women

equitable /ˈekwɪtəb(ə)l/ *adjective* **1.** fair and just **2.** applicable under the law of equity as distinguished from common or statute law

equitable interests /ˌekwɪtəb(ə)l ˈɪntrəsts/ *plural noun* interests in property which are recognised separately from rights given by law

equitable jurisdiction /ˌekwɪtəb(ə)l ˌdʒʊərɪsˈdɪkʃən/ *noun* the power of a court to enforce a person's rights

equitable lien /ˌekwɪtəb(ə)l ˈliːən/ *noun* the right of someone to hold property which legally he or she does not own until the owner pays money due

equitable mortgage /ˌekwɪtəb(ə)l ˈmɔːɡɪdʒ/ *noun* a mortgage which does not give the mortgagee a legal estate in the land mortgaged

equity /ˈekwɪti/ *noun* **1. equity law** a system of British law which developed in parallel with the common law to make the common law fairer, summarised in the maxim 'equity does not suffer a wrong to be without a remedy' **2.** the right to receive dividends as part of the profit of a company in which you own shares

equity of redemption /ˌekwɪti əv rɪ ˈdempʃən/ *noun* the right of a mortgagor to redeem the estate by paying off the principal and interest

equivocal /ɪˈkwɪvək(ə)l/ *adjective* not clearly expressed, or ambiguous ○ *The court took the view that the defendant's plea was equivocal.*

error /ˈerə/ *noun* a mistake ○ *He made an error in calculating the total.* □ **errors and omissions excepted** words written on an invoice to show that the company has no responsibility for mistakes in the invoice. Abbreviation **e. & o.e.**

error rate /ˈerə reɪt/ *noun* the number of mistakes per thousand entries or per page

escalate /ˈeskəleɪt/ *verb* to increase at a constant rate

escalation of prices /ˌeskəˈleɪʃ(ə)n əv praɪss/ *noun US* a constant increase in prices

escalator clause /ˈeskəleɪtə klɔːz/ *noun* a clause in a contract allowing for regular price increases because of increased costs

escape /ɪˈskeɪp/ *verb* **1.** to get away from a place of detention ○ *Three prisoners escaped by climbing over the wall.* **2.** to avoid something that is unpleasant ○ *He escaped with a reprimand.* ○ *They narrowly escaped prosecution.* ■ *noun* an act of getting away from a place of detention □ **to make your escape** to leave or escape from somewhere

escape clause /ɪˈskeɪp klɔːz/ *noun* a clause in a contract which allows one of the parties to avoid carrying out the terms of the contract under some conditions without penalty

escrow /ˈeskrəʊ/ *noun* a deed which the parties to it deliver to an independent person who hands it over only when specific conditions have been fulfilled □ **in escrow** held in safe keeping by a third party □ **document held in escrow** a document given to a third party to keep and to pass on to someone when, e.g., money has been paid

escrow account /ˈeskrəʊ əˌkaʊnt/ *noun US* an account where money is held until something happens such as a contract being signed or goods being delivered

ESOL /ˈiːsɒl/ *abbreviation* English for Speakers of Other Languages

espionage /ˈespiənɑːʒ/ *noun* the activity of spying

Esq. *noun* **1.** sometimes written after the name of a man instead of using 'Mr' **2.** *US* sometimes written after the name of a male or female lawyer ► full form **Esquire**

essence of contract /ˌes(ə)ns əv ˈkɒntrækt/ *noun* a fundamental term of a contract. Also called **condition of contract**

establish /ɪˈstæblɪʃ/ *verb* **1.** to set up, to make or to open something ○ *The company has established a branch in Australia.* ○ *The business was established in Scotland in 1823.* **2.** to decide what is correct or true ○ *The police are trying to establish his movements on the night of the murder.* ○ *It is an established fact that the car could not have been used because it was out of petrol.*

established use /ɪˈstæblɪʃt juːz/ *noun* the use of land for a specific purpose which is recognised by a local authority because the land has been used for this purpose for some time

establishment /ɪˈstæblɪʃmənt/ *noun* □ **the Establishment** powerful and important people who run the country and its government

establishment charges /ɪˈstæblɪʃmənt ˌtʃɑːdʒɪz/ *plural noun* in a company's accounts, the cost of staff and property

establishment officer /ɪˌstæblɪʃmənt ˈɒfɪsə/ *noun* a civil servant in charge of personnel in a government department

estate /ɪˈsteɪt/ *noun* **1.** an interest in or right to hold and occupy land **2.** all the property that is owned by a person, especially a person who has recently died ○ *His estate was valued at £100,000* or *he left estate valued at £100,000.* □ **estate duty**, **estate tax** *US* tax on property left by a person now dead

estate agency /ɪˈsteɪt ˌeɪdʒənsi/ *noun* an office which arranges for the sale of property

estate agent /ɪˈsteɪt ˌeɪdʒənt/ *noun* the person in charge of an estate agency

estate duty /ɪˈsteɪt ˌdjuːti/ *noun US* a tax paid on the property left by a dead person

estop /əˈstɒp/ *verb* to stop someone doing something, e.g. exercising a right

estoppel /ɪˈstɒp(ə)l/ *noun* a rule of evidence whereby someone is prevented from denying or asserting a fact in legal proceedings

estoppel by conduct /ɪˌstɒp(ə)l baɪ kənˈdʌkt/ *noun* the rule that no one can deny things which he or she has done or failed to do which have had an effect on other persons' actions if that person has acted in a way which relied on the others' behaviour

estoppel by deed /ɪˌstɒp(ə)l baɪ ˈdiːd/ *noun* the rule that a person cannot deny having done something which is recorded in a deed

estoppel of record /ɪˌstɒp(ə)l əv ˈrekɔːd/ *noun* the rule that a person cannot reopen a matter which has already been decided by a court

estovers /ɪˈstəʊvəz/ *plural noun* the ancient right of a tenant to take wood and timber from land which he or she rents

estreat /ɪˈstriːt/ *verb* to get a copy of a record of bail or a fine awarded by a court

estreated recognisance /ɪˌstriːtɪd rɪˈkɒgnɪz(ə)ns/ *noun* recognisance which is forfeited because the person making it has not come to court

et al. /et ˈæl/, **et alia** *phrase* a Latin phrase meaning 'and others' or 'and other things'

ethics /ˈeθɪks/ *noun* a system of moral principles which dictate how a person or community should behave

ethics board /ˈeθɪks bɔːd/ *noun* a group who debate ethical issues in relation to an existing or potential new law

ethnic /ˈeθnɪk/ *adjective* referring to a specific nation or race

ethnic group /ˈeθnɪk gruːp/ *noun* a group of people with the same background and culture, different from those of other groups

ethnic minority /ˌeθnɪk maɪˈnɒrɪti/ *noun* a group of people of one race in a country where most people are of another race

etiquette /ˈetɪket/ *noun* the set of rules governing the way people should behave, such as the way in which a solicitor or barrister behaves towards clients in court

et seq., **et sequentes** *phrase* a Latin phrase meaning 'and the following'

EU *abbreviation* European Union

EULA *abbreviation* end user licence agreement

Euro /ˈjʊərəʊ/ *noun* the main currency unit of the European Union, used as local currency in most Member States since 2002

Euro-constituency /ˌjʊərəʊ kənˈstɪtjʊənsi/ *noun* a constituency which elects an MEP to the European Parliament

Eurocrat /ˈjʊərəʊkræt/ *noun* a bureaucrat working in the European Union or the European Parliament (*informal*)

European Atomic Energy Community Treaty /ˌjʊərəpiːən əˌtɒmɪk ˌenədʒi kəˌmjuːnəti ˈtriːti/ *noun* a treaty established in 1957 to develop nuclear energy within the Common Market. Abbreviation **EURATOM**

European Commission /ˌjʊərəpiːən kəˈmɪʃ(ə)n/ *noun* the main executive body of the European Union, made up of members nominated by each Member State

European Communities /ˌjʊərəpiːən kəˈmjuːnɪtiz/ *plural noun* same as **European Community**

European Community /ˌjʊərəpiːən kə ˈmjuːnɪti/ *noun* the collective body formed by the merger in 1967 of the administrative networks of the European Atomic Energy Community, the European Coal and Steel Community, and the European Economic Community. Abbreviation **EC**. Also called **European Communities** (NOTE: The Treaty on European Union made it the official title of the European Economic Community (EEC).)

European Convention on Human Rights /ˌjʊərəpiːən kənˌvenʃ(ə)n ɒn ˌhjuːmən ˈraɪts/ *noun* a convention signed by all members of the Council of Europe covering the rights of all its citizens

COMMENT: The key provisions are now incorporated by the Human Rights Act 1998, which came into force in the UK in October 2000. The convention recognises property rights, religious rights, the right of citizens to privacy, the due process of law and the principle of legal review. Note that the European Convention on Human Rights does not form part of English law.

European Council /ˌjʊərəpiːən ˈkaʊns(ə)l/ *noun* a group formed by the heads of government of the Member States of the European Union (NOTE: Do not confuse with the **Council of the European Union**.)

COMMENT: The president of the European Council is the head of the Member State which is currently president of the Council of Ministers.

European Court of Human Rights /ˌjʊərəpiːən kɔːt əv ˌhjuːmən ˈraɪts/ *noun* a court considering the rights of citizens of states which are parties to the European Convention for the Protection of Human Rights. ◊ **European Convention on Human Rights** (NOTE: Its formal name is the **European Court for the Protection of Human Rights**.)

European Court of Justice /ˌjʊərəpiːən ˌkɔːt əv ˈdʒʌstɪs/ *noun* a court set up to see that the principles of law as laid out in the Treaty of Rome are observed and applied correctly in the European Union. Abbreviation **ECJ**. Also called **Court of Justice of the European Communities**

COMMENT: The Court is responsible for settling disputes relating to European Community Law, and also acting as a last Court of Appeal against judgments in individual Member States. The ECJ has 15 judges and 8 Advocates General; these are appointed by the governments of Member States for a period of six years. The judges come from all the Member States, and bring with them the legal traditions of each state. The court can either meet as a full court, or in chambers where only two or three judges are present. The court normally conducts its business in French, though if an action is brought before the court by or against a Member State, that Member State can choose the language in which the case will

be heard. The Court can hear actions against institutions, actions brought either by the Commission or by a Member State against another Member State. The Court also acts as Court of Appeal for appeals from the Court of First Instance. The court also interprets legislation and as such acts in a semi-legislative capacity.

European Parliament /ˌjʊərəpiːən ˈpɑːləmənt/ *noun* the parliament of members elected in each Member State of the European Union, representing the peoples of each Member State

COMMENT: The members of the European Parliament (**MEPs**) are elected by constituencies in the 25 Member States. The number of MEPs per country depends on the size of the state they come from: the largest member state, Germany, has 99 MEPs, and the smallest, Luxembourg, has only 6. The European Parliament has the duty to supervise the working of the European Commission, and can if necessary, decide to demand the resignation of the entire Commission, although it cannot demand the resignation of an individual commissioner. The Parliament takes part in making the legislation of the EU, especially by advising on new legislation being proposed by the Commission.

European Social Fund /ˌjʊərəˌpiːən ˈsəʊʃ(ə)l/ *noun* an EU initiative to help disadvantaged people by improving their employability and skills, e.g. by providing training or childcare support

European Union /ˌjʊərəpiːən ˈjuːniən/ *noun* a group of European nations that form a single economic community and have agreed on social and political cooperation (NOTE: It was established by the Treaty on European Union in 1992 and increased to 27 members in 2007.)

euthanasia /ˌjuːθəˈneɪziə/ *noun* the act of killing a very sick or very old person to end to his or her suffering

evade /ɪˈveɪd/ *verb* to try to avoid something □ **to evade tax** to try illegally to avoid paying tax

evasion /ɪˈveɪʒ(ə)n/ *noun* **1.** the practice of avoiding something that you should do **2.** something said in order to hide the truth ○ *His account was full of lies and evasions.*

evasive /ɪˈveɪsɪv/ *adjective* trying to avoid □ **to give evasive answers** to try to avoid answering questions directly

evict /ɪˈvɪkt/ *verb* to force someone, especially a tenant to leave a property ○ *All the tenants were evicted by the new landlords.*

eviction /ɪ'vɪkʃən/ *noun* the act of forcing someone, especially a tenant, to leave a property

evidence /'evɪd(ə)ns/ *noun* facts which help to prove or disprove something at a trial ○ *All the evidence points to arson.* □ **to give evidence against someone** to be a witness and make a statement in a court case suggesting that the defendant is guilty □ **to plant evidence** to put items at the scene of a crime after the crime has taken place, so that a person is incriminated and can be arrested □ **to turn Queen's evidence, to turn state's evidence** *US* to confess to a crime and then act as witness against the other criminals involved, in the hope of getting a lighter sentence ■ *verb* to show ○ *the lack of good will, as evidenced by the defendant's behaviour in the witness stand*

evidence in chief /,evɪd(ə)ns ɪn 'tʃiːf/ *noun* the questioning of a witness by the party who called them (NOTE: The opposite is **cross-examination**.)

ex /eks/ *noun* a former married or unmarried partner ○ *still in contact with her ex* ■ *preposition* out of, or from ■ *prefix* **1.** former ○ *an ex-convict* ○ *She claimed maintenance from her ex-husband.* **2.** not, or without

examination /ɪg,zæmɪ'neɪʃ(ə)n/ *noun* **1.** the process of asking someone questions to find out facts, e.g. the questioning of a prisoner by a magistrate. ◊ **cross-examination 2.** an act looking at something very carefully to see if it is acceptable

examination in chief /ɪg,zæmɪ 'neɪʃ(ə)n ɪn tʃiːf/ *noun* same as **direct examination**

examine /ɪg'zæmɪn/ *verb* to look at someone or something very carefully to see if it can be accepted ○ *The customs officials asked to examine the inside of the car.* ○ *The police are examining the papers from the managing director's safe.*

examining justice /ɪg,zæmɪnə 'dʒʌstɪs/ *noun* a magistrate who hears a case when it is presented for the first time, and decides if there should be a prosecution

excepted /ɪk'septɪd/ *adverb* not including

excepted persons /ɪk,septɪd 'pɜːs(ə)ns/ *plural noun* types of employees listed in a company's insurance policy as not being covered by the insurance

excepted powers /ɪk,septɪd 'paʊəz/ *plural noun* legislative powers which remain indefinitely with a central authority and are not passed on in devolution. ◊ **reserved powers, transferred powers**

exception /ɪk'sepʃən/ *noun* **1.** something which is not included with others ○ *All the accused were acquitted with the exception of Jones who was sent to prison for three months.* **2.** an objection raised to the ruling of a judge □ **to take exception to something** to object to something, to protest against something ○ *Counsel for the defence took exception to the witness' remarks.* ○ *He has taken exception to the reports of the trial in the newspapers.*

exceptional items /ɪk,sepʃən(ə)l 'aɪtəmz/ *plural noun* items in a balance sheet which do not appear there each year

excess /ɪk'ses/ *noun* **1.** the amount which is more than what is allowed □ **excess alcohol in the blood** more alcohol in the blood than a driver is permitted to have □ **in excess of** above, more than ○ *quantities in excess of twenty-five kilos* **2.** the amount to be paid by the insured as part of any claim made under the terms of an insurance policy ○ *She has to pay a £50 excess, and the damage came to over £1,000.*

excess of jurisdiction /ɪk,ses əv ,dʒʊərɪs'dɪkʃən/ *noun* a case where a judge or magistrate has exceeded his or her powers

excess profits /,ekses 'prɒfɪts/ *plural noun* profits which are more than is considered to be normal

excess profits tax /,ekses 'prɒfɪts tæks/ *noun* a tax on profits which are higher than what is thought to be normal

exchange /ɪks'tʃeɪndʒ/ *verb* **1.** □ **to exchange an article for another** to give one thing in place of something else **2.** □ **to exchange contracts** to hand over a contract when buying or selling a property (done by both buyer and seller at the same time)

exchange controls /ɪks'tʃeɪndʒ kən ,trəʊlz/ *plural noun* government restrictions on changing the local currency into foreign currency ○ *The government imposed exchange controls to stop the rush to buy dollars.*

Exchange Equalisation Account /ɪks,tʃeɪndʒ ,iːkwəlaɪ'zeɪʃ(ə)n ə,kaʊnt/ *noun* an account with the Bank of England used by the government when buying or selling foreign currency to influence the exchange rate for the pound

exchange of contracts /ɪks,tʃeɪndʒ əv 'kɒntrækts/ *noun* a point in the conveyance of a property when the solicitors for the buyer and seller hand over the contract of sale which then becomes binding

exchange premium /ɪks'tʃeɪndʒ ˌpriːmiəm/ *noun* an extra cost above the normal rate for buying foreign currency ○ *The dollar is at a premium.*

exchanger /ɪks'tʃeɪndʒə/ *noun* somebody who buys and sells foreign currency

exchange rate /ɪks'tʃeɪndʒ reɪt/ *noun* the rate at which one currency is exchanged for another

exchange transaction /ɪks'tʃeɪndʒ trænˌzækʃən/ *noun* the purchase or sale of foreign currency

Exchequer /ɪks'tʃekə/ *noun* a fund of all the money received by the government of the UK from taxes and other revenues. ◊ **Chancellor**

excise *noun* /'eksaɪz/ same as **excise duty** ■ *verb* /ɪk'saɪz/ to cut out ○ *The chairman ordered the remarks to be excised from the official record.*

excise duty /'eksaɪz ˌdjuːti/, **excise tax** /'ɪksaɪz tæks/ *noun* a tax on the sale of goods such as alcohol and petrol which are produced in the country, or a tax on imports where the duty was not paid on entry into the country

exclude /ɪk'skluːd/ *verb* **1.** to keep something out, or not include something ○ *She was excluded from the trip because of her bad behaviour.* **2.** to remove someone from a group ○ *He complained about being excluded from the short list.* **3.** to officially tell a student that they cannot attend a school, either temporarily or permanently, because of very bad behaviour

excluding /ɪk'skluːdɪŋ/ *preposition* not including ○ *The regulations apply to members of the public, excluding those serving in the emergency services.* □ **not excluding** including ○ *Government servants, not excluding judges, are covered by the Bill.*

exclusion /ɪk'skluːʒ(ə)n/ *noun* **1.** something which is not included **2.** a situation where someone is prevented from entering or taking part in something **3.** the situation where a student is officially prevented from attending school, either temporarily or permanently, because of very bad behaviour □ **to the exclusion of** focusing only on one particular thing or person and ignoring anything or anyone else ○ *His wife complained he had spent all his time working to the exclusion of family life.*

exclusion clause /ɪk'skluːʒ(ə)n klɔːz/ *noun* a clause in an insurance policy or con-

tract which says which items are not covered by the policy and gives details of circumstances in which the insurance company will refuse to pay

exclusion order /ɪkˌskluːʒ(ə)n 'ɔːdə/ *noun* formerly, a court order in matrimonial proceedings which stopped a wife or husband from going into the matrimonial home (NOTE: It is now replaced by an **occupation order**.)

exclusion zone /ɪk'skluːʒ(ə)n ˌzəʊn/ *noun* an area, usually an area of sea near a country, which the military forces of other countries are not allowed to enter

exclusive /ɪk'skluːsɪv/ *adjective* **1.** □ **to have the exclusive rights to something** to be the only person or company who has the rights to something **2.** □ **exclusive of** not including

exclusive agreement /ɪkˌskluːsɪv ə'griːmənt/ *noun* an agreement where a person or firm is made sole agent for a product in a market

Exclusive Economic Zone /ɪk ˌskluːsɪv ˌiːkənɒmɪk 'zəʊn/ *noun* the part of the sea that extends up to 200 nautical miles beyond a country's coastline, which may only be exploited for its natural resources by that country. Abbreviation **EEZ**

exclusive licence /ɪkˌskluːsɪv 'laɪs(ə)ns/ *noun* a licence where the licensee is the only person to be able to enjoy the licence

exclusivity /ˌeksklu:'sɪvɪti/ *noun* the exclusive right to market a product

ex-con /eks 'kɒn/ *noun* same as **ex-convict** (*informal*)

ex-convict /eks 'kɒnvɪkt/ *noun* someone who was imprisoned for a crime but has served their sentence and been released

ex-directory /ˌeks daɪ'rektəri/ *adjective* having a telephone number which is not available to the general public for reasons of privacy

execute /'eksɪkjuːt/ *verb* **1.** to carry out an order **2.** to carry out (the terms of a contract) **3.** to seal (a deed) **4.** to kill someone who has been sentenced to death by a court ○ *He was executed by firing squad.*

executed consideration /ˌeksɪkjuːtɪd kənˌsɪdə'reɪʃ(ə)n/ *noun* a consideration where one party has made a promise in exchange for which the other party has done something for him or her

execution /ˌeksɪˈkjuːʃ(ə)n/ *noun* **1.** the carrying out of a court order or of the terms of a contract **2.** the seizure and sale of goods belonging to a debtor **3.** the killing of someone who has been sentenced to death by a court

executioner /ˌeksɪˈkjuːʃ(ə)nə/ *noun* somebody who executes people who have been sentenced to death

executive /ɪɡˈzekjʊtɪv/ *adjective* **1.** putting decisions into action **2.** referring to the branch of government which puts laws into effect **3.** *US* referring to the President of the USA as head of government ■ *noun* a person such as a manager or director who takes decisions in an organisation ◇ **the Executive** *US* **1.** the section of a government which puts into effect the laws passed by Parliament **2.** the president

executive clemency /ɪɡˌzekjʊtɪv ˈklemənsi/ *noun US* a pardon granted by the President

executive detention /ɪɡˌzekjʊtɪv dɪˈtenʃən/ *noun* the act of holding suspected terrorists, illegal immigrants, etc., in custody for a limited period

executive director /ɪɡˌzekjʊtɪv daɪˈrektə/ *noun* a director who works full-time in the company

executive document /ɪɡˌzekjʊtɪv ˌdɒkjʊˈment/ *noun US* a document such as a treaty sent by the President of the USA to the Senate for ratification

executive order /ɪɡˌzekjʊtɪv ˈɔːdə/ *noun US* an order by the president of the USA or of a state governor

executive power /ɪɡˌzekjʊtɪv ˈpaʊə/ *noun* the right to act as director or to put decisions into action

executive privilege /ɪɡˌzekjʊtɪv ˈprɪvɪlɪdʒ/ *noun US* the privilege of the President of the USA not to reveal matters which he or she considers secret

executor /ɪɡˈzekjʊtə/ *noun* someone who is appointed by a person making his or her will to make sure that it is carried out correctly ◇ *He was named executor of his brother's will.*

executorship /ɪɡˈzekjʊtəʃɪp/ *noun* the position of being an executor

executory /ɪɡˈzekjʊt(ə)ri/ *adjective* still being carried out

executory consideration /ɪɡˌzekjʊt(ə)ri kənˌsɪdəˈreɪʃ(ə)n/ *noun* a consideration where one party makes a promise in exchange for a counter-promise from the other party

exemplary /ɪɡˈzempləri/ *adjective* being so good that it serves as an example to others ◇ *Her conduct in the case was exemplary.*

exemplary damages /ɪɡˌzempləri ˈdæmɪdʒɪz/ *plural noun* an extra award of damages which aims to punish the defendant's actions in addition to compensating the harm done to the claimant

exemplary sentence /ɪɡˌzempləri ˈsentəns/ *noun* a particularly harsh sentence which aims at deterring others from committing the same type of crime

exempt /ɪɡˈzempt/ *adjective* **1.** not covered by a law □ **exempt from tax, tax-exempt** not required to pay tax **2.** not forced to obey a law ■ *verb* to free something from having tax paid on it, or free someone from having to pay tax ◇ *Non profit-making organisations are exempted from tax.* ◇ *Food is exempted from sales tax.* ◇ *The government exempted trusts from tax.*

exempt information /ɪɡˌzempt ˌɪnfəˈmeɪʃ(ə)n/ *noun US* information which may be kept secret from the public because if it were disclosed it might be unfair to an individual or harmful to the authorities ◇ *The council resolved that the press and public be excluded for item 10 as it involved the likely disclosure of exempt information.*

exemption /ɪɡˈzempʃ(ə)n/ *noun* the act of exempting something from a law or obligation ◇ *Police officers have a legal exemption from having to observe speed limits.* □ **exemption from tax, tax exemption** the situation of not being required to pay tax ◇ *As a non profit-making organization you can claim tax exemption.*

exemption clause /ɪɡˈzempʃ(ə)n klɔːz/ *noun* a clause in a contract exempting a party from some liabilities

exempt supplies /ɪɡˌzempt səˈplaɪz/ *plural noun* sales of goods or services on which VAT does not have to be paid

exercise /ˈeksəsaɪz/ *noun* the use of powers, skills or official rights ◇ *A court can give directions to a local authority as to the exercise of its powers in relation to children in care.* ■ *verb* to use or to put something into practice □ **to exercise your discretion** to decide on which of several possible ways to act ◇ *The magistrates exercised their discretion and let the accused off with a suspended sentence.* □ **to exercise an option** to carry out something which you have been given the power to do ○ *He exercised his option to acquire sole marketing rights for the product.* ○ *Not many shareholders exercised their option to buy the new issue of shares.*

ex gratia /ˌeks ˈgreɪʃə/ *phrase* a Latin phrase meaning 'as a favour' □ **an ex gratia payment** a payment made as a gift, with no obligations

exhibit /ɪgˈzɪbɪt/ *noun* any object which is shown as evidence to a court

exile /ˈeksaɪl/ *noun* **1.** the punishment of being sent to live in another country ○ *The ten members of the opposition party were sent into exile.* **2.** somebody who has been sent to live in another country as a punishment ■ *verb* to send someone to live in another country as a punishment ○ *He was exiled for life.*

ex officio /ˌeks əˈfɪʃiəʊ/ *phrase* a Latin phrase meaning 'because of an office held' ○ *The treasurer is ex officio a member* or *an ex officio member of the finance committee.*

exonerate /ɪgˈzɒnəreɪt/ *verb* to remove any blame from a person previously accused of an offence ○ *The judge exonerated the driver from all responsibility for the accident.*

exoneration /ɪgˌzɒnəˈreɪʃ(ə)n/ *noun* the act of exonerating

ex parte /ˌeks ˈpɑːti/ *phrase* a Latin phrase meaning 'on behalf of', or 'on the part of one side only'; pursued by one party only ○ *The wife applied ex parte for an ouster order against her husband.* □ **an ex parte application** an application made to a court where only one side is represented and no notice is given to the other side (often where the application is for an injunction). ◊ **inter partes**

expatriate *noun* /eksˈpætriət/ somebody who lives abroad ○ *There is a large expatriate community* or *a large community of expatriates in Geneva.* ■ *verb* /eksˈpætrieɪt/ to force someone to leave the country where he or she is living

expatriation /eksˌpætriˈeɪʃ(ə)n/ *noun* the act of leaving the country where you are living

expectancy /ɪkˈspektənsi/, **expectation** /ˌekspekˈteɪʃ(ə)n/ *noun* the hope that you will inherit something

expectation of life /ˌekspekˈteɪʃ(ə)n əv laɪf/ *noun* the number of years a person is likely to live

expectations /ˌekspekˈteɪʃ(ə)nz/ ♦ **legitimate expectations**

expenditure /ɪkˈspendɪtʃə/ *noun* the amount of money spent

expert /ˈekspɜːt/ *noun* somebody who knows a lot about something ○ *The company asked a financial expert for advice* or *asked for expert financial advice.* □ **expert in the field** someone who knows a lot about the subject being discussed

expert evidence /ˌekspɜːt ˈevɪd(ə)ns/ *noun* evidence given by an expert witness

expert's report /ˌekspɜːtz rɪˈpɔːt/ *noun* a report written by an expert, usually for a court case

expert witness /ˌekspɜːt ˈwɪtnəs/ *noun* a witness who is a specialist in a subject and is asked to give his or her opinion on technical matters

expiration /ˌekspəˈreɪʃ(ə)n/ *noun* the end of something ○ *expiration of an insurance policy* ○ *to repay before the expiration of the stated period* □ **on expiration of the lease** when the lease comes to an end

expire /ɪkˈspaɪə/ *verb* to come to an end ○ *The lease expires in 2010.* ○ *My passport has expired.*

expiry /ɪkˈspaɪəri/ *noun* the end of something ○ *expiry of an insurance policy*

expiry date /ɪkˈspaɪəri deɪt/ *noun* **1.** the date when something will end, such as the last date for exercising an option **2.** the last date on which a credit card can be used

explicit /ɪkˈsplɪsɪt/ *adjective* which is clearly stated ○ *His explicit intention was to leave his house to his wife.*

explicitly /ekˈsplɪsɪtli/ *adverb* in a clear way ○ *The contract explicitly prohibits sale of the goods in Europe.*

export *noun* /ˈekspɔːt/ the sending of goods to a foreign country to be sold ■ *verb* /ɪkˈspɔːt/ to send goods abroad to be sold ○ *Most of the company's products are exported to the USA.*

export licence /ˈekspɔːt ˌlaɪs(ə)ns/ *noun* a permit which allows a company to send products abroad to be sold

export permit /ˈekspɔːt ˌpɜːmɪt/ *noun* an official document which allows goods to be exported

export trade /ˈekspɔːt treɪd/ *noun* the business of selling to other countries

ex post facto /ˌeks pəʊst ˈfæktəʊ/ *phrase* a Latin phrase meaning 'after the event': used to indicate that a law will apply retroactively

exposure /ɪkˈspəʊʒə/ *noun* the act of showing something which was hidden ○ *the* *report's exposure of corruption in the police force*

expressio unius est exclusio alterius /ɪkˌspresiəʊ ˌuːniəs est ɪksˌkluːziəʊ ɔːlˈteriəs/ *phrase* a Latin phrase meaning 'the mention that one thing is included implies that another thing is excluded': a rule that assumes that specific items not mentioned in a list are not covered by that law or contract

expressly /ɪkˈspresli/ *adverb* clearly in words ○ *The contract expressly forbids sales to the United States.* ○ *The franchisee is expressly forbidden to sell goods other than those supplied by the franchiser.*

express malice /ɪkˌspres ˈmælɪs/ *noun US* the intention to kill someone

express term /ɪkˈspres tɜːm/ *noun* a term in a contract which is agreed by both parties and clearly stated, i.e. either written or spoken. Compare **implied term**

expropriation /ɪksˌprəʊpriˈeɪʃ(ə)n/ *noun* **1.** the action of the state in taking private property for public use without paying compensation **2.** *US* the action of the state in taking private property for public use and paying compensation to the former owner (NOTE: The British equivalent is **compulsory purchase**.)

expunge /ɪkˈspʌndʒ/ *verb* to remove information from a record ○ *Inadmissible hearsay evidence was expunged from the report.*

extended credit /ɪkˌstendɪd ˈkredɪt/ *noun* credit allowing the borrower a longer time to pay

extended family /ɪkˌstendɪd ˈfæm(ə)li/ *noun* a group of related people, including distant relatives and close friends

extended sentence /ɪkˌstendɪd ˈsentəns/ *noun* a sentence which is made longer than usual because the criminal poses a significant danger to the public

extension /ɪkˈstenʃən/ *noun* the act of allowing more time for an activity □ **an extension of credit** an allowance of more time to pay back money that is owed □ **extension of a contract** a further period of time after a contract has finished □ **extension of time** an allowance by court of more time in which to do or complete something ○ *The defendant applied for an extension of time in which to serve her defence.*

extenuating circumstances /ɪkˌstenjueɪtɪŋ ˈsɜːkəmstənsɪz/ *plural noun* factors which excuse a crime in some way

extenuation /ɪkˌstenjuˈeɪʃ(ə)n/ *noun* □ **in extenuation of something** in order to excuse something ○ *Counsel pleaded the accused's age in extenuation of his actions.*

external audit /ɪkˌstɜːn(ə)l ˈɔːdɪt/ *noun* an audit carried out by an independent auditor

external auditor /ɪkˌstɜːn(ə)l ˈɔːdɪtə/ *noun* an independent person who audits the company's accounts

extinguishment /ɪkˈstɪŋgwɪʃmənt/ *noun* the act of cancelling a right or a power, especially the right to sue for non-payment once payment has been made

extort /ɪkˈstɔːt/ *verb* to get money, promises or a confession from someone by using threats ○ *He extorted £20,000 from local shopkeepers.*

extortion /ɪkˈstɔːʃ(ə)n/ *noun* the activity of getting money by threats

extortionate credit bargain /ɪkˌstɔːʃ(ə)nət ˈkredɪt ˌbɑːgɪn/ *noun* a transaction whereby money is lent at a very high rate of interest, thereby rendering the transaction illegal

extortionist /ɪkˈstɔːʃ(ə)nɪst/ *noun* someone who extorts money from people

extortion racket /ɪkˌstɔːʃ(ə)n ˈrækɪt/ *noun* a racket to make money by threatening people

extra- /ekstrə/ *prefix* outside

extra-authority payments /ˌekstrə ɔː ˌθɒrɪti ˈpeɪmənts/ *noun* payments made to another authority for services provided by that authority

extract *noun* /ˈekstrækt/ a printed document which is part of a larger document ○ *The solicitor sent an extract of the deeds.* ■ *verb* /ɪkˈstrækt/ to get something such as information or a promise from someone by force, threats or close questioning ○ *The confession was extracted under torture.* ○ *The magistrate extracted an admission from the witness that she had not seen the accident.*

extradite /ˈekstrədaɪt/ *verb* to bring an arrested person from another country to your country because he or she is wanted for trial for a crime committed in your country ○ *He was arrested in France and extradited to stand trial in Germany.*

extradition /ˌekstrəˈdɪʃ(ə)n/ *noun* the act of extraditing ○ *The USA is seeking the extradition of the leader of the drug gang.*

extradition treaty /ˌekstrəˈdɪʃ(ə)n ˌtriːti/ *noun* an agreement between two countries that a person arrested in one country can be sent to the other to stand trial for a crime committed there

extra-judicial /ˌekstrə dʒuˈdɪʃ(ə)l/ *adjective* outside the usual authority of the law

extraordinary items /ɪkˈstrɔːd(ə)n(ə)ri ˌaɪtəm/ *plural noun* items in accounts which do not appear each year and need to be noted

extraordinary rendition /ɪk ˌstrɔːd(ə)n(ə)ri renˈdɪʃ(ə)n/ *noun* the extra-judicial transfer of a person from one state to another

extra-territoriality /ˌekstrə ˌterɪtɔːri ˈælɪti/ *noun* (*of diplomats*) being outside the territory of the country where you are living, and so not subject to its laws

extra-territorial waters /ˌekstrə ˌterɪtɔːriəl ˈwɔːtəz/ *plural noun* international waters, outside the jurisdiction of any one country

extremism /ɪkˈstriːmɪz(ə)m/ *noun* ideas and practices that favour very strong action, even including the use of violence

extremist /ɪkˈstriːmɪst/ *noun* a person in favour of very strong, sometimes violent methods, regarded as unreasonable by most other people ■ *adjective* in favour of very strong, sometimes violent methods ○ *extremist political parties*

extrinsic evidence /eksˌtrɪnsɪk ˈevɪd(ə)ns/ *noun* evidence used in the interpretation of a document which is not found in the document itself. Compare **intrinsic evidence**

ex turpi causa non oritur actio /ˌeks ˌtʊəpi ˌkaʊzə nɒn ˌɒrɪtə ˈæktiəʊ/ *phrase* a Latin phrase meaning 'from a base cause no action can proceed': it is not legally possible to enforce an illegal contract

eye witness /ˌaɪ ˈwɪtnəs/ *noun* a person who saw something such as an accident or a crime happen ■ *adjective* **eye-witness** given by an eye witness ○ *She gave an eye-witness account of the bank hold-up.*

F

face /feɪs/ *verb* □ **to face a charge** to appear in court and be charged with a crime ○ *He faces three charges relating to firearms.*

facie ♦ prima facie

facsimile /fæk'sɪmɪli/, **facsimile copy** /fæk,sɪmɪli 'kɒpi/ *noun* an exact copy of a document

fact /fækt/ *noun* something which is true and real, especially something which has been proved by evidence in court ○ *The chairman of the tribunal asked to see all the facts on the income tax claim.* □ **in fact, in point of fact** really

faction /'fækʃən/ *noun* a group of people within a larger organisation such as a political party who have different views or aims from the other members (*sometimes as criticism*) ○ *Arguments broke out between different factions at the party conference.* ○ *The Prime Minister has the support of most factions in the party.*

factional /'fækʃən(ə)l/ *adjective* referring to factions ○ *Factional infighting has weakened the party structure.*

facto ♦ de facto, ipso facto

factoring /'fæktərɪŋ/ *noun* the activity of selling debts to a debt factor

factors of production /,fæktəz əv prə'dʌkʃən/ *noun* the three things needed to produce a product (land, labour and capital)

Faculty of Advocates /,fæk(ə)lti əv 'ædvəʊkəts/ *noun* the legal body to which Scottish barristers belong

failing prompt payment /,feɪlɪŋ prɒmpt 'peɪmənt/ *phrase* if the payment is not made on time

failure to appear /,feɪljə tə ə'pɪə/ *noun* a failure to come to court when expected (NOTE: The case may continue in the absence of one of the parties, but not of both.)

fair /feə/ *adjective* honest or correct

fair comment /,feə 'kɒment/ *noun* a defence to a charge of defamation on a matter of public interest asserting that the statement in question was true, fair and honestly made

fair dealing /,feə 'diːlɪŋ/ *noun* the ability to copy small sections of a work under copyright for personal use

fair dismissal /,feə dɪs'mɪs(ə)l/ *noun* the situation when an employee is deemed to have been dismissed from their employment for a lawful reason (NOTE: The lawful reasons are: (1) capability; (2) qualifications or conduct; (3) redundancy; (4) illegality; (5) some other substantial reason (SOSR).)

fair price /,feə 'praɪs/ *noun* a good price for both buyer and seller

fair rent /,feə 'rent/ *noun* reasonable rent for a property, bearing in mind the size and type of property and its situation

fair trade /,feə 'treɪd/ *noun* an international business system where countries agree not to charge import duties on items imported from their trading partners

fair trading /,feə 'treɪdɪŋ/ *noun* a way of carrying business which is reasonable and does not harm the consumer

fair use /,feə 'juːs/ *noun* the use which can be legally made of a quotation from a copyright text without the permission of the copyright owner

fair value /,feə 'væljuː/ *noun* a price paid by a buyer who knows the value of what he or she is buying, to a seller who also knows the value of what he or she is selling, i.e. neither is cheating the other

fair wear and tear /,feə weər ən 'teə/ *noun* acceptable damage caused by normal use ○ *The insurance policy covers most damage, but not fair wear and tear to the machine.*

faith /feɪθ/ *noun* □ **to have faith in something, someone** to believe that something or a person is good or will work well □ **in good faith** in an honest way □ **to act in good faith** to act honestly □ **to act in bad faith** to act dishonestly □ **to buy something in good faith** to buy something honestly, in the course of an honest transaction ○ *He bought the car in good faith, not knowing it had been stolen.*

fake /feɪk/ *noun* a copy made for criminal purposes ○ *The shipment came with fake documentation.* ■ *verb* to make an imitation for criminal purposes ○ *They faked a break-in to make the police believe the documents had been stolen.*

fall /fɔːl/ *verb* **1.** to happen on a particular day or date ○ *The national holiday falls on a Monday.* **2.** to become ○ *Her husband fell ill and couldn't work.* □ **to fall due on** to become ready to be paid on a particular date ○ *The bill fell due on the last day of March.* □ **to fall foul of** to get into trouble with someone, or break the law ○ *His plan fell foul of the local authorities.* ○ *The venture quickly fell foul of the law.* □ **to fall under someone's influence** to become strongly influenced by someone else, especially to do something wrong ◇ **fall in with someone** to become associated with someone, especially someone who is a bad influence ◇ **fall outside** not to belong to a particular area of knowledge or activity ○ *That question falls outside my specialist knowledge.* ◇ **fall within** to belong to a particular area of knowledge or activity ○ *Does this fall within the terms of the agreement?*

false /fɔːls/ *adjective* not true or not correct ○ *to make a false entry in the record* □ **by** *or* **under false pretence(s)** by doing or saying something to trick someone ○ *He was sent to prison for obtaining money by false pretences.*

false accounting /ˌfɔːls əˈkaʊntɪŋ/ *noun* the notifiable offence of changing, destroying or hiding financial records for money, punishable by up to seven years' imprisonment

false description of contents /fɔːls dɪˌskrɪpʃən əv kənˈtents/ *noun* wrongly stating the contents of a packet to trick customers into buying it

falsehood /ˈfɔːlshʊd/ *noun* a deliberately incorrect statement

false imprisonment /ˌfɔːls ɪmˈprɪz(ə)nmənt/ *noun* the unlawful detainment of an individual which restricts their right to freedom of movement to leave an area, rather than actually being put in prison

false positive /ˌfɔːls ˈpɒzɪtɪv/ *noun* an incorrect result occurring when data about a person is matched against a checklist

false representation /fɔːls ˌreprɪzenˈteɪʃ(ə)n/ *noun US* the offence of making a wrong statement which misleads someone

false weight /ˌfɔːls ˈweɪt/ *noun* a weight on shop scales which is wrong and so cheats customers

falsification of accounts /fɔːlsɪfɪˌkeɪʃ(ə)n əv əˈkaʊnts/ *noun* the action of making false entries in a record or of destroying a record

falsify /ˈfɔːlsɪfaɪ/ *verb* to change something to make it wrong □ **to falsify accounts** to change or destroy a record

family /ˈfæm(ə)li/ *noun* **1.** a group of people who are related by birth or marriage **2.** a group of organised Mafia gangsters (*slang*)

Family Division /ˌfæm(ə)li dɪˈvɪʒ(ə)n/ *noun* one of the three divisions of the High Court which deals with divorce cases and cases involving parents and children

family law /ˈfæm(ə)li lɔː/ *noun* law relating to families or to the rights and duties of the members of a family

family life /ˈfæm(ə)li laɪf/ *noun* quiet enjoyment of a private life with one's family, which is considered a basic human right. ◊ **emergency protection order, threshold criteria**

COMMENT: The right to family life is enshrined in Article 8 of the European Convention of Human Rights and was introduced into UK law by the Human Rights Act 1998. Interference in this right is allowed on the grounds of 'protection of public health, morals or national security', but must be proportionate.

FAS *abbreviation* Financial Assistance Scheme

fast track /ˈfɑːst træk/ *noun* a case management system normally applied to personal injury claims involving sums between £1000 and £15,000, and other civil claims for sums between £5,000 and £15,000

COMMENT: The timetable for the fast track is given in the directions for the case. A typical timetable starts from the date of the notice of allocation, and gives four weeks to disclosure, 10 weeks for the exchange of experts' reports, 20 weeks for the court to send out listing questionnaires and 30 weeks to the hearing; the trial must not last more than one day, and such issues as liability and quantum may be decided separately.

fast-track /ˌfɑːst ˈtræk/ *adjective* moving forward at a faster rate ○ *There is a new fast-track procedure for hearing claims.*

fatal /ˈfeɪt(ə)l/ *adjective* causing a death ○ *He took a fatal dose of drugs.* ○ *There were six fatal accidents in the first week of the year.*

fatwa /ˈfætwə/ *noun* a pronouncement according to Muslim religious law

COMMENT: The most famous fatwa was that issued in 1989 declaring that author Salman Rushdie should be killed for the blasphemous views expressed in his book The Satanic Verses.

FBI /ˌef biː ˈaɪ/ *abbreviation* Federal Bureau of Investigation

feasant ♦ **damage feasant**

feasibility /ˌfiːzəˈbɪlɪti/ *noun* the likelihood or possibility that something can be done or accomplished ○ *We looked into the feasibility of questioning all 200 eye witnesses.*

Federal Bureau of Investigation

/ˌfed(ə)rəl ˌbjuərəʊ əv ɪnˌvestɪˈɡeɪʃ(ə)n/ *noun US* the section of the US Department of Justice which investigates crimes against federal law and subversive acts in the USA. Abbreviation **FBI**

federal courts /ˈfed(ə)rəl kɔːt/ *noun US* the national courts of the USA, as opposed to state courts

federal laws /ˈfed(ə)rəl kɔːt/ *noun US* the laws of the USA, as opposed to state laws

Federal Reserve Bank /ˌfed(ə)rəl rɪ ˈzɜːv ˌbæŋk/ *noun US* one of the twelve central banks in the USA which are owned by the state and directed by the Federal Reserve Board

Federal Reserve Board /ˌfed(ə)rəl rɪ ˈzɜːv bɔːd/ *noun US* a government organisation which runs the central banks in the USA

fee /fiː/ *noun* **1.** the money paid for work carried out by a professional person such as an accountant, doctor or lawyer ○ *a barrister's fees* ○ *We charge a small fee for our services.* **2.** the money paid for something ○ *admission fee* ○ *registration fee* **3.** ownership of land which may be inherited

fee simple /ˌfiː ˈsɪmpəl/ *noun* freehold ownership of land with no restrictions to it ○ *to hold an estate in fee simple*

fee tail /ˈfiː teɪl/ *noun* a legal interest in land which is passed on to the owner's direct descendants, and which cannot be passed to anyone else (NOTE: The creation of these interests is no longer possible.)

felonious /fəˈləʊniəs/ *adjective* criminal ○ *He carried out a felonious act.*

felony /ˈfeləni/ *noun* an old term for a serious crime ○ *to commit a felony* (NOTE: It is still used in the expression **treason felony**.)

feme covert /ˌfem ˈkəʊvət/ *phrase* a French phrase meaning 'married woman'

feme sole /ˌfem ˈsəʊl/ *phrase* a French phrase meaning 'unmarried woman'

fence /fens/ *noun* somebody who receives and sells stolen goods (*informal*) ■ *verb* to receive stolen goods to sell

feudal society /ˌfjuːd(ə)l səˈsaɪəti/ *noun* a society where each class or level has a duty to serve the class above it

fiat /ˈfiːæt/ *noun* a Latin word meaning 'let it be done': an order or decree for some legal act to be carried out

fiat justitia /ˌfiːæt dʒʌsˈtɪsiə/ *phrase* a Latin phrase meaning 'let justice be done'

fiat money /ˈfiːæt ˌmʌni/ *noun* coins or notes which are not worth much as paper or metal, but are said by the government to have a value

fiction of law /ˌfɪkʃən əv ˈlɔː/ *noun* the act of assuming something to be true, even if it is not proved to be so, which is a procedural device of courts to avoid problems caused by statute

fictitious /fɪkˈtɪʃəs/ *adjective* not existing, and sometimes intended to deceive people

fictitious assets /fɪkˌtɪʃəs ˈæsets/ *plural noun* assets which do not really exist, but are entered as assets to balance the accounts

fide ♦ **bona fide purchaser**, **bona fides**

fiduciary /fɪˈdjuːʃjəri/ *adjective* acting as trustee for someone else, or being in a position of trust ○ *A company director owes a fiduciary duty to the company.* □ **to act in a fiduciary capacity** to act as a trustee ■ *noun* a trustee

fieri facias /ˌfaɪraɪ ˈfeɪʃiæs/ *phrase* a Latin phrase meaning 'make it happen.' ◊ **writ of fieri facias**

fi. fa. ♦ **fieri facias**

FIFO /ˈfaɪfəʊ/ *abbreviation* first in first out

Fifth Amendment /ˌfɪfθ əˈmendmənt/ *noun US* an amendment to the constitution of the USA, which says that no person can be forced to give evidence which might incriminate himself or herself □ **to plead the Fifth Amendment, to take the Fifth**

Amendment to refuse to give evidence to a court, tribunal or committee, because the evidence might incriminate you

file /faɪl/ *noun* **1.** documents kept for reference, either on paper or as data on a computer ○ *The police keep a file of missing vehicles.* ○ *Look up her description in the missing persons' file.* □ **to place something on file** to keep a record of something □ **to keep someone's name on file** to keep someone's name on a list for reference **2.** a cardboard holder for documents, which can fit in the drawer of a filing cabinet ○ *Put these letters in the unsolved cases file.* ○ *Look in the file marked 'Scottish police forces'.* ■ *verb* **1.** □ **to file documents** to put documents in order so that they can be found easily **2.** to make an official request □ **to file a petition in bankruptcy** to ask officially to be made bankrupt, to ask officially for someone else to be made bankrupt **3.** to send a document to court ○ *When a defendant is served with particulars of claim he can file a defence.* **4.** to register something officially ○ *to file an application for a patent* ○ *to file a return to the tax office*

file copy /ˈfaɪl ˌkɒpi/ *noun* a copy of a document which is filed in an office for reference

filing /ˈfaɪlɪŋ/ *noun* the delivery of a legal document to the court office by hand, post, fax, etc.

final demand /ˌfaɪn(ə)l dɪˈmɑːnd/ *noun* the last reminder from a supplier, after which he or she will sue for payment

final discharge /ˌfaɪn(ə)l ˈdɪstʃɑːdʒ/ *noun* the final payment of what is left of a debt

final dividend /ˌfaɪn(ə)l ˈdɪvɪdend/ *noun* a dividend paid at the end of a year

final hearing /ˌfaɪn(ə)l ˈhɪərɪŋ/ *noun* the actual hearing of a case in the small claims track, which aims at being informal and rapid

final judgment /ˌfaɪn(ə)l ˈdʒʌdʒmənt/ *noun* a judgment which is awarded at the end of an action after trial. Compare **interlocutory judgment**

Finance Act /ˈfaɪnæns ækt/ *noun* an annual Act of the British Parliament which gives the government power to raise taxes as proposed in the budget (NOTE: Use **under** when referring to an Act of Parliament: *a creditor seeking a receiving order under the Bankruptcy Act.*)

finance charge /ˈfaɪnæns tʃɑːdʒ/ *noun* **1.** the cost of borrowing money **2.** an additional charge made to a customer who asks for extended credit

finance company /ˈfaɪnæns ˌkʌmp(ə)ni/ *noun* a company which provides money for hire-purchase

finance corporation /ˈfaɪnæns ˌkɔːpəreɪʃ(ə)n/ *noun* a company which provides money for hire purchase

Finance Minister /ˌfaɪnæns ˈmɪnɪstə/ *noun* a government minister responsible for finance (both taxation and expenditure)

financial /faɪˈnænʃəl/ *adjective* referring to money or finance ○ *He has a financial interest in the company.* □ **to make financial provision for someone** to arrange for someone to receive money to live on (by attachment of earnings, etc.)

financial assistance /faɪˌnænʃəl əˈsɪstəns/ *noun* help in the form of money

Financial Assistance Scheme /faɪˌnænʃəl əˈsɪstəns ˌskiːm/ *noun* a Government fund giving support payments to former members of pension schemes which have become insolvent. Abbreviation **FAS**

financial commitments /faɪˌnænʃəl kəˈmɪtmənts/ *plural noun* money which is owed to someone for bills or purchases

financial derivative /faɪˌnænʃəl dəˈrɪvətɪv/ *noun* a tradeable financial instrument based on an asset's underlying value

financial provision order /faɪˌnænʃəl prəˈvɪʒ(ə)n ˌɔːdə/ *noun* an order which, during the course of family proceedings, is made on or after the granting of a decree of divorce or annulment, providing for a financial settlement between the parties, or a lump sum

financial relief /faɪˌnænʃ(ə)l rɪˈliːf/ *noun* any or all of the following orders available during family proceedings: maintenance pending suit orders, financial provision orders, property adjustment orders and court orders for maintenance during marriage

COMMENT: Maintenance for children of a marriage falls outside of the jurisdiction of the court and must be made to the Child Support Agency directly, the only exception being when the children of the marriage have special needs or are adopted.

financial review /faɪˌnænʃəl rɪˈvjuː/ *noun* an examination of an organisation's finances

Financial Services and Markets Act 2000 /faɪˌnænʃəl ˌsɜːvɪsɪz ən ˈmɑːkɪts ækt tuː ˌθaʊzənd/ *noun* the act that regulates all financial markets within the UK. Abbreviation **FSMA**

Financial Services Authority /faɪ ˌnænʃəl ˈsɜːvɪsɪz ɔːˌθɒrəti/ *noun* the body that regulates financial services in the UK

financial statement /faɪˌnænʃəl ˈsteɪtmənt/ *noun* a document which shows the financial situation of a company at the end of an accounting period and the transactions which have taken place during that period

find /faɪnd/ *verb* **1.** to get something which was not there before ○ *to find backing for a project* **2.** to make a legal decision in court ○ *The tribunal found that both parties were at fault.* ○ *The court found the accused guilty on all charges.* □ **to find for the defendant** to decide that the defendant was right □ **to find against the defendant** to decide that the defendant was not right

finder's fee /ˈfaɪndəz fiː/ *noun* a fee paid to a person who finds a client for another

findings /ˈfaɪndɪŋz/ *noun* a decision reached by a court □ **the findings of a commission of enquiry** the conclusions of the commission

fine /faɪn/ *noun* a sum of money ordered to be paid by a defendant as punishment on conviction for an offence ○ *The court sentenced him to pay a £25,000 fine.* ○ *We had to pay a £10 parking fine.* ○ *The sentence for dangerous driving is a £1,000 fine or two months in prison.* ■ *verb* to order a defendant who has been convicted of an offence to pay a sum of money as punishment ○ *to fine someone £2,500 for obtaining money by false pretences*

COMMENT: When imposing a fine the court is must look into the financial circumstances of the offender, and must ensure that it also reflects the severity of the offence committed.

fingerprint /ˈfɪŋɡəprɪnt/ *noun* a mark left on a surface by fingers, from which a person may be identified ○ *They found his fingerprints on the murder weapon.* ○ *The court heard evidence from a fingerprint expert.* □ **to take someone's fingerprints** to take a copy of a person's fingerprints so that he or she can be identified in future ■ *verb* to take someone's fingerprints ○ *The police fingerprinted the suspect after charging him.*

fingertip search /ˈfɪŋɡətɪp ˌsɜːtʃ/ *noun* a very careful search of a crime scene and the surrounding area carried out by hand in the hope of finding evidence

fire /faɪə/ *noun* **1.** a potentially dangerous situation in which something is burning ○ *The shipment was damaged in the fire on board the cargo boat.* ○ *Half the stock was destroyed in the warehouse fire.* □ **to catch fire** to start to burn ○ *The papers in the waste paper basket caught fire.* **2.** the act of shooting □ **to open fire** to start to shoot ■ *verb* **1.** to shoot a gun ○ *He fired two shots at the crowd.* **2.** □ **to fire someone** to dismiss someone from a job ○ *The new managing director fired half the sales force.*

firearm /ˈfaɪərɑːm/ *noun* a gun or other weapon used to shoot

firearms certificate /ˌfaɪəɑːmz sə ˈtɪfɪkət/ *noun* an official document saying that someone has permission to own a gun

firebomb /ˈfaɪəbɒm/ *noun* a large or small explosive weapon containing incendiary materials, which causes a fire ■ *verb* to use a firebomb to cause damage ○ *The shop was firebombed by vandals.*

fire certificate /ˈfaɪə səˌtɪfɪkət/ *noun* a document from the municipal fire department to say that a building is properly protected against fire

fire damage /ˈfaɪə ˌdæmɪdʒ/ *noun* damage to land caused by a fire

fire-damaged goods /ˌfaɪə ˌdæmɪdʒd ˈɡʊdz/ *plural noun* goods which have been damaged in a fire

fire escape /ˈfaɪər ɪˌskeɪp/ *noun* a door or stairs which allow staff to get out of a building which is on fire

fire-raiser /ˈfaɪə ˌreɪzə/ *noun* same as **arsonist**

fire-raising /ˈfaɪə ˌreɪzɪŋ/ *noun* same as **arson**

fire regulations /ˈfaɪə ˌreɡjʊleɪʃ(ə)nz/ *plural noun* local or national regulations which owners of buildings used by the public have to obey in order to be granted a fire certificate

firing squad /ˈfaɪərɪŋ skwɒd/ *noun* a group of soldiers who execute someone by shooting

firm /fɜːm/ *noun* a partnership or any other business which is not a company ○ *a firm of accountants* ○ *an important publishing firm* ○ *He is a partner in a law firm.* (NOTE: Firm is often used when referring to incorporated companies, but this is not correct.) ■ *verb* to remain at a price and seem likely to go up ○ *The shares firmed at £1.50.*

First Amendment /ˌfɜːst ə ˈmen(d)mənt/ *noun* US the first amendment to the Constitution of the USA, guaranteeing freedom of speech and religion

first degree murder /fɜːst dɪˌgriː ˈmɜːdə/ *noun US* the premeditated and deliberate killing of a person

COMMENT: In the US, the penalty for first degree murder can be death.

first in first out /ˌfɜːst ɪn ˌfɜːst ˈaʊt/ *noun* **1.** a redundancy policy, where the people who have been working longest are the first to be made redundant **2.** an accounting policy where stock is valued at the price of the oldest purchases

first offence /ˌfɜːst əˈfens/ *noun* the fact of committing an offence for the first time, which makes it less likely to result in a prison sentence in the case of summary offences

first offender /ˌfɜːst əˈfendə/ *noun* somebody who has committed an offence for the first time

first option /ˌfɜːst ˈɒpʃən/ *noun* the right to be the first to have the possibility of deciding or having something

FISA *abbreviation* Foreign Intelligence Surveillance Act

FISA court /ˌef aɪ es eɪ ˈkɔːt/ *noun* a US court composed of a rotating panel of federal judges that reviews in secret prosecutors' requests to tap the phones of suspected spies and terrorists and to carry out searches

fiscal measures /ˌfɪskəl ˈmeʒəz/ *plural noun* tax changes made by a government to improve the working of the economy

fishing expedition /ˈfɪʃɪŋ ˌekspɪdɪʃ(ə)n/ *noun* the use of the pre-hearing disclosure of documents to try to find other documents belonging to the defendant which the claimant does not know about and which might help him or her with the claim (*informal*)

fit /fɪt/ *adjective* physically or mentally able to do something ○ *The solicitor stated that his client was not fit to stand trial.*

fitness for purpose /ˌfɪtnəs fə ˈpɜːpəs/ *noun* an implied contractual term that goods sold will be of the necessary standard to be used for the purpose for which they were bought

fittings /ˈfɪtɪŋz/ ♦ **fixtures and fittings**

fixed capital /ˌfɪkst ˈkæpɪt(ə)l/ *noun* capital in the form of buildings and machinery

fixed charge /ˌfɪkst ˈtʃɑːdʒ/ *noun* a charge over a particular asset or property

fixed costs /ˌfɪkst ˈkɒsts/ *plural noun* **1.** a set amount of money to which a claimant is entitled in legal proceedings **2.** the cost of producing a product, which does not increase with the amount of product made, e.g. rent

fixed deposit /ˌfɪkst dɪˈpɒzɪt/ *noun* a deposit which pays a stated interest over a set period

fixed expenses /ˌfɪkst ɪkˈspensɪz/ *plural noun* money which is spent regularly, e.g. rent, electricity, or telephone costs

fixed income /ˌfɪkst ˈɪnkʌm/ *noun* an income such as from an annuity which does not change in amount from year to year

fixed interest /ˌfɪkst ˈɪntrəst/ *noun* interest which is paid at a set rate

fixed-interest investments /ˌfɪkst ˌɪntrəst ɪnˈvestmənts/ *plural noun* investments producing an interest which does not change

fixed-price agreement /ˌfɪkst ˈpraɪs əˌgriːmənt/ *noun* an agreement where a company provides a service or a product at a price which stays the same for the whole period of the agreement

fixed-price contract /ˌfɪkst ˈpraɪs ˈkɒntrækt/ *noun* a contract for work done in which the contractor will receive a pre-agreed fee on completion. Compare **cost-plus contract** (NOTE: The fee is based on the original estimate and doesn't account for any subsequent increase in the cost of labour and materials.)

fixed rate /ˌfɪkst ˈreɪt/ *noun* a charge which cannot be changed

fixed scale of charges /ˌfɪkst skeɪl əv ˈtʃɑːdʒɪz/ *plural noun* a rate of charging which cannot be altered

fixed term /ˌfɪkst ˈtɜːm/ *noun* a period which is fixed when a contract is signed and which cannot be changed afterwards

fixture /ˈfɪkstʃə/ *noun* an item such as a sink or lavatory which is permanently attached to a property and which passes to a new owner with the property itself

fixtures and fittings /ˌfɪkstʃəz ən ˈfɪtɪŋz/ *plural noun* objects in a property which are sold with the property, including both objects which are permanently fixed and those which can be removed

flag /flæg/ *verb* □ **to flag a ship** to give a ship the right to fly a flag, by registering it. ◊ **reflag** ◊ **to fly a flag 1.** to attach the flag in an obvious position to show that your ship belongs to a certain country ○ *a ship* *flying the British flag* **2.** to act in a certain way to show that you are proud of belonging to a certain country or working for a certain company ○ *The Trade Minister has gone to the World Fair to fly the flag.* ○ *He is only attending the conference to fly the flag for the company.*

flag of convenience /ˌflæg əv kən
'viːniəns/ *noun* the flag of a country which may have no ships of its own but allows ships of other countries to be registered in its ports

flagrant /ˈfleɪgrənt/ *adjective* clear and obvious ○ *a flagrant case of contempt of court* ○ *a flagrant violation of human rights*

flagrante ♦ in flagrante delicto

flat rate /ˌflæt ˈreɪt/ *noun* a charge which always stays the same ○ *We pay a flat rate for electricity each quarter.* ○ *He is paid a flat rate of £2 per thousand.*

floating charge /ˌfləʊtɪŋ tʃɑːdʒ/ *noun* a charge over assets that change on a day to day basis

flood risk area /ˈflʌd rɪsk ˌeəriə/ *noun* an area of land designating as being at risk of flooding by a local authority under the Environmental Agency

flotation /fləʊˈteɪʃ(ə)n/ *noun* the act of a private company offering its shares for sale and becoming a public company

flout /flaʊt/ *verb* to break or act go against a rule or the law ○ *By selling alcohol to minors, the shop is deliberately flouting the law.*

flyposting /ˈflaɪpəʊstɪŋ/ *noun* the practice of displaying posters wherever possible, often illegally

f.o.b. /ˈefəʊˈbiː/ *abbreviation* free on board

follow /ˈfɒləʊ/ *verb* to act in accordance with a rule ○ *The court has followed the precedent set in the 1972 case.*

football banning order /ˈfʊtbɔːl
ˌbænɪŋ ˌɔːdə/ *noun* a civil order which excludes a person from a particular place, usually a football ground, because they are a known football hooligan

football disorder /ˈfʊtbɔːl dɪsˌɔːdə/ *noun* acts of hooliganism and public disorder at large public events such as football matches

forbear /fɔːˈbeə/ *verb* □ **to forbear from doing something** not to do something which you intended to do ○ *He forbore from taking any further action.*

forbearance /fɔːˈbeərəns/ *noun* an act of not doing something, such as enforcing payment of a debt, which could have been done

force /fɔːs/ *noun* **1.** physical strength or violence **2.** influence or effect □ **to be in force** to be operating or working ○ *The rules have been in force since 1946.* □ **to come into force** to start to operate or work ○ *The new procedures will come into force on January 1st.* □ **to have the force of law** to impose legal rights and obligations ○ *The new regulations have the force of law.*

forced sale /ˌfɔːst ˈseɪl/ *noun* a sale which takes place because a court orders it or because it is the only way to avoid insolvency

force majeure /ˌfɔːs mæˈʒɜː/ *noun* something which happens which is out of the control of the parties who have signed a contract, such as a war or a storm, and which prevents the contract being fulfilled. ◊ **act of God**

forcible /ˈfɔːsɪb(ə)l/ *adjective* using force

forcible entry /ˌfɔːsɪb(ə)l ˈentri/ *noun* formerly, the criminal offence of entering a building or land and taking possession of it by force

forcible feeding /ˌfɔːsɪb(ə)l ˈfiːdɪŋ/ *noun* the act of giving food by force to a prisoner on hunger strike

foreclose /fɔːˈkləʊz/ *verb* to take possession of a property because the owner cannot repay money which he or she has borrowed using the property as security ○ *to foreclose on a mortgaged property*

foreclosure /fɔːˈkləʊʒə/ *noun* the act of foreclosing

foreclosure order absolute /fɔː
ˌkləʊʒə ˌɔːdə ˈæbsəluːt/ *noun* a court order giving the mortgagee full rights to the property

foreclosure order nisi /fɔːˌkləʊʒə
ˌɔːdə ˈnaɪsaɪ/ *noun* a court order which makes a mortgagor pay outstanding debts to a mortgagee within a specified period of time

foreign /ˈfɒrɪn/ *adjective* not belonging to one's own country ○ *Foreign cars have flooded our market.* ○ *We are increasing our trade with foreign countries.*

foreign currency /ˌfɒrɪn ˈkʌrənsi/ *noun* the currency of another country

foreign exchange broker /ˌfɒrɪn ɪks
ˈtʃeɪndʒ ˌbrəʊkə/ *noun* somebody who deals on the foreign exchange market

foreign exchange dealing /ˌfɒrɪn ɪks
'tʃeɪndʒ ˌdiːlɪŋ/ *noun* the activity of buying
and selling foreign currencies

foreign exchange market /ˌfɒrɪn ɪks
'tʃeɪndʒ ˌmɑːkɪt/ *noun* dealings in foreign
currencies

foreign exchange reserves /ˌfɒrɪn
ɪks'tʃeɪndʒ rɪˌzɜːvz/ *plural noun* foreign
money held by a government to support its
own currency and pay its debts

foreign exchange transfer /ˌfɒrɪn ɪks
'tʃeɪndʒ ˌtrænsfɜː/ *noun* the sending of
money from one country to another

foreign goods /ˌfɒrɪn 'ɡʊdz/ *plural noun*
goods produced in other countries

foreign investments /ˌfɒrɪn ɪn
'vestmənts/ *plural noun* money invested in
other countries

foreign money order /ˌfɒrɪn 'mʌni
ˌɔːdə/ *noun* money order in a foreign currency which is payable to someone living in
a foreign country

Foreign Office /'fɒrɪn ˌɒfɪs/, **Foreign
and Commonwealth Office** /ˌfɒrɪn ən
ˌkɒmənwelθ 'ɒfɪs/ *noun* the British government department dealing with relations
with other countries

foreign policy /ˌfɒrɪn 'pɒlisi/ *noun* a
policy followed by a country when dealing
with other countries

foreign rights /ˌfɒrɪn 'raɪtz/ *plural noun*
legal entitlement to sell something in a foreign country

Foreign Service /ˌfɒrɪn 'sɜːvɪs/ *noun* a
government department responsible for a
country's representation in other countries

foreign trade /ˌfɒrɪn 'treɪd/ *noun* trade
with other countries

foreman of the jury /ˌfɔːmən əv ðə
'dʒʊəri/ *noun* a person elected by the other
jurors, who chairs the meetings of a jury and
pronounces the verdict in court afterwards

forensic /fə'rensɪk/ *adjective* referring to
courts, the law, pleading a case or punishing
crime

forensic accountant /fəˌrenzɪk ə
'kauntənt/ *noun* someone who analyses
accounting evidence ○ *The forensic
accountant demonstrated that the money
entered the defendant's bank account.*

forensic accounting /fəˌrensɪk ə
'kauntɪŋ/ *noun* analysis of accounting evidence for the purposes of investigation and
legal proceedings

forensic evidence /fəˌrenzɪk 'evɪdəns/
noun legally-admissible evidence from

forensic science, such as DNA identification or fingerprints

forensic medicine /fəˌrensɪk
'med(ə)s(ə)n/ *noun* medical science concerned with solving crimes against people

forensic science /fəˌrensɪk 'saɪəns/
noun science used in solving legal problems
and criminal cases

foresee /fɔː'siː/ *verb* to guess or assess
correctly what is going to happen in the
future (NOTE: **foreseeing – foresaw – has
foreseen**)

foreseeability /fɔːˌsiːə'bɪlɪti/ *noun* the
likelihood that an event could be reasonably
predicted to happen

foreseeability test /fɔːˌsiːə'bɪliti ˌtest/
noun a test for calculating liability on the
part of a person who should have foreseen
the consequences of his or her action, especially in cases of negligence

forfeit /'fɔːfɪt/ *noun* the removal of something as a punishment □ **to be declared forfeit** to be taken away in punishment for
some crime ○ *The goods were declared forfeit.* ■ *verb* to have something taken away as
a punishment □ **to forfeit a deposit** to lose
a deposit because you have decided not to
buy the item

forfeit clause /'fɔːfɪt klɔːz/ *noun* a
clause in a contract which says that goods or
a deposit will be forfeited if the contract is
not obeyed

forfeiture /'fɔːfɪtʃə/ *noun* the act of for-
feiting a property or a right

forfeiture rule /'fɔːfɪtʃə ruːl/ *noun* the
unwritten rule that someone who has unlawfully killed another person should not benefit from the dead person's will

forge /fɔːdʒ/ *verb* to copy something such
as a document or banknote illegally to use
as if it were real ○ *He tried to enter the
country with forged documents.* ○ *She
wanted to pay the bill with a forged £10
note.*

forgery /'fɔːdʒəri/ *noun* **1.** the crime of
making an illegal copy of something such as
a document or banknote to use as if it were
real ○ *He was sent to prison for forgery.* **2.**
an illegal copy ○ *The signature was proved
to be a forgery.*

forgery and uttering /ˌfɔːdʒəri ən
'ʌtərɪŋ/ *noun* the notifiable offence of forg-
ing and then using an official document
such as a prescription for drugs

fori ♦ **lex fori**

form /fɔːm/ *noun* an official printed piece of paper with blank spaces which have to be filled in with information ○ *a customs declaration form* ○ *a pad of order forms* ○ *You have to fill in form A20.*

forma /ˈfɔːmə/ ♦ **pro forma**

formal /ˈfɔːm(ə)l/ *adjective* clearly and legally written ○ *to make a formal application* ○ *to send a formal order*

formality /fɔːˈmælɪti/ *noun* a formal procedure, thing which has to be done to obey the law or because it is the custom ○ *The chairman dispensed with the formality of reading the minutes.*

formally /ˈfɔːməli/ *adverb* in a formal way ○ *We have formally applied for planning permission for the new shopping precinct.*

form of words /ˌfɔːm əv ˈwɜːdz/ *plural noun* words correctly laid out for a legal document

forthwith /fɔːθˈwɪθ/ *adverb* immediately

fortiori ♦ **a fortiori**

forum /ˈfɔːrəm/ *noun* a place where matters are discussed or examined ○ *The magistrates' court is not the appropriate forum for this application.*

forward /ˈfɔːwəd/ *adverb* **1.** □ **to date an invoice forward** to put a later date than the present one on an invoice **2.** □ **to buy forward** to buy foreign currency, gold or commodities before you need them, in order to be certain of the exchange rate □ **to sell forward** to sell foreign currency, commodities, etc., for delivery at a later date **3.** □ **balance brought forward** the balance which is entered in an account at the end of a period or page and is then taken to be the starting point of the next period or page ■ *verb* □ **to forward something to someone** to send something to someone □ **please forward** words written on an envelope, asking the person receiving it to send it on to the person whose name is written on it

foster /ˈfɒstə/ *verb* to look after and bring up a child who is not your own

foster child /ˈfɒstə tʃaɪld/ *noun* a child who is cared for by someone other than its natural or adopted parents

foster home /ˈfɒstə həʊm/ *noun* a home where a foster child is brought up

foster parent /ˌfɒstə ˈmʌðə/ *noun* a woman or man who looks after a child and brings it up

foul bill of lading /ˌfaʊl bɪl əv ˈleɪdɪŋ/ *noun* a bill of lading which says that the goods were in bad condition when received by the shipper

419 fraud /ˌfɔː wʌn ˈnaɪn ˌfrɔːd/ *noun* an e-mail scam in which the victim is convinced to pay administrative costs for a forthcoming business opportunity, which never materialises (NOTE: The term is named after the section of the Nigerian penal code which outlaws it.)

fourth quarter /ˌfɔːθ ˈkwɔːtə/ *noun* a period of three months from October to the end of the year ○ *The instalments are payable at the end of each quarter.* ○ *The first quarter's rent is payable in advance.*

frais ♦ **sans frais**

frame /freɪm/ *verb* to arrange for someone to appear to be guilty (*informal*) □ **to be framed** to be innocent, but be in a situation which has been arranged in such a way that you appear guilty

franchise /ˈfræntʃaɪz/ *noun* **1.** a right granted to someone to do something, especially the right to vote in local or general elections **2.** a licence to trade using a brand name and paying a royalty for it ○ *He has bought a printing franchise* or *a hot dog franchise.* ■ *verb* to sell licences for people to trade using a brand name and paying a royalty ○ *His sandwich bar was so successful that he decided to franchise it.*

franchisee /ˌfræntʃaɪˈziː/ *noun* somebody who runs a franchise

franchiser /ˈfræntʃaɪzə/ *noun* somebody who licenses a franchise

franchising /ˈfræntʃaɪzɪŋ/ *noun* the act of selling a licence to trade as a franchise ○ *He runs his sandwich chain as a franchising operation.*

franchisor /ˈfræntʃaɪzə/ *noun* same as **franchiser**

franco /ˈfræŋkəʊ/ *adverb* free

fraud /frɔːd/ *noun* **1.** harming someone by obtaining their property or money after making them believe something which is not true ○ *He got possession of the property by fraud.* ○ *He was accused of frauds relating to foreign currency.* □ **to obtain money by fraud** to obtain money by saying or doing something to cheat someone **2.** the act of deceiving someone in order to make money ○ *She was convicted of a series of frauds against insurance companies.*

Fraud Squad /ˈfrɔːd skwɒd/ *noun* a department of a police force which deals with cases of fraud

fraudster /ˈfrɔːdstə/ *noun* a criminal who obtains money or other advantage by deceiving someone

fraudulent /ˈfrɔːdjʊlənt/ *adjective* dishonest, aiming to deceive people

fraudulent conveyance /ˌfrɔːdjʊlənt kənˈveɪəns/ *noun* an act of putting a property into someone else's possession to avoid it being seized to pay creditors

fraudulently /ˈfrɔːdjʊləntli/ *adverb* not honestly ○ *goods imported fraudulently*

fraudulent misrepresentation /ˌfrɔːdjʊlənt mɪsˌreprɪzenˈteɪʃ(ə)n/ *noun* a false statement made to deceive someone, or persuade someone to enter into a contract

fraudulent preference /ˌfrɔːdjʊlənt ˈpref(ə)rəns/ *noun* payment made by an insolvent company to a particular creditor in preference to other creditors

fraudulent trading /ˌfrɔːdjʊlənt ˈtreɪdɪŋ/ *noun* the activity of carrying on the business of a company, knowing that the company is insolvent

fraudulent transaction /ˌfrɔːdjʊlənt trænˈzækʃən/ *noun* a transaction which aims to cheat someone

free /friː/ *adjective, adverb* **1.** not costing any money ○ *He was given a free ticket to the exhibition.* ○ *The price includes free delivery.* ○ *Goods are delivered free.* □ **free of charge** with no payment to be made **2.** not in prison □ **to set someone free** to let someone leave prison ○ *The crowd attacked the police station and set the three prisoners free.* **3.** with no restrictions □ **free of tax, tax-free** with no tax having to be paid □ **free of duty, duty-free** with no duty to be paid **4.** not occupied ○ *Are there any tables free in the restaurant?* ○ *The solicitor will be free in a few minutes.* ○ *The hearing was delayed because there was no courtroom free.* ■ *verb* to release someone from a responsibility or from prison ○ *Will the new law free owners from responsibility to their tenants?* ○ *The new president freed all political prisoners.*

free circulation of goods /ˌfriː ˌsɜːkjʊ ˈleɪʃ(ə)n əv gʊdz/ *plural noun* free movement of goods from one country to another without import quotas or other restrictions

free collective bargaining /ˌfriː kə ˌlektɪv ˈbɑːgɪnɪŋ/ *noun* negotiations between employers and workers' representatives over wages and conditions

free competition /ˌfriː ˌkɒmpəˈtɪʃ(ə)n/ *noun* the situation of being free to compete without government interference

free currency /ˌfriː ˈkʌrənsi/ *noun* a currency which a government allows to be bought or sold without restriction

freedom /ˈfriːdəm/ *noun* **1.** not being held in custody ○ *The president gave the accused man his freedom.* **2.** the ability to do something without restriction

freedom of assembly /ˌfriːdəm əv ə ˈsembli/ *noun* the right of being able to meet other people in a group without being afraid of prosecution, provided that you do not break the law

freedom of association /ˌfriːdəm əv əsəʊsiˈeɪʃ(ə)n/ *noun* the right of being able to join together in a group with other people without being afraid of prosecution, provided that you do not break the law

freedom of information /ˌfriːdəm əv ˌɪnfəˈmeɪʃ(ə)n/ *noun* the principle of allowing citizens access to information held by government bodies and other bodies, enshrined in the Freedom of Information Act 2000

freedom of movement /ˌfriːdəm əv ˈmuːvmənt/ *noun* (*in the EU*) the fundamental right of citizens within the EU to be able to move to other EU countries to seek work

COMMENT: Freedom of movement has been extended to three types of people who are not economically active: students, retired people and people with sufficient private income.

freedom of speech /ˌfriːdəm əv ˈspiːtʃ/ *noun* the right of being able to say what you want without being afraid of prosecution, provided that you do not break the law

freedom of the press /ˌfriːdəm əv ðə ˈpres/ *noun* the right of being able to write and publish what you wish in a newspaper, or on radio or TV, without being afraid of prosecution, provided that you do not break the law

freedom of thought, conscience and religion /ˌfriːdəm əv ˌθɔːt ˌkɒnʃəns ən rɪˈlɪdʒən/ *noun* the absolute right of the individual to hold whatsoever belief or religion, without restriction

COMMENT: It is found in Article 9 of the European Convention of Human Rights and was introduced into UK law by the Human Rights Act 1998. The freedom to manifest these beliefs is subject to limitations, which are imposed if it is considered to be interfering with the public interest.

free for adoption /ˌfriː fər əˈdɒpʃ(ə)n/ *adjective* describes a child whose parents or guardians have given up their parental rights or had them removed by the court

freehold /'fri:həʊld/ *noun* the absolute right to hold land or property for an unlimited time without paying rent

freeholder /'fri:həʊldə/ *noun* somebody who holds a freehold property

freehold property /'fri:həʊld ˌprɒpəti/ *noun* property which the owner holds in freehold

free movement /ˌfri: 'mu:vmənt/ *noun* same as **freedom of movement**

free on board /ˌfri: ɒn 'bɔ:d/ *noun US* **1.** an international contract whereby the seller promises to deliver goods on board ship and notify the buyer of delivery, and the buyer arranges freight, pays the shipping cost and takes the risk once the goods have passed onto the ship **2.** a contract for sale whereby the price includes all the seller's costs until the goods are delivered to a certain place ▸ abbreviation **f.o.b.**

free pardon /ˌfri: 'pɑ:d(ə)n/ *noun* a pardon given to a convicted person where both the sentence and conviction are recorded as void

freeware /'fri:weə/ *noun* software which is subject to copyright restrictions, but is available free of charge

freeze /fri:z/ *verb* to order a person not to move money or sell assets ○ *The court ordered the company's bank account to be frozen.*

freezing injunction /ˌfri:zɪŋ ɪn 'dʒʌŋkʃən/ *noun* a court order to freeze the assets of a defendant or of a person who has gone overseas or of a company based overseas to prevent them being taken out of the country (NOTE: The injunction can apply to assets within the jurisdiction of the court, or on a worldwide basis. Since the introduction of the Civil Procedure Rules, this term has replaced **Mareva injunction.**)

freight charges /'freɪt ˌtʃɑ:dʒɪz/ *plural noun* money charged for carrying goods

fresh pursuit /ˌfreʃ pə'sju:t/ *noun* the act of chasing a thief, etc., to get back what has been stolen

friend /frend/ ♦ **litigation friend, next friend**

frisk /frɪsk/ *verb* to search someone by passing your hands over his or her clothes to see if that person is carrying a weapon or a package

frivolous complaint /ˌfrɪvələs kəm 'pleɪnt/ *noun* a complaint or action which is not brought for a serious reason

frolic /'frɒlɪk/ *noun* □ **frolic of his own** a situation where an employee does damage outside the normal course of employment, for which his or her employer cannot be held vicariously liable

front /frʌnt/ *noun* an organisation or company which serves to hide criminal activity ○ *His ice-cream shop was just a front for an extortion racket.*

front organisation /'frʌnt ˌɔ:gənaɪzeɪʃ(ə)n/ *noun* an organisation which appears to be neutral, but is in fact an active supporter of a political party or is actively engaged in illegal trade

frozen /'frəʊz(ə)n/ ♦ **freeze**

frozen assets /ˌfrəʊz(ə)n 'æsets/ *plural noun* assets of a company which cannot be sold because someone has a claim against them

frustrate /frʌ'streɪt/ *verb* to prevent something, especially the terms of a contract, being fulfilled

frustration /frʌ'streɪʃ(ə)n/ *noun* a situation where the terms of a contract cannot possibly be fulfilled, e.g. when the contract requires the use of something which is destroyed

FSMA *abbreviation* Financial Services and Markets Act 2000

fugitive /'fju:dʒɪtɪv/ *noun* a person who has done something illegal and is trying to avoid being found by the police

fugitive offender /ˌfju:dʒɪtɪv ə'fendə/ *noun* somebody running away from the police who, if he or she is caught, is sent back to the place where the offence was committed

fulfil /fʊl'fɪl/ *verb* to do everything which is promised in a contract ○ *The company has fulfilled all the terms of the agreement.*

full costs /ˌfʊl 'kɒsts/ *plural noun* **1.** all the legal costs involved in pursuing or defending a charge ○ *The judge found against the plaintiff and ordered him to pay full costs.* **2.** all the costs of manufacturing a product, including both fixed and variable costs

full cover /ˌfʊl 'kʌvə/ *noun* insurance against all types of risk

full payment /ˌfʊl 'peɪmənt/ *noun* payment for all money owed

full rate /ˌfʊl 'reɪt/ *noun* full charge, with no reductions

full repairing lease /ˌfʊl rɪˈpeərɪŋ ˌliːs/ *noun* a lease where the tenant has to pay for all repairs to the property

full title /ˌfʊl ˈtaɪt(ə)l/ *noun* the complete title of an Act of Parliament

full trial /ˌfʊl ˈtraɪəl/ *noun* a properly organised trial according to the correct procedure

functus officio /ˌfʌnktəs ɒˈfɪʃiəʊ/ *phrase* a Latin phrase meaning 'no longer having power or jurisdiction' because the power has been exercised ○ *The justices' clerk asserted that the justices were functi officio.* (NOTE: The plural is **functi officio**.)

fund /fʌnd/ *noun* □ **to convert funds to one's own use** to use someone else's money for yourself

fundamental breach /ˌfʌndəˈment(ə)l briːtʃ/ *noun* a breach of an essential or basic term of a contract by one party, entitling the other party to treat the contract as terminated

fund pool /ˈfʌnd puːl/ *noun* a pool of money which must be set aside in an insolvency case for the benefit of ordinary creditors

funds /fʌndz/ *plural noun* money available for a purpose

Funeral Payment /ˈfjuːnərəl ˌpeɪmənt/ *noun* a loan given by the Government to someone on income support who has to arrange a funeral for a close relative or friend, repayable out of the deceased's estate (NOTE: This is made out of the Government's **Social Fund**.)

fungible goods /ˈfʌndʒəb(ə)l gʊdz/, **fungibles** *plural noun* goods which are replaceable or substitutable for goods of the same value

furandi ♦ **animus furandi**

furnished lettings /ˌfɜːnɪʃt ˈletɪŋs/ *noun* furnished property to let

further information /ˌfɜːðər ˌɪnfə ˈmeɪʃ(ə)n/ *noun* a request made by a party through the court for another party to provide more details which will help clarify the case (NOTE: The second party may refuse to respond for various reasons. Since the introduction of the Civil Procedure Rules, this term has replaced **interrogatories**.)

future estate /ˌfjuːtʃə ɪˈsteɪt/ *noun* an old term for the possession and enjoyment of an estate at some time in the future

future interest /ˌfjuːtʃə ˈɪntrəst/ *noun* an interest in property which will be enjoyed in the future

fuzz /fʌz/ *noun* the police (*slang*)

G

gag /gæg/ *verb* to try to stop someone talking or writing ○ *The government was accused of using the Official Secrets Act as a means of gagging the press.*

gagging order /'gægɪŋ ˌɔːdə/ *noun* an order preventing a piece of information from being published if it is against the law, particularly human rights laws

gain /geɪn/ *noun* an increase in profit, price or value □ **for financial gain** in order to make money

gallery /'gæləri/ *noun* the seats above and around the benches in the House of Commons and House of Lords, where the public and journalists sit □ **to clear the galleries** to ask for all visitors to leave the Chamber

gallows /'gæləʊz/ *plural noun* a wooden support from which criminals are executed by hanging

game licence /ˌgeɪm 'laɪs(ə)ns/ *noun* an official permit which allows someone to sell game

game of chance /ˌgeɪm əv 'tʃɑːns/ *noun* a game such as roulette where the result depends on luck

gaming licence /'geɪmɪŋ ˌlaɪs(ə)ns/ *noun* an official permit which allows someone or a club to organise games of chance

gang /gæŋ/ *noun* a group of criminals working together ○ *a drugs gang* ○ *a gang of jewel thieves*

gangland /'gæŋlænd/ *noun* all gangs considered as a group □ **a gangland murder** the murder of a gangster by another gangster

gangster /'gæŋstə/ *noun* somebody who is a member of a gang of criminals ○ *The police shot three gangsters in the bank raid.*

gaol /dʒeɪl/ *noun* a prison. ◊ **jail** ■ *verb* to put someone in prison

gaoler /'dʒeɪlə/ *noun* somebody who works in a prison or who is in charge of a prison. ◊ **jailer**

garnish /'gɑːnɪʃ/ *verb* to tell a debtor to pay his or her debts, not to the creditor, but to a creditor of the creditor who has a judgment

garnishee proceedings /ˌgɑːniːˈʃiː prəˌsiːdɪŋz/ *noun* a court proceedings against a debtor leading to a garnishee order

garnishment /'gɑːnɪʃmənt/ *noun* a legal summons or warning concerning the taking of a debtor's property or wages to satisfy a debt

gas chamber /'gæs ˌtʃeɪmbə/ *noun* a room in which a convicted prisoner is executed by poisonous gas

gavel /'gæv(ə)l/ *noun* a small wooden hammer used by a judge to call for order or to mark the conclusion of a trial

gazump /gə'zʌmp/ *verb* □ **to be gazumped** to have your offer to buy a house cancelled at a late stage because someone offered more money before exchange of contracts

gazumping /gə'zʌmpɪŋ/ *noun* **1.** (*of a buyer*) the act of offering more money for a house than another buyer has done, so as to be sure of buying it **2.** the act of removing a house from a sale which has been agreed, so as to accept a higher offer

GBH *abbreviation* grievous bodily harm

gearing /'gɪərɪŋ/ *noun* the ratio of a company's debt to its equity

gender reassignment /'dʒendə riːə ˌsaɪnmənt/ *noun* surgery and hormonal treatments which physically change a person's gender

COMMENT: Persons undergoing gender reassignment have the right to apply for legal recognition of their acquired gender under the Gender Recognition Act of 2004.

Gender Recognition Act /ˌdʒendə ˌrekəg'nɪʃ(ə)n ˌækt/ *noun* an Act which gives persons who have undergone gender reassignment the right to apply for legal recognition of this

Gender Recognition Certificate /ˌdʒendə ˌrekəgˈnɪʃ(ə)n səˌtɪfɪkət/ *noun* a certificate which constitutes legal recognition of a person's acquired gender

general amnesty /ˌdʒen(ə)rəl ˈæmnəsti/ *noun* a pardon granted to all prisoners

general damages /ˌdʒen(ə)rəl ˈdæmɪdʒɪz/ *plural noun* damages awarded by court to compensate for a loss which cannot be calculated, e.g. an injury

general lien /ˌdʒen(ə)rəl ˈliːən/ *noun* the holding of goods or property until a debt has been paid

general office /ˈdʒen(ə)rəl ˌɒfɪs/ *noun* the main administrative office of a company

Geneva Convention /dʒɪˌniːvə kən ˈvenʃ(ə)n/ *noun* an international treaty relating to immigration and the granting of asylum

Geneva Conventions for the Protection of Victims of War /dʒɪˌniːvə kən ˌvenʃ(ə)nz fə ðə prəˌtekʃ(ə)n əv ˈvɪktɪmz/ *noun* an international treaty relating to the treatment of civilians and other non-combatants

Geneva Conventions on Negotiable Instruments /dʒɪˌniːvə kənˌvenʃ(ə)nz ɒn nɪˌgəʊʃiəb(ə)l ˈɪnstrʊmənts/ *noun* an international treaty relating to international bills of exchange, cheques, letters of credit, etc.

gentleman's agreement /ˈdʒent(ə)lmənz əˌgriːmənt/, **gentlemen's agreement** *US noun* a verbal agreement between two parties who trust each other (NOTE: A gentleman's agreement is not usually enforceable by law.)

genuine /ˈdʒenjuɪn/ *adjective* true or real ○ *a genuine Picasso* ○ *a genuine leather purse* □ **the genuine article** the real thing, not an imitation

genuine dispute /ˌdʒenjuɪn dɪˈspjuːt/ *noun* a real conflict between parties ○ *The ECJ refused to hear the reference because it considered there was no genuine dispute between the parties.*

genuineness /ˈdʒenjuɪnnəs/ *noun* the fact of not being an imitation

genuine occupational requirement /ˌdʒenjuɪn ˌɒkjʊpeɪʃ(ə)nəl rɪˈkaɪəmənt/ *noun* a quality which a person would need to be able to do a job. Abbreviation **GOR**

COMMENT: It can be used as a defence against allegations of discrimination. For example, for a person employed to model women's clothes, the employer could argue

that being female is a genuine occupational requirement for the job.

genuine purchaser /ˌdʒenjuɪn ˈpɜːtʃɪsə/ *noun* someone who is really interested in buying

geographic profiling /dʒiːəˌɡræfɪk ˈprəʊfaɪlɪŋ/ *noun* the science of predicting where a criminal lives, based on where and when the crimes were committed, based on the principle that most crimes are carried out relatively locally

geoprofiling /ˈdʒiːəʊˌprəʊfaɪlɪŋ/ *noun* same as **geographic profiling**

germane /dʒɜːˈmeɪn/ *adjective* referring to, or relevant to ○ *The argument is not germane to the motion.*

get /get/, **gett** *noun* a divorce according to Jewish religious custom, where the husband agrees to a divorce which his wife has requested

gift /ɡɪft/ *noun* a transfer of property made from one person to another for no charge ■ *verb* to give

COMMENT: A gift is irrevocable.

gift inter vivos /ˌɡɪft ɪntə ˈviːvəʊs/ *noun* a present given by a living person to another living person

Gillette defence /dʒɪˈlet dɪˌfens/ *noun* a defence against a claim for infringement of patent, by which the defendant claims that they were using the process before it was patented

COMMENT: Called after the case of *Gillette v. Anglo American Trading.*

gloss /ɡlɒs/ *noun* **1.** a note which explains or gives a meaning to a word or phrase **2.** an interpretation given to a word or phrase ■ *verb* □ **to gloss over** to cover up a mistake or fault ○ *The report glosses over the errors made by the officials in the department.*

godfather /ˈɡɒdfɑːðə/ *noun* a Mafia boss (*slang*)

going concern /ˌɡəʊɪŋ kənˈsɜːn/ *noun* a business which is actively trading, without threat of liquidation

going equipped for stealing /ˌɡəʊɪŋ ɪ ˌkwɪpd fə ˈstiːlɪŋ/ *noun* the notifiable offence of carrying tools which could be used for burglary

golden rule /ˌɡəʊld(ə)n ˈruːl/ *noun* a rule that when interpreting a statute, the court should interpret the wording of the statute to give the closest effect to the one Parliament intended when passing the law

good behaviour /ˌɡʊd bɪˈheɪvjə/ *noun* a way of behaving that is peaceful and lawful ○ *The magistrates bound him over to be of good behaviour.* ○ *She was sentenced to four years in prison, but was released early for good behaviour.*

good cause /ˌgʊd ˈkɔːz/ *noun* a reason which is accepted in law ○ *The court asked the accused to show good cause why he should not be sent to prison.* (NOTE: not used with 'the')

good consideration /gʊd kənˌsɪdəˈreɪʃ(ə)n/ *noun* consideration with relation to a contract which is acceptable

COMMENT: For consideration to be considered 'good', it must a) have an economic value; b) have not yet been paid or completed at the time of making the contract; and c) not be an already-existing contractual or legal obligation.

good faith /ˌgʊd ˈfeɪθ/ *noun* general honesty □ **in good faith** in an honest way □ **to act in good faith** to act honestly □ **to buy something in good faith** to buy something honestly, in the course of an honest transaction ○ *He bought the car in good faith, not knowing that it had been stolen.*

goods /gʊdz/ *plural noun* items which can be moved and are for sale □ **goods (held) in bond** goods held by customs until duty has been paid

goods and chattels /ˌgʊdz ən ˈtʃæt(ə)lz/ *plural noun* movable property

goods train /ˈgʊdz treɪn/ *noun* a train for carrying freight

good title /ˌgʊd ˈtaɪt(ə)l/ *noun* a title to a property which gives the owner full rights of ownership

goodwill /gʊdˈwɪl/ *noun* the good reputation of a business and its contacts with its customers, e.g. the name of the product which it sells or its popular appeal to customers ○ *She paid £10,000 for the goodwill of the shop and £4,000 for the stock.*

COMMENT: Goodwill can include the trading reputation, the patents, the trade names used, the value of a 'good site', etc., and is very difficult to establish accurately. It is an intangible asset, and so is not shown as an asset in a company's accounts, unless it figures as part of the purchase price paid when acquiring another company.

GOR *abbreviation* genuine occupational requirement

governing law /ˌgʌvənɪŋ ˈlɔː/ *noun* the law which will determine how the parties' rights and obligations under a contract should be interpreted ○ *The governing law of the contract is the law of England.*

government contractor /ˌgʌv(ə)nmənt kənˈtræktə/ *noun* a company which supplies goods or services to the government on contract

government-controlled /ˈgʌv(ə)nmənt kənˌtrəʊld/ *noun* ruled by a government

government economic indicators /ˌgʌv(ə)nmənt ˌiːkənɒmɪk ˈɪndɪkeɪtəz/ *plural noun* figures which show how the country's economy is going to perform in the short or long term

government-regulated price /ˌgʌv(ə)nmənt ˌregjʊleɪtɪd ˈpraɪs/ *noun* a price which is imposed by the government

gown /gaʊn/ *noun* a long black item of clothing worn by a lawyer, judge, etc., over normal clothes when appearing in court. ◊ **silk**

grace /greɪs/ *noun* a favour shown by granting a delay □ **period of grace** an amount of time allowed before a debt must be paid □ **two weeks' grace** two weeks allowed before a debt must be paid

graduated pension scheme /ˌgrædʒueɪtɪd ˈpenʃən skiːm/ *noun* a pension scheme where the benefit is calculated as a percentage of the salary of each person in the scheme

graft /grɑːft/ *noun* the corruption of officials (*informal*)

grand jury /ˌgrænd ˈdʒʊri/ *noun US* a group of 12–24 jurors who meet before a trial to decide if an indictment should be issued to start criminal proceedings

grand larceny /ˌgrænd ˈlɑːs(ə)ni/ *noun US* the theft of goods valued at more than a specified price

grant /grɑːnt/ *noun* **1.** the act of giving something to someone permanently or temporarily by a written document, where the object itself cannot be physically transferred ○ *The government made a grant of land to settlers.* **2.** a legal document recording a transaction in which something is transferred from one person to another **3.** money given by the government, local authority or other organisation to help pay for something ○ *The institute has a government grant to cover the cost of the development programme.* ○ *Many charities give grants for educational projects.* ■ *verb* to agree to give someone something or allow someone to do something ○ *The local authority granted the company an interest-free loan to start up the new factory.* ○ *He was granted parole.* ○ *The government*

*granted an amnesty to all political prison-
ers.*

grant-aided scheme /ˌɡrɑːnt ˈeɪdɪd
skiːm/ *noun* a scheme which is backed by
funds from the government

grantee /ɡrɑːnˈtiː/ *noun* somebody who
is assigned an interest in a property or who
receives a grant

grant-in-aid /ˌɡrɑːnt ɪn ˈeɪd/ *noun*
money given by central government to local
government to help pay for a project

grant of letters of administration
/ˌɡrɑːnt əv ˌletəz əv ədˌmɪnɪˈstreɪʃ(ə)n/
noun the giving of documents to adminis-
trators to enable them to administer the
estate of a dead person who has not made a
will

grant of probate /ˌɡrɑːnt əv ˈprəʊbeɪt/
noun an official document proving that a
will is genuine, given to the executors so
that they can act on the terms of the will

grantor /ɡrɑːnˈtɔː/ *noun* a person who
assigns an interest in a property, especially
to a lender, or who makes a grant

grass /ɡrɑːs/ *noun* a criminal who gives
information to the police about other criminals. ◊ **supergrass** ■ *verb* □ **to grass on
someone** to give information to the police
about someone

grass roots /ˌɡrɑːs ˈruːts/ *noun* the ordinary members of society or of a political
party ○ *He wants to appeal to the grass
roots.* ■ *adjective* **grass-roots** referring to
the grass roots ○ *What is the grass-roots
reaction to the constitutional changes?* ○
*The party has considerable support at
grass-roots level.*

grata ♦ **persona non grata**

gratia ♦ **ex gratia**

gratis /ˈɡrɑːtɪs/ *adverb* not costing anything, or without paying anything ○ *We got
into the exhibition gratis.*

gratuitous /ɡrəˈtjuːɪtəs/ *adjective* **1.**
without justifiable cause ○ *scenes containing gratuitous sex and violence* **2.** without
money being offered

gratuitous promise /ɡrəˌtjuːɪtəs
ˈprɒmɪs/ *noun* a promise that cannot be
enforced because no money has been
involved

Gray's Inn /ˌɡreɪz ˈɪn/ *noun* one of the
four Inns of Court in London

GRC *abbreviation* Gender Recognition
Certificate

Great Seal /ˌɡreɪt ˈsiːl/ *noun* a seal kept
by the Lord Chancellor, used for sealing

important public documents on behalf of
the Queen

Green Book /ˌɡriːn ˈbʊk/ *noun* the book
of procedural rules of the County Courts

green card /ˌɡriːn ˈkɑːd/ *noun* a registration card for a non-US citizen going to live
permanently in the USA

green form /ˈɡriːn fɔːm/ *noun* formerly,
the form upon which an application for both
legal advice and financial assistance (legal
aid) could be made □ **the green form
scheme** a scheme where a solicitor will give
advice to someone free of charge or at a
reduced rate, if the client has filled in the
green form

greenhouse gas /ˈɡriːnhaʊs ɡæs/ *noun*
a gas that contributes to the undesirable
warming of the Earth's atmosphere. ◊ **Kyoto
Agreement**

Green Paper /ˌɡriːn ˈpeɪpə/ *noun* a
report from the British government on proposals for a new law to be discussed in Parliament

grey economy /ˈɡreɪ ɪˌkɒnəmi/ *noun*
businesses operating semi-legally, e.g.
staffed by illegal immigrants or immigrants
who are not permitted to work

grievance /ˈɡriːv(ə)ns/ *noun* a complaint
made by an employee to the employers

grievous bodily harm /ˌɡriːvəs ˈbɒdɪli
hɑːm/ *noun* the crime of causing serious
physical injury to someone. Abbreviation
GBH

grooming /ˈɡruːmɪŋ/ *noun* the act of
establishing a relationship with a child for
the purposes of sexual contact

gross /ɡrəʊs/ *adjective* **1.** (*of a sum of
money*) without deductions **2.** serious

gross earnings /ˌɡrəʊs ˈɜːnɪŋz/ *noun*
total earnings before tax and other deductions

gross indecency /ˌɡrəʊs ɪnˈdiːs(ə)nsi/
noun the former offence of having unlawful
sexual contact between men or with a child,
which falls short of full sexual intercourse
(NOTE: It was repealed as an offence by the
Sexual Offences Act 2003, along with **buggery**.)

gross negligence /ˌɡrəʊs ˈneɡlɪdʒəns/
noun the act showing very serious neglect
of duty towards other people

gross receipts /ˌɡrəʊs rɪˈsiːts/ *plural
noun* the total amount of money received
before expenses are deducted

gross weight /ˌɡrəʊs ˈweɪt/ *noun* the
weight of both the container and its contents

ground landlord /ˈɡraʊnd ˌlændlɔːd/ noun a person or company which owns the freehold of a property which is then leased and subleased

ground lease /ˈɡraʊnd liːs/ noun the first lease on a freehold building

ground rent /ˈɡraʊnd rent/ noun rent paid by a lessee to the ground landlord. Also called **rentcharge**

grounds /ɡraʊndz/ plural noun basic reasons ○ Does he have good grounds for complaint? ○ There are no grounds on which we can be sued. ○ What are the grounds for the claim for damages?

guarantee /ˌɡærənˈtiː/ noun **1.** a legal document which promises that an item purchased is of good quality and will work properly ○ certificate of guarantee or guarantee certificate ○ The guarantee lasts for two years. ○ The dishwasher is sold with a two-year guarantee. □ **to be under guarantee** to be still covered by the maker's certificate of guarantee **2.** a promise made by someone that they will do something such as pay another person's debts if the other person fails to do it. Compare **indemnity** (NOTE: In English law, a guarantee must usually be in writing; the person making a guarantee is secondarily liable if the person who is primarily liable defaults.) **3.** something given as a security ○ to leave share certificates as a guarantee ■ verb to give a promise that something will happen □ **to guarantee a debt** to promise that you will pay a debt incurred by someone else if that person fails to pay it □ **to guarantee an associated company** to promise that an associate company will pay its debts □ **to guarantee a bill of exchange** to promise to pay a bill □ **to be guaranteed for twelve months** to be guaranteed to work well for twelve months, with a promise of repairs free of charge if it breaks down within that period

guarantor /ˌɡærənˈtɔː/ noun somebody who guarantees a debt □ **to stand guarantor for someone** to promise to pay someone's debts

guaranty /ˈɡær(ə)ntiː/ noun US same as **guarantee**

guard /ɡɑːd/ noun **1.** somebody whose job is to protect people or property ○ There were three guards on duty at the door of the bank or three bank guards were on duty. ○ The prisoner was shot by the guards as he tried to escape. **2.** the state of being protected by a guard ○ The prisoners were brought into the courtroom under armed guard. ■ verb to prevent someone being harmed or from escaping ○ The building is guarded by a fence and ten guard dogs. ○ The prisoners are guarded night and day.

guardian /ˈɡɑːdiən/ noun an adult person or an authority such as the High Court appointed by law to act on behalf of someone such as a child who cannot act on his or her own behalf

guardian ad litem /ˌɡɑːdiən æd ˈliːtəm/ noun somebody who acts on behalf of a minor who is a defendant in a court case

Guardian's Allowance /ˈɡɑːdiənz ə ˌlaʊəns/ noun a payment given by the Government to someone who is the main guardian of a child, but not their natural or adoptive parent (NOTE: The person need not be the child's legal guardian.)

guardianship /ˈɡɑːdiənʃɪp/ noun the state of being a guardian

guardianship order /ˈɡɑːdiənʃɪp ˌɔːdə/ noun a court order appointing a local authority to be the guardian of a child

guerrilla /ɡəˈrɪlə/ noun an armed person who is not a regular soldier who engages in unofficial war ○ The train was attacked by guerrillas.

guidelines /ˈɡaɪdlaɪnz/ plural noun unofficial suggestions from the government or some other body as to how something should be done ○ The government has issued guidelines on increases in wages and prices. ○ The Law Society has issued guidelines to its members on dealing with rape cases. ○ The Secretary of State can issue guidelines for expenditure. ○ The Lord Justice said he was not laying down guidelines for sentencing.

guillotine /ˈɡɪlətiːn/ noun a machine formerly used in France for executing criminals by cutting off their heads ■ verb to execute someone by cutting his or her head off with a guillotine

guilt /ɡɪlt/ noun being guilty, the state of having committed a crime or done some other legal wrong □ **to admit your guilt** to admit that you have committed a crime

guilt by association /ɡɪlt baɪ əˌsəʊsi ˈeɪʃ(ə)n/ noun the presumption that a person is guilty because of his or her connection with a guilty person

guilty /ˈɡɪlti/ adjective **1.** finding after a trial that a person has done something which is against the law ○ He was found guilty of libel. ○ The company was guilty of evading the VAT regulations. □ **to find**

someone guilty, **to return a verdict of guilty, to return a guilty verdict** (*of a judge or jury*) to say at the end of the trial that the accused is guilty **2.** □ **to plead guilty** (*of an accused person*) to say at the beginning of a trial that you did commit the crime of which you are accused □ **to plead not guilty** to say at the beginning of a trial that you did not commit the crime of which you are accused ○ *The accused pleaded not guilty to the charge of murder, but pleaded guilty to the lesser charge of manslaughter.*

gun /gʌn/ *noun* a weapon used for shooting ○ *The police are not allowed to carry guns.* ○ *They shouted to the robbers to drop their guns.*

gun court /'gʌn kɔːt/ *noun US* a court that hears only those cases that deal with gun-related crimes

gun crime /'gʌn kraɪm/ *noun* offences involving firearms

gun down /ˌgʌn 'daʊn/ *verb* to kill someone with a gun ○ *He was gunned down in the street outside his office.* (NOTE: **gunned – gunning**)

gun lobby /'gʌn ˌlɒbi/ *noun* organisations which support the right of the individual to own guns legally

gunman /'gʌnmən/ *noun* a man who carries and uses a gun ○ *The security van was held up by three gunmen.*

gunpoint /'gʌnpɔɪnt/ *noun* □ **at gunpoint** with a gun pointing at you ○ *He was forced at gunpoint to open the safe.*

gunshot /'gʌnʃɒt/ *noun* the result of shooting with a gun ○ *He died of gunshot wounds.*

gypsy /'dʒɪpsi/ *noun* a member of the Roma ethnic group, traditionally nomadic

H

habeas corpus /ˌheɪbiəs ˈkɔːpəs/ *phrase* a Latin phrase meaning 'may you have the body': a legal remedy against being wrongly imprisoned

habendum /hæˈbendəm/ *noun* a section of a conveyance which gives details of how the property is to be assigned to the purchaser, using the words 'to hold'

habitual /həˈbɪtʃuəl/ *adjective* (*of a person*) doing something frequently □ **habitual criminal, habitual offender** a person who has been convicted of a similar crime at least twice before □ **habitual drunkard** somebody who drinks alcohol so frequently that he or she is almost always dangerous or incapable

habitual residence /həˌbɪtʃuəl ˈrezɪd(ə)ns/ *noun* **1.** the fact of living normally in a place **2.** the place where someone normally lives

hack /hæk/ *verb* to gain access illegally to a computer system or program

hacking /ˈhækɪŋ/ *noun* wrongfully gaining access to information stored on a computer, an offence under the Computer Misuse Act 1990

Hague conventions /ˈheɪɡ kənˌvenʃ(ə)nz/ *plural noun* international agreements regarding the definition of war, and the barring of the use of chemical and biological weapons. ◊ **Geneva Convention**

hallmark /ˈhɔːlmɑːk/ *noun* a mark put on gold or silver items to show that the metal is of the correct quality ■ *verb* to put a hallmark on a piece of gold or silver ○ *a hallmarked spoon*

hand /hænd/ *noun* **1.** □ **by hand** using the hands, not a machine □ **to send a letter by hand** to ask someone to carry and deliver a letter personally, not sending it through the post **2.** □ **in hand, on hand** *US* kept in reserve **3.** □ **goods left on hand** goods which have not been sold and are left with the retailer or producer **4.** □ **out of hand** immediately, without taking time to think ○ *The justices dismissed his evidence out of hand.* **5.** □ **to hand** here, present ○ *I have the invoice to hand.* **6.** □ **to change hands** to be sold to a new owner ○ *The shop changed hands for £100,000.*

handcuff /ˈhændkʌf/ *verb* to put handcuffs on someone

handcuffed /ˈhændkʌfd/ *adjective* secured by handcuffs ○ *The accused appeared in court handcuffed to two policemen.*

handcuffs /ˈhændkʌfs/ *plural noun* two metal rings chained together which are locked round the wrists of someone who is being arrested

hand down /ˌhænd ˈdaʊn/ *verb* **1.** to pass property from one generation to another ○ *The house has been handed down from father to son since the 19th century.* **2.** □ **to hand down a verdict** to announce a verdict

handgun /ˈhændɡʌn/ *noun* a small gun which is carried in the hand ○ *The police found six handguns when they searched the car.*

handling /ˈhændlɪŋ/ *noun* the management of a situation or the movement and transfer of goods □ **handling stolen goods** the notifiable offence of receiving or selling things which you know to have been stolen

COMMENT: Handling stolen goods is a more serious crime than theft, and the penalty can be higher.

hand over /ˌhænd ˈəʊvə/ *verb* to pass something to someone ○ *She handed over the documents to the lawyer.*

hands-free kit /ˌhændz ˈfriː ˌkɪt/ *noun* a device with speakers or earphones that makes it possible to use a mobile phone while driving (NOTE: It is currently illegal in the UK to use a hand-held mobile phone while driving.)

hand up /ˌhænd ˈʌp/ *verb* to pass to someone who is in a higher place ○ *The exhibit was handed up to the judge.*

handwriting /'hændraɪtɪŋ/ *noun* **1.** writing produced with a pen or pencil and not with a machine □ **in your own handwriting** written by you by hand **2.** a particular way of committing a crime which identifies a criminal (*slang*)

handwriting expert /,hændraɪtɪŋ 'ekspɜːt/ *noun* somebody who is able to identify somebody by examining his or her handwriting

hang /hæŋ/ *verb* to execute someone by hanging him or her by a rope round the neck. ◊ **hung** (NOTE: **hanging – hanged** (not **hung**).)

hanging /'hæŋɪŋ/ *noun* the act of executing someone by hanging ○ *The hangings took place in front of the prison.*

hangman /'hæŋmən/ *noun* a man who executes criminals by hanging them

Hansard /'hænsɑːd/ *noun* the official published reports of debates that take place in Parliament

COMMENT: Official records of the discussion of a Bill are sometimes used to help interpret the 'spirit' of the law that was passed.

harass /'hærəs, hə'ræs/ *verb* to worry or to bother someone, especially by continually checking up on them

harassment /'hærəsmənt, hə'ræsmənt/ *noun* the action of harassing someone ○ *He complained of police harassment* or *of harassment by the police.*

harassment restraining order /,hærəsmənt rɪ'streɪnɪŋ ,ɔːdə/ *noun* same as **restraining order**

harbour /'hɑːbə/ *verb* to give shelter and protection to a criminal

hard /hɑːd/ *adjective* □ **to drive a hard bargain** to be a difficult negotiator □ **to strike a hard bargain** to agree a deal where the terms are favourable to you

hard bargain /,hɑːd 'bɑːgɪn/ *noun* a bargain with difficult terms

hard cash /,hɑːd 'kæʃ/ *noun* money in notes and coins which is ready at hand ○ *He paid out £100 in hard cash for the chair.*

hardened criminal /,hɑːdənd 'krɪmɪn(ə)l/ *noun* a criminal who has committed many crimes and who will never go straight

hard labour /,hɑːd 'leɪbə/ *noun* formerly, the punishment of sending someone to prison to do hard manual labour

harmonise /'hɑːmənaɪz/, **harmonize** *verb* (*in the EU*) to try to make things such

as tax rates or VAT rates the same in all Member States

hate crime /'heɪt kraɪm/ *noun* criminal behaviour motivated by prejudice or hatred on the grounds of race, ethnicity, religion, gender, sexuality or disability

H-block /'eɪtʃ blɒk/ *noun* a building in a prison built with a central section and two end wings, forming the shape of the letter H

head lease /'hed liːs/ *noun* the first lease given by a freeholder to a tenant

head licence /'hed ,laɪs(ə)ns/ *noun* the first licence given by the owner of a patent or copyright to someone who will use it

headnote /'hednəʊt/ *noun* a note at the beginning of a law report, giving a summary of the case

head of damage /,hed əv 'dæmɪdʒ/ *noun* an item of damage in a pleading or claim

head of government /,hed əv 'gʌv(ə)nmənt/ *noun* the leader of a country's government

heads of agreement /,hedz əv ə 'griːmənt/ *noun* a draft agreement containing the most important points but not all the details

Health and Safety at Work Act /,helθ ən ,seɪfti ət 'wɜːk ,ækt/ *noun* an Act of Parliament which regulates that employers must do to make sure that their employees are kept healthy and safe at work

hear /hɪə/ *verb* **1.** to sense a sound with the ears ○ *You can hear the printer in the next office.* ○ *The traffic makes so much noise that I cannot hear my phone ringing.* **2.** to have a letter or a phone call from someone ○ *We have not heard from them for some time.* ○ *We hope to hear from the lawyers within a few days.* **3.** to listen to the arguments in a court case ○ *The judge heard the case in chambers.* ○ *The case will be heard next month.* ○ *The court has heard the evidence for the defence.* **4.** □ **hear! hear!** words used in a meeting to show that you agree with the person speaking

hearing /'hɪərɪŋ/ *noun* **1.** a case which is being heard by a committee, tribunal or court of law ○ *The hearing about the planning application lasted ten days.* □ **hearing in private** a court case which is heard with no member of the public present **2.** the process of a case being considered by an official body ○ *He asked to be given a hearing by the full council so that he could state his case.*

hearsay evidence /ˌhɪəseɪ ˈevɪd(ə)ns/
noun evidence by a witness who has heard
it from another source, but did not witness
the acts personally

COMMENT: Hearsay evidence may not be
given as much weight by the court as direct
witness evidence. If a party intends to rely
on hearsay evidence, they must serve
notice to that effect.

heavily /ˈhevɪli/ adverb □ **he had to borrow heavily to pay the fine** he had to borrow a lot of money

heavy /ˈhevi/ adjective severe or harsh ○
The looters were given heavy jail sentences.
○ She was sentenced to pay a heavy fine. ■
noun a strong man employed to frighten
people (slang)

heir /eə/ noun somebody who receives or
will receive property when someone dies ○
His heirs split the estate between them.

heir apparent /ˌeər əˈpærənt/ noun an
heir who will certainly inherit if a particular
person dies before him or her

heiress /ˈeəres/ noun a female heir

heirloom /ˈeəluːm/ noun a piece of family
property such as silver, a painting or a jewel
which has been handed down for several
generations ○ The burglars stole some family heirlooms.

heir presumptive /ˌeə prɪˈzʌmptɪv/
noun an heir who will inherit if a person
dies at this moment, but whose inheritance
may be altered in the future

heirs, successors and assigns /ˌeəz
sək ˌsesəz ənd əˈsaɪnz/ plural noun people
who are eligible to profit from a person's
estate on their death

heirs and assigns /ˌeəz sək ˌsesəz ənd
əˈsaɪnz/ plural noun people who profit from
a person's estate on their death according to
the will

heist /haɪst/ noun same as **hold-up**
(slang)

henceforth /hensˈfɔːθ/, **henceforward**
US /hensˈfɔːwəd/ adverb from this time on
○ Henceforth the company shall be known
as 'Balls Plc'.

here- /hɪə/ prefix this time, or this place

hereafter /hɪərˈɑːftə/ adverb from this
time or point on

hereby /hɪəˈbaɪ/ adverb in this way ○ We
hereby revoke the agreement of January 1st
1982.

hereditament /ˌherɪˈdɪtəmənt/ noun
property, including land, belongings and
intellectual rights which form part of a person's estate and can be inherited

hereditary /həˈredɪt(ə)ri/ adjective **1.**
handed down, or legally capable of being
handed down, through generations by inheritance **2.** holding a right, function or property by right of inheritance

hereditary office /həˌredɪt(ə)ri ˈɒfɪs/
noun an official position which is inherited

herein /ˌhɪərˈɪn/ adverb in this document
○ the conditions stated herein ○ see the reference herein above

hereinafter /ˌhɪərɪnˈɑːftə/ adverb stated
later in this document ○ the conditions hereinafter listed

hereof /ˌhɪərˈɒv/ adverb of this □ **in confirmation hereof we attach a bank statement** to confirm this we attach a bank statement

hereto /ˌhɪəˈtuː/ adverb to this ○ according to the schedule of payments attached
hereto □ **as witness hereto** as a witness of
this fact □ **the parties hereto** the parties to
this agreement

heretofore /ˈhɪətəˌfɔː/ adverb previously
or earlier ○ the parties heretofore acting as
trustees

hereunder /ˌhɪərˈʌndə/ adverb under this
heading, or below this phrase ○ see the documents listed hereunder

herewith /hɪəˈwɪð/ adverb together with
this letter ○ please find the cheque enclosed
herewith

Her Majesty's Court Service /ˌhɜː
ˌmædʒəstiz ˈkɔːt ˌsɜːvɪs/ noun a division
of the DCA responsible for the administration of justice in, and the courts of, England
and Wales. Abbreviation **HMCS**

Her Majesty's government /ˌhɜː
ˌmædʒəstiz ˈgʌv(ə)nmənt/ noun the official title of the British government

Her Majesty's pleasure /ˌhɜː
ˌmædʒəstiz ˈpleʒə/ noun □ **detention at or
during Her Majesty's pleasure** imprisonment for an indefinite period, until the
Home Secretary decides that a prisoner can
be released

Her Majesty's Revenue & Customs
/ˌhɜː ˌmædʒəstiz ˌrevənjuː ən ˈkʌstəmz/
noun the government department responsible for taxation and border protection,
formed in April 2005 following the merger
of Inland Revenue and Customs and Excise.
Abbreviation **HMRC**

Her Majesty's Stationery Office /ˌhɜː
ˌmædʒəstiz ˈsteɪʃ(ə)n(ə)ri ˌɒfɪs/ noun an
information service with responsibility for
publishing and making available Acts of

Parliament, now part of the Office of Public Sector Information. Abbreviation **HMSO**

hidden asset /ˌhɪd(ə)n ˈæset/ *noun* an asset which is valued in the company's accounts at much less than its true market value

hidden reserves /ˌhɪd(ə)n rɪˈzɜːvz/ *plural noun* illegal reserves which are not declared in the company's balance sheet

High Court /ˌhaɪ ˈkɔːt/, **High Court of Justice** /ˌhaɪ kɔːt əv ˈdʒʌstɪs/ *noun* the main civil court in England and Wales, based on the six circuits

High Court of Justiciary /ˌhaɪ kɔːt əv dʒʌˈstɪʃiəri/ *noun* the supreme criminal court of Scotland

high judicial office /haɪ dʒuːˌdɪʃ(ə)l ˈɒfɪs/ *noun* an important position in the legal system, e.g. Lord Chancellor, a High Court judge, etc.

high office /ˌhaɪ ˈɒfɪs/ *noun* an important position or job

high official /ˌhaɪ əˈfɪʃ(ə)l/ *noun* an important person in a government department

high seas /ˌhaɪ ˈsiːz/ *plural noun* the part of the sea which is further than three miles or five kilometres from a coast, and so is under international jurisdiction (NOTE: usually used with 'the': *an accident on the high seas*)

High Sheriff /ˌhaɪ ˈʃerɪf/ *noun* a senior representative appointed by the government in a county

high treason /ˌhaɪ ˈtriːz(ə)n/ *noun* a formal way of referring to treason

highway /ˈhaɪweɪ/ *noun* a road or path with a right of way which anyone may use

Highway Code /ˌhaɪweɪ ˈkəʊd/ *noun* the rules which govern the behaviour of people and vehicles using roads

COMMENT: The Highway Code is not itself part of UK law.

hijack /ˈhaɪdʒæk/ *noun* the act of taking control by force of a plane, ship, train, bus or lorry which is moving ○ *The hijack was organised by a group of opponents to the government.* ■ *verb* to take control by force of a moving plane, ship, train, bus or lorry, with passengers on board ○ *The plane was hijacked by six armed terrorists.* ○ *The bandits hijacked the lorry and killed the driver.*

hijacker /ˈhaɪdʒækə/ *noun* somebody who hijacks a vehicle

hijacking /ˈhaɪdʒækɪŋ/ *noun* the act of taking control of a moving plane, ship, train,

bus or lorry by force ○ *The hijacking took place just after the plane took off.* ○ *There have been six hijackings so far this year.*

Hilary /ˈhɪləri/ *noun* **1.** one of the four sittings of the law courts **2.** one of the four law terms

HIP *abbreviation* Home Information Pack

hire purchase agreement /ˌhaɪə ˈpɜːtʃəs əˌɡriːmənt/ *noun* a contract to pay for something by instalments

hire-purchase company /ˌhaɪə ˈpɜːtʃɪs ˌkʌmp(ə)ni/ *noun* a company which provides money for hire purchase (NOTE: The US term is **installment plan**.)

hirer /ˈhaɪrə/ *noun* somebody who hires something

hit and run /ˌhɪt ən ˈrʌn/ *noun* a situation where a vehicle hits someone and continues without stopping

hit man /ˈhɪt mæn/ *noun* a person who will kill someone for a fee (*slang*)

HMCS *abbreviation* Her Majesty's Court Service

HMRC *abbreviation* Her Majesty's Revenue & Customs

HMSO *abbreviation* Her Majesty's Stationary Office

hoax /həʊks/ *noun* an action which is designed to trick someone into believing something □ **hoax phone call** a call to inform the police or fire service of a dangerous situation which does not exist

hoc ♦ ad hoc

hold /həʊld/ *verb* **1.** to keep someone in custody ○ *The prisoners are being held in the police station.* ○ *Twenty people were held in the police raid.* ○ *She was held for six days without being able to see her lawyer.* **2.** to give as a formal decision ○ *The court held that there was no case to answer.* ○ *The appeal judge held that the defendant was not in breach of his statutory duty.* (NOTE: **holding – held**)

holder /ˈhəʊldə/ *noun* **1.** somebody who owns or keeps something ○ *the holder of an insurance policy* or *a policy holder* ○ *She is a British passport holder* or *she is the holder of a British passport.* **2.** the person to whom a cheque is made payable and who has possession of it **3.** somebody who is holding a bill of exchange or promissory note **4.** something which keeps or protects something

holder in due course /ˌhəʊldə ɪn djuː ˈkɔːs/ *noun* somebody who takes a bill, promissory note or cheque before it becomes overdue or is dishonoured

holding /ˈhəʊldɪŋ/ *noun* a ruling given by a court of law, especially one that decides a legal issue raised by a particular case

holding charge /ˈhəʊldɪŋ tʃɑːdʒ/ *noun* a minor charge brought against someone so that he or she can be held in custody while more serious charges are being prepared

holding over /ˌhəʊldɪŋ ˈəʊvə/, **holdover** US /ˈhəʊldəʊvə/ *noun* a situation where a person who had a lease for a period continues to occupy the property after the end of the lease

hold out /ˌhəʊld ˈaʊt/ *verb* □ **to hold out for** to ask for something and refuse to act until you get what you asked for ○ *He held out for a 50% discount.*

hold to /ˈhəʊld tuː/ *verb* not to allow something to change □ **to hold someone to an agreement** to insist that someone stick to the terms of an agreement

hold up /ˌhəʊld ˈʌp/ *verb* **1.** to go into a bank, stop a lorry, etc., in order to steal money ○ *Six gunmen held up the bank* or *the security van.* **2.** to stay at a high level ○ *Share prices have held up well.* ○ *Sales held up during the tourist season.* **3.** to delay ○ *The shipment has been held up at the customs.* ○ *Payment will be held up until the contract has been signed.*

hold-up /ˈhəʊld ʌp/ *noun* **1.** the act of holding up a bank, etc. ○ *The gang committed three armed hold-ups on the same day.* **2.** a delay ○ *The traffic congestion caused hold-ups for people on their way to work.*

HOLMES2 /ˌhəʊlmz ˈtuː/ *noun* a police database system which is used in the investigation of major crimes, and also to record information on the casualties of large-scale accidents. Full form **Home Office Large Major Enquiry System 2**

holograph /ˈhɒləɡrɑːf/ *noun* a document written by hand

holographic will /ˌhɒləɡrɑːf ˌwɪl/, **holograph will** *noun* a will, written out by hand, and not necessarily witnessed

home court /ˈhəʊm kɔːt/ *noun* the County Court for the district in which a defendant lives or has his or her address for service (NOTE: The US term is **domestic court**.)

Home Information Pack /ˌhəʊm ˌɪnfə ˈmeɪʃ(ə)n ˌpæk/ *noun* a set of documents containing information on a property, which every person who wants to sell a home must

make available for potential buyers from 1 June 2007. Abbreviation **HIP**

homeless person /ˌhəʊmləs ˈpɜːs(ə)n/ *noun* a person with no fixed accommodation (NOTE: A person in this situation may be eligible for the provision of accommodation by a local council.)

home market /ˌhəʊm ˈmɑːkɪt/ *noun* the market in the country where the selling company is based

Home Office /ˈhəʊm ˌɒfɪs/ *noun* a British government ministry dealing with internal affairs including security, terrorism and immigration (NOTE: In 2007 its duties pertaining to the prison and probation services were passed to the new **Ministry of Justice**.)

Home Office Large Major Enquiry System 2 *noun* full form of **HOLMES2**

Home Office pathologist /həʊm ˌɒfɪs pəˈθɒlədʒɪst/ *noun* an official government pathologist employed by the Home Office to examine corpses

Home Secretary /ˌhəʊm ˈsekrət(ə)ri/ *noun* a member of the British government, the minister in charge of the Home Office, dealing with law and order, the police and prisons

COMMENT: In most countries the government department dealing with the internal order of the country is called the Ministry of the Interior, with a Minister of the Interior in charge.

homestead /ˈhəʊmsted/ *noun* US the house and land where a family lives

COMMENT: A homestead cannot be the subject of a sale by court order to satisfy creditors.

home trade /ˌhəʊm ˈtreɪd/ *noun* trade in the country where a company is based

homicidal /ˌhɒmɪˈsaɪd(ə)l/ *adjective* (*of a person*) likely or wanting to commit murder

homicide /ˈhɒmɪsaɪd/ *noun* **1.** the accidental or illegal killing of a person ○ *He was found guilty of homicide.* ○ *The homicide rate has doubled in the last ten years.* **2.** murder

COMMENT: Homicide covers the crimes of murder, manslaughter and infanticide.

Homicide Squad /ˈhɒmɪˌsaɪd skwɒd/ *noun* US a department of a police force which deals with cases of murder

honest /ˈɒnɪst/ *adjective* not lying or cheating □ **to play the honest broker** to act for the parties in a negotiation to try to help them agree to a solution

honestly /'ɒnɪstli/ *adverb* acting in an open and truthful way

honesty /'ɒnɪsti/ *noun* the fact of being open and truthful ○ *The court praised the witness for her honesty in informing the police of the crime.*

honorarium /ˌɒnə'reəriəm/ *noun* a sum of money paid to a professional person such as an accountant or a lawyer which is less than a full fee

honour /'ɒnə/ *verb* to accept and pay a cheque or bill of exchange □ **to honour a debt** to pay a debt because it is owed and is correct □ **to honour a signature** to pay something because the signature is correct

hoodlum /'hu:dləm/ *noun US* a gangster

hooligan /'hu:lɪgən/ *noun* somebody who behaves violently in public ○ *The police put up barriers to prevent the football hooligans from damaging property.*

hooliganism /'hu:lɪgənɪz(ə)m/ *noun* violent behaviour □ **football hooliganism** violent behaviour by football supporters in connection with football matches

hopper /'hɒpə/ *noun US* a box where bills are put after being introduced in the House of Representatives

horse-trading /'hɔːs ˌtreɪdɪŋ/ *noun* bargaining between groups of people to obtain a general agreement for something ○ *After a period of horse-trading, the committee agreed on the election of a member of one of the smaller parties as Chairman.*

hospital block /'hɒspɪt(ə)l blɒk/ *noun* the section of a prison which contains the hospital

hospital order /ˌhɒspɪt(ə)l 'ɔːdə/ *noun* a court order confining someone who has been found not guilty by reason of insanity to hospital for treatment

hostage /'hɒstɪdʒ/ *noun* a person captured by an enemy or by criminals and kept until your demands are met ○ *The terrorists released three hostages.* □ **to take someone hostage** to capture a person and keep them in this way ○ *The bandits found the bank manager hiding and took him hostage.* ○ *She was taken hostage by the guerillas.*

hostile /'hɒstaɪl/ *adjective* not friendly

hostile witness /ˌhɒstaɪl 'wɪtnəs/ *noun* a witness called by a party, whose evidence goes unexpectedly against that party, and who can then be cross-examined by his or her own side as if giving evidence for the other side ○ *She was ruled a hostile witness by the judge.*

hot /hɒt/ *adjective* stolen or illegal (*informal*) ○ *hot jewels* ○ *a hot car*

hotchpot /'hɒtʃpɒt/ *noun* the act of bringing together into one fund money to be distributed under a will

hotchpot rule /'hɒtʃpɒt ruːl/ *noun* the rule that money passed to one child during his or her lifetime by a deceased person should be counted as part of the total estate to be distributed to all the children in the case where the person died intestate

hot money /ˌhɒt 'mʌni/ *noun* **1.** money which is moved from country to country to get the best interest rates **2.** stolen money, or money which has been obtained illegally

hot pursuit /ˌhɒt pə'sjuːt/ *noun* the right in international law to chase a ship into international waters, or to chase suspected criminals across an international border into another country

house /haʊz/ *noun* one of the two parts of the British Parliament (the House of Commons and the House of Lords) ○ *The minister brought a matter to the attention of the House.*

house arrest /'haʊs əˌrest/ *noun* the situation of being ordered by a court to stay in your house and not to leave it ○ *The opposition leader has been under house arrest for six years.*

housebreaker /'haʊsbreɪkə/ *noun US* a burglar, a person who breaks into houses and steals things

housebreaking /'haʊsbreɪkɪŋ/ *noun US* same as **burglary**

household effects /ˌhaʊshəʊld ɪ'fekts/ *plural noun* furniture and other items used in a house, and moved with the owner when he or she moves house

householder /'haʊshəʊldə/ *noun* somebody who occupies a private house

House of Commons /ˌhaʊs əv 'kɒmənz/ *noun* **1.** the lower house of the British Parliament, made up of 659 elected members **2.** the lower house of a legislature (as in Canada)

COMMENT: Members of the House of Commons (called MPs) are elected for five years, which is the maximum length of a Parliament. Bills can be presented in either the House of Commons or House of Lords, and sent to the other chamber for discussion and amendment. All bills relating to revenue must be introduced in the House of Commons, and most other bills are introduced there also.

House of Lords /ˌhaʊs əv 'lɔːdz/ *noun* the non-elected upper house of Parliament in the United Kingdom, made up of life peers, some hereditary peers and some bishops

COMMENT: The composition of the House of Lords was changed by the House of Lords Act; hereditary peers no longer sit there by right, although 92 remain, elected by their own party or crossbench (non-party) groups, or as Deputy Speakers, Committee Chairs, or to fill two hereditary royal appointments, the Earl Marshal and the Lord Great Chamberlain. As a court, the decisions of the House of Lords are binding on all other courts, and the only appeal from the House of Lords is to the European Court of Justice. The judicial functions of the House of Lords are scheduled to be transferred to a new **Supreme Court of the United Kingdom** in 2009.

House of Representatives /ˌhaʊs əv reprɪˈzentətɪvz/ *noun* **1.** *US* the lower house of the Congress of the United States, made up of 435 elected members **2.** the lower house of a legislature (as in Australia)

COMMENT: The members of the US House of Representatives (called Congressmen) are elected for two years. All bills relating to revenue must originate in the House of Representatives; otherwise bills can be proposed in either the House or the Senate and sent to the other chamber for discussion and amendment.

house property /ˈhaʊs ˌprɒpəti/ *noun* private houses, not shops, offices or factories

housing benefit /ˈhaʊzɪŋ ˌbenɪfɪt/ *noun* financial help with rent payments given by local councils to someone who is on a low income

human error /ˌhjuːmən ˈerə/ *noun* a mistake made by a person, not by a machine

human rights /ˌhjuːmən ˈraɪts/ *plural noun* the rights of individual men and women to basic freedoms such as freedom of association, freedom of speech

Human Rights Act /ˌhjuːmən ˈraɪts ˌækt/ *noun* legislation introduced into domestic law for the whole of the UK in October 2000, in order to comply with the obligations set out in European Convention of Human Rights

COMMENT: The Human Rights Act 1998, in force since October 2000, incorporated into UK law the European Convention for the Protection of Human Rights and Fundamental Freedoms. The Convention rights may now be relied on by litigants in the UK without the need to take a case to the European Court of Human Rights in Strasbourg. The Act creates a statutory duty that all laws,

past or present, must be interpreted in a way that is compatible to the Convention.

humble address /ˌhʌmbəl əˈdres/ *noun* a formal communication from one or both Houses of Parliament to the Queen

hung /hʌŋ/ *adjective* with no majority

hunger strike /ˈhʌŋɡə straɪk/ *noun* a protest, often by a prisoner, where the person refuses to eat until his or her demands have been met ○ *He went on hunger strike until the prison authorities allowed him to receive mail.*

hung jury /ˌhʌŋ ˈdʒʊəri/ *noun* a jury which cannot arrive at a unanimous or majority verdict

hung parliament /ˌhʌŋ ˈpɑːləmənt/ *noun* a parliament where no single party has enough votes to form a government

hunting ban /ˈhʌntɪŋ bæn/ *noun* legislation stating that it is illegal to hunt foxes using dogs

hurdle /ˈhɜːd(ə)l/ *noun* something which prevents something happening ○ *The defendant will have to overcome two hurdles if his appeal is to be successful.*

hush money /ˈhʌʃ ˌmʌni/ *noun* money paid to someone to stop him or her talking (*informal*)

hustings /ˈhʌstɪŋz/ *noun* □ **at the hustings** at a parliamentary election

COMMENT: The hustings were formerly the booths where votes were taken, or the platform on which candidates stood to speak, but now the word is used simply to mean 'an election'.

Hybrid Bill /ˈhaɪbrɪd bɪl/ *noun* a term used to refer to a Public Bill which affects the private interests of a particular person or organisation

hybrid offence /ˌhaɪbrɪd əˈfens/ *noun* an offence which can be tried either by magistrates or by a judge and jury

hypothecation /haɪˌpɒθəˈkeɪʃ(ə)n/ *noun* **1.** the use of property such as securities as collateral for a loan, without transferring legal ownership to the lender, as opposed to a mortgage, where the lender holds the title to the property **2.** the action of earmarking money derived from specific sources for related expenditure, e.g. investing the taxes from private cars or petrol sales solely in public transport

hypothetical question /ˌhaɪpəθetɪk(ə)l ˈkwestʃ(ə)n/ *noun* a question about a possible rather than an actual situation which is posed for discussion during a decision-making process

I

IBA *abbreviation* International Bar Association

ibid /'ɪbɪd/, **ibidem** *adverb* just the same, or in the same place in a book

ICC *abbreviation* **1.** International Criminal Court **2.** International Chamber of Commerce

IC code /,aɪ 'siː ,kəʊd/ *noun* a code given over police radio which describes a suspect's ethnicity

id /ɪd/, **idem** /'ɪdem/ *pronoun* the same thing, or the same person

ID *abbreviation* identity

identification /aɪ,dentɪfɪ'keɪʃ(ə)n/ *noun* the act of identifying someone or something

identification parade /aɪ,dentɪfɪ'keɪʃ(ə)n pə,reɪd/ *noun* same as **identity parade**

identify /aɪ'dentɪfaɪ/ *verb* to say who someone is or what something is ○ *She was able to identify her attacker.* ○ *Passengers were asked to identify their suitcases.* ○ *The dead man was identified by his fingerprints.*

Identikit /aɪ'dentɪkɪt/ *noun* a trademark for a method of making a picture of a criminal from descriptions given by witnesses, using pieces of photographs and drawings of different types of faces ○ *The police issued an identikit picture of the mugger.* (NOTE: Now replaced by **Photofit pictures.**)

identity /aɪ'dentɪti/ *noun* who someone is □ **to change one's identity** to assume a different name, change one's appearance, etc. (usually done to avoid being recognised) □ **to ask for proof of identity** to ask someone to prove they are really the person they say they are □ **case of mistaken identity** a situation where a person is wrongly thought to be someone else

identity authentication /aɪ'dentɪti ɔː ,θentɪkeɪʃ(ə)n/ *noun* the act of verifying a person's identity, e.g. by checking biometric data

identity card /aɪ'dentɪti kɑːd/, **ID card** /,aɪ 'diː ,kɑːd/ *noun* a card issued by the UK government to an individual for identification purposes

identity of parties /aɪ,dentɪti əv 'pɑːtiz/ *noun* a situation where the parties in different actions are the same

identity parade /aɪ'dentɪti pə,reɪd/ *noun* an arrangement where a group of people including a suspect stand in a line at a police station so that a witness can point out the person whom he or she recognises

identity theft /aɪ'dentɪti θeft/ *noun* the theft of personal data such as the details of someone's credit card

ignorance /'ɪɡnərəns/ *noun* lack of knowledge

ignorantia legis non excusat, ignorantia legis neminem excusat, ignorantia legis haud excusat *phrase* a Latin phrase meaning 'ignorance of the law is not an excuse for anyone': the principle that even if someone does not know that he or she has committed an offence, it does not make the offence any the less

IIDB *abbreviation* Industrial Injuries Disablement Benefit

ILEX /'aɪleks/ *abbreviation* Institute of Legal Executives

illegal /ɪ'liːɡ(ə)l/ *adjective* not legal in criminal law ○ *the illegal carrying of arms* ○ *Illegal immigrants are deported.*

illegal alien /ɪ,liːɡ(ə)l 'eɪliən/ *noun* a person who is not a citizen of a country but is living there illegally, e.g. on an expired visa

illegal contract /ɪ,liːɡ(ə)l 'kɒntrækt/ *noun* a contract which cannot be enforced in law, e.g. a contract to commit a crime

illegal immigrant /ɪ,liːɡ(ə)l 'ɪmɪɡrənt/ *noun* somebody who enters a country to live permanently without having the permission of the government to do so

illegality /ˌɪliːˈgælɪti/ *noun* the fact of being illegal

illegitimacy /ˌɪlɪˈdʒɪtɪməsi/ *noun* the state of being illegitimate

illegitimate /ˌɪlɪˈdʒɪtɪmət/ *adjective* **1.** against the law **2.** born to parents who are not married to each other

COMMENT: A child born in this way has the right to claim the property of its parents should they die intestate.

illicit /ɪˈlɪsɪt/ *adjective* not allowed by the law or by other rules ○ *illicit sale of alcohol* ○ *the trade in illicit alcohol*

ILO *abbreviation* International Labour Organization

IMF *abbreviation* International Monetary Fund

imitation /ˌɪmɪˈteɪʃ(ə)n/ *noun* something which copies another □ **beware of imitations** be careful not to buy low quality goods which are made to look like other more expensive items

imitation firearm /ˌɪmɪteɪʃ(ə)n ˈfaɪrɑːm/ *noun* an object which looks like a firearm and could be used to intimidate people, but is not functional

immaterial /ˌɪməˈtɪəriəl/ *adjective* not relevant or important □ **immaterial evidence** evidence that is not relevant to a particular case

immemorial /ˌɪməˈmɔːriəl/ *adjective* so old it cannot be remembered □ **from time immemorial** for so long that no one can remember when it started ○ *Villagers said that there had been a footpath across the field from time immemorial.*

immemorial existence /ˌɪməmɔːriəl ɪɡˈzɪstəns/ *noun* the period before 1189, the date from which events are supposed to be remembered. ◊ **legal memory**

immigrant /ˈɪmɪɡrənt/ *noun* somebody who moves to this country to live permanently

immigrate /ˈɪmɪɡreɪt/ *verb* to move to this country to live permanently. Compare **emigrate**

immigration /ˌɪmɪˈɡreɪʃ(ə)n/ *noun* an act of moving into a country to live permanently

Immigration Laws /ˌɪmɪˈɡreɪʃ(ə)n lɔːz/ *plural noun* legislation regarding immigration into a country

immigration officer /ˌɪmɪˈɡreɪʃ(ə)n ˌɒfɪsə/ *noun* an official at an airport or port, whose job is to check the passports and visas of people entering the country

immoral earnings /ɪˌmɒrəl ˈɜːnɪŋz/ *plural noun* money earned from prostitution

immovable /ɪˈmuːvəb(ə)l/ *adjective* being unable to be moved

immovable property /ɪˌmuːvəb(ə)l ˈprɒpəti/ *noun* houses and other buildings on land, as well as land itself

immunity /ɪˈmjuːnɪti/ *noun* protection from arrest or prosecution □ **to be granted immunity from prosecution** to be told you will not be prosecuted

COMMENT: Immunity from prosecution is granted to magistrates, counsel and witnesses as regards their statements in judicial proceedings. Families and servants of diplomats may be covered by diplomatic immunity. In the USA, immunity is the protection of members of Congress against being sued for libel or slander for statements made on the floor of the House (in the UK this is called **privilege**).

impanel /ɪmˈpæn(ə)l/ *verb US* same as **empanel**

impartial /ɪmˈpɑːʃ(ə)l/ *adjective* not biased or prejudiced ○ *to give someone a fair and impartial hearing* ○ *A judgment must be impartial.*

impartiality /ɪmˌpɑːʃiˈælɪti/ *noun* the state of being impartial ○ *The newspapers doubted the impartiality of the judge.*

impartially /ɪmˈpɑːʃ(ə)li/ *adverb* not showing any bias or favour towards someone ○ *The adjudicator has to decide impartially between the two parties.*

impeach /ɪmˈpiːtʃ/ *verb* **1.** formerly, to charge a person with treason before Parliament **2.** *US* to charge a head of state with treason **3.** *US* to charge any government official with misconduct **4.** *US* to discredit a witness

impeachment /ɪmˈpiːtʃmənt/ *noun US* **1.** a charge of treason brought against a head of state **2.** a charge of misconduct against any public official

impersonate /ɪmˈpɜːsəneɪt/ *verb* to pretend to be someone else ○ *He gained entrance to the house by impersonating a local authority inspector.*

impersonation /ɪmˌpɜːsəˈneɪʃ(ə)n/ *noun* the activity of pretending to be someone else in order to deceive people ○ *He was charged with impersonation of a police officer.*

impleader /ɪmˈpliːdə/ *noun US* a procedure to join a third party to an original action, undertaken either by the plaintiff or the defendant (NOTE: The British equivalent is **third party proceedings**.)

implication /ˌɪmplɪˈkeɪʃ(ə)n/ *noun* **1.** the possible effect of an action ○ *What will the implications of this decision be?* **2.** an involvement with a crime or something that is morally wrong ○ *The newspaper revealed his implication in the affair of the stolen diamonds.* **3.** a suggestion that something such as a criticism or accusation is true although it has not been expressed directly ○ *I resent the implication that I knew anything about the report in advance.*

implicit /ɪmˈplɪsɪt/ *adjective* implied rather than clearly stated

implied /ɪmˈplaɪd/ *adjective* being presumed to exist or which can be established by circumstantial evidence

implied contract /ɪmˌplaɪd kənˈtrækt/ *noun* an agreement which is considered to be a contract, because the parties intended it to be a contract or because the law considers it to be a contract

implied malice /ɪmˌplaɪd ˈmælɪs/ *noun* the intention to commit grievous bodily harm on someone

implied term /ɪmˈplaɪd tɜːm/ *noun* a term in a contract which is not expressly written or spoken but which is understood to exist. Compare **express term**

implied terms and conditions /ɪmˌplaɪd tɜːmz ən kənˈdɪʃ(ə)nz/ *plural noun* terms and conditions which are not written in a contract, but which are legally taken to be present in the contract

implied trust /ɪmˌplaɪd ˈtrʌst/ *noun* a trust which is implied by the intentions and actions of the parties

imply /ɪmˈplaɪ/ *verb* to suggest that something may be true without stating it clearly ○ *Counsel implied that the witness had not in fact seen the accident take place.* ○ *Do you wish to imply that the police acted improperly?*

import licence /ˈɪmpɔːt ˌlaɪs(ə)ns/ *noun* a permit which allows a company to bring a particular type of product into a country

import permit /ˈɪmpɔːt ˌpɜːmɪt/ *noun* an official document which allows goods to be imported

import quota /ˈɪmpɔːt ˌkwəʊtə/ *noun* a fixed quantity of a particular type of goods which the government allows to be imported

import surcharge /ˈɪmpɔːt ˌsɜːtʃɑːdʒ/ *noun* an extra charge on imported goods

import trade /ˈɪmpɔːt treɪd/ *noun* the business of buying from other countries

importune /ˌɪmpəˈtjuːn/ *verb* to ask someone to have sexual relations (NOTE: Used of prostitutes looking for clients, or of men looking for prostitutes.)

importuning /ˌɪmpəˈtjuːnɪŋ/ *noun* the crime of asking someone to have sexual relations with you for money

impose /ɪmˈpəʊz/ *verb* **1.** to ask someone to pay a fine ○ *The court imposed a fine of £100.* ○ *They tried to impose a ban on smoking outside bars.* **2.** to put a tax or a duty on goods ○ *The government imposed a special duty on oil.* ○ *The customs have imposed a 10% tax increase on electrical items.*

imposition /ˌɪmpəˈzɪʃ(ə)n/ *noun* the introduction of something such as a rule or tax

impossibility of performance /ɪmˌpɒsəbɪlɪti əv pəˈfɔːməns/ *noun* a situation where a party to a contract is unable to perform his or her part of the contract

impound /ɪmˈpaʊnd/ *verb* to take something away and keep it until a tax is paid or until documents are checked to see if they are correct ○ *The customs impounded the whole cargo.*

impounding /ɪmˈpaʊndɪŋ/ *noun* the act of taking something and keeping it

imprison /ɪmˈprɪz(ə)n/ *verb* to put someone in prison ○ *He was imprisoned by the secret police for six months.*

imprisonment /ɪmˈprɪz(ə)nmənt/ *noun* the punishment of being put in prison ○ *The penalty for the first offence is a fine of £200 or six weeks' imprisonment.* □ **term of imprisonment** the time which a prisoner has to spend in prison ○ *He was sentenced to the maximum term of imprisonment.*

COMMENT: Life imprisonment is a term of many years, but in the UK not necessarily for the rest of the prisoner's life. The judge should recommend the minimum length of term (the **tariff**) at the time of sentencing. See Supplement for more detail.

improper /ɪmˈprɒpə/ *adjective* not correct, not as it should be

improperly /ɪmˈprɒpəli/ *adverb* not correctly ○ *The police constable's report was improperly made out.* ○ *She was accused of acting improperly in going to see the prisoner's father.*

impunity /ɪmˈpjuːnɪti/ *noun* □ **with impunity** without punishment ○ *No one can flout the law with impunity.*

imputation /ˌɪmpjuːˈteɪʃ(ə)n/ *noun* a suggestion that someone has done something wrong

imputation of malice /ˌɪmpjuːteɪʃ(ə)n əv ˈmælɪs/ *noun* the suggestion that someone acted out of malice

impute /ɪmˈpjuːt/ *verb* to suggest □ **to impute a motive to someone** to suggest that someone had a motive in acting as he or she did

in absentia /ˌɪn æbˈsenʃə/ *adverb* without someone being present ○ *She was tried and sentenced to death in absentia.*

inadmissible /ˌɪnədˈmɪsɪb(ə)l/ *adjective* not able to be used in court as evidence

inalienable /ɪnˈeɪliənəb(ə)l/ *adjective* which cannot be taken away □ **inalienable rights** rights which cannot be taken away from a person or transferred to someone else

inapplicable /ˌɪnəˈplɪkəb(ə)l/ *adjective* being unable to be applied ○ *The government argued that the national legislation had not been applied and was inapplicable in this case.*

Inc *abbreviation* incorporated

in camera /ˌɪn ˈkæm(ə)rə/ *adverb* with no members of the public permitted to be present ○ *The case was heard in camera.* (NOTE: Since the introduction of the Civil Procedure Rules, this term has been replaced by **in private**.)

incapable /ɪnˈkeɪpəb(ə)l/ *adjective* not able ○ *He was incapable of fulfilling the terms of the contract.* ○ *A child is considered legally incapable of committing a crime.*

incapacitant /ˌɪnkəˈpæsɪtənt/ *noun* same as **electroshock weapon**

incapacity /ˌɪnkəˈpæsɪti/ *noun* the state of not being legally able to do something ○ *The court had to act because of the incapacity of the trustees.*

incapacity benefit /ˌɪnkəˈpæsɪti ˌbenɪfɪt/ *noun* financial help given by the Government to someone who is unable to work because of a disability or long-term illness

incapax ♦ **doli capax**

incarcerate /ɪnˈkɑːsəreɪt/ *verb* to put in prison ○ *He was incarcerated for the murder of his wife.*

incarceration /ɪnˌkɑːsəˈreɪʃ(ə)n/ *noun* the act of putting a criminal in prison

incendiary /ɪnˈsendiəri/ *adjective* referring to a fire which has been deliberately started ○ *incendiary weapons*

inception /ɪnˈsepʃən/ *noun* a beginning ○ *Some people believe that subsidiarity has existed in the Community ever since its inception.*

incest /ˈɪnsest/ *noun* a notifiable offence of having sexual intercourse with a close relative such as a daughter, son, mother or father

in chambers /ɪn ˈtʃeɪmbəz/ *adverb* in the office of a judge and not in a courtroom ○ *The judge heard the application in chambers.*

inchoate /ɪnˈkəʊət/ *adjective* just beginning to form but not complete

inchoate instrument /ɪnˌkəʊət ˈɪnstrumənt/ *noun* a document which is not complete

inchoate offences /ɪnˌkəʊət əˈfenss/ *plural noun* offences such as incitement, attempt or conspiracy to commit a crime even though the crime itself may not have been committed

incidence /ˈɪnsɪd(ə)ns/ *noun* how often something happens ○ *a high incidence of accidents relating to drunken drivers* ○ *The incidence of cases of rape has increased over the last years.*

incident /ˈɪnsɪd(ə)nt/ *noun* something which happens at a particular time, e.g. a crime, accident or violent event ○ *Three incidents were reported when police vehicles were attacked by a crowd.* ■ *adjective* □ **incident to something** depending on something else

incident room /ˈɪnsɪd(ə)nt ruːm/ *noun* a special room in a police station set up to deal with a particular crime or accident

incident tape /ˈɪnsɪd(ə)nt teɪp/ *noun* wide yellow and black tape that is used to isolate an area and keep people away from a crime scene (NOTE: The US term is **crime scene tape**.)

incite /ɪnˈsaɪt/ *verb* to encourage, persuade or advise someone to commit a crime

incitement /ɪnˈsaɪtmənt/ *noun* the crime of encouraging, persuading or advising someone to commit a crime

COMMENT: It is not necessary for a crime to have been committed for incitement to be proved.

incitement to racial hatred /ɪn ˌsaɪtmənt tə ˌreɪʃ(ə)l ˈheɪtrɪd/ *noun* the offence of encouraging people by words, actions or writing to attack others because of their race

income /'ɪnkʌm/ *noun* money that a person receives as salary, dividend or interest □ **income from rents** money received from allowing other people to use property such as offices, houses or land that you own

income support /'ɪnkʌm səˌpɔːt/ *noun* financial help given by the state to families with low incomes (NOTE: An individual must not work more than sixteen hours a week in order to qualify.)

income tax /'ɪnkʌm tæks/ *noun* a tax on salaries and wages, calculated at different rates according to how much you earn

incompetency /ɪn'kɒmpɪt(ə)nsi/ *noun* the state of not being legally competent to do something

incompetent /ɪn'kɒmpɪt(ə)nt/ *adjective* **1.** unable to carry out duties to the required standard ○ *The sales manager is quite incompetent.* ○ *The company has an incompetent deputy MD.* **2.** not legally able to do something ○ *He is incompetent to sign the contract.*

incorporate /ɪn'kɔːpəreɪt/ *verb* **1.** to bring something in to be part of something else, e.g. to make a document part of another document ○ *Income from the 1998 acquisition is incorporated into the accounts.* ○ *The list of markets is incorporated into the main contract.* **2.** to form a registered company ○ *a company incorporated in the USA* ○ *an incorporated company* ○ *J. Doe Incorporated*

incorporation /ɪnˌkɔːpəˈreɪʃ(ə)n/ *noun* the act of incorporating a company

incorporeal /ˌɪnkɔːˈpɔːriəl/ *adjective* not having physical form, so being unable to be touched

incorporeal chattels /ˌɪnkɔːpɔːriəl 'tʃæt(ə)lz/ *plural noun* items such as patents and copyrights which have intellectual rather than physical existence

incorporeal hereditament /ˌɪnkɔːpɔːriəl ˌherɪ'dɪtəmənts/ *noun* a hereditament which does not physically exist, such as a patent or copyright. Compare **corporeal hereditament**

incorrigible /ɪn'kɒrɪdʒɪb(ə)l/ *adjective* unwilling to change one's bad behaviour

incriminate /ɪn'krɪmɪneɪt/ *verb* to show that a person has committed a criminal act ○ *He was incriminated by the recorded message he sent to the victim.*

incriminating /ɪn'krɪmɪneɪtɪŋ/ *adjective* which shows that someone has committed a crime ○ *Incriminating evidence was found in his car.*

incumbent /ɪn'kʌmbənt/ *adjective* □ **to be incumbent on** or **upon a person** to be something that a person has to do, because it is their duty ○ *It is incumbent on us to check our facts before making an accusation.* ○ *It is incumbent upon justices to give some warning of their doubts about a case.* ■ *noun* somebody who holds an official position ○ *There will be no changes in the governor's staff while the present incumbent is still in office.*

incumbrance /ɪn'kʌmbrəns/ *noun* same as **encumbrance**

incur /ɪn'kɜː/ *verb* to make yourself liable to □ **to incur the risk of a penalty** to make it possible that you risk paying a penalty □ **to incur costs** to do something which means that you will have to pay costs □ **to incur heavy costs** to make yourself liable to pay large sums of money

incuriam ♦ **per incuriam**

indebted /ɪn'detɪd/ *adjective* owing money to someone ○ *to be indebted to a property company*

indebtedness /ɪn'detɪdnəs/ *noun* the amount of money owed by someone

indecency /ɪn'diːs(ə)nsi/ *noun* the state of being offensive and shocking to most people □ **gross indecency** the former offence of having unlawful sexual contact between men or with a child, which falls short of full sexual intercourse

indecent /ɪn'diːs(ə)nt/ *adjective* **1.** offensive and shocking to most people, especially in relation to sexual matters **2.** not polite and considerate □ **indecent haste** unsuitably fast action ○ *They accepted the suggestion of compensation with indecent haste.*

indecent assault /ɪnˌdiːsənt ə'sɔːlt/ *noun* the crime of assaulting a person together with an indecent act or proposal

indecent exposure /ɪnˌdiːs(ə)nt ɪk 'spəʊʒə/ *noun* an offence in which a person shows his or her sexual organs in a public place

indefeasible right /ˌɪndɪfiːzɪb(ə)l 'raɪt/ *noun* a right which cannot be made void

indefensible /ˌɪndɪ'fensɪb(ə)l/ *adjective* **1.** impossible to justify or pardon ○ *The court rules that your actions were indefensible.* **2.** invalid ○ *The defendant's arguments are indefensible.* **3.** vulnerable to attack ○ *The country's borders are indefensible since the coup.*

indemnification /ɪnˌdemnɪfɪˈkeɪʃən/ noun payment for damage

indemnify /ɪnˈdemnɪfaɪ/ verb to pay for damage suffered ○ *to indemnify someone for a loss*

indemnity /ɪnˈdemnɪti/ noun **1.** compensation for a loss or a wrong **2.** a statement of liability to pay compensation for a loss or for a wrong in a transaction to which you are a party ○ *She had to pay an indemnity of £100.* Compare **guarantee.** ◊ **letter of indemnity** (NOTE: The person making an indemnity is primarily liable and can be sued by the person with whom he makes the transaction.) **3.** (*in civil cases*) the right of someone to recover from a third party the amount which is liable to be paid

indenture /ɪnˈdentʃə/ noun a deed made between two or more parties ■ **indentures** a contract by which a trainee craftsman works for a master for some years to learn a trade ■ verb to enter into a trainee contract in order to learn a trade ○ *He was indentured to a builder.*

independence /ˌɪndɪˈpendəns/ noun freedom from the rule, control or influence of others ○ *All teenagers need some independence.* ○ *Britain granted her colonies independence in the years after the Second World War.*

independent /ˌɪndɪˈpendənt/ adjective not controlled by anyone else

Independent Police Complaints Commission /pəˌliːs kəmˈpleɪnts kəˌmɪti/ noun a non-departmental government body which investigates complaints made by members of the public against the police. Abbreviation **IPCC**

independent rights /ˌɪndɪˈpendənt raɪts/ plural noun the rights of employed people, students, retired people and people with private incomes, to enter, live and work in a EU country

indict /ɪnˈdaɪt/ verb to charge someone with a crime ○ *She was indicted for murder.*

indictable offence /ɪnˌdaɪtəb(ə)l əˈfens/ noun formerly, a serious offence which could be tried in the Crown Court (NOTE: Now called **notifiable offence**.)

indictment /ɪnˈdaɪtmənt/ noun a written statement of the details of the crime with which someone is charged in the Crown Court ○ *The clerk to the justices read out the indictment.*

indirect discrimination /ˌɪndaɪrekt ˌsekjʊəl dɪsˌkrɪmɪˈneɪʃ(ə)n/ noun discrimination caused by the application of a general principle, where the result is that some people are treated unfairly

indirect sexual discrimination /ˌɪndaɪrekt ˌsekjʊəl dɪsˌkrɪmɪˈneɪʃ(ə)n/ noun an instance of sexual discrimination that is covert, where employment conditions are such that it would be difficult for one sex to fulfil them. ◊ **direct sexual discrimination**

COMMENT: An example of indirect sexual discrimination would be where promotion is based on continuous employment, meaning that a woman taking maternity leave be less likely to get promoted than a man where all else is equal.

individual exemption /ˌɪndɪvɪdʒuəl ɪgˈzempʃ(ə)n/ noun an exemption granted to a person or small business, exempting them from specific obligations

individual retirement account /ˌɪndɪvɪdʒuəl rɪˈtaɪəmənt əˌkaʊnt/ noun US a privately-managed pension plan, to which individuals can make contributions which are separate from a company pension plan. Abbreviation **IRA** (NOTE: The British equivalent is a **personal pension plan**.)

individual voluntary arrangement /ˌɪndɪvɪdʒuəl ˌvɒlənt(ə)ri əˈreɪndʒmənt/ noun a court approved scheme between a person and his or her creditors which determines how the debts will be discharged, used as an alternative to bankruptcy. Abbreviation **IVA**

indorse /ɪnˈdɔːs/ verb same as **endorse**

indorsement /ɪnˈdɔːsmənt/ noun same as **endorsement**

induce /ɪnˈdjuːs/ verb to help persuade someone to do something ○ *He was induced to steal the plans by an offer of a large amount of money.*

inducement /ɪnˈdjuːsmənt/ noun something which helps to persuade someone to do something ○ *They offered him a company car as an inducement to stay.*

inducement to break contract /ɪn ˌdjuːsmənt tə breɪk ˈkɒntrækt/ noun the tort of persuading someone to break a contract he or she has entered into

industrial /ɪnˈdʌstriəl/ adjective relating to work

industrial accident /ɪnˌdʌstriəl ˈæksɪd(ə)nt/ noun an accident which takes place at work

industrial arbitration tribunal /ɪn
ˌdʌstriəl ˌɑːbɪˈtreɪʃ(ə)n traɪˌbjuːn(ə)l/
noun a court which decides in industrial disputes ○ *to accept the ruling of the arbitration board*

industrial development /ɪnˌdʌstriəl
dɪˈveləpmənt/ *noun* the planning and
building of new industries in special areas

industrial dispute /ɪnˌdʌstriəl dɪ
ˈspjuːt/ *noun* an argument between
employers and employees

industrial espionage /ɪnˌdʌstriəl
ˈespiənɑːʒ/ *noun* the activity of trying to
find out the secrets of a competitor's work
or products, usually by illegal means

industrial estate /ɪnˈdʌstriəl ɪˌsteɪt/
noun an area of land near a town specially
for factories and warehouses

industrial injuries /ɪnˌdʌstriəl
ˈɪndʒəriz/ *plural noun* injuries caused to
employees at work

**Industrial Injuries Disablement
Benefit** /ɪnˌdʌstriəl ˌɪndʒəriz dɪs
ˈeɪb(ə)lmənt ˌbenɪfɪt/ *noun* financial help
given by the Government to people who
have become disabled because of an accident at work or an illness caused by their job
(e.g. by exposure to asbestos or radiation).
Abbreviation **IIDB**

industrial property /ɪnˌdʌstriəl
ˈprɒpəti/ *noun* an item with intellectual
rather than physical existence such as a patent, trademark or company name which is
owned by a company

industrial relations /ɪnˌdʌstriəl rɪ
ˈleɪʃ(ə)nz/ *plural noun* relations between
management and workers

industrial tribunal /ɪnˌdʌstriəl traɪ
ˈbjuːn(ə)l/ *noun* same as **employment tribunal**

in esse /ˌɪn ˈeseɪ/ *phrase* a Latin phrase
meaning 'in being': refers to a child which
has been born. Compare **in posse**

infant /ˈɪnfənt/ *noun* a person aged less
than eighteen years (NOTE: This is an old
term, now replaced by **minor**.)

infanticide /ɪnˈfæntɪsaɪd/ *noun* the notifiable offence of killing a child, especially
the killing of a child by its mother before it
is 12 months old

infer /ɪnˈfɜː/ *verb* to reach an opinion
about something ○ *He inferred from the letter that the accused knew the murder victim.*
○ *Counsel inferred that the witness had not
been present at the time of the accident.*

inferior court /ɪnˈfɪəriə kɔːt/ *noun* a
lower court such as a magistrates' court or
County Court

in flagrante delicto /ɪn fləˌɡrænti dɪ
ˈlɪktəʊ/ *phrase* a Latin phrase meaning
'(caught) in the act of committing a crime'

influence peddling /ˈɪnfluəns ˌpedlɪŋ/
noun the act of offering to use personal
influence, especially political power, for
payment in order to help a person or group
achieve something

inform /ɪnˈfɔːm/ *verb* **1.** to tell someone
officially ○ *I regret to inform you that your
tender was not acceptable.* ○ *We are pleased
to inform you that your offer has been
accepted.* ○ *We have been informed by the
Department of Trade that new tariffs are
coming into force.* **2.** □ **to inform on someone** to tell the police that someone has committed a crime

informant /ɪnˈfɔːmənt/ *noun* a person
who gives information to someone secretly
○ *Is your informant reliable?*

in forma pauperis /ˌɪn ˌfɔːmə
ˈpɔːpəris/ *phrase* a Latin phrase meaning
'as a poor person': formerly used to allow a
person to bring an action even if he or she
could not afford to pay the costs of the case
(NOTE: The has been replaced by **Legal
Aid**.)

information /ˌɪnfəˈmeɪʃ(ə)n/ *noun* **1.** the
details which explain something ○ *to disclose a piece of information* ○ *to answer a
request for information* ○ *Have you any
information on* or *about deposit accounts?*
○ *I enclose this leaflet for your information.*
□ **disclosure of confidential information**
telling someone information which should
be secret **2.** the details of a crime drawn up
by the clerk and given to a magistrate □ **laying (an) information** starting criminal proceedings in a magistrates' court by informing the magistrate of the offence

information bureau /ˌɪnfəˈmeɪʃ(ə)n
ˌbjʊərəʊ/ *noun* an office where someone
can answer questions from members of the
public

information officer /ˌɪnfəˈmeɪʃ(ə)n
ˌɒfɪsə/ *noun* **1.** a person whose job is to give
information about a company, an organisation or a government department to the public **2.** a person whose job is to give information to other departments in the same organization

informed /ɪnˈfɔːmd/ *adjective* having the
latest information ○ *The police requested*

that they be kept informed if the stalker contacted her again.

informed consent /ɪnˌfɔːmd kənˈsent/ *noun* an agreement that an operation can be carried out which is given by a patient or the guardians of a patient after they have been given all the information they need to make the decision

informer /ɪnˈfɔːmə/ *noun* somebody who gives information to the police about a crime or about criminals

infraction /ɪnˈfrækʃən/ *noun US* a minor offence

infringe /ɪnˈfrɪndʒ/ *verb* to break a law or a right □ **to infringe a copyright** to copy a copyright text illegally □ **to infringe a patent** to make a product which works in the same way as a patented product and not pay a royalty to the patent holder

infringement /ɪnˈfrɪndʒmənt/ *noun* an act of breaking a law or a right

infringement of copyright /ɪnˌfrɪndʒmənt əv ˈkɒpɪraɪt/ *noun* the act of illegally copying a work without proper permission or the consent of the copyright owner

infringement of patent /ɪnˌfrɪndʒmənt əv ˈpeɪtənt/ *noun* the act of illegally using, making or selling an invention which is patented without the permission of the patent holder

infringer /ɪnˈfrɪndʒə/ *noun* a person who infringes a right such as a copyright

infringing goods /ɪnˌfrɪndʒɪŋ ˈɡʊdz/ *plural noun* goods which are made in infringement of a copyright or patent

inherit /ɪnˈherɪt/ *verb* to acquire something from a person who has died ○ *When her father died she inherited the shop.* ○ *He inherited £10,000 from his grandfather.*

inheritance /ɪnˈherɪt(ə)ns/ *noun* property which is received by someone from a person who has died

inheritance tax /ɪnˈherɪt(ə)ns tæks/ *noun* a tax levied on property received by inheritance or legal succession, calculated according to the value of the property received

inheritor /ɪnˈherɪtə/ *noun* somebody who receives something from somebody who has died

iniquity /ɪnˈɪkwɪti/ *noun* **1.** immoral or illegal behaviour □ **den of iniquity** a place where illegal or immoral behaviour regularly takes place **2.** injustice

initial /ɪˈnɪʃ(ə)l/ *adjective* happening at the beginning of something ■ *verb* to write your initials on a document to show you have read it and approved ○ *to initial an amendment to a contract* ○ *Please initial the agreement at the place marked with an X.*

initial capital /ɪˌnɪʃ(ə)l ˈkæpɪt(ə)l/ *noun* capital which is used to start a business ○ *He started the business with initial capital of only £500.*

initio ♦ **ab initio**

injunction /ɪnˈdʒʌŋkʃ(ə)n/ *noun* **1.** a court order that requires someone involved in a legal action to do something or refrain from doing something ○ *He got an injunction preventing the company from selling his car.* ○ *The company applied for an injunction to stop their competitor from marketing a similar product.* □ **interlocutory injunction**, **temporary injunction** an injunction which is granted until a case comes to court **2.** a command or order, especially from someone in a position of authority

injure /ˈɪndʒə/ *verb* to hurt someone ○ *Two employees were injured in the fire.*

injured party /ˌɪndʒəd ˈpɑːti/ *noun* a party in a court case which has been harmed by another party

injurious /ɪnˈdʒʊəriəs/ *adjective* being capable of causing injury

injurious falsehood /ɪnˌdʒʊəriəs ˈfɔːlshʊd/ *noun* the tort of making a wrong statement about someone so as to harm their reputation, usually in relation to their business or property

injury /ˈɪndʒəri/ *noun* **1.** violation of a person's rights **2.** hurt caused to a person

injury benefit /ˈɪndʒəri ˌbenɪfɪt/ *noun* money paid to an employee who has been hurt at work

injustice /ɪnˈdʒʌstɪs/ *noun* a situation in which justice has not been done ○ *She complained about the injustice of not being allowed to see her lawyer.*

inland freight charges /ˌɪnlənd ˈfreɪt ˌtʃɑːdʒɪz/ *plural noun* charges for carrying goods from one part of the country to another

Inland Revenue /ˌɪnlənd ˈrevənjuː/ *noun* a former government department dealing with income tax, now part of HM Revenue and Customs

in loco parentis /ˌɪn ˌləʊkəʊ pəˈrentɪs/ *phrase* a Latin phrase meaning 'in the place of a parent' ○ *The court is acting in loco parentis.*

Inner Temple /ˌɪnə 'temp(ə)l/ one of the four Inns of Court in London. ◊ **Inns of Court**

innocence /'ɪnəs(ə)ns/ *noun* the state of being innocent ○ *He tried to establish his innocence.*

innocent /'ɪnəs(ə)nt/ *adjective* not guilty of a crime ○ *The accused was found to be innocent.* ○ *In English law, the accused is presumed to be innocent until he is proved to be guilty.*

innominate term /ɪ'nɒmɪnət tɜːm/ *noun* a term of a contract which can be treated either as a condition or a warranty, depending upon the seriousness of the consequences of its breach

Inns of Court /ˌɪnz əv 'kɔːt/ *plural noun* four societies in London, of which the members are lawyers and are called to the bar as barristers (NOTE: The Four Inns are called **Gray's Inn**, **Lincoln's Inn**, **Middle Temple** and **Inner Temple**. The names should each properly begin with 'The Honourable Society of…', although these is rarely observed in speech.)

innuendo /ˌɪnju'endəʊ/ *noun* spoken words which are defamatory because they have a double meaning ○ *An apparently innocent statement may be defamatory if it contains an innuendo.*

in personam /ɪn pɜː'səʊnæm/ *phrase* a Latin phrase meaning 'against a person' □ **action in personam** a court case in which one party claims that the other should do some act or should pay damages. ◊ **in rem**

in posse /ˌɪn 'eseɪ/ *phrase* a Latin phrase meaning 'in potential': refers to a child which has been conceived but not yet born. Compare **in esse**

in private /ɪn 'praɪvət/ *adverb* **1.** with no members of the public permitted to be present ○ *The case was heard in private.* (NOTE: Since the introduction of the Civil Procedure Rules, this term has replaced **in camera** or **in chambers**.) **2.** away from other people ○ *He asked to see the managing director in private.*

input tax /'ɪnpʊt tæks/ *noun* VAT paid on goods or services bought

inquest /'ɪŋkwest/ *noun* an inquiry by a coroner into a death

COMMENT: An inquest has to take place where death is violent or unexpected, where death could be murder or manslaughter,

where a person dies in custody and when police are involved.

inquire /ɪn'kwaɪə/, **enquire** /ɪŋ'kwaɪə/ *verb* **1.** to ask questions about something ○ *The police are inquiring into his background.* (NOTE: also spelled **enquire**) **2.** to conduct an official investigation into something

inquiry /ɪn'kwaɪəri/, **enquiry** /ɪn'kwaɪri/ *noun* a question about something ○ *The police are making inquiries into the whereabouts of the stolen car.* □ **to help police with their inquiries** to be taken to the police station for questioning

COMMENT: Anyone who helps the police with their inquiries voluntarily has the right to leave the police station when he or she wants, unless they are arrested as a result of information given. Refusal to go along to the police station voluntarily can also be grounds for arrest.

inquisitorial procedure /ɪn ˌkwɪzɪtɔːriəl prə'siːdʒə/ *noun* in countries where Roman law is applied, a procedure by which an examining magistrate has the duty to investigate a case and produce the evidence. Compare **accusatorial procedure**

inquorate /ɪn'kwɔːreɪt/ *adjective* without a quorum, i.e. without the minimum number of people present who are required to make the transaction legal ○ *The meeting was declared inquorate and had to be abandoned.*

in re /ɪn 'reɪ/ *phrase* a Latin phrase meaning 'concerning' or 'in the case of'

in rem /ɪn 'rem/ *phrase* a Latin phrase meaning 'against a thing' □ **action in rem** a court case in which one party claims property or goods in the possession of the other. ◊ **in personam**

insane /ɪn'seɪn/ *adjective* suffering from a state of mind which makes it impossible for a person to know that they are doing wrong and so cannot be held responsible for their actions

insanity /ɪn'sænɪti/ *noun* the state of being mentally unfit and so not responsible for your actions

COMMENT: Insanity can be used as a defence in both civil and criminal cases. Where a person is found to be insane in a criminal case, a verdict of 'not guilty by reason of insanity' is returned and a **hospital order** or **guardianship order** issued.

inside /ɪn'saɪd/ *adjective* known or carried out by people who belong to a particular group or organisation □ **inside information** *or* **knowledge** special knowledge about something because of working for an organisation or being part of a particular group ■ *adjective, adverb* in prison (*slang*) ○ *He spent six months inside in 1996.*

inside job /ˈɪnˌsaɪd dʒɒb/ *noun* a crime which has been committed on a company's property by one of the employees of the company

insider /ɪnˈsaɪdə/ *noun* a person who works in an organisation and therefore knows its secrets

insider dealing /ɪnˌsaɪdə ˈdiːlɪŋ/ *noun* the illegal buying or selling of shares by staff of a company or other persons who have secret information about the company's plans

insolvency /ɪnˈsɒlvənsi/ *noun* the state of not being able to pay debts □ **to be in a state of insolvency** of a company, to be unable to pay its debts

insolvency practitioner /ɪnˈsɒlvənsi prækˌtɪʃ(ə)nə/ *noun* a person (usually an accountant or solicitor) authorised by the Insolvency Service to act as a liquidator or administrator

Insolvency Service /ɪnˈsɒlvənsi ˌsɜːvɪs/ *noun* an agency of the Department of Trade and Industry which administers the affairs of bankrupts

insolvent /ɪnˈsɒlvənt/ *adjective* not able to pay debts ○ *The company was declared insolvent.* (NOTE: **insolvent** and **insolvency** are general terms, but are usually applied to companies; individuals or partners are usually described as **bankrupt** once they have been declared so by a court.)

inspect /ɪnˈspekt/ *verb* to examine in detail ○ *to inspect a machine* or *a prison* ○ *to inspect the accounts of a company* □ **to inspect products for defects** to look at products in detail to see if they have any defects

inspection /ɪnˈspekʃ(ə)n/ *noun* **1.** the close and careful examination of something ○ *to make an inspection* or *to carry out an inspection of a prison* □ **to carry out a tour of inspection** to visit various places, offices or factories to inspect them □ **to issue an inspection order** to order a defendant to allow a claimant to inspect documents, where the claimant thinks the defendant has not disclosed all relevant documents **2.** the examination of documents after disclosure ○ *Inspection was ordered to take place seven days after disclosure.*

inspection stamp /ɪnˈspekʃən stæmp/ *noun* a stamp placed on something to show it has been inspected

inspector /ɪnˈspektə/ *noun* **1.** an official who inspects □ **inspector of taxes, tax inspector** an official who examines tax returns and decides how much tax people should pay **2.** a rank in the police force above a sergeant and below chief inspector

Inspectorate of Prisons /ɪnˌspekt(ə)rət əv ˈprɪzənz/ *noun* a section of the Prison Service which deals with the inspection of prisons to see that they are being run correctly and efficiently

instance /ˈɪnstəns/ *noun* **1.** a particular example or case ○ *In this instance we will overlook the delay.* **2.** ♦ **court of first instance**

in statu quo ante /ɪn ˌstætuː ˈkwəʊ/ *phrase* a Latin phrase meaning 'in the state things were in before': refers to a request for everything to be restored to its previous state after the rescission of a contract

institute /ˈɪnstɪtjuːt/ *verb* to start something ○ *to institute proceedings against someone*

institution /ˌɪnstɪˈtjuːʃ(ə)n/ *noun* **1.** an organisation or society set up for a particular purpose □ **the Community institutions** (*in the EU*) the four bodies which legally form the European Community – the Commission, the Council, the European Parliament and the European Court of Justice **2.** a widely-accepted mechanism of social order to which people conform ○ *the institution of marriage*

institutional /ˌɪnstɪˈtjuːʃ(ə)n(ə)l/ *adjective* referring to an institution, especially a public body □ **institutional racism** racist policies of an organisation which perpetuate inequality among staff, or compromise the service that it offers to its customers

institutionalised /ˌɪnstɪˈtjuːʃ(ə)nəlaɪzd/ *adjective* **1.** unable to live independently after having been in prison, hospital or other institution for a long time **2.** happening so often that it is considered to be normal even though wrong or harmful ○ *institutionalised racism*

instruct /ɪnˈstrʌkt/ *verb* **1.** to give an order to someone □ **to instruct someone to do something** to tell someone officially to do something ○ *He instructed the credit controller to take action.* **2.** □ **to instruct a solicitor** to give information to a solicitor and to ask him or her to start legal proceedings on your behalf □ **to instruct a barris-**

ter (*of a solicitor*) to give a barrister all the details of a case which he or she will plead in court

instructions /ɪnˈstrʌkʃənz/ *plural noun* **1.** order which tells what should be done or how something is to be used ○ *He gave instructions to his stockbroker to sell the shares immediately.* □ **to await instructions** to wait for someone to tell you what to do □ **to issue instructions** to tell everyone what to do □ **in accordance with, according to instructions** as the instructions show □ **failing instructions to the contrary** unless different instructions are given **2.** the details of a case given by a client to a solicitor, or by a solicitor to a barrister

instructions to the jury /ɪnˌstrʌkʃənz tə ðə ˈdʒʊəri/ *noun US* a speech by a judge at the end of a trial where he or she reviews all the evidence and arguments and notes important points of law for the benefit of the jury (NOTE: The British term is **summing up**.)

instrument /ˈɪnstrʊmənt/ *noun* **1.** a tool or piece of equipment ○ *The technical staff have instruments to measure the output of electricity.* **2.** a legal document

insulting behaviour /ɪnˌsʌltɪŋ bɪ ˈheɪvjə/ *noun* the offence of shouting or making rude signs in a way which shows that you are insulting someone

insurable /ɪnˈʃʊərəb(ə)l/ *adjective* being able to be insured

insurable interest /ɪnˌʃʊərəb(ə)l ˈɪntrəst/ *noun* an interest which a person taking out an insurance policy must have in what is being insured

insurance /ɪnˈʃʊərəns/ *noun* an agreement that in return for regular small payments, a company will pay compensation for loss, damage, injury or death □ **to take out an insurance against fire** to pay a premium so that if a fire happens, compensation will be paid

insurance broker /ɪnˈʃʊərəns ˌbrəʊkə/ *noun* somebody who sells insurance to clients

insurance claim /ɪnˈʃʊərəns kleɪm/ *noun* a request to an insurance company to pay for damages or for loss

insurance cover /ɪnˈʃʊərəns ˌkʌvə/ *noun* protection guaranteed by an insurance policy

insurance policy /ɪnˈʃʊərəns ˌpɒlɪsi/ *noun* a document which shows the conditions of an insurance contract

insurance premium /ɪnˈʃʊərəns ˌpriːmiəm/ *noun* a payment made by the insured person or a company to an insurance company

insurance rates /ɪnˈʃʊərəns reɪts/ *plural noun* the amount of premium which has to be paid per £1,000 of insurance

insure /ɪnˈʃʊə/ *verb* to have a contract with a company where, if regular small payments are made, the company will pay compensation for loss, damage, injury or death ○ *to insure a house against fire* ○ *to insure baggage against loss* ○ *to insure against bad weather* ○ *to insure against loss of earnings* ○ *He was insured for £100,000.* □ **the life insured** the person whose life is covered by a life assurance □ **the sum insured** the largest amount which an insurer will pay under the terms of an insurance

insurer /ɪnˈʃʊərə/ *noun* a company which insures someone or something (NOTE: For life insurance, British English prefers to use **assurer**.)

intangible /ɪnˈtændʒɪb(ə)l/ *adjective* being unable to be touched

intangible assets /ɪnˌtændʒɪb(ə)l ˈæsets/ *plural noun* assets which have a value, but which have no physical presence, e.g. goodwill, a patent or a trademark. Compare **tangible assets**

integrity /ɪnˈtegrɪti/ *noun* the original state of something which has not been adapted or changed in any way ○ *The electronic signature confirms the integrity of the document.*

intellectual /ˌɪntɪˈlektʃuəl/ *adjective* belonging to the mind

intellectual property /ˌɪntɪlektʃuəl ˈprɒpəti/ *noun* something such as a copyright, patent or design which someone has created or produced that no-one else can legally copy, use or sell

intellectual property rights /ˌɪntɪlektʃuəl ˈprɒpəti ˌraɪts/ *plural noun* the rights of ownership of something such as a copyright, patent or design. Abbreviation **IPR**

intelligible /ɪnˈtelɪdʒɪb(ə)l/ *adjective* able to be easily understood ○ *A key is required to make an encrypted message intelligible.*

intend /ɪnˈtend/ *verb* to plan to do something ○ *The company intends to sue for damages.* ○ *We intend to offer jobs to 250 unemployed young people.*

intended murder /ɪnˌtendɪd ˈmɜːdə/ *noun US* a murder which was planned in advance

intent /ɪnˈtent/ *noun* **1.** the state of mind of a person when they commit a crime. ◊ **mens rea 2.** what a person wants or means to happen when they do something such as enter into a contract □ **intent of a law** what Parliament intended when it made a law, used to help interpret the wording in relation to a particular case

intention /ɪnˈtenʃən/ *noun* **1.** the wish or plan to do something ○ *He was accused of perjury with the intention of incriminating his employer.* **2.** the belief that something will happen as the result of an action **3.** the meaning of the words in a document such as a will which may not be the same as what the maker of the document had actually written

> COMMENT: Intention to create a legal relationship is one of the essential elements of a contract.

intentional /ɪnˈtenʃən(ə)l/ *adjective* deliberate ○ *an act of intentional cruelty*

intentional homelessness /ɪnˌtenʃ(ə)nəl ˈhəʊmləsnəs/ *adjective* a situation in which a person has chosen to become homeless, with the result that their local authority has no duty to provide them with accommodation

intentionally /ɪnˈtenʃən(ə)li/ *adverb* deliberately ○ *She gave an intentionally misleading account of what happened.*

inter alia /ˌɪntə ˈeɪliə/ *phrase* a Latin phrase meaning 'among other things'

inter alios /ˌɪntər ˈeɪliəʊs/ *phrase* a Latin phrase meaning 'among other people': used to indicate one of several parties to a legal document

intercept /ˌɪntəˈsept/ *verb* to stop something as it is passing ○ *We have intercepted a message from one of the enemy agents in London.*

interception /ˌɪntəˈsepʃən/ *noun* the action of intercepting a message

inter-company comparisons /ˌɪntə ˌkʌmp(ə)ni kəmˈpærɪs(ə)nz/ *plural noun* comparing the results of one company with those of another in the same product area

inter-company dealings /ˌɪntə ˌkʌmp(ə)ni ˈdiːlɪŋz/ *plural noun* dealings between two companies in the same group

interdict /ˈɪntədɪkt/ *noun* (*in Scotland*) a ban, a written court order telling someone not to do something

interest /ˈɪntrəst/ *noun* **1.** a charge to be paid for borrowing money, usually calculated as a percentage of the amount borrowed ○ *The building society charges interest of 13% on its credit card.* **2.** money paid as income on investments or loans ○ *to receive interest at 5%* ○ *The bank pays 10% interest on deposits.* **3.** a right, title or legal share in something ○ *He has interests overseas.* □ **to declare an interest** to state in public that you have a right or title to something or a connection with it which means that you are not impartial **4.** special attention ○ *The police showed a lot of interest in the abandoned car.* ◊ **public interest** □ **to somebody's interest** which might interest somebody ○ *I have information which might be to your interest.* ■ *plural noun* **interests** □ **to be in somebody's best interests** to be the right thing to do in order to benefit or protect somebody ○ *The judge ruled that it was in the child's best interests to remain with his natural mother.* ■ *verb* to attract someone's attention ○ *He tried to interest several companies in his new invention.* □ **interested in** paying attention to ○ *The managing director is interested only in increasing profitability.*

interest-bearing deposits /ˌɪntrəst ˌbeərɪŋ dɪˈpɒzɪts/ *plural noun* deposits which produce interest

interest charges /ˈɪntrəst ˌtʃɑːdʒɪz/ *plural noun* the fees payable for borrowing money, usually a set percentage of how much is borrowed

interested party /ˌɪntrestɪd ˈpɑːti/ *noun* a person or company with a financial interest in a company

interest-free credit /ˌɪntrəst friː ˈkredɪt/, **interest-free loan** /ˈɪntrəst friː ləʊn/ *noun* credit or a loan where no interest is paid by the borrower

interest in remainder /ˌɪntrəst ɪn rɪ ˈmeɪndə/ *noun* an interest in land which will come into someone's possession when another person's interest ends

interest rate /ˈɪntrəst reɪt/ *noun* a percentage charge to be paid for borrowing money

interfere /ˌɪntəˈfɪə/ *verb* to get involved with something which is not your concern

interference /ˌɪntəˈfɪərəns/ *noun* the process of deliberately getting involved with something that is not your concern □ **interference with vehicles** an offence where someone tries to break into a vehicle with the intention of stealing it, or part of it, or of stealing its contents

interfere with /ˌɪntəˈfɪə wɪð/ *verb* **1.** to act in a way that stops something happening or developing ○ *He was accused of interfering with the course of justice.* **2.** to use or try to use something that does not belong to you or to which you have no right, especially if damage is caused ○ *He had been seen interfering with the lock.* **3.** to persuade someone such as a witness or a juror to give false information or change their opinion **4.** to touch a child in a sexual way

interim /ˈɪntərɪm/ *adjective* intended to happen or be used only until something more permanent is available ○ *He was ordered to make interim payments.* □ **in the interim** meanwhile, for the time being

interim dividend /ˌɪntərɪm ˈdɪvɪdend/ *noun* a dividend paid at the end of a half-year

interim injunction /ˌɪntərɪm ɪnˈdʒʌŋkʃən/ *noun* an injunction which prevents someone from doing something until the case is heard

interim order /ˌɪntərɪm ˈɔːdə/ *noun* an order given which has effect while a case is still being heard

interim payment /ˌɪntərɪm ˈpeɪmənt/ *noun* a part payment of a dividend or of money owed

interim relief /ˌɪntərɪm rɪˈliːf/ *noun* same as **interim remedy**

interim remedy /ˌɪntərɪm ˈremədi/ *noun* an action by a court to grant relief to a party while a claim is being processed, and even after judgment has been given

COMMENT: Interim remedies include interim injunctions, freezing injunctions, search orders, inspection of property, interim payments, etc.

interim report /ˌɪntərɪm rɪˈpɔːt/ *noun* **1.** a report from a commission which is not final **2.** a financial report given at the end of a half-year

interlocutory /ˌɪntəˈlɒkjʊt(ə)ri/ *adjective* **1.** temporary or provisional **2.** happening at a court hearing which takes place before full trial

interlocutory injunction /ˌɪntəlɒkjʊt(ə)ri ɪnˈdʒʌŋkʃ(ə)n/ *noun* an injunction which is granted for the period until a case comes to court

interlocutory judgment /ˌɪntəlɒkjʊt(ə)ri ˈdʒʌdʒmənt/ *noun* a judgment given during the course of an

action before full trial. Compare **final judgment**

interlocutory matter /ˌɪntəlɒkjʊt(ə)ri ˈmætə/ *noun* a subsidiary dispute which is dealt with before full trial

interlocutory proceedings /ˌɪntəlɒkjʊt(ə)ri prəˈsiːdɪŋz/ *plural noun* court hearings that take place before the full trial

intermeddle /ˌɪntəˈmed(ə)l/ *verb* to deal in someone's affairs ○ *If an executor pays the debts of an estate, this can be considered intermeddling, and thus is acceptance of the office of executor.*

intermediary /ˌɪntəˈmiːdiəri/ *noun* somebody who is the link between parties who do not agree or who are negotiating ○ *He refused to act as an intermediary between the two directors.*

intern /ɪnˈtɜːn/ *verb* to put someone in prison or other place of detainment without trial, usually for political reasons

internal /ɪnˈtɜːn(ə)l/ *adjective* referring to the inside □ **internal affairs** the way in which a country deals with its own citizens ○ *it is not usual for one country to criticize the internal affairs of another*

internal audit /ɪnˌtɜːn(ə)l ˈɔːdɪt/ *noun* an audit carried out by a department inside the company

internal auditor /ɪnˌtɜːn(ə)l ˈɔːdɪtə/ *noun* a member of staff who audits a company's accounts

international /ˌɪntəˈnæʃ(ə)nəl/ *adjective* working between countries

International Bar Association /ˌɪntənæʃ(ə)nəl ˈbɑː əˌsəʊsieɪʃ(ə)n/ *noun* an international lawyers' organisation formed to promote international law. Abbreviation **IBA**

International Chamber of Commerce /ˌɪntənæʃ(ə)nəl ˌtʃeɪmbər əv ˈkɒmɜːs/ *noun* a world business organisation, with a division based in Paris which administers international arbitrations. Abbreviation **ICC**

International Court of Justice /ˌɪntənæʃ(ə)nəl ˌkɔːt əv ˈdʒʌstɪs/ *noun* the court of the United Nations, which sits in the Hague, Netherlands

International Criminal Court /ˌɪntə ˈnæʃ(ə)nəl ˈkrɪmɪn(ə)l kɔːt/ *noun* an independent permanent court which tries persons accused of the most serious crimes of international concern. Abbreviation **ICC**

International Labour Organization /ˌɪntənæʃ(ə)nəl ˈleɪbə ˌɔːɡənaɪzeɪʃ(ə)n/ noun a section of the United Nations which tries to improve working conditions and workers' pay in member countries. Abbreviation **ILO**

international law /ˌɪntənæʃ(ə)nəl ˈlɔː/ noun law governing relations between countries

international lawyer /ˌɪntənæʃ(ə)nəl ˈlɔːjə/ noun a person who specialises in international law

international politics /ˌɪntənæʃ(ə)nəl ˈpɒlɪtɪks/ plural noun relationships between governments of different political parties and systems

international waters /ˌɪntənæʃ(ə)nəl ˈwɔːtəz/ plural noun the part of the sea which is beyond territorial waters and does not fall under any country's jurisdiction. Also called **high seas**, **mare liberum**

> COMMENT: Crimes committed in international waters fall under the jurisdiction of the country under whose flag the ship is sailing. In cases of piracy or people smuggling, any country can exercise its jurisdiction.

internee /ˌɪntɜːˈniː/ noun somebody who is interned

internment /ɪnˈtɜːnmənt/ noun the act of being putting someone in prison or other place of detention without trial

inter partes /ˌɪntə ˈpɑːteɪz/ phrase a Latin phrase meaning 'between the parties': a case heard where both parties are represented ○ The court's opinion was that the case should be heard inter partes as soon as possible. ◊ **ex parte**

interpleader /ˌɪntəˈpliːdə/ noun a court action started by a person who holds property which is claimed by two or more people, or by a person who may be sued by two different parties (NOTE: Do not confuse with the US term **impleader**.)

Interpol /ˈɪntəpɒl/ noun an international police organisation whereby the member countries co-operate in solving crimes ○ They warned Interpol that the criminals might be disguised as women.

interpret /ɪnˈtɜːprɪt/ verb **1.** to say what you think a law or precedent means ○ The role of the ECJ is to interpret a law, while the role of the national court is to apply it. ○ Courts in Member States cannot give authoritative rulings on how community law should be interpreted. **2.** to translate what someone has said into another language ○ My assistant knows Greek, so he will interpret for us.

interpretation /ɪnˌtɜːprɪˈteɪʃ(ə)n/ noun what someone thinks is the meaning of a law or precedent ○ Interpretation of the Treaty has been entrusted to the European Court of Justice. □ **to put an interpretation on something** to make something have a different meaning ○ His ruling puts quite a different interpretation on the responsibility of trustees.

Interpretation Act /ɪnˌtɜːprɪˈteɪʃ(ə)n ækt/ noun an Act of Parliament which rules how words used in other Acts of Parliament are to be understood

interpretation clause /ɪnˌtɜːprɪˈteɪʃ(ə)n klɔːz/ noun a clause in a contract stating the meaning to be given to terms in the contract

interpreter /ɪnˈtɜːprɪtə/ noun somebody who translates what someone has said into another language ○ The witness could not speak English, so the court had to appoint an interpreter.

interpretive /ɪnˈtɜːrprɪtɪv/ adjective (in the EU) referring to interpretation ○ There is an interpretive obligation on Member States to interpret national laws in a way which accords with the aims and objectives of the directives of the EU.

interregnum /ˌɪntəˈreɡnəm/ noun **1.** a period between the death or deposition of one monarch and the accession of the next **2.** a period during which no-one is at the head of an organisation or area until a new leader is appointed

interrogate /ɪnˈterəɡeɪt/ verb to ask questions in a severe manner ○ The prisoners were interrogated for three hours.

interrogation /ɪnˌterəˈɡeɪʃ(ə)n/ noun severe questioning ○ He confessed to the crime during his interrogation. ○ Under interrogation, she gave the names of her accomplices.

interrogator /ɪnˈterəɡeɪtə/ noun somebody who questions suspects

interrogatories /ˌɪntəˈrɒɡət(ə)riz/ plural noun questions put in writing during a civil action by one side to the other and which have to be answered on oath (NOTE: Since the introduction of the Civil Procedure Rules, this term has been replaced by **further information**.)

in terrorem /ɪn teˈrɔːrem/ phrase a Latin phrase meaning 'in order to cause fear': used when a threat is implied in a contract, e.g. by suggesting that a right will be forfeited if a party takes an undesirable course of action

interrupt /ˌɪntəˈrʌpt/ *verb* to try to speak or to shout when someone else is talking

intervene /ˌɪntəˈviːn/ *verb* **1.** to come between people or things so as to make a change □ **to intervene in a dispute** to try to settle a dispute **2.** to become a party to an action

intervener /ˌɪntəˈviːnə/ *noun* somebody who intervenes in an action to which he or she was not originally a party

intervention /ˌɪntəˈvenʃən/ *noun* an act made to make a change ○ *the government's intervention in the foreign exchange markets* ○ *the central bank's intervention in the banking crisis* □ **to stage an intervention** to force somebody to get help for their addictions or change their destructive lifestyle

interview /ˈɪntəvjuː/ *noun* a meeting between a suspect and one or more police officers, who ask him or her questions

COMMENT: Suspects must be cautioned before an interview takes place. The interview should be recorded and the record must be shown to the suspect at the end of the interview. If there is any possibility that the police have threatened the suspect so as to get a confession, that confession will not be admitted in court.

interview room /ˈɪntəvjuː ruːm/ *noun* a room where a person is asked questions or is interviewed

inter vivos /ˌɪntə ˈviːvəʊs/ *phrase* a Latin phrase meaning 'among living people'

COMMENT: An inter vivos transfer of property can be used as a way of passing property to someone without using a will; it does not necessarily take effect when someone dies, but can be put into effect as soon as it is signed.

intestacy /ɪnˈtestəsi/ *noun* dying without having made a will

intestate /ɪnˈtestət/ *adjective* □ **to die intestate** to die without having made a will

COMMENT: When someone dies intestate, the property automatically goes to the surviving marital partner, unless there are children.

intestate succession /ɪnˌtestət səkˈseʃ(ə)n/ *noun* the rules which apply when someone dies without having made a will

intimidate /ɪnˈtɪmɪdeɪt/ *verb* to frighten someone to make him or her do something, or to prevent him or her from doing something ○ *The accused was said to have intimidated the witnesses.*

intimidation /ɪnˌtɪmɪˈdeɪʃ(ə)n/ *noun* the act of frightening someone to make them do something or to prevent them from doing something

intoxicated /ɪnˈtɒksɪkeɪtɪd/ *adjective* showing the effects of having drunk alcohol

intoxication /ɪnˌtɒksɪˈkeɪʃ(ə)n/ *noun* the state of being drunk

in transit /ɪn ˈtrænzɪt/ *adverb* □ **goods in transit** goods being carried from one place to another

intra vires /ˌɪntrə ˈvaɪriːz/ *phrase* a Latin phrase meaning 'within the permitted powers' ○ *The minister's action was ruled to be intra vires.* ◊ **ultra vires**

intrinsic evidence /ɪnˌtrɪnsɪk ˈevɪd(ə)ns/ *noun* evidence used to interpret a document which can be found in the document itself. Compare **extrinsic evidence**

invalid /ˈɪnvəlɪd/ *adjective* **1.** not legally effective ○ *a claim which has been declared invalid* ○ *The permit is out-of-date and therefore invalid.* ○ *National courts cannot find EU legislation to be invalid.* **2.** not based on the facts that are known ○ *an invalid argument*

invalidate /ɪnˈvælɪdeɪt/ *verb* to make something invalid ○ *Because the company has been taken over, the contract has been invalidated.*

invalidation /ɪnˌvælɪˈdeɪʃən/ *noun* the act of making something invalid

invalidity /ˌɪnvəˈlɪdɪti/ *noun* the fact of not being valid ○ *the invalidity of the contract*

invasion of privacy /ɪnˌveɪʒ(ə)n əv ˈprɪvəsi/ *noun* action which causes disturbance to someone's private life, e.g. being followed intrusively by newspaper reporters

inventory /ˈɪnvənt(ə)ri/ *noun* a complete list of all the things occurring in something such as a house for sale, an office for rent, or the estate of a deceased person ■ *verb* to make a list of the contents of a property

invest /ɪnˈvest/ *verb* to put money into something such as a bank or a company where it is expected to increase in value ○ *He invested all his money in a shop.* ○ *She was advised to invest in real estate.*

investigate /ɪnˈvestɪgeɪt/ *verb* to examine something which may be wrong

investigation /ɪnˌvestɪˈgeɪʃ(ə)n/ *noun* an examination to find out what is wrong ○ *to conduct an investigation into irregularities in share dealings*

investigator /ɪn'vestɪgeɪtə/ *noun* somebody who investigates ○ *a government investigator*

investor /ɪn'vestə/ *noun* a person or company which invests money

invitation /ˌɪnvɪ'teɪʃ(ə)n/ *noun* the act of asking someone to do something □ **invitation to treat** the act of asking someone to make an offer to buy, e.g. by putting items for sale in a shop window

invite /ɪn'vaɪt/ *verb* to ask someone to do something (NOTE: The fact of inviting somebody onto your property means that you are responsible for their safety under the Occupier's Liability Act 1957.)

invitee /ˌɪnvaɪ'tiː/ *noun* somebody who has accepted an invitation to go into a property

involuntarily /ɪn'vɒlənt(ə)rəli/ *adverb* not willingly ○ *The accused's defence was that she acted involuntarily.*

involuntary /ɪn'vɒlənt(ə)ri/ *adjective* not done willingly

involuntary conduct /ɪnˌvɒlənt(ə)ri kən'dʌkt/ *noun* conduct beyond a person's control, offered as a defence to a criminal charge

involuntary manslaughter /ɪnˌvɒlənt(ə)ri 'mænslɔːtə/ *noun* the killing of someone without having intended to do so, through recklessness or criminal negligence

IOU /ˌaɪ əʊ 'juː/ *noun* a signed document promising that you will pay back money borrowed ○ *to pay a pile of IOUs* Full form **I owe you**

IPCC *abbreviation* Independent Police Complaints Commission

IPR *abbreviation* intellectual property rights

ipso facto /ˌɪpsəʊ 'fæktəʊ/ *phrase* a Latin phrase meaning 'by this very fact' or 'the fact itself shows' ○ *The writing of the letter was ipso facto an admission of guilt.* ○ *He was found in the vehicle at the time of the accident and ipso facto was deemed to be in charge of it.*

ipso jure /ˌɪpsəʊ 'dʒʊəreɪ/ *phrase* a Latin phrase meaning 'by the operation of the law': used to describe a situation in which an automatic change of the legal situation takes place as a consequence of some other action (NOTE: For example, a partnership contract may be dissolved ipso jure if one of the partners is found guilty of misconduct.)

irreconcilable /ɪˌrekən'saɪləb(ə)l/ *adjective* so opposed that agreement is not possible □ **irreconcilable differences** strong disagreement between a husband and wife which leads to divorce

irrecoverable /ˌɪrɪ'kʌv(ə)rəb(ə)l/ *adjective* being impossible to get back

irrecoverable debt /ɪrɪˌkʌv(ə)rəb(ə)l 'det/ *noun* a debt which will never be paid

irredeemable /ɪrɪ'diːməb(ə)l/ *adjective* being impossible to redeem

irredeemable bond /ɪrɪˌdiːməb(ə)l 'bɒnd/ *noun* a bond which has no date of maturity and which therefore provides interest but can never be redeemed at full value

irredentism /ˌɪrɪ'dentɪz(ə)m/ *noun* the act of trying to get back a colony or territory which has been lost to another country or which is felt to belong to the country because of similar language, culture, etc.

irredentist /ˌɪrɪ'dentɪst/ *noun* somebody who wants a territory returned

irregular /ɪ'regjʊlə/ *adjective* not following the usual rules, or not done in the way regarded as being correct ○ *irregular documentation* ○ *This procedure is highly irregular.*

irregularity /ɪˌregjʊ'lærɪti/ *noun* a situation in which the usual rules or ways of doing something have not been followed (*often plural*) ○ *to investigate irregularities in the share dealings*

irrelevant /ɪ'reləvənt/ *adjective* not relevant or important to what is being considered

irresistible impulse /ˌɪrɪzɪstəb(ə)l 'ɪmpʌls/ *noun* a strong wish to do something which you cannot resist because of insanity

irretrievable /ˌɪrɪ'triːvəb(ə)l/ *adjective* which cannot be brought back to its former state □ **irretrievable breakdown of a marriage** a situation in which the two spouses can no longer live together, where the marriage cannot be saved and therefore divorce proceedings can be started

irrevocable /ɪ'revəkəb(ə)l/ *adjective* being impossible to change

irrevocable acceptance /ɪˌrevəkəb(ə)l ək'septəns/ *noun* an acceptance which cannot be withdrawn

irrevocable letter of credit /ɪˌrevəkəb(ə)l ˌletər əv 'kredɪt/ *noun* a letter of credit which cannot be cancelled or changed

irritancy /'ɪrɪtənsi/ *noun* in Scotland, the forfeiture of a right through failure to abide by the law or an agreement, as occurs, e.g., when a tenant fails to pay rent due

IRS *abbreviation US* Internal Revenue Service

Islamic finance /ɪz,læmɪk 'faɪnæns/ *noun* a loan or mortgage with repayment terms that comply with the Sharia prohibition on paying or receiving interest

Islamic Law /ɪz'læmɪk lɔː/ *noun* the law of Muslim countries set out in the Koran and the teachings of the prophet Muhammad. ◊ **Sharia law** (NOTE: The law itself cannot be changed, but it can be interpreted in different ways.)

isolation /,aɪsə'leɪʃ(ə)n/ *noun* **1.** the state of being separated from other people **2.** □ **in isolation** kept on your own away from other people ○ *He had been kept in isolation for several weeks.*

isolationist /,aɪsə'leɪʃ(ə)nɪst/ *noun* somebody who believes that his or her country should not get involved in the affairs of other countries, and especially should not fight wars to protect other countries

issuance /'ɪʃuəns/ *noun* the act of issuing ○ *Upon issuance of the order, the bailiffs seized the property.*

issue /'ɪʃuː/ *noun* **1.** a subject that is discussed or argued about ○ *safety issues* ◊ **collateral issue** □ **at issue** under discussion as the most important aspect of a subject ○ *The point at issue is the ownership of the property.* □ **to have issues with something** to disagree or have problems with something (*informal*) ○ *I have issues with the idea of*

completely free access. □ **to make an issue of something** to treat something as more important than it is ○ *I don't want to make an issue of it, but I thought her information could have been more detailed.* □ **to take issue with someone** *or* **over something** to disagree with someone or about something ○ *I have to take issue with you over the handling of the case.* ○ *Barristers took issue over the proposals to change the system.* **2.** a legal matter in a dispute between two parties **3.** a child or children of a parent ○ *He had issue two sons and one daughter.* ○ *She died without issue.* ○ *They have no issue.* **4.** the act of giving something to someone or making something available ○ *The issue of new parking permits is expected soon.* **5.** the act of filing a Claim Form at court, in order to begin court proceedings against a defendant ■ *verb* to announce or give something officially ○ *to issue a letter of credit* ○ *The Secretary of State issued guidelines for expenditure.* ○ *He issued writs for libel in connection with allegations made in a Sunday newspaper.*

itemise /'aɪtəmaɪz/, **itemize** *verb* to make a detailed list of things ○ *Itemising the sales figures will take about two days.*

itemised account /,aɪtəmaɪzd ə'kaʊnt/ *noun* a detailed record of money paid or owed

item of expenditure /,aɪtəm əv ɪk'spendɪtʃə/ *noun* something such as goods or a service which has been paid for and appears in the accounts

IVA *abbreviation* individual voluntary arrangement

J

J /dʒeɪ/ *abbreviation* Justice ○ *Smith J said he was not laying down guidelines for sentencing.* (NOTE: often put after the name of a High Court judge: **Smith J** is spoken as 'Mr Justice Smith')

JAC *abbreviation* Judicial Appointments Commission

jactitation /ˌdʒæktɪˈteɪʃ(ə)n/ *noun* the act of maliciously boasting that something is true at the expense of another person

jactitation of marriage /ˌdʒæktɪteɪʃ(ə)n əv ˈmærɪdʒ/ *noun* the act of boasting that you are married to someone when you are not (NOTE: This is an archaic term and rarely used.)

jail /dʒeɪl/ *noun* a place where criminals are kept before trial or after they have been convicted ○ *He spent ten years in jail.* ■ *verb* to put someone in prison ○ *She was jailed for three years.* ○ *He was jailed for manslaughter.* (NOTE: also spelled **gaol** in British English)

jailbird /ˈdʒeɪlbɜːd/ *noun* somebody who is in prison or who has often been sent to prison

jailbreak /ˈdʒeɪlbreɪk/ *noun* escape from prison

jailer /ˈdʒeɪlə/ *noun* somebody who works in a jail or who is in charge of a jail

jaywalker /ˈdʒeɪwɔːkə/ *noun US* somebody who walks across a street at a place which is not a proper crossing place

jaywalking /ˈdʒeɪwɔːkɪŋ/ *noun US* the offence of walking across a street at a place which is not a proper crossing point for pedestrians

jeopardise /ˈdʒepədaɪz/, **jeopardize** *verb* to be likely to harm ○ *Her arrest for drunken driving may jeopardise her work as a doctor specialising in child care.*

jeopardy /ˈdʒepədi/ *noun* □ **to be in jeopardy** to be in danger of punishment or of harm. ◊ **double jeopardy**

Job Centre /ˈdʒɒb ˌsentə/ *noun* a government office which lists and helps to fill jobs which are vacant

Job Grant /ˈdʒɒb grɑːnt/ *noun* a one-off payment made by the Government to somebody who is going into work (of at least 16 hours per week) after a period receiving unemployment benefits

job openings /ˈdʒɒb ˌəʊp(ə)nɪŋ/ *plural noun* jobs which are empty and need filling

jobseeker's allowance /ˌdʒɒbsiːkəz əˈlaʊəns/ *noun* financial help given by the Government to someone who is unemployed and currently seeking work (NOTE: Sometimes informally called **the dole**: *to claim the dole*; *to be on the dole*.)

John Doe /ˌdʒɒn ˈdəʊ/ *noun US* a name used as an example in fictitious cases

join /dʒɔɪn/ *verb* □ **to join someone to an action** to attach someone's name as one of the parties to an action

joinder /ˈdʒɔɪndə/ *noun* the act of bringing together several actions or several parties in one action. ◊ **misjoinder, nonjoinder**

joint /dʒɔɪnt/ *adjective* **1.** with two or more organisations or people linked together **2.** of two or more people who work together or who are linked ○ *joint beneficiary* ○ *joint managing director* ○ *joint owner* ○ *joint signatory* ■ *noun* a place or building (*slang*) □ **to case a joint** to look at a building carefully before deciding how to break into it

joint and several /ˌdʒɔɪnt ən ˈsev(ə)rəl/ *adjective* as a group together and also separately

joint and several liability /ˌdʒɔɪnt ən ˌsev(ə)rəl ˌlaɪəˈbɪlɪti/ *noun* a situation where two or more parties share a single liability, and each party is also liable for the whole claim

joint commission of inquiry /ˌdʒɔɪnt kəˌmɪʃ(ə)n əv ɪnˈkwaɪəri/ *noun* a commission with representatives of various organisations on it

joint committee /ˌdʒɔɪnt kəˈmɪti/ *noun* a committee formed of equal numbers of members of the House of Commons and House of Lords

joint discussions /ˌdʒɔɪnt dɪˈskʌʃ(ə)nz/ *plural noun* discussions between employers and employees before something is done

joint heir /ˌdʒɔɪnt ˈeə/ *noun* somebody who is an heir with someone else

joint liability /dʒɔɪnt ˌlaɪəˈbɪlɪti/ *noun* a situation where two or more parties share a single liability

jointly /ˈdʒɔɪntli/ *adverb* together with one or more other people ○ *to own a property jointly* ○ *to manage a company jointly* ○ *They are jointly liable for damages.* □ **jointly and severally liable** liable both as a group and as individuals

joint management /ˌdʒɔɪnt ˈmænɪdʒmənt/ *noun* management by two or more people

joint ownership /ˌdʒɔɪnt ˈəʊnəʃɪp/ *noun* a situation where two or more persons own the same property

joint resolution /ˌdʒɔɪnt ˌrezəˈluːʃ(ə)n/ *noun US* a Bill which has been passed by both House and Senate, and is sent to the President for signature

joint tenancy /ˌdʒɔɪnt ˈtenənsi/ *noun* a situation where two or more persons acquire an interest in a property together, where if one of the joint tenants dies, his or her share goes to those surviving. ◊ **tenancy in common**

joint tortfeasors /ˌdʒɔɪnt tɔːtˈfiːzəz/ *plural noun* two or more people who are responsible and liable for a tort

jointure /ˈdʒɔɪntʃə/ *noun* the estate settled on a spouse (traditionally the wife) after the death of the other

joint venture /ˌdʒɔɪnt ˈventʃə/ *noun* a very large business partnership where two or more companies join together as partners for a limited period

joy ride /ˈdʒɔɪ ˌraɪdɪŋ/ *noun* a reckless, high-speed drive that tests the prowess of the driver, usually in a stolen car

joyriding /ˈdʒɔɪraɪdɪŋ/ *noun* the offence of stealing a car and driving it dangerously at high speed

JP *abbreviation* justice of the peace (NOTE: The plural is **JPs**.)

judge /dʒʌdʒ/ *noun* **1.** an official who presides over a court and in civil cases decides which party is in the right ○ *a County Court judge* ○ *a judge in the Divorce Court* ○ *The judge sent him to prison for embezzlement.* (NOTE: In the UK it is planned to transfer the appointment of judges to a Judicial Appointments Board.) **2.** one of the fifteen members of the European Court of Justice, appointed by the Member States ■ *verb* to decide ○ *He judged it was time to call an end to the discussions.*

COMMENT: In England, judges are appointed by the Lord Chancellor on the recommendation of the Judicial Appointments Committee. The minimum requirement is that one should be a barrister or solicitor of ten years' standing. The majority of judges are barristers, but they cannot practise as barristers. Recorders are practising barristers who act as judges on a part-time basis. The appointment of judges is not a political appointment, and judges remain in office unless they are found guilty of gross misconduct. Judges cannot be Members of Parliament. In the USA, state judges can be appointed by the state governor or can be elected; in the federal courts and the Supreme Court, judges are appointed by the President, but the appointment has to be approved by Congress.

Judge Advocate-General /ˌdʒʌdʒ ˌædvəkət ˈdʒen(ə)rəl/ *noun* a lawyer appointed by the state to advise on all legal matters concerning the army

Judge Advocate-General of the Forces /ˌdʒʌdʒ ˌædvəkət ˌdʒen(ə)rəl əv ðə ˈfɔːsɪz/ *noun* a lawyer appointed by the state to advise on all legal matters concerning the Army and Air Force

Judge Advocate of the Fleet /ˌdʒʌdʒ ˌædvəkət əv ðə ˈfliːt/ *noun* a lawyer appointed by the state to advise on all legal matters concerning the Royal Navy

judge in chambers /ˌdʒʌdʒ ɪn ˈtʃeɪmbəz/ *noun* a judge who hears a case in private rooms without the public being present and not in open court

Judges' Rules /ˌdʒʌdʒɪz ˈruːlz/ *noun* an informal set of rules governing how the police may question a suspect

judgment /ˈdʒʌdʒmənt/, **judgement** *noun* an official decision of a court (NOTE: The spelling **judgment** is preferred in most legal contexts in the UK) □ **to pronounce judgment, to give one's judgment on something** to give an official or legal decision about something □ **to enter judgment, to take judgment** to record an official judgment on a case □ **to enter judgment for the claimant** to make a legal judgment that the claimant's claim is accepted □ **to enter judgment against the claimant** to make a legal judgment that the claimant's claim is not accepted □ **to enter judgment in default** to take judgment because the defendant failed to defend the case

judgment by default /ˌdʒʌdʒmənt baɪ dɪˈfɔːlt/ *noun* a judgment without trial against a defendant who fails to respond to a claim

judgment creditor /ˈdʒʌdʒmənt ˌkredɪtə/ *noun* somebody who has been given a court order making a debtor pay a debt

judgment debtor /ˈdʒʌdʒmənt ˌdetə/ *noun* somebody who has been ordered by a court to pay a debt

judgment-proof /ˈdʒʌdʒmənt pruːf/ *adjective US* of a person, financially insolvent and so incapable of paying debts even if ordered to do so by law

judgment summons /ˌdʒʌdʒmənt ˈsʌmənz/ *noun* a summons by a court to enforce a court order, such as ordering a judgment debtor to pay or to go to prison

judicata ♦ **res judicata**

judicature /ˈdʒuːdɪkətʃə/ *noun* administration of justice □ **judicature paper** thick heavy paper on which court documents are engrossed. ◊ **Supreme Court**

judice ♦ **sub judice**

judicial /dʒuːˈdɪʃ(ə)l/ *adjective* **1.** referring to a judge or the law □ **the Judicial Committee of the House of Lords** the highest appeal court in England and Wales **2.** done in a court or by a judge

Judicial Appointments Commission /dʒuːˌdɪʃ(ə)l əˈpɔɪntmənts kəˌmɪʃ(ə)n/ *noun* a non-departmental public body set up in 2006 under the Constitutional Reform Act, which makes recommendations on the appointment of judges to the Lord Chancellor. Abbreviation **JAC**

Judicial Committee of the House of Lords /dʒuːˌdɪʃ(ə)l kəˌmɪti əv ðə ˌhaʊs əv ˈlɔːdz/ *noun* the highest court of appeal in both civil and criminal cases in England and Wales

Judicial Committee of the Privy Council /dʒuːˌdɪʃ(ə)l kəˌmɪti əv ðə ˌprɪvi ˈkaʊnsəl/ *noun* the appeal court for appeals from courts outside the UK, such as the courts of some Commonwealth countries

judicial immunity /dʒuːˌdɪʃ(ə)l ɪˈmjuːnɪti/ *noun* a safety from prosecution granted to judges when acting in a judicial capacity

judicial notice /dʒuːˌdɪʃ(ə)l ˈnəʊtɪs/ *noun* facts and matters which a judge is presumed to know, so that evidence does not have to be produced to prove them ○ *The court took judicial notice of the fact that the 3-month old baby was not capable of walking.*

judicial precedent /dʒuːˌdɪʃ(ə)l ˈpresɪd(ə)nt/ *noun* a precedent set by a court decision, which can be reversed only by a higher court

judicial processes /dʒuːˌdɪʃ(ə)l ˈprəʊsesɪz/ *plural noun* the ways in which the law works

judicial review /dʒuːˌdɪʃ(ə)l rɪˈvjuː/ *noun* a reassessment or re-examination by judges of a decision or proceeding by a lower court or a government department

judicial separation /dʒuːˌdɪʃ(ə)l ˌsepəˈreɪʃ(ə)n/ *noun* same as **legal separation**

judiciary /dʒʊˈdɪʃəri/ *noun* □ **the judiciary** all judges, the court system, the judicial power in general

jump /dʒʌmp/ ♦ **bail**

junior /ˈdʒuːniə/ *adjective* younger or lower in rank □ **John Smith, Junior** the younger John Smith (i.e. the son of John Smith, Senior) ■ *noun* **1.** a barrister who is not a Queen's Counsel **2.** a barrister appearing with a leader ► also called **junior barrister**

junior clerk /ˌdʒuːniə ˈklɑːk/ *noun* a clerk, usually a young person, who has lower status than a senior clerk

junior executive /ˌdʒuːniə ɪɡˈzekjʊtɪv/ *noun* a less important manager in a company

junior partner /ˌdʒuːniə ˈpɑːtnə/ *noun* somebody who has a small part of the shares in a partnership

jurat /ˈdʒʊəræt/ *noun* words at the end of an affidavit, showing the details of when and by whom it was sworn

juridical /dʒʊˈrɪdɪk(ə)l/ *adjective* referring to the law or to judges

jurisdiction /ˌdʒʊərɪsˈdɪkʃən/ *noun* legal power over someone or something □ **within the jurisdiction of the court** in the legal power of a court □ **outside the jurisdiction of the court** not covered by the legal power of the court □ **to refuse to recognise the jurisdiction of the court** to say that you do not believe that a court has the legal right to try you

jurisdictional /ˌdʒʊərɪs'dɪkʃənəl/ *adjective* referring to a court's jurisdiction

jurisprudence /ˌdʒʊərɪs'pruːdəns/ *noun* the study of the law and the legal system

jurist /'dʒʊərɪst/ *noun* a person who has specialised in the study and practice of law

juristic /ˌdʒʊə'rɪstɪk/ *adjective* according to the practice of law

juror /'dʒʊərə/ *noun* a member of a jury

jury /'dʒʊəri/ *noun* a group of twelve citizens who are sworn to decide whether someone is guilty or not guilty on the basis of the evidence they hear in court □ **to be called for jury service** to be officially summoned to serve on a jury □ **'members of the jury'** the proper way to address a jury in court □ **the foreman of the jury** the chief juror, elected by the other jurors, who chairs the discussions of the jury and pronounces the verdict in court afterwards

COMMENT: Juries are used in criminal cases, and in some civil actions, notably actions for libel. They are also used in some coroner's inquests. The role of the jury is use their common sense to decide if the verdict should be for or against the accused. Jurors have no knowledge of the law and follow the explanations given to them by the judge. See Supplement for further explanation of eligibility for jury service.

jury box /'dʒʊəri bɒks/ *noun* a place where the jury sit in the courtroom

Jury Central Summoning Bureau /ˌdʒʊəri ˌsentr(ə)l 'sʌmənɪŋ ˌbjʊərəʊ/ *noun* the organisation responsible for arranging jury service in the UK

juryman /'dʒʊərimən/ *noun* a member of a jury (NOTE: The plural is **jurymen**.)

jury room /'dʒʊəri ruːm/ *noun* a room where a jury meet to discuss the trial and reach a verdict

jury service /'dʒʊəri ˌsɜːvɪs/ *noun* the duty which each citizen has of serving on a jury if asked to do so

jury vetting /ˌdʒʊəri 'vetɪŋ/ *noun* the examination of each of the proposed members of a jury to see if he or she is qualified to be a juror

jus /dʒʌs/ *noun* a Latin word meaning 'law' or 'right'

jus accrescendi /ˌdʒʌs ˌækre'sendi/ ♦ **survivorship**

just /dʒʌst/ *adjective* fair or right □ **to show just cause** to show a reason which is

fair and acceptable in law □ **just war** a war which is considered to be morally defensible

justice /'dʒʌstɪs/ *noun* **1.** fair treatment under the law □ **to administer justice** to bring about justice through the application of the law □ **to bring a criminal to justice** to find a criminal and charge him or her with an offence **2.** a magistrate **3.** a judge **4.** the title given to a High Court judge ○ *Mr Justice Adams*

justice gap /'dʒʌstɪs gæp/ *noun* a situation in which fewer people are being convicted for crimes than are statistically likely to be guilty ○ *Only 5.6% of reported rape cases last year resulted in a conviction, revealing a huge justice gap.*

justice of the peace /ˌdʒʌstɪs əv ðə 'piːs/ *noun* a magistrate or local judge. Abbreviation **JP**

justices' chief executive /ˌdʒʌstɪsɪz ˌtʃiːf ɪg'zekjʊtɪv/ *noun* a senior administrator appointed by a magistrates' courts committee to run the courts in an area, but not to give legal advice

justices' clerk /ˌdʒʌstɪsɪz 'klɑːk/ *noun* an official of a magistrates' court who gives advice to the justices on law, practice or procedure

justiciable /dʒʌs'tɪʃəb(ə)l/ *adjective* referring to a legal principle which can be subject to laws ○ *Some people question whether subsidiarity is justiciable.*

justiciary /dʒʌs'tɪʃəri/ *noun* all judges

justifiable /'dʒʌstɪfaɪəb(ə)l/ *adjective* excusable

justifiable homicide /ˌdʒʌstɪfaɪəb(ə)l 'hɒmɪsaɪd/ *noun* the act of killing a person for an acceptable reason such as self-defence

justification /ˌdʒʌstɪfɪ'keɪʃ(ə)n/ *noun* an acceptable reason for doing something □ **in justification** as an acceptable excuse for something ○ *In justification, the accused claimed that the burglar had attacked him with an axe.* ○ *He wrote a letter in justification of his decision.* ○ *The defendant entered defence of justification.* □ **with some justification** having a good reason for something ○ *She claimed, with some justification, that she could not have known about the change as the letter had gone to the wrong address.*

justify /'dʒʌstɪfaɪ/ *verb* to give an excuse for □ **the end justifies the means** if the result is right, the means used to reach it are acceptable

justitia ♦ fiat justitia

juvenile /'dʒuːvənaɪl/ *noun, adjective* same as **minor**

Juvenile Court /'dʒuːvəˌnaɪl kɔːt/ *noun* a court which tries young offenders ○ *The appeal court quashed the care order made by the juvenile court.* (NOTE: The **Juvenile Court** is now called the **Youth Court**.)

juvenile delinquent /ˌdʒuːvənaɪl dɪ'lɪŋkwənt/ *noun* a young criminal who commits minor crimes, especially against property

juvenile offender /ˌdʒuːvənaɪl ə'fendə/ *noun* the former term for a young person tried in a Juvenile Court (NOTE: Now replaced by **young offender**.)

K

kangaroo court /ˌkæŋgəˈruː kɔːt/ *noun* an unofficial and illegal court set up by a group of people

KC *abbreviation* King's Counsel

Keeper of the Great Seal /ˌkiːpər əv ðiː ˌgreɪt ˈsiːl/ *noun* the Lord Chancellor

Keogh plan /ˈkiːəʊ ˌplæn/ *noun US* a private pension programme which allows self-employed businessmen and professionals to set up pension plans for themselves

kerb crawling /ˌkɜːb ˈkrɔːlɪŋ/ *noun* driving slowly in order to importune women standing on the pavement

key money /ˈkiː ˌmʌni/ *noun* a premium paid when taking over the keys of a flat or office which you are renting

kickback /ˈkɪkbæk/ *noun* an illegal commission paid to someone, especially a government official, who helps in a business deal

kidnap /ˈkɪdnæp/ *verb* to take away someone and keep them somewhere against their will, usually asking for money to be paid or conditions to be met before they can be released

kidnapper /ˈkɪdnæpə/ *noun* somebody who kidnaps someone

kidnapping /ˈkɪdnæpɪŋ/ *noun* the notifiable offence of taking away a person by force

kill /kɪl/ *verb* to make someone die ○ *He was accused of killing his girlfriend with a knife.*

killer /ˈkɪlə/ *noun* somebody who kills ○ *The police are searching for the girl's killer.*

kin /kɪn/ *plural noun* relatives or close members of the family. ◊ **next of kin**

King's Counsel /ˌkɪŋz ˈkaʊnsəl/ *noun* abbreviation **KC**. ♦ **Queen's Counsel**

kleptomania /ˌkleptəʊˈmeɪniə/ *noun* a mental illness which makes someone steal things

kleptomaniac /ˌkleptəʊˈmeɪniæk/ *noun* somebody who steals things because he or she suffers from kleptomania

knock-for-knock agreement /ˌnɒk fə ˌnɒk əˈgriːmənt/ *noun* an agreement between two insurance companies that they will not take legal action against each other, and that each will pay the claims of their own clients

knowingly /ˈnəʊɪŋli/ *adverb* deliberately ○ *It was charged that he knowingly broke the Official Secrets Act by publishing the document in his newspaper.*

know-your-client /ˌnəʊ jɔː ˈklaɪənt/ *noun* the principle that a solicitor or other professional should have reasonable knowledge of their client's identity, to guard against fraud or money laundering. Abbreviation **KYC**

KYC *abbreviation* know-your-client

Kyoto Agreement, Kyoto Protocol *noun* a United Nations treaty on climate change, which imposes mandatory limits on its signatory nations for the emission of greenhouse gases. ◊ **carbon permit**, **emissions trading**

L

labour /'leɪbə/ *noun* **1.** heavy work □ **to charge for materials and labour** to charge for both the materials used in a job and also the hours of work involved **2.** \the workforce in general □ **skilled labour** workers who have special knowledge or qualifications

labour-intensive industry /ˌleɪbər ɪn ˌtensɪv 'ɪndəstri/ *noun* an industry which needs large numbers of employees or where labour costs are high in relation to turnover

labour law /'leɪbə lɔː/, **labour laws** /'leɪbə lɔːz/, **labour legislation** /ˌleɪbə ˌledʒɪ'sleɪʃ(ə)n/ *noun US* law relating to the employment of workers

laches /'lætʃɪz/ *noun* in equity law, unreasonable delay or neglect in asserting a legal right. ◊ **doctrine of laches**

lading /'leɪdɪŋ/ ♦ **bill of lading**

Lady Day /'leɪdi deɪ/ *noun* 25th March, one of the quarter days when rent is paid for land

laissez-faire /ˌleɪseɪ 'feə/, **laisser-faire** *noun* the principle that a governing body should do nothing to manipulate or control economic activity ○ *Laissez-faire policies meant that fewer women were rising to positions of power in the company.*

land /lænd/ *noun* an area of ground that somebody owns and may use for some purpose

COMMENT: Under English law, the ownership of all land is vested in the Crown; individuals or other legal persons may however hold estates in land, the most important of which are freehold estates (which amount to absolute ownership) and leasehold estates (which last for a fixed period of time). Ownership of land usually confers ownership of everything above and below the land. The process of buying and selling land is 'conveyancing'. Any contract transferring land or any interest in land must be in writing. Interests in land can be disposed of by a will.

land agent /'lænd ˌeɪdʒənt/ *noun* somebody who manages a farm or large area of land for someone

land certificate /'lænd səˌtɪfɪkət/ *noun* a document which shows who owns a piece of land, and whether there are any charges on it

land charges /'lænd ˌtʃɑːdʒɪz/ *plural noun* covenants, mortgages, etc., which are attached to a piece of land

landing charges /'lændɪŋ ˌtʃɑːdʒɪz/ *plural noun* payment for putting goods on land and for customs duties

landing order /'lændɪŋ ˌɔːdə/ *noun* a permit which allows goods to be unloaded into a bonded warehouse without paying customs duty

landlady /'lændleɪdi/ *noun* a woman who owns a property which is let

landlord /'lændlɔːd/ *noun* a person or company which owns a property which is let

Landlord and Tenant Act /ˌlændlɔːd ən 'tenənt ˌækt/ *noun* an Act of Parliament which regulates the letting of property

landmark decision /ˌlændmɑːk dɪ 'sɪʒ(ə)n/ *noun* a legal or legislative decision which creates an important legal precedent

landowner /'lændəʊnə/ *noun* somebody who owns large areas of land

land register /'lænd ˌredʒɪstə/ *noun* a register of land, showing who owns it and what buildings are on it

land registration /'lænd redʒɪ ˌstreɪʃ(ə)n/ *noun* a system of registering land and its owners

Land Registry /'lænd ˌredʒɪstri/ *noun* the British government office where details of land and its ownership are kept

lands /lændz/ *plural noun* large areas of land owned by a single owner

Lands Tribunal /'lɑːndz traɪˌbjuːn(ə)l/ *noun* a court which deals with compensation claims relating to land

land tax /'lænd tæks/ *noun* a tax on the amount of land owned

lapse /læps/ *noun* **1.** □ **a lapse of time** a period of time which has passed **2.** the ending of a right, a privilege or an offer, e.g. the termination of an insurance policy because the premiums have not been paid **3.** the failure of a legacy because the beneficiary has died before the testator ■ *verb* to stop being valid or effective □ **to let an offer lapse** to allow time to pass so that an offer is no longer valid □ **lapsed passport** a passport which is out of date

lapsed legacy /,læpst 'legəsi/ *noun* a legacy which cannot be put into effect because the person who should have received it died before the person who made the will

lapsed policy /læpst 'pɒlisi/, **lapsed insurance policy** /læpst ɪn,ʃʊərəns 'pɒlisi/ *noun* insurance which is no longer valid because the premiums have not been paid

larceny /'lɑːs(ə)ni/ *noun* the crime of stealing goods which belong to another person ○ *She was convicted of larceny.*

COMMENT: Larceny no longer exists in English law, having been replaced by the crime of **theft**.

last /lɑːst/ *adjective, adverb* coming at the end of a series ○ *Out of a queue of twenty people, I was served last.* ○ *This is our last board meeting before we move to our new offices.* ○ *This is the last case that the magistrates will hear before lunch.*

last in first out /,lɑːst ɪn ,fɜːst 'aʊt/ *phrase* **1.** in a redundancy situation, the dismissal of the people who have been most recently appointed before people who have longer service **2.** an accounting method where stock is valued at the price of the latest purchases ▸ abbreviation **LIFO**

last will and testament /,lɑːst ,wɪl ən 'testəmənt/ *noun* a document by which a person says what they want to happen to their property when they die

late /leɪt/ *adjective* **1.** after the time stated or agreed ○ *We apologise for the late start of this meeting.* □ **to carry a penalty for late delivery** to incur a fine if delivery is later than the agreed date **2.** at the end of a period of time **3.** dead ○ *She inherited a fortune from his late uncle.*

late completion /,leɪt kəm'pliːʃ(ə)n/ *noun* a situation in which the seller of property fails to complete the contract at the agreed time

latent /'leɪt(ə)nt/ *adjective* existing but not obvious or visible

latent ambiguity /,leɪt(ə)nt ,æmbɪ'gjuːɪti/ *noun* a word or phrase in a contract which can mean two or more things, but which does not appear to be misleading at first

latent defect /,leɪt(ə)nt 'diːfekt/ *noun* a fault which cannot be seen immediately

launder /'lɔːndə/ *verb* to transfer illegal or stolen money into an ordinary bank account, usually by a complex process to avoid detection (*slang*) ○ *The proceeds of the robbery were laundered through a bank in the Caribbean.*

law /lɔː/ *noun* **1.** a written or unwritten rule by which a country is governed and the activities of people and organisations are controlled ○ *A law has to be passed by Parliament.* ○ *The government has proposed a new law to regulate the sale of goods on Sundays.* **2.** □ **contract law, the law of contract** laws relating to agreements □ **to go to law** to start legal proceedings about something ○ *We went to law to try to regain our property.* □ **to take someone to law** to sue someone □ **inside the law, within the law** obeying the laws of a country □ **against the law, outside the law** not according to the laws of a country ○ *Dismissing an employee without reason is against the law.* ○ *The company is operating outside the law.* □ **in law** according to the law ○ *What are the duties in law of a guardian?* □ **to break the law** to do something which is against the law ○ *You will be breaking the law if you try to take that computer out of the country without an export licence.* **3.** a general rule **4.** □ **the law** the police and the courts (*informal*) ○ *The law will catch up with him in the end.* ○ *If you don't stop making that noise I'll have the law on you.* □ **the long arm of the law** the ability of the police to catch criminals and deal with crime

COMMENT: A law in the UK is an Act of Parliament which has received the Royal Assent, or, in the US, an Act of Congress which has been signed by the President or which has been passed by Congress over the President's veto. See Supplement for discussion of the process of passing a law.

law and order /,lɔː ənd 'ɔːdə/ *noun* a situation where the laws of a country are being obeyed by most people ○ *There was a breakdown of law and order following the assassination of the president.*

lawbreaker /'lɔː,breɪkə/ *noun* somebody who breaks the law

law-breaking /'lɔː ˌbreɪkɪŋ/ *noun* the act of doing something which is against the law

Law Centre /'lɔː ˌsentə/ *noun* a local office with full-time staff who advise on points of law and represent clients free of charge

Law Commission /'lɔː kəˌmɪʃ(ə)n/ *noun* a permanent committee which reviews English law and recommends changes to it

law court /'lɔː kɔːt/ *noun* a place where trials are held

law enforcement /'lɔː ɪnˌfɔːsmənt/ *noun* the activity of making sure that laws are obeyed

law enforcement officers /'lɔːr ɪn ˌfɔːsmənt ˌɒfɪsəz/ *plural noun* people who have the official role of making sure that people obey the law, e.g. police officers

lawful /'lɔːf(ə)l/ *adjective* according to the law

lawful interception /ˌlɔːf(ə)l ˌɪntə ˈsep(ə)n/ *noun* the interception of communications such as telephone or e-mail signals by an authority in accordance with the law

lawfully /'lɔːfəli/ *adverb* acting within the law

lawful practice /ˌlɔːf(ə)l ˈpræktɪs/ *noun* action which is permitted by the law

lawful trade /ˌlɔːf(ə)l ˈtreɪd/ *noun* trade which is allowed by law

lawless /'lɔːləs/ *adjective* not controlled by the law or by the police ○ *The magistrates criticised the lawless behaviour of the football crowd.*

lawlessness /'lɔːləsnəs/ *noun* the state of being lawless ○ *The government is trying to fight lawlessness in large cities.*

law library /'lɔː ˌlaɪbrəri/ *noun* a library that specialises in the provision of books about the law, often to support university and college departments training lawyers

Law List /'lɔː lɪst/ *noun* an annual published list of barristers and solicitors

Law Lords /'lɔː lɔːdz/ *plural noun* members of the House of Lords who are or were judges, including the Lord Chancellor and the Lords of Appeal in Ordinary

law-making /'lɔː ˌmeɪkɪŋ/ *noun* the process of making of laws ○ *Parliament is the law-making body in Great Britain.*

lawman /'lɔːmæn/ *noun US* a policeman (NOTE: The plural is **lawmen**.)

Law Officers /'lɔː ˌɒfɪsəz/ *plural noun* members of the British government, but not members of the Cabinet: the Attorney-General and Solicitor-General in England and Wales, and the Lord Advocate and Solicitor-General in Scotland

COMMENT: The Law Officers advise the government and individual ministries on legal matters. The Attorney-General will prosecute in trials for serious crimes.

law of property /ˌlɔː əv ˈprɒpəti/ *noun* a branch of the law dealing with the rights of ownership

law of succession /ˌlɔː əv səkˈseʃ(ə)n/ *noun* law relating to how property shall pass to others when the owner dies

law of supply and demand /ˌlɔː əv sə ˌplaɪ ən dɪˈmɑːnd/ *noun* the general rule that the amount of a product which is available is related to the needs of possible customers

law of the sea /ˌlɔː əv ðə ˈsiː/ *noun* same as **Admiralty law**

law reform /ˌlɔː rɪˈfɔːm/ *noun* the continuing process of revising laws to make them better suited to the needs of society

Law Reports /'lɔː rɪˌpɔːts/ *plural noun* regular reports of new cases and legislation

law school /'lɔː skuːl/ *noun US* a school where lawyers are trained

Law Society /ˌlɔː səˈsaɪəti/ *noun* an organisation of solicitors in England and Wales, which represents the profession (NOTE: In January 2007 the Law Society's regulatory function was transferred to the **Solicitors Regulation Authority**.)

Laws of Oleron /ˌlɔːz əv ˈɒlərɒn/ *plural noun* the first maritime laws, drawn up in 1216 and used as a base for subsequent international laws

lawsuit /'lɔːsuːt/ *noun US* a case brought to a court by a private person □ **to bring a lawsuit against someone** to tell someone to appear in court to settle an argument □ **to defend a lawsuit** to appear in court to state your case

lawyer /'lɔːjə/ *noun* a person who has studied law and can act for people on legal business

lay /leɪ/ *verb* □ **to lay down** to state clearly ○ *The conditions are laid down in the document.* ○ *The guidelines lay down rules for dealing with traffic offences.* ■ *adjective* not belonging to a specific profession

lay assessor /'leɪ əˌsesə/ *noun* a person who is not a lawyer who has technical knowledge of a subject and advises a court on specialised matters

lay magistrate /ˌleɪ ˈmædʒɪstreɪt/ *noun* an unpaid magistrate who is not usually a qualified lawyer. Compare **stipendiary magistrate**

layperson /ˈleɪmən/, **layman, laywoman** *noun* somebody who does not belong to the legal profession (NOTE: The plural is **laymen.**)

lay reader /ˈleɪ ˌriːdə/ *noun* someone who needs to understand technical information but doesn't have specialist knowledge of the subject ○ *This document should be accessible to the lay reader.*

lay representative /leɪ ˌreprɪˈzentətɪv/ *noun* a person representing someone in a case in the small claims track who is not a solicitor, barrister or legal executive

LBO *abbreviation* leveraged buy-out

LC *abbreviation* Lord Chancellor

L/C *abbreviation* letter of credit

LCIA *abbreviation* London Court of International Arbitration

LCJ *abbreviation* Lord Chief Justice

lead /liːd/ *noun* a piece of information which may help solve a crime ○ *The police are following up several leads in the murder investigation.* ■ *verb* **1.** to be the first or in front ○ *The company leads the market in cheap computers.* **2.** to be the main person in charge of a group **3.** to be the main person in a team of barristers appearing for one side in a case ○ *The prosecution is led by J.M. Jones, QC.* ○ *Mr Smith is leading for the Crown.* **4.** to start to do something such as present a case in court ○ *Mr Jones led for the prosecution.* ○ *The Home Secretary will lead for the Government in the emergency debate.* **5.** to bring evidence before a court **6.** to try to make a witness answer a question in court in a specific way ○ *Counsel must not lead the witness.* (NOTE: **leading – led – has led**)

leader /ˈliːdə/ *noun* **1.** somebody who manages or directs others ○ *She is the leader of the trade delegation to Nigeria.* ○ *The minister was the leader of the party of lawyers on a tour of American courts.* **2.** the main barrister, usually a QC, in a team appearing for one side in a case **3.** a product which sells best

leading /ˈliːdɪŋ/ *adjective* **1.** most important ○ *Leading shareholders in the company forced a change in management policy.* ○ *They are the leading company in the field.* **2.** suggesting a particular answer or designed to make a person respond in a particular way. ◊ **leading question**

leading cases /ˌliːdɪŋ ˈkeɪsɪz/ *plural noun* important cases which have set precedents

leading counsel /ˌliːdɪŋ ˈkaʊnsəl/ *noun* the main barrister, usually a QC, in a team appearing for one side in a case

leading question /ˌliːdɪŋ ˈkweʃtʃən/ *noun* a question put by a barrister to a witness which strongly suggests to the witness what the answer ought to be, e.g. a question which can only be answered 'Yes' or 'No'

COMMENT: Leading questions may be asked during cross-examination or during examination in chief.

leak /liːk/ *noun* the unofficial passing of information which has not yet been published, by officials, MPs or employees to newspapers, TV or radio stations, or other public forums ○ *The government is investigating the latest leak of documents relating to the spy trial.* ■ *verb* to make secret information public without being authorised to do so ○ *The details of the plan have been leaked to the press to test public reaction.*

leapfrog appeal /ˈliːpfrɒg əˌpiːl/ *noun* an appeal from a decision of the High Court which bypasses the Court of Appeal and goes straight to the House of Lords

lease /liːs/ *noun* **1.** a written contract for letting or renting of a building, a piece of land or a piece of equipment for a period of time on payment of a fee □ **the lease runs out in 2020** the lease comes to an end in 2020 □ **on expiration of the lease** when the lease comes to an end. ◊ **demise 2.** □ **to hold an oil lease in the North Sea** to have a lease on a section of the North Sea to explore for oil ■ *verb* **1.** to let or rent offices, land or machinery for a period ○ *to lease offices to small firms* ○ *to lease equipment* **2.** to use an office, land or machinery for a time and pay a fee to the landlord or lessor ○ *to lease an office from an insurance company* ○ *All our company cars are leased.*

lease back /ˌliːs ˈbæk/ *verb* to sell a property or machinery to a company and then take it back on a lease ○ *They sold the office building to raise cash, and then leased it back for twenty-five years.*

lease-back /ˈliːs bæk/ *noun* an arrangement by which property is sold and then taken back on a lease ○ *They sold the office building and then took it back under a lease-back arrangement.*

leasehold /ˈliːshəʊld/ *adjective, adverb* on the basis of a lease ○ *a leasehold property* ○ *to purchase a flat leasehold* ■ *noun* a property which is held for a period of time on the basis of a lease ○ *The company has some valuable leaseholds in the city centre.*

Leasehold Advisory Service /ˌliːshəʊld ədˈvaɪzəri ˌsɜːvɪs/ *noun* a UK organisation that provides free advice on the law affecting residential long leasehold property and commonhold

leasehold enfranchisement /ˌliːshəʊld ɪnˈfræntʃaɪzmənt/ *noun* the right of a leaseholder to buy the freehold of the property which he or she is leasing

leaseholder /ˈliːshəʊldə/ *noun* somebody who holds a property on a lease

leasing /ˈliːsɪŋ/ *noun* the activity of let someone use something for a period on payment of a fee ○ *The company has branched out into car leasing.* ■ *adjective* providing something on the basis of a lease ○ *to run a photocopier under a leasing arrangement* ○ *a computer-leasing company*

leave /liːv/ *noun* **1.** permission to do something ○ *Counsel asked leave of the court to show a film taken of the accident.* □ **'by your leave'** with your permission □ **leave to defend** permission from a court allowing someone to defend him or herself against an accusation **2.** a permitted period of being away from work. ◊ **maternity leave, paternity leave, sick leave** □ **leave of absence** permission to be away from work for a period for an unexpected reason □ **to go on leave, to be on leave** to be away from work on holiday ○ *She is away on sick leave* or *on maternity leave.* ■ *verb* **1.** to go away from somewhere or someone ○ *The next plane leaves at 10.20.* ○ *He left his office early to go to the meeting.* **2.** to give property to someone when you die ○ *He left his house to his wife.* ○ *I was left £5,000 by my grandmother in her will.* **3.** to resign ○ *She left her job and started up a new business.* (NOTE: **leaving – left – has left**)

left of centre /ˌleft əv ˈsentə/ *adjective* tending towards socialism

legacy /ˈlegəsi/ *noun* money or personal property excluding land given by someone to someone else in a will ○ *She received a small legacy in her uncle's will.*

COMMENT: Freehold land left to someone in a will is a **devise**.

legal /ˈliːg(ə)l/ *adjective* **1.** according to or allowed by the law ○ *The company's action was completely legal.* **2.** referring to the law □ **to take legal action, to start legal proceedings** to sue someone, to take someone to court □ **to take legal advice** to ask a law-

yer to advise about a problem in law □ **legal department** the section of a company dealing with legal matters ■ *verb* to send a story to a lawyer to check that it is safe to publish it (*informal*)

legal adviser /ˌliːg(ə)l ədˈvaɪzə/ *noun* somebody who advises clients about problems in law

legal age /ˈliːg(ə)l eɪdʒ/ *noun US* the age at which a person can sue or can be sued or can undertake business (NOTE: The UK term is **age of majority**.)

Legal Aid /ˌliːg(ə)l ˈeɪd/ *noun* a scheme whereby a person with very little money can have legal representation and advice paid for by the state (NOTE: Formerly a British Government scheme, it is now administered by the Legal Services Commission.)

Legal Aid Centre /ˌliːg(ə)l ˈeɪd ˌsentə/ *noun* formerly, a local office giving advice to clients with legal problems, assisting with Legal Aid applications and recommending clients to solicitors. ◊ **Legal Services Commission**

legal alien /ˌliːg(ə)l ˈeɪliən/ *noun* a person who is not a citizen of a country but is legally resident there

legal certainty /ˌliːg(ə)l ˈsɜːt(ə)nti/ *noun* in European law, a principle which states that vested rights are not retroactive, that legislation shall not have retrospective effect, and that the legitimate expectations of a claimant must be respected

legal charge /ˌliːg(ə)l ˈtʃɑːdʒ/ *noun* a charge created over property by a legal mortgage

legal claim /ˈliːg(ə)l kleɪm/ *noun* a statement that someone owns something legally □ **to have a legal claim to something** to have the right to establish legal ownership of something ○ *He has no legal claim to the property.*

legal costs /ˈliːg(ə)l kɒsts/ *noun* money spent on fees to lawyers

legal currency /ˌliːg(ə)l ˈkʌrənsi/ *noun* the money that is legally used in a country

legal disability /ˌliːg(ə)l ˌdɪsəˈbɪlɪti/ *noun* circumstances which make a person ineligible to stand trial □ **under a legal disability** being ineligible to stand trial because of a legal disability

COMMENT: Persons under a legal disability are usually considered to be those under the age of responsibility (currently 18 in the UK) and those suffering from a mental disability.

legal executive /ˌliːg(ə)l ɪɡˈzekjʊtɪv/ *noun* a clerk in a solicitor's office who is not a solicitor and is not articled to become one, but has passed the examinations of the Institute of Legal Executives

COMMENT: Legal executives deal with a lot of the background work in solicitors' offices, including probate, conveyancing, matrimonial disputes, etc. They can speak before a judge on questions which are not contested.

legal expenses insurance /ˌliːg(ə)l ɪkˌspensɪz ɪnˈʃʊərəns/ *noun* insurance which will pay the costs of a court case

legal expert /ˈliːg(ə)l ˌekspɜːt/ *noun* somebody who has a wide knowledge of the law

legal fee /ˈliːg(ə)l fiː/ *noun* a fee charged by a lawyer or conveyancer for legal services

legal holiday /ˌliːg(ə)l ˈhɒlɪdeɪ/ *noun* a day when banks and other businesses are closed

legal insanity /ˌliːg(ə)l ɪnˈsænɪti/ *noun* a state of mind which makes it impossible for a person to know that they are doing wrong and so should not be held responsible for their actions

legalisation /ˌliːgəlaɪˈzeɪʃ(ə)n/, **legalization** *noun* the process of making something legal ○ *the campaign for the legalisation of soft drugs*

legalise /ˈliːgəlaɪz/, **legalize** *verb* to make something legal

legality /lɪˈgælɪti/ *noun* the fact of being allowed by law ○ *There is doubt about the legality of the company's action in dismissing him.*

legally /ˈliːgəli/ *adverb* according to the law □ **legally responsible** responsible according to the law

legally binding /ˌliːgəli ˈbaɪndɪŋ/ *adjective* creating legal obligations ○ *A prenuptial agreement is not legally binding in the UK* ○ *The contract is legally binding on both parties.*

legal memory /ˌliːg(ə)l ˈmem(ə)ri/ *noun* the period since 1189, the accepted date to which legal title can be traced ○ *This practice has existed from before the time of legal memory.* ◊ **immemorial existence**

legal person /ˌliːg(ə)l ˈpɜːs(ə)n/ *noun* a company or corporation considered as a legal body

legal personality /ˌliːg(ə)l ˌpɜːsəˈnæləti/ *noun* existence as a body and so ability to be affected by the law

legal proceedings /ˈliːg(ə)l prəˌsiːdɪŋz/ *plural noun* a case that is brought

to court or to a tribunal ○ *The court proceedings were adjourned.*

legal representative /ˌliːg(ə)l ˌreprɪˈzentətɪv/ *noun* a barrister, solicitor, or legal executive who acts on behalf of a party in a case

legal right /ˈliːg(ə)l raɪt/ *noun* a right which exists under law

legal secretary /ˌliːg(ə)l ˈsekrət(ə)ri/ *noun* a secretary in a firm of solicitors or the legal department of a company

legal separation /ˌliːg(ə)l ˌsepəˈreɪʃ(ə)n/ *noun* a decree of a court acknowledging the separation of a married couple. Also called **divorce a mensa y toro**, **judicial separation**, **limited divorce** (NOTE: Neither person is allowed to marry again because they are not divorced.)

Legal Services Commission /ˌliːg(ə)l ˌsɜːvɪsɪz kəˈmɪʃ(ə)n/ *noun* a body set up to run the Community Legal Service and the Criminal Defence Service. Abbreviation **LSC**. Former name **Legal Aid**

Legal Services Ombudsman /ˈliːg(ə)l ˌsɜːvɪsɪz ˌɒmbədzmən/ *noun* an independent officer who investigates how well complaints against lawyers are handled by their own regulatory bodies

legal status /ˈliːg(ə)l ˌsteɪtəs/ *noun* the legal identity of a person or body such as a company or partnership

legal tender /ˌliːg(ə)l ˈtendə/ *noun* coins or notes which can be legally used to pay a debt (NOTE: Small denominations cannot be used to pay large debts.)

legal title /ˌliːg(ə)l ˈtaɪt(ə)l/ *noun* the right to be regarded as the legal owner of property

legal writer /ˌliːg(ə)l ˈraɪtə/ *noun* somebody who writes and publishes commentaries on legal problems

legatee /ˌlegəˈtiː/ *noun* somebody who receives a legacy from someone who has died

legis ◊ **corpus legis**, **ratio legis**

legislate /ˈledʒɪsleɪt/ *verb* to make a law ○ *Parliament has legislated against the sale of drugs* or *to prevent the sale of drugs.* □ **legislate for** to make a law promoting or protecting something ○ *We should be legislating for better access to health care.* □ **legislate against** to make a law banning something ○ *You can't legislate against freedom of speech.*

legislation /ˌledʒɪˈsleɪʃ(ə)n/ *noun* the set of laws that have been agreed by Parliament and are implemented by the courts ○ *We have to comply with new Health and Safety legislation.*

legislative /'ledʒɪslətɪv/ *adjective* used to make laws ○ *Parliament has a legislative function.*

legislative initiative /ˌledʒɪslətɪv ɪ'nɪʃətɪv/ *noun* the power to propose legislation

legislative veto /ˌledʒɪslətɪv 'viːtəʊ/ *noun* a clause written into legislation relating to government agencies, which states that the agency cannot act in a way that the US Congress does not approve

legislator /'ledʒɪsleɪtə/ *noun* a person who makes or passes laws as a member of a national or other legislative body

legislature /'ledʒɪslətʃə/ *noun* **1.** the part of a national or other government which makes or changes laws ○ *Members of the legislature voted against the proposal.* (NOTE: The other parts are the **executive** and the **judiciary**.) **2.** the building where a Parliament meets ○ *The protesters marched towards the State Legislature.*

legitimacy /lɪ'dʒɪtɪməsi/ *noun* **1.** the state of being legitimate ○ *The court doubted the legitimacy of his claim.* **2.** a court case to make someone legitimate

legitimate *adjective* /lɪ'dʒɪtɪmət/ **1.** allowed by law ○ *He has a legitimate claim to the property.* **2.** born to parents who are married to each other ○ *He left his property to his legitimate offspring.* ◊ **illegitimate** ■ *verb* /lɪ'dʒɪtɪmeɪt/ to make a child legitimate

legitimate expectations /lɪˌdʒɪtɪmət ˌekspek'teɪʃ(ə)nz/ *plural noun* expectations of an employee which are usual and what one might expect employees to have

legitimation /lɪˌdʒɪtɪ'meɪʃ(ə)n/, **legitimisation** /lɪˌdʒɪtɪmaɪ'zeɪʃ(ə)n/ *noun* the act of making a child legitimate, e.g. by the marriage of the parents

lend /lend/ *verb* to allow someone to use something for a period ○ *to lend something to someone* or *to lend someone something* ○ *He lent the company money* or *he lent money to the company.* ○ *She lent the company car to her daughter.* ○ *The bank lent him £50,000 to start his business.*

lender /'lendə/ *noun* somebody who lends money

lender of the last resort /ˌlendə əv ðɪ lɑːst rɪ'zɔːt/ *noun* a central bank which lends money to commercial banks

lending /'lendɪŋ/ *noun* the act of letting someone use money for a time

lending limit /'lendɪŋ ˌlɪmɪt/ *noun* a limit on the amount of money a bank can lend

lessee /le'siː/ *noun* a person who pays rent for a property he or she leases from a lessor

less-lethal weapon /ˌles ˌliːθəl 'wepən/ *noun* a weapon which is unlikely to cause lasting harm to the victim, used by the police for riot control or by private citizens for self-defence (NOTE: Pepper spray, electroshock weapons and water cannons are all types of less-lethal weapon.)

lessor /le'sɔː/ *noun* somebody who grants a lease on a property to a lessee

let /let/ *verb* **1.** to allow someone to do something ○ *The magistrate let the prisoner speak to his wife.* **2.** to lend a property such as house, office, farm to someone for a payment □ **to let an office** to allow someone to use an office for a time in return for payment of rent □ **offices to let** offices which are available to be leased by companies ■ *noun* **1.** the period of lease of a property ○ *They took the office on a short let.* **2.** □ **without let or hindrance** without any obstruction

let-out clause /'let aʊt ˌklɔːz/ *noun* a clause which allows someone to avoid doing something in a contract ○ *He added a let-out clause to the effect that the payments would be revised if the exchange rate fell by more than 5%.*

letter before action /ˌletə bɪˌfɔː 'ækʃən/ *noun* a letter written by a lawyer to give a party the chance to pay the client before he or she sues

letter of acknowledgement /ˌletər əv ək'nɒlɪdʒmənt/ *noun* a letter which says that something has been received

letter of attorney /ˌletər əv ə'tɜːni/ *noun* a document showing that someone has power of attorney

letter of comfort /ˌletər əv 'kʌmfət/ *noun* a letter supporting someone who is trying to get a loan

letter of credit /ˌletər əv 'kredɪt/ *noun* a letter from a bank authorising payment of a specific sum to a person or company, usually in another country. Abbreviation **L/C**

letter of demand /ˌletər əv dɪ'mɑːnd/ *noun US* a letter issued by a party or lawyer demanding payment before taking legal action

letter of indemnity /ˌletər əv ɪn
'demnɪti/ *noun* a letter promising payment
of compensation for a loss

letter of reference /ˌletər əv
'ref(ə)rəns/ *noun* a letter in which an
employer or former employer recommends
someone for a new job

letter of renunciation /ˌletər əv rɪ
ˌnʌnsi'eɪʃ(ə)n/ *noun* a form sent with new
shares, which allows the person who has
been allotted the shares to refuse to accept
them and so sell them to someone else

letter of request /ˌletər əv rɪ'kwest/
noun a letter to a court in another country,
asking for evidence to be taken from someone under that court's jurisdiction

letters of administration /ˌletəz əv əd
ˌmɪnɪ'streɪʃ(ə)n/ *noun* a document given
by a court to allow someone to deal with the
estate of a person who has died without
leaving a will or where the executor
appointed under the will cannot act (NOTE:
not used in the singular)

letters patent /ˌletəz 'peɪtənt/ *plural
noun* an official document from the Crown,
which gives someone the exclusive right to
make and sell an invention

letting agency /'letɪŋ ˌeɪdʒənsi/ *noun*
an agency which deals in property to let

leveraged buy-out /ˌliːvərɪdʒd
'baɪaʊt/ *noun* a situation in which a company is acquired by the use of borrowed
money. Abbreviation **LBO**

levy /'levi/ *noun* a type of tax which is col-
lected by the government or an official body
■ *verb* to seize property in accordance with
a legal ruling ○ *to levy a duty on the import
of computer parts* ○ *The government has
decided to levy a tax on imported cars.*

lex /leks/ *noun* a Latin word meaning 'law'

lex fori /ˌleks 'fɔːri/ *phrase* a Latin phrase
meaning 'the law of the place where the
case is being heard'

lex loci actus /ˌleks ˌləʊkaɪ 'æktəs/
phrase a Latin phrase meaning 'the law of
the place where the act took place'

lex loci contractus /ˌleks ˌləʊkaɪ kən
'træktəs/ *phrase* a Latin phrase meaning
'the law of the place where the contract was
made'

lex loci delicti /ˌleks ˌləʊkaɪ dɪ'lektaɪ/
phrase a Latin phrase meaning 'the law of
the place where the crime was committed'

liabilities /ˌlaɪə'bɪlɪtiz/ *plural noun* debts
of a business ○ *The balance sheet shows the
company's assets and liabilities.*

liability /ˌlaɪə'bɪlɪti/ *noun* **1.** the fact of
being legally responsible for paying for
damage or loss incurred ○ *His insurers have
admitted liability but the amount of damages has not yet been agreed.* □ **to admit
liability for something** to agree that you
are responsible for something □ **to refuse
liability for something** to refuse to agree
that you are responsible for something **2.** □
to meet your liabilities to be able to pay
your debts □ **to discharge one's liabilities
in full** to repay all debts

liability clause /ˌlaɪə'bɪlɪti klɔːz/ *noun* a
clause in the articles of association of a
company which states that the liability of its
members is limited

liable /'laɪəb(ə)l/ *adjective* **1.** legally
responsible for something ○ *The customer is
liable for breakages.* ○ *The chairman was
personally liable for the company's debts.* ○
*He was found by the judge to be liable for
the accident.* ○ *He will be found liable if he
assists a trustee to commit a dishonest
breach of trust.* **2.** officially due to pay or do
something ○ *sales which are liable to stamp
duty* ○ *Such an action renders him liable to
a fine.*

libel /'laɪb(ə)l/ *noun* **1.** a published or
broadcast statement which damages someone's character ○ *She claimed that the newspaper report was a libel.* **2.** the act of making a libel □ **action for libel**, **libel action** a
case in a law court where someone says that
another person has written a libel about him
or her ■ *verb* to damage someone's character in writing or in a broadcast (NOTE: **libel-
ling – libelled**. The US spelling is **libeling
– libeled**.)

libeller /'laɪb(ə)lə/ *noun* somebody who
has libelled someone

libellous /'laɪbələs/ *adjective* casting a
slur on someone's character ○ *She said that
the report was libellous.*

liberty /'lɪbəti/ *noun* the situation of being
free □ **at liberty** free, not in prison ○ *They
are still at liberty while waiting for charges
to be brought.* □ **liberty of the individual**
the freedom for each person to act within
the law □ **liberty of the press** the freedom
of newspapers to publish what they want
within the law without censorship □ **liberty
of the subject** the right of a citizen to be
free unless convicted of a crime which is
punishable by imprisonment

Liberty /'lɪbəti/ *noun* an organisation
which promotes the protection of civil liberties and human rights worldwide

licence /'laɪs(ə)ns/, **license** *US* /'laɪs(ə)ns/ *noun* **1.** an official document which allows someone to do something or to use something ○ *He granted his neighbour a licence to use his field.* □ **licence to sell liquor**, **liquor licence** a document given by the Magistrates' Court allowing someone to sell alcohol □ **on licence** a licence to sell alcohol for drinking on the premises, usually in a bar or restaurant **2.** permission given by someone to another person to do something which would otherwise be illegal **3.** permission for someone to leave prison before the end of his or her sentence **4.** □ **goods manufactured under licence** goods made with the permission of the owner of the copyright or patent

license /'laɪs(ə)ns/ *noun* US spelling of **licence** ■ *verb* to give someone official permission to do something ○ *licensed to sell beers, wines and spirits* ○ *to license a company to produce spare parts* ○ *He is licensed to drive a lorry.* ○ *She is licensed to run an employment agency.*

licensed conveyancer /,laɪs(ə)nst kən'veɪənsə/ *noun* a person who is licensed to carry out conveyancing work, but isn't a qualified solicitor

licensed deposit-taker /,laɪs(ə)nst dɪ'pɒzɪt ,teɪkə/ *noun* a business such as a bank which takes deposits from individuals and lends the money to others

licensed premises /,laɪs(ə)nst 'premɪsɪz/ *plural noun* a pub, restaurant, bar or shop which has a licence to sell alcohol

licensee /,laɪs(ə)n'siː/ *noun* a person who has a licence allowing them to carry out an activity such as selling alcohol or manufacturing or extracting something

licensing /'laɪs(ə)nsɪŋ/ *adjective* relating to licences

licensing agreement /'laɪs(ə)nsɪŋ ə ,griːmənt/ *noun* an agreement where a person is granted a licence to manufacture or use something

licensing hours /'laɪs(ə)nsɪŋ ,aʊəz/ *plural noun* hours of the day where alcohol can be bought to be drunk on the premises

licensing laws /'laɪs(ə)nsɪŋ ,lɔːz/ *plural noun* laws which specify where and at what times alcohol may be served and consumed

COMMENT: The licensing laws were relaxed in the UK in 2005, allowing alcohol to be served any time by an establishment holding a valid license to do so. Previously the sale of alcohol on most licensed premises was prohibited after 11pm.

licensing magistrates /,laɪs(ə)nsɪŋ 'mædʒɪstreɪts/ *plural noun* magistrates who grant licences to persons or premises for the sale of alcohol

licit /'lɪsɪt/ *adjective* legal

lie /laɪ/ *noun* a statement which is not true

lie detector /'laɪ dɪ,tektə/ *noun* a machine which detects if a person is telling the truth

lien /'liːən/ *noun* the legal right to hold someone's goods and keep them until a debt has been paid ○ *The garage had a lien on her car until she paid the repair bill.* (NOTE: You have a lien **on** an item.)

lieu /ljuː/ *noun* □ **in lieu of** instead of □ **to give someone two months' salary in lieu of notice** to give an employee money equivalent to the salary for two months' work and ask him or her to leave immediately

lie upon the table /,laɪ ə,pɒn ðə 'teɪb(ə)l/ *verb* (*of a petition*) to have been put before the House of Commons

life /laɪf/ *noun* **1.** the time when a person is alive □ **for life** for as long as someone is alive ○ *His pension gives him a comfortable income for life.* □ **the life assured**, **the life insured** the person whose life has been covered by the life assurance **2.** the period of time when something is in existence ○ *the life of a loan* ○ *during the life of the agreement* □ **shelf life of a product** the length of time when a product can stay in the shop and still be good to use

life annuity /'laɪf ə,njuːɪti/ *noun* annual payments made to someone for the rest of their life

life assurance /'laɪf ə,ʃʊərəns/ *noun* insurance which pays a sum of money when someone dies, or at a specified date if the person is still alive

life imprisonment /,laɪf ɪm 'prɪz(ə)nmənt/ *noun* the punishment of being sent to prison for a serious crime, but not necessarily for the whole of your life (NOTE: As a penalty for murder, life imprisonment lasts on average ten years in the UK)

life insurance /'laɪf ɪn,ʃʊərəns/ *noun* same as **life assurance**

life interest /,laɪf 'ɪntrəst/ *noun* a situation where someone benefits from a property as long as he or she is alive

Life in the UK test /,laɪf ɪn ðiː juː 'keɪ ,test/ *noun* a test that some immigrants are required to take in order to be naturalised as British citizens

life peer /ˈlaɪf pɪə/ *noun* a member of the House of Lords who is appointed for life and whose title does not pass to another member of the family

life preserver /ˈlaɪf prɪˌzɜːvə/ *noun* a heavy club or cosh

lifer /ˈlaɪfə/ *noun* somebody serving a life sentence (*slang*)

LIFO /ˈlaɪfəʊ/ *abbreviation* last in first out

lift /lɪft/ *verb* **1.** to take away or to remove ○ *The government has lifted the ban on imports of technical equipment.* ○ *The minister has lifted the embargo on the export of firearms.* ○ *Proceedings will continue when the stay is lifted.* **2.** to steal (*informal*)

lightning factor /ˌlaɪtnɪŋ ˈfæktə/ *noun* the possibility that even a good case may fail for an unexpected reason, which is one of the factors to be taken into account when preparing a conditional fee agreement (*informal*)

likelihood of bias /ˌlaɪklɪhʊd əv ˈbaɪəs/ *noun* the possibility that bias will occur because of a connection between a member of the court and a party in the case

limit /ˈlɪmɪt/ *noun* the point at which something ends □ **to set limits to imports, to impose limits on imports** to allow only a specific amount of goods to be imported □ **to exceed your credit limit** to borrow more money than you are allowed to do ■ *verb* to stop something from going beyond a specific point ○ *The court limited damages to £100.* □ **to limit credit** of a bank, to allow customers only a limited amount of credit

limitation /ˌlɪmɪˈteɪʃ(ə)n/ *noun* a legal restriction on the powers that someone has ○ *The contract imposes limitations on the number of cars which can be imported.*

limitation of actions /ˌlɪmɪteɪʃ(ə)n əv ˈækʃ(ə)nz/ *noun* a law which allows only a specific amount of time, usually six years, for someone to start legal proceedings in order to claim property or compensation for damage

limitation of liability /ˌlɪmɪteɪʃ(ə)n əv ˌlaɪəˈbɪlɪti/ *noun* **1.** making someone liable for only a part of the damage or loss **2.** making shareholders in a limited company liable for the debts of the company only in proportion to their shareholding

limitation period /ˌlɪmɪˈteɪʃ(ə)n ˌpɪəriəd/ *noun* a period during which someone who has a right to claim against another person must start court proceedings (NOTE:

If the claim is not made in time, this may be used as a defence argument – see **statute of limitations**.)

limited /ˈlɪmɪtɪd/ *adjective* restricted

limited divorce /ˌlɪmɪtɪd dɪˈvɔːs/ *noun* same as **legal separation**

limited liability /ˌlɪmɪtɪd ˌlaɪəˈbɪlɪti/ *noun* the legal principle that individual members of a limited liability company are liable for that company's debts only to the value of their shares

limited liability company /ˌlɪmɪtɪd ˌlaɪəbɪlɪti ˈkʌmp(ə)ni/ *noun* a company where each shareholder is responsible for repaying the company's debts only to the face value of the shares he or she owns

limited liability partnership /ˌlɪmɪtɪd ˌlaɪəbɪlɪti ˈpɑːtnəʃɪp/ *noun* a partnership which limits the personal responsibility of its partners for the firm's debts. Abbreviation **LLC**

limited market /ˌlɪmɪtɪd ˈmɑːkɪt/ *noun* a market which can take only a specific quantity of goods

limited partner /ˌlɪmɪtɪd ˈpɑːtnə/ *noun* a partner who has only limited liability for the partnership debts

limited partnership /ˌlɪmɪtɪd ˈpɑːtnəʃɪp/ *noun* a partnership where the liability of some of the partners is limited to the amount of capital they have each provided to the business while other working partners are fully liable for all the obligations of the partnership (NOTE: These partners with limited liability may not take part in the running of the business.)

limited warranty /ˌlɪmɪtɪd ˈwɒrənti/ *noun* a warranty which is limited in some way such as being valid only for a specific period of time or under special conditions of use

limiting /ˈlɪmɪtɪŋ/ *adjective* restricting ○ *a limiting clause in a contract* ○ *The short holiday season is a limiting factor on the hotel trade.*

Lincoln's Inn /ˌlɪnkənz ˈɪn/ *noun* one of the four Inns of Court in London

lineal descent /ˌlɪniəl dɪˈsent/ *noun* direct descent from parent to child

line management /ˈlaɪn ˌmænɪdʒmənt/ *noun* a type of business organisation where each manager is directly responsible for a stage in the operation of the business

liquid assets /ˌlɪkwɪd ˈæsets/ *noun* cash, or bills which can be quickly converted into cash

liquidate /'lɪkwɪdeɪt/ *verb* □ **to liquidate a company** to wind up a company, to close down a company and sell its assets □ **to liquidate a debt** to pay a debt in full □ **to liquidate assets, stock** to sell assets or stock to raise cash

liquidated damages /ˌlɪkwɪdeɪtɪd 'dæmɪdʒɪz/ *plural noun* a specific amount which has been calculated as the loss suffered

liquidation /ˌlɪkwɪ'deɪʃ(ə)n/ *noun* **1.** □ **liquidation of a debt** payment of a debt in full **2.** the closing of a company and selling of its assets □ **to go into liquidation** to be closed and all assets sold

liquidator /'lɪkwɪdeɪtə/ *noun* somebody who administers the assets and supervises the winding up of a company

liquidity /lɪ'kwɪdɪti/ *noun* the situation of having cash or assets which can easily be sold to raise cash ○ *The company was going through a liquidity crisis and had to stop payments.*

lis /lɪs/ *noun* a Latin word meaning 'lawsuit'

lis alibi pendens /ˌlɪs ˌælɪbaɪ 'pendenz/ *phrase* a Latin phrase meaning 'a legal action has been started in another place': the principle that the same case cannot be tried in two courts simultaneously

lis pendens /ˌlɪs 'pendenz/ *phrase* a Latin phrase meaning 'pending suit'

list /lɪst/ *noun* **1.** a set of several items written one after the other ○ *a list of debtors* ○ *to add an item to a list* ○ *to cross someone's name off a list* ○ *the list of cases to be heard* **2.** a particular court to which cases are allocated according to their subject **3.** a catalogue ■ *verb* **1.** to write a series of items one after the other ○ *The catalogue lists products by category.* **2.** to decide on the date at which a case will be heard ○ *The case is listed to be heard next week.*

listed building /ˌlɪstɪd 'bɪldɪŋ/ *noun* a building of special interest, often because it is old, which the owners cannot alter or demolish

listing /'lɪstɪŋ/ *noun* the action of scheduling a case to be heard on a specific date

listing hearing /ˌlɪstɪŋ 'hɪərɪŋ/ *noun* a hearing which may be held at which a court decides on the date at which a case will be heard

listing questionnaire /ˌlɪstɪŋ k(w)estʃə'neə/ *noun* a questionnaire sent by a court to the parties in a case allocated to the fast track

COMMENT: The parties must give details of things such as documents, witnesses and expert evidence in the listing questionnaire. It has to be filed with the court within 14 days and is used by the court to decide on scheduling the date when the case will be heard.

list of documents /ˌlɪst əv 'dɒkjʊ ˌments/ *noun* a list prepared by parties in a civil action giving disclosure of documents relevant to the action

litem ⧫ **ad litem**

literal rule /'lɪt(ə)rəl ruːl/ *noun* a rule that, when interpreting a statute, the court should give the words of the statute their most obvious meaning

litigant /'lɪtɪgənt/ *noun* somebody who brings a lawsuit against someone

litigant in person /ˌlɪtɪgənt ɪn 'pɜːs(ə)n/ *noun* a person bringing a lawsuit who also speaks on his or her own behalf in court without the help of a lawyer

litigate /'lɪtɪgeɪt/ *verb* to bring a lawsuit against someone to have a dispute settled

litigation /ˌlɪtɪ'geɪʃ(ə)n/ *noun* the action of bringing a lawsuit against someone to have a dispute settled ○ *He has got into litigation with the county council.*

litigation friend /ˌlɪtɪ'geɪʃ(ə)n frend/ *noun* somebody who represents a child or patient in court, and whose duty is to act in the best interests of the child or patient

litigation practitioner /ˌlɪtɪ'geɪʃ(ə)n præk,tɪʃ(ə)nə/ *noun* a lawyer who specialises in litigation

litigious /lɪ'tɪdʒəs/ *adjective* very willing to bring a lawsuit against someone to settle a disagreement

living off immoral earnings /ˌlɪvɪŋ ɒf ɪˌmɒrəl 'ɜːnɪŋz/ *noun* the offence of making a living from money obtained from prostitutes

LJ *abbreviation* Lord Justice (NOTE: written after the surname of the judge in legal reports: *Smith LJ said he was not laying down any guidelines for sentencing* but **Smith LJ** is spoken as 'Lord Justice Smith'.)

LJJ *abbreviation* lord justices

LL.B., LL.M., LL.D. *abbreviation* letters written after someone's name, showing that he or she has the degree of Bachelor of Laws, Master of Laws or Doctor of Laws

LLC /ˌel el 'siː/ *abbreviation* limited liability partnership

Lloyd's /lɔɪdz/ *noun* a central London market for underwriting insurances

Lloyd's Register /ˌlɔɪdz ˈredʒɪstə/ *noun* a classified list showing details of all the ships in the world □ **ship which is A1 at Lloyd's** a ship which is in best condition according to Lloyd's Register

Lloyd's underwriter /ˌlɔɪdz ˈʌndəraɪtə/ *noun* a member of an insurance group at Lloyd's who accepts to underwrite insurances

loan /ləʊn/ *noun* money that has been lent □ **short-term loan** a loan which has to be repaid within a short period of time □ **long-term loan** a loan which must be repaid over a long period of time ■ *verb* to lend

loan stock /ˈləʊn stɒk/ *noun* money lent to a company at a fixed rate of interest

lobby /ˈlɒbi/ *noun* a group of people or pressure group which tries to influence MPs or the passage of legislation □ **the car lobby** people who try to persuade government that cars should be encouraged and not restricted □ **the environmentalist lobby** people who try to persuade government that the environment must be protected, pollution stopped, etc.

lobbyist /ˈlɒbiɪst/ *noun* somebody who is paid to represent a pressure group

local court /ˈləʊk(ə)l kɔːt/ *noun* a court such as a magistrates' court which hears cases coming from its local area

local custom /ˌləʊk(ə)l ˈkʌstəm/ *noun* the way in which things are usually done in a particular place

loc. cit. *phrase* a Latin phrase meaning 'in the place which has been mentioned' (NOTE: used when referring to a point in a legal text: 'see also Smith J in *Jones v. Associated Steel Ltd* loc. cit. line 26')

locking up /ˌlɒkɪŋ ˈʌp/ *noun* □ **the locking up of money in stock** investing money in stock so that it cannot be used for other, possibly more profitable, investments

lock up /ˌlɒk ˈʌp/ *verb* **1.** to put someone in prison or a psychiatric hospital **2.** □ **to lock up a shop, an office** to close and lock the door at the end of the day's work □ **to lock up capital** to have capital invested in such a way that it cannot be used for other investments

lock-up /ˈlɒk ʌp/ *adjective* □ **lock-up shop** a shop which has no living accommodation which the proprietor locks at night when it is closed ■ *noun* a prison (*informal*)

loco ♦ **in loco parentis**

locum /ˈləʊkəm/, **locum tenens** /ˌləʊkəm ˈtenənz/ *noun* somebody who takes the place of another person for a time ○ *locums wanted in South London*

locus /ˈləʊkəs/ *noun* a Latin word meaning 'place'

locus sigilli /ˌləʊkəs sɪˈdʒɪlaɪ/ *phrase* a Latin phrase meaning 'place of the seal': used to show where to put the seal on a document

locus standi /ˌləʊkəs ˈstændaɪ/ *phrase* a Latin phrase meaning 'place to stand': the right to be heard in a court ○ *The taxpayer does not have locus standi in this court.*

lodge /lɒdʒ/ *verb* to deposit something such as a document officially □ **to lodge caution** to deposit a document with the Land Registry which prevents land or property being sold without notice □ **to lodge a complaint against someone** to make an official complaint about someone □ **to lodge money with someone** to deposit money with someone □ **to lodge securities as collateral** to put securities into a bank to be used as collateral for a loan

lodger /ˈlɒdʒə/ *noun* somebody who lives in a house or part of a house which is owned by a resident landlord

loitering with intent /ˌlɔɪtərɪŋ wɪð ɪnˈtent/ *noun* the offence of being in a place waiting for an opportunity to commit a crime, especially to solicit sexual relations

London Court of International Arbitration /ˌlʌndən kɔːt əv ˌɪntənæʃ(ə)nəl ˌɑːbɪˈtreɪʃ(ə)n/ *noun* an organisation based in London which administers international dispute resolutions. Abbreviation **LCIA**

London Stock Exchange /ˌlʌndən ˈstɒk ɪksˌtʃeɪndʒ/ *noun* a stock exchange based in London. Abbreviation **LSE**

long credit /ˌlɒŋ ˈkredɪt/ *noun* credit terms which allow the borrower a long time to pay

long-dated bills /ˌlɒŋ ˌdeɪtɪd ˈbɪlz/ *plural noun* bills of exchange which are payable in more than three months' time

long lease /ˌlɒŋ ˈliːs/ *noun* a lease which runs for fifty years or more ○ *to take an office building on a long lease*

long-standing customer /ˌlɒŋ ˌstændɪŋ ˈkʌstəmə/ *noun* somebody who has been a customer for many years

long tenancy /ˌlɒŋ ˈtenənsi/ *noun* tenancy for a period of more than 21 years

long-term /ˌlɒŋ ˈtɜːm/ *adjective* □ **on a long-term basis** for a long period of time

long-term debts /ˌlɒŋ tɜːm ˈdets/ *plural noun* debts which will be repaid many years later

long-term liabilities /ˌlɒŋ tɜːm ˌlaɪəˈbɪlɪtiz/ *plural noun* debts which are not due to be repaid for some years

long-term loan /ˌlɒŋ tɜːm ˈləʊn/ *noun* a loan to be repaid many years later

long title /ˌʃɔːt ˈtaɪt(ə)l/ *noun* the official name of an Act of Parliament (NOTE: It will more usually be referred to by its **short title**, which is easier to remember.)

Long Vacation /ˌlɒŋ vəˈkeɪʃ(ə)n/ *noun* the summer holiday of the law courts and universities

loophole /ˈluːphəʊl/ *noun* □ **to find a loophole in the law** to find a means of doing what you want to do, by finding a way of getting round a law which otherwise would prevent you from acting □ **to find a tax loophole** to find a means of legally not paying tax

loot /luːt/ *noun* stolen money or goods ■ *verb* to steal goods from shops, warehouses or homes during a period of unrest, disaster or lack of government control ○ *The stores were looted by a mob of hooligans.*

looter /ˈluːtə/ *noun* a person who steals valuables from shops, warehouses or homes during a period of unrest, disaster or lack of government control

looting /ˈluːtɪŋ/ *noun* the act of stealing valuable goods ○ *The police cordoned off the area to prevent looting.*

Lord Advocate /ˌlɔːd ˈædvəkət/ *noun* a member of the government who is one of the two Law Officers in Scotland

Lord Chancellor /ˌlɔːd ˈtʃɑːnsələ/ *noun* a senior functionary in the British government

Lord Chief Justice /ˌlɔːd tʃiːf ˈdʒʌstɪs/ *noun* the chief judge of the Queen's Bench Division of the High Court who is also a member of the Court of Appeal

Lord Justice /ˌlɔːd ˈdʒʌstɪs/ *noun* the title given to a judge who is a member of the House of Lords and the Court of Appeal (NOTE: It may be written abbreviated as **LJ**, or **LJJ** for the plural, after a surname: *Smith LJ* or *Jones and White LJJ*.)

Lord Justice Clerk /ˌlɔːd ˌdʒʌstɪs ˈklɑːk/ *noun* the second most important judge in the Scottish High Court of Justiciary

Lord Justice General /ˌlɔːd ˌdʒʌstɪs ˈdʒen(ə)rəl/ *noun* the chief judge in the Scottish High Court of Judiciary

Lord Lieutenant /ˌlɔːd lefˈtenənt/ *noun* the representative of the Crown in a county

Lord of Appeal /ˌlɔːd əv əˈpiːl/ *noun* a member of the House of Lords who sits when the House is acting as a Court of Appeal

Lord of Appeal in Ordinary /ˌlɔːd əv ə ˌpiːl ɪn ˈɔːd(ə)n(ə)ri/ *noun* one of eleven lords who are paid to sit as members of the House of Lords when it acts as a Court of Appeal

Lord Ordinary /ˌlɔːd ˈɔːd(ə)n(ə)ri/ *noun* a judge of first instance in the outer house of the Scottish Court of Session

Lord President /ˌlɔːd ˈprezɪdənt/ *noun* a judge of the Scottish Court of Session

Lord President of the Council /ˌlɔːd ˌprezɪdənt əv ðə ˈkaʊns(ə)l/ *noun* a senior member of the UK government, who is a member of the House of Lords and head of the Privy Council Office and has other duties allocated by the Prime Minister

Lords /lɔːdz/ *plural noun* **1.** the House of Lords ○ *The Lords voted to amend the Bill.* **2.** members of the House of Lords. ◊ **Law Lords**

lose /luːz/ *verb* **1.** not to be successful in a legal case ○ *He lost his appeal to the House of Lords.* ○ *She lost her case for compensation.* **2.** not to have something any more □ **to lose your job** to be sacked or made redundant **3.** to have less money ○ *He lost £25,000 in his father's computer company.* **4.** to drop to a lower price ○ *The dollar lost two cents against the pound.* ○ *Gold shares lost 5% on the market yesterday.* (NOTE: **losing – lost – has lost**)

loss /lɒs/ *noun* **1.** harm suffered by someone, which may be recoverable as damages ○ *Mrs Smith's claim for damages is based upon his losses arising out of the car crash.* **2.** □ **a dead loss** something that is so badly damaged that it loses all its value **3.** □ **loss in weight** goods which weigh less than when they were packed □ **loss in transport** the amount of weight which is lost while goods are being shipped

loss adjuster /ˈlɒs əˌdʒʌstə/ *noun* same as **average adjuster**

loss-leader /ˈlɒs ˌliːdə/ *noun* a product which is sold very cheaply to attract customers

lost profits /ˌlɒst ˈprɒfɪts/ *plural noun* profits which would have been made from a transaction which is the subject of an action for breach of contract

lower house /ˌləʊə ˈtʃeɪmbə/ *noun* the less important of the two houses in a bicameral system of government. Opposite **upper house**

LSC *abbreviation* Legal Services Commission

LSE *abbreviation* London Stock Exchange

lump sum /ˌlʌmp ˈsʌm/ *noun* an amount of money that is paid in one single payment, not in several small amounts ○ *He received a lump sum payment of £500.* ○ *The company offer a lump sum of £1,000 as an out-of-court settlement.*

lynch /lɪntʃ/ *verb* to execute an accused person, usually by hanging, without a trial

lynch law /ˈlɪntʃ lɔː/ *noun* the killing of accused persons by a mob without a trial

M

Maastricht Treaty /ˈmɑːstrɪkt ˌtriːti/ *noun* same as **Treaty on European Union**

Madam Chairman /ˌmædəm ˈtʃeəmən/ *noun* a way of addressing a woman who is in the chair at the meeting

mafia /ˈmæfiə/ *noun* any organised group of criminals ○ *the Russian drugs mafia*

magistrate /ˈmædʒɪstreɪt/ *noun* a usually unpaid official who tries cases in a police court

magistrates' clerk /ˈmædʒɪstreɪts klɑːk/ *noun* an official of a magistrates' court who gives advice to the magistrates on law, practice or procedure

magistrates' court /ˈmædʒɪstreɪts kɔːt/ *noun* **1.** a building where magistrates try cases **2.** a court presided over by magistrates

COMMENT: The Magistrates' Courts hear cases of petty crime, adoption, affiliation, maintenance and violence in the home; they hear almost all criminal cases. The court can commit someone for trial or for sentence in the Crown Court. A stipendiary magistrate is a qualified lawyer who usually sits alone; lay magistrates usually sit as a bench of three, and can only sit if there is a justices' clerk present to advise them.

magistrates' courts committee /ˌmædʒɪstreɪts ˌkɔːt kəˈmɪti/ *noun* a committee which organises the administration of the courts in one or more petty sessions areas

maintenance /ˈmeɪntənəns/ *noun* **1.** the activity of keeping things going or working ○ *The maintenance of law and order is in the hands of the local police force.* **2.** a payment made by a divorced or separated husband or wife to the former spouse, to help pay for living expenses and the cost of bringing up the children **3.** formerly, the crime or tort of unlawfully providing someone with money to help that person to pay the costs of suing a third party

maintenance agreement /ˌmeɪntənəns əˈɡriːmənt/ *noun* an agreement drawn up between two parents who are separating, detailing the financial arrangements which will be made to support the child

maintenance contract /ˈmeɪntənəns ˌkɒntrækt/ *noun* a contract by which a company keeps a piece of equipment in good working order

maintenance order /ˌmeɪntənəns ˈɔːdə/ *noun* a court order which orders a divorced or separated husband or wife to pay maintenance to the former spouse, or an absent parent to pay maintenance for their child

maintenance pending suit /ˌmeɪntənəns ˈpendɪŋ suːt/ *noun* maintenance obtained by a spouse in matrimonial proceedings until there is a full hearing to deal with the couple's financial affairs (NOTE: The US term is **alimony**.)

Majesty /ˈmædʒəsti/ *noun* the title given to a King or Queen ○ *his Majesty, the King* ○ *their Majesties, the King and Queen* ○ *'Your Majesty, the Ambassador has arrived'* □ **on Her Majesty's Service (OHMS)** words printed on official letters from government departments. ◊ **Her Majesty's pleasure**

majeure /mæˈʒɜː/ ♦ **force majeure**

majority /məˈdʒɒrɪti/ *noun* **1.** a larger group than any other □ **a majority of the jury** more than 50% of the jury ○ **to accept something by a majority** to accept something because more people voted to accept it than to reject it □ **a majority shareholder** person who owns more than half the shares in a company **2.** ♦ **age of majority**

majority verdict /məˌdʒɒrɪti ˈvɜːdɪkt/ *noun* a verdict reached by a jury where at least ten jurors vote for the verdict

making time of the essence /ˌmeɪkɪŋ ˌtaɪm əv ðiː ˈes(ə)ns/ *noun* a provision in a contract that makes a date stipulated impossible to challenge or overlook

maladministration /ˌmæləd.mɪnɪˈstreɪʃ(ə)n/ *noun* incompetent or illegal administration

mala in se /ˌmælə ɪn ˈseɪ/ *phrase* a Latin phrase meaning 'wrongs in themselves': acts such as murder which are thought to be inherently wrong

mala prohibita /ˌmælə prəʊˈhɪbɪtə/ *phrase* a Latin phrase meaning 'forbidden wrongs': acts such as walking on the grass in a park which are not inherently wrong, but which are crimes because they are forbidden

malfeasance /mælˈfiːz(ə)ns/ *noun* an unlawful act

malice /ˈmælɪs/ *noun* the fact of intentionally committing an act from wrong motives, or the intention to commit a crime □ **with malice aforethought** with the intention of committing a crime (especially murder)

malicious /məˈlɪʃəs/ *adjective* intending to cause harm

malicious communication /məˌlɪʃəs kəˌmjuːnɪˈkeɪʃ(ə)n/ *noun* a phone call, letter, text message or other communication which is intended to upset or harass the recipient

malicious damage /məˌlɪʃəs ˈdæmɪdʒ/ *noun* the deliberate and intentional harming of property

maliciously /məˈlɪʃəsli/ *adverb* in a malicious way, with the intention of causing harm ○ *He claimed that he had been prosecuted maliciously.*

malicious prosecution /məˌlɪʃəs ˌprɒsɪˈkjuːʃ(ə)n/ *noun* the tort of bringing charges against a person out of malice and without proper reason

malicious wounding /məˌlɪʃəs ˈwuːndɪŋ/ *noun* the offence of inflicting grievous bodily harm on someone with the purpose of causing them injury

malpractice /mælˈpræktɪs/ *noun* the tort of failing to act in a professional way according to your status

management buy-out /ˌmænɪdʒmənt ˈbaɪaʊt/ *noun* a situation in which a company is acquired by its management. Abbreviation **MBO**

mandamus /mænˈdeɪməs/ *noun* a Latin word meaning 'we command': a court order from the Divisional Court of the Queen's Bench Division, ordering a body such as a lower court or tribunal to perform a legal duty ○ *The Chief Constable applied for an order of mandamus directing the justices to rehear the case.*

mandate /ˈmændeɪt/ *noun* the authority given to a person or persons to act on behalf of the person or persons giving the authority and carry out their wishes ○ *The government has a mandate from the people to carry out the plans put forward in its manifesto.* □ **to seek a new mandate** to try to be re-elected to a position ■ *verb* /mænˈdeɪt/ to give a person or persons the authority to carry out a specific action on behalf of another person or persons and according to their wishes ○ *The government has been mandated to revise the tax system.*

mandatory /ˈmændət(ə)ri/ *adjective* obligatory

mandatory injunction /ˌmændət(ə)ri ɪnˈdʒʌŋkʃən/ *noun* an order from a court which compels someone to do something

mandatory life sentence /ˌmændət(ə)ri laɪf ˈsent(ə)ns/ *noun* the only sentence available to the courts for persons over the age of 21 found guilty of murder

manendi ♦ **animus manendi**

manifest /ˈmænɪfest/ *adjective* obvious ○ *a manifest injustice*

manipulate /məˈnɪpjʊleɪt/ *verb* to influence or control a person in a deceitful way ○ *He was accused of trying to manipulate the witness.* ■ to make false or misleading statements for your own gain ○ *She manipulated the company accounts to make it appear profitable.*

manslaughter /ˈmænslɔːtə/ *noun* the notifiable offence of killing someone without having intended to do so, or of killing someone intentionally but with mitigating circumstances ○ *He was accused of manslaughter.* ○ *She was convicted of the manslaughter of her husband.*

Mareva injunction /məˈreɪvə ɪn ˌdʒʌŋkʃ(ə)n/ *noun* formerly, a court order to freeze the assets of a person who has gone overseas or of a company based overseas to prevent them being taken out of the country (NOTE: Called after the case of *Mareva Compania Naviera SA v. International Bulk-Carriers SA*. Since the introduction of the Civil Procedure Rules, this term has been replaced by **freezing injunction**.)

margin of appreciation /ˌmɑːdʒɪn əv əˌpriːsiˈeɪʃ(ə)n/ *noun* the principle that the European Court of Justice should make allowance for local customs when deciding whether to overturn the decision of a national court

marine insurance /məˌriːn ɪnˈʃʊərəns/ *noun* insurance of ships and their cargoes

marine underwriter /məˌriːn ˈʌndəraɪtə/ *noun* somebody who insures ships and their cargoes

marital /ˈmærɪt(ə)l/ *adjective* referring to a marriage

marital acquest /ˌmærɪt(ə)l əˈkwest/ *noun* assets accumulated over the course of a marriage

marital privileges /ˌmærɪt(ə)l ˈprɪvəlɪdʒs/ *plural noun* the privilege of a spouse not to give evidence against the other spouse in some criminal proceedings

marital rape /ˈmærɪt(ə)l reɪp/ *noun* the act of a husband forcing his wife to have sexual intercourse without her consent

maritime law /ˌmærɪtaɪm ˈlɔː/ *noun* the set of laws referring to ships, ports, etc.

maritime lawyer /ˌmærɪtaɪm ˈlɔːjə/ *noun* a lawyer who specialises in legal matters concerning ships and cargoes

maritime lien /ˌmærɪtaɪm ˈliːən/ *noun* the right to seize some ship against an unpaid debt

maritime trade /ˌmærɪtaɪm ˈtreɪd/ *noun* the activity of carrying commercial goods by sea

mark /mɑːk/ *noun* a cross ('X') put on a document in place of a signature by someone who cannot write

market /ˈmɑːkɪt/ *noun* 1. □ **to pay black market prices** to pay high prices to get items which are not easily available 2. □ **a buyer's market** a market where goods are sold cheaply because there is little demand □ **a seller's market** a market where the seller can ask high prices because there is a large demand for the product 3. □ **the foreign exchange markets** market where people buy and sell foreign currencies

marketable title /ˌmɑːkɪtəb(ə)l ˈtaɪt(ə)l/ *noun* a title to a property which can be sold, i.e. it is free of major encumbrances

market capitalisation /ˌmɑːkɪt ˌkæpɪtəlaɪˈzeɪʃ(ə)n/ *noun* the value of a company calculated by multiplying the price of its shares on the Stock Exchange by the number of shares issued

market dues /ˌmɑːkɪt ˈdjuːz/ *plural noun* rent for a place in a market

market overt /ˌmɑːkɪt əʊˈvɜːt/ *noun* a street market

COMMENT: It used to be the accepted rule that a sale at a market overt gave good title to the buyer, even though the seller's title may have been defective. However, this was abolished by the Sale of Goods (Amendment) Act 1994.

market price /ˈmɑːkɪt praɪs/ *noun* the price at which a product can be sold

market value /ˌmɑːkɪt ˈvæljuː/ *noun* the value of an asset, product or company, if sold today

marksman /ˈmɑːksmən/ *noun* 1. somebody who can shoot a gun very accurately 2. a person who cannot write and who has to put an 'X' in place of a signature

mark up /ˌmɑːk ˈʌp/ *verb* □ **to mark up a bill** *US* to make changes to a bill as it goes through committee

marriage /ˈmærɪdʒ/ *noun* the act or state of being joined together as husband and wife □ **by marriage** because of being married ○ *She became a British citizen by marriage.*

marriage of convenience /ˌmærɪdʒ əv kənˈviːniəns/ *noun* a form of marriage arranged for the purpose of acquiring the nationality of a spouse or for some other financial reason

marriage settlement /ˌmærɪdʒ ˈset(ə)lmənt/ *noun* an agreement which is made before marriage where money or property is given on trust for the benefit of the future spouse

marshal /ˈmɑːʃ(ə)l/ *noun US* 1. an official who carries out the orders of a court (NOTE: The British equivalent is a **bailiff**.) 2. a federal officer with the same functions as a sheriff at state level

marshalling /ˈmɑːʃ(ə)lɪŋ/ *noun* the action of a beneficiary of an estate to recover money due to them which was paid to a creditor

Marshal of the Admiralty Court /ˌmɑːʃ(ə)l əv ði ˌædm(ə)rəlti ˌkɔːt/ *noun* an official in charge of the Admiralty Court

martial /ˈmɑːʃ(ə)l/ *adjective* relating to the armed services

martial law /ˌmɑːʃ(ə)l ˈlɔː/ *noun* rule of a country or part of a country by the army on the orders of the government when ordinary civil law has been suspended ○ *The president imposed* or *declared martial law in two provinces.* ○ *The government lifted martial law.*

mass jailbreak /mæs ˈdʒeɪlˌbreɪk/ *noun* the escape from prison of several prisoners at the same time

master /ˈmɑːstə/ *noun* **1.** an official in the Queen's Bench Division or Chancery Division of the High Court whose work is to examine and decide on preliminary matters before trial **2.** main or original □ **master copy of a file** main copy of a computer file, kept for security purposes

Master of the Rolls /ˌmɑːstə əv ðə ˈrəʊlz/ *noun* a senior judge who presides over the Civil Division of the Court of Appeal and is responsible for admitting solicitors to the Roll of Solicitors

Masters of the Bench /ˌmɑːstəz əv ðə ˈbentʃ/ *plural noun* senior members of one of the Inns of Court

material /məˈtɪəriəl/ *adjective* important or relevant ○ *material things*

material alteration /məˌtɪəriəl ˌɔːltəˈreɪʃ(ə)n/ *noun* a change made to a legal document which alters the rights or duties in it

material evidence /məˌtɪəriəl ˈevɪd(ə)ns/ *noun* evidence which has important relevance to a case

material welfare /məˌtɪəriəl ˈwelfeə/ *noun* the fact of having enough money and possessions to live comfortably ○ *The mother must be able to look after the children's material welfare.*

material witness /məˌtɪəriəl ˈwɪtnəs/ *noun* a witness whose evidence is important to the case

maternity leave /məˈtɜːnɪti liːv/ *noun* a period when a woman is away from work to have a baby, receiving maternity pay

maternity pay /məˈtɜːnɪti peɪ/ *noun* standard pay which a woman is entitled to receive when taking time off work to have a baby

COMMENT: The Work and Families Act made it possible for women to take 39 weeks of paid maternity leave. For the first 6 weeks the woman is entitled to receive 90% of her usual pay; for the remaining 33 weeks she will receive either 90% of her usual pay or the standard rate, whichever is the lower. The standard rate is currently £112.75 per week.

matricide /ˈmætrɪsaɪd/ *noun* the murder of your own mother

matrimonial /ˌmætrɪˈməʊniəl/ *adjective* referring to marriage

matrimonial causes /ˌmætrɪˈməʊniəl ˈkɔːz/ *plural noun* proceedings concerned with rights of partners in a marriage, e.g. divorce or separation proceedings

matrimonial home /ˌmætrɪˈməʊniəl həʊm/ *noun* the place where a husband and wife live together

matrimony /ˈmætrɪməni/ *noun* the state of being legally married

matter /ˈmætə/ *noun* **1.** a problem □ **it is a matter of concern to the members of the committee** the members of the committee are worried about it **2.** a question or problem to be discussed ○ *the most important matter on the agenda* ○ *We shall consider first the matter of last month's fall in prices.* ■ *verb* to be important ○ *Does it matter if one month's sales are down?*

matter of fact /ˌmætə əv ˈfækt/ *noun* a question of fact which has to be decided

matters of fact /ˌmætəz əv ˈfækt/ *plural noun* facts relevant to a case which is being tried at court

matters of law /ˌmætəz əv ˈlɔː/ *noun* the law relevant to a case which is tried at court ○ *It is a matter of law whether or not the contract is legal.*

mature /məˈtʃʊə/ *verb* to be due for payment ○ *bill which will mature in three months*

maturity /məˈtʃʊərɪti/ *noun* the time when a bill, government stock or insurance is due for payment

maxim /ˈmæksɪm/ *noun* a short phrase which formulates a principle, e.g. 'let the buyer beware'

maximum /ˈmæksɪməm/ *noun* the largest possible quantity, price or number ■ *adjective* largest possible ○ *the maximum penalty*

maximum harmonisation /ˌmæksɪməm ˌhɑːmənaɪˈzeɪʃ(ə)n/ *noun* the principle that when a Member State implements a piece of EU legislation (such as a directive or regulation), its national law may not exceed the terms of the legislation

mayhem /ˈmeɪhem/ *noun* **1.** a general riot or disturbance **2.** the violent removal of a person's arm or leg

mayoralty /ˈmeər(ə)lti/ *noun* **1.** the position of mayor **2.** the time for which someone is mayor ○ *He was accused of bribing officials during his mayoralty.*

MBO *abbreviation* management buy-out

McNaghten, McNaughten ♦ **M'Naghten Rules**

means /miːnz/ *plural noun* money which is available

measure /'meʒə/ *noun* **1.** a way of calculating size or quantity **2.** an action to achieve something, e.g. a law passed by Parliament or a statutory instrument ○ *a government measure to reduce crime in the inner cities* □ **to take measures to prevent something happening** to act to stop something happening □ **to take emergency measures** to act rapidly to stop a dangerous situation developing □ **an economy measure** action taken to try to save money or materials □ **as a precautionary measure** to prevent something taking place

measurement of profitability /,meʒəmənt əv ,prɒfɪtə'bɪlɪti/ *noun* a way of calculating how profitable something is

measure of damages /,meʒə əv 'dæmɪdʒɪz/ *noun* a calculation of how much money a court should order one party to pay another to compensate for a tort or breach

mechanical reproduction rights /mɪ ,kænɪk(ə)l ,riːprə'dʌkʃ(ə)n ,raɪts/ *plural noun* the rights to make a recording of a piece of music or a photocopy or other copy of something, usually for a fee

mechanic's lien /mɪ,kænɪks 'liːən/ ♦ lien

mediate /'miːdieɪt/ *verb* to try to make the two sides in an argument come to an agreement ○ *I tried to mediate between the manager and his staff.* ○ *The government offered to mediate in the dispute.*

mediation /,miːdi'eɪʃ(ə)n/ *noun* an attempt by a third party to make the two sides in an argument agree ○ *The employers refused an offer of government mediation.* ○ *The dispute was ended through the mediation of a disinterested party.*

medical certificate /'medɪk(ə)l sə ,tɪfɪkət/ *noun* a certificate from a doctor to show that an employee has been ill

medical inspection /'medɪk(ə)l ɪn ,spekʃ(ə)n/ *noun* the examination of a place of work to see if the conditions are safe

medicolegal /,medɪkəʊ'liːg(ə)l/ *adjective* relating to the possible legal implications of giving medical care, especially when this is faulty or negligent

meeting /'miːtɪŋ/ *noun* **1.** the coming together of a group of people **2.** □ **to hold a meeting** to organise a meeting of a group of people ○ *The meeting will be held in the committee room.* □ **to open a meeting** to start a meeting □ **to conduct a meeting** to be in the chair for a meeting □ **to close a meeting** to end a meeting □ **to put a resolution to a meeting** to ask a meeting to vote on a proposal

member /'membə/ *noun* **1.** somebody who belongs to a group or a society **2.** an organisation which belongs to a society ○ *the member countries* or *the Member States of the EU* ○ *the members of the United Nations* ○ *the member firms of the Stock Exchange*

Member of the European Parliament /,membə əv ðə ,jʊərəpiːən 'pɑːləmənt/ *noun* a person elected to represent a Euro-constituency in the European Parliament. Abbreviation **MEP**

membership organisation /'membəʃɪp ,ɔːgənaɪzeɪʃ(ə)n/ *noun* a body, usually a company limited by guarantee or an unincorporated association, set up and run by its members, often for a non-profit purpose

member state /'membə steɪt/ *noun* (*in the EU*) a state which is a member of the European Union

members' voluntary liquidation /,membəz ,vɒlənt(ə)ri ,lɪkwɪ'deɪʃ(ə)n/ *noun* the liquidation of a company by the decision of its shareholders, conducted by an insolvency practitioner. Abbreviation **MVL**

memorandum /,memə'rændəm/ *noun* a short note

memorandum of association /,memərændəm əv ə,səʊsi'eɪʃ(ə)n/ *noun* a legal document setting up a limited company and giving details of its aims, capital structure, and registered office

memorandum of satisfaction /,memərændəm əv ,sætɪs'fækʃən/ *noun* a document showing that a company has repaid a mortgage or charge (NOTE: The plural is **memoranda**.)

menace /'menɪs/ *noun* a threat or action which frightens someone □ **demanding money with menaces** the crime of getting money by threatening another person

mens rea /,mens 'reɪə/ *phrase* a Latin phrase meaning 'guilty mind': the mental state required to be guilty of committing a crime (intention, recklessness or guilty knowledge). See Comment at **crime**. Compare **actus reus**

mental /'ment(ə)l/ *adjective* referring to the mind

mental cruelty /,ment(ə)l 'kruːəlti/ *noun US* cruelty by one spouse to the other, which may harm his or her mental state (NOTE: It is grounds for divorce in the USA.)

mental disability /ˌment(ə)l ˌdɪsə'bɪlɪti/ *noun* a condition that limits a person's ability to learn and to function independently

mental disorder /ˌment(ə)l dɪs'ɔːdə/ *noun* a temporary or permanent change in a person's mental state which makes them function less effectively than they would usually

mentally /'ment(ə)li/ *adverb* in the mind

mentally ill /'ment(ə)li/ *adverb* suffering from a mental disability ○ *Mentally ill criminals are committed to special establishments.* ◊ **section**

mention /'menʃən/ *noun* a short hearing at court

mentis ♦ **compos mentis**

MEP *abbreviation* Member of the European Parliament

mercantile law /'mɜːkəntaɪl lɔː/ *noun* law relating to commerce

merchantable quality /ˌmɜːtʃəntəb(ə)l 'kwɒlɪti/ *noun* a quality of goods for sale, which are suitable for the purpose for which they are to be used and conform to the description and price given for them in the manufacturer's catalogue

merchant marine /ˌmɜːtʃənt mə'riːn/ *noun* all the commercial ships of a country

mercy /'mɜːsi/ *noun* the act of treating or punishing someone less severely than you could

mercy killing /'mɜːsi ˌkɪlɪŋ/ *noun* same as **euthanasia**

merge /mɜːdʒ/ *verb* to join together ○ *The two companies have merged.* ○ *The firm merged with its main competitor.*

merger /'mɜːdʒə/ *noun* **1.** the joining of a small estate to a large one ○ *As a result of the merger, the company is the largest in the field.* **2.** the joining together of two or more companies

merit award /'merɪt əˌwɔːd/ *noun* US extra money given to an employee because he or she has worked well

merit increase /'merɪt ˌɪnkriːs/ *noun* US an increase in pay given to someone because his or her work is good

merits of the case /ˌmerɪts əv ðə 'keɪs/ *plural noun* the main question which is at issue in an action

mesne /miːn/ *adjective* in the middle □ **action for mesne profits** action to recover money that should be paid to a landowner in place of rent by a person who is in wrongful possession

mesne process /'miːn ˌprəʊses/ *noun* a process in a legal action, which comes after the first writ but before the outcome of the action has been decided

Messenger-at-Arms /ˌmesɪndʒər æt 'ɑːmz/ *noun* an officer of the Scottish Court of Session, responsible for serving documents and enforcing court orders throughout Scotland

messuage /'meswɪdʒ/ *noun* a house where people live, and the land and buildings attached to it

meta-data /'metə ˌdeɪtə/ *noun* information about a piece of digital data

metropolitan /ˌmetrə'pɒlɪt(ə)n/ *adjective* referring to a large city

Metropolitan District Council /ˌmetrəpɒlɪt(ə)n ˌdɪstrɪkt 'kaʊns(ə)l/ *noun* a large administrative area covering an urban area in England or Wales

Metropolitan Police /ˌmetrəpɒlɪt(ə)n pə'liːs/ *noun* the police force of Greater London, which is directly responsible to the Home Secretary (NOTE: The higher ranks in the Metropolitan Police are Deputy Assistant Commissioner, Assistant Commissioner, and Commissioner.) □ **solicitor for the Metropolitan Police** a solicitor responsible for prosecutions brought by the Metropolitan Police

Metropolitan Police Commissioner /ˌmetrəpɒlɪt(ə)n pəˌliːs kə'mɪʃ(ə)nə/ *noun* the head of the Metropolitan Police, appointed directly by the Home Secretary

Michaelmas /'mɪk(ə)lməs/ *noun* **1.** 29th September, one of the quarter days when rent is payable on land **2.** one of the four sittings of the law courts **3.** one of the four law terms

Middle Temple /ˌmɪd(ə)l 'temp(ə)l/ *noun* one of the four Inns of Court in London. ◊ **Inns of Court**

Midland Circuit /ˌmɪdlənd ənd 'ɒksfəd ˌsɜːkɪt/ *noun* in the UK, one of the six circuits of the Crown Court to which barristers belong

Midsummer day /ˌmɪd'sʌmə deɪ/ *noun* 24th June, one of the four quarter days when rent is payable on land

migration /maɪ'greɪʃ(ə)n/ *noun* the moving of people from one country to another

militant /'mɪlɪtənt/ *noun* a person who uses extreme methods to actively support and work for a cause ■ *adjective* using extreme methods in supporting a cause

military police /ˌmɪlɪt(ə)ri pəˈliːs/ *noun* soldiers who act as policemen to keep order among other soldiers

minimis ♦ de minimis non curat lex

minimum /ˈmɪnɪməm/ *noun* the smallest possible quantity, price or number ○ *to keep expenses to a minimum* ○ *to reduce the risk of a loss to a minimum* ■ *adjective* smallest possible

minimum harmonisation /ˌmɪnɪməm ˌhɑːmənaɪˈzeɪʃ(ə)n/ *noun* the principle that a piece of EU legislation (such as a directive or regulation) sets a minimum threshold which each Member State's national law must comply

minimum payment /ˌmɪnɪməm ˈpeɪmənt/ *noun* the smallest payment necessary

minimum sentence /ˌmɪnɪməm ˈsentəns/ *noun* the shortest possible sentence allowed in law for an offence

minimum term /ˌmɪnɪməm ˈtɜːm/ *noun* the minimum amount of time that a prisoner must spend in jail

minimum wage /ˌmɪnɪməm ˈweɪdʒ/ *noun* the lowest hourly wage that a company can legally pay its workers

mining concession /ˈmaɪnɪŋ kənˌseʃ(ə)n/ *noun* the right to dig a mine on a piece of land which you do not own

ministerial tribunal /ˌmɪnɪstɪəriəl traɪˈbjuːn(ə)l/ *noun* a tribunal set up by a government minister to hear appeals from local tribunals

Minister of State /ˌmɪnɪstə əv ˈsteɪt/ *noun* somebody who is in charge of a section of a government department

Minister without Portfolio /ˌmɪnɪstə wɪˌðaʊt pɔːtˈfəʊliəʊ/ *noun* a minister who does not have responsibility for any particular department

Ministry of Defence /ˌmɪnɪstri əv dɪˈfens/ *noun* a government department in charge of the armed forces

Ministry of Justice /ˌmɪnɪstri əv ˈdʒʌstɪs/ *noun* the UK government department responsible for the justice system, human rights and constitutional affairs. Abbreviation **MoJ** (NOTE: It was formed in 2007, taking over the duties of the former **Department for Constitutional Affairs** and also the prison and probation service, formerly part of the **Home Office**'s remit.)

Ministry of the Interior /ˌmɪnɪstri əv ðə ɪnˈtɪəriə/ *noun* in some countries, a government department dealing with law and order, usually including the police

minor /ˈmaɪnə/ *adjective* less important ○ *minor expenditure* ○ *minor shareholders* □ **a loss of minor importance** not a very serious loss ■ *noun* a person less than eighteen years old

minority /maɪˈnɒrɪti/ *noun* **1.** the state of being less than eighteen years old ○ *A person is not liable for debts contracted during minority.* **2.** a period during which someone is less than eighteen years old **3.** a number or quantity which is less than half of the total ○ *A minority of board members opposed the chairman.* □ **in the minority** being fewer than half ○ *The small parties are in the minority on the local council.*

minute /ˈmɪnɪt/ *noun* □ **to take the minutes** to write notes of what happened at a meeting ■ *verb* to put something into the minutes of a meeting ○ *The chairman's remarks about the auditors were minuted.*

minutes of order /ˌmɪnɪts əv ˈɔːdə/ *plural noun* a draft order submitted to a court when a party wishes the court to make an order

misadventure /ˌmɪsədˈventʃə/ *noun* an accident □ **death by misadventure** accidental death ○ *The coroner's verdict was death by misadventure.*

misappropriate /ˌmɪsəˈprəʊprieɪt/ *verb* to steal or use illegally money which is not yours, but with which you have been trusted

misappropriation /ˌmɪsəprəʊpriˈeɪʃ(ə)n/ *noun* the illegal use of money by someone who is not the owner but who has been trusted to look after it

misbehaviour /ˌmɪsbɪˈheɪvjə/ *noun* bad behaviour, especially a criminal offence committed by a public official

miscarriage of justice /ˌmɪskærɪdʒ əv ˈdʒʌstɪs/ *noun* **1.** a decision wrongly or unjustly reached by a court **2.** a decision which goes against the rights of a party in a case, in such a way that the decision may be reversed on appeal

mischief rule /ˈmɪstʃɪf ruːl/ *noun* the rule that when interpreting a statute, the court should try to see what the wrong was that the statute tried to remedy and what the remedy was that Parliament has enacted

misconduct /mɪsˈkɒndʌkt/ *noun* an illegal action which can harm someone

misdeed /mɪsˈdiːd/ *noun* a crime

misdemeanour /ˌmɪsdɪˈmiːnə/ *noun* a minor crime ○ *He was charged with several misdemeanours, including driving without a valid licence and creating a disturbance.*

misdescription /ˌmɪsdɪˈskrɪpʃ(ə)n/ *noun* a false or misleading description of the subject of a contract

misdirect /ˌmɪsdaɪˈrekt/ *verb* to give wrong directions to a jury on a point of law

misdirection /ˌmɪsdɪˈrekʃ(ə)n/ *noun* the giving of wrong directions to a jury on a point of law

misfeasance /mɪsˈfiːz(ə)ns/ *noun* acting improperly or illegally in performing an action that is in itself lawful

misinterpret /ˌmɪsɪnˈtɜːprɪt/ *verb* to understand something wrongly ○ *The firefighters misinterpreted the instructions of the police.*

misinterpretation /ˌmɪsɪnˌtɜːprɪˈteɪʃ(ə)n/ *noun* a wrong interpretation or understanding of something □ **open to misinterpretation** capable of being wrongly interpreted

misjoinder /mɪsˈdʒɔɪndə/ *noun* wrongly joining someone as a party to an action

misprision /mɪsˈprɪʒ(ə)n/ *noun* generally, the situation of knowing that a crime is being committed, but doing nothing about it

misprision of treason /mɪsˌprɪʒ(ə)n əv ˈtriːz(ə)n/ *noun* the crime of knowing that treason has been committed and not reporting it

misrepresent /ˌmɪsreprɪˈzent/ *verb* to report facts wrongly

misrepresentation /ˌmɪsˌreprɪzenˈteɪʃ(ə)n/ *noun* the act of making a wrong statement with the intention of persuading someone to enter into a contract

mistake /mɪˈsteɪk/ *noun* the act of entering into a legal contract under a mistaken impression, which may affect its validity if challenged. ◊ **common mistake, mutual mistake, unilateral mistake**

mistake in venue /mɪˌsteɪk ɪn ˈvenjuː/ *noun* the starting of legal proceedings in the wrong court

mistaken identity /mɪˌsteɪkən aɪˈdentɪti/ *noun* a situation where someone is wrongly thought to be another person ○ *He was arrested for burglary, but released after it had been established that it was a case of mistaken identity.*

mistrial /ˈmɪstraɪəl/ *noun* a trial which is not valid because the proper procedure was not followed, or because the jury is hung

COMMENT: A declaration of a mistrial usually means that a **retrial** will be held.

misuse /mɪsˈjuːs/ *noun* wrong use ○ *misuse of funds*

mitigate /ˈmɪtɪɡeɪt/ *verb* to make a crime or a punishment less serious

mitigating circumstances /ˌmɪtɪɡeɪtɪŋ ˈsɜːkəmstænsɪz/ *plural noun* circumstances which make a crime less serious or which can excuse a crime

mitigation /ˌmɪtɪˈɡeɪʃ(ə)n/ *noun* a reduction of a sentence or of the seriousness of a crime ○ *In mitigation, counsel submitted evidence of his client's work for charity.* ○ *Defence counsel made a speech in mitigation.*

mitigation of damages /ˌmɪtɪɡeɪʃ(ə)n əv ˈdæmɪdʒɪz/ *noun* a reduction in the extent of damages awarded

mixed hereditaments /ˌmɪkst ˌherɪˈdɪtəmənts/ *plural noun* properties which are used for both domestic and business purposes

M'Naghten Rules /məkˌnɔːtən ˈruːlz/ *plural noun* rules which a judge applies in deciding if a person charged with a crime is insane

COMMENT: To prove insanity, it has to be shown that because of a diseased mind, the accused did not know what he was doing or did not know that his action was wrong. Based on the case of *R v. M'Naghten* (1843) in which the House of Lords considered and ruled on the defence of insanity.

mob /mɒb/ *noun US* the Mafia

mobster /ˈmɒbstə/ *noun US* a member of an organised crime group

modus operandi /ˌməʊdəs ˌɒpəˈrændiː/ *phrase* a Latin phrase meaning 'way of working': a particular way of committing crimes which can identify a criminal

modus vivendi /ˌməʊdəs vɪˈvendiː/ *phrase* a Latin phrase meaning 'way of living', an informal agreement between two or more parties such as employers and employees to exist peacefully together ○ *After years of confrontation, they finally have achieved a modus vivendi.*

moiety /ˈmɔɪəti/ *noun* half

MoJ *abbreviation* Ministry of Justice

molest /məˈlest/ *verb* to threaten violent or unwanted sexual behaviour against somebody ○ *He was accused of molesting children in the park.*

molestation /ˌməʊleˈsteɪʃ(ə)n/ *noun* the act of threatening violent behaviour towards a child or a woman, especially a spouse

molester /məˈlestə/ *noun* somebody who molests ○ *a convicted child molester*

Molotov cocktail /ˌmɒlətɒf ˈkɒkteɪl/ *noun* a crude firebomb made out of a bottle filled with petrol and a lighted rag, often used by rioters

money claim /ˈmʌni kleɪm/ *noun* a claim which involves the payment of money, e.g. a claim for repayment of a debt or a claim for damages

money laundering /ˈmʌni ˌlɔːndərɪŋ/ *noun* the act of passing illegal money into the banking system

moneylender /ˈmʌniˌlendə/ *noun* somebody who lends money at interest

money markets /ˌmʌni ˈmɑːkɪts/ *plural noun* markets for buying and selling short-term loans

money order /ˈmʌni ˌɔːdə/ *noun* a document which can be bought for sending money through the post

monies /ˈmʌniz/ *plural noun* sums of money ○ *monies owing to the company* ○ *to collect monies due*

monogamy /məˈnɒɡəmi/ *noun* a system of society where a person is allowed one spouse only. Compare **bigamy**, **polygamy**

Monopolies Commission, **Monopolies and Mergers Commission** *noun* a British body which examines takeovers and mergers to make sure that a monopoly is not being created (NOTE: US English uses **trust** more often than **monopoly**.)

monopolisation /məˌnɒpəlaɪˈzeɪʃ(ə)n/, **monopolization** *noun* the process of making a monopoly

monopolise /məˈnɒpəlaɪz/ *verb* to get control of all the supply of a product

monopoly /məˈnɒpəli/ *noun* **1.** a situation where one person or company controls all the market in the supply of a product ○ *to have the monopoly of alcohol sales* or *to have the alcohol monopoly* ○ *The company has the absolute monopoly of imports of French wine.* **2.** the right given to one person or company to control all the market in the supply of a product

monopsony /məˈnɒpsəni/ *noun* a situation where one person or company controls all the purchasing in a market

Monroe doctrine /mʌnˈrəʊ ˌdɒktrɪn/ *noun* US the principle that the USA has an interest in preventing outside interference in the internal affairs of other American states

COMMENT: So called because it was first proposed by President Monroe in 1823.

moonlight /ˈmuːnlaɪt/ *verb* to do a second job for cash, often in the evening, as well as a regular job, often not declaring the money earned to the income tax authorities (*informal*)

moonlighter /ˈmuːnlaɪtə/ *noun* somebody who moonlights

moonlighting /ˈmuːnlaɪtɪŋ/ *noun* the activity of doing a second job without telling the tax authorities ○ *He makes thousands a year from moonlighting.*

moot /muːt/ *adjective* legally insignificant because of having already been decided or settled

moot case /ˌmuːt ˈkeɪs/ *noun* a legal case to be discussed on its own, to establish a precedent

moral /ˈmɒrəl/ *adjective* referring to the difference between what is right and what is wrong ○ *the high moral standard which should be set by judges*

moral rights /ˌmɒrəl ˈraɪts/ *noun* the rights of a copyright holder to be identified as the creator of the work, not to have the work subjected to derogatory treatment, and to prevent anyone else from claiming to be the author of the work. Also called **paternity**

morals /ˈmɒrəlz/ *plural noun* standards of behaviour □ **to corrupt someone's morals** to make someone willing to commit a crime or to act against usual standards of behaviour

moratorium /ˌmɒrəˈtɔːriəm/ *noun* a temporary stop to repayments of money owed ○ *The banks called for a moratorium on payments.* (NOTE: The plural is **moratoria**.)

mortality tables /mɔːˈtæləti ˌteɪb(ə)lz/ *plural noun* charts, used by insurers, that show how long a person can be expected to live on average

mortem ♦ **post mortem**

mortgage /ˈmɔːɡɪdʒ/ *noun* **1.** an agreement where someone lends money to another person so that he or she can buy a property, the property being used as the security ○ *to take out a mortgage on a house* **2.** money lent in this way ○ *to buy a house with a £20,000 mortgage* □ **to foreclose on a mortgaged property** to take possession of a property because the owner cannot pay the interest on the money which he or she has borrowed using the property as security □ **to pay off a mortgage** to pay back the principal and all the interest on a loan to buy a property ■ *verb* to accept a loan with a property as security ○ *The house is mortgaged to the bank.* ○ *He mortgaged his house to set up in business.*

mortgage bond /ˈmɔːgɪdʒ bɒnd/ *noun* a certificate showing that a mortgage exists and that the property is security for it

mortgage debenture /ˈmɔːgɪdʒ dɪˌbentʃə/ *noun* a debenture where the lender can be repaid by selling the company's property

mortgage deed /ˈmɔːgɪdʒ diːd/ *noun* a legal document setting out the mortgage lender's interest in the property and containing the terms of the mortgage

mortgagee /ˌmɔːgəˈdʒiː/ *noun* a person or company which lends money for someone to buy a property and takes a mortgage of the property as security

mortgage payments /ˈmɔːgɪdʒ ˈpeɪmənts/, **mortgage repayments** /ˈmɔːgɪdʒ rɪˈpeɪmənts/ *plural noun* money paid each month as interest on a mortgage, together with repayment of a small part of the capital borrowed

mortgagor /ˈmɔːgɪdʒə/ *noun* somebody who borrows money, giving a property as security

mortis /ˈmɔːtɪs/ ♦ **donatio mortis causa, rigor mortis**

most favoured nation /ˌməʊst ˌfeɪvəd ˈneɪʃ(ə)n/ *noun* a country which has the best trade terms

most-favoured-nation clause /məʊst ˌfeɪvəd ˈneɪʃ(ə)n klɔːz/ *noun* an agreement between two countries that each will offer the best possible terms in commercial contracts

Mother of Parliaments /ˌmʌðə əv ˈpɑːləmənts/ *noun* the British Parliament at Westminster

motion /ˈməʊʃ(ə)n/ *noun* **1.** the action of moving **2.** a proposal which will be put to a meeting for that meeting to vote on ○ *to propose* or *to move a motion* ○ *to speak against* or *for a motion* ○ *The meeting voted on the motion.* □ **the motion was carried** the motion was approved **3.** an application to a judge in court, asking for an order in favour of the person making the application ◇ **to table a motion** *US* **1.** to put forward a proposal for discussion by putting details of it on the table at a meeting **2.** to remove a pro-

posal from discussion by a meeting for an indefinite period

motion of censure /ˌməʊʃ(ə)n əv ˈsenʃə/ *noun* a proposal from the Opposition to pass a vote to criticise the government

movable /ˈmuːvəb(ə)l/, **moveable** *adjective* being able to be moved

movable property /ˌmuːvəb(ə)l ˈprɒpəti/ *noun* chattels and other objects which can be moved, as opposed to land

movables /ˈmuːvəb(ə)lz/ *plural noun* same as **movable property**

move /muːv/ *verb* **1.** to go from one place to another ○ *The company is moving from London Road to the centre of town.* ○ *We have decided to move our factory to a site near the airport.* **2.** to propose formally that a motion be accepted by a meeting ○ *He moved that the accounts be agreed.* ○ *I move that the meeting should adjourn for ten minutes.* **3.** to make an application to the court

movements of capital /ˌmuːvmənts əv ˈkæpɪt(ə)l/ *plural noun* changes of investments from one country to another

mover /ˈmuːvə/ *noun* somebody who proposes a motion

MP /ˈem ˈpiː/ *abbreviation* Member of Parliament *or* military police

MR *abbreviation* Master of the Rolls (NOTE: usually written after the surname: *Lord Smith, MR* but spoken as 'the Master of the Rolls, Lord Smith')

Mr Big /ˌmɪstə ˈbɪg/ *noun* a criminal whose name is not known, who is the person in control of a large criminal operation (*informal*)

mug /mʌg/ *noun* (*informal*) **1.** somebody who is easily cheated **2.** a face ■ *verb* to attack and rob someone ○ *The tourists were mugged in the station.* ○ *He was accused of mugging an old lady in the street.* (NOTE: **mugging – mugged**)

mugger /ˈmʌgə/ *noun* somebody who attacks and robs someone

mugging /ˈmʌgɪŋ/ *noun* the act of attacking and robbing someone ○ *The number of muggings has increased sharply over the last few years.*

mug shot /ˈmʌg ʃɒt/ *noun* a photograph of a criminal taken after he or she has been detained, kept in the police records

mule /mjuːl/ *noun* a person who smuggles illegal drugs from one country to another by hiding them on or in their body

multiple ownership /ˌmʌltɪp(ə)l ˈəʊnəʃɪp/ *noun* a situation where something is owned by several parties

multi-track /ˈmʌlti træk/ *noun* (*in civil cases*) the case management system which applies to cases involving sums of more than £15,000 or which present particular complications

COMMENT: The multi-track is the track for most High Court actions including claims regarding professional negligence, fatal accidents, fraud, defamation and claims against the police. The timetable for a multi-track action is as follows: the court fixes a date for a case management conference, then one for listing questionnaires to be sent and filed, and finally a date for the trial.

municipal law /mjuːˈnɪsɪp(ə)l lɔː/ *noun* law which is in operation within a state. Compare **international law**

muniments /ˈmjuːnɪmənts/ *plural noun* title deeds

murder /ˈmɜːdə/ *noun* **1.** the notifiable offence of killing someone illegally and intentionally ○ *He was charged with murder.* ○ *She was found guilty of murder.* ○ *The murder rate has fallen over the last year.* **2.** an act of killing someone illegally and intentionally ○ *Three murders have been committed during the last week.* ◊ **first degree murder, second degree murder** ■ *verb* to kill someone illegally and intentionally ○ *He was accused of murdering his wife.*

murderer /ˈmɜːdərə/ *noun* somebody who commits a murder

murderess /ˈmɜːdəres/ *noun* a woman who commits a murder

mutatis mutandis /mjuːˌtɑːtiːs mjuːˈtændiːs/ *phrase* a Latin phrase meaning 'with the things having been changed that need to be changed': ○ *After negotiations, the parties signed the contract mutatis mutandis.*

mutineer /ˌmjuːtɪˈnɪə/ *noun* somebody who takes part in a mutiny

mutiny /ˈmjuːtɪni/ *noun* an agreement between two or more members of the armed forces to disobey commands of superior officers and to try to take command themselves ■ *verb* to carry out a mutiny

mutuality /ˌmjuːtʃuˈælɪti/ *noun* a state where two parties are bound contractually to each other

mutual mistake *noun* a situation in which the legality of a contract is challenged, on the grounds that both parties were mistaken about the same fact or term of contract at the time of signing

mutual wills /ˌmjuːtʃuəl ˈwɪlz/ *plural noun* wills made by two people, usually each leaving their property to the other (NOTE: Mutual wills are less capable of being revoked than normal wills.)

MVL *abbreviation* members' voluntary liquidation

N

name and shame /ˌneɪm ən ˈʃeɪm/ *verb* to publish the names of people who have broken the law or not fulfilled a duty, because it is in the public interest or as a punishment and deterrent ○ *The newspaper named and shamed the hospitals found to be unhygienic in the investigation.*

named /neɪmd/ *adjective* □ **person named in the policy** the person whose name is given on an insurance policy as the person insured

Napoleonic Code /nəˌpəʊliːɒnɪk ˈkəʊd/ *noun* a code of law introduced in France by Napoleon at the beginning of the 19th century and still influential today in many jurisdictions, especially those in South America

COMMENT: One of the key differences between the Napoleonic Code and the common law legal systems is that while the latter has a presumption of innocence, the former has a presumption of guilt.

nark /nɑːk/ *noun* a person, often a criminal, who gives information about other criminals to the police (*slang*)

national /ˈnæʃ(ə)nəl/ *adjective* referring to a particular country ■ *noun* somebody who is a citizen of a state ○ *The government ordered the deportation of all foreign nationals.* ○ *Any national of a Member State has the right to work in another Member State, under the same conditions as nationals of that state.* Compare **non-national**

National Archives /ˌnæʃ(ə)nəl ˈɑːkaɪvz/ *noun* a UK body created in April 2003 to maintain a national archive for England and Wales

National Audit Office /ˌnæʃ(ə)nəl ˈɔːdɪt ˌɒfɪs/ *noun* an independent body, headed by the Comptroller and Auditor-General, which examines the accounts of government departments

National Community Safety Plan /ˌnæʃ(ə)nəl kəˌmjuːnɪti ˈseɪfti ˌplæn/ *noun* a Home Office initiative to reduce crime and anti-social behaviour in the community. Abbreviation **NCSP**

National Crime Squad /ˌnæʃ(ə)nəl ˈkraɪm ˌskwɒd/ *noun* a section of the national police which deals with crime on a nation-wide basis and is not part of any local police force. Abbreviation **NCS**

National Criminal Intelligence Service /ˌnæʃ(ə)nəl ˌkrɪmɪn(ə)l ɪnˈtelɪdʒəns ˌsɜːvɪs/ *noun* a former central police department which kept records of criminals from national and international sources and made them available to police forces all over the country. Abbreviation **NCIS** (NOTE: The former duties of the NCIS are now discharged by the **Serious Organised Crime Agency**.)

National Insurance contributions /ˌnæʃ(ə)nəl ɪnˈʃʊərəns ˌkɒntrɪbjuːʃ(ə)nz/ *plural noun* money paid into the National Insurance scheme by the employer and the worker. Abbreviation **NIC**

nationalise /ˈnæʃ(ə)nəlaɪz/, **nationalize** *verb* to put a privately owned industry under state ownership and control

National Offender Management Service /ˌnæʃ(ə)nəl əˈfendə ˌmænɪdʒmənt ˌsɜːvɪs/ *noun* in the UK, a service which is responsible for improving the rehabilitation of offenders in order to reduce repeat offences and crime (NOTE: Formerly part of the Home Office, it was transferred to the **Ministry of Justice** in 2007.)

nation state /ˈneɪʃ(ə)n steɪt/ *noun* a country which is an independent political unit, usually formed of people with the same language and traditions

natural-born subject /ˌnætʃ(ə)rəl bɔːn ˈsʌbdʒɪkt/ *noun* a term formerly applied to a person born in the UK or a Commonwealth country who was a British citizen by birth

natural child /ˌnætʃ(ə)rəl 'tʃaɪld/ *noun* the child, especially an illegitimate child, of a particular parent

naturalisation /ˌnætʃ(ə)rəlaɪ'zeɪʃ(ə)n/, **naturalization** *noun* the granting of citizenship of a state to a foreigner ○ *She has applied for naturalisation.* ○ *You must fill in the naturalisation papers.*

COMMENT: British citizenship by way of naturalisation can be granted to a person who has lived legally in the UK for 6 years, or for 3 years as the spouse of a British citizen. They must also be judged to be 'of good character' and be able to speak English well.

naturalised /'nætʃ(ə)rəlaɪzd/, **naturalized** *adjective* having legally become a citizen of another country ○ *He is a naturalised American citizen.*

natural justice /ˌnætʃ(ə)rəl 'dʒʌstɪs/ *noun* the general principles of justice

natural law /ˌnætʃ(ə)rəl 'lɔː/ *noun* generally accepted rules of human behaviour, applied in all societies

natural parent /ˌnætʃ(ə)rəl 'peərənt/ *noun* same as **biological parent**

natural person /ˌnætʃ(ə)rəl 'pɜːs(ə)n/ *noun* a human being, as opposed to a legal or artificial 'person' such as a company ○ *In this case, the term 'establishment' is not confined to legal persons, but is extended to natural persons.*

natural right /ˌnætʃ(ə)rəl 'raɪt/ *noun* the general right that people have to live freely, usually stated in a written constitution

NCIS *abbreviation* National Criminal Intelligence Service

NCS *abbreviation* National Crime Squad

NCSP *abbreviation* National Community Safety Plan

NDA *abbreviation* non-disclosure agreement

NDPB *abbreviation* non-departmental public body

negative easement /ˌnegətɪv 'iːzmənt/ *noun* an easement where the servient owner stops the dominant owner from doing something

negative integration /ˌnegətɪv ˌɪntɪ'greɪʃ(ə)n/ *noun* integration between EU states caused by the abolition of national laws which are different from those in other states. Compare **positive integration**

negative pledge /ˌnegətɪv 'pledʒ/ *noun* an agreement not to grant any security that would conflict with security already granted

neglect /nɪ'glekt/ *noun* **1.** failure to do a duty **2.** a lack of care towards someone or something ○ *The children were suffering from neglect.* ■ *verb* **1.** to fail to do a duty ○ *She was accused of neglecting her paperwork.* **2.** to fail to take care of someone ○ *He neglected his three children.* **3.** □ **to neglect to do something** to forget or omit to do something which has to be done ○ *He neglected to return his income tax form.*

neglected /nɪ'glektɪd/ *adjective* not well looked after ○ *The local authority applied for a care order for the family of neglected children.*

negligence /'neglɪdʒəns/ *noun* **1.** failure to give proper care to something, especially a duty or responsibility, with the result that a person or property is harmed **2.** the tort of acting carelessly towards others so as to cause harm, entitling the injured party to claim damages

negligent /'neglɪdʒ(ə)nt/ *adjective* failing to give proper care or attention to something ○ *The defendant was negligent in carrying out his duties as a trustee.*

negligently /'neglɪdʒənt(ə)li/ *adverb* in a way which shows negligence ○ *The guardian acted negligently towards his ward.*

negotiability /nɪˌgəʊʃiə'bɪlɪti/ *noun* the ability of a document to be legally transferred to a person simply by being put into his or her possession

negotiable /nɪ'gəʊʃiəb(ə)l/ *adjective* **1.** able to be changed by discussion □ **not negotiable** fixed and unable to be changed ○ *The terms of the agreement are not negotiable.* **2.** able to be exchanged for money □ **not negotiable** not able to be exchanged for cash (*sometimes written on a cheque to indicate that only the person named on the cheque can cash it*)

negotiable cheque /nɪˌgəʊʃiəb(ə)l 'tʃek/ *noun* a cheque made payable to the bearer, i.e. to anyone who holds it

negotiable instrument /nɪˌgəʊʃiəb(ə)l 'ɪnstrʊmənt/ *noun* a document such as a bill of exchange or cheque which can be legally transferred to another owner simply by passing it to him or her or by endorsing it, or which can be exchanged for cash

negotiable paper /nɪˌgəʊʃiəb(ə)l 'peɪpə/ *noun* a document which can be transferred from one owner to another for money

negotiate /nɪ'gəʊʃieɪt/ *verb* □ **to negotiate with someone** to discuss a problem formally with someone, so as to reach an agreement ○ *The management refused to negotiate with the union.* □ **to negotiate terms and conditions** to discuss and agree the terms of an agreement

negotiation /nɪˌɡəʊʃiˈeɪʃ(ə)n/ *noun* a discussion of terms and conditions to reach an agreement □ **contract under negotiation** a contract which is being discussed □ **a matter for negotiation** something which must be discussed before a decision is reached □ **to enter into negotiations, to start negotiations** to start discussing a problem □ **to resume negotiations** to start discussing a problem again, after talks have stopped for a time □ **to break off negotiations** to refuse to go on discussing a problem □ **to conduct negotiations** to negotiate

negotiator /nɪˈɡəʊʃieɪtə/ *noun* somebody who discusses with the aim of reaching an agreement

neighbourhood watch /ˌneɪbəhʊd ˈwɒtʃ/ *noun* a system where the people living in an area are encouraged to look out for criminals or to report any breakdown of law and order

nemine contradicente /ˌnemɪneɪ ˌkɒntrædɪˈsenteɪ/, **nem con** /ˌnem ˈkɒn/ *phrase* a Latin phrase meaning 'with no one contradicting': a phrase used to show that no one voted against the proposal ○ *The motion was adopted nem con.*

nemo dat quod non habet /ˌneɪməʊ dæt kwɒd nɒn ˈhæbet/ *phrase* a Latin phrase meaning 'no one can give what he does not have': the rule that no one can pass or sell to another person something such as stolen goods to which he or she has no title

net /net/, **nett** *adjective, adverb* remaining after money has been deducted for tax, expenses, etc. ○ *The company's net profit was £10,000.*

net earnings /ˌnet ˈɜːnɪŋz/ *noun* total earnings after tax and other deductions

net estate /ˌnet ɪˈsteɪt/ *noun* the estate of a deceased person less administration charges and funeral costs

net gain /ˌnet ˈɡeɪn/ *noun* the total number of something gained after deducting losses ○ *The government lost twenty seats and gained thirty one, making a net gain of eleven.*

net price /ˌnet ˈpraɪs/ *noun* a price which cannot be reduced by a discount

net profit /ˌnet ˈprɒfɪt/ *noun* a result where income from sales is larger than all expenditure

neutral /ˈnjuːtrəl/ *adjective* not taking sides in a dispute

neutralism /ˈnjuːtrəlɪz(ə)m/ *noun* a state of affairs where a country does not ally itself with others in times of war

New Deal /njuː diːl/ *noun* a series of Government programmes designed to support unemployed people wanting to get back into work

new trial /ˌnjuː ˈtraɪəl/ *noun* a trial which can be ordered to take place in civil cases, when the first trial was improper in some way

next friend /ˌnekst ˈfrend/ *noun* somebody who brings an action on behalf of a minor

next of kin /ˌnekst əv ˈkɪn/ *noun* the person or persons who are most closely related to someone ○ *His only next of kin is an aunt living in Scotland.* ○ *The police have informed the next of kin of the people killed in the accident.* (NOTE: can be singular or plural)

NIC /ˌen aɪ ˈsiː/ *abbreviation* National Insurance contributions

nick /nɪk/ *noun* a police station ■ *verb* **1.** to steal **2.** to arrest

night duty /ˈnaɪt ˌdjuːti/ *noun* work done at night ○ *PC Smith is on night duty this week.*

nisi ⏵ **decree nisi, foreclosure order nisi**

nobble /ˈnɒb(ə)l/ *verb* to interfere with, bribe or influence a juror or jury (*slang*)

no-claims bonus /ˌnəʊ ˈkleɪmz ˌbəʊnəs/ *noun* the reduction of premiums paid because no claims have been made against an insurance policy

noise abatement /ˈnɔɪz əˌbeɪtmənt/ *noun* measures taken to reduce unacceptable sounds or vibrations, or to protect people from exposure to them ○ *A noise abatement notice was served on the club.*

noise nuisance /nɔɪz ˈnjuːs(ə)ns/ *noun* noise which causes inconvenience to somebody on their property

noise pollution /ˈnɔɪz pəˌluːʃ(ə)n/ *noun* unpleasant sounds which cause discomfort

nolle prosequi /ˌnɒli ˈprɒsɪkwaɪ/ *phrase* a Latin phrase meaning 'do not pursue': a power used by the Attorney-General to stop a criminal trial

nominal /ˈnɒmɪn(ə)l/ *adjective* **1.** (*of an amount*) very small ○ *We make a nominal charge for our services.* ○ *They are paying a nominal rent.* **2.** referring to the official value of something rather than the actual value ○ *property with a nominal value of £1 million* **3.** in name only ○ *He was the nominal leader of the group but his wife made all the important decisions.*

nominal damages /ˌnɒmɪn(ə)l 'dæmɪdʒɪz/ *plural noun* a very small amount of damages, awarded to show that the loss or harm suffered was technical rather than actual

nominate /'nɒmɪneɪt/ *verb* to officially suggest someone for a position or a prize ○ *He was nominated as Labour candidate.* □ **to nominate someone to a post** to appoint someone to a post without an election □ **to nominate someone as proxy** to name someone as your proxy

nominator /'nɒmɪneɪtə/ *noun* somebody who is entitled to receive money and writes a nomination

nominee /ˌnɒmɪ'niː/ *noun* **1.** a person who has been officially suggested for a position or a prize **2.** a person who is appointed to deal with financial matters on behalf of another person

nominee account /ˌnɒmɪ'niː əˌkaʊnt/ *noun* an account held on behalf of another person

non-acceptance /ˌnɒn ək'septəns/ *noun* a situation where the person who should pay a bill of exchange does not accept it

non-accidental death /ˌnɒn ˌæksɪdent(ə)l 'deθ/ *noun* death by natural causes, e.g. illness, advanced age. Compare **accidental death**

non-arrestable offence /ˌnɒn əˌrestəb(ə)l ə'fens/ *noun* a crime for which a person cannot be arrested without a warrant

COMMENT: Non-arrestable offences are usually crimes which carry a sentence of less than five years imprisonment.

non-capital crime /ə'fens/, **non-capital offence** *noun* a crime or offence for which an offender cannot be sentenced to death

non compos mentis /ˌnɒn ˌkɒmpəs 'mentɪs/ *phrase* a Latin phrase meaning 'mad' or 'not fully sane'

non-conformance /ˌnɒn kən'fɔːməns/ *noun* the act of not conforming ○ *He was criticised for non-conformance with the regulations.*

non-consummation /ˌnɒn ˌkɒnsə 'meɪʃ(ə)n/ *noun* □ **non-consummation of marriage** not having sexual intercourse (between husband and wife)

non-departmental public body /ˌnɒn ˌdiːpɑːtment(ə)l ˌpʌblɪk 'bɒdi/ *noun* a national or regional public body, working independently of the ministers to whom it is accountable, e.g. the Environmental Agency, some Royal Commissions. Abbreviation **NDPB**

non-direction /ˌnɒn daɪ'rekʃən/ *noun* (*of a judge*) the fact of not giving instructions to a jury about how to consider something

non-disclosure /ˌnɒn dɪs'kləʊʒə/ *noun* the failure to disclose information which one has a duty to disclose

non-disclosure agreement /nɒn dɪs 'kləʊʒər əˌgriːmənt/ *noun* a legal contract between two parties which forbids one from revealing information which the other does not want disclosed, such as a trade secret. Abbreviation **NDA**

non est factum *phrase* a Latin phrase meaning 'it is not his or her deed': a plea that a contract's signatory was not fully aware of what they were doing when they signed, and so cannot be held to the contract

non-executive director /nɒn ɪg ˌzekjʊtɪv daɪ'rektə/ *noun* a director who attends board meetings and gives advice, but does not work full time for a company

nonfeasance /nɒn'fiːzəns/ *noun* failure to do something which should be done by law

nonjoinder /nɒn'dʒɔɪndə/ *noun* a plea that a claimant has not joined all the necessary parties to his or her action

non-molestation order /nɒn ˌməʊle 'steɪʃ(ə)n ˌɔːdə/ *noun* an order made by a court to prevent one party, particularly a co-habitant or spouse, from threatening, attacking or making contact with the other

non-national /nɒn 'næʃ(ə)nəl/ *noun* somebody who is not a citizen of a particular state ○ *Non-nationals can be barred from working in an EU country if they do not speak the language.*

non-negotiable instrument /ˌnɒn nɪ ˌgəʊʃəb(ə)l 'ɪnstrʊmənt/ *noun* a document such as a crossed cheque which is not payable to bearer and so cannot be exchanged for cash

non-payment /ˌnɒn 'peɪmənt/ *noun* □ **non-payment of a debt** not paying a debt due

non-proliferation treaty /ˌnɒn prəˌlɪfə 'reɪʃ(ə)n ˌtriːti/ *noun* a treaty to prevent the possession and development of nuclear weapons spreading to countries which do not yet possess them

non-recurring items /ˌnɒn rɪˌkɜːrɪŋ ˈaɪtəmz/ *noun* special items in a set of accounts which appear only once

non-refundable /ˌnɒn rɪˈfʌndəb(ə)l/ *adjective* being ineligible for refund

non-resident /ˌnɒn ˈrezɪd(ə)nt/ *noun* somebody who is not considered a resident of a country for tax purposes

non-retroactivity /nɒn ˌretrəʊæk ˈtɪvɪti/ *noun* (*in the EU*) the state of not being retroactive

non-returnable /ˌnɒn rɪˈtɜːnəb(ə)l/ *adjective* being impossible to return

nonsufficient funds /nɒnsəˌfɪʃənt ˈfʌndz/ *noun US* a sum of money in an account which is less than is needed to pay a cheque which has been presented

nonsuit, nonsuited ◊ **to be nonsuit, to be nonsuited 1.** a situation in civil proceedings where a claimant fails to establish a cause of action and is forced to abandon proceedings **2.** a situation in criminal proceedings where a judge directs a jury to find the defendant not guilty

non-taxable /ˌnɒn ˈtæksəb(ə)l/ *adjective* being ineligible for tax

non-verbal evidence /nɒn ˌvɜːb(ə)l ˈevɪd(ə)ns/ *noun* evidence produced in court in the form of maps, photographs or other documents

North-Eastern Circuit, Northern Circuit /ˌnɔːθ ˈiːstən ˌsɜːkɪt/ *noun* two of the six circuits of the Crown Court to which barristers belong, with centres in Leeds and Manchester

Northern Ireland Assembly /ˌnɔːð(ə)n ˌaɪələnd əˈsembli/ *noun* the centre of devolved Government for Northern Ireland, formed in 1998 under the terms of the Good Friday Agreement

noscitur a sociis /ˌnɒskɪtə ɑː ˈsəʊsiis/ *phrase* a Latin phrase meaning 'the meaning of the words can be understood from the words around them': ambiguous words or phrases can be clarified by referring to the context in which they are used

notarial /nəʊˈteəriəl/ *adjective* referring to notaries public

notarial act /nəʊˌteəriəl ˈækt/ *noun* an act which can be carried out only by a notary public

notary /ˈnəʊtəri/ *noun* a person who is legally authorised to certify the authenticity or legitimacy of signatures and documents

notary public /ˌnəʊtəri ˈpʌblɪk/, **notary** /ˈnəʊtəri/ *noun* a lawyer, usually but not necessarily a solicitor, who has the authority to draw up and witness specific types of document and so make them official (NOTE: The plural is **notaries public**.)

note /nəʊt/ *verb* □ **to note a bill** to attach a note to a dishonoured bill of exchange, explaining why it has not been honoured

note of costs /ˌnəʊt əv ˈkɒsts/ *noun* a bill or invoice

note of hand /ˌnəʊt əv ˈhænd/ *noun* a document stating that someone promises to pay an amount of money on a specified date

not guilty /ˌnɒt ˈɡɪlti/ ♦ **guilty**

notice /ˈnəʊtɪs/ *noun* **1.** a piece of written information ○ *The company secretary pinned up a notice about the pension scheme.* **2.** information given to warn someone officially that something is going to happen, e.g. that a contract is going to end, that terms of a contract are going to be changed, that an employee will leave a job at a specific date, or that a tenant must leave the property being occupied □ **to give someone notice, to serve notice on someone** to give someone a legal notice □ **to give a tenant notice to quit, to serve a tenant with notice to quit** to inform a tenant officially that he or she has to leave the premises by a specified date □ **to hand in your notice** to inform your employers officially that you will leave your job **3.** a legal document informing someone of something □ **to give notice of appeal** to start official proceedings for an appeal to be heard **4.** knowledge of a fact

notice of allocation /ˌnəʊtɪs əv ˌæləˈkeɪʃ(ə)n/ *noun* an official letter from a court, telling the parties to which of three management tracks their case has been allocated

notice of dishonour /ˌnəʊtɪs əv dɪsˈɒnə/ *noun* a letter or document warning a person to pay a cheque or risk being sued

notice of motion /ˌnəʊtɪs əv ˈməʊʃ(ə)n/ *noun* a document telling the other party to a case that an application will be made to the court

notice of opposition /ˌnəʊtɪs əv ˌɒpəˈzɪʃ(ə)n/ *noun* a document opposing a patent application

notice of service /ˌnəʊtɪs əv ˈsɜːvɪs/ *noun* a document issued by a court to show that a claim has been served

notice period /ˌpɪəriəd əv ˈnəʊtɪs/ *noun* the time stated in the contract of employment which the employee or company has to allow between resigning or being fired and the employee actually leaving his or her job

notice to quit /ˌnəʊtɪs tə ˈkwɪt/ *noun* formal notice served by a landlord on a tenant before proceedings are started for possession

notifiable /ˈnəʊtɪfaɪəb(ə)l/ *adjective* sufficiently serious that it has to be officially recorded

notifiable disease /ˌnəʊtɪfaɪəb(ə)l dɪˈfens/ *noun* a disease of livestock which must be reported to the authorities if it is diagnosed, so that preventive measures can be taken

notifiable offence /ˌnəʊtɪfaɪəb(ə)l əˈfens/ *noun* a serious offence which can be tried in the Crown Court

not proven /ˌnɒt ˈpruːv(ə)n/ *adjective* referring to a verdict that a prosecution has not produced sufficient evidence to allow the accused to be proved guilty

notwithstanding /ˌnɒtwɪðˈstændɪŋ/ *preposition* in spite of ○ *The case proceeded notwithstanding the objections of the defendant.* ■ *adverb* despite the fact or thing previously mentioned ○ *We had to close the advice centre for lack of funds, its excellent work notwithstanding.*

novation /nəʊˈveɪʃ(ə)n/ *noun* a transaction in which a new contract is agreed by all parties to replace an existing contract, e.g. where one of the parties to the old contract is released from their liability under the old contract and this liability is assumed by a third party

no win no fee /nəʊ ˌwɪn nəʊ ˈfiː/ *noun* same as **conditional fee agreement**

NSF /ˌen es ˈef/ *abbreviation US* nonsufficient funds

nuisance /ˈnjuːs(ə)ns/ *noun* something which causes harm or inconvenience to someone or to property

null /nʌl/ *adjective* without legal value or effect □ **the contract was declared null and void** the contract was said to be no longer valid □ **to render a decision null** to make a decision useless, to cancel a decision

nullification /ˌnʌlɪfɪˈkeɪʃ(ə)n/ *noun* the act of making something invalid

nullify /ˈnʌlɪfaɪ/ *verb* to make something lose its legal value or effect

nullity /ˈnʌlɪti/ *noun* **1.** an action which is void or invalid **2.** a situation where a marriage is ruled never to have been in effective existence

nuncupative will /ˌnʌnkʌpətɪv ˈwɪl/ *noun* a will made orally in the presence of a witness, e.g. a will made by a soldier in time of war

O

oath /əʊθ/ *noun* a solemn legal promise that someone will say or write only what is true □ **to be under oath** to have sworn in court to tell the truth □ **to administer an oath to someone** to make someone swear an oath

oath of allegiance /ˌəʊθ əv əˈliːdʒəns/ *noun* an oath which is sworn to put the person under the orders or rules of a country, an army, etc ○ *all officers swore an oath of allegiance to the new president*

obiter dicta /ˌɒbɪtə ˈdɪktə/ *phrase* a Latin phrase meaning 'things which are said in passing': part of a judgment which is not essential to the decision of the judge and does not create a precedent. ◊ **ratio decidendi** (NOTE: The singular is **obiter dictum**.)

object /ˈɒbdʒekt/ *noun* purpose or aim ■ *verb* /əbˈdʒekt/ to say that you do not accept or agree with something ○ *to object to a clause in a contract* □ **to object to a juror** to ask for a juror not to be appointed because he or she may be biased

objection /əbˈdʒekʃən/ *noun* □ **to raise an objection to something** to object to something ○ *One of the parties raised an objection to the wording of the agreement.*

objective /əbˈdʒektɪv/ *noun* something which you try to do ■ *adjective* considered from a general point of view and not from that of the person involved ○ *The judge asked the jury to be objective in considering the evidence put before them.* ○ *You must be objective in assessing the performance of the staff.*

objects clause /ˈɒbdʒɪkts klɔːz/ *noun* a section in a company's memorandum of association which says what work the company will do

obligate /ˈɒblɪɡeɪt/ *verb* □ **to be obligated to do something** *especially US* to have a legal duty to do something

obligation /ˌɒblɪˈɡeɪʃ(ə)n/ *noun* **1.** a legal or moral duty to do something □ **to be**

under an obligation to do something to feel it is your duty to do something □ **to be under no contractual obligation** to have not signed any agreement □ **to fulfil one's contractual obligations** to do what is stated in a contract □ **two weeks' free trial without obligation** situation where the customer can try the item at home for two weeks without having to buy it at the end of the test **2.** a debt □ **to meet one's obligations** to pay one's debts

obligatory /əˈblɪɡət(ə)ri/ *adjective* necessary according to the law or rules ○ *Each new member of staff has to pass an obligatory medical examination.*

obligee /ˌɒblɪˈdʒiː/ *noun* somebody who is owed a duty

obligor /ˌɒblɪˈɡɔː/ *noun* somebody who owes a duty to someone

obscene /əbˈsiːn/ *adjective* likely to offend public morals and accepted standards of decency, or to deprave or corrupt someone ○ *The magazine was classed as an obscene publication.* ○ *The police seized a number of obscene films.*

obscene publication /əbˌsiːn ˌpʌblɪ ˈkeɪʃ(ə)n/ *noun* a book or magazine which is liable to deprave or corrupt someone who sees or reads it ○ *The magazine was classed as an obscene publication and seized by customs.*

obscenity /əbˈsenɪti/ *noun* the state of being obscene ○ *The magistrate commented on the obscenity of some parts of the film.*

obscenity laws /əbˈsenɪti lɔːz/ *plural noun* law relating to obscene publications or films

observance /əbˈzɜːv(ə)ns/ *noun* doing what is required by a law ○ *the government's observance of international agreements*

observe /əbˈzɜːv/ *verb* **1.** to obey a rule or a law ○ *failure to observe the correct procedure* ○ *All members of the association should observe the code of practice.* **2.** to watch or to notice what is happening ○ *Officials have been instructed to observe the conduct of the election.*

observer /əb'zɜːvə/ *noun* somebody who observes ○ *Two official observers attended the meeting.*

obsolete /'ɒbsəliːt/ *adjective* no longer being used or in force and replaced by something else ○ *The law has been made obsolete by new developments in forensic science.*

obstruct /əb'strʌkt/ *verb* to stop something progressing ○ *The parked cars are obstructing the traffic.* □ **obstructing the police** the offence of doing something which prevents a police officer carrying out his or her duty

obstruction /əb'strʌkʃən/ *noun* **1.** something which gets in the way ○ *The car caused an obstruction to the traffic.* **2.** an act of obstructing someone □ **obstruction of the police** doing anything which prevents a police officer from doing his or her duty

obstructive /əb'strʌktɪv/ *adjective* deliberately causing problems ○ *obstructive behaviour*

obtain /əb'teɪn/ *verb* **1.** to get something ○ *to obtain supplies from abroad* ○ *to obtain an injunction against a company* ○ *We find these items very difficult to obtain.* □ **to obtain a property by fraud, by deception** to trick someone into handing over possession of property □ **obtaining a pecuniary advantage by deception** the offence of deceiving someone so as to derive a financial benefit **2.** to exist, be generally accepted, or have legal status ○ *a rule obtaining in international law* ○ *This right does not obtain in judicial proceedings.*

obtaining by deception /əb,teɪnɪŋ baɪ dɪ'sepʃən/ *noun* the act of acquiring money or property by tricking someone into handing it over

obtaining credit /əb,teɪnɪŋ 'kredɪt/ *noun* an offence whereby an undischarged bankrupt obtains credit above a limit of £50

occasion /ə'keɪʒ(ə)n/ *noun* the time when something takes place ○ *The opening of the trial was the occasion of protests by the family of the accused.* ■ *verb* to make something happen ○ *He pleaded guilty to assault occasioning actual bodily harm.*

occasional /ə'keɪʒ(ə)n(ə)l/ *adjective* happening from time to time

occasional licence /ə,keɪʒ(ə)n(ə)l 'laɪs(ə)ns/ *noun* a licence to sell alcohol at a specific place and time only

occupancy /'ɒkjʊpənsi/ *noun* **1.** the act of occupying a property such as a house, office, or room in a hotel □ **with immediate occupancy** empty and available to be occupied immediately **2.** the fact of occupying a property which has no owner and so acquiring title to the property

occupant /'ɒkjʊpənt/ *noun* a person or company which occupies a property

occupation /,ɒkjʊ'peɪʃ(ə)n/ *noun* **1.** the act of occupying a property which has no owner, and so acquiring title to the property **2.** the work that someone does

occupational /,ɒkjʊ'peɪʃ(ə)nəl/ *adjective* referring to a job □ **occupational accident** an accident which takes place at work □ **occupational disease** a disease which affects people in some jobs □ **occupational hazards** dangers which apply to specific jobs

occupational pension /,ɒkjʊpeɪʃ(ə)nəl 'penʃən/ *noun* a pension which is paid by the company by which an employee has been employed

occupational pension scheme /,ɒkjʊpeɪʃ(ə)nəl 'penʃən skiːm/ *noun* a pension scheme where the employee gets a pension from the company he or she has worked for

occupation order /,ɒkjʊ'peɪʃ(ə)n ,ɔːdə/ *noun* a court order in marital proceedings which decides the rights of a spouse to use the marital home. Former name **exclusion order** (NOTE: It may exclude them entirely or allow them access to the whole or part of the home.)

occupier /'ɒkjʊpaɪə/ *noun* somebody who lives in a property

COMMENT: The occupier has the right to stay in or on a property, but is not necessarily an owner.

occupier's liability /,ɒkjʊpaɪəz ,laɪə'bɪlɪti/ *noun* the duty of an occupier to make sure that visitors to a property are not harmed

occupy /'ɒkjʊpaɪ/ *verb* to enter and stay in a property illegally ○ *The rebels occupied the Post Office.* ○ *Squatters are occupying the building.*

offence /ə'fens/ *noun* an illegal act ○ *He was charged with three serious offences.* ○ *The minister was arrested and charged with offences against the Official Secrets Act.* □ **offence triable either way** an offence which can be tried before a magistrates' court or a Crown Court

offence against property /əˌfens ə
ˌgenst ˈprɒpəti/ *noun* a criminal act which
damages or destroys property, e.g. theft, forgery or criminal damage

offence against public order /əˌfens
əˌgenst ˌpʌblɪk ˈɔːdə/ *noun* a criminal act
which disturbs the general calm of society,
e.g. riot or affray

offence against the person /əˌfens ə
ˌgenst ðə ˈpɜːs(ə)n/ *noun* a criminal act
which harms a person physically, e.g. murder or actual bodily harm

offence against the state /əˌfens ə
ˌgenst ðə ˈsteɪt/ *noun* an attack on the lawful government of a country, e.g. sedition or
treason

offend /əˈfend/ *verb* to commit a crime

offender /əˈfendə/ *noun* somebody who
commits a crime

offensive weapon /əˌfensɪv ˈwepən/
noun an object which can be used to harm a
person or property □ **carrying an offensive
weapon** the offence of holding a weapon or
something such as a bottle which could be
used as a weapon

COMMENT: Many things can be considered
as offensive weapons if they are used as
such: a brick, a bottle, a piece of wire, etc.

offer /ˈɒfə/ *noun* **1.** a statement by one
party to a contract that he or she proposes to
do something (NOTE: The offer (and acceptance by the other party) is one of the
essential elements of a contract.) **2.** □
under offer (*of a property*) having been
offered for sale, and an offer made to buy
which has been provisionally accepted □
open to offers willing to discuss changing
something that has been put forward □ **or
near offer (o.n.o.)** or an offer of a price
which is slightly less than the price asked ○
asking price: #200 o.n.o. ■ *verb* **1.** to propose something to someone, or propose to
do something ○ *to offer someone £100,000
for their house* ○ *He offered to buy the
house.* □ **to offer someone a job** to tell
someone that he or she can have a job in
your company **2.** to say that you are willing
to sell something ○ *We offered the house for
sale.*

offeree /ˌɒfəˈriː/ *noun* somebody who
receives an offer

offer of amends /ˌɒfə əv əˈmendz/ *plural noun* an offer to write an apology by
someone who has libelled another person

offeror /ˈɒfərə/ *noun* somebody who
makes an offer

offer to buy /ˌɒfə tə ˈbaɪ/ *noun* a statement that you are willing to pay a specific
amount of money to buy something ○ *to
accept an offer to buy for the car* ○ *We made
a written offer to buy for the house.*

offer to sell /ˌɒfə tə ˈsel/ *noun* a statement that you are willing to sell something

office /ˈɒfɪs/ *noun* **1.** a set of rooms where
a company works or where business is done
2. a room where someone works and does
business ○ *She has a pleasant office which
looks out over the park.* ○ *The senior partner's office is on the third floor.* **3.** □ **information office** an office where someone can
answer questions from members of the public **4.** a post or position ○ *He holds* or *performs the office of treasurer.* □ **compensation for loss of office** payment to a director
who is asked to leave a company before his
or her contract ends

office creeper /ˈɒfɪs ˌkriːpə/ *noun* a
well-dressed, well-spoken thief who pre-
tends to be someone such as a sales or repair
person and steals valuable items such as
laptop computers from offices (*slang*)

Office of Fair Trading /ˌɒfɪs əv feə
ˈtreɪdɪŋ/ *noun* the British government
department which protects consumers
against unfair or illegal business. Abbreviation **OFT**

office of profit /ˌɒfɪs əv ˈprɒfɪt/, **office
of profit under the Crown** /ˌɒfɪs əv
ˌprɒfɪt ˈʌndə ðɪ kraʊn/ *noun* a government post which disqualifies someone from
being a Member of Parliament

Office of Public Sector Information
/ˌɒfɪs əv ˌpʌblɪk ˌsektər ˌɪnfəˈmeɪʃ(ə)n/
noun a UK body responsible for public
information services in the UK, including
the publication of Acts of Parliament, and
for Crown copyright. Abbreviation **OPSI**

officer /ˈɒfɪsə/ *noun* **1.** somebody who has
an official position □ **the company officers**,
the officers of a company the main executives or directors of a company **2.** an official, usually unpaid, of a club or society ○
the election of officers of an association

officer of the court /ˌɒfɪsər əv ðə ˈkɔːt/
noun anybody who is involved in the application of the law through the court system,
such as a judge, juror or prosecutor

office security /ˌɒfɪs sɪˈkjʊərɪti/ *noun*
the means taken to protect an office against
theft of equipment, personal property or
information

official /əˈfɪʃ(ə)l/ *adjective* **1.** done
because it has been authorised by a govern-

ment department or organisation ○ *He left official documents in his car.* ○ *She received an official letter of explanation.* □ **speaking in an official capacity** speaking officially □ **to go through official channels** to deal with officials, especially when making a request **2.** done or approved by a director or by a person in authority ○ *This must be an official order – it is written on the company's notepaper.* ■ *noun* somebody working in a government department

official copy /ə,fɪʃ(ə)l ˈkɒpi/ *noun* a copy of an official document which has been sealed by the office which issued it

Official Journal /ə,fɪʃ(ə)l ˈdʒɜːn(ə)l/ *noun* a publication which lists the regulations, statutory instruments and directives of the EC

officially /əˈfɪʃ(ə)li/ *adverb* openly, on the record ○ *Officially he knows nothing about the problem, but unofficially he has given us a lot of advice about it.*

official mediator /ə,fɪʃ(ə)l ˈmiːdieɪtə/ *noun* a government official who tries to make the two sides in an industrial dispute agree

Official Receiver /ə,fɪʃ(ə)l rɪˈsiːvə/ *noun* a government official who is appointed to close down a company which is in liquidation or deal with the affairs of a bankrupt

official referee /ə,fɪʃ(ə)l ,refəˈriː/ *noun* a judge with specialist knowledge who is appointed by the High Court to try complicated, usually technical, cases

official return /ə,fɪʃ(ə)l rɪˈtɜːn/ *noun* an official report or statement

official secret /ə,fɪʃ(ə)l ˈsiːkrət/ *noun* a piece of information which is classified as important to the state and which it is a crime to reveal

Official Secrets Act /ə,fɪʃ(ə)l ˈsiːkrəts ,ækt/ *noun* an Act of Parliament which governs the publication of secret information relating to the state

Official Solicitor /ə,fɪʃ(ə)l səˈlɪsɪtə/ *noun* a solicitor who acts in the High Court for parties who have no-one to act for them, usually because they are under a legal disability

officio /əˈfɪʃɪəʊ/ ♦ **ex officio, functus officio**

off-licence /ˈɒf ,laɪs(ə)ns/ *noun* **1.** a licence to sell alcohol for drinking away from the place where you buy it **2.** a shop which sells alcohol for drinking at home

offspring /ˈɒfsprɪŋ/ *noun* a child or children of a parent ○ *His offspring inherited the estate.* ○ *They had two offspring.* (NOTE: **Offspring** is both singular and plural.)

off the record /,ɒf ðə ˈrekɔːd/ *adverb* unofficially or in private ○ *He made some remarks off the record about the rising crime figures.*

OFT *abbreviation* Office of Fair Trading

Old Bailey /,əʊld ˈbeɪli/ *noun* the central Criminal Court in London

old lag /,əʊld ˈlæg/ *noun* a criminal who has served many (short) prison sentences, one who will never go straight (*informal*)

ombudsman /ˈɒmbʊdzmən/ *noun* an official who investigates complaints by the public against government departments or other large organisations

COMMENT: There are in fact several ombudsmen: the main one is the Parliamentary Commissioner, but there are also others, such as the Health Service Commissioner, who investigates complaints against the Health Service, and the Local Ombudsman who investigates complaints against local authorities, the Banking Ombudsman, who investigates complaints against banks, etc. In 1990, a Legal Services Ombudsman was appointed to investigate complaints against non-legal professional people who supply legal services, such as conveyancing. Although an ombudsman will make his recommendations to the department concerned, and may make his recommendations public, he has no power to enforce them. The Parliamentary Commissioner may only investigate complaints which are addressed to him through an MP; the member of the public first brings his complaint to his MP, and if the MP cannot get satisfaction from the department against which the complaint is made, then the matter is passed to the Ombudsman.

omission /əʊˈmɪʃ(ə)n/ *noun* failure to do something that you should do □ **lie of omission** the fact of deliberately misleading someone by leaving out important parts of a story

one minute speech /,wʌn ˈmɪnət ,spiːtʃ/ *noun US* a short speech by a member of the House of Representatives on any subject at the beginning of the day's business

onus /ˈəʊnəs/ *noun* responsibility for doing something difficult

onus probandi *phrase* a Latin phrase meaning 'burden of proof'. ◊ **burden of proof**

op. cit. /ˌɒp ˈsɪt/ *phrase* a Latin phrase meaning 'in the work mentioned' (NOTE: used when referring to a legal text: 'see Smith LJ in *Jones v. Amalgamated Steel Ltd* op. cit. p. 260')

open /ˈəʊpən/ *adjective* □ **in open court** in a courtroom with members of the public present ■ *verb* to begin speaking ○ *Counsel for the prosecution opened with a description of the accused's family background.* □ **to open negotiations** to begin negotiating

open account /ˌəʊpən əˈkaʊnt/ *noun* an amount owed with no security offered

open cheque /ˌəʊpən ˈtʃek/ *noun* a cheque which is not crossed and can be exchanged for cash anywhere

open court /ˈəʊpən kɔːt/ *noun* a court where the hearings are open to the public

open credit /ˌəʊpən ˈkredɪt/ *noun* bank credit given to good customers without security up to a maximum sum

open-ended /ˌəʊpən ˈendɪd/, **open-end** US /ˌəʊpən ˈend/ *adjective* with no fixed limit, or with some items not specified ○ *an open-ended agreement*

open hearing /ˌəʊpən ˈhɪərɪŋ/ *noun* a hearing that the public and journalists may attend

opening /ˈəʊp(ə)nɪŋ/ *noun* □ **a market opening** the possibility of starting to do business in a new market ■ *adjective* happening at the beginning of something ○ *the judge's opening remarks* ○ *the opening speech from the defence counsel or from the Home Secretary*

open policy /ˌəʊpən ˈpɒlɪsi/ *noun* a marine insurance policy, where the value of what is insured is not stated

open prison /ˌəʊpən ˈprɪz(ə)n/ *noun* a prison with minimum security where category 'D' prisoners can be kept

open verdict /ˌəʊpən ˈvɜːdɪkt/ *noun* a verdict in a coroner's court which does not decide how the dead person died ○ *The court recorded an open verdict on the two fatalities.*

operandi ♦ **modus operandi**

operating /ˈɒpəreɪtɪŋ/ *noun* the general running of a business or of a machine

operating budget /ˈɒpəreɪtɪŋ ˌbʌdʒɪt/ *noun* income and expenditure which is expected to be incurred over a period of time

operating costs /ˈɒpəreɪtɪŋ kɒsts/ *plural noun* costs of the day-to-day organisation of a company

operating loss /ˈɒpəreɪtɪŋ lɒs/ *noun* a loss made by a company in its usual business

operation /ˌɒpəˈreɪʃ(ə)n/ *noun* □ **in operation** working, being used ○ *The system will be in operation by June.* ○ *The new system came into operation on June 1st.*

operational /ˌɒpəˈreɪʃ(ə)nəl/ *adjective* □ **to become operational** to begin working

operational budget /ˌɒpəreɪʃ(ə)nəl ˈbʌdʒɪt/ *noun* expenditure which is expected to be made in running a business, office or other organisation such as a police force

operational costs /ˌɒpəreɪʃ(ə)nəl ˈkɒsts/ *plural noun* the costs of running a business or a police force

operational planning /ˌɒpəreɪʃ(ə)nəl ˈplænɪŋ/ *noun* the activity of planning how something is to be run

operational research /ˌɒpəreɪʃ(ə)nəl rɪˈsɜːtʃ/ *noun* a study of a method of working to see if it can be made more efficient and cost-effective

operations review /ˌɒpəˈreɪʃ(ə)nz rɪˌvjuː/ *noun* an assessment of the way in which a company or department works to see how it can be made more efficient and profitable

operative words /ˌɒp(ə)rətɪv ˈwɜːdz/ *plural noun* words in a conveyancing document which transfer the land or create an interest in the land

opinion /əˈpɪnjən/ *noun* **1.** □ **to be of the opinion** to believe or to think ○ *The judge was of the opinion that if the evidence was doubtful the claim should be dismissed.* **2.** a piece of expert advice ○ *to ask an adviser for his opinion on a case* ○ *The lawyers gave their opinion.* ○ *Counsel prepared a written opinion.* **3.** a judgment delivered by a court, especially the House of Lords **4.** (*in the EU*) an opinion of the European Community which is not legally binding

opinion poll /əˈpɪnjən pəʊl/ *noun* the activity of asking a sample group of people what they feel about something in order to assess the opinion of the whole population

opponent /əˈpəʊnənt/ *noun* somebody who is against you or who votes against what you propose ○ *The prosecution tried to discredit their opponents in the case.*

oppose /əˈpəʊz/ *verb* **1.** to try to stop something happening ○ *We are all opposed to the takeover.* ○ *Counsel for the claimant opposed the defendant's application for an* *adjournment.* □ **to oppose bail** to say that bail should not be granted to the accused **2.** to vote against something ○ *A minority of board members opposed the motion.*

opposition /ˌɒpəˈzɪʃ(ə)n/ *noun* strong disagreement with a suggestion or plan, often including action to try to change or stop it ○ *There was considerable opposition to the plan for reorganising the divorce courts.* ○ *The voters showed their opposition to the government by voting against the proposal in the referendum.*

OPSI *abbreviation* Office of Public Sector Information

option /ˈɒpʃən/ *noun* an offer to someone of the right to enter into a contract at a later date □ **option to purchase** giving someone the possibility to buy something within a period of time or when a specific event happens □ **to grant someone a six-month option on a product** to allow someone six months to decide if he or she wants to be the agent for a product, or if he or she wants to manufacture the product under licence □ **to take up an option, to exercise an option** to accept the option which has been offered and to put it into action ○ *He exercised his option* or *he took up his option to acquire sole marketing rights to the product.* □ **to leave your options open** to be able to decide what to do when the time is right □ **to take the soft option** to decide to do something which involves the least risk, effort or problems

opt-out request /ˈɒpt aʊt rɪˌkwest/ *noun* a reply to a commercial e-mail asking for your address to be taken off their mailing list

COMMENT: By law, all commercial e-mails must include a valid e-mail address to which to send opt-out requests.

oral /ˈɔːrəl/ *adjective* spoken

oral evidence /ˌɔːrəl ˈevɪd(ə)ns/ *noun* spoken evidence, as opposed to written evidence

orally /ˈɔːrəli/ *adverb* in speech, not in writing

order /ˈɔːdə/ *noun* **1.** a general state of calm, where everything is working as planned and ruled ○ *There was a serious breakdown of law and order.* □ **offence against public order, public order offence** a riot, street fight, etc. **2.** □ **orders** legislation made by ministers, under powers delegated to them by Act of Parliament, but which still have to be ratified by Parliament before coming into force **3.** □ **to call a meet-**

-ing to order to start proceedings officially □ **to bring a meeting to order** to get a meeting back to discussing the agenda again (after an interruption) **4.** □ **pay to Mr Smith or order** pay money to Mr Smith or as he orders □ **pay to the order of somebody** pay money directly into somebody's bank account

order book /ˈɔːdə bʊk/ *noun* a list showing the House of Commons business for the term of Parliament

Order in Council /ˌɔːdə ɪn ˈkaʊns(ə)l/ *noun* legislation approved by the Queen in Council, which is allowed by an Act of Parliament and does not have to be ratified by Parliament

order of certiorari /ˌɔːdə əv ˌsɜːʃiə ˈreəraɪ/ *noun* an order which transfers a case from a lower court to the High Court for investigation into its legality ○ *He applied for judicial review by way of certiorari.* ○ *The court ordered certiorari following judicial review, quashing the order made by the juvenile court.*

order of committal /ˌɔːdə əv kə ˈmɪt(ə)l/ *noun* same as **committal order**

order of discharge /ˌɔːdə əv ˈdɪstʃɑːdʒ/ *noun* a court order releasing a person from bankruptcy

order paper /ˌɔːdə ˈpeɪpə/ *noun* the agenda of business to be discussed each day in the House of Commons

ordinance /ˈɔːdɪnəns/ *noun* **1.** a special decree of a government **2.** *US* a rule made by a municipal authority, and effective only within the jurisdiction of that authority

ordinarily /ˈɔːd(ə)n(ə)rɪli/ *adverb* normally or usually

ordinarily resident /ˌɔːd(ə)n(ə)rɪli ˈrezɪd(ə)nt/ *noun* someone who is usually resident in a particular country

ordinary /ˈɔːd(ə)n(ə)ri/ *adjective* normal or not special ○ *He wore jeans and an ordinary black t-shirt.*

ordinary creditor /ˌɔːd(ə)n(ə)ri ˈkredɪtə/ *noun* a creditor who is neither a secured nor a preferential creditor, e.g. an unsecured creditor

organised crime /ˌɔːgənaɪzd ˈkraɪm/ *noun* criminal activities which are run as a business, with groups of specialist criminals, assistants, security staff, etc., all run by a group of directors or by a boss

organised labour /ˌɔːgənaɪzd ˈleɪbə/ *noun* all the employees who are members of trade unions

original /əˈrɪdʒən(ə)l/ *noun* the first copy made ○ *Send the original and file two copies.*

original evidence /əˌrɪdʒən(ə)l ˈevɪd(ə)ns/ *noun* evidence given by a witness, based on facts which he or she knows to be true as opposed to hearsay

originate /əˈrɪdʒɪneɪt/ *verb* to begin to exist

originating application /əˌrɪdʒɪneɪtɪŋ ˌæplɪˈkeɪʃ(ə)n/ *noun* a way of beginning some types of case in the County Court

originating summons /əˌrɪdʒɪneɪtɪŋ ˈsʌmənz/ *noun* a summons whereby a legal action is commenced, usually in the Chancery Division of the High Court in cases relating to land or the administration of an estate

orphan /ˈɔːf(ə)n/ *noun* a child whose parents have died

ostensible /ɒˈstensɪb(ə)l/ *adjective* appearing to be something, but not really so

ostensible partner /ɒˌstensɪb(ə)l ˈpɑːtnə/ *noun* a person who appears to be a partner in a business by allowing his or her name to be used but really has no interest

otherwise /ˈʌðəwaɪz/ *adverb* in another way ○ *John Smith, otherwise known as 'the Butcher'.* □ **except as otherwise stated** except where it is stated in a different way □ **unless otherwise agreed** unless different terms are agreed

oust /aʊst/ *verb* to officially remove somebody from their position or from a property that they are legally occupying ○ *He was ousted from his position as director after charges of misconduct.* Compare **eject**

ouster /ˈaʊstə/ *noun* the official removal of an occupier from a property or an employee from their post ○ *Critics protested against the president's ouster of the Chief Justice for misconduct.*

ouster order /ˈaʊstər ˌɔːdə/ *noun* a court order ejecting an occupier from a property, used especially in matrimonial proceedings against a violent spouse ○ *He had to apply for an ouster order.* ○ *The judge made an ouster order.*

Outer House /ˈaʊtə haʊz/ *noun* part of the Scottish Court of Session, formed of five judges

outlaw /ˈaʊtlɔː/ *noun* an old term for a person who was thrown out of society as a punishment ■ *verb* to say that something is unlawful ○ *The government has proposed a bill to outlaw drinking in public.*

outline planning permission /ˌaʊt(ə)laɪn ˈplænɪŋ pəˌmɪʃ(ə)n/ *noun* general permission to build a property on a piece of land, but not final because there are no details provided

out of court /ˌaʊt əv ˈkɔːt/ *adverb, adjective* without going to court to end a dispute □ **to reach a settlement out of court** to settle a dispute between two parties privately without continuing a court case

out of pocket /ˌaʊt əv ˈpɒkɪt/ *adjective, adverb* having paid out money personally □ **out-of-pocket expenses** the amount of money to pay an employee back for his or her own money which has been spent on company business

output tax /ˈaʊtpʊt tæks/ *noun* VAT charged by a company on goods or services sold

outright /ˌaʊtˈraɪt/ *adverb, adjective* completely □ **to purchase something outright** to buy something completely, including all rights in it

outside /ˈaʊtsaɪd/ *adjective, adverb* not in a prison or institution □ **on the outside** outside a prison or institution ○ *They need help with returning to life on the outside.*

outside dealer /ˌaʊtsaɪd ˈdiːlə/ *noun* somebody who is not a member of the Stock Exchange but is allowed to trade

outside director /ˌaʊtsaɪd daɪˈrektə/ *noun* a director who is not employed by the company

outstanding /aʊtˈstændɪŋ/ *adjective* not yet paid or completed □ **matters outstanding** questions which have not yet been settled

outstanding debts /aʊtˌstændɪŋ ˈdets/ *plural noun* debts which are waiting to be paid

outstanding offences /aʊtˌstændɪŋ ə ˈfensz/ *plural noun* offences for which a person has not yet been convicted, which can be considered at the same time as a similar offence for which he or she faces sentence

Oval Office /ˌəʊvəl ˈɒfɪs/ *noun* the room in the White House which is the personal office of the President of the United States (NOTE: also used to mean the President himself: *The Oval Office was not pleased by the attitude of the Senate.*)

overall majority /ˌəʊvərɔːl məˈdʒɒrɪti/ *noun* same as **absolute majority**

overdue /ˌəʊvəˈdjuː/ *adjective* having not been paid on time □ **to be three weeks**

overdue to have been due to be paid three weeks ago

overreaching /ˌəʊvəˈriːtʃɪŋ/ *noun* a legal principle where an interest in land is replaced by a direct right to money

override /ˌəʊvəˈraɪd/ *verb* **1.** to be more important than something else ○ *They believe public safety overrides individual preference.* **2.** to use official power to change someone else's decision ○ *The appeal court overrode the decision of the lower court.*

COMMENT: If the President of the USA disapproves of a bill sent to him by Congress for signature, he can send it back with objections within ten days of receiving it. Then if the Congress votes with a two-thirds majority in both Houses to continue with the bill, the bill becomes law and the President's veto is overridden.

overrider /ˈəʊvəraɪdə/, **overriding commission** /ˌəʊvəraɪdɪŋ kəˈmɪʃ(ə)n/ *noun* a special extra commission which is above all other commissions

overriding interest /ˌəʊvəraɪdɪŋ ˈɪntrəst/ *noun* an interest which comes before that of another party ○ *His wife established an overriding interest in the property against the bank's charge on it.* (NOTE: **overriding – overrode – has overridden**)

Overriding Objective /ˌəʊvəraɪdɪŋ əb ˈdʒektɪv/ *noun* the fundamental goal of the Civil Procedure Rules, which is to enable the court system to deal with cases justly

overrule /ˌəʊvəˈruːl/ *verb* **1.** (*of a higher court*) to reverse a previous court's decision on a case ○ *The Supreme Court can overrule any other court in the USA.* **2.** to use your power to not allow something asked for ○ *Mr Smith tried to object but his objection was overruled by the chairman.* ○ *Community law must overrule national constitutions of Member States.* □ **objection overruled** the judge does not uphold counsel's objection

overt /əʊˈvɜːt/ *adjective* clear and obvious

overt act /əʊˈvɜːt ækt/ *noun* an act which is obviously aimed at committing a criminal offence

overturn /ˌəʊvəˈtɜːn/ *verb* to cancel a judgment on appeal

own /əʊn/ *verb* to have or to possess □ **a wholly-owned subsidiary** a subsidiary which belongs completely to the parent company □ **a state-owned industry** an industry which is nationalised

owner /ˈəʊnə/ *noun* somebody who owns something □ **goods sent at owner's risk** a situation where it is the owner of the goods who has to insure them while they are being shipped

owner-occupier /ˌəʊnər ˈɒkjʊpaɪə/ *noun* somebody who owns the property which he or she occupies

ownership /ˈəʊnəʃɪp/ *noun* the act of owning something

oyez /əʊˈjez/ *verb* a French word meaning 'hear!': used at the beginning of some types of official proceedings

P

pack /pæk/ *verb* to fill a group such as a committee or a jury with members who are sympathetic to your views ○ *The left-wing group packed the general purposes committee with activists.*

pact /pækt/ *noun* a formal agreement between two parties or countries ○ *The countries in the region signed a non-aggression pact.* ○ *The two minority parties signed an electoral pact not to oppose each other in specific constituencies.*

paedophile /'piːdəfaɪl/ *noun* a person who is sexually attracted to children, especially prepubescents

pais ♦ estoppel

palimony /'pælɪməni/ *noun* the money that a court orders a man to pay regularly to a woman with whom he has been living and from whom he has separated

pan- /pæn/ *prefix* meaning 'covering all'

pandering /'pændərɪŋ/ *noun* the crime of attempting to solicit customers for prostitutes

panel /'pæn(ə)l/ ♦ **empanel**

Papal Nuncio /ˌpeɪp(ə)l 'nʌnsiəʊ/ *noun* an ambassador sent by the Pope to a country

paper /'peɪpə/ *noun* **1.** an outline report ○ *The Treasurer asked his deputy to write a paper on new funding.* ○ *The planning department prepared a paper for the committee on the possible uses of the site.* ◊ **Green Paper**, **White Paper 2.** □ **papers** documents ○ *The solicitor sent me the relevant papers on the case.* ○ *The police have sent the papers on the fraud to the Director of Public Prosecutions.* ○ *He has lost the customs papers.* ○ *The office is asking for the VAT papers.* **3.** □ **on paper** as explained in writing, but not tested in practice ○ *On paper the system is ideal, but we have to see it working before we will sign the contract.* **4.** documents such as bills of exchange or promissory notes which can represent money **5.** □ **paper money**, **paper currency** banknotes **6.** a newspaper

paper loss /ˌpeɪpə 'lɒs/ *noun* the loss made when an asset has fallen in value but has not been sold

paper profit /ˌpeɪpə 'prɒfɪt/ *noun* the profit made when an asset has increased in value but has not been sold

paralegal /ˌpærə'liːg(ə)l/ *adjective* related to, but not part of, the law ■ *noun* somebody with no legal qualifications who works in a lawyer's office

paramount /'pærəmaʊnt/ *adjective* most important or significant ○ *The children's safety is of paramount importance.*

parasitic rights /ˌpærə'sɪtɪk raɪts/ *noun* (*in the EU*) the rights of persons to live in a EU country if they are dependent for their means of living on persons who have the right to reside and to have employment

pardon /'pɑːd(ə)n/ *noun* the action of forgiving an offence by a Parliament or by a monarch ■ *verb* to forgive an offence ○ *The political prisoners were pardoned by the president.*

COMMENT: Not the same as 'quashing' a conviction, which means that the conviction has been made void; both 'pardoning' and 'quashing' have the same effect.

parens patriae /ˌpærenz 'pætriiː/ *phrase* a Latin phrase meaning 'parent of the nation', referring to a king, queen or other head of state as the sovereign and guardian of children or people suffering from a legal disability

parent /'peərənt/ *noun* the father or mother of a child ■ *adjective* controlling or owning ○ *parent company*

parental responsibility /pəˌrent(ə)l rɪˌspɒnsɪ'bɪlɪti/ *noun* a concept introduced by the Children's Act 1989, which encompasses all the rights, duties and responsibilities that by law a parent of a child is entitled to have. Former name **custody**

COMMENT: Parental responsibility is automatically acquired by both parents if married and in cases of unmarried couples, given to the mother alone. An unmarried father is able to acquire parental responsibility by consent of the mother or by obtaining a parental responsibility order which is issued by a court.

parent company /ˈpeərənt ˌkʌmp(ə)ni/ *noun* a company which owns more than half of another company's shares

parentis ♦ **in loco parentis**

pari passu /ˌpæri ˈpæsuː/ *phrase* a Latin phrase meaning 'on a equal footing': equally and fairly

COMMENT: A bankrupt's creditors are often said to be paid 'pari passu', meaning that each receives a fair proportion of the estate according to the amount of credit that they gave.

parity /ˈpærɪti/ *noun* the fact of being equal □ **the female staff want parity with the men** they want to have the same rates of pay and conditions as the men □ **the pound fell to parity with the dollar** the pound fell to a point where one pound equalled one dollar

parking dispensation /ˈpɑːkɪŋ ˌdɪspenseɪʃ(ə)n/ *noun* temporary permission to park in a place or at a time normally outlawed under existing parking restrictions

parking offence /ˈpɑːkɪŋ əˌfens/ *noun* an offence caused when parking a vehicle, e.g. parking on yellow lines, or too near to street corners or pedestrian crossings

parliament /ˈpɑːləmənt/ *noun* an elected group of representatives who form the legislative body which votes the laws of a country ■ **Parliament** in the UK, the legislative body formed of the House of Commons and House of Lords

parliamentary /ˌpɑːləˈment(ə)ri/ *adjective* referring to parliament

parliamentary agent /ˌpɑːləment(ə)ri ˈeɪdʒ(ə)nt/ *noun* a person, usually a solicitor or barrister, who advises private individuals who wish to promote a Bill in Parliament

Parliamentary Commissioner /ˌpɑːlə ˌment(ə)ri kəˈmɪʃ(ə)nə/, **Parliamentary Commissioner for Administration** /ˌpɑːləment(ə)ri kəˌmɪʃ(ə)nə fər ədmɪnɪ ˈstreɪʃ(ə)n/ *noun* the official who investigates complaints by the public against government departments. Also called **ombudsman**

parliamentary counsel /ˌpɑːləment(ə)ri ˈkaʊnsəl/ *noun* a solicitor who is responsible for drafting Bills going before Parliament

Parliamentary privilege /ˌpɑːləment(ə)ri ˈprɪvɪlɪdʒ/ *noun* the right of a Member of Parliament or Member of the House of Lords to speak freely to the House without possibility of being sued for slander

parol /pəˈrəʊl/ *adjective* done by speaking

parol agreement /pəˈrəʊl əˌgriːmənt/ *noun* a simple contract, informal or oral contract

parole /pəˈrəʊl/ *noun* **1.** allowing a prisoner to leave prison for a short time, on condition that he or she behaves well ○ *He was given a week's parole to visit his mother in hospital.* **2.** permission for a prisoner who has behaved well to be released from prison early on condition that he or she continues to behave well ○ *After six month's good conduct in prison she is eligible for parole.* ○ *He was let out on parole and immediately burgled a house.* ■ *verb* to allow a prisoner to leave prison before the end of their sentence on condition that he or she behaves well ○ *If you're lucky you will be paroled before Christmas.*

parole board /pəˈrəʊl bɔːd/ *noun* a group of people who advise the Home Secretary if a prisoner should be released on parole before the end of his or her sentence

parolee /pəˈrəʊliː/ *noun US* a prisoner who is let out on parole

parol evidence /pəˈrəʊl ˌevɪdəns/ *noun* evidence in the form of spoken communication □ **parol evidence rule** the principle that oral communications between the parties which take place before a contract is written up do not constitute part of the contract

part /pɑːt/ *noun* **1.** a piece or section ○ *Part of the shipment was damaged.* ○ *Part of the staff is on overtime.* ○ *Part of the expenses will be refunded.* **2.** one of the sections of an Act, Bill, or other official document (*below*) **3.** □ **in part** not completely ○ *to contribute in part to the costs* ○ *to pay the costs in part*

Part 20 claim /ˌpɑːt ˈtwenti ˌkleɪm/ *noun* any claim other than the main claim filed by a claimant against a defendant in the particulars of claim

COMMENT: Part 20 claims include counterclaims by a defendant against a claimant, or against other persons who are not parties to the case, or a claim by another person against any other person. These claims are dealt with under Part 20 of the new Civil Procedure Rules, hence the name.

Part 36 offer, Part 36 payment *noun* an offer or payment made by a defendant (the offeror) to a claimant (the offeree) to settle all or part of a claim after proceedings have started (NOTE: These offers or payments do not apply to the small claims procedure.)

parte ♦ **ex parte**, **inter partes**, **audi alteram partem**

part exchange /ˌpɑːt ɪksˈtʃeɪndʒ/ *noun* giving an old product as part of the payment for a new one

partial /ˈpɑːʃ(ə)l/ *adjective* **1.** not complete □ **he was awarded partial compensation for the damage to his house** he was compensated for part of the damage **2.** showing unfair support for one person or group compared with others ○ *The defendant complained that the judge was partial.*

partial defence /ˌpɑːʃ(ə)l dɪˈfens/ *noun* a defence which is not enough to acquit the defendant, but which can reduce their charge to a lesser one (NOTE: The three established defences to a charge of murder are **self-defence**, **provocation** and **suicide pact**.)

partial intestacy /ˌpɑːʃ(ə)l ɪnˈtestəsi/ *noun* a situation where a person dies leaving a will which does not cover all his or her estate

partial loss /ˈpɑːʃ(ə)l lɒs/ *noun* a situation where only part of the insured property has been damaged or lost

particular /pəˈtɪkjʊlə/ ♦ **particulars**

particular average /pəˌtɪkjʊlə ˈæv(ə)rɪdʒ/ *noun* a situation where part of a shipment is lost or damaged and the insurance costs are borne by the owner of the lost goods and not shared among all the owners of the shipment

particular lien /pəˌtɪkjʊlə ˈliːən/ *noun* the right of a person to keep possession of another person's property until debts relating to that property have been paid

particulars /pəˈtɪkjʊləz/ *plural noun* **1.** a statement of the facts of a case made by a party in civil proceedings or a County Court pleading setting out the claimant's claim □ **request for further and better particulars** a pleading served by one party on another in civil proceedings, asking for information about the other party's claim or defence **2.** detailed information about something ○ *The inspector asked for particulars of the missing car.* □ **to give full particulars of something** to list all the known details about something

particulars of claim /pəˌtɪkjʊləz əv ˈkleɪm/ *noun* a document containing details of a claimant's case and the relief sought

against the defendant (NOTE: Since the introduction of the Civil Procedure Rules, this term has replaced **statement of claim**.)

COMMENT: Particulars of claim are usually included in the claim form filed by the claimant. They should give a statement of the facts of the claim, together with details of interest or damages claimed. They must include the following if they are to form part of the claim to be pleaded: details of fraud, illegality, breach of trust, default, or unsoundness of mind on the part of the defendant.

partition /pɑːˈtɪʃ(ə)n/ *noun* the division of land which is held by joint tenants or tenants in common

partly-secured creditors /ˌpɑːtli sɪ ˌkjʊəd ˈkredɪtəz/ *plural noun* creditors whose debts are not fully covered by the value of the security

partner /ˈpɑːtnə/ *noun* somebody who works in a firm and has a share in it with other partners ○ *He became a partner in a firm of solicitors.*

partnership /ˈpɑːtnəʃɪp/ *noun* a company set up by two or more people who put money into the business and share the financial risks and profits □ **to offer someone a partnership**, **to take someone into partnership with you** to have a working business and bring someone in to share it with you □ **to dissolve a partnership** to bring a partnership to an end

partnership at will /ˌpɑːtnəʃɪp ət ˈwɪl/ *noun* a partnership with no fixed time limit stated

part-owner /ˌpɑːt ˈəʊnə/ *noun* somebody who owns something jointly with one or more other persons

part-ownership /ˌpɑːt ˈəʊnəʃɪp/ *noun* a situation where two or more persons own the same property

part payment /ˌpɑːt ˈpeɪmənt/ *noun* the payment of part of an amount which is owed

part performance /ˌpɑːt pəˈfɔːməns/ *noun* a situation where a party has carried out part of a contract, but not complied with all the terms of it

party /ˈpɑːti/ *noun* a person or group of people involved in a legal dispute, legal agreement or crime ○ *One of the parties to the suit has died.* ○ *The company is not a party to the agreement.* □ **to be party to something** to be involved in a legal action ○ *How important is this case to those persons who are not party to it?*

party and party costs /ˌpɑːtɪ ən ˌpɑːtɪ ˈkɒsts/ *plural noun* the normal basis for assessment of costs, which includes all costs incurred in the other party's case

party wall /ˌpɑːtɪ ˈwɔːl/ *noun* a wall which separates two adjoining properties such as houses or land and belongs to both owners equally

pass /pɑːs/ *noun* a permit allowing someone to go into a building ○ *You need a pass to enter the ministry offices.* ○ *All members of staff must show their passes.* ■ *verb* **1.** to vote to approve ○ *The finance director has to pass an invoice before it is paid.* ○ *The loan has been passed by the board.* □ **to pass a resolution** to vote to agree to a resolution **2.** to vote to make a law ○ *Parliament passed the Bill which has now become law.* **3.** □ **to pass sentence on someone** to give a convicted person the official legal punishment ○ *The jury returned a verdict of guilty, and the judge will pass sentence next week.*

PASS /pɑːs/ *noun* a Home Office accreditation scheme for identity cards which are used to prove someone's age, e.g. for the purposes of buying alcohol. Full form **Proof-of-Age Standards Scheme**

passenger manifest /ˌpæsɪndʒə ˈmænɪfest/ *noun* a list of passengers on a ship or plane

passing off /ˌpɑːsɪŋ ˈɒf/ *noun* the action of trying to sell goods by giving the impression that they have been made by someone else, using that other person's reputation to make a sale

pass off /ˌpɑːs ˈɒf/ *verb* □ **to pass something off as something else** to pretend that it is another thing in order to cheat a customer

pass over /ˌpɑːs ˈəʊvə/ *verb* to avoid using someone who has been appointed, and use someone else instead

COMMENT: The appointed executor of a will can be officially passed over in favour of someone else is if he or she has disappeared, is serving a life sentence in prison or has some personal interest in the estate.

passport /ˈpɑːspɔːt/ *noun* an official document proving that someone is a citizen of a country, which has to be shown when travelling from one country to another ○ *We had to show our passports at the customs post.* ○ *His passport is out of date.* ○ *The passport officer stamped my passport.*

passport holder /ˌpɑːspɔːt ˈhəʊldə/ *noun* somebody who holds a passport ○ *She is a British passport holder.*

passport section /ˌpɑːspɔːt ˈsekʃən/ *noun* the part of an embassy which deals with passport inquiries

patent /ˈpeɪtənt, ˈpætənt/ *noun* an official document showing that a person has the exclusive right to make and sell an invention ○ *to take out a patent for a new type of light bulb* ○ *to apply for a patent for a new invention* ○ *He has received a grant of patent for his invention.* □ **to file a patent application** to apply for a patent □ **patent applied for, patent pending** words on a product showing that the inventor has applied for a patent for it □ **to forfeit a patent** to lose a patent because payments have not been made □ **to infringe a patent** to make a product which works in the same way as a patented product and not pay a royalty to the patent holder ■ *verb* □ **to patent an invention** to register an invention with the patent office to prevent other people from copying it ■ *adjective* very obvious ○ *The prisoner's statement is a patent lie.*

COMMENT: To qualify for a patent an invention must be new and not previously disclosed, it must be an advance on previous inventions, it must be able to be manufactured and it must not involve anything excluded from patent cover. Things excluded from patent cover include scientific theories (because they are confidential information), games and computer programs (which are covered by copyrights), medical treatments, some newly developed plants, animals and other biological processes. When a patent is granted, it gives the patentee a monopoly on his or her invention for 20 years.

patentability /ˌpætəntəˈbɪlɪti/ *noun* the eligibility of an invention to be patented

patentable /ˈpeɪtəntəb(ə)l/ *adjective* able to be the subject of a patent ○ *Computer programs are not patentable because they are covered by copyright.*

patent agent /ˈpeɪtənt ˌeɪdʒənt/ *noun* somebody who advises on patents and applies for patents on behalf of clients

patent defect /ˌpeɪtənt dɪˈfekt/ *noun* an obvious defect

patented /ˈpeɪtəntɪd, ˈpætəntɪd/ *adjective* being protected by a patent

patentee /ˌpeɪtənˈtiː/ *noun* somebody who has been granted a patent

patent examiner /ˌpeɪtənt ɪgˈzæmɪnə/ *noun* an official who checks patent applications to see if the inventions are really new

patent holder /ˌpeɪtənt ˈhəʊldə/ *noun* somebody who has been granted a patent

patent number /ˌpeɪtənt ˈnʌmbə/ *noun* a reference number given to a patented invention

patent office /ˈpeɪtənt ˌɒfɪs/ *noun* a government office which grants patents and supervises them

patent pending /ˌpeɪtənt ˈpendɪŋ/ *noun* a phrase printed on a product to show that its inventor has applied for a grant of patent but has not yet received it

patent proprietor /ˌpeɪtənt prəˈpraɪətə/ *noun* a person who holds a patent

patent rights /ˈpeɪtənt raɪts/ *plural noun* rights which an inventor holds under a patent

patent specification /ˌpeɪtənt ˌspesɪfɪˈkeɪʃ(ə)n/ *noun* the full details of an invention which is the subject of a patent application

paternity /pəˈtɜːnɪti/ *noun* **1.** the act of being a father **2.** the moral right of a copyright holder to be identified as the creator of the work

paternity action /pəˌtɜːnɪti ˈækʃən/, **suit** /suːt/ *noun* a lawsuit brought by the mother of a child to establish the father's legal paternity, so that he can be made to pay maintenance

paternity leave /məˈtɜːnɪti liːv/ *noun* a period when a man is away from work because his partner is about to have, or has had a baby

COMMENT: The current length of statutory paternity leave in the UK is 2 weeks.

pathologist /pəˈθɒlədʒɪst/ *noun* a doctor who specialises in pathology, especially a doctor who examines corpses to find out the cause of death

patrial /ˈpeɪtriəl/ *noun* a person who has the right to live in the UK because they have close family ties with the country

patricide /ˈpætrɪsaɪd/ *noun* the murder of your own father

Patriot Act /ˈpætriət ˌækt/ *noun* in the USA, a set of federal anti-terrorism measures that allows lower standards of probable cause to be accepted for obtaining intelligence warrants against suspected spies and terrorists

patrol /pəˈtrəʊl/ *noun* a group of people who walk through an area to see what is happening □ **a police patrol** a group of policemen who are patrolling an area □ **on patrol** monitoring an area to see what is happening ○ *We have six squad cars on patrol in the centre of the town.* □ **on foot**

patrol patrolling an area on foot, not in a car ■ *verb* to walk regularly through an area to see what is happening ○ *Groups of riot police were patrolling the centre of the town.*

patrol car /pəˈtrəʊl kɑː/ *noun* a car used by police on patrol

patrolman /pəˈtrəʊlmən/ *noun US* the lowest rank of policeman ○ *Patrolman Jones was at the scene of the accident.*

patronage secretary /ˌpætrənɪdʒ ˈsekrət(ə)ri/ *noun* an official of the Prime Minister's staff who deals with appointments to posts

pauperis ♦ **in forma pauperis**

pawn /pɔːn/ *verb* □ **to pawn a watch** to leave a watch with a pawnbroker who gives a loan against it

pawnbroker /ˈpɔːnbrəʊkə/ *noun* somebody who lends money at a fixed rate of interest in exchange for articles of personal property that are left as security

pawnshop /ˈpɔːnʃɒp/ *noun* a pawnbroker's shop

pawn ticket /ˈpɔːn ˌtɪkɪt/ *noun* a receipt given by the pawnbroker for the object left in pawn

pay /peɪ/ *noun* a salary, wage, or money given to someone for work done ■ *verb* **1.** to give money to buy an item or a service □ **to pay in advance** to give money before you receive the item bought or before the service has been completed □ **to pay in instalments** to give money for an item by giving small amounts regularly □ **to pay cash** to pay the complete sum in cash □ **to pay costs** to pay the costs of a court case □ **to pay on demand** to pay money when it is asked for, not after a period of credit □ **to pay a dividend** to give shareholders a part of the profits of a company □ **to pay interest** to give money as interest on money borrowed or invested **2.** to give an employee money for work done ○ *The employees have not been paid for three weeks.* ○ *We pay good wages for skilled employees.* ○ *How much do they pay you per hour?* □ **to be paid by the hour** to get money for each hour worked □ **to be paid at piece-work rates** to get money calculated on the number of pieces of work finished

payable /ˈpeɪəb(ə)l/ *adjective* being due to be paid □ **payable in advance** being payable before the goods are delivered □ **payable on delivery** being payable when the goods are delivered □ **payable on demand** being payable when payment is asked for □

payable at sixty days being payable by sixty days after the date of invoice □ **payable to bearer** of a cheque, which will be paid to the person who has it, not to any particular name written on it □ **charges payable by the tenant** charges for which the tenant is responsible

pay as you earn /ˌpeɪ əz juː ˈɜːn/ noun a tax system by which income tax is deducted from the salary before it is paid to the worker. Abbreviation **PAYE** (NOTE: The US term is **pay-as-you-go.**)

pay-as-you-go /ˌpeɪ əz juː ˈɡəʊ/ noun **1.** US same as **pay as you earn 2.** a system of summarily assessing costs in a trial

pay back /ˌpeɪ ˈbæk/ verb to give money back to someone ○ I lent her £50 and she promised to pay me back in a month. ○ He has never paid me back the money he borrowed.

payback /ˈpeɪbæk/ noun the repayment of money which has been borrowed

payback clause /ˈpeɪbæk klɔːz/ noun a clause in a contract which states the terms for repaying a loan

payback period /ˈpeɪbæk ˌpɪəriəd/ noun the period of time over which a loan is to be repaid or an investment is to pay for itself

pay cheque /ˈpeɪ tʃek/ noun a salary cheque given to an employee

pay down /ˌpeɪ ˈdaʊn/ verb □ **to pay money down** to make a deposit ○ He paid £50 down and the rest in monthly instalments.

PAYE abbreviation pay as you earn

payee /peɪˈiː/ noun somebody who receives money from someone, the person whose name is on a cheque or bill of exchange

pay in /ˌpeɪ ˈɪn/, **into** /ˈɪntə, ˈɪntʊ, ˈɪntuː/ verb □ **to pay in, to pay money into court** (of a defendant) to deposit money with the court at the beginning of a case, to try to satisfy the claimant's claim

paying party /ˌpeɪɪŋ ˈpɑːti/ noun the party in a case who is liable to pay costs (NOTE: The other party is the **receiving party.**)

payment /ˈpeɪmənt/ noun **1.** the transfer of money from one person to another to satisfy a debt or obligation ○ payment in cash or cash payment ○ payment by cheque □ **payment on account** paying part of the money owed before a bill is delivered ○ The solicitor asked for a payment of £100 on account. □ **payment on invoice** paying money as soon as an invoice is received **2.** money paid

payment into court /ˌpeɪmənt ˈɪntə kɔːt/ noun the depositing of money by the defendant into the court before the case starts, to try to satisfy the claimant's claim

COMMENT: If at trial the claimant fails to recover more than the amount the defendant has paid in, he or she will have to pay the defendant's costs from the date of the payment into court.

pay negotiations /ˈpeɪ nɪɡəʊʃiˌeɪʃ(ə)nz/ plural noun discussions between employers and employees about pay increases

pay off /ˌpeɪ ˈɒf/ verb **1.** to finish paying money which is owed ○ to pay off a mortgage ○ to pay off a loan **2.** to pay all the money owed to someone and terminate his or her employment ○ When the company was taken over the factory was closed and all the employees were paid off.

payoff /ˈpeɪɒf/ noun money paid to finish paying something which is owed

pay restraint /ˈpeɪ rɪˌstreɪnt/ noun the activity of keeping increases in wages under control

pay up /ˌpeɪ ˈʌp/ verb to give money which is owed ○ The company paid up only when we sent them a letter from our solicitor. ○ He finally paid up six months late.

PC abbreviation police constable or Privy Council or Privy Councillor (NOTE: The plural is **PCs.**)

PCC abbreviation Press Complaints Commission

PDs abbreviation practice directions

pecuniary /pɪˈkjuːniəri/ adjective referring to money □ **obtaining a pecuniary advantage by deception** crime of tricking someone into handing over money □ **he gained no pecuniary advantage** he made no financial gain

pecuniary default judgment /pɪˌkjuːniəri dɪˌfɔːlt ˈdʒʌdʒmənt/ noun a judgment without trial against a defendant who fails to respond to a claim, which gives the claimant the money claimed including interest

pecuniary legacy /pɪˌkjuːniəri ˈleɡəsi/ noun a legacy in the form of money

pedestrian precinct /pəˌdestriən ˈpriːsɪŋkt/ noun part of a town which is closed to traffic so that people can walk about and shop

peer /pɪə/ *noun* somebody who is in the same group or rank as another □ **a jury of one's peers** a jury formed of laypersons, who are normal members of society

peer group /'pɪə ˌgruːp/ *noun* a group of persons of the same level or rank ○ *Children try to behave like other members of their peer group.*

penal /'piːn(ə)l/ *adjective* referring to punishment

penal code /'piːn(ə)l kəʊd/ *noun* a set of laws governing crime and its punishment

penal colony /ˌpiːn(ə)l 'kɒləni/ *noun* a prison camp in a distant place, where prisoners are sent for long periods

penal institution /'piːn(ə)l ˌɪnstɪtjuːʃ(ə)n/ *noun* a place such as a prison where convicted criminals are kept

penalise /'piːnəlaɪz/, **penalize** *verb* to punish someone for doing something wrong, especially by fining them ○ *to penalise a supplier for late deliveries* ○ *They were penalised for bad service.*

penal laws /'piːn(ə)l lɔːs/ *plural noun* system of punishments relating to different crimes

penal servitude /ˌpiːn(ə)l 'sɜːvɪtjuːd/ *noun* a former punishment by imprisonment with hard labour

penal system /ˌpiːn(ə)l 'sɪstəm/ *noun* same as **penal laws**

penalty /'pen(ə)lti/ *noun* a punishment such as a fine which is imposed if something is not done or if a law is not obeyed ○ *The penalty for carrying an offensive weapon is a fine of £2,000 and three months in prison.*

penalty clause /'pen(ə)lti klɔːz/ *noun* a clause in a contract that imposes a penalty for non-compliance with its terms, which does not comprise liquidated damages and is therefore unenforceable

COMMENT: Penalty clauses in a contract are sometimes unenforceable.

penalty points /ˌtɒtɪŋ 'ʌp/ *plural noun* a system of marking a person's driving license each time they commit a traffic offence

COMMENT: Each traffic offence incurs or 'earns' a particular number of points. For example, a person convicted of driving a vehicle in a dangerously poor condition will likely earn 3 points on their license, whereas the crime of failing to stop after an accident will incur between 5 and 10 points. If the driver gets more than 12 points on their licence in a 3 year period (under the **totting**

up** system), they are liable to be disqualified from driving.

pendens ♦ **lis pendens**

pendente lite /pen,denteɪ 'laɪteɪ/ *phrase* a Latin phrase meaning 'during the lawsuit.' ◊ **alimony**

pending /'pendɪŋ/ *adjective* waiting

pending action /ˌpendɪŋ 'ækʃən/ *noun* a court action that has not yet been heard

pending suit /'pendɪŋ suːt/ *adverb* while a lawsuit is being heard

penitentiary /ˌpenɪ'tenʃəri/ *noun US* a large prison ○ *the Pennsylvania State Penitentiary*

penology /piː'nɒlədʒi/ *noun* the study of sentences in relation to crimes

pensionable age /ˌpenʃənəb(ə)l 'eɪdʒ/ *noun* the age after which someone can take a pension

pension contributions /'penʃən kɒntrɪˌbjuːʃ(ə)nz/ *plural noun* money paid by a company or employee into a pension fund

pension entitlement /'penʃən ɪnˌtaɪt(ə)lmənt/ *noun* the amount of pension which someone has the right to receive when he or she retires

pension fund /'penʃən fʌnd/ *noun* money which provides pensions for retired members of staff

pension plan /'penʃən plæn/ *noun* a plan worked out by an insurance company which arranges for an employee to pay part of his or her salary over many years and receive a regular payment on retirement

peppercorn rent /ˌpepəkɔːn 'rent/ *noun* a very small or nominal rent ○ *to pay a peppercorn rent* ○ *to lease a property for* or *at a peppercorn rent*

pepper spray /'pepə spreɪ/ *noun* a weapon in the form of a spray which irritates the eyes, nose and mouth, sometimes causing temporary blindness

COMMENT: The main agent in pepper spray in capsaicin, a compound found in chilli peppers. It is used for self-defence and riot control purposes.

per annum /pər 'ænəm/ *adverb* in each year ○ *The rent is £2,500 per annum.* ○ *What is their turnover per annum?*

per autre vie /ˌpɜːr ˌəʊtrə 'viː/ *phrase* a French phrase meaning 'for the lifetime of another person'

per capita /pə 'kæpɪtə/ *adjective, adverb* **1.** divided among beneficiaries individually. Compare **per stirpes 2.** for each person □

per capita expenditure the total money spent divided by the number of people involved

percentage increase /pə,sentɪdʒ ˈɪnkriːs/ *noun* an increase in costs above base costs, which is negotiated as part of a conditional fee agreement

per contra /,pɜː ˈkɒntrə/ *noun* a phrase that shows that a contra entry has been made

per curiam /pɜː ˈkjuːriəm/ *phrase* a Latin phrase meaning 'by a court': a decision correctly made by a court, which can be used as a precedent

per diem /,pɜː ˈdiːem/ *phrase* a Latin phrase meaning 'for each day': a small amount of money allocated by a company to each employee for daily expenses

peremptory challenge /pə,rempt(ə)ri ˈtʃælɪndʒ/ *noun* an objection made about a juror without stating any reason

perfect right /,pɜːfɪkt ˈraɪt/ *noun* a correct and legally acceptable right

perform /pəˈfɔːm/ *verb* to carry out a task or duty, or something which is required in a contract

performance /pəˈfɔːməns/ *noun* **1.** the way in which someone or something acts □ **as a measure of the company's performance** as a way of judging if the company's results are good or bad □ **performance of personnel against objectives** how well personnel have worked against the measures set **2.** the activity of carrying out of something, such as a duty or the terms of a contract

performance bond /pəˈfɔːməns bɒnd/ *noun* a sum of money deposited as a guarantee that you will carry out the terms of a contract

performance review /pəˈfɔːməns rɪˌvjuː/ *noun* a yearly interview between an employer and each employee to discuss how the employee has worked during the year

performing right /pəˈfɔːmɪŋ raɪt/ *noun* the right to allow the playing of a copyright piece of music

peril /ˈperɪl/ *noun* danger, especially a possible accident covered by an insurance policy □ **perils of the sea, maritime perils** accidents which can happen at sea

per incuriam /,pɜː ɪnˈkjuːriəm/ *phrase* a Latin phrase meaning 'because of lack of care': a decision wrongly made by a court which does not therefore set a precedent

periodic /,pɪəriˈɒdɪk/, **periodical** /,pɪəriˈɒdɪk(ə)l/ *adjective* happening regularly from time to time

periodical payments /,pɪəriɒdɪk(ə)l ˈpeɪmənts/ *plural noun* regular payments, e.g. maintenance paid to a divorced spouse

periodic tenancy /,pɪəriɒdɪk ˈtenənsi/ *noun* a tenancy where the tenant rents for several short periods but not for a fixed length of time

period of qualification /,pɪəriəd əv ,kwɒlɪfɪˈkeɪʃ(ə)n/ *noun* the time which has to pass before something qualifies for something

period of validity /,pɪəriəd əv vəˈlɪdɪti/ *noun* the length of time for which a document is valid

perjure /ˈpɜːdʒə/ *verb* □ **to perjure yourself** to tell lies when you have made an oath to say what is true

perjury /ˈpɜːdʒəri/ *noun* the notifiable offence of telling lies when you have made an oath to say what is true in court ○ *He was sent to prison for perjury.* ○ *She appeared in court on a charge of perjury* or *on a perjury charge.*

permissive waste /pə,mɪsɪv ˈweɪst/ *noun* damage to a property which is caused by a tenant not carrying out repairs

permit *noun* /ˈpɜːmɪt/ an official document which allows someone to do something ■ *verb* /pəˈmɪt/ to allow someone to do something ○ *This document permits the export of twenty-five computer systems.* ○ *The ticket permits three people to go into the exhibition.*

per my et per tout /pɜː maɪ ,iː ˈtiː taʊt/ *phrase* a French phrase meaning 'by half and by all': used to indicate the relationship between joint tenants

perpetrate /ˈpɜːpɪtreɪt/ *verb* to commit a crime

perpetrator /ˈpɜːpɪtreɪtə/ *noun* a person who does something harmful or dishonest, especially a person who commits a crime

perpetuity /,pɜːpɪtˈjuːɪti/ *noun* □ **in perpetuity** for ever

per pro /,pɜː ˈprəʊ/ a Latin phrase meaning 'with the authority of' □ **to sign per pro someone** to sign on behalf of, and with the authority of, someone

per procurationem /pə ,prɒkjʊræsɪˈəʊnəm/ *phrase* a Latin phrase meaning 'with the authority of'

per quod /pɜː ˈkwɒd/ *phrase* a Latin phrase meaning 'by which' or 'whereby'

per se /ˌpɜː ˈseɪ/ *phrase* a Latin phrase meaning 'on its own' or 'alone'

persistent offender /pəˌsɪstənt əˈfendə/ *noun* a person who has been convicted of a crime at least three times before and is likely to commit the crime again

person /ˈpɜːs(ə)n/ *noun* a man or woman ○ *insurance policy which covers a named person* □ **the persons named in the contract** the people whose names are given in the contract □ **to be witnessed by a third person** of a document, to be witnessed by someone who is not named in the document □ **in person** himself or herself

persona /pəˈsəʊnə/ *noun* something such as a company which owns property

personal /ˈpɜːs(ə)n(ə)l/ *adjective* **1.** referring to one person □ **personal service** the act of giving legal documents to someone as part of a legal action, e.g. serving someone with a writ **2.** private ○ *I want to see the director on a personal matter.*

personal action /ˌpɜːs(ə)n(ə)l ˈækʃən/ *noun* **1.** a legal action brought by a person himself or herself **2.** the common law term for an action against a person arising out of a contract or tort

personal allowances /ˌpɜːs(ə)n(ə)l əˈlaʊəns/ *plural noun* part of a person's income which is not taxed ○ *allowances against tax* or *tax allowances*

personal assets /ˌpɜːs(ə)n(ə)l ˈæsets/ *plural noun* moveable assets which belong to a person

personal chattels /ˌpɜːs(ə)n(ə)l ˈtʃæt(ə)lz/ *noun* household things such as furniture, clothes, or cars which belong to a person and which are not land

personal conduct /ˌpɜːs(ə)n(ə)l kənˈdʌkt/ *noun* the way in which a person acts in society

COMMENT: Personal conduct can be used as a reason for excluding a national of another EU state from entering a country and taking up work.

personal effects /ˌpɜːs(ə)n(ə)l ɪˈfekts/ *plural noun* personal belongings

personal estate /ˌpɜːs(ə)n(ə)l ɪˈsteɪt/ *noun* the set of things, excluding land, which belong to someone and can be inherited by their heirs

personal income /ˌpɜːs(ə)n(ə)l ˈɪnkʌm/ *noun* income received by an individual person before tax is paid

personal injury /ˌpɜːs(ə)n(ə)l ˈɪndʒəri/ *noun* injury to the body suffered by the victim of an accident

personal injury claim /ˈpɜːs(ə)n ˌɪndʒəriz/ *noun* a claim for compensation made by someone who has suffered an injury as a result of an accident

personal property /ˌpɜːs(ə)n(ə)l ˈprɒpəti/ *noun* property which belongs to one person, excluding land and buildings, but including money, goods, securities, etc.

personal representative /ˌpɜːs(ə)n(ə)l ˌreprɪˈzentətɪv/ *noun* **1.** a person who is the executor of a will or the administrator of the estate of a deceased person. Abbreviation **PR 2.** a person appointed to deal with the estate of a person who dies intestate

COMMENT: The personal representative holds the property on trust, pays any liabilities and expenses, and invests money until such time as the estate is distributed.

personalty /ˈpɜːs(ə)n(ə)lti/ *noun* personal property or chattels as opposed to land

personam ♦ **action**

persona non grata /pəˌsəʊnə nɒn ˈɡrɑːtə/ *noun* a foreign person who is not acceptable to a government (*used especially of diplomats*)

personation /ˌpɜːsəˈneɪʃ(ə)n/ *noun* the crime of fraudulently pretending to be someone else

per stirpes /pɜː ˈstɜːpiːz/ *phrase* a Latin phrase meaning 'by branches': used in wills where the entitlement is divided among branches of a family rather than among individuals (which is 'per capita')

persuasive precedent /pəˌsweɪsɪv ˈpresɪd(ə)nt/, **persuasive authority** /ɔː ˈθɒrɪti/ *noun* a precedent which a judge is not obliged to follow but is of importance in reaching a judgment. Compare **binding precedent**

pertain /pəˈteɪn/ *verb* □ **to pertain to** to refer to or to relate to ○ *the law pertaining to public order*

perverse verdict /pəˌvɜːs ˈvɜːdɪkt/ *noun* a verdict by a jury which goes against what anyone would usually feel to be the right decision, or which goes against the direction of the judge

pervert /pəˈvɜːt/ *verb* to change or to interfere □ **perverting the course of justice** the offence of trying to influence the outcome of a trial by falsifying evidence, perjury, bribery, intimidation of witnesses etc.

COMMENT: Perverting the course of justice is a notifiable offence.

petition /pə'tɪʃ(ə)n/ *noun* **1.** a written application to a court □ **to file a petition in bankruptcy** to ask officially to be made bankrupt, to ask officially for someone else to be made bankrupt **2.** a written request accompanied by a list of signatures of people supporting it ○ *They presented a petition with a million signatures to Parliament, asking for the law to be repealed.* ■ *verb* to make an official request ○ *He petitioned the government for a special pension.* ○ *The marriage had broken down and the wife petitioned for divorce.*

petitioner /pə'tɪʃ(ə)nə/ *noun* somebody who puts forward a petition

petty crime /ˌpeti 'kraɪm/ *noun* small crimes which are not very serious

petty jury /ˌpeti 'dʒʊəri/ *noun mainly US* an ordinary jury of twelve jurors

petty larceny /ˌpeti 'lɑːs(ə)ni/ *noun* minor thefts

petty sessions /ˌpeti 'seʃ(ə)nz/ *plural noun* an old name for the magistrates' court

petty-sessions area /ˌpeti ˌseʃ(ə)n(ə)dɪ'vɪʒ(ə)n/, **petty sessional division** /ˌpeti ˌseʃ(ə)nz 'eəriə/ *noun* an area of the country covered by a magistrates' courts committee for administration purposes

COMMENT: England and Wales are divided into 45 petty sessions areas.

petty theft /ˌpeti 'θeft/ *noun* the theft of small items or small amounts of money

petty thief /ˌpeti 'θiːf/ *noun* somebody who steals small items or small amounts of money

PFI *abbreviation* private finance initiative

phishing /'fɪʃɪŋ/ *noun* the act of sending emails purportedly from legitimate enterprises, which trick recipients into surrendering private information for the purposes of identity theft

Photofit /'fəʊtəʊfɪt/ a trademark for a method of making a picture of a criminal from descriptions given by witnesses, using pieces of photographs of different types of faces ○ *The police issued an Photofit picture of the mugger.*

physician-assisted suicide /fɪˌzɪʃ(ə)n əˌsɪstɪd 'suːɪsaɪd/ *noun* an act of euthanasia carried out by a doctor, e.g. by administering a drug or withdrawing life-saving treatment

picker /'pɪkə/ *noun* a person in a team of pickpockets who performs the act of picking the victim's pocket while the others cause distractions (*slang*) Compare **runner**

pickpocket /'pɪkpɒkɪt/ *noun* somebody who steals things from people's pockets

pilfer /'pɪlfə/ *verb* to steal small objects or small amounts of money

pilferage /'pɪlfərɪdʒ/, **pilfering** /'pɪlfərɪŋ/ *noun* the offence of stealing small amounts of money or small items

pilferer /'pɪlfərə/ *noun* somebody who steals small objects or small amounts of money

pimp /pɪmp/ *verb* to organise prostitutes and earn money from their activities (NOTE: This is an offence in the UK) ■ *noun* somebody who earns money in this way

pinch /pɪntʃ/ *verb* (*informal*) **1.** to steal **2.** to arrest

piracy /'paɪrəsi/ *noun* **1.** a robbery at sea, by attacking ships **2.** the activity of copying patented inventions or copyright works ○ *laws to ban book piracy*

pirate /'paɪrət/ *noun* **1.** somebody who attacks a ship at sea to steal cargo **2.** somebody who copies a patented invention or a copyright work and sells it ○ *a pirate copy of a book* □ **pirate radio station** a radio station which broadcasts without a licence from outside a country's territorial waters ■ *verb* to copy a copyright work ○ *a pirated book* or *a pirated design* ○ *The drawings for the new dress collection were pirated in the Far East.*

pith and marrow /ˌpɪθ ən 'mærəʊ/ *noun* the doctrine that a patent can be applied to separate parts of an invention or process as well as to a single invention itself

placement /'pleɪsmənt/ *noun* the activity of finding work for someone

place of performance /ˌpleɪs əv pə 'fɔːməns/ *noun* a place where a contract is to be performed

plagiarise /'pleɪdʒəraɪz/, **plagiarize** *verb* to copy the text of a work created by someone else and pass it off as your own

plagiarism /'pleɪdʒərɪz(ə)m/ *noun* the activity of copying the text of a work created by someone else and passing it off as your own

plainclothes /'pleɪnkləʊðz/ *adjective* (*of a police officer*) working in ordinary clothes, not in uniform ○ *A group of plainclothes police went into the house.* ○ *A plainclothes detective travelled on the train.*

plaint /pleɪnt/ *noun* a claim brought by one party (the claimant) against another party (the defendant)

plaintiff /ˈpleɪntɪf/ *noun* somebody who starts an action against someone in the civil courts. Compare **defendant** (NOTE: Since the introduction of the Civil Procedure Rules, this term has been replaced by **claimant**.)

plaint note /ˈpleɪnt nəʊt/ *noun* a note issued by a County Court at the beginning of a County Court action

planned economy /ˌplænd ɪˈkɒnəmi/ *noun* a system where the government plans all business activity

planning authority /ˈplænɪŋ ɔːˌθɒrəti/ *noun* a local body which gives permission for changes to be made to existing buildings or for new use of land

planning department /ˈplænɪŋ dɪˌpɑːtmənt/ *noun* a section of a local government office which deals with requests for planning permission

planning inquiry /ˈplænɪŋ ɪnˌkwaɪri/ *noun* a hearing before a government inspector relating to the decision of a local authority in planning matters

planning permission /ˈplænɪŋ pəˌmɪʃ(ə)n/ *noun* an official document allowing a person or company to plan new buildings on empty land or to alter existing buildings □ **outline planning permission** general permission to build a property on a piece of land, but not the final approval because there are no details given ○ *He was refused planning permission.* ○ *We are waiting for planning permission before we can start building.* ○ *The land is to be sold with outline planning permission for four houses.*

plant /plɑːnt/ *verb* □ **to plant evidence** to put items at the scene of a crime after the crime has taken place, so that a person is incriminated and can be arrested

plastic bullet /ˌplæstɪk ˈbʊlɪt/ *noun* same as **baton round**

plea /pliː/ *noun* **1.** in civil law, an answer made by a defendant to the case presented by the claimant **2.** in criminal law, a statement made by a person accused in court in answer to the charge □ **to enter a plea** to answer a charge by stating whether you are guilty or not guilty □ **to enter a plea of not guilty** to answer the charge by stating that you are not guilty

plea bargaining /ˈpliː ˌbɑːɡɪnɪŋ/ *noun* an arrangement where the accused pleads guilty to some charges and the prosecution drops other charges

plead /pliːd/ *verb* **1.** to make an allegation in legal proceedings ○ *If fraud is to be pleaded as part of a claim, details of it must be given in the particulars of claim.* **2.** to answer a charge in a criminal court □ **fit to plead** mentally capable of facing trial □ **to plead guilty** to say at the beginning of a trial that you did commit the crime of which you are accused □ **to plead not guilty** to say at the beginning of a trial that you did not commit the crime of which you are accused **3.** to speak on behalf of a client in court

pleader /ˈpliːdə/ *noun* somebody who pleads a case in court ○ *The pleader of the defence must deal with each allegation made in the particulars of claim.*

pleading /ˈpliːdɪŋ/ *noun* the action of speaking in court on someone's behalf

pleadings /ˈpliːdɪŋz/ *plural noun* documents setting out the claim of the claimant or the defence of the defendant, or giving the arguments which the two sides will use in proceedings ○ *The damage is itemised in the pleadings.* ○ *The judge found that the claimant's pleadings disclosed no cause of action.* ○ *Pleadings must be submitted to the court when the action is set down for trial.* (NOTE: Since the introduction of the Civil Procedure Rules, this term has been replaced by **statements of case**.)

plea in mitigation /ˌpliː ɪn ˌmɪtɪˈɡeɪʃ(ə)n/ *noun* a statement in court on behalf of a guilty party to persuade the court to impose a lenient sentence

pleasure /ˈpleʒə/ ♦ **Her Majesty's pleasure**

pledge /pledʒ/ *noun* **1.** the transfer of objects or documents to someone as security for a loan **2.** an object given by someone such as a pawnbroker as security for a loan □ **to redeem a pledge** to pay back a loan and interest and so get back the security ■ *verb* **1.** to transfer objects or property to someone as security for a loan **2.** to make a solemn promise ○ *The Government pledged to reform the justice system.*

pledgee /ˌpledʒˈiː/ *noun* somebody who receives objects or documents as security for money lent

pledger /ˈpledʒə/ *noun* somebody who gives objects or documents as security for money borrowed

plenary /ˈpliːnəri/ *adjective* full or complete

plenary power /ˈpliːnəri ˌpaʊə/ *noun* absolute power of a governing body

plenary session /ˈpliːnəri ˌseʃ(ə)n/ noun a session of a legislature that all members attend

plenipotentiary /ˌplenɪpəˈtenʃəri/ noun an official person acting on behalf of a government in international affairs

pluralism /ˈplʊərəlɪz(ə)m/ noun a system allowing different political or religious groups to exist in the same society

pluralist state /ˌplʊərəlɪst ˈsteɪt/ noun a state where various political pressure groups can exist and exert influence over the government

PNC abbreviation Police National Computer

poaching /ˈpəʊtʃɪŋ/ noun **1.** the crime of killing game which belongs to another person or trespassing on someone's land to kill game **2.** the activity of persuading employees to leave their current company and join another

pocket veto /ˌpɒkɪt ˈviːtəʊ/ noun US a veto by the President of a bill after Congress has adjourned

COMMENT: Normally the President has ten days to object to a bill which has been passed to him by Congress; if Congress adjourns during that period, the President's veto kills the bill.

point /pɔɪnt/ noun a question relating to a matter □ **to take a point** to agree that the point made by another speaker is correct □ **point taken**, **I take your point** I agree that what you say is valid □ **in point of fact** really or actually

point duty /ˈpɔɪnt ˌdjuːti/ noun the work of a policeman or traffic warden to direct the traffic at a crossroads

point of fact /ˌpɔɪnt əv ˈfækt/ noun a question which has to be decided regarding the facts of a case

point of law /ˌpɔɪnt əv ˈlɔː/ noun a question relating to the law as applied to a case ○ Counsel raised a point of law.

point of order /ˌpɔɪnt əv ˈɔːdə/ noun a question relating to the way in which a meeting is being conducted ○ He raised a point of order. ○ On a point of order, Mr Chairman, can this committee approve its own accounts? ○ The meeting was adjourned on a point of order.

poison /ˈpɔɪz(ə)n/ noun a substance which can kill if eaten or drunk ○ She killed the old lady by putting poison in her tea. ■ verb to kill someone, or make them very ill, using poison ○ He was not shot, he was poisoned.

poison-pen letter /ˌpɔɪz(ə)n pen ˈletə/ noun an anonymous letter containing defamatory allegations about someone

poison pill defence /ˌpɔɪz(ə)n ˈpɪl dɪˌfens/ noun a strategy used by a company to discourage a hostile takeover by another company

police /pəˈliːs/ noun a group of people who keep law and order in a country or town ○ The police have cordoned off the town centre. ○ The government is relying on the police to keep law and order during the elections. ○ The bank robbers were picked up by the police at the railway station.

COMMENT: Under English law, a police officer is primarily an ordinary citizen who has certain powers at common law and by statute. The police are organised by area, each area functioning independently with its own police force. London, and the area round London, is policed by the Metropolitan Police Force under the direct supervision of the Home Secretary. Outside London, each police force is answerable to a local police authority, although day-to-day control of operations is vested entirely in the Chief Constable.

police authority /pəˌliːs ɔːˈθɒrɪti/ noun a local committee which supervises a local police force

police bail /pəˌliːs ˈbeɪl/ noun bail granted by the police from police custody

COMMENT: Release under police bail does not cost the accused any money, but he or she will be obliged to return at a set time and date to answer their bail. Any person not answering their bail, or breaching a condition of their bail, may be rearrested,

police brutality /pəˌliːs bruːˈtælɪti/ noun excessive force, violence or threats used by police officers in the course of their duty

Police Commissioner /pəˌliːs kəˈmɪʃ(ə)nə/ noun the highest rank in some police forces

Police Community Support Officer /pəˌliːs kəˌmjuːnɪti səˈpɔːt ˌɒfɪsə/ noun a person whose job is to patrol the streets, especially in cities, providing assistance to the public, dealing with incidents of nuisance and anti-social behaviour which don't require full police powers, and issuing some fixed penalty notices to offenders. Abbreviation **PCSO**. Also called **community support officer**

Police Complaints Authority /pəˌliːs kəmˈpleɪnts ˌɔːrɪti/ noun a former organisation which investigated complaints made by members of the public against the police (NOTE: It was replaced in 2004 by the **Independent Police Complaints Commission (IPCC)**.)

police constable /pə'li:s ˌkʌnstəb(ə)l/ *noun* an ordinary member of the police ○ *Police Constables Smith and Jones are on patrol.* ○ *The sergeant and six police constables searched the premises.* (NOTE: Usually abbreviated to **PC**.)

police cordon /pə,li:s 'kɔ:d(ə)n/ *noun* a line of barriers and police officers put round an area to prevent anyone moving in or out of the area

police court /pə'li:s kɔ:t/ *noun* a magistrates' court

police force /pə'li:s fɔ:s/ *noun* a group of policemen organised in a certain area ○ *The members of several local police forces have collaborated in the murder hunt.* ○ *The London police force is looking for more recruits.* ◊ **detective**, **Metropolitan Police**

COMMENT: The ranks in a British police force are: **Police Constable, Police Sergeant, Inspector, Chief Inspector, Superintendent, Chief Superintendent, Assistant Chief Constable, Deputy Chief Constable and Chief Constable.**

police headquarters /pə,li:s hed'kwɔ:təz/ *noun* the main offices of a police force

police inspector /pə,li:s ɪn'spektə/ *noun* a rank in the police force above a sergeant

policeman /pə'li:smən/ *noun* a man who is a member of the police (NOTE: The plural is **policemen**.)

Police National Computer /pə,li:s ˌnæf(ə)nəl kəm'pju:tə/ *noun* a national database used by UK police forces and law enforcement agencies, which holds details of criminal records and stolen property

police officer /pə'li:s ˌɒfɪsə/ *noun* a member of the police

police precinct /pə,li:s 'pri:sɪŋ(k)t/ *noun* US a section of a town with its own police station

police protection /pə,li:s prə'tekʃən/ *noun* the services of the police to protect someone who might be harmed ○ *The minister was given police protection.*

police sergeant /pə,li:s 'sɑ:dʒənt/ *noun* a rank in the police force above constable and below inspector

police station /pə'li:s ˌsteɪʃ(ə)n/ *noun* a local office of a police force

police superintendent /pə,li:s ˌsu:pərɪn'tendənt/ *noun* a high rank in a police force, above Chief Inspector and below Chief Superintendent

policewoman /pə'li:swʊmən/ *noun* a female member of a police force (NOTE: The plural is **policewomen**.)

policing /pə'li:sɪŋ/ *noun* the activity of keeping law and order in a place, using the police force

policy holder /'pɒlɪsi ˌhəʊldə/ *noun* somebody who is insured by an insurance company

political crime /pə,lɪtɪk(ə)l 'kraɪm/ *noun* a crime such as an assassination committed for a political reason

political prisoner /pə,lɪtɪk(ə)l 'prɪz(ə)nə/ *noun* a person kept in prison because he or she is an opponent of the political party in power

poll /pəʊl/ *noun* a survey asking people how they feel about something □ **to poll a sample of the population** to ask a sample group of people what they feel about something □ **to poll the members of the club on an issue** to ask the members for their opinion on an issue

pollutant /pə'lu:t(ə)nt/ *noun* a substance or agent which pollutes ○ *Discharge pipes take pollutants away from the coastal area into the sea.*

pollute /pə'lu:t/ *verb* to discharge harmful substances into the environment naturally, accidentally or deliberately

polluter /pə'lu:tə/ *noun* a person or company which causes pollution ○ *Certain industries are major polluters of the environment.*

polluter pays principle /pə,lu:tə 'peɪz ˌprɪnsəp(ə)l/ *noun* the principle that if pollution occurs, the person or company responsible should be required to pay for the consequences of the pollution and for avoiding it in future

pollution /pə'lu:ʃ(ə)n/ *noun* the presence of harmful substances in the environment, especially when produced by human activity

pollution charges /pə'lu:ʃ(ə)n tʃɑ:dʒɪz/ *plural noun* the cost of repairing or stopping environmental pollution

pollution control /pə'lu:ʃ(ə)n kən,trəʊl/ *noun* any of various means of limiting pollution

Pollution Prevention and Control /pə,lu:ʃ(ə)n prɪ,venʃ(ə)n ən kən'trəʊl/

noun a policy designed to control and reduce pollution caused by industrial practices. ◊ **Best Available Techniques**

polygamous /pə'lɪgəməs/ *adjective* referring to polygamy □ **a polygamous society** a society where men are allowed to be married to more than one wife at the same time

polygamy /pə'lɪgəmi/ *noun* the state of having more than one wife. Compare **bigamy, monogamy**

polygraph /'pɒlɪɡrɑːf/ *noun* a machine which tells if a person is lying by recording physiological changes which take place while the person is being interviewed. Also called **lie detector**

popular vote /ˌpɒpjʊlə 'vəʊt/ *noun* a vote of the people

pornographer /pɔː'nɒɡrəfə/ *noun* a person who makes and distributes obscene publications or books

pornography /pɔː'nɒɡrəfi/ *noun* obscene publications or films

porridge /'pɒrɪdʒ/ *noun* imprisonment (*slang*) □ **to do porridge** to serve a term of imprisonment

portion /'pɔːʃ(ə)n/ *noun* money or property given to a young person to provide money for them as income

port of registry /ˌpɔːt əv 'redʒɪstri/ *noun* the port where a ship is registered

position /pə'zɪʃ(ə)n/ *noun* a job or role in an organisation ○ *to apply for a position as manager* ○ *We have several positions vacant.* ○ *All the vacant positions have been filled.* ○ *She retired from her position in the accounts department.*

position of trust /pə,zɪʃ(ə)n əv 'trʌst/ *noun* a job where an employee is trusted by his or her employer to look after money, confidential information, etc.

positive discrimination /ˌpɒzɪtɪv dɪsˌkrɪmɪ'neɪʃ(ə)n/ *noun* discrimination in favour of one category of workers, such as women, to enable them to be more equal ○ *The council's policy of positive discrimination has ensured that more women are appointed to senior posts.*

positive integration /ˌnegətɪv ˌɪntɪ'ɡreɪʃ(ə)n/ *noun* integration between EU states created by the universal adoption of new EU laws. Compare **negative integration**

positive vetting /ˌpɒzɪtɪv 'vetɪŋ/ *noun* a thorough examination of a person before

that person is allowed to work with classified information

possess /pə'zes/ *verb* to own or to be in occupation of or to be in control of ○ *The company possesses property in the centre of the town.* ○ *He lost all he possessed when his company was put into liquidation.*

possession /pə'zeʃ(ə)n/ *noun* **1.** control over property **2.** physically holding something which does not necessarily belong to you □ **to have something in your possession** to be holding something □ **unlawful possession of drugs** the offence of having drugs

possession in law /pə,zeʃ(ə)n ɪn 'lɔː/ *noun* ownership of land or buildings without actually occupying them

possessive action /pə,zesɪv 'ækʃən/ *noun* an action to regain possession of land or buildings

possessory /pə'zesəri/ *adjective* referring to possession of property

possessory title /pə,zesəri 'taɪt(ə)l/ *noun* a title to land acquired by occupying it continuously, usually for twelve years

post /pəʊst/ *verb* to pay a bond or bail for someone

post- /pəʊst/ *prefix* after

postal vote /'pəʊst(ə)l vəʊt/ *noun* a vote that is posted instead of being made in person, usually because the voter cannot get to the polling station

post-contract /ˌpəʊst 'kɒntrækt/ *adjective* taking place after a contract has been signed

posteriori ♦ a posteriori

posthumous /'pɒstjʊməs/ *adjective* **1.** happening after someone's death ○ *posthumous publication of her book* **2.** born after the death of a father ○ *a posthumous child*

posthumous pardon /ˌpɒstjʊməs 'pɑːdən/ *noun* a pardon granted to a person after they have died

post mortem /ˌpəʊst 'mɔːtəm/ *noun* an examination of the body of a dead person to see how he or she died ○ *The post mortem was carried out* or *was conducted by the police pathologist.*

post obit bond /ˌpəʊst 'əʊbɪt ˌbɒnd/ *noun* an agreement where a borrower will repay a loan when he or she receives money as a legacy from someone

post-traumatic stress disorder /ˌpəʊst trɔːˌmætɪk 'stres dɪsˌɔːdə/ *noun* a psychological condition affecting people who have suffered severe emotional trauma as a result of a bad experience

power /'pauə/ *noun* **1.** strength, ability or capacity **2.** authority or legal right ○ *the powers of a local authority in relation to children in care* ○ *the powers and duties conferred on the tribunal by the statutory code* ○ *The president was granted wide powers under the constitution.* □ **the full power of the law** the full force of the law when applied ○ *We will apply the full power of the law to regain possession of our property.* **3.** a powerful country or state ○ *one of the important military powers in the region*

power of advancement /ˌpauə əv əd 'vɑːnsmənt/ *noun* the power of a trustee to advance funds from a trust to a beneficiary

power of appointment /ˌpauər əv ə 'pɔɪntmənt/ *noun* a power given to one person such as a trustee to dispose of property belonging to another

power of attorney /ˌpauər əv ə'tɜːni/ *noun* an official power giving someone the right to act on someone else's behalf in legal matters ○ *His solicitor was granted power of attorney.*

power of search /ˌpauər əv 'sɜːtʃ/ *noun* the authority to search premises, which is given to the police and some other officials such as Customs officers

power politics /ˌpauə 'pɒlɪtɪks/ *noun* the threat to use economic or military force by one country to try to get other countries to do what it wants

practice /'præktɪs/ *noun* **1.** a way of doing things ○ *His practice was to arrive at work at 7.30 and start counting the cash.* **2.** a way of working in court **3.** the business premises and clients of a professional person ○ *She has set up in practice as a solicitor* or *a patent agent.* ○ *He is a partner in a country solicitor's practice.* **4.** the carrying on of a profession ○ *He has been in practice for twenty years.*

practice directions /ˌpræktɪs daɪ 'rekʃənz/ *plural noun* notes made by judges as to how specific procedures or formalities should be carried out. Abbreviation **PDs**

practice form /'præktɪs fɔːm/ *noun* a form which lays out practice in a specific case

Practice Master /ˌpræktɪs 'mɑːstə/ *noun* the Master on duty in the High Court, who will hear solicitors without appointment and give directions in relation to the general conduct of proceedings

practise /'præktɪs/ *verb* to work in a profession, especially law or medicine ○ *He is a practising solicitor.*

practising certificate /ˌpræktɪsɪŋ sə 'tɪfɪkət/ *noun* a certificate from the Law Society allowing someone to work as a solicitor

praecipe /'priːsɪpi/ *noun* a written request addressed to a court, asking that court to prepare and issue a document such as a writ of execution or a witness summons

pray /preɪ/ *verb* to ask □ **to pray in aid** to rely on something when pleading a case ○ *I pray in aid the Statute of Frauds.*

prayer /preə/ *noun* words at the end of a petition or pleading, which summarise what the litigant is asking the court to do

pre-action /priː 'ækʃən/ *adjective* before an action starts

pre-action practice /priː ˌækʃən 'præktɪs/ *noun* the way of working before a case comes to court

pre-action protocol /priː ˌækʃən 'prəutəkɒl/ *noun* rules contained within the Civil Procedure Rules setting out steps that parties should take before the commencement of legal proceedings ○ *The claimant has complied with the relevant pre-action protocol.*

preamble /priː'æmb(ə)l/ *noun* the first words in an official document such as a contract, introducing the document and setting out the main points in it

precatory /'prekət(ə)ri/ *adjective* requesting

precatory words /ˌprekət(ə)ri 'wɜːdz/ *noun* in a document such as a will, words which ask for something to be done

precedent /'presɪd(ə)nt/ *noun* something such as a judgment which has happened earlier than the present, and which can be a guide to what should be done in the present case □ **to set a precedent** to make a decision in court which will show other courts how to act in future □ **to follow a precedent** to decide in the same way as an earlier decision in the same type of case ○ *The court followed the precedent set in 1926.*

COMMENT: Although English law is increasingly governed by statute, the doctrine of precedent still plays a major role. The decisions of higher courts bind lower courts, except in the case of the Court of Appeal, where the court has power to change a previous decision reached per incuriam. Cases can be distinguished by the courts where the facts seem to be sufficiently different.

precept /'priːsept/ *noun* **1.** a warrant or writ that is issued by a legal authority **2.** an order for the payment of money

precepting body /ˌpriːseptɪŋ 'bɒdi/ *noun* an organisation which levies a precept

preclude /prɪ'kluːd/ *verb* to forbid or to prevent ○ *The High Court is precluded by statute from reviewing such a decision.* ○ *This agreement does not preclude a further agreement between the parties in the future.*

pre-contract /ˌpriː 'kɒntrækt/ *noun* a contract made in advance to prevent a subsequent contract ■ *verb* to make a contract or enter into an agreement in advance

predecease /ˌpriːdɪ'siːs/ *verb* to die before someone ○ *He predeceased his father.* ○ *His estate is left to his daughter, but should she predecease him, it will be held in trust for her children.*

predecessor /'priːdɪsesə/ *noun* somebody who had a job or position before someone else ○ *He took over from his predecessor last May.* ○ *She acquired her predecessor's list of clients.*

pre-emption /ˌpriː 'empʃən/ *noun* the right of first refusal to purchase something before it is sold to someone else

pre-emption clause /priː 'empʃən ˌklɔːz/ *noun* a clause in a private company's articles of association which requires any shares offered for sale to be offered first to existing shareholders

prefer /prɪ'fɜː/ *verb* **1.** to pay one creditor before any others **2.** to bring something before a court □ **to prefer charges** to charge someone with an offence

preference /'pref(ə)rəns/ *noun* **1.** something which is preferred **2.** the payment of one creditor before other creditors

preferential /ˌprefə'renʃəl/ *adjective* showing that something is preferred more than another

> COMMENT: In the case of a company liquidation, preferential debts are debts owed to the government or its agencies and include PAYE owed to the Inland Revenue, VAT, social security contributions, contributions to state pensions schemes.

preferential creditor /ˌprefərenʃ(ə)l 'kredɪtə/ *noun* a creditor who must be paid first if a company is in liquidation

preferential debt /ˌprefərenʃ(ə)l 'det/ *noun* a debt which is paid before all others

preferential duty /ˌprefərenʃ(ə)l 'djuːti/ *noun* a special low rate of tax

preferential payment /ˌprefərenʃ(ə)l 'peɪmənt/ *noun* payment made to one creditor before others

preferential terms /ˌprefə'renʃ(ə)l tɜːms/ *plural noun* terms in an agreement which are better than usual ○ *He was accused of offering preferential terms to his friends and family.*

preferment of charges /prɪˌfɜːmənt əv 'tʃɑːdʒɪz/ *noun* the act of charging someone with a criminal offence

preferred creditor /prɪˌfɜːd 'kredɪtə/ *noun* a creditor who must be paid first if a company is in liquidation

preferred shares /prɪˌfɜːd 'ʃeəz/ *plural noun* shares which receive their dividend before all other shares, and which are repaid first (at face value) if the company is in liquidation

prejudge /priː'dʒʌdʒ/ *verb* to judge an issue before having heard the evidence ○ *Do not prejudge the issue – hear what defence counsel has to say.*

prejudice /'predʒʊdɪs/ *noun* **1.** an unreasonable view of someone or something based on feelings or opinions rather than facts ○ *She was accused of prejudice in her hiring practices.* **2.** harm done to someone □ **without prejudice** a phrase spoken or written in letters when attempting to negotiate a settlement, meaning that the negotiations cannot be referred to in court or relied upon by the other party if the discussions fail □ **to somebody's prejudice** causing harm to somebody ○ *If you don't have proper evidence to back up your claim, it will be to your prejudice.* □ **to act to the prejudice of a claim** to do something which may harm a claim ■ *verb* to harm ○ *to prejudice someone's claim*

preliminary /prɪ'lɪmɪn(ə)ri/ *adjective* happening before other things as an introduction or in preparation

preliminary discussion /prɪˌlɪmɪn(ə)ri dɪ'skʌʃ(ə)n/ *noun* a discussion or meeting which takes place before the main discussion or meeting starts

preliminary hearing /prɪˌlɪmɪn(ə)ri 'hɪərɪŋ/ *noun* **1.** court proceedings where the witnesses and the defendant are examined to see if there are sufficient grounds for the case to proceed **2.** in the small claims track, a hearing to decide if special directions should be issued, or if the statement of case should be struck out **3.** court proceedings to try a specific issue rather than the whole case

preliminary inquiries /prɪˌlɪmɪn(ə)ri ɪnˈkwaɪərɪz/ *plural noun* investigation by the solicitor for the purchaser of a property addressed to the vendor's solicitor, concerning the vendor's title to the property

preliminary investigation /prɪˌlɪmɪn(ə)ri ɪnˌvestɪˈɡeɪʃ(ə)n/ *noun* examination of the details of a case by a magistrate who then has to decide if the case should be committed to a higher court for trial

preliminary reference /prɪˌlɪmɪn(ə)ri ˈref(ə)rəns/ *noun* a reference from a court in a Member State of the European Union to the European Court of Justice on a question of interpretation of EU law

COMMENT: The aim of a preliminary reference is to ensure that the laws are interpreted uniformly throughout the EU, and that all national courts are familiar with it. The ECJ has used preliminary references as a means of extending the scope of EU law.

preliminary ruling /prɪˌlɪmɪn(ə)ri ˈruːlɪŋ/ *noun* a provisional decision of the European Court of Justice

premeditated /priːˈmedɪteɪtɪd/ *adjective* having been thought about carefully or which has been planned ○ *a premeditated murder* ○ *The crime was premeditated.*

premeditation /ˌpriːmedɪˈteɪʃ(ə)n/ *noun* the activity of thinking about and planning a crime such as murder

premises /ˈpremɪsɪz/ *plural noun* **1.** a building and the land it stands on □ **office premises** a building which houses an office □ **lock-up premises** a shop which is locked up at night when the owner goes home □ **on the premises** in the building ○ *There is a doctor on the premises at all times.* **2.** things that have been referred to previously (NOTE: used at the end of a pleading: *In the premises the defendant denies that he is indebted to the claimant as alleged or at all.*)

premium /ˈpriːmiəm/ *noun* **1.** a sum of money paid by one person to another, especially one paid regularly **2.** the amount to be paid to a landlord or a tenant for the right to take over a lease ○ *a flat to let with a premium of £10,000* ○ *annual rent: £8,500 – premium: £25,000* **3.** an extra charge

prenuptial agreement /prɪˌnʌpʃ(ə)l əˈɡriːmənt/ *noun* an agreement made before marriage describing how shared assets should be divided in the event of divorce

COMMENT: Currently prenuptial agreements are not legally enforceable in the UK

prerogative /prɪˈrɒɡətɪv/ *noun* a special right which someone has

prerogative of mercy /prɪˌrɒɡətɪv əv ˈmɜːsi/ *noun* the power (used by the Home Secretary) to commute or remit a sentence

prerogative order /prɪˌrɒɡətɪv ˈɔːdə/ *noun* a writ from the High Court, which requests a body to do its duty, or not to do some act, or to conduct an inquiry into its own actions

prerogative powers /prɪˌrɒɡətɪv ˈpaʊəs/ *plural noun* special powers used by a government, acting in the name of the King or Queen, to do something such as declare war, or nominate judges or ministers without needing to ask Parliament to approve the decision

prescribe /prɪˈskraɪb/ *verb* to lay down rules ○ *The law prescribes heavy penalties for sexual offences.*

prescribed limits /prɪˌskraɪbd ˈlɪmɪts/ *plural noun* limits which are set down in legislation, e.g. the limit on the amount of alcohol a driver is allowed to drink and still drive

prescribed rights /prɪˌskraɪbd ˈraɪts/ *plural noun* rights which a person can claim because they have been enjoying them for a long period of time

prescription /prɪˈskrɪpʃən/ *noun* the act of acquiring a right or exercising a right over a period of time

present /ˈprez(ə)nt/ *noun* □ **these presents** this document itself □ **know all men by these presents** be informed by this document ■ *verb* to bring or send and show a document □ **to present a bill for acceptance** to send a bill for payment by the person who has accepted it □ **to present a bill for payment** to send a bill to be paid

presentation /ˌprez(ə)nˈteɪʃ(ə)n/ *noun* the process or an act of offering or showing information for other people to consider or make a decision about ○ *The presentation of the case took several days.* □ **on presentation of** by showing ○ *admission only on presentation of this pass*

presentment /prɪˈzentmənt/ *noun* the act of showing a document ○ *presentment of a bill of exchange*

preservation order /ˌprezəˈveɪʃ(ə)n ˌɔːdə/ *noun* a court order which prevents a building from being demolished or a tree from being cut down

preside /prɪˈzaɪd/ *verb* to be chairman ○ *to preside over a meeting* ○ *The meeting was* *held in the committee room, Mr Smith presiding.*

presidential-style /ˌprezɪˈdenʃəl ˌstaɪl/ *adjective* working in a similar way to the United States presidency □ **presidential-style government** governing in the same way as a President of the USA, who is not a member of the elected legislature □ **presidential-style campaign** an election campaign which concentrates on the person of the leader of the party, and not on the party's policies ○ *The Prime Minister was accused of running a presidential-style election campaign.*

President of the Family Division /ˌprezɪdənt əv ðə ˈfæm(ə)li dɪˌvɪʒ(ə)n/ *noun* a judge who is responsible for the work of the Family Division of the High Court

presiding judge /prɪˌzaɪdɪŋ ˈdʒʌdʒ/ *noun* a High Court judge who is responsible for a main Crown Court in a circuit

press /pres/ *verb* □ **to press charges against someone** to say formally that someone has committed a crime ○ *He was very angry when his neighbour's son set fire to his car, but decided not to press charges.*

Press Complaints Commission /ˌpres kəmˈpleɪnts kəˌmɪʃ(ə)n/ *noun* a voluntary body concerned with the self-regulation of the press. Abbreviation **PCC**

press conference /ˈpres ˌkɒnf(ə)rəns/ *noun* a meeting where reporters from newspapers and TV are invited to ask a minister questions, to hear the result of a court case, etc.

press coverage /ˈpres ˌkʌv(ə)rɪdʒ/ *noun* reports about something in the newspapers, on TV, etc. ○ *The company had good media coverage for the launch of its new model.*

press release /ˈpres rɪˌliːs/ *noun* a sheet giving news about something which is sent to newspapers and TV and radio stations so that they can use the information

pressure group /ˈpreʃə gruːp/ *noun* a group of people with similar interests, who try to influence government policies

pressure politics /ˌpreʃə ˈpɒlɪtɪks/ *noun* an attempt to change a government's policies by political pressure

presume /prɪˈzjuːm/ *verb* to suppose something is correct ○ *The court presumes the maintenance payments are being paid on time.* ○ *The company is presumed to be still solvent.* ○ *We presume the shipment has*

been stolen. ○ *Two sailors are missing, presumed drowned.*

COMMENT: In English law, the accused is presumed to be innocent until proven to be guilty, and presumed to be sane until proven to be insane.

presumption /prɪˈzʌmpʃən/ *noun* something which is assumed to be correct, because it is based on other facts

presumption of advancement /prɪ ˌzʌmpʃən əv ədˈvɑːnsmənt/ *noun* the legal principle that, in certain circumstances, a transfer of money or property from one person to another is intended as a gift (e.g. from a husband to a wife)

presumption of death /prɪˌzʌmpʃən əv ˈdeθ/ *noun* a situation where a person has not been seen for seven years and is presumed to be legally dead

presumption of innocence /prɪ ˌzʌmpʃən əv ˈɪnəs(ə)ns/ *noun* the act of assuming that someone is innocent, until they have been proved guilty

presumptive evidence /prɪˌzʌmptɪv ˈevɪd(ə)ns/ *noun* circumstantial evidence

pretrial /priːˈtraɪəl/ *adjective* before a trial starts

pretrial detention /priːˌtraɪəl dɪ ˈtenʃən/ *noun US* the situation of being kept in prison until your trial starts (NOTE: The British equivalent is **remanded in custody**.)

pretrial release /priːˌtraɪəl rɪˈliːs/ *noun US* the release of an accused person pending his or her return to court to face trial (NOTE: The British equivalent is **bail**.)

pretrial review /priːˌtraɪəl rɪˈvjuː/ *noun* a meeting of the parties before a civil action to examine what is likely to arise during the action, so that ways can be found of making it shorter and to reduce costs

prevail /prɪˈveɪl/ *verb* □ **to prevail upon someone to do something** to persuade someone to do something ○ *Counsel prevailed upon the judge to grant an adjournment.*

prevaricate /prɪˈværɪkeɪt/ *verb* not to give a clear and straightforward answer to a question

prevention /prɪˈvenʃən/ *noun* the act of stopping something from taking place □ **the prevention of terrorism** stopping terrorist acts taking place

prevention of corruption /prɪˌvenʃən əv kəˈrʌpʃən/ *noun US* activity undertaken to stop corruption taking place

prevention of terrorism /prɪˌvenʃən əv ˈterərɪz(ə)m/ *noun* measures used to prevent terrorism, such as increased police powers to arrest and detain suspected persons

preventive /prɪˈventɪv/ *adjective* trying to stop something happening □ **to take preventive measures against theft** to try to stop things from being stolen

preventive detention /prɪˌventɪv dɪˈtenʃən/ *noun* formerly, the imprisonment of someone who frequently committed a specific crime, so as to prevent them from doing it again (NOTE: Now replaced by **extended sentences**.)

previous /ˈpriːviəs/ *noun* a previous conviction or convictions for criminal offences

price controls /ˈpraɪs kənˌtrəʊlz/ *plural noun* legal measures to prevent prices rising too fast

price fixing /ˈpraɪs ˌfɪksɪŋ/ *noun* an illegal agreement between companies to charge the same price for competing products

pricing /ˈpraɪsɪŋ/ *noun* the activity of giving a price to a product

pricing policy /ˈpraɪsɪŋ ˌpɒlisi/ *noun* a company's policy in setting prices for its products

primacy /ˈpraɪməsi/ *noun* supremacy, one of the twin pillars of EU law. ◊ **supremacy**

prima facie /ˌpraɪmə ˈfeɪʃi/ *phrase* a Latin phrase meaning 'on the face of it' or 'as things seem at first' □ **there is a prima facie case to answer** one side in a case has shown that there is a case to answer, and so the action should be proceeded with

primarily /praɪˈmer(ə)li/ *adverb* in the first place ○ *He is primarily liable for his debts.* ◊ **secondarily**

primary caregiver /ˌpraɪməri ˈkeəgɪvə/ *noun* the person who is primarily responsible for looking after someone's health, safety and comfort, especially that of a child

primary evidence /ˌpraɪməri ˈevɪd(ə)ns/ *noun* the most reliable type of evidence, e.g. original documents, or evidence from eye witnesses

primary legislation /ˌpraɪməri ˌledʒɪˈsleɪʃ(ə)n/ *noun* legislation of the Member States of the European Union, as opposed to legislation of the EU itself

primary residence /ˌpraɪməri ˈrezɪd(ə)ns/ *noun* the place where a person

usually lives, used when calculating tax or applying for a mortgage

prime /praɪm/ *adjective* most important ○ *Her safety is of prime concern.* ■ *verb* to make ready for use ○ *He had primed the gun ready for use.*

prime bills /ˌpraɪm ˈbɪlz/ *plural noun* bills of exchange which do not involve any risk

prime rate /ˈpraɪm reɪt/ *noun* the best rate of interest at which a bank lends to its customers

primogeniture /ˌpraɪməʊˈdʒenɪtʃə/ *noun* a former rule that the oldest son inherits all his father's estate

principal /ˈprɪnsɪp(ə)l/ *noun* **1.** the initial sum of money invested or borrowed, before interest or any other revenue is added, or the remainder of that sum after payments have been made **2.** a person who is responsible for something, especially someone who is in charge of a company or someone who commits a crime **3.** someone for whom a representative or proxy acts in a legal matter

principle /ˈprɪnsɪp(ə)l/ *noun* a general point or rule that is used as the basis of the way something is done □ **in principle** in agreement with a general rule ■ *plural noun* **principles** personally-held beliefs and moral standards of behaviour □ **to be against your principles** to go against what you believe to be the correct way to act

printed matter /ˈprɪntɪd ˌmætə/ *noun* books, newspapers, advertising material, etc.

prior /ˈpraɪə/ *adjective* earlier □ **without prior knowledge** without knowing before

prior agreement /ˌpraɪə əˈgriːmənt/ *noun* an agreement which was reached earlier

prior charge /ˌpraɪə ˈtʃɑːdʒ/ *noun* a charge which ranks before others

priori ♦ **a priori**

prison /ˈprɪz(ə)n/ *noun* **1.** a safe building where criminals can be kept locked up after they have been convicted or while they await trial ○ *The government has ordered the construction of six new prisons.* ○ *This prison was built 150 years ago.* **2.** a place where prisoners are kept as a punishment ○ *She was sent to prison for six years.* ○ *They have spent the last six months in prison.* ○ *He escaped from prison by climbing over the wall.* (NOTE: no plural for sense 2, which is also usually written without the article: *in prison*; *out of prison*; *sent to prison*.)

prison chaplain /ˌprɪz(ə)n 'tʃæplɪn/ *noun* a priest or minister who works in a prison

prisoner /'prɪz(ə)nə/ *noun* somebody who is in prison

prisoner at the bar /ˌprɪz(ə)nə ət ðə 'bɑː/ *noun* a prisoner who is being tried in court

prisoner of war /ˌprɪz(ə)nə əv 'wɔː/ *noun* a member of the armed forces captured and put in prison by the enemy in time of war

prisoner on remand /ˌprɪz(ə)nə ɒn rɪ 'mɑːnd/ *noun* a prisoner who has been told to reappear in court at a later date

prison governor /'prɪz(ə)n ˌgʌv(ə)nə/ *noun* the person in charge of a prison

prison officer /'prɪz(ə)n ˌɒfɪsə/ *noun* a member of staff in a prison

privacy /'prɪvəsi/ *noun* a private life

private /'praɪvət/ *adjective* **1.** belonging to a single person, not a company or the state ○ *private property* **2.** secret, not shared with others ○ *His private belief was that she was guilty.*

Private Bill /'praɪvət bɪl/ *noun* a Bill or Act relating to a particular person, corporation or institution

private business /ˌpraɪvət 'bɪznɪs/ *noun* a business dealing with the members of a group or matters which cannot be discussed in public ○ *The committee held a special meeting to discuss some private business.*

private carrier /ˌpraɪvət 'kæriə/ *noun* a firm which carries goods or passengers, but which is not contractually bound to offer the service to anyone

private client /ˌpraɪvət 'klaɪənt/ *noun* a client dealt with by a professional person or by a salesperson as an individual person, not as a company

private detective /ˌpraɪvət dɪ'tektɪv/ *noun* a person who for a fee will try to find missing people, keep watch on someone, or find out information

private effects /ˌpraɪvət ɪ'fekts/ *plural noun* goods which belong to someone and are used by him or her

private eye /ˌpraɪvət 'aɪ/ *noun* somebody who for a fee will try to solve mysteries, to find missing persons or to keep watch on someone (*informal*)

private finance initiative /ˌpraɪvət 'faɪnæns ɪ,nɪʃətɪv/ *noun* the practice of funding government projects by having

them set up and run by private companies on long-term contracts. Abbreviation **PFI**

private law /'praɪvət lɔː/ *noun* a law such as the law of contract relating to relations between individual people

private letter /ˌpraɪvət 'letə/ *noun* a letter which deals with personal matters

Private Member's Bill /ˌpraɪvət 'membəz ˌbɪl/ *noun* a Bill which is drafted and proposed as legislation in the House of Commons by an ordinary Member of Parliament, not by a government minister on behalf of the government

private nuisance /ˌpraɪvət 'njuːs(ə)ns/ *noun* a nuisance which causes harm or damage to a particular person or their rights

private ownership /ˌpraɪvət 'əʊnəʃɪp/ *noun* a situation where a company is owned by private shareholders

private property /ˌpraɪvət 'prɒpəti/ *noun* property which belongs to a private person, not to the public

private prosecution /ˌpraɪvət ˌprɒsɪ 'kjuːʃ(ə)n/ *noun* a prosecution for a criminal act, brought by an ordinary member of the public and not by the police

privatise /'praɪvətaɪz/, **privatize** *verb* to sell a nationalised industry to private shareholders

privilege /'prɪvɪlɪdʒ/ *noun* **1.** protection from the law given in some circumstances. ◊ **Crown privilege, professional privilege** **2.** the right of a party not to disclose a document, or to refuse to answer questions, on the ground of some special interest **3.** *US* the order of priority □ **motion of the highest privilege** a motion which will be discussed first, before all other motions

privileged /'prɪvɪlɪdʒd/ *adjective* protected by privilege

privileged communication /ˌprɪvɪlɪdʒd kə,mjuːnɪ'keɪʃ(ə)n/ *noun* a letter which could be libellous, but which is protected by privilege, e.g. a letter from a client to his or her lawyer

privileged meeting /ˌprɪvɪlɪdʒd 'miːtɪŋ/ *noun* a meeting where what is said will not be repeated outside

privileged questions /ˌprɪvɪlɪdʒd 'kwestʃ(ə)ns/ *plural noun US* order of priority of motions to be discussed

privileged will /'prɪvɪlɪdʒd wɪl/ *noun* a will which is not made in writing and is not signed or witnessed, e.g. a will made by a soldier on the battlefield or a seaman while at sea

COMMENT: Privileged wills are not like ordinary wills, in that they may be oral, or if written, need not be signed or witnessed. It is sufficient that the intention of the testator was made clear at the time.

privity /'prɪvɪti/ *noun* a legally recognised relationship between two parties, e.g. between members of a family, between an employer and employees, or between others who have entered into a contract together

privity of contract /ˌprɪvɪti əv 'kɒntrækt/ *noun* a relationship between the parties to a contract, which makes the contract enforceable as between them

Privy Council /ˌprɪvi 'kaʊnsəl/ *noun* a body of senior advisers who advise the Queen on specific matters

COMMENT: The Privy Council is mainly formed of members of the cabinet, and former members of the cabinet. It never meets as a group, but three Privy Councillors need to be present when the Queen signs Orders in Council.

Privy Councillor /ˌprɪvi 'kaʊnsələ/ *noun* a member of the Privy Council

prize /praɪz/ *noun* formerly, an enemy ship or cargo captured in war

prize court /'praɪz kɔːt/ *noun* formerly, a court set up to rule on the ownership of prize ships

pro /prəʊ/ *preposition* for or on behalf of

probable cause /ˌprɒbəb(ə)l 'kɔːz/ *noun US* the fact of believing that it is likely that a crime has been committed and by an identified person, which is a necessary part of police stop and search procedures

probate /'prəʊbeɪt/ *noun* legal acceptance that a document, especially a will, is valid □ **to be granted probate** to be told officially that a will is valid

Probate Registry /'prəʊbeɪt ˌredʒɪstri/ *noun* a court office which deals with the granting of probate

probation /prə'beɪʃ(ə)n/ *noun* **1.** a legal system for dealing with criminals, often young offenders, where they are not sent to prison provided that they continue to behave well under the supervision of a probation officer ○ *She was sentenced to probation for one year.* **2.** a period when a new employee is being tested before being confirmed as having a permanent job ◇ **on probation 1.** being tested ○ *to take someone on probation* **2.** being under a probation order from a court

probationer /prə'beɪʃ(ə)nə/ *noun* somebody who has been put on probation

probation officer /prə'beɪʃ(ə)n ˌɒfɪsə/ *noun* an official of the social services who supervises young people on probation

probation order /prəˌbeɪʃ(ə)n 'ɔːdə/ *noun* a court order putting someone on probation

probative /'prəʊbətɪv/ *adjective* relating to proof

probative value /'prəʊbətɪv ˌvæljuː/ *noun US* the value of an item as evidence in a trial

problem area /'prɒbləm ˌeəriə/ *noun* an area of work which is difficult to manage ○ *Drug-related crime is a problem area in large cities.*

procedural /prə'siːdʒərəl/ *adjective* referring to legal procedure

procedural judge /prə'siːdʒərəl dʒʌdʒ/ *noun* a judge who deals with the management of a case, its allocation to a particular track, etc.

procedural law /prə'siːdʒərəl lɔː/ *noun* law relating to how the civil or criminal law is administered by the courts. Compare **substantive law**

procedural problem /prəˌsiːdʒərəl 'prɒbləm/ *noun* a question concerning procedure ○ *The hearing was held up while counsel argued over procedural problems.*

procedure /prə'siːdʒə/ *noun* a way in which something is done, especially the correct or agreed way to deal with something ○ *to follow the proper procedure* ○ *to criticise police procedures*

proceed /prə'siːd/ *verb* to continue doing something ○ *The negotiations are proceeding slowly.* □ **to proceed against someone** to start a legal action against someone □ **to proceed with something** to go on doing something

proceedings /prə'siːdɪŋz/ *plural noun* □ **to institute or to start proceedings against someone** to start a legal action against someone

proceedings in tort /prəˌsiːdɪŋz ɪn 'tɔːt/ *plural noun* court action for damages for a tort

process *noun* /'prəʊses/ **1.** the way in which a court acts to assert its jurisdiction **2.** the writs issued by a court to summon a defendant to appear in court **3.** a legal procedure □ **the due process of the law** the formal work of a fair legal action ■ *verb* /prəʊ 'ses/ to deal with something in the usual routine way ○ *to process an insurance claim*

○ *The incident room is processing information received from the public.*

processing /'prəʊsesɪŋ/ *noun* □ **the processing of a claim for insurance** putting a claim for compensation through the usual office routine in the insurance company

process-server /'prəʊses ˌsɜːvə/ *noun* a person who delivers legal documents such as a writ or summons to people in person

proctor /'prɒktə/ *noun* (*in a university*) an official who is responsible for keeping law and order

procurationem ◆ per procurationem

Procurator Fiscal /ˌprɒkjʊreɪtə 'fɪsk(ə)l/ *noun* (*in Scotland*) a law officer who decides whether an alleged criminal should be prosecuted

procure /prə'kjʊə/ *verb* to get someone to do something, especially to arrange for a woman to provide sexual intercourse for money

procurer /prə'kjʊərə/ *noun* somebody who procures women

procuring /prə'kjʊəmənt/, **procurement** *noun* the notifiable offence of getting a woman to provide sexual intercourse for money

product liability /ˌprɒdʌkt laɪə'bɪlɪti/ *noun* the liability of the maker of a product for negligence in the design or production of the product

proferentem ◆ contra proferentem

profession /prə'feʃ(ə)n/ *noun* **1.** work which needs special learning over a period of time **2.** a group of specialised workers □ **the legal profession** all lawyers □ **the medical profession** all doctors

professional /prə'feʃ(ə)nəl/ *adjective* **1.** referring to one of the professions ○ *The accountant sent in his bill for professional services.* ○ *We had to ask our lawyer for professional advice on the contract.* □ **professional qualifications** documents showing that someone has successfully finished a course of study which allows them to work in their chosen profession **2.** expert ■ *noun* a person with special skills and qualifications in a particular subject

professional misconduct /prə ˌfeʃ(ə)nəl mɪs'kɒndʌkt/ *noun* behaviour by a professional person such as a lawyer, accountant or doctor which the body which regulates that profession considers to be wrong, e.g. an action by a solicitor which is considered wrong by the Law Society

professional negligence /prə ˌfeʃ(ə)nəl 'neglɪdʒəns/ *noun* grounds for an action against a professional (such as a solicitor or an accountant) based on their failure to exercise due care and skill in their work

professional privilege /prə,feʃ(ə)nəl 'prɪvɪlɪdʒ/ *noun* confidentiality of communications between a client and his or her lawyer

profit /ˌprɒfi æ 'prɒndrə/ *noun* **1.** the right to take natural resources such as game, fish or firewood from another person's land. Also called **profit à prendre 2.** money gained from a sale which is more than the money spent on making the item sold

profit after tax /ˌprɒfɪt ɑːftə 'tæks/ *noun* the profit made by a company after tax has been deducted

profit and loss account /ˌprɒfɪt ən 'lɒs ə,kaʊnt/ *noun* a statement of a company's expenditure and income over a period of time, almost always one calendar year, showing whether the company has made a profit or loss

profit à prendre /ˌprɒfi æ 'prɒndrə/ *noun* same as **profit**

profit before tax /ˌprɒfɪt bɪfɔː 'tæks/ *noun* the profit of a company after expenses have been deducted but before tax has been calculated

profiteer /ˌprɒfɪ'tɪə/ *noun* somebody who makes too much profit, especially when goods are rationed or in short supply

pro forma /ˌprəʊ 'fɔːmə/ *phrase* a Latin phrase meaning 'for the sake of form' □ **pro forma (invoice)** an invoice sent to a buyer before the goods are sent, so that payment can be made or that business documents can be produced □ **pro forma letter** a formal letter which informs a court of a decision of another court

progress report /'prəʊgres rɪ,pɔːt/ *noun* a document which describes what progress has been made

prohibit /prəʊ'hɪbɪt/ *verb* to say that something must not happen ○ *Parking is prohibited in front of the garage.* ○ *The law prohibits the sale of alcohol to minors.*

prohibited degrees /prəʊ,hɪbɪtɪd dɪ 'griːs/ *plural noun* the relationships which make it illegal for a man and woman to marry, e.g. father and daughter

prohibited goods /prəʊ,hɪbɪtɪd 'gʊdz/ *plural noun* goods which are not allowed to be imported

prohibition /ˌprəʊɪˈbɪʃ(ə)n/ *noun* **1.** the act of forbidding something **2.** a High Court order forbidding a lower court from doing something which exceeds its jurisdiction

prohibitory injunction /prəˌhɪbɪt(ə)ri ɪnˈdʒʌŋkʃən/ *noun* an order from a court preventing someone from doing an illegal act

promisee /ˌprɒmɪˈsiː/ *noun* somebody to whom a promise is made

promisor /ˌprɒmɪˈsɔː/ *noun* somebody who makes a promise

promissory /ˈprɒmɪsəri/ *adjective* promising

promissory estoppel /ˌprɒmɪsəri ɪˈstɒp(ə)l/ *noun* □ **doctrine of promissory estoppel** the principle that a person may not withdraw a promise made to another, if that other person has reasonably relied on it and acted upon it to their cost

promote /prəˈməʊt/ *verb* **1.** to introduce a new Bill into Parliament **2.** to encourage something to grow ○ *illegal websites promoting terrorism*

promoter /prəˈməʊtə/ *noun* somebody who introduces a new Bill into Parliament

prompt /prɒmpt/ *verb* to tell someone what to say ○ *The judge warned counsel not to prompt the witness.*

proof /pruːf/ *noun* **1.** evidence which shows that something is true □ **proof beyond reasonable doubt** proof that no reasonable person could doubt (the proof needed to convict a person in a criminal case) **2.** the statement or evidence of a creditor to show that he or she is owed money by a bankrupt or by a company in liquidation

proofing /ˈpruːfɪŋ/ *noun* □ **proofing of witnesses** the act of looking into witnesses' statements

Proof-of-Age Standards Scheme /ˌpruːf əv eɪdʒ ˈstændədz ˌskiːm/ *noun* full form of **PASS**

proof of debt /ˌpruːf əv ˈdet/ *noun* proceedings for a creditor to claim payment from a bankrupt's assets

proof of evidence /ˌpruːf əv ˈevɪd(ə)ns/ *noun* a written statement of what a witness intends to say in court

proof of identification /ˌpruːf əv aɪˌdentɪfɪˈkeɪʃ(ə)n/ *noun* **1.** proving that something is what the evidence says it is **2.** proving that someone is who they say they are ○ *Everyone has to provide proof of identification before they can leave the country.*

proof of service /ˌpruːf əv ˈsɜːvɪs/ *noun* proof that that legal documents have been delivered to someone

property /ˈprɒpəti/ *noun* **1.** things that are owned by someone ○ *They have no respect for other people's property.* ○ *He was known to be a receiver of stolen property.* **2.** land and buildings ○ *He owns a lot of property in the north.* **3.** a building such as a house, shop or factory ○ *There are several properties for sale in the centre of the town.* ■ *adjective* relating to land and buildings ○ *a rise in property prices*

proportionality /prəˌpɔːʃ(ə)ˈnælɪti/ *noun* **1.** the principle that a government or local authority can only act if the action is in proportion to the aim which is to be achieved, the aim being to protect the rights of ordinary citizens **2.** the principle that a legal action can only take place if the costs are proportionate to the aim to be achieved ○ *The requirement of proportionality may be a reason for a party to refuse to respond to a request for further information.*

proportionate /prəˈpɔːʃ(ə)nət/ *adjective* directly related to or in proportion to something

proposal form /prəˈpəʊz(ə)l fɔːm/ *noun* an official document with details of a property or person to be insured which is sent to the insurance company when asking for an insurance

propose /prəˈpəʊz/ *verb* □ **to propose to** to say that you intend to do something ○ *I propose to repay the loan at £20 a month.*

proprietary drug /prəˌpraɪət(ə)ri ˈdrʌg/ *noun* a drug which is made by a particular company and marketed under a brand name

proprietary right /prəˈpraɪət(ə)ri raɪt/ *noun* the right of someone who owns a property

proprietor /prəˈpraɪətə/ *noun* the owner of a property

proprietorship /prəˈpraɪətəʃɪp/ *noun* the fact of being the proprietor of land

proprietorship register /prəˈpraɪətəʃɪp ˌredʒɪstə/ *noun* a land register which shows the details of owners of land

proprietress /prəˈpraɪətrəs/ *noun* a female owner

pro rata /ˌprəʊ ˈrɑːtə/ *adjective, adverb* at a rate which changes proportionally according to the size, length or importance of something else ○ *to pay someone pro rata* □ **to pay somebody pro rata** to pay somebody according to the number of hours that they work □ **pro rata liability** the liability of debtors only for their own proportion of a debt

prorogation /ˌprəʊrəˈɡeɪʃ(ə)n/ *noun* the end of a session of Parliament

prorogue /prəˈrəʊɡ/ *verb* to end a session of Parliament ○ *Parliament was prorogued for the summer recess.*

proscribe /prəʊˈskraɪb/ *verb* to ban □ **proscribed organisation, proscribed political party** an organisation or political party which has been banned

prosecute /ˈprɒsɪkjuːt/ *verb* **1.** to bring someone to court to answer a criminal charge ○ *She was prosecuted for embezzlement.* **2.** to speak against the accused person on behalf of the party bringing the charge ○ *Mr Smith is prosecuting, and Mr Jones is appearing for the defence.*

prosecution /ˌprɒsɪˈkjuːʃ(ə)n/ *noun* **1.** the act of bringing someone to court to answer a charge ○ *his prosecution for embezzlement* ◊ **Crown Prosecution Service, Director of Public Prosecutions 2.** a party who brings a criminal charge against someone ○ *The costs of the case will be borne by the prosecution.* **3.** the group of lawyers representing the party who brings a criminal charge against someone

prosecution counsel /ˌprɒsɪˈkjuːʃ(ə)n ˌkaʊnsəl/ *noun* a lawyer acting for the prosecution

prosecution witness /ˌprɒsɪˈkjuːʃ(ə)n ˌwɪtnəs/ *noun* a person called by the prosecution side to give evidence against the defendant or the accused

prosecutor /ˈprɒsɪkjuːtə/ *noun* somebody who brings criminal charges against someone

prosequi ♦ nolle prosequi

prospectus /prəˈspektəs/ *noun* a document issued by a company for the purposes of a flotation

prostitute /ˈprɒstɪtjuːt/ *noun* somebody who provides sexual intercourse in return for payment

prostitution /ˌprɒstɪˈtjuːʃ(ə)n/ *noun* the activity of providing sexual intercourse in return for payment

COMMENT: The legal status of prostitution varies from country to country. It is an offence punishable by death in some Muslim countries, whereas in Holland it is not only legal but officially regulated and licensed by the authorities, with tax payable on earnings. In the UK the act of prostitution is not officially illegal, but soliciting, kerb-crawling, benefiting from the prostitution of others (**pimping**) and owning or running a brothel are all outlawed.

protect /prəˈtekt/ *verb* to defend something against harm ○ *The employees are protected from unfair dismissal by government legislation.* ○ *You can protect your intellectual property by applying for a patent.* (NOTE: You protect someone **from** something or **from having** something done to him or her.)

protected person /prəˌtektɪd ˈpɜːs(ə)n/ *noun* an important person such as a President or Prime Minister who has special police protection

protected tenancy /prəˌtektɪd ˈtenənsi/ *noun* a tenancy where the tenant is protected from eviction

protection /prəˈtekʃən/ *noun* the fact of being safe and defended from harm

protection order /prəˈtekʃən ˌɔːdə/ *noun* a court order which protects someone from harm, e.g. a non-molestation order or occupation order. ◊ **associated persons**

protection racket /prəˌtekʃən ˈrækɪt/ *noun* an illegal organisation where people demand money from someone such as a small businessperson to pay for 'protection' against criminal attacks

protective /prəˈtektɪv/ *adjective* shielding from potential danger

protective custody /prəˌtektɪv ˈkʌstədi/ □ **to take someone into protective custody** to put someone in a safe place, e.g. police station cells, to protect him or her from being harassed or attacked ○ *The witness was put in protective custody* ○ *They took his children into protective custody because of his aggressive behaviour.*

protective tariff /prəˌtektɪv ˈtærɪf/ *noun* a tariff which tries to ban imports to stop them competing with local products

pro tem /ˌprəʊ ˈtem/, **pro tempore** *adverb* for a short time

protest *noun* /ˈprəʊtest/ **1.** a statement or action to show that you do not approve of something ○ *to make a protest against high prices* □ **in protest at** showing that you do not approve of something ○ *The staff occupied the offices in protest at the low pay offer.* □ **to do something under protest** to do something, but say that you do not approve of it **2.** an official document from a notary public which notes that a bill of exchange has not been paid ■ *verb* /prə ˈtest/ **1.** □ **to protest against something** to say that you do not approve of something ○ *The retailers are protesting against the ban on imported goods.* **2.** □ **to protest a bill** to draw up a document to prove that a bill of exchange has not been paid

protester /prə'testə/ *noun* someone who makes their opposition to something public

protest march /'prəʊtest mɑːtʃ/ *noun* a demonstration where protesters march through the streets

protest strike /'prəʊtest straɪk/ *noun* a strike in protest at a particular grievance

protocol /'prəʊtəkɒl/ *noun* **1.** a draft memorandum. ◊ **pre-action protocol 2.** a list of things which have been agreed. ◊ **pre-action protocol 3.** correct diplomatic behaviour □ **to follow protocol** to do things in the correct diplomatic way

provable /'pruːvəb(ə)l/ *adjective* being able to be proved

provable debts /ˌpruːvəb(ə)l 'dets/ *plural noun* debts which a creditor can prove against a bankrupt estate

prove /pruːv/ *verb* to show beyond all doubt that something is true ○ *CCTV images prove that he was in the building at the time of the robbery.* □ **to prove your innocence** to show beyond any doubt that you are innocent □ **to prove a debt** to show that a bankrupt owes you money □ **to prove a will** to show that a will is valid and obtain a grant of probate

proven /'pruːv(ə)n/ *adjective* □ **not proven** (*in Scotland*) a verdict that the prosecution has not produced sufficient evidence to prove the accused to be guilty

provide /prə'vaɪd/ *verb* **1.** □ **to provide for something** to allow for something which may happen in the future ○ *These expenses have not been provided for* ○ *The contract provides for an annual increase in charges.* □ **to provide for someone** to put aside money to give someone enough to live on ○ *He provided for his daughter in his will.* **2.** □ **to provide someone with something** to supply something to someone ○ *The defendant provided the court with a detailed account of his movements.* ○ *Duress provides no defence to a charge of murder.*

provided that /prə'vaɪdɪd ðæt/, **providing** /prə'vaɪdɪŋ/ *conjunction* on condition that ○ *The judge will sentence the convicted man next week provided (that)* or *providing the psychiatrist's report is received in time.*

COMMENT: The words 'provided always that' are used to indicate a **proviso** in a deed.

province /'prɒvɪns/ *noun* □ **the Province** Northern Ireland

provision /prə'vɪʒ(ə)n/ *noun* **1.** □ **to make provision for** to see that something is allowed for in the future □ **to make financial provision for someone** to arrange for someone to receive money to live on (by attachment of earnings, etc.) **2.** money put aside in accounts in case it is needed in the future ○ *The company has made a £2m provision for bad debts.* **3.** a legal condition □ **the provisions of a Bill** conditions listed in a Bill before Parliament □ **to make provision to something** in a contract, to put in terms which take something into account

provisional /prə'vɪʒ(ə)n(ə)l/ *adjective* temporary, not final or permanent ○ *They wrote to give their provisional acceptance of the contract.*

provisional damages /prəˌvɪʒ(ə)n(ə)l 'dæmɪdʒɪz/ *plural noun* damages claimed by a claimant while the case is still being heard

provisional injunction /prəˌvɪʒ(ə)n(ə)l ɪn'dʒʌŋkʃən/ *noun* a temporary injunction granted until a full court hearing can take place

provisional licence /prəˌvɪʒ(ə)n(ə)l 'laɪs(ə)ns/ *noun* a temporary driving licence for people who have not yet passed a driving test

provisional liquidator /prəˌvɪʒ(ə)n(ə)l 'lɪkwɪdeɪtə/ *noun* an official appointed by a court to protect the assets of a company which is the subject of a winding up order

proviso /prə'vaɪzəʊ/ *noun* **1.** a condition on which somebody does something ○ *He is taking the job with the proviso that his salary can be renegotiated in six months' time.* **2.** a condition in a contract or deed (NOTE: A proviso usually begins with the phrase 'provided always that': *The carrier shall be liable for the value of the goods carried, provided always that this value has been properly declared.*)

provocateur ♦ **agent provocateur**

provocation /ˌprɒvə'keɪʃ(ə)n/ *noun* incitement to commit a crime or carry out an action which you had not intended to do, which is a defence to a charge of murder ○ *He acted under provocation.*

provoke /prə'vəʊk/ *verb* to make someone do something or to make something happen ○ *The strikers provoked the police to retaliate.* ○ *The murders provoked a campaign to increase police protection for poli-*

ticians. (NOTE: You provoke someone **to do** something.)

proxy /ˈprɒksi/ *noun* **1.** a document which gives someone the power to act on behalf of someone else ○ *to sign by proxy* **2.** somebody who acts on behalf of someone else ○ *to act as proxy for someone*

PSBR *abbreviation* public sector borrowing requirement

public /ˈpʌblɪk/ *adjective* **1.** referring to all the people in general □ **the public, the general public** the people in general □ **in public** in front of everyone **2.** referring to the government or the state

public administration /ˌpʌblɪk əd ˌmɪnɪˈstreɪʃ(ə)n/ *noun* **1.** the means whereby government policy is carried out **2.** the people responsible for carrying out government policy

publication /ˌpʌblɪˈkeɪʃ(ə)n/ *noun* **1.** the act of making something public either in speech or writing ○ *Publication of Cabinet papers takes place after thirty years.* **2.** the act of making a libel known to the general public **3.** a printed work shown to the public

Public Bill /ˌpʌblɪk ˈbɪl/ *noun* an ordinary Bill relating to a matter applying to the public in general, introduced by a government minister

public disorder /ˌpʌblɪk dɪsˈɔːdə/ *noun* same as **civil disorder**

public domain /ˌpʌblɪk dəʊˈmeɪn/ *noun* the body of intellectual property which is available free of copyright restrictions, usually because copyright has expired

public expenditure /ˌpʌblɪk ɪk ˈspendɪtʃə/ *noun* the spending of money by local or central government

public funds /ˌpʌblɪk ˈfʌndz/ *plural noun* government money available for expenditure

public interest /ˌpʌblɪk ˈɪntrəst/ *noun* the usefulness of a piece of information to the public, in matters concerning national security, fraud, medical malpractice, etc., used as a defence against charges of passing on confidential information or of invasion of privacy

COMMENT: Public interest implies that the actions of someone or information held by someone might affect the public in some way: if a newspaper discloses that a group of companies are fixing prices so as not to compete with each other, this disclosure might be held to be in the public interest. If a TV programme reveals that a Member of Parliament apparently took drugs, then this might be held to be in the public interest.

public law /ˌpʌblɪk ˈlɔː/ *noun* laws which refer to people in general such as administrative and constitutional law

public monopoly /ˌpʌblɪk məˈnɒpəli/ *noun* a situation where the state is the only supplier of a product or service

public nuisance /ˌpʌblɪk ˈnjuːs(ə)ns/ *noun* a criminal act which causes harm or damage to members of the public in general or to their rights

public opinion /ˌpʌblɪk əˈpɪnjən/ *noun* what people think about something

public order /ˌpʌblɪk ˈɔːdə/ *noun* a situation were the general public is calm and there are no riots

public ownership /ˌpʌblɪk ˈəʊnəʃɪp/ *noun* a situation where an industry is nationalised

public place /ˌpʌblɪk ˈpleɪs/ *noun* a place such as a road or park where the public have a right to be

public policy /ˌpʌblɪk ˈpɒlɪsi/ *noun* the policy of the government of a Member State of the European Union which protects its nationals, and which can be used to exclude nationals of other EU states from entering the country to take up work (NOTE: This excuse cannot be used to exclude people for economic reasons.)

public procurement /ˌpʌblɪk prə ˈkjʊəmənt/ *noun* the purchase of goods and services by a government, dealt with in the UK by the Office of Government Commerce

public prosecutor /ˌpʌblɪk ˈprɒsɪkjuːtə/ *noun* a government official who brings charges against alleged criminals (NOTE: In the UK, it is the **Director of Public Prosecutions**.)

public sector borrowing requirement /ˌpʌblɪk ˌsektə ˌbɒrəʊɪŋ rɪ ˈkwaɪəmənt/ *noun* the amount of money which a government has to borrow to pay for its own spending. Abbreviation **PSBR**

Public Trustee /ˌpʌblɪk ˌtrʌˈstiː/ *noun* an official who is appointed as a trustee of an individual's property

puisne /ˈpjuːni/ *adjective* less important, inferior in rank

puisne judge /ˌpjuːni ˈdʒʌdʒ/ *noun* a High Court judge

puisne mortgage /ˌpjuːni ˈmɔːɡɪdʒ/ *noun* a mortgage where the deeds of the property have not been deposited with the lender

punish /'pʌnɪʃ/ *verb* to make someone pay the penalty for a crime which he or she has committed ○ *It's likely he'll be punished severely for his offences.*

punishable /'pʌnɪʃəb(ə)l/ *adjective* able to be punished ○ *crimes punishable by imprisonment*

punishment /'pʌnɪʃmənt/ *noun* **1.** the act of punishing someone **2.** treatment of someone as a way of making them suffer for their crime ○ *The punishment for treason is death.*

punitive damages /,pju:nɪtɪv 'dæmɪdʒɪz/ *plural noun* heavy damages which punish the defendant for the loss or harm caused to the claimant, awarded to show that the court feels the defendant has behaved badly towards the claimant. Also called **exemplary damages**

pupil /'pju:p(ə)l/ *noun* a trainee barrister, undergoing a year-long training period before qualification

pupillage /'pju:pɪlɪdʒ/ *noun* a training period of one year after completing studies at university and passing all examinations, which a person has to serve before he or she can practise independently as a barrister

pur autre vie /,pu:ə ,əʊtrə 'vi:/ ♦ **per autre vie**

purchase order /'pɜ:tʃɪs ,ɔ:də/ *noun* an official paper which places an order for something

purchaser /'pɜ:tʃɪsə/ *noun* a person or company that buys something

purge /pɜ:dʒ/ *verb* □ **to purge one's contempt**, **to purge a contempt of court** to do something such as make an apology to show that you are sorry for the lack of respect you have shown

purpose /'pɜ:pəs/ *noun* an aim, plan or intention □ **on purpose** intentionally ○ *She hid the knife on purpose.* □ **for the purposes of** in order to achieve something ○ *We need the crime number for the purposes of claiming on our insurance.*

purposive /'pɜ:pəsɪv/ *adjective* referring to the purpose behind something ○ *a purposive interpretation of the Treaty on European Union*

pursuant to /pə'sju:ənt tə/ *adverb* relating to or concerning ○ *matters pursuant to Article 124 of the EC treaty* ○ *pursuant to the powers conferred on the local authority*

pursue /pə'sju:/ *verb* to continue with something such as the proceedings in court

pursuer /pə'sju:ə/ *noun* in Scotland, a plaintiff in a lawsuit, who brings a case against the defendant

pursuit /pə'sju:t/ ♦ **fresh pursuit**, **hot pursuit**

purview /'pɜ:vju:/ *noun* the general scope of an Act of Parliament

put /pʊt/ *verb* to place or to fix □ **to put a proposal to the vote** to ask a meeting to vote for or against the proposal □ **to put a proposal to the board** to ask the board to consider a suggestion

put aside /,pʊt ə'saɪd/ *verb* to decide to cancel an order, judgment or decision

putative father /,pju:tətɪv 'fɑ:ðə/ *noun* a man who is supposed to be or who a court decides must be the father of an illegitimate child

put away /,pʊt ə'weɪ/ *verb* to send to prison ○ *He was put away for ten years.*

put down /,pʊt 'daʊn/ *verb* **1.** to make a deposit ○ *to put down money on a house* **2.** to write an item in an account book ○ *to put down a figure for expenses*

put in /,pʊt 'ɪn/ *verb* □ **to put in a bid for something** to offer (usually in writing) to buy something □ **to put in a claim for damage**, **loss** to ask an insurance company to pay for damage or loss

put into /,pʊt 'ɪntʊ/ *verb* □ **to put money into a business** to invest money in a business

put on /,pʊt 'ɒn/ *verb* □ **to put an item on the agenda** to list an item for discussion at a meeting □ **to put an embargo on trade** to forbid trade

pyramiding /'pɪrəmɪdɪŋ/ *noun* illegally using new investors' deposits to pay the interest on the deposits made by existing investors

pyramid scheme /'pɪrəmɪd ,seliŋ/ *noun* a confidence trick which fools people into making a small investment, thinking that they will receive a large pay-out at a later stage

COMMENT: In a pyramid scheme, each investor pays in a small amount to join and is asked to recruit several new members to do the same, These new members join at the bottom, pushing earlier investors to the top of the 'pyramid' at which point they should receive a proportion of the total money invested. However, the scheme very quickly becomes unsustainable and collapses, as it relies on an endless supply of new investors.

Q

QB¹ *abbreviation* Queen's Bench

QB², **QBD** *abbreviation* Queen's Bench Division

QC *abbreviation* Queen's Counsel (NOTE: written after the surname of the lawyer: **W. Smith QC**. Note also that the plural is written **QCs**.)

qua /kwɑː/ *conjunction* as or acting in the capacity of ○ *a decision of the Lord Chancellor qua head of the judiciary*

qualified /'kwɒlɪfaɪd/ *adjective* **1.** having passed special examinations in a subject ○ *She is a qualified solicitor.* □ **highly qualified** with very good results in examinations ○ *All our staff are highly qualified.* ○ *They employ twenty-six highly qualified legal assistants.* **2.** with some reservations or conditions ○ *qualified acceptance of a bill of exchange* ○ *The plan received qualified approval from the board.*

qualified accounts /ˌkwɒlɪfaɪd ə 'kaʊnts/ *plural noun* accounts which have been commented on by the auditors because they contain something with which the auditors do not agree

qualified auditors' report /ˌkwɒlɪfaɪd 'ɔːdɪtəz rɪˌpɔːt/ *noun* a report from a company's auditors which points out areas in the accounts with which the auditors do not agree or about which they are not prepared to express an opinion

qualified privilege /ˌkwɒlɪfaɪd 'prɪvɪlɪdʒ/ *noun* protection from being sued for defamation, which is given to someone only if it can be proved that the statements were made without malice

qualified title /ˌkwɒlɪfaɪd 'taɪt(ə)l/ *noun* a title to a property which is not absolute because there is some defect

qualify /'kwɒlɪfaɪ/ *verb* **1.** □ **to qualify for** to be in the right position for or to be entitled to ○ *He does not qualify for Legal Aid.* ○ *She qualifies for unemployment benefit.* **2.** □ **to qualify as** to follow a specialised course and pass examinations so that you can do a particular job ○ *She has qualified as an accountant.* ○ *He will qualify as a solicitor next year.* **3.** to change or clarify a statement ○ *He qualified his statement by stating this he did not actually see the perpetrator's face.*

qualifying period /'kwɒlɪfaɪɪŋ ˌpɪəriəd/ *noun* a time which has to pass before something qualifies as suitable for something ○ *There is a six month qualifying period before you can get a grant from the local authority.*

quantum /'kwɒntəm/ *noun* an amount of damages ○ *Liability was admitted by the defendants, but the case went to trial because they could not agree the quantum of damages.*

quantum meruit /ˌkwæntʊm 'meruɪt/ *phrase* a Latin phrase meaning 'as much as he has deserved': a rule that, when claiming for breach of contract, a party is entitled to payment for work done

quarantine /'kwɒrəntiːn/ *noun* a period when a ship, animal or person newly arrived in a country has to be kept away from others in case there is a danger of carrying diseases ○ *The animals were put in quarantine on arrival at the port.* ○ *Quarantine restrictions have been lifted on imported animals from that country.* (NOTE: used without **the**: *The dog was put in quarantine* or *was held in quarantine* or *was released from quarantine*.) ■ *verb* to put in quarantine ○ *The ship was searched and all the animals on it were quarantined.*

quarter /'kwɔːtə/ *noun* a period of three months

quarter day /'kwɔːtə deɪ/ *noun* the day at the end of a quarter, when rents should be paid

COMMENT: In England the quarter days are 25th March (Lady Day), 24th June (Midsummer Day), 29th September (Michaelmas Day) and 25th December (Christmas Day).

quarterly /'kwɔːtəli/ *adjective, adverb* happening every three months, i.e. four times a year ○ *There is a quarterly charge for electricity.* ○ *The bank sends us a quarterly statement.* ○ *We agreed to pay the rent quarterly* or *on a quarterly basis.*

Quarter Sessions /'kwɔːtə ˌseʃ(ə)nz/ *plural noun* the old name for the criminal court replaced by the Crown Court

quash /kwɒʃ/ *verb* **1.** to stop something from continuing **2.** to announce officially that a decision is incorrect and cannot be accepted ○ *The appeal court quashed the verdict.* ○ *He applied for judicial review to quash the order.* ○ *A conviction obtained by fraud or perjury by a witness will be quashed.*

quashing order /'kwɒʃɪŋ ˌɔːdə/ *noun* an order made by a superior court to an inferior one, ordering that a case be referred to the superior court for review

quasi- /kweɪzaɪ/ *prefix* partly ○ *a quasi-official body* ○ *a quasi-judicial investigation*

quasi-contract /ˌkweɪzaɪ 'kɒntrækt/ *noun* same as **implied contract**

Queen's Bench /ˌkwiːnz 'bentʃ dɪ ˌvɪʒ(ə)n/ *noun* full form of **QB**

Queen's Bench Division /ˌkwiːnz 'bentʃ/ *noun* one of the main divisions of the High Court. Abbreviation **QBD**

Queen's Counsel /ˌkwiːnz 'kaʊnsəl/ *noun* a professional status for senior barristers and solicitors, recognised by the Crown. Abbreviation **QC**

COMMENT: The appointment of new QCs was temporarily suspended in 2003 pending a review into the selection process. Appointments are now made annually by an independent selection panel comprising both lawyers and non-lawyers, endorsed by the Law Society and Bar Council and overseen by the Secretary of State for Constitutional Affairs.

Queen's evidence /ˌkwiːnz 'evɪd(ə)ns/ *noun* □ **to turn Queen's evidence** to confess to a crime and then act as witness against the other criminals involved, in the hope of getting a lighter sentence

Queen's Proctor /ˌkwiːnz 'prɒktə/ *noun* a solicitor acting for the Crown in matrimonial and probate cases

Queen's Speech /ˌkwiːnz 'spiːtʃ/ *noun* a speech made by the Queen at the opening of a session of Parliament, which outlines the government's plans for legislation

COMMENT: The Queen's Speech is not written by the Queen herself, but by her ministers, and she is not responsible for what is in the speech.

question /'kwestʃ(ə)n/ *noun* **1.** a sentence which needs an answer ○ *Counsel asked the witness questions about his bank accounts.* ○ *Counsel for the prosecution put three questions to the police inspector.* ○ *The market research team prepared a series of questions to test the public's attitude to problems of law and order.* **2.** a problem ○ *He raised the question of the cost of the lawsuit.* ○ *The main question is that of time.* ○ *The tribunal discussed the question of redundancy payments.* ■ *verb* **1.** to ask questions ○ *The police questioned the accounts staff for four hours.* ○ *She questioned the chairman about the company's investment policy.* **2.** to query or to suggest that something may be wrong ○ *Counsel questioned the reliability of the witness' evidence.* ○ *The accused questioned the result of the breathalyser test.*

questioning /'kwestʃ(ə)nɪŋ/ *noun* the action of asking someone questions ○ *The man was taken to the police station for questioning.* ○ *During questioning by the police, she confessed to the crime.* ○ *The witness became confused during questioning by counsel for the prosecution.*

questionnaire /ˌkwestʃə'neə/ *noun* a printed list of questions given to people to answer

question of fact /ˌkwestʃ(ə)n əv 'fækt/ *noun* a fact relevant to a case which is tried at court

question of law /ˌkwestʃ(ə)n əv 'lɔː/ *noun* the law relevant to a case which is tried at court

question of privilege /ˌkwestʃ(ə)n əv 'prɪvɪlɪdʒ/ *noun* a matter which refers to the House or a member of it

quickie /'kwɪki/, **quickie divorce** /ˌkwɪki dɪ'vɔːs/ *noun* a divorce which is processed rapidly through the court by use of the special procedure

quid pro quo /ˌkwɪd prəʊ 'kwəʊ/ *phrase* a Latin phrase meaning 'one thing for another': an action done in return for something done or promised

quiet enjoyment /ˌkwaɪət ɪn'dʒɔɪmənt/ *noun* the right of an occupier to occupy property peacefully under a tenancy without the landlord or anyone else interfering with that right

quit /kwɪt/ *verb* to leave rented accommodation

quo ♦ **quid pro quo**, **status quo**

quorate /ˈkwɔːreɪt/ *adjective* having a quorum ○ *The resolution was invalid because the shareholders' meeting was not quorate.* ◊ **inquorate**

quorum /ˈkwɔːrəm/ *noun* the minimum number of people who have to be present at a meeting to make it valid □ **to have a quorum** to have enough people present for a meeting to go ahead ○ *Do we have a quorum?* ○ *The meeting was adjourned since there was no quorum.*

quota system /ˈkwəʊtə ˌsɪstəm/ *noun* a system where imports, exports or supplies are regulated by fixing maximum amounts

quote /kwəʊt/ *verb* to repeat a reference number ○ *In reply please quote this number: PC 1234.*

quoted company /ˌkwəʊtɪd ˈkʌmp(ə)ni/ *noun* a company whose shares are listed on the Stock Exchange

quo warranto /ˌkwəʊ wæˈrəntəʊ/ *phrase* a Latin phrase meaning 'by what authority': an action which questions the authority of someone

q.v., quod vide *phrase* a Latin phrase meaning 'which see': used to direct a reader to another part of a technical text for further information

R

R /ɑː/ abbreviation Regina or Rex (NOTE: used in reports of cases where the Crown is a party: *R. v. Smith Ltd*)

race /reɪs/ noun a group of people with distinct physical characteristics or culture who are considered to be different from other groups

race relations /ˌreɪs rɪˈleɪʃ(ə)nz/ plural noun the relationships between different racial groups in a country

racial /ˈreɪʃ(ə)l/ adjective referring to race

racial discrimination /ˌreɪʃ(ə)l dɪsˌkrɪmɪˈneɪʃ(ə)n/ noun unfair treatment of someone because of their racial background

racial hatred /ˌreɪʃ(ə)l ˈheɪtrɪd/ noun a violent dislike of someone because of their racial background

racial prejudice /ˌreɪʃ(ə)l ˈpredʒʊdɪs/ noun an unreasonably hostile attitude towards someone because of their racial background

racial profiling /ˌreɪʃ(ə)l ˈprəʊfaɪlɪŋ/ noun the alleged policy of some police officers to stop and question members of some ethnic groups more than others without reasonable cause

racial segregation /ˌreɪʃ(ə)l ˌsegrɪˈgeɪʃ(ə)n/ noun a policy of keeping people of different races separate in society, especially in such areas as education, housing, transport or leisure activities

racism /ˈreɪsɪz(ə)m/, **racialism** /ˈreɪʃ(ə)lɪz(ə)m/ noun a belief in racist ideas or actions based on racist ideas ○ *The minority groups have accused the council of racism in their allocation of council houses.*

racist /ˈreɪsɪst/, **racialist** /ˈreɪʃ(ə)lɪst/ adjective believing that people from other racial groups are different and should receive different and usually inferior treatment ■ noun somebody with racist ideas

racket /ˈrækɪt/ noun an illegal business which makes a lot of money by fraud ○ *He runs a cheap ticket racket.* ⟡ **protection**

racketeer /ˌrækɪˈtɪə/ noun somebody who runs a racket

racketeering /ˌrækɪˈtɪərɪŋ/ noun the activity of running an illegal racket

rack rent /ˈræk rent/ noun **1.** full yearly rent of a property let on a normal lease **2.** a very high rent

raid /reɪd/ noun a sudden attack or search ○ *Six people were arrested in the police raid on the club.* ■ verb to make a sudden attack or search ○ *The police have raided several houses in the town.* ○ *Drugs were found when the police raided the club.*

raison d'état /ˌreɪzɒn deɪˈtæ/ noun the reason for a political action, which says that an action is justified because it is for the common good

COMMENT: Raison d'état is open to criticism because it can be used to justify acts such as the abolition of individual rights, if the general good of the people may seem to require it at the time.

ransom /ˈræns(ə)m/ noun money paid to abductors to get back someone who has been abducted ○ *The daughter of the banker was held by kidnappers who asked for a ransom of £1m.* □ **to hold someone to ransom** to keep someone secretly until a ransom is paid ■ verb to pay money so that someone is released ○ *She was ransomed by her family.*

ransom note /ˈræns(ə)m nəʊt/ noun a message sent by kidnappers asking for a ransom to be paid

rap /ræp/ noun a criminal charge brought against somebody

rape /reɪp/ noun the notifiable offence of forcing a person to have sexual intercourse without their consent ○ *He was brought to court and charged with rape.* ○ *The incidence of cases of rape has increased over the last years.* ■ verb to force a person to have sexual intercourse without their consent

rapporteur /ˌræpɔː'tɜː/ *noun* one of the judges in the European Court of Justice who is assigned to a particular case and whose job it is to examine the written applications and the defence to them, and then prepare a report on the case before the court starts oral hearings

rapprochement /ræ'prɒʃmɒŋ/ *noun* a French word meaning 'coming closer': used to refer to a situation where two parties reach an understanding after a period of tension ○ *Political commentators have noted the rapprochement which has been taking place since the old president died.*

rate /reɪt/ *verb* □ **to rate someone highly** to value someone, to think someone is very good

rateable value /ˌreɪtəb(ə)l 'væljuː/ *noun* the value of a property as a basis for calculating local taxes

rate of inflation /ˌreɪt əv ɪn'fleɪʃ(ə)n/ *noun* a percentage increase in prices over the period of one year

rate of return /ˌreɪt əv rɪ't3ːn/ *noun* the amount of interest or dividend which comes from an investment, shown as a percentage of the money invested

rates /reɪts/ *plural noun* local tax on property

ratification /ˌrætɪfɪ'keɪʃ(ə)n/ *noun* official approval of something which then becomes legally binding

ratify /'rætɪfaɪ/ *verb* to approve officially something which has already been agreed ○ *The treaty was ratified by Congress.* ○ *The agreement has to be ratified by the board.* ○ *Although the directors had acted without due authority, the company ratified their actions.*

ratio decidendi /ˌrætɪəʊ ˌdeɪsɪ'dendi/ *phrase* a Latin phrase meaning 'reason for deciding': the main part of a court judgment setting out the legal principles applicable to the case and forming the binding part of the judgment to which other courts must pay regard. ◊ **obiter dicta**

ratio legis /ˌrætɪəʊ 'ledʒɪs/ *phrase* a Latin phrase meaning 'reason of the law': the principle behind a law

RCJ *abbreviation* Royal Courts of Justice

re /riː/ *preposition* about, concerning, or referring to ○ *re: your inquiry of May 29th* ○ *re: Smith's memorandum of yesterday* ○ *re: the agenda for the AGM* □ **in re** concerning, in the case of ○ *in re Jones & Co. Ltd* ◊ **res**

re- /riː/ *prefix* again

rea ◆ **mens rea**

reading /'riːdɪŋ/ *noun* **1.** □ **First Reading, Second Reading, Third Reading** the three stages of discussion of a Bill in Parliament **2.** (*in the EU*) an examination in detail of proposed legislation by the European Parliament

COMMENT: First Reading is the formal presentation of the Bill when the title is read to MPs; Second Reading is the stage when MPs have printed copies of the Bill and it is explained by the Minister proposing it, there is a debate and a vote is taken; the Bill is then discussed in Committee and at the Report Stage; Third Reading is the final discussion of the Bill in the whole House of Commons or House of Lords. European legislation is placed before the European Parliament for discussion. This is the First Reading, and can be decided by a simple majority in the Parliament. If the Council of the European Union sets out a common position on proposed legislation and communicates this to Parliament, Parliament will consider the proposal and may approve it by an absolute majority of its members.

ready money /ˌredi 'mʌni/ *noun* money which is immediately available

real /rɪəl/ *adjective* **1.** not imitation □ **in real terms** actually or really ○ *Sales have gone up by 3% but with inflation running at 5% that is a fall in real terms.* **2.** referring to things as opposed to persons **3.** referring to land, especially freehold land

real estate /'rɪəl ɪˌsteɪt/ *noun* land or buildings considered from a legal point of view

real income /ˌrɪəl 'ɪnkʌm/ *noun* income which is available for spending after tax and any other deductions have been made

realisable assets /ˌrɪəlaɪzəb(ə)l 'æsets/ *plural noun* assets which can be sold for money

realisation /ˌrɪəlaɪ'zeɪʃ(ə)n/ *noun* the process of making something happen □ **the realisation of a project** putting a plan into action

realisation of assets /ˌrɪəlaɪzeɪʃ(ə)n əv 'æsets/ *noun* the selling of assets for money

realise /'rɪəlaɪz/, **realize** *verb* **1.** to make something become real □ **to realise a project** to put a project into action **2.** to sell something to produce money ○ *to realise property* or *assets* ○ *The sale realised £100,000.*

realpolitik /reɪˈɑːlpɒlɪtɪk/ *noun* a German word meaning 'politics based on real and practical factors and not on moral ideas'

realty /ˈrɪəlti/ *noun* property, real estate or legal rights to land

reasonable /ˈriːz(ə)nəb(ə)l/ *adjective* fair and sensible ○ *The magistrates were very reasonable when she explained that the driving licence was necessary for her work.* □ **no reasonable offer refused** we will accept any offer which is not too low

reasonable doubt /ˌriːz(ə)nəb(ə)l ˈdaʊt/ *noun* □ **beyond reasonable doubt** a phrase describing the almost certain proof needed to convict a person in a criminal case ○ *The prosecution in a criminal case has to establish beyond reasonable doubt that the accused committed the crime.*

reasonable financial provision /ˌriːz(ə)nəb(ə)l faɪˌnænʃəl prəˈvɪʒ(ə)n/ *noun* a provision which relatives and dependants of a deceased person may ask a court to provide in cases where the deceased died intestate, or where no provision was made for them under the will. Abbreviation **RFP**

reasonable force /ˌriːz(ə)nəb(ə)l ˈfɔːs/ *noun* the least amount of force needed to do something ○ *The police were instructed to use reasonable force in dealing with the riot.*

reasonable man /ˈriːz(ə)nəb(ə)l mæn/ *noun* an imaginary person with average judgement and intelligence, who is used as a reference point for usually expected standards of social behaviour

reasoned /ˈriːz(ə)nd/ *adjective* carefully thought out and explained ○ *reasoned argument*

rebel /ˈreb(ə)l/ *noun* somebody who fights against the government or against people in authority ○ *Anti-government rebels have taken six towns.* ○ *Rebel councillors forced a vote.* ■ *verb* to fight against authority ○ *Some teachers have threatened to rebel against the new procedures.* ○ *It's natural for teenagers to rebel but this has got out of hand.* (NOTE: **rebelling – rebelled**)

rebut /rɪˈbʌt/ *verb* to contradict or to go against ○ *He attempted to rebut the assertions made by the prosecution witness.* (NOTE: **rebutting – rebutted**)

rebuttable /rɪˈbʌtəb(ə)l/ *adjective* being able to be rebutted

rebuttal /rɪˈbʌt(ə)l/ *noun* the act of rebutting

recall¹ /rɪˈkɔːl/ *verb* to remember ○ *The witness could not recall having seen the papers.*

recall² /rɪˈkɔːl/ *noun* a request for someone to come back again ■ *verb* to ask someone to come back ○ *MPs are asking for Parliament to be recalled to debate the financial crisis.* ○ *The witness was recalled to the witness box.*

recd *abbreviation* received

receipt /rɪˈsiːt/ *verb* to stamp or sign something such as a document to show that it has been received or an invoice to show that it has been paid

receipt in due form /rɪˌsiːt ɪn djuː ˈfɔːm/ *noun* a correctly written receipt

receipts /rɪˈsiːts/ *plural noun* money taken in sales ○ *to itemise receipts and expenditure* ○ *Receipts are down against the same period of last year.*

receivable /rɪˈsiːvəb(ə)l/ *adjective* being able to be received

receivables /rɪˈsiːvəb(ə)lz/ *plural noun* money which is owed to a company

receive /rɪˈsiːv/ *verb* □ **receiving stolen goods** the crime of taking in and disposing of property which you know to be stolen

receiver /rɪˈsiːvə/ *noun* **1.** someone appointed by a court to manage a business or property that is involved in a legal process such as bankruptcy **2.** somebody who receives stolen goods and disposes of them

receiver of wrecks /rɪˌsiːvər əv ˈreks/ *noun* an official of the Department of Trade who deals with legal problems of wrecked ships within his or her area

receivership /rɪˈsiːvəʃɪp/ *noun* administration of a company by a receiver □ **to go into receivership** of a company, to be put into the hands of a receiver

receiving /rɪˈsiːvɪŋ/ *noun* the act of taking something which has been delivered □ **receiving stolen property** the crime of taking in and disposing of goods which are known to be stolen

receiving clerk /rɪˈsiːvɪŋ klɑːk/ *noun* an official who works in a receiving office

receiving department /rɪˈsiːvɪŋ dɪˌpɑːtmənt/ *noun* the section of a company which deals with goods or payments which are received by the company

receiving office /rɪˈsiːvɪŋ ˌɒfɪs/ *noun* an office where goods or payments are received

receiving order /rɪˈsiːvɪŋ ˌɔːdə/ *noun* a court order made placing the Official

Receiver in charge of a person's assets before a bankruptcy order is made

receiving party /rɪˌsiːvɪŋ ˈpɑːti/ *noun* a party who is entitled to be paid costs (NOTE: The other party is the **paying party**.)

recess /rɪˈses/ *noun* **1.** a period when the court does not meet, but is not formally adjourned **2.** a period when an official body is not sitting ○ *The last meeting before the summer recess will be on 23rd July.* ■ *verb* not to meet, but without formally adjourning ○ *The Senate recessed at the end of the afternoon.*

recidivist /rɪˈsɪdɪvɪst/ *noun* a criminal who commits a crime again

reciprocal /rɪˈsɪprək(ə)l/ *adjective* according to an arrangement by which each party involved agrees to benefit the other in the same way

reciprocal holdings /rɪˌsɪprək(ə)l ˈhəʊldɪŋz/ *plural noun* a situation where two companies own shares in each other to prevent takeover bids

reciprocal trade /rɪˌsɪprək(ə)l ˈtreɪd/ *noun* trade between two countries

reciprocal wills /rɪˈsɪprək(ə)l wɪlz/ *plural noun* wills in which two people, usually husband and wife, leave their property to each other

reciprocate /rɪˈsɪprəkeɪt/ *verb* to do the same thing to someone as he or she has just done to you ○ *They offered us an exclusive agency for their cars and we reciprocated with an offer of the agency for our buses.*

reciprocity /ˌresɪˈprɒsɪti/ *noun* an arrangement which applies from one party to another and vice versa

recitals /rɪˈsaɪt(ə)lz/ *plural noun* an introduction to a deed or conveyance which sets out the main purpose and the parties to it

reckless /ˈrekləs/ *adjective* taking a risk knowing that the action may be dangerous

reckless driving /ˌrekləs ˈdraɪvɪŋ/ *noun* the offence of driving a vehicle in such a way that it may cause damage to property or injure people, where the driver is unaware of causing a risk to other people

recklessly /ˈrekləsli/ *adverb* taking risks and being unaware of the likely effect on other people ○ *The company recklessly spent millions of pounds on a new factory.* ○ *He was accused of acting recklessly.*

recklessness /ˈrekləsnəs/ *noun* the act of taking risks

reclaim /rɪˈkleɪm/ *verb* to claim back money which has been paid earlier

reclassification /ˌriːklæsɪfɪˈkeɪʃ(ə)n/ *noun* the act of changing the class of a drug, making possessing or dealing it a greater or lesser crime than before

recognisance /rɪˈkɒgnɪz(ə)ns/ *noun* an obligation undertaken by someone to a court that he, she or someone else will appear in the court at a later date to answer charges, or if not, will pay a penalty ○ *He was bound over on his own recognizance of £4,000.*

recognise /ˈrekəgnaɪz/, **recognize** *verb* **1.** to know someone or something because you have seen or heard them before ○ *She recognised the man who attacked her.* ○ *I recognised his voice before he said who he was.* ○ *Do you recognise the handwriting on the letter?* **2.** to approve something as being legal □ **to recognise a government** to say that a government which has taken power in a foreign country is the legal government of that country □ **the prisoner refused to recognise the jurisdiction of the court** the prisoner said that he or she did not believe that the court had the legal right to try them

recognised agent /ˌrekəgnaɪzd ˈeɪdʒənt/ *noun* an agent who is approved by the company for which he or she acts

recommendation /ˌrekəmenˈdeɪʃ(ə)n/ *noun* a piece of advice about how something should be done ○ *He was sentenced to life imprisonment, with a recommendation that he should serve at least twenty years.* ○ *He was released on the recommendation of the Parole Board* or *on the Parole Board's recommendation.*

recommendations /ˌrekəmenˈdeɪʃ(ə)nz/ *noun* a decision of the European Community which is not legally binding

recommittal /ˌriːkəˈmɪt(ə)l/ *noun* US the act of sending a bill back to a committee for further discussion

reconcile /ˈrekənsaɪl/ *verb* to make two accounts or statements agree ○ *to reconcile one account with another* ○ *to reconcile the accounts*

reconciliation /ˌrekənsɪliˈeɪʃ(ə)n/ *noun* the act of making two accounts, parties or statements agree

reconciliation statement /ˌrekənsɪliˈeɪʃ(ə)n ˌsteɪtmənt/ *noun* a statement which explains why two accounts do not agree

reconsider /ˌriːkənˈsɪdə/ *verb* to think again ○ *The applicant asked the committee to reconsider its decision to refuse the* *application.* □ **motion to reconsider a vote** *US* a motion at the end of a discussion of any bill, but especially one passed with a close vote, so that a second vote has to be taken to settle the matter

reconstruction of a crime /ˌriːkən ˈstrʌkʃən əv eɪ kraɪm/ *noun* recreating a crime using actors, in order to try to get witnesses to remember details of it

reconsultation /riːˌkɒnsəlˈteɪʃ(ə)n/ *noun* the act of consulting again, as when the Council of the European Union looks again at proposed legislation, taking into account objections raised by the European Parliament

reconvict /ˌriːkənˈvɪkt/ *verb* to convict someone again who has previously been convicted of a crime

reconviction /ˌriːkənˈvɪkʃ(ə)n/ *noun* the conviction of someone who has been previously convicted of a crime ○ *The reconviction rate is rising.* □ **reconviction rates** how many criminals are being convicted for the second time or more

record /ˈrekɔːd/ *noun* **1.** a report of something which has happened, especially an official transcript of a court action ○ *The chairman signed the minutes as a true record of the last meeting.* □ **a matter of record** something which has been written down and can be confirmed □ **for the record** a phrase used to officially note something that has been done □ **to set the record straight** to correct a mistake or wrong impression □ **on record** taken as the official version of events ○ *The chairman is on record as saying that profits are set to rise.* **2.** a description of what has happened in the past ○ *the clerk's record of service* or *service record* ○ *the company's record in industrial relations* **3.** a result which is better or higher than anything before □ **record crime figures, record losses, record profits** crime figures, losses or profits which are higher than ever before ■ *verb* /rɪˈkɔːd/ to note or to report ○ *The company has recorded another year of increased sales.* ○ *Your complaint has been recorded and will be investigated.* ○ *The court recorded a plea of not guilty.* ○ *The coroner recorded a verdict of death by misadventure.*

recorder /rɪˈkɔːdə/ *noun* a part-time judge of the Crown Court

Recorder of London /rɪˌkɔːdə əv ˈlʌndən/ *noun* the chief judge of the Central Criminal Court

records /ˈrekɔːdz/ *plural noun* documents which give information ○ *The names of customers are kept in the company's records.* ○ *We find from our records that our invoice number 1234 has not been paid.*

recours ♦ **sans recours**

recourse /rɪˈkɔːs/ *noun* □ **to decide to have recourse to the courts** to decide in the end to start legal proceedings

recover /rɪˈkʌvə/ *verb* **1.** to get back something which has been lost ○ *to recover damages from the driver of the car* ○ *to start a court action to recover property* ○ *He never recovered his money.* ○ *The initial investment was never recovered.* **2.** to get better or to rise ○ *She's still recovering after the attack.* ○ *The stock market fell in the morning, but recovered during the afternoon.*

recoverable /rɪˈkʌv(ə)rəb(ə)l/ *adjective* being possible to get back ○ *Your costs may be recoverable if you win your case.*

recovery /rɪˈkʌv(ə)ri/ *noun* **1.** the process of getting back something which has been lost or stolen ○ *to start an action for recovery of property* ○ *We are aiming for the complete recovery of the money invested.* **2.** the movement upwards of shares or of the economy ○ *the recovery of the economy after a recession* ○ *The economy showed signs of a recovery.*

rectification /ˌrektɪfɪˈkeɪʃ(ə)n/ *noun* the process of making changes to a document or register to make it correct

rectify /ˈrektɪfaɪ/ *verb* **1.** to make changes to a document to make it correct ○ *The court rectified its mistake.* **2.** to make something correct

recusal /rɪˈkjuːz(ə)l/ *noun* the disqualification of a judge or jury because of bias

red bag /ˌred ˈbæg/ *noun* the bag in which a barrister carries his or her gown, given them by a QC. ◊ **blue bag**

red box /ˌred ˈbɒks/ *noun* a large briefcase covered in red leather in which government papers are delivered to ministers

redeem /rɪˈdiːm/ *verb* **1.** to pay back all the principal and interest on a loan, a debt or a mortgage **2.** □ **to redeem a bond** to sell a bond for cash

redeemable /rɪˈdiːməb(ə)l/ *adjective* being possible to sell for cash

redemption /rɪˈdempʃən/ *noun* **1.** the repayment of a loan □ **redemption before due date** paying back a loan before the date when repayment is due **2.** the repayment of a debt or a mortgage

redemption date /rɪ'dempʃən deɪt/ noun the date on which a loan, etc., is due to be repaid

redemption value /rɪ'dempʃən ˌvæljuː/ noun the value of a security when redeemed

red tape /ˌred 'teɪp/ noun **1.** a red ribbon used to tie up a pile of legal documents ○ *The application has been held up by red tape.* **2.** unhelpful rules which slow down administrative work

reduced /rɪ'djuːst/ adjective lower ○ *He received a reduced sentence on appeal.*

redundancy /rɪ'dʌndənsi/ noun a state where someone is no longer employed, because the job being done is no longer needed

redundancy payment /rɪ'dʌndənsi ˌpeɪmənt/ noun a payment made to an employee to compensate for losing his or her job

redundant /rɪ'dʌndənt/ adjective **1.** more than is needed **2.** useless **3.** something which is no longer needed ○ *a redundant clause in a contract* ○ *This law is now redundant.* ○ *The new legislation has made clause 6 redundant.* **4.** □ **to make someone redundant** to decide that an employee is not needed any more

redundant staff /rɪˌdʌndənt 'stɑːf/ noun staff who have lost their jobs because they are not needed any more

re-entry /ˌriː 'entri/ noun the act of going back into a property

re-examination /ˌriː ɪɡˌzæmɪ'neɪʃən/ noun the activity of asking a witness more questions after cross-examination by counsel for the other party

re-examine /ˌriːɪɡ'zæmɪn/ verb **1.** to look again at something ○ *The judge decided to re-examine the evidence.* **2.** (of a barrister) to ask his or her own witness more questions after the witness has been cross-examined by counsel for the other party

refer /rɪ'fɜː/ verb **1.** to mention, deal with or write about something ○ *referring to the court order dated June 4th* ○ *We refer to your letter of May 26th.* ○ *He referred to an article which he had seen in 'The Times'.* □ **the schedule before referred to** the schedule which has been mentioned before **2.** to pass a problem on to someone else to decide ○ *to refer a question to a committee* ○ *We have referred your complaint to the tribu-*

nal. **3.** □ **'refer to drawer'** words written on a cheque which a bank refuses to pay **4.** (in the EU) to pass a case to the ECJ for a ruling (NOTE: **referring – referred**)

referee /ˌrefə'riː/ noun **1.** somebody who can give a report on someone's character, ability or speed of work, etc. ○ *to give someone's name as referee* ○ *She gave the name of her boss as a referee.* ○ *When applying please give the names of three referees.* **2.** somebody to whom a problem is passed for a decision ○ *The question of maintenance payments is with a court-appointed referee.*

reference /'ref(ə)rəns/ noun **1.** the act of passing a problem to a someone for his or her opinion **2.** a comment that mentions someone or something □ **with reference to** used to introduce something that will be talked or written about ○ *with reference to your letter of 18th August* **3.** the numbers or letters given to a document which make it possible to find it after it has been filed ○ *our reference: SJ/JA 134* ○ *Thank you for your letter (reference MA 25.2).* ○ *Please quote this reference in all correspondence.* ○ *When replying please quote reference GS/km 264.* **4.** a written report on someone's character, ability, etc. ○ *to write someone a reference* or *to give someone a reference* ○ *to ask applicants to supply references* **5.** □ **to hear a reference** (of the ECJ) to discuss a legal point which has been referred to them □ **to make a reference** (of a national court) to ask the ECJ to decide on a legal point. ◊ **preliminary reference 6.** somebody who reports on someone's character, ability, etc. ○ *to give someone's name as reference* ○ *Please use me as a reference if you wish.*

referral /rɪ'fɜːrəl/ noun **1.** the act of passing a problem on to someone else for a decision ○ *the referral of the case to the planning committee* **2.** (in the EU) the action of referring a case to the ECJ

reflag /riː'flæɡ/ verb to register a ship in a different country, giving it the right to fly a different flag

reform /rɪ'fɔːm/ noun a change made to something to make it better ○ *They have signed an appeal for the reform of the remand system.* ○ *The reform in the legislation was intended to make the court procedure more straightforward.* ■ verb to change something to make it better ○ *The group is pressing for the prison system to be reformed.* ○ *The prisoner has committed so many crimes of violence that he will never be reformed.* □ **reformed criminal** a person who has committed crimes in the past, but will not offend again

refrain /rɪˈfreɪn/ *verb* □ **to refrain from something** to agree not to do something which you were doing previously ○ *He was asked to give an undertaking to refrain from political activity.*

refresher /rɪˈfreʃə/ *noun* a fee paid to counsel for the second and subsequent days of a hearing ○ *Counsel's brief fee was £1,000 with refreshers of £250.*

regard /rɪˈɡɑːd/ *noun* □ **having regard to, as regards, regarding** concerning a particular subject ○ *having regard to the opinion of the European Parliament* ○ *Regarding the second of the accused, the jury was unable to reach a majority verdict.*

regarding /rɪˈɡɑːdɪŋ/ *preposition* concerning a particular subject ○ *I wrote last week regarding my appointment.*

regardless /rɪˈɡɑːdləs/ *adverb* □ **regardless of** without concerning ○ *Such conduct constitutes contempt of court regardless of intent.* ○ *The court takes a serious view of such crimes, regardless of the age of the accused.*

regime /reɪˈʒiːm/ *noun* (*sometimes as criticism*) **1.** a type of government ○ *Under a military regime, civil liberties may be severely curtailed.* **2.** a period of rule ○ *Life was better under the previous regime.*

Regina /rɪˈdʒaɪnə/ *noun* a Latin word meaning 'the Queen': the Crown or state, as a party in legal proceedings (NOTE: In written reports, usually abbreviated to **R**: *the case of R. v. Smith.*)

register /ˈredʒɪstə/ *noun* an official list ○ *to enter something in a register* ○ *to keep a register up to date* ■ *verb* to write something in an official list or record ○ *to register a company* ○ *to register a sale* ○ *to register a property* ○ *to register a trademark* ○ *to register a marriage* or *a death*

registered /ˈredʒɪstəd/ *adjective* having been noted on an official list □ **a company's registered office** the address of a company which is officially registered with the Registrar of Companies and to which specific legal documents must normally be sent

registered company /ˌredʒɪstəd ˈkʌmp(ə)ni/ *noun* a company which has been properly formed and incorporated

Registered European Lawyer /ˌredʒɪstəd ˌjʊərəpiən ˈlɔːjə/ *noun* a lawyer from an EU Member State registered with the Solicitors Regulation Authority to practice in England and Wales. Abbreviation **REL**

registered land /ˈredʒɪstəd lænd/ *noun* land which has been registered with the land registry

registered office /ˌredʒɪstəd ˈɒfɪs/ *noun* in Britain, the office address of a company which is officially registered with the Companies' Registrar and to which legal documents must normally be sent

registered trade mark /ˌredʒɪstəd ˈtreɪd ˌmɑːk/ *noun* a name, design or other feature which identifies a commercial product, has been registered by the maker and cannot be used by other makers ○ *You cannot call your beds 'Soft and kumfi' – it is a registered trademark.*

registered user /ˌredʒɪstəd ˈjuːzə/ *noun* a person or company which has been officially given a licence to use a registered trademark

register of charges /ˌredʒɪstə əv ˈtʃɑːdʒɪz/ *noun* an index of charges affecting land

register of debentures /ˌredʒɪstə əv dɪˈbentʃʊəz/ *noun* a list of debentures over a company's assets

register of directors /ˌredʒɪstər əv daɪˈrektəz/ *noun* an official list of the directors of a company which has to be sent to the Registrar of Companies

register of electors /ˌredʒɪstər əv ɪˈlektəz/ *noun* an official list of names and addresses of people living in a specific area who are eligible to vote in local or national elections

Register Office /ˌredʒɪstə ˈɒfɪs/ *noun* a local office where records of births, marriages and deaths are kept and where civil marriages can be performed

Register of Judgments, Orders and Fines /ˌredʒɪstə əv ˌdʒʌdʒmənts ˌɔːdəz ən ˈfaɪnz/ *noun* a national office that holds a register of all UK county court and High Court judgments

registrar /ˌredʒɪˈstrɑː/ *noun* **1.** somebody who keeps official records **2.** an official of a court who can hear preliminary arguments in civil cases **3.** the head of the registry of the European Court of Justice, who is the manager of the court and maintains the files of all pleadings

Registrar-General /ˌredʒɪstrɑːˈdʒen(ə)rəl/ *noun* an official who is responsible for the process of registering all births, marriages and deaths

Registrar of Companies /ˌredʒɪstrɑː əv ˈkʌmp(ə)niz/ *noun* an official who keeps a record of all incorporated companies, the details of their directors and financial state

registrar of trademarks /ˌredʒɪstrɑː əv ˌtreɪdˈmɑːks/ *noun* an official who keeps a record of all trademarks

registration /ˌredʒɪˈstreɪʃ(ə)n/ *noun* the act of having something noted on an official list ○ *registration of a trademark*

registration fee /ˌredʒɪˈstreɪʃ(ə)n fiː/ *noun* **1.** money paid to have something registered **2.** money paid to attend a conference

registration number /ˌredʒɪˈstreɪʃ(ə)n ˌnʌmbə/ *noun* the official number of something which has been registered such as a car

registry /ˈredʒɪstri/ *noun* **1.** a place where official records are kept **2.** the registering of a ship **3.** (*in the EU*) an office which administers the ECJ

regulate /ˈregjuleɪt/ *verb* **1.** to adjust something so that it works well or is correct **2.** to change or maintain something by law □ **to regulate something by supply and demand** to increase or decrease the amount of something according to supply and demand

regulation /ˌregjuˈleɪʃ(ə)n/ *noun* the act of making sure that something will work well ○ *the regulation of trading practices*

regulations /ˌregjuˈleɪʃ(ə)nz/ *plural noun* **1.** rules made by ministers, which then have to be submitted to Parliament for approval ○ *the new government regulations on standards for electrical goods* ○ *safety regulations which apply to places of work* ○ *regulations concerning imports and exports* **2.** rules laid down by the Council or Commission of the European Communities, according to the European Union treaties, which are binding on all Member States of the EU without any implementing legislation being passed. Compare **directive**

COMMENT: Regulations are binding on people in general as citizens of Member States of the EU; they have a direct effect on all Member States and on all citizens of Member States.

regulatory /ˈregjulət(ə)ri/ *adjective* making something work according to law ○ *The independent radio and television companies are supervised by a regulatory body.* ○ *Complaints are referred to several regulatory bodies.*

regulatory system /ˈregjulət(ə)ri ˌsɪstəm/ *noun* a system of laws, procedures and supervisory bodies governing the production and sale of something

rehabilitate /ˌriːəˈbɪlɪteɪt/ *verb* to help a criminal become a responsible member of society again

rehabilitation /ˌriːəbɪlɪˈteɪʃ(ə)n/ *noun* the process of making someone fit to be a member of society again □ **rehabilitation of offenders** the principle whereby a person convicted of a crime and being of good character after a period of time is treated as if he or she had not had a conviction

rehabilitation period /ˌriːəbɪlɪˈteɪʃ(ə)n ˌpɪəriəd/ the length of time that an offender must pass without reoffending after their sentence is served

COMMENT: Under the Rehabilitation of Offenders Act 1974, a person who is convicted of an offence, and then completes their rehabilitation period without committing any other offence, is not required to reveal that he has a previous conviction (the conviction is considered **spent**.)

rehear /riːˈhɪə/ *verb* to hear a case again when the first hearing was in some way invalid

rehearing /riːˈhɪərɪŋ/ *noun* the hearing of a case again

reinsurance /ˌriːɪnˈʃʊərəns/ *noun* insurance where a second insurer (the reinsurer) agrees to cover part of the risk insured by the first insurer

reject /rɪˈdʒekt/ *verb* **1.** to refuse to accept something ○ *The appeal was rejected by the House of Lords.* ○ *The magistrate rejected a request from the defendant.* **2.** to say that something is not satisfactory

rejection /rɪˈdʒekʃən/ *noun* a refusal to accept ○ *the rejection of the defendant's request* ○ *the rejection of the appeal by the tribunal*

rejoinder /rɪˈdʒɔɪndə/ *noun* formerly, a plea served in answer to a claimant's reply

REL *abbreviation* Registered European Lawyer

related /rɪˈleɪtɪd/ *adjective* connected, linked, being of the same family ○ *offences related to drugs* or *drug-related offences* ○ *the law which relates to drunk driving*

related company /rɪˌleɪtɪd ˈkʌmp(ə)ni/ *noun* a company which is partly owned by another company

relation /rɪˈleɪʃ(ə)n/ *noun* **1.** □ **in relation to** referring to or connected with ○ *documents in relation to the case* ○ *the court's* *powers in relation to children in care* **2.** a procedure by which, for legal purposes, an act is deemed to have been done at an earlier time than was actually the case ■ *plural noun* **1. relations** links with other people or other groups. ◊ **industrial relations 2.** □ **to enter into relations with someone** to start discussing a business deal with someone □ **to break off relations with someone** to stop dealing with someone

relation back /rɪˈleɪʃ(ə)n bæk/ *noun* the ability of the administrator of an estate to take action to recover funds which were removed from the estate in the interval between the death and the grant of administration

relationship of care /rɪˌleɪʃ(ə)nʃɪp əv ˈkeə/ *noun* a situation in which one person is caring for another with a mental disability, often a spouse or family member

relator /rɪˈleɪtə/ *noun* a private person who suggests to the Attorney-General that proceedings should be brought, usually against a public body

release /rɪˈliːs/ *noun* **1.** an act of setting someone free, or allowing someone to leave prison **2.** the abandoning of rights by someone in favour of someone else ■ *verb* **1.** to free someone or something, or allow someone to leave prison ○ *The president released the opposition leader from prison.* ○ *Customs released the goods against payment of a fine.* □ **to release someone from a debt** to make someone no longer liable for a debt □ **to release someone from a contract** to make someone no longer bound by a contract **2.** to make something public ○ *The company released information about the new mine in Australia.* ○ *The government has refused to release figures for the number of unemployed women.*

release on licence /rɪˌliːs ɒn ˈlaɪs(ə)ns/ *noun* permission to leave prison on parole ○ *The appellant will be released on licence after eight months.*

release on recognizance /rɪˌliːs ɒn rɪ ˈkɒɡnɪz(ə)ns/ *noun US* the release of an accused person, provided that he or she promises to come back to court when asked to do so. Abbreviation **ROR**

relevance /ˈreləv(ə)ns/ *noun* a connection with a subject being discussed ○ *Counsel argued with the judge over the relevance of the documents to the case.*

relevant /ˈreləv(ə)nt/ *adjective* having to do with what is being discussed ○ *The question is not relevant to the case.* ○ *Which is*

the relevant government department? ○ *Can you give me the relevant papers?*

reliable /rɪˈlaɪəb(ə)l/ *adjective* being trustworthy ○ *He is a reliable witness* or *the witness is completely reliable.* ○ *The police have reliable information about the gang's movements.*

relief /rɪˈliːf/ *noun* a remedy sought by a claimant in a legal action ○ *The relief the claimant sought was an injunction and damages.*

rem /rem/ ◆ **in rem**

remainder /rɪˈmeɪndə/ *noun* **1.** something left behind ○ *The remainder of the stock will be sold off at half price.* **2.** what is left of an estate, or the right to an estate which will return to the owner at the end of a lease ■ *verb* □ **to remainder stock** to sell unsold stock off cheaply

remainderman /rɪˈmeɪndəmən/ *noun* somebody who receives the remainder of an estate

remand /rɪˈmɑːnd/ *noun* the act of sending a prisoner away for a time when a case is adjourned to be heard at a later date ■ *verb* **1.** to send a prisoner away to reappear later to answer a case which has been adjourned □ **to be remanded in custody** to be sent to prison while waiting for trial □ **to be remanded on bail** to be allowed to go free on payment of bail while waiting for trial **2.** *US* to send a case back to a lower court after a higher court has given an opinion on it

remand centre /rɪˈmɑːnd ˌsentə/ *noun* a special prison for keeping young persons who have been remanded in custody

remedy /ˈremədi/ *noun* a way of repairing harm or damage suffered ○ *The claimant is seeking remedy through the courts.* ■ *verb* to help repair harm or damage

remission /rɪˈmɪʃ(ə)n/ *noun* the reduction of a prison sentence ○ *He was sentenced to five years, but should serve only three with remission.* ○ *She got six months' remission for good behaviour.*

remit *noun* /ˈriːmɪt/ an area of responsibility given to someone ○ *This department can do nothing on the case as it is not part of our remit* or *it is beyond our remit.* ■ *verb* /rɪ ˈmɪt/ **1.** to reduce a prison sentence **2.** to send money ○ *to remit by cheque* (NOTE: **remitting – remitted**)

remittance /rɪˈmɪt(ə)ns/ *noun* money that is sent ○ *Please send remittances to the treasurer.* ○ *The family lives on a weekly remittance from their father in the USA.*

remote /rɪˈməʊt/ *adjective* too far to be connected ○ *The court decided that the damage was too remote to be recoverable by the claimant.*

remoteness /rɪˈməʊtnəs/ *noun* the fact of not being connected or relevant to something □ **remoteness of damage** the legal principle that damage that is insufficiently connected or foreseeable by a defendant should not make the defendant liable to the claimant

remuneration certificate /rɪˌmjuːnə ˈreɪʃ(ə)n səˌtɪfɪkət/ *noun* a certificate issued by the Solicitors Regulation Authority approving the level of a solicitor's fees

render /ˈrendə/ *verb* **1.** to provide something **2.** to make someone or something become something ○ *Failure to observe the conditions of bail renders the accused liable to arrest.* ○ *The state of health of the witness renders his appearance in court impossible.* **3.** to officially announce a judgment or verdict ○ *The jury rendered a guilty verdict.*

rendition /renˈdɪʃ(ə)n/ *noun* the transfer of a person from one state to another, e.g. by extradition, deportation or extraordinary rendition

renew /rɪˈnjuː/ *verb* to grant something again so that it continues for a further period of time ○ *to renew a bill of exchange* or *to renew a lease* □ **to renew a subscription** to pay a subscription for another year □ **to renew an insurance policy** to pay the premium for another year's insurance

renewal /rɪˈnjuːəl/ *noun* the act of renewing ○ *renewal of a lease* or *of a subscription* or *of a bill* ○ *The lease is up for renewal next month.* ○ *When is the renewal date of the bill?*

renewal notice /rɪˈnjuːəl ˌnəʊtɪs/ *noun* a note sent by an insurance company asking the insured person to renew the insurance

renewal premium /rɪˈnjuːəl ˌpriːmiəm/ *noun* a premium to be paid to renew an insurance

renounce /rɪˈnaʊns/ *verb* to give up a right or a planned action ○ *The government has renounced the use of force in dealing with international terrorists.*

rent /rent/ *noun* money paid, or occasionally a service provided, in return for using something such as an office, house, factory, car or piece of equipment for a period of time

rent action /ˈrent ˌækʃən/ *noun* proceedings to obtain payment of rent owing

rental /ˈrent(ə)l/ *noun* money paid to use something such as an office, house, factory, car or piece of equipment for a period of time

rental income /ˈrent(ə)l ˌɪnkʌm/ *noun* income from letting property

rent allowance /ˈrent əˌlaʊəns/ *noun* same as **housing benefit**

rental value /ˈrent(ə)l ˌvæljuː/ *noun* the full value of the rent for a property if it were charged at the current market rate, i.e. calculated between rent reviews

rentcharge /ˈrenttʃɑːdʒ/ *noun* same as **ground rent**

rent controls /ˈrent kənˌtrəʊlz/ *plural noun* government regulation of rents charged by landlords

rent rebate /ˈrent ˌriːbeɪt/ *noun* same as **housing benefit**

rent review /ˈrent rɪˌvjuː/ *noun* an increase in rent which is carried out during the term of a lease (NOTE: Most leases allow for rent to be reviewed every three or five years.)

rent tribunal /ˈrent traɪˌbjuːn(ə)l/ *noun* a court which adjudicates in disputes about rents and awards fair rents

renunciation /rɪˌnʌnsiˈeɪʃ(ə)n/ *noun* the act of giving up a right, especially the ownership of shares

reoffend /ˌriːəˈfend/ *verb* to commit an offence again ○ *He came out of prison and immediately reoffended.*

reoffender /ˌriːəˈfendə/ *noun* somebody who commits an offence again

reopen /riːˈəʊpən/ *verb* **1.** to start investigating a case again ○ *After receiving new evidence, the police have reopened the murder inquiry.* **2.** to start an activity such as a hearing or inquiry again ○ *The hearing reopened on Monday afternoon.*

reorganisation /riːˌɔːɡənaɪˈzeɪʃ(ə)n/, **reorganization** *noun* the action of organising a company in a different way (NOTE: In the USA, a bankrupt company applies to be treated under Chapter 11 to be protected from its creditors while it is being reorganised.)

repairer's lien /rɪˈpeərəz ˌliːn/ *noun* the right of someone who has been carrying out repairs to keep the goods until the repair bill has been paid

Reparation Order /ˌrepəˈreɪʃ(ə)n ˌɔːdə/ *noun* a community order which requires the offender to put right the damage they have done, e.g. by cleaning up graffiti

repatriate /riːˈpætrieɪt/ *verb* to force someone to leave the country he or she is living in and go back to their country of birth

repatriation /riːˌpætriˈeɪʃ(ə)n/ *noun* **1.** the act of forcing someone to return to their own country **2.** the return of foreign investments, profits, etc., to the home country of their owner

repeal /rɪˈpiːl/ *noun* the act of saying that a law is no longer valid ○ *pressing for the repeal of the Immigration Act* ■ *verb* to say officially that a law no longer has legal authority ○ *The Bill seeks to repeal the existing legislation.* ○ *Member States must repeal national legislation which conflicts with Community legislation.*

> COMMENT: Since the UK does not have a written constitution, all EC law has to be incorporated into UK law by acts of Parliament. Since no act of one parliament can be considered binding on another parliament, these acts can in theory be repealed by subsequent parliaments. No parliament can bind subsequent parliaments to the principle of the supremacy of EC law.

repeat /rɪˈpiːt/ *verb* □ **to repeat an offence** to commit an offence again

repeat offender /rɪˌpiːt əˈfendə/ *noun* somebody who commits an offence more than once

repetition /ˌrepɪˈtɪʃ(ə)n/ *noun* the act of repeating something ○ *Repetition of a libel is an offence.*

replevin /rɪˈplevɪn/ *noun* an action brought to obtain possession of goods which have been seized, by paying off a judgment debt

reply /rɪˈplaɪ/ *noun* **1.** a written statement by a claimant in a civil case in answer to the defendant's defence (NOTE: The reply must be filed at the same time as the claimant files his allocation questionnaire.) **2.** a speech by prosecution counsel or counsel for the claimant which answers claims made by the defence ■ *verb* **1.** to answer claims made by an opponent **2.** to give an opposing view in a discussion

repo *abbreviation* repurchase agreement

report /rɪˈpɔːt/ *noun* **1.** a statement describing what has happened or describing a state of affairs ○ *to make a report* or *to present a report* or *to send in a report* ○ *The court heard a report from the probation officer.* ○ *The chairman has received a report from the insurance company.* □ **the company's annual report** a document sent each year by the chairman of a company, explaining what the company has done during the year □ **the treasurer's report** document from the honorary treasurer of a society to explain the financial state of the society to its members **2.** □ **a report in a newspaper, a newspaper report** an article or news item **3.** an official document from a government committee ○ *The government has issued a report on the problems of inner city violence.* ■ *verb* **1.** to make a statement describing something ○ *The probation officer reported on the progress of the two young criminals.* ○ *He reported the damage to the insurance company.* ○ *We asked the bank to report on his financial status.* **2.** to broadcast an account of events on television or radio or publish it in a newspaper □ **reporting restrictions were lifted** journalists were allowed to report details of the case

reported case /rɪˌpɔːtɪd ˈkeɪs/ *noun* a case which has been reported in the Law Reports because of its importance as a precedent

reporting restrictions /rɪˌpɔːtɪŋ rɪˈstrɪkʃ(ə)ns/ *plural noun* restrictions on information about a case which can be reported in newspapers

repossess /ˌriːpəˈzes/ *verb* to take back an item which someone is buying under a hire-purchase agreement or a property which someone is buying under a mortgage because the purchaser cannot continue the repayments

repossession /ˌriːpəˈzeʃ(ə)n/ *noun* the act of repossessing something, such as taking possession of a mortgaged property where the purchaser cannot continue the mortgage repayments

represent /ˌreprɪˈzent/ *verb* **1.** to state or to show ○ *He was represented as a man of great honour.* **2.** to act on behalf of someone ○ *The defendant is represented by his solicitor.*

representation /ˌreprɪzenˈteɪʃ(ə)n/ *noun* **1.** a statement, especially a statement made to persuade someone to enter into a contract **2.** □ **to make representations** to complain **3.** the process of being represented by a solicitor □ **to have legal representation** to have a lawyer to represent you in court **4.** a system where the people of a country elect representatives to a Parliament which governs the country

Representation of the People Act /ˌreprɪzenteɪʃ(ə)n əv ðə ˈpiːp(ə)l ˌækt/

noun an Act of Parliament which states how elections must be organised

representative /ˌreprɪˈzentətɪv/ *noun* somebody who represents another person ○ *The court heard the representative of the insurance company.*

reprieve /rɪˈpriːv/ *noun* temporarily stopping the carrying out of a sentence or court order ■ *verb* to stop a sentence or order being carried out ○ *He was sentenced to death but was reprieved by the president.*

reprimand /ˈreprɪmɑːnd/ *noun* an official criticism ○ *The police officer received an official reprimand after the inquiry into the accident.* ■ *verb* to criticise someone officially ○ *He was reprimanded by the magistrate.*

reproduction /ˌriːprəˈdʌkʃ(ə)n/ *noun* the process of making a copy of something ○ *The reproduction of copyright material without the permission of the copyright holder is banned by law.*

republication /riːˌpʌblɪˈkeɪʃ(ə)n/ *noun* the action of publishing a will again

republish /riːˈpʌblɪʃ/ *verb* to make an existing will valid again from the date of republication (NOTE: This makes possessions acquired since the will was originally made fall within the dispositions of the will.)

repudiate /rɪˈpjuːdieɪt/ *verb* to refuse to accept □ **to repudiate an agreement, a contract** to refuse to perform one's obligations under an agreement or contract

repudiation /rɪˌpjuːdiˈeɪʃ(ə)n/ *noun* **1.** a refusal to accept **2.** a refusal to perform one's obligations under an agreement or contract

repurchase agreement /riːˈpɜːtʃɪs əˌɡriːmənt/ *noun* an agreement whereby someone sells securities for cash and agrees to repurchase those securities for a greater sum of cash at some later date. Abbreviation **repo**

reputable /ˈrepjʊtəb(ə)l/ *adjective* with a good reputation ○ *a reputable firm of accountants* ○ *We use only reputable carriers.*

reputation /ˌrepjʊˈteɪʃ(ə)n/ *noun* the opinion of someone or something held by other people ○ *company with a reputation for quality* ○ *She has a reputation for being difficult to negotiate with.*

request for arbitration /rɪˌkwest fər ˌɑːbɪˈtreɪʃ(ə)n/ *noun* a document used to commence arbitration proceedings, the equivalent of a Claim Form in litigation

requesting state /rɪˈkwestɪŋ steɪt/ *noun* a state which is seeking the extradition of someone from another state

requisition /ˌrekwɪˈzɪʃ(ə)n/ *verb* to take private property into the ownership of the state for the state to use ○ *The army requisitioned all the trucks to carry supplies.*

requisition on title /ˌrekwɪzɪʃ(ə)n ɒn ˈtaɪt(ə)l/ *noun* a request to the vendor of a property for details of the title to the property

res /rez/ *noun* a Latin word meaning 'thing' or 'matter'

resale price maintenance /riːˌseɪl ˈpraɪs ˌmeɪntənəns/ *noun* a system where the price for an item is fixed by the manufacturer and the retailer is not allowed to sell it for a lower price. Abbreviation **RPM**

> COMMENT: This system applies in the UK to certain products only, such as newspapers.

rescind /rɪˈsɪnd/ *verb* to revoke a contract and return the parties to their former positions before the contract ○ *to rescind a contract* or *an agreement* ○ *The committee rescinded its earlier resolution on the use of council premises.*

rescission /rɪˈsɪʒ(ə)n/ *noun* **1.** the cancellation of a contract **2.** *US* an item in an appropriation bill which cancels money previously appropriated but not spent

research institute /rɪˈsɜːtʃ ˌɪnstɪtjuːt/ *noun* an organisation set up to do research

reservation /ˌrezəˈveɪʃ(ə)n/ *noun* the act of keeping something back □ **reservation of title clause** a clause in a contract whereby the seller provides that title to the goods does not pass to the buyer until the buyer has paid for them. ◊ **Romalpa clause**

reserve /rɪˈzɜːv/ *noun* a supply of something that might be needed in future □ **in reserve** kept to be used at a later date ■ *verb* **1.** to ask for a room, table or seat to be kept free for you ○ *I want to reserve a table for four people.* ○ *Can you reserve a seat for me on the train to Glasgow?* **2.** to keep something back □ **to reserve one's defence** not to present any defence at a preliminary hearing, but to wait until full trial □ **to reserve judgment** not to pass judgment immediately, but keep it back until later so that the judge has time to consider the case □ **to reserve the right to do something** to indicate that you consider that you have the right to do something, and intend to use that right in the future ○ *He reserved the right to cross-examine witnesses.* ○ *We reserve the* *right to appeal against the tribunal's decision.*

reserve currency /rɪˈzɜːv ˌkʌrənsi/ *noun* a strong currency held by other countries to support their own weaker currencies

reserved powers /rɪˌzɜːvd ˈpaʊəz/ *plural noun* legislative powers which remain with a central authority, but may be passed on to a devolved Government at a later date. ◊ **excepted powers, transferred powers**

reserve for bad debts /rɪˌzɜːv fə ˌbæd ˈdets/ *noun* money kept by a company to cover debts which may not be paid

reserve fund /rɪˈzɜːv fʌnd/ *noun* profits in a business which have not been paid out as dividend but which have been ploughed back into the business

res gestae /ˌreɪz ˈdʒestaɪ/ *phrase* a Latin phrase meaning 'things which have been done'

residence /ˈrezɪd(ə)ns/ *noun* **1.** a place where someone lives ○ *He has a country residence where he spends his weekends.* **2.** the act of living or operating officially in a country

residence order /ˈrezɪd(ə)ns ˌɔːdə/ *noun* a court order determining where a child must live

residence permit /ˈrezɪd(ə)ns ˌpɜːmɪt/ *noun* an official document allowing a non-resident to live in a country ○ *He has applied for a residence permit.* ○ *She was granted a residence permit for one year.*

COMMENT: In the European Union, a residence permit is a document which permits the holder to live in a country while not being a citizen of that country. Normally a residence permit is valid for five years and can be renewed automatically. A residence permit is not withdrawn if the person becomes unemployed involuntarily, although voluntary unemployment may result in it being withdrawn.

resident /ˈrezɪd(ə)nt/ *adjective* living or operating in a country ○ *The company is resident in France.* □ **person ordinarily resident in the UK** somebody who normally lives in the UK ■ *noun* a person living in a country

resident alien /ˌrezɪd(ə)nt ˈeɪliən/ *noun* an alien who has permission to live in a country without having citizenship

residual /rɪˈzɪdjuəl/ *noun* **residuals** payments made to a performer for repeated broadcasts of their work (NOTE: This is not the same thing as a **royalty**, which is paid for reproduction of a copyrighted piece of

intellectual property.) ■ *adjective* remaining after everything else has gone

residuary /rɪˈzɪdjuəri/ *adjective* referring to what is left

residuary body /rɪˈzɪdjuəri ˌbɒdi/ *noun* a body set up to administer the ending of a local authority and to manage those of its functions which have not been handed over to other authorities

residuary devise /rɪˌzɪdjuəri dɪˈvaɪz/ *noun* a devise made to someone of what is left of the testator's property after other devises have been made and taxes have been paid

residuary devisee /rɪˌzɪdjuəri ˌdiːvaɪ ˈziː/ *noun* somebody who receives the rest of the land when the other bequests have been made

residuary estate /rɪˌzɪdjuəri ɪˈsteɪt/ *noun* **1.** the estate of a deceased person which has not been bequeathed in the will **2.** what remains of an estate after the debts have been paid and bequests have been made

residuary legacy /rɪˌzɪdjuəri ˈlegəsi/ *noun* a legacy of what remains of an estate after debts, taxes and other legacies have been paid

residuary legatee /rɪˌzɪdjuəri ˌlegəˈtiː/ *noun* somebody who receives the rest of the personal property after specific legacies have been made

residue /ˈrezɪdjuː/ *noun* what is left over, especially what is left of an estate after debts and bequests have been made ○ *After paying various bequests the residue of his estate was split between his children.*

resign /rɪˈzaɪn/ *verb* to leave a job ○ *He resigned from his post as treasurer.* ○ *He has resigned with effect from July 1st.* ○ *She resigned as Education Minister.*

resignation /ˌrezɪɡˈneɪʃ(ə)n/ *noun* the act of giving up a job ○ *The newspaper published the Minister's letter of resignation and the Prime Minister's reply.* ○ *He wrote his letter of resignation to the chairman.* □ **to hand in, to give in, to send in one's resignation** to resign from a job

res ipsa loquitur /ˌreɪz ˌɪpsə ˈlɒkwɪtə/ *phrase* a Latin phrase meaning 'the matter speaks for itself': a situation where the facts seem so obvious, that it is for the defendant to prove he or she was not negligent rather than for the claimant to prove his or her claim

resisting arrest /rɪˌzɪstɪŋ əˈrest/ *noun* the offence of refusing to allow yourself to be arrested

res judicata /ˌreɪz ˌdʒuːdɪˈkætə/ *phrase* a Latin phrase meaning 'matter on which a judgment has been given': the principle that the same case cannot be tried again, unless on appeal

resolution /ˌrezəˈluːʃ(ə)n/ *noun* the action of solving a dispute ○ *The aim of the small claims track is the rapid resolution of disputes.*

respect /rɪˈspekt/ *noun* □ **with respect to, in respect of** concerning ○ *his right to an indemnity with respect to earlier payments* ○ *The defendant counterclaimed for loss and damage in respect of a machine sold to him by the claimant.*

respondeat superior /rɪˌspɒndeɪæt su ˈperiɔː/ *phrase* a Latin phrase meaning 'let the superior be responsible': the rule that a principal is responsible for actions of the agent or the employer for actions of the employee

respondent /rɪˈspɒndənt/ *noun* **1.** the other side in a case which is the subject of an appeal **2.** a person against whom an order is sought by an application notice **3.** somebody who answers a petition, especially one who is being sued for divorce ▸ ◊ **co-respondent**

responsible for /rɪˈspɒnsɪb(ə)l fɔː/ *adjective* being in charge of or being in control of ○ *The tenant is responsible for all repairs to the building.* ○ *The consignee is held responsible for the goods he has received on consignment.* ○ *She was responsible for a series of thefts from offices.*

responsible government /rɪ ˌspɒnsɪb(ə)l ˈɡʌv(ə)nmənt/ *noun* a form of government which acts in accordance with the wishes of the people and which is accountable to Parliament for its actions

responsible to someone /rɪ ˌspɒnsɪb(ə)l tə ˈsʌmwʌn/ *noun* being under someone's authority ○ *Magistrates are responsible to the Lord Chancellor.*

restitutio in integrum /restiˌtuːtiəʊ ɪn ɪnˈteɡrəm/ *phrase* a Latin phrase meaning 'returning everything to the state as it was before': the principle that the amount of damages awarded should restore the claimant to the position that they would be in had the tort not been committed

restitution /ˌrestɪˈtjuːʃ(ə)n/ *noun* **1.** the return of property which has been illegally obtained ○ *The court ordered the restitution*

of assets to the company. **2.** compensation or payment for damage or loss

restitution order /ˌrestɪˈtjuːʃ(ə)n ˌɔːdə/ *noun* a court order asking for property to be returned to someone

restrain /rɪˈstreɪn/ *verb* **1.** to control or to hold someone back ○ *The prisoner fought and had to be restrained by two policemen.* **2.** to tell someone not to do something ○ *The court granted the claimant an injunction restraining the defendant from breaching copyright.*

restraining order /rɪˈstreɪnɪŋ ˌɔːdə/ *noun* a court order which tells a defendant not to do something while the court is still taking a decision ■ an order to stay away from another person, which may be granted under the Protection from Harassment Act 1997

restraint of trade /rɪˌstreɪnt əv ˈtreɪd/ *noun* **1.** a situation where an employee is not allowed to move to another job in the same trade because the experience acquired with the present employer might be sensitive or unfairly beneficial to the new employer **2.** an attempt by companies to fix prices, create monopolies or reduce competition, which could affect free trade

restriction /rɪˈstrɪkʃ(ə)n/ *noun* something that limits what can happen or what someone can do □ **to impose restrictions on imports** to start limiting imports □ **to lift credit restrictions** to allow credit to be given freely □ **reporting restrictions were lifted** journalists were allowed to report details of the case

restrictive covenant /rɪˌstrɪktɪv ˈkʌvənənt/ *noun* a clause in a contract which prevents someone from doing something

COMMENT: Examples of restrictive covenants could be a clause in a contract of employment which prevents the employee from going to work for a competitor, or a clause in a contract for the sale of a property which prevents the purchaser from altering the building.

restrictive practices /rɪˌstrɪktɪv ˈpræktɪsɪz/ *plural noun* illegal ways of working which exclude free competition in relation to the supply of goods or labour in order to maintain high prices or wages

Restrictive Practices Court /rɪ ˌstrɪktɪv ˈpræktɪsɪz ˌkɔːt/ *noun* a court which decides in cases of restrictive practices

resulting trust /rɪˌzʌltɪŋ 'trʌst/ *noun* a trust that arises by operation of law whereby the equitable benefit of the property transfers results back to the settler, e.g. because the purpose for which the settler intended the trust property to be used has come to an end

retail /'riːteɪl/ *noun* the sale of small quantities of goods to individual customers

retailer /'riːteɪlə/ *noun* a person who runs a business that sells goods to the public

retain /rɪ'teɪn/ *verb* □ **to retain a lawyer to act for you** to agree with a lawyer that he or she will act for you (and pay a fee in advance)

retainer /rɪ'teɪnə/ *noun* **1.** a fee paid to a barrister **2.** money paid in advance to someone when they are not actively working for you so that they will work for you on the occasions when they are needed ○ *We pay him a retainer of £1,000 per annum.*

retiral /rɪ'taɪərəl/ *noun Scotland, US* same as **retirement**

retire /rɪ'taɪə/ *verb* **1.** to stop working permanently ○ *She retired with a £6,000 pension.* ○ *The chairman of the company retired at the age of 65.* ○ *The shop is owned by a retired policeman.* **2.** to make an employee stop working permanently ○ *They decided to retire all staff over 50 years of age.* **3.** to come to the end of an elected term of office ○ *The treasurer retires after six years.* ○ *Two retiring directors offer themselves for re-election.* **4.** to go away from a court for a period of time ○ *The magistrates retired to consider their verdict.* ○ *The jury retired for four hours.*

retirement /rɪ'taɪəmənt/ *noun* **1.** the act of retiring from work □ **to take early retirement** to leave work before the usual age **2.** (*of a jury*) the act of leaving a courtroom to consider a verdict

retirement age /rɪ'taɪəmənt eɪdʒ/ *noun* the age at which people retire (NOTE: In the UK, this is now 65 for both men and women.)

retirement pension /rɪ'taɪəmənt ˌpenʃən/ *noun* a state pension given to a man who is over 65 or woman who is over 60

retirement plan /rɪ'taɪəmənt plæn/ *noun* a plan set up to provide a person for someone when he or she retires

retiring age /rɪ'taɪərɪŋ eɪdʒ/ *noun* same as **retirement age**

retrial /'riːˌtraɪəl/ *noun* a new hearing of a case that has been previously tried without a verdict being reached ○ *The Court of Appeal ordered a retrial.*

retroactive /ˌretrəʊ'æktɪv/ *adjective* taking effect from a time in the past ○ *They received a pay rise retroactive to last January.*

retroactively /ˌretrəʊ'æktɪvli/ *adverb* going back to a time in the past

retrocession /ˌretrəʊ'seʃ(ə)n/ *noun* further reinsurance taken on by a reinsurer on a large assumed risk

retrospective /ˌretrəʊ'spektɪv/ *adjective* going back in time ○ *Legislation is enacted with the presumption that it should not be retrospective.* □ **with retrospective effect** applying to a past period

retrospective legislation /ˌretrəʊspektɪv ˌledʒɪ'sleɪʃ(ə)n/ *noun* an Act of Parliament which applies to the period before the Act was passed

retrospectively /ˌretrəʊ'spektɪvli/ *adverb* in a retrospective way ○ *The ruling is applied retrospectively.*

retry /ˌriː'traɪ/ *verb* to try a case a second time ○ *The court ordered the case to be retried.*

return /rɪ't3ːn/ *noun* □ **to make a return to the tax office, to make an income tax return** to send a statement of income to the tax office □ **to fill in a VAT return** to complete the form showing VAT income and expenditure

return on investment /rɪˌt3ːn ɒn ɪn'vestmənt/ *noun* profit shown as a percentage of money invested

reus ♦ **actus reus**

revenue expenditure /'revənjuː ɪk ˌspendɪtʃə/ *noun* the day-to-day costs of a council such as salaries and wages, maintenance of buildings, etc.

revenue officer /'revənjuː ˌɒfɪsə/ *noun* somebody working in a government tax office

reversal /rɪ'v3ːs(ə)l/ *noun* **1.** the change of a decision to the opposite ○ *the reversal of the High Court ruling by the Court of Appeal* **2.** a change from being profitable to unprofitable ○ *The company suffered a reversal in the Far East.*

reverse /rɪ'v3ːs/ *adjective* opposite, in the opposite direction ■ *verb* to change a decision to the opposite one ○ *The Appeal Court reversed the decision of the High Court.*

reverse takeover /rɪ,vɜːs 'teɪkəʊvə/ *noun* a takeover where the company which has been taken over ends up owning the company which has taken it over

reversion /rɪ'vɜːʃ(ə)n/ *noun* the return of property to an original owner when a lease expires □ **to have the reversion of an estate** to receive an estate when the present lease ends or when the present owner dies

reversionary /rɪ'vɜːʃ(ə)n(ə)ri/ *adjective* referring to property which passes to another owner on the death of the present one

reversionary annuity /rɪ,vɜːʃ(ə)n(ə)ri ə'njuːɪti/ *noun* an annuity paid to someone on the death of another person

reversionary right /rɪ,vɜːʃ(ə)n(ə)ri 'raɪt/ *noun* the right of a writer's heir to his or her copyrights after his or her death

revert /rɪ'vɜːt/ *verb* to go back to the previous state or owner ○ *The property reverts to its original owner in 2010.*

review /rɪ'vjuː/ *noun* a general examination of something again ○ *to conduct a review of sentencing policy* ○ *The coroner asked for a review of police procedures.* ■ *verb* to examine something generally ○ *A committee has been appointed to review judicial salaries.* ○ *The High Court has reviewed the decision.*

revise /rɪ'vaɪz/ *verb* to change a document, decision or opinion in some way ○ *The judge revised his earlier decision not to consider a submission from defence counsel.*

revision /rɪ'vɪʒ(ə)n/ *noun* the act of changing something ○ *The Lord Chancellor has proposed a revision of the divorce procedures.*

revival /rɪ'vaɪv(ə)l/ *noun* the act of making a will that has been revoked but not destroyed valid again

revive /rɪ'vaɪv/ *verb* to make a revoked will become valid again

revocable /'revəkəb(ə)l/ *adjective* being able to be revoked. Opposite **irrevocable**

revocandi ♦ animus revocandi

revocation /,revəʊ'keɪʃ(ə)n/ *noun* the act of cancelling a permission, right, agreement, offer or will

revoke /rɪ'vəʊk/ *verb* to cancel a permission, right, agreement, offer or will ○ *to revoke a clause in an agreement* ○ *The treaty on fishing rights has been revoked.*

COMMENT: A will may be revoked by marriage, by writing another will which changes the dispositions of the first one, or by destroying the will intentionally.

reward /rɪ'wɔːd/ *noun* a payment given to someone who does a service such as finding something which has been lost or giving information about something ○ *She offered a £50 reward to anyone who found her watch.* ○ *The police have offered a reward for information about the man seen at the bank.*

Rex /reks/ *noun* a Latin word meaning 'the King': the Crown or state, as a party in legal proceedings (NOTE: In written reports, usually abbreviated to **R**: *the case of R. v. Smith.*)

RFP *abbreviation* reasonable financial provision

rider /'raɪdə/ *noun* **1.** a clause added to a document such as contract or report **2.** *US* a clause attached to a bill, which may have nothing to do with the subject of the bill, but which the sponsor hopes will help the bill to pass into law more easily

right /raɪt/ *noun* a legal or moral entitlement to something ○ *the right of renewal of a contract* ○ *She has a right to the property.* ○ *He has no right to the patent.* ○ *The staff have a right to know what the company is doing.*

rightful /'raɪtf(ə)l/ *adjective* legally correct

rightful claimant /,raɪtf(ə)l 'kleɪmənt/ *noun* somebody who has a legal claim to something

rightful owner /,raɪtf(ə)l 'əʊnə/ *noun* the legal owner

Right Honourable /,raɪt 'ɒn(ə)rəb(ə)l/ *noun* the title given to members of the Privy Council (NOTE: usually written **Hon.**: *the Hon. Member; the Rt. Hon. William Smith, M.P.*)

right of abode /,raɪt əv ə'bəʊd/ *noun* the right to live in a country

right of audience /,raɪt əv 'ɔːdiəns/ *noun* the right to speak to a court, which can be used by the parties in the case or their legal representatives ○ *A barrister has right of audience in any court in England and Wales.*

COMMENT: Solicitors have a right of audience in a limited number of courts. Solicitor-advocates have the same rights of audience as barristers.

right of establishment /,raɪt əv ɪ'stæblɪʃmənt/ *noun* the right of an EU citizen to live and work in any EU country

right of first refusal /ˌraɪt əv fɜːst rɪ
ˈfjuːzəl/ *noun* the right to make an offer to
buy a property after other others have been
submitted and with the knowledge of the
value of those other offers

right of pre-emption /ˌraɪt əv priː
ˈempʃ(ə)n/ *noun* the right to make an offer
to buy property before it is offered to others

right of redemption /ˌraɪt əv rɪ
ˈdempʃ(ə)n/ *noun* the right to buy back
property that has been lost through non-
payment of debt by later paying off the debt

right of re-entry /ˌraɪt əv riˈentri/ *noun*
1. the right of a landlord to take back possession of the property if the tenant breaks
his or her agreement **2.** the right of a person
resident in a country to go back into that
country after leaving it for a time

right of reply /ˌraɪt əv rɪˈplaɪ/ *noun* the
right of someone to answer claims made by
an opponent ○ *He demanded the right of
reply to the newspaper allegations.*

right of silence /ˌraɪt əv ˈsaɪləns/ *noun*
the right of an accused not to say anything
when charged with a criminal offence

right of survivorship /ˌraɪt əv sə
ˈvaɪvəʃɪp/ *noun* a right of the survivor of a
joint tenancy to the estate rather than of the
heirs of the deceased tenant (NOTE: The right
of survivorship is also called by its Latin
name: *jus accrescendi*.)

right of way /ˌraɪt əv ˈweɪ/ *noun* the right
to go lawfully along a path on another person's land

rights management /ˈraɪts
ˌmænɪdʒmənt/ *noun* methods of enforcing
copyright on works by issuing usage
licences and preventing unauthorised copying

right to enter /ˌraɪt tə ˈentə/ *noun* the
right of a EU citizen to go into another EU
country to look for work

right to light /ˌraɪt tə ˈlaɪt/ *noun* the right
of the owner of a building to contest the
building of new neighbouring structures
which would block their natural light. Also
called **ancient lights**

right to reside /ˌraɪt tə rɪˈzaɪd/ *noun*
one of the fundamental rights of citizens
and workers in the European Union, the
right of living in any another EU Member
State

rigor mortis /ˌrɪɡə ˈmɔːtɪs/ *phrase* a
Latin phrase meaning 'stiffening of the
dead': a state where a dead body becomes
stiff some time after death, which can allow

a pathologist to estimate the time of death in
some cases

ring /rɪŋ/ *verb* to alter chassis or engine
numbers on a car, so as to falsify its origin
(*slang*)

riot /ˈraɪət/ *noun* a notifiable offence when
three or more people meet illegally and plan
to use force to achieve their aims or to
frighten the public ■ *verb* to form an illegal
group to use force

riot control /ˈraɪət kənˌtrəʊl/ *noun*
methods used by police for containing and
subduing large groups of people engaged in
a riot (NOTE: These methods may include
the use of batons, riot shields and less-
lethal weapons such as pepper spray or a
water cannon.)

rioter /ˈraɪətə/ *noun* somebody who takes
part in a riot ○ *Rioters attacked the banks
and post offices.*

riotous assembly /ˌraɪətəs əˈsemblɪ/
noun formerly, a meeting of twelve or more
people who come together to use force to
achieve their aims or frighten other people

riot police /ˈraɪət pəˌliːs/, **riot squad**
noun police officers who are specially
armed and trained in riot control

riot shield /ˈraɪət ʃiːld/ *noun* a clear,
lightweight shield used by riot police,
which protects against physical attack and
thrown objects

riotsquad helmet /ˈraɪətˌskwɒd
ˌhelmɪt/ *noun* a helmet with a visor which
protects the head from thrown objects, used
by riot police

riparian /rɪˈpeəriən/ *adjective* referring to
the bank of a river

riparian rights /raɪˈpeəriən ˌraɪts/ *plural
noun* the rights that apply to people who
own land on the bank of a river, e.g. the right
to fish in the river

risk /rɪsk/ *noun* **1.** possible harm, loss or
chance of danger □ **at risk** in a situation
where something bad or dangerous is likely
to happen ○ *His careless driving had put his
passengers as well as other road-users at
risk.* ○ *The school was known to be at risk of
flooding.* □ **at owner's risk** a situation in
which goods shipped or stored are the
responsibility of the owner, not of the shipping company or storage company □ **to run
a risk *or* run the risk of something** to be
likely to suffer harm ○ *She knew she was
running a risk in not reporting the accident.*
○ *In allowing him to retain his passport, the
court runs the risk of the accused leaving
the country.* **2.** loss or damage against which

you are insured □ **to be a bad risk** for it to be likely that an insurance company will have to pay out compensation as far as you are concerned

road rage /ˈrəʊd ˌreɪdʒ/ *noun* a violent attack by a driver on another car or its driver, caused by anger at the way the other driver has been driving ○ *There have been several incidents of road rage lately.* ○ *In the latest road rage attack, the driver leapt out of his car and knocked a cyclist to the ground.*

road tax /ˈrəʊd tæks/ *noun* an annual tax levied on cars and other vehicles

rob /rɒb/ *verb* to steal something from someone, usually violently ○ *They robbed a bank in London and stole a car to make their getaway.* ○ *The gang robbed shopkeepers in the centre of the town.* (NOTE: **robbing – robbed**. Note also that you rob someone of something.)

robber /ˈrɒbə/ *noun* somebody who robs people

robbery /ˈrɒbəri/ *noun* **1.** the offence of stealing something from someone using force or threatening to use force **2.** the act of stealing something with violence ○ *He committed three petrol station robberies in two days.*

robbery with violence /ˌrɒbəri wɪð ˈvaɪələns/ *noun* the offence of stealing goods and harming someone at the same time

rogatory letter /ˈrɒɡət(ə)ri ˌletə/ *noun* a letter of request to a court in another country, asking for evidence to be taken from someone under that court's jurisdiction

rolling contract /ˌrəʊlɪŋ ˈkɒntrækt/ *noun* **1.** a contract for a period of more than one year that is renewed annually for the same period, subject to a favourable review **2.** a contract that is open-ended and runs until one of the contracting parties cancels it

Roll of Solicitors /ˌrəʊl əv səˈlɪsɪtəz/ *noun* a list of solicitors approved to practice by the Solicitors Regulation Authority

roll over /ˌrəʊl ˈəʊvə/ *verb* □ **to roll over credit** to make credit available over a continuing period

Romalpa clause /rəʊˈmɒlpə ˌklɔːz/ *noun* a clause in a contract, whereby the seller provides that title to the goods does not pass to the buyer until the buyer has paid for them

COMMENT: Called after the case of *Aluminium Industrie Vaassen BV v. Romalpa Ltd.*

Roman law /ˈrəʊmən lɔː/ *noun* the set of laws which existed in the Roman Empire

COMMENT: Roman law is the basis of the laws of many European countries but has had only negligible and indirect influence on the development of English law.

Rome Convention /ˌrəʊm kənˈvenʃ(ə)n/ *noun* a copyright convention signed in Rome, covering the rights of record producers, musical performers, broadcasters and television companies, etc.

root of title /ˌruːt əv ˈtaɪt(ə)l/ *noun* the basic title deed which proves that a vendor has the right to sell a property

ROR *abbreviation US* release on recognizance

rough copy /ˌrʌf ˈkɒpi/ *noun* a draft of a document which is expected to have changes made to it before it is complete

rough draft /ˌrʌf ˈdrɑːft/ *noun* a plan of a document which may have changes made to it before it is complete

rough justice /ˌrʌf ˈdʒʌstɪs/ *noun* legal processes which are not always very fair

round table conference /ˌraʊnd ˌteɪb(ə)l ˈkɒnf(ə)rəns/ *noun* a conference at which each party at the meeting is of equal status to the others ○ *The government is trying to get the rebel leaders to come to the conference table.*

rout /raʊt/ *noun* the offence of gathering together of people to do some unlawful act

Royal Assent /ˌrɔɪəl əˈsent/ *noun* the act of signing of bill by the Queen, confirming that the bill is to become law as an Act of Parliament

Royal Commission /ˌrɔɪəl kəˈmɪʃ(ə)n/ *noun* a group of people specially appointed by a minister to examine and report on a major problem

Royal Courts of Justice /ˌrɔɪəl ˌkɔːts əv ˈdʒʌstɪs/ *noun* the central civil court in London, where serious claims covering fatal accidents, professional negligence, defamation, and claims against the police are heard. Abbreviation **RCJ**

Royal pardon /ˌrɔɪəl ˈpɑːd(ə)n/ *noun* a pardon whereby a person convicted of a crime is forgiven and released

Royal prerogative /ˌrɔɪəl prɪˈrɒɡətɪv/ *noun* a special right belonging only to a king or queen such as the right to appoint ministers or end a session of Parliament

royalty /ˈrɔɪəlti/ *noun* money paid to an inventor, writer, or the owner of land for the right to use his or her property ○ *Oil royal-*

ties make up a large proportion of the country's revenue. ○ *He is receiving royalties from his invention.* (NOTE: It is usually an agreed percentage of sales or an amount per sale.)

rozzer /ˈrɒzə/ *noun* a policeman (*informal*)

RPM *abbreviation* resale price maintenance

RSC *abbreviation* Rules of the Supreme Court

rule /ruːl/ *noun* **1.** a general order of conduct which says how things should be done ○ *The debate followed the rules of procedure used in the British House of Commons.* □ **to work to rule** to work strictly according to the rules agreed by the company and union, and therefore to work very slowly **2.** *US* a special decision made by the Rules Committee which states how a particular bill should be treated in the House of Representatives **3.** the way in which a country is governed ○ *The country has had ten years of military rule.* □ **the rule of law** the principle of government that all persons and bodies and the government itself are equal before and answerable to the law and that no person shall be punished without trial **4.** a decision made by a court □ **Rule in X v. X** the legal principle that emerged from case X v. X. ■ *verb* **1.** to give an official decision ○ *We are waiting for the judge to rule on the admissibility of the defence evidence.* ○ *The commission of inquiry ruled that the company was in breach of contract.* **2.** to govern

a country ○ *The country is ruled by a group of army officers.*

rule against perpetuities /ˌruːl əˌgenst ˌpɜːpɪtˈjuːɪtiz/ *noun* a rule that an interest can only last for a period of no more than 21 years

rule of evidence /ˌruːl əv ˈevɪd(ə)ns/ *noun* a rule established by law which determines the type of evidence which a court will consider and how such evidence must be given

Rules of the Supreme Court /ˌruːlz əv ðə suˌpriːm ˈkɔːt/ *plural noun* rules governing practice and procedure in the Supreme Court. Abbreviation **RSC**. ◊ **Civil Procedure Rules**, **County Court Rules**, **White Book**

ruling /ˈruːlɪŋ/ *noun* a decision made by someone with official authority such as a judge, magistrate, arbitrator or chairman ○ *According to the ruling of the court, the contract was illegal.* ■ *adjective* **1.** in power or in control ○ *the ruling Democratic Party* ○ *The actions of the ruling junta have been criticised in the press.* **2.** most important ○ *The ruling consideration is one of cost.* **3.** in operation at the moment ○ *We invoiced at ruling prices.*

runner /ˈrʌnə/ *noun* a member of a gang of pickpockets who takes the items stolen and runs away with them to a safe place (*slang*)

S

sabotage /'sæbətɑːʒ/ *noun* malicious damage done to machines or equipment ○ *Several acts of sabotage were committed against radio stations.* (NOTE: no plural; for the plural say **acts of sabotage**)

sack /sæk/ *noun* □ **to get the sack** to be dismissed from a job ■ *verb* □ **to sack someone** to dismiss someone from a job ○ *He was sacked after being late for work.*

sacking /'sækɪŋ/ *noun* dismissal from a job ○ *The scandal led to the sacking of several employees.*

safe /seɪf/ *noun* a heavy metal box which cannot be opened easily, in which valuable items such as documents or money can be kept ○ *Put the documents in the safe.* ○ *We keep the petty cash in the safe.* ■ *adjective* **1.** out of danger □ **to keep something in a safe place** to put something in a place where it cannot be stolen or destroyed **2.** referring to a judgment of a court which is well-based and is not likely to be quashed on appeal ○ *The court of appeal found that the original conviction was not safe.* ◊ **unsafe**

safe deposit /'seɪf dɪ,pɒzɪt/ *noun* a safe in a bank vault where you can leave jewellery or documents

safe deposit box /,seɪf dɪ'pɒzɪt ,bɒks/ *noun* a small box which you can rent to keep jewellery or documents in a bank's safe

safeguard /'seɪfgɑːd/ *noun* an action or plan for doing something that prevents something unwanted from happening ○ *The proposed legislation will provide a safeguard against illegal traders.* ■ *verb* to protect someone or something against something unwanted happening ○ *The court acted to safeguard the interests of the shareholders.* ○ *The management had failed to safeguard their employees against exposure to the hazard.*

safekeeping /,seɪf 'kiːpɪŋ/ *noun* care and protection ○ *We put the documents into the bank for safekeeping.*

safety /'seɪfti/ *noun* the situation of being free from danger or risk □ **to take safety precautions, safety measures** to act to make sure something is safe

safety margin /'seɪfti ,mɑːdʒɪn/ *noun* time or space allowed for something to be safe

safety measures /'seɪfti ,meʒəz/ *plural noun* actions to make sure that something is or will be safe

safety regulations /'seɪfti ,regjʊleɪʃ(ə)nz/ *plural noun* rules to make a place of work safe for the employees

salary /'sæləri/ *noun* payment for work made to an employee with a contract of employment, especially in a professional or office job (NOTE: The plural is **salaries**.)

sale /seɪl/ *noun* **1.** the act of selling or transferring an item or a property from one owner to another in exchange for a consideration, usually in the form of money **2.** □ **for sale** ready to be sold □ **to offer something for sale, to put something up for sale** to announce that something is ready to be sold ○ *They put the factory up for sale.* **3.** the selling of goods at specially low prices ○ *The shop is having a sale to clear old stock.* ○ *The sale price is 50% of the normal price.*

sale and lease-back /,seɪl ən 'liːs bæk/ *noun* a situation where a company sells a property to raise cash and then leases it back from the purchaser

Sale of Goods Act /,seɪl əv 'gʊdz ,ækt/ *noun* an Act of Parliament which regulates the selling of goods but not land, copyrights or patents

COMMENT: Under the Sale Of Goods Act, goods sold by a trader to a consumer must be **as described, of satisfactory quality** and **fit for purpose**. A consumer will be able to claim compensation (in the form of a repair, replacement or refund) if these conditions are not met, unless they were made aware of the defect before buying, or have accepted the goods or failed to return them in good time after discovering the defect (**affirmation**).

sale or return /ˌseɪl ɔː rɪˈtɜːn/ *noun* a system which allows unsold goods to be delivered to a person, who then has the right to keep the goods for a specified time while deciding whether or not to purchase them

sales description /ˈseɪlz dɪˌskrɪpʃ(ə)n/ *noun* the description given of goods sold to a consumer

COMMENT: Under the Sale Of Goods Act, the goods sold must correspond to their sales description, as well as being fit for purpose and of satisfactory quality.

salvage /ˈsælvɪdʒ/ *noun* **1.** the right of a person who saves a ship from being wrecked or cargo from a ship which has been wrecked in order to receive compensation **2.** goods saved from a wrecked ship or from a fire or other accident ○ *a sale of flood salvage items* ■ *verb* to save goods or a ship from being wrecked ○ *We are selling off a warehouse full of salvaged goods.*

salvage agreement /ˌsælvɪdʒ əˈgriːmənt/ *noun* an agreement between the captain of a sinking ship and a salvage crew, giving the terms on which the ship will be saved

salvage vessel /ˈsælvɪdʒ ˌves(ə)l/ *noun* a ship which specialises in saving other ships and their cargoes

same-sex couple /ˌseɪm seks ˈkʌp(ə)l/ *noun* a couple who are either both men or both women (NOTE: Same-sex couples are entitled to legally register a **civil partnership** in the UK)

sample /ˈsɑːmpəl/ *noun* a small part of something taken to show what the whole is like ○ *They polled a sample group of voters.* ■ *verb* to take a small part of something and examine it ○ *The suspect's urine was sampled and the test proved positive.*

sanction /ˈsæŋkʃən/ *noun* **1.** an official order to do something ○ *You will need the sanction of the local authorities before you can knock down the office block.* ○ *The payment was made without official sanction.* **2.** *US* punishment by a court for failure to comply with an order (NOTE: If the sanction is payment of costs, the party in default may obtain relief by appealing.) **3.** a punishment for an act which goes against what is generally accepted behaviour □ **(economic) sanctions** restrictions on trade with a country in order to influence its political situation or in order to make its government

change its policy ○ *to impose sanctions on a country* or *to lift sanctions* ■ *verb* to approve or permit something officially ○ *The board sanctioned the expenditure of £1.2m on the development plan.*

sane /seɪn/ *adjective* mentally well ○ *Was he sane when he made the will?*

sanity /ˈsæniti/ *noun* the ability to make rational decisions

sans frais /ˌsænz ˈfreɪs/ *phrase* a French phrase meaning 'with no expense'

sans recours /ˌsænz rəˈkuːəz/ *phrase* a French phrase meaning 'with no recourse': used to show that someone such as an agent acting for a principal in endorsing a bill is not responsible for paying it

SAP *abbreviation* Sentencing Advisory Panel

satisfaction /ˌsætɪsˈfækʃən/ *noun* **1.** the acceptance of money or goods by an injured party who then cannot make any further claim **2.** payment or goods given to someone in exchange for that person's agreement to stop a claim

satisfactory quality /ˌsætɪsfæktəri ˈkwɒliti/ *noun* an implied contractual term that goods sold will be free of defects

satisfy /ˈsætɪsfaɪ/ *verb* **1.** to convince someone that something is correct ○ *When opposing bail the police had to satisfy the court that the prisoner was likely to try to leave the country.* **2.** to fulfil or to carry out fully ○ *Has he satisfied all the conditions for parole?* ○ *The company has not satisfied all the conditions laid down in the agreement.* ○ *We cannot produce enough to satisfy the demand for the product.*

scaffold /ˈskæfəʊld/ *noun* a raised platform on which executions take place

scale /skeɪl/ *noun* □ **large scale** working with large amounts of investment, staff, etc. □ **small scale** working with small amounts of investment, staff, etc. □ **to start in business on a small scale** to start in business with a small staff, few products or little investment ■ *verb* □ **to scale up** to increase in proportion □ **to scale down, to scale up** to lower in proportion ○ *The police decided to scale down the investigation.*

scale of charges /ˌskeɪl əv ˈtʃɑːdʒɪz/ *noun* a list showing prices for various goods or services offered

scale of salaries /ˌskeɪl əv ˈsæləriz/ *noun* a list of salaries showing different levels of pay in different jobs in the same company

scam /skæm/ *noun* a dishonest plan to deceive someone, especially in order to obtain money (*informal*)

scene /si:n/ *noun* where something has happened □ **scene of the crime** the place where a crime occurred ○ *Perpetrators often return to the scene of the crime.*

scene-of-crime /ˌsi:n əv ˈkraɪm/ *adjective* relating or belonging to the part of the police force responsible for collecting forensic evidence at crime scenes

scenes à faire *phrase* a French phrase meaning 'scenes to be made': the principles that elements of a book, film or piece of music cannot be copyrighted if they are characteristic of the work's genre

schedule /ˈʃedjuːl/ *noun* **1.** a plan of the times when something will happen □ **to be ahead of schedule** to be early □ **to be on schedule** to be on time □ **to be behind schedule** to be late ○ *I am sorry to say that we are three months behind schedule.* **2.** a list of details, often in the form of an appendix to a legal or legislative document ○ *the schedule of markets to which a contract applies* ○ *see the attached schedule* or *as per the attached schedule* ○ *the schedule before referred to* **3.** a list ○ *We publish our new schedule of charges.* (NOTE: For the schedules applying to drugs, see **drug**.) ■ *verb* **1.** to list officially ○ *scheduled prices* or *scheduled charges* **2.** to plan the time when something will happen ○ *The building is scheduled for completion in May.*

Schedule A /ˌʃedjuːl ˈeɪ/ *noun* a schedule to the Finance Acts under which tax is charged on income from land or buildings

Schedule B /ˌʃedjuːl ˈbiː/ *noun* a schedule to the Finance Acts under which tax is charged on income from woodlands

Schedule C /ˌʃedjuːl ˈsiː/ *noun* a schedule to the Finance Acts under which tax is charged on profits from government stock

Schedule D /ˌʃedjuːl ˈdiː/ *noun* a schedule to the Finance Acts under which tax is charged on income from trades, professions, interest and other earnings which do not come from employment

Schedule F /ˌʃedjuːl ˈef/ *noun* a schedule to the Finance Acts under which tax is charged on income from dividends

scheme of arrangement /ˌskiːm əv ə ˈreɪndʒmənt/ *noun* a scheme drawn up by an individual offering ways of paying debts and so avoiding bankruptcy proceedings

scire facias /ˌsaɪəri ˈfeɪʃiæs/ *phrase* a Latin phrase meaning 'you should make (it)

known': a writ that requires a defendant to appear in court to show why the plaintiff should not be permitted to take a specific legal step

scope /skəʊp/ *noun* the limits covered by something ○ *The question does not come within the scope of the authority's powers.* ○ *The Bill plans to increase the scope of the tribunal's authority.*

Scotland Yard /ˌskɒtlənd ˈjɑːd/ *noun* the headquarters of the Metropolitan Police in London

Scottish Parliament /ˈskɒtɪʃ ˈpɑːləmənt/ *noun* the centre of devolved government for Scotland, made up of elected members

screw /skruː/ *noun* a prison warder (*slang*)

scrip /skrɪp/ *noun* a certificate showing that someone owns shares in a company

scuttle /ˈskʌt(ə)l/ *verb* to sink a ship deliberately by making holes in the bottom of it

seal /siːl/ *noun* **1.** a piece of wax or red paper attached to a document to show that it is legally valid **2.** a stamp printed or marked on a document to show that it is valid **3.** a mark put on a document by a court to show that it has been correctly issued by that court ○ *The document bears the court's seal and is admissible in evidence.* **4.** a piece of paper, metal or wax attached to close something, so that it can be opened only if the paper, metal or wax is removed or broken ■ *verb* **1.** to close something tightly ○ *The documents were sent in a sealed box.* **2.** (*of a court*) to attach a mark to a document to show that it has been issued by that court ○ *A court must seal a claim form when it is issued.* **3.** to attach a seal ○ *Customs sealed the shipment.* **4.** to stamp something with a seal

sealed instrument /ˌsiːld ˈɪnstrʊmənt/ *noun* a contract which has been signed and sealed

sealed tender /ˌsiːld ˈtendə/ *noun* tenders sent in sealed envelopes, which will all be opened together at a specified time

seal off /ˌsiːl ˈɒf/ *verb* to put barriers across a street or an entrance to prevent people from going in or out ○ *Police sealed off all roads leading to the courthouse.*

search /sɜːtʃ/ *noun* an act of examining a place to try to find something. ◊ **power of search** ■ *verb* to examine a place or a person to try to find something ○ *The agent searched his files for a record of the sale.* ○

All drivers and their cars are searched at the customs post. ○ *The police searched the area round the house for clues.* □ **to stop and search** to stop a person in a public place and search them for weapons, implements used for burglary, stolen articles, etc.

search order /'sɜːtʃ ˌɔːdə/ *noun* an order by a court in a civil case allowing a party to inspect and photocopy or remove a defendant's documents, especially where the defendant might destroy evidence (NOTE: The search should be done in the presence of an independent solicitor. Since the introduction of the Civil Procedure Rules, this term has replaced **Anton Piller order**.)

search warrant /'sɜːtʃ ˌwɒrənt/ *noun* an official document signed by a magistrate allowing the police to enter premises and look for persons suspected of being criminals, objects which are believed to have been stolen, or dangerous or illegal substances

secede /sɪ'siːd/ *verb* to break away from an organisation or a federation ○ *The American colonies seceded from Great Britain in 1776 and formed the USA.*

secession /sɪ'seʃ(ə)n/ *noun* the act of seceding

second /'sekənd/ *verb* □ **to second a motion** to agree to support a motion after it has been proposed by the proposer, but before a vote is taken ○ *The motion is proposed by Mr Smith, seconded by Mr Jones.*

secondarily /ˌsekən'deərɪli/ *adverb* in second place ○ *The person making a guarantee is secondarily liable if the person who is primarily liable defaults.* ◊ **primarily**

secondary /'sekənd(ə)ri/ *adjective* second in importance

secondary action /ˌsekənd(ə)ri 'ækʃən/ *noun* the picketing of another factory or place of work which is not directly connected with a strike to prevent it supplying a striking factory or receiving supplies from it

secondary banks /ˌsekənd(ə)ri 'bæŋks/ *plural noun* companies which provide money for hire-purchase deals

secondary evidence /ˌsekənd(ə)ri 'evɪd(ə)ns/ *noun* evidence which is not the main proof, e.g. copies of documents and not the original documents themselves (NOTE: Secondary evidence can be admitted in a legal investigation if there is no primary evidence available.)

secondary legislation /ˌsekənd(ə)ri ˌledʒɪ'sleɪʃ(ə)n/ *noun* legislation passed by

the European Union, as opposed to primary legislation passed by the Member States themselves

second degree murder /ˌsekənd dɪ ˌgriː 'mɜːdə/ *noun US* the unlawful killing of a person without premeditation and not committed at the same time as rape or robbery

second mortgage /ˌsekənd 'mɔːgɪdʒ/ *noun* a further mortgage on a property which is already mortgaged (NOTE: The first mortgage has prior claim.)

second quarter /ˌsekənd 'kwɔːtə/ *noun* a period of three months from April to the end of June

Second Reading /ˌsekənd 'riːdɪŋ/ *noun* **1.** a detailed presentation of a Bill in the House of Commons by the responsible minister, followed by a discussion and vote **2.** *US* a detailed examination of a Bill in the House of Representatives, before it is passed to the Senate

seconds /'sekəndz/ *plural noun* goods sold which are known to be of substandard quality, e.g. because of a manufacturing fault

COMMENT: Consumers have the same statutory rights when purchasing seconds as when purchasing normal goods; however, the standards of **satisfactory quality** may be somewhat lower.

secret agent /ˌsiːkrət 'eɪdʒənt/ *noun* somebody who tries to find out information in secret about other countries, other governments or other armed forces

Secretary-General /ˌsekrətri 'dʒen(ə)rəl/ *noun* a main administrator in a large organisation such as the United Nations or a political party

Secretary of State for Constitutional Affairs /ˌsekrət(ə)ri əv steɪt fə ˌkɒnstɪtjuːʃ(ə)nl ə'feəz/ *noun* the UK government minister formerly in charge of the Department of Constitutional Affairs (NOTE: The post is now known as the **Secretary of State for Justice**.)

Secretary of State for Defence /ˌsekrət(ə)ri əv steɪt fə dɪ'fens/ *noun* a government minister in charge of the armed forces. Also called **Defence Secretary**

Secretary of State for Justice /ˌsekrət(ə)ri əv steɪt fə 'dʒʌstɪs/ *noun* the UK government minister in charge of the Ministry of Justice (NOTE: The Secretary of State for Justice also holds the post of **Lord Chancellor**.)

Secretary of the Treasury /ˌsekrət(ə)ri əv ðə ˈtreʒəri/ *noun US* a senior member of the government in charge of financial affairs

Secretary to the Senate /ˌsekrətri tə ðə ˈsenət/ *noun US* the head of the administrative staff in the Senate

secret police /ˌsiːkrət pəˈliːs/ *noun* police officers who work in secret, especially dealing with people working against the state

section /ˈsekʃən/ *noun* part of an Act of Parliament or bylaw ○ *He does not qualify for a grant under section 2 of the Act.* (NOTE: When referring to a section of an act, it is abbreviated to **s**: *s 24 LGA*.) ■ *verb* to order somebody to be confined in a psychiatric hospital under the Mental Health Act

secure /sɪˈkjʊə/ *adjective* **1.** safe from danger or harm ○ *The documents should be kept in a secure place.* ○ *The police and army have made the border secure.* **2.** firmly fastened or held ■ *verb* □ **to secure a loan** to pledge a property or other assets as a security for a loan

secured creditor /sɪˌkjʊəd ˈkredɪtə/ *noun* a person who is owed money by someone and holds a mortgage or charge on that person's property as security

secured debts /sɪˌkjʊəd ˈdet/ *plural noun* debts which are guaranteed by assets

secured loan /sɪˌkjʊəd ˈləʊn/ *noun* a loan which is guaranteed by the borrower giving valuable property as security

secure tenant /sɪˌkjʊə ˈtenənt/ *noun* a tenant of a local authority who has the right to buy the freehold of the property he or she rents at a discount

security /sɪˈkjʊərɪti/ *noun* **1.** safety from danger or harm **2.** the state of being protected **3.** a guarantee that someone will repay money borrowed □ **to stand security for someone** to guarantee that if the person does not repay a loan, you will repay on their behalf

security for costs /sɪˌkjʊərɪti fə ˈkɒsts/ *noun* a guarantee that a party in a dispute will pay costs ○ *The master ordered that the claimant should deposit £2,000 as security for the defendant's costs.*

COMMENT: Where a foreign claimant or a company which may become insolvent brings proceedings against a defendant, the defendant is entitled to apply to the court for an order that the proceedings be stayed unless the claimant deposits money to secure the defendant's costs if the claimant fails in his action.

security of tenure /sɪˌkjʊərɪti əv ˈtenjə/ *noun* the right to keep a position or rented accommodation, provided that conditions are met

security printer /sɪˈkjʊərɪti ˌprɪntə/ *noun* a printer who prints paper money or sensitive material such as government documents

sedition /sɪˈdɪʃ(ə)n/ *noun* the crime of doing acts or speaking or publishing words which bring the royal family or the government into hatred or contempt and encourage civil disorder

COMMENT: Sedition is a lesser crime than treason.

seditious /sɪˈdɪʃəs/ *adjective* provoking sedition

seek /siːk/ *verb* **1.** to ask for ○ *a creditor seeking a receiving order under the Bankruptcy Act* ○ *They are seeking damages for loss of revenue.* ○ *The applicant sought judicial review to quash the order.* ○ *The Bill requires a social worker to seek permission of the Juvenile Court.* □ **to seek an interview** to ask if you can see someone ○ *She sought an interview with the minister.* **2.** to look for someone or something ○ *The police are seeking a tall man who was seen near the scene of the crime.* ○ *Two men are being sought by the police.* **3.** to try to do something ○ *The local authority is seeking to place the ward of court in accommodation.* (NOTE: **seeking – sought – has sought**)

segregate /ˈsegrɪgeɪt/ *verb* to separate or keep apart, especially to keep different ethnic groups in a country apart ○ *Single-sex schools segregate boys from girls.*

seised /siːzd/, **seized** *adjective* the fact of having ownership of land □ **to be seised of property** to be legally in possession of property

seisin /ˈsiːzɪn/, **seizin** *noun* **1.** the legal freehold possession of land (*feudal law*) **2.** the act of taking legal freehold possession of land **3.** land that is wholly and legally owned, especially land taken possession of legally

seize /siːz/ *verb* to take hold of something, to take possession of something ○ *Police raided the property and seized thousands of pounds worth of stolen property.*

seizure /ˈsiːʒə/ *noun* the act of taking possession of something ○ *The court ordered the seizure of the shipment or of the company's funds.*

self-defence /ˌself dɪˈfens/ *noun* actions or skills that you use to try to protect yourself when attacked ○ *He pleaded that he had acted in self-defence when he had hit the mugger.*

> COMMENT: This can be used as a defence to a charge of a crime of violence, where the defendant pleads that his actions were attributable to defending him or herself rather than to a desire to commit violence.

self-incrimination /ˌself ɪnˌkrɪmɪˈneɪʃ(ə)n/ *noun* the act of incriminating yourself, of saying something which shows you are guilty □ **right against self-incrimination** the right not to say anything, when questioned by the police, in case you may say something which could incriminate you

sell /sel/ *verb* to transfer the ownership of property to another person in exchange for money ○ *to sell cars* or *to sell refrigerators* ○ *to sell something on credit* ○ *They have decided to sell their house.* ○ *They tried to sell their house for £100,000.* ○ *Her house is difficult to sell.* ○ *Their products are easy to sell.* □ **to sell forward** to sell foreign currency, commodities, etc., for delivery at a later date

seller /ˈselə/ *noun* **1.** somebody who sells ○ *There were few sellers in the market, so prices remained high.* **2.** something which sells ○ *This book is a good seller.*

selling price /ˈselɪŋ praɪs/ *noun* the price at which someone is willing to sell

selling rights /ˈselɪŋ raɪts/ *plural noun* the legal right to sell specific goods or services

semble /ˈsemb(ə)l/ *noun* a French word meaning 'it appears': a word used in discussing a court judgment where there is some uncertainty about what the court intended

semi-autonomous /ˌsemi ɔːˈtɒnəməs/ *noun* with a limited amount of autonomy

senate /ˈsenət/ *noun* **1.** an upper house of a legislative body **2.** **Senate** *US* the upper house of the American Congress ○ *The US Senate voted against the proposal.* ○ *The Secretary of State appeared before the Senate Foreign Relations Committee.* **3.** the ruling body of a university, college or other institution

> COMMENT: The US Senate has 100 members, each state electing two senators by popular vote. Bills may be introduced in the Senate, with the exception of bills relating to finance. The Senate has the power to ratify treaties and to confirm presidential appointments to federal posts.

senator /ˈsenətə/, **Senator** *noun* a member of a senate (NOTE: written with a capital letter when used as a title: *Senator Jackson*)

senatorial /ˌsenəˈtɔːriəl/ *adjective* referring to a senate or to senators

senatorial courtesy /ˌsenəˌtɔːriəl ˈkɜːtəsi/ *noun US* acknowledgement of the importance of the Senate, e.g. the convention that the President consults senators about appointments to federal posts in their states

seniority /ˌsiːniˈɒrɪti/ *noun* **1.** the state of being older or more important than someone else □ **in order of seniority** arranged from the oldest or most important to the youngest or least important **2.** the fact of having been employed in a job for longer than someone else (NOTE: This is a legitimate reason for an employee to earn more pay than another, even if the two jobs are the same.)

senior manager /ˌsiːniə ˈmænɪdʒə/ *noun* a manager or director who has a higher rank than others

senior partner /ˌsiːniə ˈpɑːtnə/ *noun* somebody who has a large part of the shares in a partnership

sentence /ˈsentəns/ *noun* a legal punishment given by a court to a convicted person ○ *He received a three-year jail sentence.* ○ *The two men accused of rape face sentences of up to six years in prison.* □ **to pass sentence** to give a convicted person the official legal punishment ○ *The jury returned a verdict of manslaughter and the judge will pass sentence next week.* ■ *verb* to give someone an official legal punishment ○ *The judge sentenced him to six months in prison* or *he was sentenced to six months' imprisonment.* ○ *The accused was convicted of murder and will be sentenced next week.* Compare **convict**

sentencer /ˈsentənsə/ *noun* a person such as a judge who can pass a legal sentence on someone

sentencing /ˈsentənsɪŋ/ *noun* the act of giving a judicial sentence to a defendant

Sentencing Advisory Panel /ˈsentənsɪŋ ədˌvaɪz(ə)ri ˌpæn(ə)l/ *noun* a body which undertakes research on sentencing and advises the Sentencing Guidance Council. Abbreviation **SAP**

Sentencing Guidance Council /ˈsentənsɪŋ ˌgaɪdəns ˌkaʊns(ə)l/ *noun* a body which produces official guidelines on appropriate sentencing for various crimes, acting on advice from the Sentencing Advisory Panel. Abbreviation **SGC**

separate property /ˌsep(ə)rət ˈprɒpəti/ noun US property owned by a husband and wife before their marriage. Compare **community property**

separation /ˌsepəˈreɪʃ(ə)n/ noun **1.** an agreement between a husband and wife to live apart from each other **2.** US the act of leaving a job by resigning, retiring, being fired or made redundant **3.** the act of keeping things separate from each other

COMMENT: In the USA, the three parts of the power of the state are kept separate and independent: the President does not sit in Congress; Congress cannot influence the decisions of the Supreme Court, etc. In the UK, the powers are not separated, because Parliament has both legislative powers (it makes laws) and judicial powers (the House of Lords acts as a court of appeal); the government (the executive) is not independent and is responsible to Parliament which can outvote it and so cause a general election. In the USA, members of government are not members of Congress, though their appointment has to be approved by Senate; in the UK, members of government are usually Members of Parliament, although some are members of the House of Lords.

separation of powers /ˌsepəreɪʃ(ə)n əv ˈpaʊəs/ noun a system in which the power in a state is separated between the legislative body which passes laws, the judiciary which enforces the law, and the executive which runs the government

seq ♦ et seq.

sequester /sɪˈkwestə/, **sequestrate** /ˈsiːkwɪstreɪt, sɪˈkwestreɪt/ verb to take and keep property because a court has ordered it

sequestration /ˌsiːkweˈstreɪʃ(ə)n/ noun the taking and keeping of property on the order of a court, especially seizing property from someone who is in contempt of court ○ His property has been kept under sequestration.

sequestrator /ˈsiːkwɪstreɪtə, sɪˈkwestreɪtə/ noun somebody who takes and keeps property on the order of a court

seriatim /ˌsɪəriˈeɪtɪm/ adverb a Latin word meaning 'one after the other in order'

Serious Fraud Office /ˌsɪəriəs ˈfrɔːd ˌɒfɪs/ noun a government department in charge of investigating fraud in companies involving amounts over £1,000,000. Abbreviation **SFO**

Serious Organised Crime Agency /ˌsɪəriəs ˌɔːɡənaɪzd ˈkraɪm ˌeɪdʒənsi/ noun a non-departmental public body set up to deal with serious crime, including drug and people trafficking, money laundering and cybercrime. Abbreviation **SOCA**

Serjeant ♦ Common Serjeant

serve /sɜːv/ verb **1.** to deal with (a customer), to do a type of work □ **to serve articles** to work in a solicitor's office as a trainee □ **to serve on a jury** to act as a member of a jury **2.** to give someone a legal document that requires them to do something ○ They were served notice to quit the premises in two months' time. □ **to serve someone with a Claim Form**, **to serve a Claim Form on someone** to give someone an official notice of impending civil proceedings against them **3.** to spend a period of time in prison after being sentenced to imprisonment ○ He served six months in a local jail. ○ She still has half her sentence to serve. □ **to serve time** to spend a period of time in prison for a particular crime ○ Her brother has served time for robbery.

service /ˈsɜːvɪs/ noun □ **service (of process)**, **personal service** the delivery of a document such as a writ or summons to someone in person or to his or her legal representative □ **to acknowledge service** to confirm that a legal document such as a claim form has been received

COMMENT: The Civil Procedure Rules give five methods of service of documents: (i) personal service (i.e. physically to the person themselves); (ii) by first-class post; (iii) by sending or leaving the document at an address for service; (iv) by sending the document through a document exchange; (v) by fax or other electronic means, though this method is only used in certain circumstances, such as sending documents to a legal representative. Note also that under these rules, documents are prepared and usually served by the court itself and not by one or other of the parties concerned.

service by an alternative method serving a legal document on someone other than by the legally prescribed method, e.g. by posting it to the last known address, or by advertising (NOTE: Since the introduction of the Civil Procedure Rules, this term has replaced **substituted service**.)

service charge /ˈsɜːvɪs tʃɑːdʒ/ noun **1.** a charge made by a landlord to cover general work done to the property such as cleaning stairs or collecting rubbish **2.** a charge made in a restaurant for serving the customer

service contract /ˈsɜːvɪs ˌkɒntrækt/ *noun* same as **contract of employment**

servient /ˈsɜːviənt/ *adjective* being less important

servient owner /ˌsɜːviənt ˈəʊnə/ *noun* the owner of land over which someone else has a right to use a path. Compare **dominant owner**

servient tenement /ˌsɜːviənt ˈtenəmənt/ *noun* land over which the owner grants an easement to the owner of another property. Compare **dominant tenement**

session /ˈseʃ(ə)n/ *noun* **1.** the period when a group of people meets ○ *The morning session will be held at 10.30 a.m.* **2.** the period during which formal meetings of a body are being held ○ *The Act was passed in the last session of Parliament* or *the last Parliamentary session.* □ **in session** taking place and carrying out the usual activities

COMMENT: The Parliamentary session starts in October with the Opening of Parliament and the Queen's Speech. It usually lasts until August. In the USA, a new congressional session starts on the 3rd of January each year.

sessional Select Committee /ˌseʃ(ə)n(ə)l sɪˌlekt kəˈmɪti/ *noun* a Select Committee set up at the beginning of each session of parliament ○ *the Select Committee on Defence* or *the Defence Select Committee*

sessions /ˈseʃ(ə)nz/ *plural noun* court

set /set/ *noun* □ **set (of chambers)** a series of offices for a group of barristers who work together

set aside /ˌset əˈsaɪd/ *verb* to decide not to apply a decision, or to cancel an order, judgment or step taken by a party in legal proceedings ○ *The arbitrator's award was set aside on appeal.*

set down /ˌset ˈdaʊn/ *verb* to arrange for a trial to take place by putting it on one of the lists of trials ○ *Pleadings must be submitted to the court when the action is set down for trial.*

set forth /ˌset ˈfɔːθ/ *verb* to put down in writing ○ *The argument is set forth in the document from the European Court.*

set-off /ˈset ɒf/ *noun* a counterclaim by a defendant which should be deducted from the sum being claimed by the claimant

set out /ˌset ˈaʊt/ *verb* **1.** to put down in writing ○ *The claim is set out in the*

enclosed document. ○ *The figures are set out in the tables at the back of the book.* **2.** to try to do something ○ *Counsel for the prosecution has set out to discredit the defence witness.*

settle /ˈset(ə)l/ *verb* **1.** □ **to settle an account** to pay what is owed □ **to settle a claim** to agree to pay what is asked for ○ *The insurance company refused to settle his claim for storm damage.* **2.** to reach a settlement □ **to settle out of court** to reach an agreement privately without continuing the court case **3.** □ **to settle property on someone** to arrange for land to be passed to trustees to keep for the benefit of future owners **4.** to write something such as a contract out in its final form ○ *Counsel is instructed to settle the defence.*

settled land /ˌset(ə)ld ˈlænd/ *noun* land which is subject of a settlement

settlement /ˈset(ə)lmənt/ *noun* **1.** the payment of a bill, debt or claim □ **to offer a discount for quick settlement** to reduce the price of something if the customer pays quickly **2.** an agreement reached after discussion or negotiation □ **to effect a settlement between two parties** to bring two parties together and make them agree to a settlement □ **to accept something in full settlement** to accept money or service from a debtor and agree that it covers all the claim **3.** an agreement reached without completing legal proceedings **4.** a document recording a conveyance of property **5.** a restriction in a will that ensures that property stays in the ownership of the family of the deceased, or ensures that the property is held in trust for the deceased's family and that they receive any income from the sale of it

settlement day /ˈset(ə)lmənt deɪ/ *noun* the day when accounts have to be settled

settle on /ˈset(ə)l ɒn/ *verb* to leave property to someone when you die ○ *He settled his property on his children.*

settlor /ˈset(ə)lə/ *noun* somebody who settles property on someone

sever /ˈsevə/ *verb* to split off from the rest ○ *The property was severed from the rest of his assets and formed a specific legacy to his friend.*

severable /ˈsev(ə)rəb(ə)l/ *adjective* being able to be divided off from the rest ○ *the deceased's severable share of a joint property*

several /ˈsev(ə)rəl/ *adjective* **1.** some ○ *Several judges are retiring this year.* ○ *Several of our clients have received long prison* *sentences.* **2.** separate ○ *The tenants have several liability for the rent.* ◊ **joint and several**

severally /ˈsev(ə)rəli/ *adverb* separately or not jointly □ **they are jointly and severally liable** they are liable both together as a group and as individuals

several tenancy /ˌsev(ə)rəl ˈtenənsi/ *noun* the holding of property by a number of people, each separately and not jointly with any other person

severance /ˈsev(ə)rəns/ *noun* **1.** the ending of a joint tenancy **2.** the ending of a contract of employment

severance pay /ˈsev(ə)rəns peɪ/ *noun* money paid as compensation to someone who is losing his or her job

sexual /ˈsekʃuəl/ *adjective* relating to the two sexes

sexual assault /ˌsekʃuəl əˈsɒlt/ *noun* the offence of forcing sexual contact on someone without their consent

sexual discrimination /ˌsekʃuəl dɪskrɪmɪˈneɪʃ(ə)n/ *noun* the unfair treatment of someone because of their sex, either before or after entering a contract of employment or during the course of their employment. ◊ **indirect sexual discrimination**

sexual intercourse /ˌsekʃuəl ˈɪntəkɔːs/ *noun* a sexual act between a man and a woman ○ *Sexual intercourse with a girl under sixteen is an offence.*

sexual offence /ˌsekʃuəl əˈfens/ *noun* a criminal act involving sexual activity, e.g. rape, incest

SFO *abbreviation* Serious Fraud Office

SGC *abbreviation* Sentencing Guidance Council

shadow director /ˈʃædəʊ daɪˌrektə/ *noun* a person not formally appointed as a director of a company, but whose instructions the company follows

sham /ʃæm/ *adjective* false or not true

sham marriage /ˌʃæm ˈmærɪdʒ/ *noun* a legal marriage which is entered into for the purposes of obtaining a visa or citizenship

shareholder /ˈʃeəhəʊldə/ *noun* somebody who owns shares in a company

shareholders' agreement /ˌʃeəhəʊldəz əˈgriːmənt/ *noun* an agreement showing the rights of shareholders in a company

share option /ˈʃeər ˌɒpʃən/ *noun* the right to buy or sell shares at a specific price

at a time in the future (NOTE: Sometimes offered to new employees as a benefit of the post.)

shareware /ˈʃeəweə/ *noun* software which is subject to copyright restrictions, but is available free of charge for a trial period prior to purchase

Sharia law /ʃəˈriːə lɔː/ *noun* Islamic religious law

sharp practice /ˌʃɑːp ˈpræktɪs/ *noun* a way of doing business which is not honest or fair, but is not illegal

Shelter /ˈʃeltə/ *noun* a housing and homelessness charity

sheriff /ˈʃerɪf/ *noun* **1.** US an official in charge of justice in a county (NOTE: At federal level, the equivalent is a **marshal**.) **2.** (*in Scotland*) the chief judge in a district

Sheriff Court /ˈʃerɪf kɔːt/ *noun* in Scotland, one of the lower courts for civil and criminal cases, presided over by a sheriff

sheriff officer /ˈʃerɪf ˌɒfɪsə/ *noun* in Scotland, a legal officer who serves under a sheriff and is empowered to take possession of a debtor's property, forcibly if necessary, to serve writs and to make arrests

sheriff's sale /ˈʃerɪfs ˌseɪl/ *noun* a public sale of the goods of a person whose property has been seized by the courts because he or she has defaulted on payments

shipper /ˈʃɪpə/ *noun* a person who sends goods or who organises the sending of goods for other customers

shipping agent /ˈʃɪpɪŋ ˌeɪdʒənt/ *noun* a company which specialises in the sending of goods

shipping company /ˈʃɪpɪŋ ˌkʌmp(ə)ni/ *noun* a company which owns ships

shipwreck /ˈʃɪprek/ *noun* the action of sinking or badly damaging a ship

shoplifter /ˈʃɒplɪftə/ *noun* somebody who steals goods from shops ○ *At Christmas time gangs of shoplifters target the stores in Oxford Street.*

shoplifting /ˈʃɒplɪftɪŋ/ *noun* the offence of stealing goods from shops, by taking them when the shop is open and not paying for them

Short Cause List /ˌʃɔːt ˈkɔːz ˌlɪst/ *noun* the set of cases to be heard in the Queen's Bench Division which the judge thinks are not likely to take very long to hear

shorthand writer /ˌʃɔːthænd ˈraɪtə/ *noun* somebody who takes down in shorthand evidence or a judgment given in court

shorthold tenancy /ˌʃɔːthəʊld ˈtenənsi/ *noun* a protected tenancy for a limited period of less than five years

short lease /ˌʃɔːt ˈliːs/ *noun* a lease which runs for up to two or three years ○ *to rent office space on a twenty-year lease* ○ *We have a short lease on our current premises.*

short sharp shock /ˌʃɔːt ˌʃɑːp ˈʃɒk/ *noun* formerly, a type of punishment for young offenders where they were subjected to harsh discipline for a short period in a detention centre

short title /ˌʃɔːt ˈtaɪt(ə)l/ *noun* the usual name by which an Act of Parliament is known, which is shorter and easier to remember than the long title

show of hands /ˌʃəʊ əv ˈhændz/ *noun* a way of casting votes where people show how they vote by raising their hands ○ *The motion was carried on a show of hands.*

shrink-wrap licence /ˈʃrɪŋk ræp ˈlaɪs(ə)ns/ *noun* **1.** a manufacturer's licence applied to software sold to a customer under which the manufacturer grants only limited warranty over the product **2.** a contract entered into when buying a piece of software, in which the act of opening the secure packaging constitutes agreement to enter the contract (NOTE: Alternatively, confirmation can be asked for during the software's installation on a computer.)

COMMENT: In general, the customer does not own the software he has bought, and the manufacturer has no liability for damages consequent on using the product.

SI *abbreviation* statutory instrument

sic /sɪk/ *noun* used to show that this was the way a word was actually written in the document in question even if it looks like a mistake ○ *The letter stated 'my legal adviser intends to apply for attack (sic) of earnings'.*

sick leave /ˈsɪk liːv/ *noun* a period when an employee is away from work because of illness

sight draft /ˈsaɪt drɑːft/ *noun* a bill of exchange which is payable when it is presented

signatory /ˈsɪgnət(ə)ri/ *noun* a person who signs an official document such as a contract ○ *You have to get the permission of all the signatories to the agreement if you want to change the terms.*

signature /ˈsɪgnɪtʃə/ *noun* **1.** someone's name or initials written by that person in their own recognisable handwriting, used to

authorise documents ○ *a pile of letters waiting for the managing director's signature* ○ *The contract has been engrossed ready for signature.* ○ *A will needs the signature of the testator and two witnesses.* ○ *All the company's cheques need two signatures.* ◊ **electronic signature 2.** the action of signing a document ○ *Are the letters ready for signature yet?*

silk /sɪlk/ *noun* □ **a silk** a Queen's Counsel (*informal*) □ **to take silk** to become a QC

similiter /sɪˈmɪlɪtə/ *adverb* a Latin word meaning 'similarly' or 'in a similar way': a short reply from one party in a trial agreeing to a request made by the other party

simple contract /ˌsɪmpəl ˈkɒntrækt/ *noun* a contract which is not under seal, but is made orally or in writing. Compare **contract under seal**

sine die /ˌsiːni ˈdiːeɪ/ *phrase* a Latin phrase meaning 'with no day' □ **the hearing was adjourned sine die** the hearing was adjourned without saying when it would meet again

sine qua non /ˌsɪni kwɑː ˈnɒn/ *phrase* a Latin phrase meaning 'without which nothing': a condition without which something cannot work ○ *Agreement by the management is a sine qua non of all employment contracts.*

sinking fund /ˈsɪŋkɪŋ fʌnd/ *noun* a fund built up out of amounts of money put aside regularly to meet a future need

sit-down protest /ˈsɪt daʊn ˌprəʊtest/ *noun* an action by members of the staff who occupy their place of work and refuse to leave

sitting /ˈsɪtɪŋ/ *noun* a meeting of a court, tribunal or parliament (NOTE: There are four sittings in the legal year: **Michaelmas, Hilary, Easter** and **Trinity**.)

sittings /ˈsɪtɪŋz/ *plural noun* periods when courts sit

sitting tenant /ˌsɪtɪŋ ˈtenənt/ *noun* a tenant who is living in a house when the freehold or lease is sold

situate /ˈsɪtʃueɪtɪd/, **situated** *adjective* in a specific place ○ *a freehold property situated in the borough of Richmond*

situations vacant /ˌsɪtʃueɪʃ(ə)nz ˈveɪkənt/ *plural noun* a list of jobs which are available

skeleton argument /ˈskelɪtən ˌɑːgjumənt/ *noun* a document summarising what an advocate will say in a hearing, now required by the CPR

skimming /'skɪmɪŋ/ *noun* the crime of fraudulently reusing the electronic information from a bank card used in a previous transaction

slander /'slɑːndə/ *noun* an untrue spoken statement which damages someone's character. ◊ **defamation of character** □ **action for slander**, **slander action** a case in a law court where someone says that another person has slandered him or her ■ *verb* □ **to slander someone** to damage someone's character by saying untrue things about him or her. Compare **libel**

slanderous /'slɑːnd(ə)rəs/ *adjective* being slander ○ *He made slanderous statements about the Prime Minister on television.*

SLAPP *abbreviation* the practice of companies taking out large, expensive lawsuits against their critics, who cannot possibly compete and are forced to back down. Full form **Strategic Lawsuits Against Public Participation**

slip /slɪp/ *noun* **1.** a slip of paper used for a particular purpose ○ *a voting slip* **2.** a small mistake ○ *He made a couple of slips in repeating what he had said the day before.*

slip law /'slɪp lɔː/ *noun* US a law published for the first time after it has been approved, printed on a single sheet of paper or as a small separate booklet

slip rule /'slɪp ruːl/ *noun* the name for one of the Rules of the Supreme Court allowing minor errors to be corrected on pleadings

small claim /ˌsmɔːl 'kleɪm/ *noun* a claim for less than £5000 in the County Court

small claims court /ˌsmɔːl 'kleɪmz ˌkɔːt/ *noun* a court which deals with disputes over small amounts of money

small claims track /ˌsmɔːl 'kleɪmz ˌtræk/ *noun* the case management system which applies to claims under £5,000

COMMENT: The aim of the small claims track is to deal with disputes as rapidly as possible, especially where the litigants appear in person. Lawyers are discouraged, but lay representatives can appear. There is only a limited right of appeal in this track.

small print /'smɔːl prɪnt/ *noun* information printed at the end of a contract or other official document in smaller letters than the rest of the text, often containing important details that might be overlooked

smash and grab /ˌsmæʃ ən 'græb/ *noun* a robbery committed by breaking a

shop window in order to steal the goods on display

smoking ban /'sməʊkɪŋ bæn/ *noun* legislation stating that it is no longer permitted to smoke in public places

COMMENT: In the UK legislation banning smoking in enclosed public areas came into force in Scotland in March 2006, in Wales and Northern Ireland in April 2007, and in England in July 2007.

smoking gun /ˌsməʊkɪŋ 'gʌn/ *noun* a crucial piece of evidence

smuggle /'smʌg(ə)l/ *verb* to take goods into or out of a country without declaring them to Revenue and Customs ○ *They had to smuggle the spare parts into the country.*

smuggler /'smʌglə/ *noun* somebody who smuggles

smuggling /'smʌglɪŋ/ *noun* the offence of taking goods illegally into or out of a country, without paying any tax ○ *He made his money in arms smuggling.*

snatch squad /'snætʃ skwɒd/ *noun* a group of police officers trained to find and arrest the leaders of groups causing public disorder (*informal*)

snatch theft /'snætʃ θeft/ *noun* the theft of an item of personal property such as a bag or mobile phone in a public place

SOCA *abbreviation* Serious Organised Crime Agency

social advantage /ˌsəʊʃ(ə)l əd'vɑːntɪdʒ/ *noun* a benefit which some people are given, e.g. a bus pass given to a retired person or a special loan given to a family with many children

social class /ˌsəʊʃ(ə)l 'klɑːs/ *noun* a group of people who have a position in society

Social Fund /'səʊʃ(ə)l fʌnd/ *noun* a Government fund which provides grants and loans to help people with general living expenses

social ownership /ˌsəʊʃ(ə)l 'əʊnəʃɪp/ *noun* a situation where an industry is nationalised and run by a board appointed by the government

social worker /'səʊʃ(ə)l ˌwɜːkə/ *noun* somebody who works in a social services department, visiting and looking after people who need help

SOCO /'sɒkəʊ/ *noun* a police officer responsible for collecting forensic evidence. Full form **scene-of-crime officer**

sodomy /'sɒdəmi/ *noun* same as **buggery**

soft loan /'sɒft ləʊn/ *noun* a loan from a company to an employee or from one government to another with no interest payable

software licence /'sɒftweə ˌlaɪs(ə)ns/ *noun* permission to use a piece of copyrighted software, with attendant rights and restrictions

sole /səʊl/ *adjective* only ○ *He is the sole owner of the property.*

solemn /'sɒləm/ *adjective* **1.** formal and serious ○ *He made a solemn promise to reform his behaviour.* **2.** ♦ **solemn procedure**

solemn and binding agreement /ˌsɒləm ən ˌbaɪndɪŋ ə'griːmənt/ *noun* an agreement which is not legally binding, but which all parties are supposed to obey

solemn procedure /ˌsɒləm prə'siːdʒə/ *noun* in Scotland, a criminal hearing in a Sheriff Court that takes place with a jury

sole owner /ˌsəʊl 'əʊnə/ *noun* a person who owns a business and has no partners

sole trader /ˌsəʊl 'treɪdə/ *noun* a person who runs a business, usually without partners, but has not registered it as a company

solicit /sə'lɪsɪt/ *verb* **1.** □ **to solicit orders** to ask for orders, to try to get people to order goods **2.** to ask for something immoral, especially to offer to provide sexual intercourse for money

soliciting /sə'lɪsɪtɪŋ/ *noun* the offence of offering to provide sexual intercourse for money

solicitor /sə'lɪsɪtə/ *noun* a lawyer who has passed the examinations of the Law Society and has a valid certificate to practise, who gives advice to members of the public and acts for them in legal matters, and who may have right of audience in some courts □ **to instruct a solicitor** to give orders to a solicitor to act on your behalf □ **the Official Solicitor** a solicitor who acts in the High Court for parties who have no one to act for them, usually because they are under a legal disability

COMMENT: Solicitors of ten years standing can be appointed as judges. Solicitor-advocates are fully qualified solicitors who have taken additional advocacy exams and have the same rights of audience as barristers.

Solicitor-General /səˌlɪsɪtə 'dʒen(ə)rəl/ *noun* one of the law officers, a Member of the House of Commons and deputy to the Attorney-General

Solicitor-General for Scotland /sə ˌlɪsɪtə ˌdʒen(ə)rəl fə 'skɒtlənd/ *noun* a junior law officer in Scotland

solicitors' charges /sə'lɪsɪtəz ˌtʃɑːdʒɪz/ *plural noun* payments to be made to solicitors for work done on behalf of clients

Solicitors Regulation Authority /sə ˌlɪsɪtəz ˌregjʊ'leɪʃ(ə)n ɔːˌθɒrɪti/ *noun* the official regulatory body for solicitors in England and Wales. Abbreviation **SRA**

solitary confinement /ˌsɒlɪt(ə)ri kən 'faɪnmənt/ *noun* the practice of keeping someone alone in a cell, without being able to see or speak to other prisoners ○ *He was kept in solitary confinement for six months.*

solus agreement /ˌsəʊləs ə'griːmənt/ *noun* an agreement where one party is linked only to the other party, especially an agreement where a retailer buys all their stock from a single supplier

solvency /'sɒlv(ə)nsi/ *noun* the ability of a company to pay all debts. ◊ **insolvency**

solvent /'sɒlv(ə)nt/ *adjective* having enough money to pay debts ○ *When he bought the company it was barely solvent.* ■ *noun* a powerful glue

solvent abuse /'sɒlvənt əˌbjuːs/ *noun* the activity of sniffing solvent, which acts as a hallucinatory drug

SOSR *abbreviation* some other substantial reason

sought /sɔːt/ ♦ **seek**

sound /saʊnd/ *adjective* reliable, effective or thorough ○ *The company's financial situation is very sound.* ○ *The solicitor gave us some very sound advice.* ○ *The evidence brought forward by the police is not very sound.* □ **of sound mind** sane, mentally well ○ *He was of sound mind when he wrote the will.*

soundness /'saʊndnəs/ *noun* the fact of being reliable and effective

source /sɔːs/ *noun* a place where something comes from ○ *source of income* ○ *You must declare income from all sources to the Inland Revenue.* □ **to tax income at source** to remove tax before the income is paid

South-Eastern Circuit /saʊθ ˌiːst(ə)n 'sɜːkɪt/ *noun* one of the six circuits of the Crown Court to which barristers belong, with its centre in London

sovereign /'sɒvrɪn/ *noun* the king or queen as head of state ○ *The sovereign's head appears on coins and stamps.* ■ *adjective* having complete freedom to govern itself

COMMENT: The agreement of the sovereign is needed to pass an Act of Parliament, although once the Bill has been approved by the House of Commons and House of Lords it is usually given royal assent as a matter of course.

sovereign immunity /ˌsɒvrɪn ɪ'mjuːnɪti/ *noun* immunity of a foreign head of state or former head of state from prosecution outside his or her country for crimes committed inside his or her country in the course of exercising public function

sovereign rights /ˌsɒvrɪn 'raɪts/ *noun* the rights of a state, which are limited by the application of EU law

spam /spæm/ *noun* unsolicited bulk emails

Speaker /'spiːkə/ *noun* somebody who presides over a meeting of a parliament

COMMENT: In the House of Commons, the speaker is an ordinary Member of Parliament chosen by the other members; the equivalent in the House of Lords is the Lord Chancellor. In the US Congress, the speaker of the House of Representatives is an ordinary congressman, elected by the other congressmen; the person presiding over meetings of the Senate is the Vice-President.

Speaker's Chaplain /ˌspiːkəz 'tʃæplɪn/ *noun* a priest who reads prayers at the beginning of each sitting of the House of Commons

special agent /ˌspeʃ(ə)l 'eɪdʒənt/ *noun* **1.** a person who represents someone in a particular matter **2.** a person who does secret work for a government

Special Branch /'speʃ(ə)l brɑːnʃ/ *noun* a department of the British police which deals with terrorism

special constable /ˌspeʃ(ə)l 'kʌnstəb(ə)l/ *noun* a part-time policeman who works mainly at weekends or on important occasions

special damages /ˌspeʃ(ə)l 'dæmɪdʒɪz/ *plural noun* damages awarded by court to compensate for a loss such as the expense of repairing something, which can be calculated (NOTE: They are noted at the end of a report on a case as: *Special damages: £100; General damages: £2,500.*)

special deposits /ˌspeʃ(ə)l dɪ'pɒzɪts/ *plural noun* large sums of money which banks have to deposit with the Bank of England

special directions /ˌspeʃ(ə)l daɪ'rekʃənz/ *plural noun* instructions given by a court in a specific case, which are additional to the standard instructions

special endorsement /ˌspeʃ(ə)l ɪn'dɔːsmənt/ *noun* full details of a claim involving money, land or goods which a claimant is trying to recover

specialise /'speʃəlaɪz/ *verb* **1.** to study one particular subject ○ *He specialised in employment cases.* **2.** to produce one thing in particular ○ *The company specialises in electronic components.* (NOTE: **specialised -specialising**)

special procedure /ˌspeʃ(ə)l prə'siːdʒə/ *noun* a special system for dealing quickly with undefended divorce cases whereby the parties can obtain a divorce without the necessity of a full trial

special resolution /ˌspeʃ(ə)l ˌrezə'luːʃ(ə)n/ *noun* a resolution of the members of a company which is only valid if it is approved by 75% of the votes cast at a meeting

COMMENT: 21 days' notice that a special resolution will be put to a meeting must be given. A special resolution might deal with an important matter, such as a change to the company's articles of association, a change of the company's name, or of the objects of the company.

special sessions /ˌspeʃ(ə)l 'seʃ(ə)ns/ *plural noun* a sitting of a Magistrates' Court which is held in addition to the usual scheduled sittings, e.g. because of there being a high volume of cases to hear

specialty contract /ˌspeʃ(ə)lti kən'trækt/ *noun* a contract made under seal

specific devise /spəˌsɪfɪk dɪ'vaɪz/ *noun* a devise of a specified property made to someone

specific disclosure /spəˌsɪfɪk dɪs'kləʊʒə/ *noun* an order by a court for a party to disclose specific documents or to search for them and disclose them if they are found to exist

specific legacy /spəˌsɪfɪk 'legəsi/ *noun* a legacy of a specific item to someone in a will

specific performance /spəˌsɪfɪk pə'fɔːməns/ *noun* a court order to a party to carry out his or her obligations in a contract

specimen /'spesɪmɪn/ *noun* something which is given as a sample

specimen signature /ˌspesɪmɪn 'sɪɡnətʃə/ *noun* a copy of a signature which is sent to a bank so that they can authenticate the signatures on company cheques

speeding /'spiːdɪŋ/ *noun* an offence committed when driving a vehicle faster than the speed limit ○ *He was booked for speeding.*

spent conviction /ˌspent kənˈvɪkʃən/ *noun* a conviction for which an accused person has been sentenced in the past

COMMENT: Under the Rehabilitation of Offenders Act, a conviction becomes **spent** when the sentence has been served and a particular period of time (calculated in relation to the sentence) has passed. It is illegal for an employer to discriminate against a potential employee on the grounds of a spent conviction, and it should not be referred to in future legal proceedings.

sphere of influence /ˌsfɪə əv ˈɪnfluəns/ *noun* an area of the world where a very strong country can exert powerful influence over other states ○ *Some Latin American states fall within the USA's sphere of influence.*

splendid isolation /ˌsplendɪd ˌaɪsəˈleɪʃ(ə)n/ *noun* a policy whereby a country refuses to link with other countries in treaties

spoil /spɔɪl/ *verb* to make a ballot paper invalid by filling it in incorrectly

spoils of war /ˌspɔɪlz əv ˈwɔː/ *plural noun* goods or valuables taken by an army from an enemy

spoilt ballot paper /ˌspɔɪlt ˈbælət ˌpeɪpə/ *noun* a voting paper which has not been filled in correctly by the voter

spokesperson /ˈspəʊksˌpɜːs(ə)n/ *noun* somebody who speaks in public on behalf of a group

spousal abuse /ˈspaʊsəl əˌbjuːs/ *noun* physical or mental abuse between a husband and wife

spouse /spaʊs/ *noun* **1.** a husband or wife **2.** a person who is married to another person

springing use /ˌsprɪŋɪŋ ˈjuːs/ *noun* a use which will come into effect if something happens in the future

spy /spaɪ/ *noun* somebody who tries to find out secrets about another country ○ *He spent many years as a spy for the enemy.* ○ *He was arrested as a spy.* ■ *verb* **1.** to watch another country secretly to get information ○ *She was accused of spying for the enemy.* **2.** to see

squad /skwɒd/ *noun* **1.** a special group of police **2.** a special group of soldiers or workers

squad car /ˈskwɒd kɑː/ *noun* a police patrol car

square measure /ˌskweə ˈmeʒə/ *noun* area in square feet or metres, calculated by multiplying width and length

squat /skwɒt/ *verb* to occupy premises belonging to another person unlawfully and without title or without paying rent (NOTE: **squatting – squatted**)

squatter /ˈskwɒtə/ *noun* somebody who squats in someone else's property

squatter's rights /ˈskwɒtəz ˌraɪts/ *plural noun* rights of a person who is squatting in another person's property to remain in unlawful possession of premises until ordered to leave by a court

COMMENT: If a squatter has lived on the premises for a long period (over 12 years) and the owner has not tried to evict him or her, he or she may have rights over the premises.

squeal /skwiːl/ *verb* to inform the police about other criminals (*slang*)

squire /ˈskwaɪə/ *noun US* a local legal official such as a magistrate

SRA *abbreviation* Solicitors Regulation Authority

SSP *abbreviation* Statutory Sick Pay

stabvest /ˈstæbvest/ *noun* a padded waistcoat, designed to protect a police or security officer against attacks with knives

stakeholder /ˈsteɪkhəʊldə/ *noun* **1.** someone with a personal interest in how something happens **2.** a person or group of people who have invested in and own part of a business **3.** a person who holds money impartially, such as money deposited by one of the parties to a wager, until it has to be given it up to another party

stakeholder pension /ˈsteɪkhəʊldə ˌpenʃən/ *noun* a pension scheme available to employees through their employer, although the employer does not have to contribute any funds to it

stalker /ˈstɔːkə/ *noun* someone who commits the act of stalking ○ *She obtained a restraining order against her stalker.*

stalking /ˈstɔːkɪŋ/ *noun* repeatedly harassing someone, which may constitute an offence under the Protection from Harassment Act 1997

stamp duty /ˈstæmp ˌdjuːti/ *noun* a tax on documents recording legal activities such as the conveyance of a property to a new owner or the contract for the purchase of shares

stand /stænd/ *noun* **1.** an active campaign against something ○ *the government's stand against racial prejudice* ○ *The police chief criticised the council's stand on law and order.* **2.** the position of a member of Congress on a question (either for or against) **3.**

□ **to take the stand** to go into the witness box to give evidence ■ *verb* **1.** to offer yourself as a candidate in an election ○ *He stood as a Liberal candidate in the General Election.* ○ *He is standing against the present deputy leader in the leadership contest.* ○ *She was persuaded to stand for parliament.* ○ *He has stood for office several times, but has never been elected.* **2.** to exist, to be in a state ○ *The report stood referred to the Finance Committee.* (NOTE: **standing – stood**)

standard /ˈstændəd/ *noun* the normal quality or normal conditions against which other things are judged □ **up to standard** of acceptable quality

standard agreement /ˌstændəd əˈɡriːmənt/ *noun* a normal printed contract form

standard directions /ˌstændəd daɪˈrekʃənz/ *plural noun* directions as laid out in the practice direction for a particular track

standard disclosure /ˌstændəd dɪsˈkləʊʒə/ *noun* a statement by a party about the existence of documents which will support his or her case, or which will support the case of the other party

standard form contract /ˌstændəd fɔːm ˈkɒntrækt/ *noun* a contract which states the conditions of carrying out a common commercial arrangement such as chartering a ship

standard letter /ˌstændəd ˈletə/ *noun* a letter which is sent with only minor changes to various correspondents

standard rate /ˈstændəd reɪt/ *noun* a general level of tax such as the level of income tax which is paid by most taxpayers or the level of VAT which is levied on most goods and services

standard scale /ˌstændəd ˈskeɪl/ *noun* a system which specifies the amount that an offender may be fined if found guilty of a particular crime

standi ♦ **locus standi**

stand in for /ˌstænd ˈɪn fɔː/ *verb* to take the place of someone ○ *Mr Smith is standing in for the chairman who is away on holiday.*

standing /ˈstændɪŋ/ *adjective* permanent ■ *noun* good reputation ○ *the financial standing of a company*

standing committee /ˈstændɪŋ kəˌmɪti/ *noun* a permanent committee which deals with matters not given to other committees, e.g. a parliamentary committee

which examines Bills not sent to other committees

standing orders /ˌstændɪŋ ˈɔːdəz/ *plural noun* rules or regulations which control the conduct of any official institution or committee

stand over /ˌstænd ˈəʊvə/ *verb* to adjourn ○ *The case has been stood over to next month.*

Star Chamber /ˈstɑː ˌtʃeɪmbə/ *noun* formerly, a royal court which tried cases without a jury

stare decisis /ˌstɑːreɪ dɪˈsaɪsɪs/ *phrase* a Latin phrase meaning 'stand by preceding decisions': the principle that courts must abide by precedents set by judgments made in higher courts

state /steɪt/ *noun* **1.** a semi-independent section of a federal country such as the USA **2.** the government of a country □ **offence against the state** an act of attacking the lawful government of a country, e.g. sedition, treason ■ *verb* to say clearly ○ *The document states that all revenue has to be declared to the tax office.*

state capital /ˌsteɪt ˈkæpɪt(ə)l/ *noun* the main town in a state or province

State Capitol /ˌsteɪt ˈkæpɪt(ə)l/ *noun* in the USA, a building which houses the State legislature in the main city of a state

state-controlled /ˈsteɪt kənˌtrəʊld/ *adjective* run by the state ○ *state-controlled television*

state enterprise /ˌsteɪt ˈentəpraɪz/ *noun* a company run by the state

stateless person /ˌsteɪtləs ˈpɜːs(ə)n/ *noun* somebody who is not a citizen of any state

statement /ˈsteɪtmənt/ *noun* **1.** a formal account of what happened or what was seen at a particular time, given to the police who are investigating a crime □ **to make a statement** to give details of something to the police □ **to make a false statement** to give wrong details to the police about something that happened or was seen **2.** the presentation of information about something **3.** an announcement of something in public ○ *The company issued a statement denying the allegations.* **4.** a document that shows the amount of money in a bank account or information about business accounts ○ *a financial statement* ○ *a monthly statement*

statement of account /ˌsteɪtmənt əv ə ˈkaʊnt/ *noun* a list of invoices and credits and debits sent by a supplier to a customer at the end of each month

statement of affairs /ˌsteɪtmənt əv əˈfeəz/ *noun* an official statement made by an insolvent company, listing its assets and liabilities

statement of claim /ˌsteɪtmənt əv ˈkleɪm/ *noun* formerly, a document containing details of a claimant's case and the relief sought against the defendant (NOTE: Since the introduction of the Civil Procedure Rules, this term has been replaced by **particulars of claim**.)

Statement of Means /ˌsteɪtmənt əv ˈmiːnz/ *noun* a statement showing the financial position of the claimant, attached to an application for Legal Aid

statement of truth /ˌsteɪtmənt əv ˈtruːθ/ *noun* a statement attached to a claim form or the particulars of a claim by which the claimant or defendant states that he or she believes that the facts given are true (NOTE: If it can be proved that the statement was signed without believing it to be true, the claimant is guilty of contempt of court.)

statement of value /ˌsteɪtmənt əv ˈvæljuː/ *noun* a document filed by the claimant as part of a claim, detailing the value of the claim, or a document filed by the defendant giving an estimate of value in reply to the claim

statements of case /ˌsteɪtmənts əv ˈkeɪs/ *plural noun* documents relating to a claim, including the claim form, the particulars of claim, the defence and counterclaim, the reply and the defence to the counterclaim (NOTE: Since the introduction of the Civil Procedure Rules, this term has replaced **pleadings**.)

state of indebtedness /ˌsteɪt əv ɪnˈdetɪdnəs/ *noun* the state of owing money

state of repair /ˌsteɪt əv rɪˈpeə/ *noun* the physical condition of something ○ *The house was in a bad state of repair when he bought it.*

State of the Union message /steɪt əv ðə ˌjuːnjən ˈmesɪdʒ/ *noun US* an annual speech by the President of the USA which summarises the political situation in the country

state pension /ˌsteɪt ˈpenʃən/ *noun* a standard pension paid by the Government

COMMENT: To be eligible for a state pension you must have reached pensionable age, and have made National Insurance payments throughout your working life. Currently the pensionable age for men is 65 and a 'working life' is 49 years or more. Women born before 1950 qualify at the age of 60 with a working life of 44 years; after this the age and length of service requirements increase by one year per annum. For birth dates after 1954, the same requirements apply as for men.

States of the Union /ˌsteɪts əv ðə ˈjuːnjən/ *plural noun* the states joined together to form the United States of America

statistical discrepancy /stəˌtɪstɪk(ə)l dɪˈskrepənsi/ *noun* the amount by which two sets of figures differ

statistics /stəˈtɪstɪks/ *plural noun* the study of facts in the form of figures ○ *He asked for the birth statistics for 1998.* ○ *Council statistics show that the amount of rented property in the borough has increased.* ○ *Government trade statistics show that exports to the EC have fallen over the last six months.*

status inquiry /ˈsteɪtəs ɪnˌkwaɪəri/ *noun* a request for a check on a customer's credit rating

status quo /ˌsteɪtəs ˈkwəʊ/ *noun* the state of things as they are now ○ *The contract does not alter the status quo.*

status quo ante /ˌsteɪtəs ˌkwəʊ ˈænti/ *noun* the situation as it was before

statute /ˈstætʃuːt/ *noun* an established written law, especially an Act of Parliament

statute-barred /ˌstætʃuːt ˈbɑːd/ *adjective* being unable to take place because the time laid down in the statute of limitations has expired

statute book /ˈstætʃuːt bʊk/ *noun* all laws passed by Parliament which are still in force

statute of limitations /ˌstætʃuːt əv ˌlɪmɪˈteɪʃ(ə)nz/ *noun* a law which allows only a certain amount of time (usually six years) for someone to start legal proceedings to claim property or compensation for damage, etc. ◊ **doctrine of laches**

statutorily /ˈstætʃʊt(ə)rɪli/ *adverb* by statute ○ *a statutorily protected tenant*

statutory /ˈstætʃʊt(ə)ri/ *adjective* fixed by law or by a statute ○ *powers conferred on an authority by the statutory code* ○ *There is a statutory period of probation of thirteen weeks.* ○ *The authority has a statutory obligation to provide free education to all children.*

statutory body /ˈstætʃʊt(ə)ri ˌbɒdi/ *noun* an organisation with the legal authority to take action in respect of a particular area of life

statutory books /ˌstætʃʊt(ə)ri ˈbʊks/ plural noun official registers which a company must keep

statutory declaration /ˌstætʃʊt(ə)ri ˌdekləˈreɪʃ(ə)n/ noun **1.** a statement made to the Registrar of Companies that a company has complied with certain legal conditions **2.** a declaration signed and witnessed for official purposes

statutory duty /ˌstætʃʊt(ə)ri ˈdjuːti/ noun a duty which someone must perform and which is laid down by statute

statutory holiday /ˌstætʃʊt(ə)ri ˈhɒlɪdeɪ/ noun a holiday which is fixed by law

statutory instrument /ˌstætʃʊt(ə)ri ˈɪnstrʊmənt/ noun an order with the force of law made under authority granted to a minister by an Act of Parliament. Abbreviation **SI**

statutory legacy /ˌstætʃʊt(ə)ri ˈlegəsi/ noun the amount of money which is distributed to a surviving spouse of a person who dies intestate and has other surviving relatives but no surviving children

statutory rights /ˌstætʃʊt(ə)ri ˈraɪts/ plural noun rights enjoyed by consumers of goods under the Sale of Goods Act

Statutory Sick Pay /ˌstætʃʊt(ə)ri ˈsɪk ˌpeɪ/ noun standard pay given by an employer to an employee who is too ill to work, for up to a maximum of 28 weeks. Abbreviation **SSP**

statutory trust /ˌstætʃʊt(ə)ri ˈtrʌst/ noun an arrangement for holding property on behalf of the children of a person who has died intestate

statutory undertakers /ˌstætʃʊt(ə)ri ˌʌndəˈteɪkəz/ plural noun bodies formed by statute and having legal duties to provide services such as gas, electricity or water

statutory will /ˌstætʃʊt(ə)ri ˈwɪl/ noun a will made on behalf of a person who is judged unable to do so themselves on the instructions of the Court of Protection

stay /steɪ/ noun the temporary stopping of an order made by a court ○ *The stay was extended for a further four weeks.* ■ verb to stop an action temporarily ○ *The defendant made an application to stay the proceedings until the claimant gave security for costs.* ○ *One of the parties asked for the action to be stayed for a month to allow for a settlement to be attempted.*

stay away order /ˌsteɪ əˈweɪ ˌɔːdə/ noun a court order that tells someone to have no contact or communication with another person

stay of execution /ˌsteɪ əv eksɪˈkjuːʃ(ə)n/ noun a temporary prevention of someone from enforcing a judgment ○ *The court granted the company a two-week stay of execution.*

stay of proceedings /ˌsteɪ əv prəˈsiːdɪŋz/ noun the stopping of a case which is being heard ○ *Proceedings will continue when the stay is lifted.*

steal /stiːl/ verb to take something which does not belong to you ○ *Two burglars broke into the office and stole the petty cash.* ○ *One of our managers left to form her own company and stole the list of our clients' addresses.* ○ *One of our biggest problems is stealing in the wine department.*

stealing /ˈstiːlɪŋ/ noun the crime of taking property which belongs to someone else □ **going equipped for stealing** the notifiable offence of carrying tools which could be used for burglary

steaming /ˈstiːmɪŋ/ noun an offence committed by a group of youths, usually unarmed, who rush down a street or through a public place such as a train carriage, stealing items and harassing people

stenographer /stəˈnɒɡrəfə/ noun an official person who can write in shorthand and so take records of what is said in court

step- /step/ prefix showing a family relationship through a parent who has married again

stepfather /ˈstepfɑːðə/ noun a man who has married a child's mother but is not the natural father of the child

stepmother /ˈstepmʌðə/ noun a woman who has married a child's father but is not the natural mother of the child

stepparent /ˈstepˌpeərənt/ noun a stepfather or stepmother

stinger /ˈstɪŋə/ noun a device covered in spikes that can be thrown across a road to puncture a car's tyres if the police want to stop someone

stipendiary magistrate /staɪˌpendiəri ˈmædʒɪstreɪt/ noun a magistrate who is a qualified lawyer and who receives a salary. Compare **lay magistrate** (NOTE: Now called **District Judge** or **Senior District Judge**.)

stipulate /ˈstɪpjʊleɪt/ verb to demand that a condition be put into a contract ○ *to stipulate that the contract should run for five years* ○ *to pay the stipulated charges* ○ *The company failed to pay on the stipulated* *date* or *on the date stipulated in the contract.* ○ *The contract stipulates that the seller pays the buyer's legal costs.*

stipulation /ˌstɪpjʊˈleɪʃ(ə)n/ *noun* a condition in a contract

stirpes ♦ **per stirpes**

stirpital /ˈstɜːpɪt(ə)l/ *adjective* referring to an entitlement which is divided among branches of a family rather than among individuals ○ *The judge placed a stirpital construction on the rule that children of a deceased person dying intestate must bring interest received from that person into hotchpot.*

stock /stɒk/ *noun* □ **in stock, out of stock** available or not available in the warehouse or store

Stock Exchange /ˈstɒk ɪksˌtʃeɪndʒ/ *noun* a place where stocks and shares are bought and sold ○ *He works on the Stock Exchange.* ○ *Shares in the company are traded on the Stock Exchange.*

stock movements /ˈstɒk ˌmuːvmənts/ *plural noun* passing of stock into or out of the warehouse

stock option /ˈstɒk ˌɒpʃən/ *noun* same as **share option**

stock valuation /ˌstɒk ˌvæljuˈeɪʃ(ə)n/ *noun* estimation of the value of stock at the end of an accounting period

stolen goods /ˌstəʊlən ˈɡʊdz/ *plural noun* goods which have been stolen □ **handling stolen goods, receiving stolen goods** the offence of dealing with goods (receiving them or selling them) which you know to have been stolen

stop and search /stɒp ən sɜːtʃ/, **stop and frisk** *US* /stɒp ən frɪsk/ *noun* the power held by a police officer to stop anyone and search them, even though there is no evidence that the person has committed any offence

storm damage /ˈstɔːm ˌdæmɪdʒ/ *noun* damage to property caused by a storm

straight /streɪt/ *adjective* not dishonest □ **to play straight, to act straight with someone** to act honestly with someone □ **to go straight** to stop criminal activities

stranger crime /ˈstreɪndʒə ˌkraɪm/ *noun* a violent crime in which the attacker is someone whom the victim does not know

Strategic Lawsuits Against Public Participation /strəˌtiːdʒɪk ˌlɔːsuːts ə ˌɡenst ˌpʌblɪk pɑːˌtɪsɪˈpeɪʃ(ə)n/ *noun* full form of **SLAPP**

street crime /ˈstriːt kraɪm/ *noun* criminal activity in a public place, especially an urban area, especially theft of personal possessions or cars, or the illegal possession or use of firearms

strict liability /strɪkt ˌlaɪəˈbɪlɪti/ *noun* total liability for an offence which has been committed whether you are at fault or not

strife /straɪf/ *noun* violent public arguments and disorder

strike /straɪk/ *noun* **1.** the activity of stopping work because of an inability to reach agreement with management or because of orders from a union **2.** □ **to take strike action** to go on strike ■ *verb* **1.** to stop working because there is no agreement with management ○ *to strike for higher wages* or *for shorter working hours* ○ *to strike in protest against bad working conditions* **2.** to hit someone or something ○ *Two policemen were struck by bottles.* ○ *He was struck on the head by a cosh.* **3.** □ **to strike from the record** to remove words from the written minutes of a meeting because they are incorrect or offensive ○ *The chairman's remarks were struck from the record.*

strike off /ˌstraɪk ˈɒf/ *verb* to delete a name or item from a list or record □ **to strike someone off the rolls** to stop a solicitor from practising by removing his or her name from the Roll of Solicitors

strike out /ˈstraɪk aʊt/ *verb* **1.** to delete a word or words from a document □ **to strike out the last word** *US* way of getting permission of the chair to speak on a question, by moving that the last word of the amendment or section being discussed should be deleted, so that it no longer forms part of the case ○ *to strike out a pleading* or *a statement of case* ○ *A party can apply for a statement of case to be struck out if it is not verified.* ○ *A court may strike out a statement of case if it appears that the statement shows no grounds for bringing the claim.*

strip search /ˈstrɪp sɜːtʃ/ *noun* the searching of a person after he or she has removed their clothes (NOTE: Strip searches should be carried out by a doctor or nurse, or at least by a police officer of the same sex as the person being searched.)

stun gun /ˈstʌn ɡʌn/ *noun* same as **electroshock weapon**

sub- /sʌb/ *prefix* less important

sub-agency /ˈsʌb ˌeɪdʒənsi/ *noun* a small agency which is part of a large agency

sub-agent /ˈsʌb ˌeɪdʒənt/ *noun* somebody who is in charge of a sub-agency

sub-clause /ˌsʌb ˈklɔːz/ *noun* part of a clause in a Bill being considered by Parliament, which will become a sub-section when the Bill becomes an Act

sub-committee /ˈsʌb kəˌmɪti/ *noun* a small committee which reports on a special subject to a main committee ○ *He is chairman of the finance sub-committee.*

subcontract *noun* /ˈsʌbˌkɒntrækt/ a contract between the main contractor for a whole project and another firm who will do part of the work ○ *They have been awarded the subcontract for all the electrical work in the new building.* ○ *We will put the electrical work out to subcontract.* ■ *verb* /ˌsʌbkən ˈtrækt/ to agree with a company that they will do part of the work for a project ○ *The electrical work has been subcontracted to Smith Ltd.*

subcontractor /ˈsʌbkənˌtræktə/ *noun* a company which has a contract to do work for a main contractor

subject /ˈsʌbdʒɪkt/ *noun* 1. what something is concerned with ○ *The subject of the action was the liability of the defendant for the claimant's injuries.* 2. somebody who is a citizen of a country and bound by its laws ○ *He is a British subject.* ○ *British subjects do not need visas to visit EU countries.* □ **liberty of the subject** the right of a citizen to be free unless convicted of a crime which is punishable by imprisonment

subject to /ˈsʌbdʒɪkt tə/ *adjective* 1. depending on □ **subject to approval** only if it is approved □ **subject to contract** only when a proper contract has been signed □ **subject to availability** only if the goods are available 2. being liable for something □ **subject to tax** liable for tax

sub judice /ˌsʌb ˈdʒuːdɪsi/ *phrase* a Latin phrase meaning 'under the law': being considered by a court and so not decided

COMMENT: Cases which are sub judice cannot be mentioned in the media or in Parliament if the mention is likely to prejudice the trial, and so would constitute contempt of court.

sublease *noun* /ˈsʌbliːs/ a lease from a tenant to another tenant ■ *verb* /sʌbˈliːs/ to lease a leased property from another tenant ○ *They subleased a small office in the centre of town.*

sublessee /ˌsʌbleˈsiː/ *noun* a person or company which holds a property on a sublease

sublessor /ˌsʌbleˈsɔː/ *noun* a tenant who lets a leased property to another tenant

sublet /sʌbˈlet/ *verb* to let a leased property to another tenant ○ *We have sublet part of our office to a financial consultancy.* (NOTE: **subletting – sublet – has sublet**)

submission /səbˈmɪʃ(ə)n/ *noun* 1. a statement made to a judge or other person considering a case ○ *The court heard the submission of defence counsel that there was no case to answer.* 2. a document outlining a proposal given to someone who has to make a decision about it ○ *The deadline for submissions is the end of June.* 3. the process of presenting something for consideration 4. the state of giving in or having to obey someone

submit /səbˈmɪt/ *verb* 1. to put something forward to be examined ○ *to submit a proposal to the committee* ○ *She submitted a claim to the insurers.* 2. to plead an argument in court ○ *Counsel submitted that the defendant had no case to answer.* ○ *It was submitted that the right of self-defence can be available only against unlawful attack.* 3. to agree to be ruled by something ○ *He refused to submit to the jurisdiction of the court.* (NOTE: **submitting – submitted**)

subornation of perjury /ˌsʌbɔːˈneɪʃ(ə)n əv ˈpɜːdʒəri/ *noun* the offence of getting someone to commit perjury

subpoena /səˈpiːnə/ *noun* a Latin word meaning 'under penalty': a court order requiring someone to appear in court ■ *verb* to order someone to appear in court ○ *The finance director was subpoenaed by the prosecution.*

subpoena ad testificandum /səˌpiːnə æd ˌtestɪfɪˈkændəm/ *phrase* a Latin phrase meaning 'under penalty to testify': a court order requiring someone to appear as a witness (NOTE: Since the introduction of the Civil Procedure Rules, this term has been replaced by **witness summons**.)

subpoena duces tecum *phrase* a Latin phrase meaning 'under penalty to bring with you': a court order requiring someone to appear as a witness and bring with them documents relevant to the case (NOTE: Since the introduction of the Civil Procedure Rules, this term has been replaced by **witness summons**.)

subrogation /ˌsʌbrəʊˈgeɪʃ(ə)n/ *noun* a legal principle whereby someone stands in the place of another person and acquires that person's rights and is responsible for that person's liabilities

sub-section /ˈsʌb ˌsekʃən/ *noun* a part of a section of a document such as an Act of Parliament ○ *You will find the information in sub-section 3 of Section 47.*

subsequent /ˈsʌbsɪkwənt/ *adjective* following because of something ○ *his arrest and subsequent imprisonment*

subsidiarity /səbˌsɪdiˈærɪti/ *noun* the principle that the EU shall only decide on matters which are better decided at EU level than at the level of the individual Member States and that other matters shall be left to each Member State to decide (NOTE: Subsidiarity only operates in those areas where the EU does not have exclusive jurisdiction.)

subsidiary /səbˈsɪdiəri/ *adjective* related to, but less important than, something else ○ *He faces one serious charge and several subsidiary charges arising out of the main charge.*

subsidiary company /səbˌsɪdiəri ˈkʌmp(ə)ni/ *noun* a company which is owned by a parent company

subsidise /ˈsʌbsɪdaɪz/, **subsidize** *verb* to help by giving money ○ *The government has refused to subsidise the car industry.*

subsidised accommodation /ˌsʌbsɪdaɪzd əˌkɒməˈdeɪʃ(ə)n/ *noun* cheap accommodation which is partly paid for by someone else such as an employer or a local authority

substance /ˈsʌbstəns/ *noun* **1.** a drug, solvent, gas or other material on which someone can become dependent or which can cause harm ○ *regulations on the transport of dangerous substances such as corrosive chemicals* ○ *illegal substances* ◊ **controlled drug 2.** the real basis of a report or argument ○ *There is no substance to the stories about his resignation.*

substance abuse /ˈsʌbstəns əˌbjuːs/ *noun* the practice of drinking too much alcohol or using illegal drugs or other substances

substantial interference /səbˌstænʃ(ə)l ˌɪntəˈfɪərəns/ *noun* any action legally regarded as constituting a major breach of the rights of another individual

substantive /səbˈstæntɪv/ *adjective* real or actual

substantive law /ˌsʌbstəntɪv ˈlɔː/ *noun* all laws including common law and statute law which deal with legal principles (as opposed to procedural law which refers to the procedure for putting law into practice). Compare **procedural law**

substantive offence /ˌsʌbstəntɪv əˈfens/ *noun* an offence which has actually taken place

substitute /ˈsʌbstɪtjuːt/ *noun* somebody or something which takes the place of someone or something else ■ *verb* **1.** to take the place of something else **2.** to put something in the place of something else ○ *They made an application to substitute a party, but the claimant refused his consent.*

substituted service /ˌsʌbstɪtjuːtɪd ˈsɜːvɪs/ *noun* serving a legal document on someone other than by the legally prescribed method, e.g. by posting it to the last known address, or by advertising in the press (NOTE: Since the introduction of the Civil Procedure Rules, this term has been replaced by **service by an alternative method**.)

substitution /ˌsʌbstɪˈtjuːʃ(ə)n/ *noun* an act of putting something or someone in the place of something else ○ *The substitution of a party may take place if the court agrees that the original party was named by mistake.*

substitutionary /ˌsʌbstɪˈtjuːʃ(ə)n(ə)ri/ *adjective* acting as a substitute ○ *He made a will leaving everything to his wife, but with the substitutionary provision that if she died before him, his estate devolved on their children.*

subtenancy /sʌbˈtenənsi/ *noun* an agreement to sublet a property

subtenant /sʌbˈtenənt/ *noun* a person or company to which a property has been sublet

subversive /səbˈvɜːsɪv/ *adjective* acting secretly against the government ○ *The police is investigating subversive groups in the student organisations.*

success fee /səkˈses fiː/ *noun* same as **conditional fee agreement**

succession /səkˈseʃ(ə)n/ *noun* the act of acquiring property or title from someone who has died

successor /səkˈsesə/ *noun* somebody who takes over from someone ○ *Mr Smith's successor as chairman will be Mr Jones.*

sue /sjuː/ *verb* to start legal proceedings against someone to get compensation for a wrong ○ *to sue someone for damages* ○ *He is suing the company for £50,000 compensation.*

sufferance /'sʌfərəns/ *noun* an agreement to something which is not stated, but assumed because no objection has been raised ○ *He has been allowed to live in the house on sufferance.*

suffrage /'sʌfrɪdʒ/ *noun* the right to vote in elections

suggestion box /sə'dʒestʃən bɒks/ *noun* a place in a company where members of staff can put forward their ideas for making the company more efficient and profitable

suicide /'suːɪsaɪd/ *noun* **1.** the act of killing yourself ○ *The police are treating the death as suicide, not murder.* □ **to commit suicide** to kill yourself ○ *After shooting his wife, he committed suicide in the bedroom.* **2.** somebody who has committed suicide

COMMENT: It is a notifiable offence in the UK to help somebody commit suicide.

suicide bomber /'suːɪsaɪd ˌbɒmə/ *noun* a person who deliberately allows himself or herself to be killed in the process of committing a terrorist crime

suicide pact /'suːɪsaɪd pækt/ *noun* an agreement between two or more people that they will all commit suicide at the same time (NOTE: 'Suicide pact' is a partial defence to a charge of murder. If it is upheld, the offence will be downgraded to **voluntary manslaughter.**)

sui generis /ˌsuːaɪ 'dʒenərɪs/ *phrase* a Latin phrase meaning 'of its own right': being in a class of its own

sui juris /ˌsuːaɪ 'dʒʊərɪs/ *phrase* a Latin phrase meaning 'in one's own right': legally able to make contracts and sue others or be sued. Compare **alieni juris**

suit /suːt/ *noun* a civil legal case

sum /sʌm/ *verb* □ **to sum up** (*of a judge*) to speak at the end of a trial and review all the evidence and arguments for the benefit of the jury

summarily /'sʌmərɪli/ *adverb* immediately ○ *Magistrates can try a case summarily or refer it to the Crown Court.*

summarise /'sʌməraɪz/ *verb* to write or give a short account of what has been said or what happened (NOTE: **summarised** – **summarising**)

summary /'sʌməri/ *noun* a short account of what has happened or of what has been written ○ *The chairman gave a summary of his discussions with the German delegation.* ○ *The police inspector have a summary of*

events leading to the raid on the house. ■ *adjective* happening immediately

summary arrest /ˌsʌməri ə'rest/ *noun* an arrest without a warrant

summary assessment /ˌsʌməri ə'sesmənt/ *noun* an immediate costs award made by a judge

summary conviction /ˌsʌməri kən'vɪkʃən/ *noun* a conviction by a magistrate sitting without a jury

summary dismissal /ˌsʌməri dɪs'mɪs(ə)l/ *noun* the dismissal of an employee without giving the notice stated in the contract of employment

summary judgment /ˌsʌməri 'dʒʌdʒmənt/ *noun* the hearing of a case on an expedited basis (NOTE: This can be decided by the court itself or can be applied for by a party believing the opposing party has no real chance of succeeding with the case.)

summary jurisdiction /ˌsʌməri ˌdʒʊərɪs'dɪkʃən/ *noun* the power of a magistrates' court to try a case without a jury or to try a case immediately without referring it to the Crown Court

summary offence /ˌsʌməri ə'fens/ *noun* a minor crime which can be tried only in a magistrates' court

summary trial /ˌsʌməri 'traɪəl/ *noun* the trial of a petty offence by magistrates

summing up /ˌsʌmɪŋ 'ʌp/ *noun* a speech by a judge at the end of a trial, reviewing all the evidence and arguments and noting important points of law for the benefit of the jury (NOTE: The US term is **instructions**.)

summit conference /ˌsʌmɪt 'kɒnf(ə)rəns/ *noun* the meeting of two or more heads of government ○ *The summit conference or summit meeting was held in Geneva.* ○ *The matter will be discussed at next week's summit of the EC leaders.*

summon /'sʌmən/ *verb* to call someone to come ○ *He was summoned to appear before the committee.*

summons /'sʌmənz/ *noun* an official command from a court requiring someone to appear in court to be tried for a criminal offence or to defend a civil action

sunshine law /'sʌnʃaɪn ˌlɔː/ *noun* a law forcing public bodies to hold meetings that are open to the public, or 'in the sunshine'

super /'suːpə/ *noun* same as **police superintendent**

supergrass /'suːpəgrɑːs/ *noun* a person, usually a criminal, who gives information to the police about a large number of criminals (*slang*)

supervision order /ˌsuːpəˈvɪʒ(ə)n ˌɔːdə/ *noun* a court order for a young offender to be placed under the supervision of the probation service

supplemental /ˌsʌplɪˈmentəl/ *adjective* being additional to something

supplementary /ˌsʌplɪˈment(ə)ri/ *adjective* additional

supply /səˈplaɪ/ *noun* the act of selling or making available something that is wanted or needed ■ *verb* to sell or make something available, especially something illegal such as drugs (NOTE: The maximum sentence for supplying a Class A drug is life imprisonment.)

supply and demand /səˌplaɪ ən dɪ ˈmaːnd/ *noun* the amount of a product which is available at a specific price and the amount which is wanted by customers at that price

Supply Bill /səˈplaɪ bɪl/ *noun* a Bill for providing money for government requirements

supply price /səˈplaɪ praɪs/ *noun* the price at which something is provided

suppress /səˈpres/ *verb* **1.** to hide documents **2.** to prevent evidence being given

suppressio veri /səˌpresiəʊ ˈveraɪ/ *phrase* a Latin phrase meaning 'suppressing the truth': an act of not mentioning some important fact

supra /ˈsuːprə/ *adverb* above

supremacy /sʊˈpreməsi/ *noun* **1.** a situation where one person or group is much more powerful than any other □ **the supremacy of Parliament** the principle that the UK Parliament can both pass and repeal laws **2.** the feeling that the ethnic group you belong to is superior to other groups **3.** one of the twin pillars of EU law, by which it cannot be overridden by national laws even if the national laws existed before the EU law. ◊ **direct effect** (NOTE: It is based on all forms of EU law, i.e. treaty articles, community acts and agreements with third parties.)

Supreme Court /sʊˌpriːm ˈkɔːt/ *noun* **1.** the highest federal court in the USA and other countries **2.** □ **Supreme Court of Judicature of England and Wales** the collective name for the Court of Appeal, the High Court of Justice and the Crown Courts in England and Wales **3.** □ **Supreme Court of the United Kingdom** in the United Kingdom, a court that is planned as a

replacement for the Law Lords committee as the highest court in the land

COMMENT: The Constitutional Reform Act provided for the future creation of a **Supreme Court of the United Kingdom**. It will take over the judicial functions of the Law Lords, as well as some functions of the Privy Council, and be situated in Parliament Square in Westminster. It is scheduled to open in 2009. When this takes effect, the current Supreme Court of Judicature of England and Wales will be renamed the **Senior Courts of England and Wales**.

surcharge /ˈsɜːtʃɑːdʒ/ *noun* **1.** an extra charge **2.** a penalty for incurring expenditure without authorisation

Sure Start Maternity Grant /ˌʃʊə staːt məˈtɜːnɪti ˌgraːnt/ *noun* a one-off payment made by the Government to new or expectant parents on income support, to help with the cost of having a baby (NOTE: This is made out of the Government's Social Fund.)

surety /ˈʃʊərəti/ *noun* **1.** somebody who guarantees that someone will do something, especially by paying to guarantee that someone will keep the peace ○ *to stand surety for someone* **2.** something such as money, deeds or share certificates deposited as security for a loan

surrender /səˈrendə/ *noun* the abandonment of legal rights, especially the giving up of a lease or an insurance policy before it has expired ■ *verb* to give in a document or a right ○ *The court ordered him to surrender his passport.* ○ *She surrendered her rights to the piece of land.* ○ *The contract becomes null and void when these documents are surrendered.*

surrender value /səˈrendə ˌvæljuː/ *noun* money which an insurer will pay if an insurance policy is given up before it matures

surrogate /ˈsʌrəgət/ *noun* a person appointed to act in place of someone else

surrogate mother /ˌsʌrəgət ˈmʌðə/ *noun* a woman who has a child by artificial insemination for a couple when the wife cannot become pregnant, with the intention of handing the child over to them when it is born

surveillance /səˈveɪləns/ *noun* the activity of keeping careful watch on someone to find out what they are doing ○ *The diplomats were placed under police surveillance.* ○ *Surveillance at international airports has been increased.*

surveillance device /sə'veɪləns dɪ
ˌvaɪs/ *noun* same as **bug**

survive /sə'vaɪv/ *verb* to live longer than
another person ○ *He survived his wife.* ○ *She
is survived by her husband and three children.* □ **to leave your estate to your surviving relatives** to leave your estate to relatives
who are still alive

surviving spouse /sə,vaɪvɪŋ 'spaʊs/
noun the living husband or wife of a person
who has died, who is usually the beneficiary
of the estate, even if the dead person died
intestate (NOTE: If there are living children,
then the spouse takes the personal chattels, a statutory sum as legacy, and interest
in half the remaining estate.)

survivor /sə'vaɪvə/ *noun* someone who
lives longer than another person

survivorship /sə'vaɪvəʃɪp/ *noun* the
state of being the survivor of two or more
people who hold a joint tenancy on a property

SUS law /'sʌs lɔː/ *noun* formerly, a law
which allowed the police to stop and arrest
a person whom they suspected of having
committed an offence

suspect *noun* /'sʌspekt/ somebody
whom the police think has committed a
crime ○ *The police have taken six suspects
into custody.* ○ *The police are questioning
the suspect about his movements at the time
the crime was committed.* ■ *verb* /sə'spekt/
to believe that something is the case ○ *He
was arrested as a suspected spy.* ○ *The
police suspect that the thefts were committed by a member of the shop's staff.* (NOTE:
You suspect someone **of** committing a
crime.)

suspend /sə'spend/ *verb* **1.** to stop something happening for a period of time ○ *We
have suspended payments while we are
waiting for news from our agent.* ○ *The
hearings have been suspended for two
weeks.* ○ *Work on the preparation of the
case has been suspended.* **2.** to stop someone working for a period of time ○ *She was
suspended on full pay while the police
investigations were proceeding.* **3.** to punish
a student by refusing to allow him or her to
attend school or college ○ *Three boys were
suspended from school for fighting.*

suspended sentence /sə,spendɪd
'sentəns/ *noun* a sentence of imprisonment
which a court orders shall not take effect
unless the offender commits another crime

suspension /sə'spenʃən/ *noun* the act of
stopping something for a time ○ *suspension
of payments* ○ *suspension of deliveries*

suspicion /sə'spɪʃ(ə)n/ *noun* a feeling
that something is the case ○ *I had a suspicion that he was guilty.* □ **on suspicion**
because of a feeling that someone has committed a crime ○ *He was arrested on suspicion of being an accessory to the crime.*

suspicious /sə'spɪʃəs/ *adjective* which
makes someone suspect ○ *The police are
dealing with the suspicious package found
in the car.* ○ *Suspicious substances were
found in the man's pocket.*

sustain /sə'steɪn/ *verb* to agree with the
validity of a statement made by counsel □
objection sustained the judge upholds
counsel's objection

swear /sweə/ *verb* to promise that what
you will say will be the truth ○ *He swore to
tell the truth.* □ **'I swear to tell the truth,
the whole truth and nothing but the
truth'** words used when a witness takes the
oath in court

swear in /,sweə 'ɪn/ *verb* to make someone take an oath before taking up a position
○ *He was sworn in as a Privy Councillor.*

swearing-in /,sweərɪŋ 'ɪn/ *noun* the act
of making someone take an oath before taking up a position

swindle /'swɪnd(ə)l/ *noun* an illegal deal
in which someone is cheated out of his or
her money ■ *verb* to cheat someone out of
his or her money ○ *He made £50,000 by
swindling small shopkeepers.* ○ *The gang
swindled the bank out of £1.5m.*

swindler /'swɪndlə/ *noun* somebody who
swindles

syllabus /'sɪləbəs/ *noun US* a headnote
giving a short summary of a case

T

table /'teɪb(ə)l/ *noun* □ **to let a bill lie on the table** *US* not to proceed with discussion of a bill, but to hold it over to be debated later ◊ **to lay a bill on the table** *US* **1.** to present a bill to the House of Commons for discussion **2.** to kill debate on a bill in the House of Representatives ◊ **to table a motion** *US* **1.** to put forward a proposal for discussion by putting details of it on the table at a meeting **2.** to remove a motion from consideration for an indefinite period

Table A-F Regulations /ˌteɪb(ə)l 'eɪ/ *noun* model memoranda and articles of association for limited, unlimited and public companies, set out in the Companies Act 1985 (NOTE: The Companies Act 1985 is due to be reformed by the Companies Act 2006, although its provisions have not yet come into force.)

tabs /tæbz/ *plural noun* bands of white cloth worn by a barrister round his or her neck, instead of a tie

tacit /'tæsɪt/ *adjective* agreed but not stated ◊ *He gave the proposal his tacit approval.* ◊ *The committee gave its tacit agreement to the proposal.*

tail /teɪl/ ◆ **fee tail**

take in /ˌteɪk 'ɪn/ *verb* to trick someone into believing something that is not true ◊ *We were taken in by his promise of quick profits.*

taken without owner's consent full form of **TWOC**

take out /ˌteɪk 'aʊt/ *verb* □ **to take out a patent for an invention** to apply for and receive a patent □ **to take out insurance against theft** to pay a premium to an insurance company, so that if a theft takes place the company will pay compensation

take over /ˌteɪk 'əʊvə/ *verb* **1.** to start to do something in place of someone else ◊ *Miss Black took over from Mr Jones on May 1st.* ◊ *The new chairman takes over on July 1st.* **2.** □ **to take over a company** to buy a business by offering to buy most of its shares ◊ *The company was taken over by a large international corporation.*

takeover /'teɪkəʊvə/ *noun* the activity of one business buying another

takeover bid /'teɪkəʊvə bɪd/ *noun* an offer to buy all or a majority of the shares in a company so as to control it □ **to make a takeover bid for a company** to offer to buy a majority of the shares in a company □ **to withdraw a takeover bid** to say that you no longer offer to buy most of the shares in a company

Takeover Panel /'teɪkəʊvə ˌpæn(ə)l/ *noun* a non-statutory body which examines takeovers and applies the City Code on Takeovers and Mergers

talaq /'tælæk/ *noun* an Islamic form of divorce where the husband may divorce his wife unilaterally by an oral declaration made three times

tamper /'tæmpə/ *verb* □ **to tamper with something** to interfere with something in a harmful way ◊ *The police were accused of tampering with the evidence.* ◊ *The charges state that she had tampered with the wheels of the victim's car.* □ **to tamper with the jury** to attempt to influence a jury

tangible assets /ˌtændʒɪb(ə)l 'æsets/ *plural noun* assets which exist in the physical world, e.g. machinery, buildings, furniture or jewellery. Compare **intangible assets**

tariff /'tærɪf/ *noun* the minimum period of time which a life prisoner must serve in prison

TASER, Taser a trademark for a type of electroshock weapon resembling a gun

tax /tæks/ *noun* **1.** money taken compulsorily by the government or by an official body to pay for government services **2.** □ **to levy a tax, to impose a tax** to make a tax payable ◊ *The government has imposed a 15% tax on petrol.* □ **to lift a tax** to remove a tax □ **tax deducted at source** tax which is removed from a salary, interest payment or dividend payment before the money is paid out □ **tax loophole** a legal means of not paying tax □ **tax planning** planning one's financial affairs so that one pays as little tax as possible ■ *verb* **1.** to impose a tax on something, or make someone pay a tax ○ *to tax businesses at 50%* ○ *Income is taxed at 29%.* ○ *These items are heavily taxed.* **2.** to have the costs of a legal action assessed by the court ○ *The court ordered the costs to be taxed if not agreed.* **3.** to assess the bill presented by a Parliamentary agent

tax abatement /'tæks ə,beɪtmənt/ *noun* the reduction of tax

taxable /'tæksəb(ə)l/ *adjective* being able to be taxed □ **taxable items** items on which a tax has to be paid

taxable income /,tæksəb(ə)l 'ɪnkʌm/ *noun* income on which a person has to pay tax

tax advantage /'tæks əd,vɑːntɪdʒ/ *noun* a special tax reduction accorded to some classes of taxpayers such as those with low pay

tax allowances /'tæks ə,laʊənsɪz/ *plural noun* part of one's income which a person is allowed to earn and not pay tax on

taxation of costs /tæk,seɪʃ(ə)n əv 'kɒsts/ *noun* formerly, the assessment of the costs of a legal action by the Taxing Master (NOTE: Since the introduction of the Civil Procedure Rules, this term has been replaced by **assessment of costs**.)

tax avoidance /'tæks ə,vɔɪd(ə)ns/ *noun* a legal attempt to minimise the amount of tax to be paid

tax code /'tæks kəʊd/ *noun* a number given to indicate the amount of tax allowances a person has

tax concession /'tæks kən,seʃ(ə)n/ *noun* a reduction in the amount of tax that has to be paid

tax consultant /'tæks kən,sʌltənt/ *noun* somebody who gives advice on tax problems

tax court /'tæks kɔːt/ *noun US* a tribunal which hears appeals from taxpayers against the Internal Revenue Service

tax credit /'tæks ,kredɪt/ *noun* payments made by the Government to people to help with everyday costs, which change according to personal circumstances. ◊ **Child Tax Credit, Working Tax Credit**

tax-deductible /,tæks dɪ'dʌktɪb(ə)l/ *adjective* being possible to deduct from an income before tax is calculated □ **these**

expenses are not tax-deductible tax has to be paid on these expenses

tax deductions /'tæks dɪ,dʌkʃənz/ *plural noun US* **1.** money removed from a salary to pay tax **2.** business expenses which can be claimed against tax

taxed costs /,tæksd 'kɒsts/ *plural noun* varying amount of costs which can be awarded in legal proceedings

tax evasion /'tæks ɪ,veɪʒ(ə)n/ *noun* illegally trying not to pay tax

tax-exempt /,tæks ɪg'zempt/ *adjective* **1.** (*of a person or organisation*) not required to pay tax **2.** (*of income or goods*) not subject to tax

tax exemption /'tæks ɪg,zempʃən/ *noun US* **1.** the state of being free from the obligation to pay tax **2.** a part of income which a person is allowed to earn and not pay tax on

tax-free /,tæks 'friː/ *adjective* on which tax does not have to be paid

tax haven /'tæks ,heɪv(ə)n/ *noun* a country where taxes levied on foreigners or foreign companies are low

tax holiday /'tæks ,hɒlɪdeɪ/ *noun* the period when a new business is exempted from paying tax

Taxing Master /,tæksɪŋ 'mɑːstə/ *noun* an official of the Supreme Court who assesses the costs of a court action (NOTE: Since the introduction of the Civil Procedure Rules, this term has been replaced in some contexts by **costs judge**.)

taxing officer /,tæksɪŋ 'ɒfɪsə/ *noun* a person appointed by the House of Commons to assess the charges presented by a Parliamentary agent

tax inspector /'tæks ɪn,spektə/ *noun* an official of the Inland Revenue who examines tax returns and decides how much tax someone should pay

taxpayer /'tækspeɪə/ *noun* a person or company which has to pay tax ○ *basic taxpayer or taxpayer at the basic rate*

tax point /'tæks pɔɪnt/ *noun* **1.** the date when goods are supplied and VAT is charged **2.** the date at which a tax begins to be applied

tax relief /'tæks rɪ,liːf/ *noun* a reduction in the amount of tax that has to be paid

tax return /'tæks rɪ,tɜːn/ *noun* a completed tax form, with details of income and allowances

TD *abbreviation* Teachta Dala

Teachta Dala /ˌtɪæxtə ˈdælə/ *noun* a member of the lower house of the parliament of the Republic of Ireland, the Dáil. Abbreviation **TD**

tear gas /ˈtɪə gæs/ *noun* same as **pepper spray**

technical /ˈteknɪk(ə)l/ *adjective* referring to a specific legal point, using a strictly legal interpretation ○ *Nominal damages were awarded as the harm was judged to be technical rather than actual.*

technicality /ˌteknɪˈkælɪti/ *noun* a fine or obscure detail of legal procedure which may influence the outcome of a case, often used pejoratively ○ *The Appeal Court rejected the appeal on a technicality.* ○ *He was let off on a technicality.*

teleological /ˌtiːliəˈlɒdʒɪk(ə)l/ *adjective* referring to the final purpose of something ○ *The ECJ uses a teleological approach to legislation.*

telephone hearing /ˌtelɪfəʊn ˈhɪərɪŋ/ *noun* a hearing conducted by telephone and recorded on tape, using a telephone conferencing system

telephone tapping /ˈtelɪfəʊn ˌtæpɪŋ/ *noun* same as **lawful interception**

tem /tem/ ♦ **pro tem**

Temple ♦ **Inns of Court**

temporary employment /ˌtemp(ə)rəri ɪmˈplɔɪmənt/ *noun* full-time work which does not last for more than a few days or weeks

tenancy /ˈtenənsi/ *noun* **1.** an agreement by which a person can occupy a property **2.** the period during which a person has an agreement to occupy a property **3.** the period during which a barrister occupies chambers

tenancy at sufferance /ˌtenənsi ət ˈsʌf(ə)rəns/ *noun* a situation where a previously lawful tenant is still in possession of property after the termination of the lease

tenancy at will /ˌtenənsi ət ˈwɪl/ *noun* a situation where the owner of a property allows a tenant to occupy it as long as either party wishes

tenancy in common /ˌtenənsi ɪn ˈkɒmən/ *noun* a situation where two or more persons jointly lease a property and each can leave his or her interest to an heir on their death

tenant /ˈtenənt/ *noun* a person or company which rents a house, flat or office in which to live or work ○ *The tenant is liable for repairs.*

tenant at will /ˌtenənt ət ˈwɪl/ *noun* a tenant who holds a property at the will of the owner

tenant for life /ˌtenənt fə ˈlaɪf/ *noun* somebody who can occupy a property for life

tenant for years /ˌtenənt fə ˈjɪəz/ *noun* a tenant who has been so for a period of several years and who has certain rights by law

tender /ˈtendə/ *noun* □ **tender before claim** the defence that the defendant offered the claimant the amount of money claimed before the claimant started proceedings. Also called **defence before claim** ■ *verb* **1.** □ **to tender for a contract** to put forward an estimate of cost for work in order to secure a contract ○ *to tender for the construction of a hospital* **2.** □ **to tender one's resignation** to give in one's resignation

tenderer /ˈtendərə/ *noun* a person or company which tenders for work ○ *The company was the successful tenderer for the project.*

tenement /ˈtenəmənt/ *noun* **1.** property which is held by a tenant **2.** in Scotland, a building which is divided into rented flats

tenens /ˈtenənz/ ♦ **locum**

tenure /ˈtenjə/ *noun* **1.** the right to hold property or a position **2.** the time when a position is held ○ *during his tenure of the office of chairman*

term /tɜːm/ *noun* **1.** a period of time ○ *the term of a lease* ○ *to have a loan for a term of fifteen years* ○ *during his term of office as chairman* ○ *The term of the loan is fifteen years.* □ **term of years** a fixed period of several years (of a lease) **2.** point at which a contract or agreement ends **3.** □ **terms** conditions or duties which have to be carried out as part of a contract, arrangements which have to be agreed before a contract is valid ○ *He refused to agree to some of the terms of the contract.* ○ *By* or *under the terms of the contract, the company is responsible for all damage to the property.* **4.** a part of a legal year when courts are in session (NOTE: The four law terms are Easter, Hilary, Michaelmas and Trinity.) **5.** a word or phrase which has a particular meaning ○ *Counsel used several technical terms which the prisoner didn't understand.*

term deposit /ˈtɜːm dɪˌpɒzɪt/ *noun* money invested for a fixed period which gives a higher rate of interest than normal

terminable /ˈtɜːmɪnəb(ə)l/ *adjective* being possible to terminate

terminate /'tɜːmɪneɪt/ *verb* **1.** to bring something to an end ○ *to terminate an agreement* ○ *His employment was terminated.* **2.** to come to an end ○ *An offer terminates on the death of the offeror.*

termination /ˌtɜːmɪ'neɪʃ(ə)n/ *noun* **1.** bringing to an end ○ *the termination of an offer* or *of a lease* ○ *to appeal against the termination of a foster order* **2.** *US* the act of leaving a job by resigning, retiring, or being fired or made redundant

termination clause /ˌtɜːmɪ'neɪʃ(ə)n klɔːz/ *noun* a clause which explains how and when a contract can be terminated

term insurance /'tɜːm ɪnˌʃʊərəns/ *noun* life assurance which covers a person's life for a fixed period of time

term loan /'tɜːm ləʊn/ *noun* a loan for a fixed period of time

term shares /'tɜːm ʃeəz/ *plural noun* a type of building society deposit for a fixed period of time at a higher rate of interest

terms of employment /ˌtɜːmz əv ɪm'plɔɪmənt/ *plural noun* conditions set out in a contract of employment

terms of payment /ˌtɜːmz əv 'peɪmənt/ *plural noun* conditions for paying something

terms of reference /ˌtɜːmz əv 'ref(ə)rəns/ *plural noun* areas which a committee or an inspector can deal with ○ *Under the terms of reference of the committee, it cannot investigate complaints from the public.* ○ *The tribunal's terms of reference do not cover traffic offences.*

terms of sale /ˌtɜːmz əv 'seɪl/ *plural noun* same as **conditions of sale**

territorial /ˌterɪ'tɔːriəl/ *adjective* referring to land □ **territorial claims** claims to own land which is part of another country

territoriality /ˌterɪtɔːri'ælɪti/ *noun* the principle that a country has jurisdiction only over its own territory. ◊ **extra-territorial waters** /ˌterɪtɔːriəl 'wɔːtəz/ *plural noun* the part of the sea up to 12 nautical miles from the coast of a country, which is owned by that country and governed by its laws ○ *They were caught trespassing in territorial waters.* □ **outside territorial waters** in international waters, where a single country's jurisdiction does not apply

territory /'terɪt(ə)ri/ *noun* an area of land over which a government has control ○ *Their government has laid claim to part of our territory.*

terrorism /'terərɪz(ə)m/ *noun* the use of violent actions such as assassination or bombing for political reasons ○ *The act of terrorism was condemned by the Minister for Justice.*

Terrorism Act /'terərɪz(ə)m ækt/ *noun* legislation which seeks to prevent terrorism

COMMENT: The Act increases police powers to search, arrest and detain persons suspected of terrorism before charging them, and also creates several new offences including **encouragement to terrorism**, committing an **act preparatory to terrorism** and training or being trained in terrorist methods.

terrorist /'terərɪst/ *noun* somebody who commits a violent act for political reasons ○ *The bomb was planted by a terrorist group* or *by a group of terrorists.* ○ *Six people were killed in the terrorist attack on the airport.*

terrorist training /ˌterərɪst 'treɪnɪŋ/ *noun* the offence of providing training to potential terrorists, or undergoing such training

testacy /'testəsi/ *noun* the condition of having made a legally valid will

testamentary /ˌtestə'mentəri/ *adjective* referring to a will

testamentary capacity /testəˌmentəri kə'pæsɪti/ *noun* the legal ability of someone to make a will

testamentary disposition /testəˌmentəri ˌdɪspə'zɪʃ(ə)n/ *noun* the passing of property to someone in a will

testamentary freedom /testəˌmentəri 'friːdəm/ *noun* freedom to dispose of your property in a will as you want

testate /'testeɪt/ *adjective* having made a will ○ *Did he die testate?* ◊ **intestate**

testator /te'steɪtə/ *noun* someone who has made a will

COMMENT: A testator must be able to make a will: he or she must be of sound mind (i.e. must know what it means to make a will, what property he or she owns, and who it is being left to); must approve of the will (for example, in cases where a will is prepared for a testator by someone else), and must be acting freely (not coerced or tricked into making a fraudulent will).

test case /'test keɪs/ *noun* a legal action where the decision will fix a principle which other cases can follow

test certificate /'test səˌtɪfɪkət/ *noun* a certificate to show that something has passed a test

testify /'testɪfaɪ/ *verb* to give evidence in court

testimonium clause /ˌtestɪ'məʊniəm ˌklɔːz/ *noun* the last section of a document such as a will or conveyance which shows how it has been witnessed

COMMENT: The testimonium clause usually begins with the words: 'in witness whereof I have set my hand'.

testimony /'testɪməni/ *noun* an oral statement given by a witness in court about what happened ○ *She gave her testimony in a low voice.*

test of effectiveness /ˌest əv ɪ 'fektɪvnəs/ *noun* in the European Union, a test to show if an action is more effective when taken by a Member State than when taken centrally (NOTE: It is one of the tests used to decide on **subsidiarity**.)

test of scale /ˌtest əv 'skeɪl/ *noun* in the European Union, a test to show if an action is more effective when taken centrally than when taken by a Member State (NOTE: It is one of the tests used to decide on **subsidiarity**.)

TEU *abbreviation* Treaty on European Union

textbook /'tekstbʊk/ *noun* a book of legal commentary which can be cited in court

theft /θeft/ *noun* **1.** the crime of taking of property which belongs to someone else with the intention of permanently depriving that person of it ○ *to take out insurance against theft* ○ *We have brought in security guards to protect the store against theft.* ○ *The company is trying to reduce losses caused by theft.* **2.** the act of stealing ○ *There has been a wave of thefts from newsagents.*

COMMENT: Types of theft which are notifiable offences are: theft from the person of another; theft in a dwelling; theft by an employee; theft of mail, pedal cycle or motor vehicle; theft from vehicles, from a shop or from an automatic machine or meter.

there- /ðeə/ *prefix* that thing

thereafter /ðeər'ɑːftə/ *adverb* after that

thereby /ðeə'baɪ/ *adverb* by that

therefor /ðeə'fɔː/ *adverb* for that

therefrom /ðeə'frʌm/ *adverb* from that

therein /ðeər'ɪn/ *adverb* in that

thereinafter /ˌðeərɪn'ɑːftə/ *adverb* afterwards listed in that document

thereinbefore /ˌðeərɪnbɪ'fɔː/ *adverb* mentioned before in that document

thereinunder /ˌðeərɪn'ʌndə/ *adverb* mentioned under that heading

thereof /ðeər'ɒv/ *adverb* of that □ **in respect thereof** regarding that thing

thereto /ðeə'tuː/ *adverb* to that

theretofore /ˌðeətʊ'fɔː/ *adverb* before that time

therewith /ðeə'wɪð/ *adverb* with that

thief /θiːf/ *noun* somebody who steals or who takes property which belongs to someone else ○ *Thieves broke into the office and stole the petty cash.*

third party /ˌθɜːd 'pɑːti/ *noun* **1.** any person other than the two main parties involved in proceedings or contract □ **in the hands of a third party** being dealt with by someone who is not one of the main interested parties **2.** the other person involved in an accident

Third Party Debt Order /ˌθɜːd ˌpɑːti 'det ˌɔːdə/ *noun* an order compelling someone who owes money to pay a third-party creditor of their original creditor

third party insurance /ˌθɜːd pɑːti ɪn 'ʃʊərəns/ *noun* insurance which pays compensation if someone who is not the insured person incurs loss or injury

third party notice /θɜːd ˌpɑːti 'nəʊtɪs/ *noun* a pleading served by a defendant on another party joining that party to an existing court action

third party proceedings /θɜːd ˌpɑːti prə'siːdɪŋz/ *plural noun* the introduction of a third party into a case by the defendant, or by the claimant in the case of a counterclaim (NOTE: The US term is **impleader**.)

third quarter /ˌθɜːd 'kwɔːtə/ *noun* a period of three months from July to the end of September

Third Reading /ˌθɜːd 'riːdɪŋ/ *noun* a final discussion and vote on a Bill in Parliament

threat /θret/ *noun* **1.** spoken or written words which say that something unpleasant may happen to someone, and which frighten that person **2.** an action or situation that could be harmful or dangerous ○ *The introduction of ID cards might be regarded as a threat to civil liberties.*

threaten /'θret(ə)n/ *verb* to tell someone or imply to them that you intend to cause them harm ○ *He threatened to take the tenant to court* or *to have the tenant evicted.* ○ *She complained that her husband had threatened her with a knife.* □ **threatening behaviour** acting in a way which threatens someone

threshold criteria /'θreʃhəʊld kraɪ
ˌtɪərɪə/ *plural noun* the conditions that need
to be met before the social services of a
local authority can begin care proceedings

COMMENT: The aim of the threshold criteria
is to establish whether the child is suffering
or likely to suffer significant harm if left in the
care of its natural parents, indicating that the
child is beyond parental control. Since the
introduction of the Human Rights Act 1998,
the court must be satisfied that such an
order does not contravene Article 8, which
guarantees a right to family life. Conse-
quently, the court must be satisfied that any
intervention is proportionate to the legitimate aim of protecting family life.

ticket touting /'tɪkɪt ˌtaʊtɪŋ/ *noun* the
act of buying tickets to an event and selling
them on at a profit, illegal in some circumstances

tied cottage /ˌtaɪd 'kɒtɪdʒ/ *noun* a house
owned by an employer and let to an
employee for the period of his or her
employment

tie up /ˌtaɪ 'ʌp/ *verb* **1.** to invest money in
such a way that it cannot be used for other
purposes **2.** to place legal restrictions on the
selling or alienation of property

time-bar /'taɪm bɑː/ *verb* to stop someone
doing something such as exercising a right
because a set time limit has expired (NOTE:
time-barring – time-barred)

time charter /'taɪm ˌtʃɑːtə/ *noun* an
agreement to charter a ship for a fixed
period

time limit /'taɪm ˌlɪmɪt/ *noun* the maximum time which can be taken to do something

time limitation /'taɪm lɪmɪˌteɪʃ(ə)n/
noun the amount of time which is available

time policy /'taɪm ˌpɒlɪsi/ *noun* a marine
insurance policy which runs for a fixed
period of time

time summons /'taɪm ˌsʌmənz/ *noun* a
summons issued to apply to the court for
more time in which to serve a pleading

tip off /ˌtɪp 'ɒf/ *verb* □ **to tip someone off**
to warn someone (*informal*) ○ *We think he
tipped the burglars off that the police were
outside.* ○ *She tipped them off that a police
investigation was about to take place.*

tip-off /''tɪp ɒf/ *noun* a piece of useful
information, given secretly (*informal*) ○ *Acting on a tip-off from a member of the public,
customs officials stopped the truck.* ○ *The
police received a tip-off about a bomb in the*

building. ○ *The police raided the club after
a tip-off from a member of the public.*

tipstaff /'tɪpstɑːf/ *noun* an official of the
Supreme Court who is responsible for
arresting persons in contempt of court

title /'taɪt(ə)l/ *noun* **1.** the right to hold
goods or property ○ *She has no title to the
property.* **2.** a document proving a right to
hold a property □ **to have a clear title to
something** to have a right to something with
no limitations or charges **3.** the name of a
bill which comes before Parliament or of an
Act of Parliament

title deeds /'taɪt(ə)l ˌdiːdz/ *plural noun* a
document showing who owns a property

token charge /ˌtəʊkən 'tʃɑːdʒ/ *noun* a
small charge which does not cover the real
costs ○ *A token charge is made for heating.*

token payment /'təʊkən ˌpeɪmənt/
noun a small payment to show that a payment is being made

token rent /ˌtəʊkən 'rent/ *noun* a very
low rent payment to show that a rent is
being asked

toll /təʊl/ *verb US* to suspend a law for a
period

top security prison /tɒp sɪˌkjʊərɪti
'prɪz(ə)n/ *noun* a prison with very strict
security where category 'A' prisoners are
kept

tort /tɔːt/ *noun* a civil wrong done by one
person to another and entitling the victim to
claim damages □ **action in tort** a case
brought by a claimant who alleges he or she
has suffered damage or harm caused by the
defendant

tortfeasor /tɔːt'fiːzə/ *noun* somebody
who has committed a tort

tortious /'tɔːʃəs/ *adjective* referring to a
tort □ **tortious act** a wrong, an act which
damages someone □ **tortious liability** liability for harm caused by a breach of duty

torture /'tɔːtʃə/ *verb* to hurt someone
badly so as to force him or her to give information

torturer /'tɔːtʃərə/ *noun* somebody who
tortures

total intestacy /ˌtəʊt(ə)l ɪn'testəsi/
noun a state where a person has not made a
will, or where a previous will has been
revoked

total loss /ˌtəʊt(ə)l 'lɒs/ *noun* same as
dead loss

toties quoties /ˌtəʊʃiːz 'kwəʊʃiːz/
phrase a Latin phrase meaning 'as often as
necessary' ○ *He may delegate his duties*

toties quoties during the course of his employment.

totting up /ˌtɒtɪŋ ˈʌp/ *noun* the procedure of adding together all penalty points incurred for traffic offences in the last three years (NOTE: If the points add up to 12 or more, the driver will be liable to be disqualified.)

town planner /ˌtaʊn ˈplænə/ *noun* a person who supervises the design of a town, the way the streets and buildings in a town are laid out and how the land in a town used

town planning /ˌtaʊn ˈplænɪŋ/ *noun* the activity of supervising the design of a town and the use of land in a town

trace /treɪs/ *noun* a tiny amount of something ○ *We found traces of an illegal drug in his bloodstream.* ■ *verb* to look for someone or something ○ *We have traced the missing documents.* ○ *The police traced the two men to a hotel in London.*

tracing action /ˌtreɪsɪŋ ˈækʃən/ *noun* a court action begun to trace money or the proceeds of a sale

track /træk/ *noun* one of three management systems by which a court case is processed: namely the small claims track, the fast track or the multi-track

track record /ˈtræk ˌrekɔːd/ *noun* the success or failure of someone in the past ○ *He has a good track record as a detective.* ○ *The company has no track record in the computer market.*

trade /treɪd/ *noun* **1.** the business of buying and selling **2.** □ **trade references** traders who have done business with a company and can report on their experience **3.** all the people or companies dealing in the same type of product ○ *He is in the secondhand car trade.* ○ *She is very well known in the clothing trade.*

trade agreement /ˈtreɪd əˌgriːmənt/ *noun* an international agreement between countries over general terms of trade

trade association /ˈtreɪd əˌsəʊsieɪʃ(ə)n/ *noun* a group which joins together companies in the same type of business

trade description /ˌtreɪd dɪˈskrɪpʃən/ *noun* a description of a product to attract customers

Trade Descriptions Act /ˌtreɪd dɪ ˈskrɪpʃənz ækt/ *noun* an Act of Parliament which limits the way in which products can be described so as to protect consumers from wrong descriptions made by the makers

trade dispute /ˈtreɪd dɪˌspjuːt/ *noun* **1.** an international dispute over trade matters **2.** a dispute between management and workers over conditions of employment or union membership

trade fixtures /ˌtreɪd ˈfɪkstʃəz/ *plural noun* equipment attached to a property by a tenant so that they can exercise their trade, which may be removed at the end of the tenancy

Trades Union Congress /ˌtreɪdz ˈjuːnjən ˌkɒŋgres/ *noun* a central organisation for all British trade unions. Abbreviation **TUC** (NOTE: Although **Trades Union Congress** is the official name for the organisation, **trade union** is more common than **trades union**.)

trade terms /ˈtreɪd tɜːmz/ *plural noun* special discount for people in the same trade

trade union /ˌtreɪd ˈjuːnjən/ *noun* an organisation which represents workers who are its members in discussions with management about wages and conditions of work

trading loss /ˌtreɪdɪŋ ˈlɒs/ *noun* a situation where the company's receipts are less than its expenditure

trading profit /ˈtreɪdɪŋ ˌprɒfɪt/ *noun* a result where the company' receipts are higher than its expenditure

Trading Standards Department /ˌtreɪdɪŋ ˈstændədz dɪˌpɑːtmənt/ *noun* a department of a council which deals with weighing and measuring equipment used by shops and other consumer matters. Also called **Weights and Measures Department**

trading standards officer /ˌtreɪdɪŋ ˈstændədz ˌɒfɪsə/ *noun* an official in charge of a council's Trading Standards Department

traffic /ˈtræfɪk/ *verb* to buy and sell something illegally ○ *He was charged with trafficking in drugs.*

traffic calming /ˈtræfɪk ˌkɑːmɪŋ/ *noun* measures for reducing traffic impact in built-up areas, such as speed cameras or a congestion charge scheme

trafficking /ˈtræfɪkɪŋ/ *noun* the activity of dealing in illegal goods ○ *drug trafficking* □ **trafficking in persons** the illegal practice of finding and using human beings for unpaid, often unpleasant, work in situations their circumstances prevent them from leaving

traffic offences /'træfɪk əˌfensɪz/ *plural noun* offences committed by drivers of vehicles

traffic police /'træfɪk pəˌliːs/ *noun* a section of the police concerned with problems on the roads

traffic warden /'træfɪk ˌwɔːdən/ *noun* a person whose job is to regulate the traffic under the supervision of the police, especially to deal with cars which are illegally parked

trainee /treɪ'niː/ *noun* a young person who is learning a skill or job

traineeship /treɪ'niːʃɪp/ *noun* the period during which someone is working in a solicitor's office to learn the law

trainee solicitor /treɪˌniː səˈlɪsɪtə/ *noun* someone who is bound by a training contract to work in a solicitor's office for some years to learn the law (NOTE: This term has officially replaced **articled clerk**.)

training contract /ˌtreɪnɪŋ 'kɒntrækt/ *noun* a contract under which a trainee works in a solicitor's office to learn the law (NOTE: This term has officially replaced **articles**.)

training levy /'treɪnɪŋ ˌlevi/ *noun* a tax to be paid by companies to fund the government's training schemes

training officer /'treɪnɪŋ ˌɒfɪsə/ *noun* somebody who deals with the training of staff

transact /træn'zækt/ *verb* □ **to transact business** to carry out a piece of business

transaction /træn'zækʃən/ *noun* a transfer or exchange of items between two people, often a transfer of goods in exchange for money

transaction at an undervalue /ˌtrænzækʃ(ə)n æt ən ˌʌndə'væljuː/ *noun* a gift or a transfer of property for less than it is worth, which may be challenged by a liquidator or administrator

transcript /'trænskrɪpt/ *noun* a record in full of something noted in shorthand or of recorded speech ○ *The judge asked for a full transcript of the evidence.* ○ *Transcripts of cases are available in the Supreme Court Library.*

transfer /træns'fɜː/ *noun* /'trænsfɜː/ **1.** the movement of someone or something to a new place **2.** the movement of the hearing of a case to another court ■ *verb* to pass to someone else

transferable /træns'fɜːrəb(ə)l/ *adjective* being able to be passed to someone else □

the ticket is not transferable the ticket cannot be given or lent to someone else to use

transferee /ˌtrænzfə'riː/ *noun* somebody to whom property or goods are transferred

transfer of property /ˌtrænsfɜːr əv 'prɒpəti/ *noun* the movement of the ownership of property from one person to another

transferor /træns'fɜːrə/ *noun* somebody who transfers goods or property to another

transferred powers /trænsˌfɜːd 'pauəz/ *plural noun* legislative powers which are devolved from a central authority to a local one. ◊ **excepted powers**, **reserved powers**

transgender /trænz'dʒendə/ *adjective* living as a member of the opposite gender

transit /'trænzɪt/ ♦ **in transit**

transparency /træns'pærənsi/ *noun* the state of being open and easy to understand ○ *Too many different decision-making processes can cause a lack of transparency.*

transparent /træns'pærənt/ *adjective* **1.** completely obvious ○ *Her explanation was a transparent lie.* **2.** open and honest about official actions ○ *The government insists on the importance all its actions being transparent.*

transsexual /trænz'sekʃuəl/ *noun* a person who wants to live and be identified and accepted as a member of the opposite gender

COMMENT: Transsexual persons can undergo **gender reassignment**, which qualifies them for legal recognition as their chosen gender.

travel document /'træv(ə)l ˌdɒkjumənt/ *noun* a document proving identity and/or permitting travel, such as a passport or visa

traverse /trə'vɜːs/ *noun* denial in a pleading by one side in a case that the facts alleged by the other side are correct

treason /'triːz(ə)n/ *noun* a notifiable offence of betraying one's country, usually by helping the enemy in time of war ○ *He was accused of treason.* ○ *Three men were executed for treason.*

treasonable /'triːz(ə)nəb(ə)l/ *adjective* being considered as treason ○ *He was accused of making treasonable remarks.*

treason felony /ˌtriːz(ə)n 'feləni/ *noun* the notifiable offence of planning to remove a King or Queen, or of planning to start a war against the United Kingdom

treasure /ˈtreʒə/ *noun* gold, silver or jewels, especially when found or stolen ○ *buried treasure*

COMMENT: Treasure is now classified as objects made of at least 10% gold or silver and over 300 years old, whether they have been buried intentionally or simply lost. It also covers other items of value such as pottery. Anyone finding treasure has to report it to the local coroner, but since the Treasure Act 1996 they will only receive a reward if a museum wants to acquire the object. The reward is based on an independent expert's valuation. The owner of the land where the object was found is also eligible for a reward. They may also be allowed to keep the object if a museum does not want to pay for it.

treasure trove /ˌtreʒə ˈtrəʊv/ *noun* treasure which has been hidden by someone in the past and has been discovered, but cannot be returned to the original owner because he or she cannot be found

treasury /ˈtreʒəri/ *noun* the UK Government department which is responsible for the country's financial and economic policy □ **the Treasury Benches** front benches in the House of Commons where the government ministers sit

COMMENT: In most countries, the government's finances are the responsibility of the Ministry of Finance, headed by the Finance Minister. In the UK, the Treasury is headed by the Chancellor of the Exchequer.

treasury bonds /ˈtreʒəri bɒndz/ *plural noun* bonds issued by the Treasury of the USA

Treasury counsel /ˌtreʒəri ˈkaʊnsəl/ *noun* a barrister who pleads in the Central Criminal Court on behalf of the Director of Public Prosecutions

Treasury Solicitor /ˌtreʒəri səˈlɪsɪtə/ *noun* the solicitor who is the head of the Government's legal department in England and Wales and legal adviser to the Cabinet Office and other government departments

treaty /ˈtriːti/ *noun* **1.** a written legal agreement between countries ○ *commercial treaty* ○ *cultural treaty* **2.** a formal written agreement, especially between two or more countries □ **to sell (a house) by private treaty** to sell (a house) to another person not by auction

Treaty of Accession /ˌtriːti əv əkˈseʃn/ *noun* the treaty whereby the UK joined the EU

Treaty of Rome /ˌtriːti əv ˈrəʊm/ *noun* the treaty which established the European Economic Community (later amended to the **European Community**) in 1957

Treaty on European Union /ˌtriːti ɒn ˌjʊərəpiːən ˈjuːnjən/ *noun* the treaty which created the European Union, with three main pillars: the European Community, the Common Foreign and Security Policy, and the Common Home Affairs and Justice Policy. Abbreviation **TEU**. Also called **Maastricht Treaty**

COMMENT: The TEU established a committee of the regions; the Court of Auditors became part of the Community; more emphasis was put on cooperation in culture, education, etc.; the European Parliament had a greater role than before; capital can move freely between Member States.

trespass /ˈtrespəs/ *noun* the tort of interfering with the land or goods of another person (NOTE: Trespass on someone's property is not a criminal offence.) □ **trespass to goods** the tort of harming, stealing or interfering with goods which belong to someone else □ **trespass to land** the tort of interfering with, going on someone's property or putting things or animals on someone's property without permission □ **trespass to the person** the tort of harming someone by assault or false imprisonment ■ *verb* to offend by going on to property without the permission of the owner

trespasser /ˈtrespəsə/ *noun* somebody who commits trespass by going onto land without the permission of the owner

triable /ˈtraɪəb(ə)l/ *adjective* referring to an offence for which a person can be tried in a court □ **offence triable either way** an offence which can be tried before the Magistrates' Court or before the Crown Court

triad /ˈtraɪæd/ *noun* a secret Chinese criminal organisation

trial /ˈtraɪəl/ *noun* **1.** a criminal or civil court case heard before a judge ○ *The trial lasted six days.* ○ *The judge ordered a new trial when one of the jurors was found to be the accused's brother.* □ **to stand trial, to be on trial** to be tried for an offence in a court □ **to commit someone for trial** to send someone to a court to be tried **2.** a test to see if something is good ◇ **on trial 1.** being tested ○ *The product is on trial in our laboratories.* **2.** before a court

trial balance /ˈtraɪəl ˌbæləns/ *noun* a draft adding of debits and credits to see if they balance

trial bundle /ˌtraɪəl ˈbʌnd(ə)l/ *noun* all the documents brought together by the claimant for a trial in a ring binder

trial by jury /ˌtraɪəl baɪ ˈdʒʊəri/ *noun* proceedings where an accused is tried by a jury and judge

trial by media /ˌtraɪəl baɪ ˈmiːdiə/ *noun* a situation in which a person undergoing legal proceedings is portrayed by the media in a way that damages their reputation, regardless of the verdict reached in court

trial judge /ˈtraɪəl dʒʌdʒ/ *noun* a judge who is hearing a trial

trial location /ˌtraɪəl ləʊˈkeɪʃ(ə)n/ *noun* a place where a trial is to be held

trial period /ˌtraɪəl ˈpɪəriəd/ *noun* the time when a customer can test a product before buying it

trial sample /ˈtraɪəl ˌsɑːmpəl/ *noun* a small piece of a product used for testing

trial timetable /ˌtraɪəl ˈtaɪmteɪb(ə)l/ *noun* a detailed timetable of a hearing, set out in the listing directions, including information such as the length of time allowed for speeches and for cross-examination of witnesses

trial window /ˌtraɪəl ˈwɪndəʊ/ *noun* a period of three weeks during which a trial is scheduled to take place

tribunal /traɪˈbjuːn(ə)l/ *noun* **1.** a specialist court outside the judicial system which examines special problems and makes judgments **2.** the arbitrator or arbitrators who adjudicate in an arbitration

trier of fact /ˌtraɪə əv ˈfækt/ *noun US* a person such as a member of a jury whose role it is to find out the true facts about a case

Trinity /ˈtrɪnɪti/ *noun* **1.** one of the four sittings of the law courts **2.** one of the four law terms

Trinity House /ˌtrɪnɪti ˈhaʊz/ *noun* a body which superintends lighthouses and pilots in some areas of the British coast

trover /ˈtrəʊvə/ *noun* an action to recover property which has been converted, or goods which have been taken or passed to other parties

true /truː/ *adjective* correct or accurate □ **true copy** exact copy ○ *I certify that this is a true copy.* ○ *The document has been certified as a true copy.*

true bill /ˌtruː ˈbɪl/ *noun* the verdict by a grand jury that an indictment should proceed

trust /trʌst/ *noun* **1.** a feeling of confidence that something is correct, will work, etc. □ **to take something on trust** to accept something without examining it to see if it is correct **2.** the duty of looking after goods, money or property which someone (the beneficiary) has passed to you (the trustee) ○ *He left his property in trust for his grandchildren.* **3.** the management of money or property for someone ○ *They set up a family trust for their grandchildren.* **4.** *US* a small group of companies which control the supply of a product ■ *verb* □ **to trust someone with something** to give something to someone to look after ○ *Can he be trusted with all that cash?*

trust company /ˈtrʌst ˌkʌmp(ə)ni/ *noun US* an organisation which supervises the financial affairs of private trusts, executes wills, and acts as a bank to a limited number of customers

trust deed /ˈtrʌst diːd/ *noun* a document which sets out the details of a trust

trustee /trʌˈstiː/ *noun* a person who has charge of money or property in trust ○ *the trustees of the pension fund*

trustee in bankruptcy /trʌˌstiː ɪn ˈbæŋkrʌptsi/ *noun* somebody who is appointed by a court to run the affairs of a bankrupt and pay his or her creditors

trusteeship /trʌˈstiːʃɪp/ *noun* the position of being a trustee ○ *The territory is under United Nations trusteeship.*

trust for sale /ˌtrʌst fə ˈseɪl/ *noun* a trust whereby property is held but can be sold and the money passed to the beneficiaries

trust fund /ˈtrʌst fʌnd/ *noun* assets such as money, securities or property that are held in trust for someone

trust territory /ˌtrʌst ˈterɪt(ə)ri/ *noun* a territory which is being administered by another country under a trusteeship agreement

trusty /ˈtrʌsti/ *noun* a prisoner who is trusted by the prison warders (*slang*)

truth in sentencing /ˌtruːθ ɪn ˈsentənsɪŋ/ *noun* the principal, often enforced by government legislation, that convicted criminals should serve the full sentence they have been given and not become eligible for early parole

try /traɪ/ *verb* to hear a civil or criminal trial ○ *He was tried for murder and sentenced to life imprisonment.* ○ *The court is not competent to try the case.*

TUC *abbreviation* Trades Union Congress

turnkey operation /ˈtɜːnkiː ɒpəˌreɪʃ(ə)n/ *noun* a contract where a company takes all responsibility for building, fitting and staffing for a building such as a school, hospital or factory so that it is completely ready for the purchaser to take over at an agreed date

turn over /ˌtɜːn ˈəʊvə/ *verb* to have a specific amount of sales ○ *We turn over £2,000 a week.*

twoc /twɒk/ *verb* to take a car and drive it away without the owner's permission (*slang*)

TWOC /twɒk/ *noun* the offence of taking a vehicle and driving it away without the owner's permission. Full form **taken without owner's consent** (NOTE: It is not necessary to prove that the offender intended to permanently deprive the owner of the vehicle, as with the crime of **theft**.)

twocced /twɒkt/ *adjective* of a car, taken and driven away without the owner's permission (*slang*) (NOTE: This piece of police slang is a back-formation from **TWOC**.)

twoccer /ˈtwɒkə/ *noun* a person who takes cars and drives them away without the owner's permission (*slang*) (NOTE: This piece of police slang is a back-formation from **TWOC**.)

U

uberrimae fidei /uːˌberɪmiː ˈfaɪdeɪ/ *phrase* a Latin phrase meaning 'of total good faith': the state which should exist between parties to some types of legal relationship such as partnerships or insurance ○ *An insurance contract is uberrimae fidei.*

UCC *abbreviation* Universal Copyright Convention

ulterior motive /ʌlˌtɪəriə ˈməʊtɪv/ *noun* a reason for doing something which is not immediately connected with the action, but is done in anticipation of its result and so is an act of bad faith

ultimate consumer /ˌʌltɪmət kən ˈsjuːmə/ *noun* the person who actually uses a product

ultimate owner /ˌʌltɪmət ˈəʊnə/ *noun* the real or true owner

ultimatum /ˌʌltɪˈmeɪtəm/ *noun* a statement to someone that unless something is done within a period of time a punishment will follow (NOTE: The plural is **ultimatums** or **ultimata**.)

ultra vires /ˌʌltrə ˈvaɪriːz/ *phrase* a Latin phrase meaning 'beyond powers.' ◊ **intra vires** □ **an ultra vires action** an action which exceeds someone's legal powers

umpire /ˈʌmpaɪə/ *noun* a person called in to decide when two arbitrators cannot agree

unadmitted /ˌʌnədˈmɪtɪd/ *adjective* (*of a member of staff of a solicitor's office*) not having been admitted as a solicitor

unanimous /juːˈnænɪməs/ *adjective* where everyone votes in the same way ○ *There was a unanimous vote against the proposal.* ○ *They reached unanimous agreement.* □ **unanimous verdict** a verdict agreed by all the jurors ○ *The jury reached a unanimous verdict of not guilty.*

unanimously /juːˈnænɪməsli/ *adverb* with everyone agreeing ○ *The appeal court decided unanimously in favour of the defendant.*

unascertained /ˌʌnæsəˈteɪnd/ *adjective* not identified ○ *Title to unascertained goods cannot pass to the buyer until the goods have been ascertained.*

unborn /ʌnˈbɔːn/ *adjective* referring to a child still in the mother's body and not yet born

unchallenged /ʌnˈtʃælɪndʒd/ *adjective* not questioned or argued about

unclean ♦ clean hands

unconditional /ˌʌnkənˈdɪʃ(ə)nəl/ *adjective* with no conditions attached ○ *unconditional acceptance of the offer by the board* ○ *On the claimant's application for summary judgment the master gave the defendant unconditional leave to defend.*

unconfirmed /ˌʌnkənˈfɜːmd/ *adjective* having not been confirmed ○ *There are unconfirmed reports that a BBC reporter has been arrested.*

unconstitutional /ˌʌnkɒnstɪ ˈtjuːʃ(ə)n(ə)l/ *adjective* **1.** being not according to the constitution of a country ○ *Legislation which is contrary to European Community regulations is declared unconstitutional.* ○ *The Appeal Court ruled that the action of the Attorney-General was unconstitutional.* **2.** being not allowed by the rules of an organisation ○ *The chairman ruled that the meeting was unconstitutional.*

uncontested /ˌʌnkənˈtestɪd/ *adjective* being not contested or defended ○ *an uncontested divorce case* or *election*

uncrossed cheque /ˌʌnkrɒst ˈtʃek/ *noun* a cheque which does not have two lines across it and can be exchanged for cash anywhere

undefended /ˌʌndɪˈfendɪd/ *adjective* referring to a case in which the defendant does not acknowledge service and does not appear at the court to defend the case ○ *an undefended divorce case*

under-age /ˌʌndər ˈeɪdʒ/ *adjective* done while younger than the legal age limit ○ *under-age sex*

under-age drinking /ˌʌndər eɪdʒ ˈdrɪŋkɪŋ/ *noun* the act of drinking alcohol while under the legal age (currently 16 in the UK)

undercover agent /ˌʌndəkʌvə ˈeɪdʒənt/ *noun* someone acting secretly to get information or catch criminals

underground press /ˈʌndəgraʊnd ˌpres/ *noun* illegal newspapers published in a country where publications are censored

underlease /ˈʌndəliːs/ *noun* a lease from a tenant to another tenant

underlet /ˈʌndəlet/ *verb* to let a property which is held on a lease

undermentioned /ˌʌndəˈmenʃ(ə)nd/ *adjective* mentioned lower down in a document

undersheriff /ˈʌndəˌʃerɪf/ *noun* a person who is second to a High Sheriff and deputises for him or her

undersigned /ˌʌndəˈsaɪnd/ *noun* somebody who has signed a letter □ **we, the undersigned** we, the people who have signed below

understanding /ˌʌndəˈstændɪŋ/ *noun* a private agreement ○ *The two parties came to an understanding about the division of the estate.* □ **on the understanding that** on condition that, provided that ○ *We accept the terms of the contract, on the understanding that it has to be ratified by the full board.*

undertake /ˌʌndəˈteɪk/ *verb* to promise to do something ○ *to undertake an investigation of the fraud* ○ *The members of the jury have undertaken not to read the newspapers.* ○ *He undertook to report to the probation office once a month.* (NOTE: **undertaking – undertook – has undertaken**)

undertaking /ˈʌndəteɪkɪŋ/ *noun* **1.** a business ○ *a commercial undertaking* **2.** a promise to do something that has legal force ○ *They have given us a written undertaking that they will not infringe our patent.* ○ *The judge accepted the defendant's undertaking not to harass the claimant.*

undertenant /ˌʌndəˈtenənt/ *noun* somebody who holds a property on an underlease

underworld /ˈʌndəwɜːld/ *noun* the world of criminals ○ *The police has informers in the London underworld.* ○ *The indications are that it is an underworld killing.*

underwrite /ˌʌndəˈraɪt/ *verb* **1.** to accept responsibility for □ **to underwrite an**

insurance policy to accept liability for the payment of compensation according to the policy **2.** to agree to pay for costs ○ *The government has underwritten the development costs of the building.* (NOTE: **underwriting – underwrote – has underwritten**)

underwriter /ˈʌndəraɪtə/ *noun* somebody who accepts liability for an insurance

undesirable alien /ˌʌndɪzaɪrəb(ə)l ˈeɪliən/ *noun* a person who is not a citizen of a country, and who the government considers should not be allowed to stay in the country ○ *He was deported as an undesirable alien.*

undischarged bankrupt /ˌʌndɪstʃɑːdʒd ˈbæŋkrʌpt/ *noun* somebody who has been declared bankrupt and has not been released from that state

undisclosed /ˌʌndɪsˈkləʊzd/ *adjective* not identified

undisclosed principal /ˌʌndɪskləʊzd ˈprɪnsɪp(ə)l/ *noun* a principal who has not been identified by his or her agent

COMMENT: The doctrine of the undisclosed principal means that the agent may be liable to be sued as well if the principal's identity is discovered.

undue influence /ˌʌndju ˈɪnfluəns/ *noun* wrongful pressure put on someone which prevents that person from acting independently

unemployment benefit /ˌʌnɪm ˈplɔɪmənt ˌbenɪfɪt/ *noun* financial help given by the government to someone who is unemployed

unenforceable /ˌʌnɪnˈfɔːsəb(ə)l/ *adjective* unable to be enforced

unequivocal /ˌʌnɪˈkwɪvək(ə)l/ *adjective* clear and not ambiguous in any way

unfair /ʌnˈfeə/ *adjective* not just or reasonable

unfair competition /ˌʌnfeə ˌkɒmpə ˈtɪʃ(ə)n/ *noun* an attempt to do better than another company by using methods such as importing foreign products at very low prices or by wrongly criticising a competitor's products

unfair contract term /ˌʌnfeə ˈkɒntrækt tɜːm/ *noun* a term in a contract which is held by law to be unjust

unfair credit relationship /ˌʌnfeə ˈkredɪt rɪˌleɪʃ(ə)nʃɪp/ *noun* a relationship between a lender and a borrower which breaches the Consumer Credit Act 2006, e.g. because the interest rate is extortionate or because the lender is not transparent about its charges

unfair dismissal /ˌʌnfeə dɪsˈmɪs(ə)l/ *noun* the act of removing someone from a job in a way that appears not to be reasonable such as dismissing someone who wants to join a union

COMMENT: An employee can complain of unfair dismissal to an employment tribunal.

unfit to plead /ʌnˌfɪt tə ˈpliːd/ *noun* mentally not capable of being tried

uni- /juːni/ *prefix* meaning single

Uniform Commercial Code /ˌjuːnɪfɔːm kəˌmɜːʃ(ə)l ˈkəʊd/ *noun* in the USA, a set of uniform laws governing commercial transactions

unilateral /ˌjuːnɪˈlæt(ə)rəl/ *adjective* on one side only, or done by one party only ○ *They took the unilateral decision to cancel the contract.*

unilateral contract /ˌjuːnɪlæt(ə)rəl ˈkɒntrækt/ *noun* a contract which can be entered into by anybody who responds to an offer or opportunity, e.g. by buying a product

unilaterally /ˌjuːnɪˈlæt(ə)rəli/ *adverb* by one party only ○ *They cancelled the contract unilaterally.*

unilateral mistake /ˌjuːnɪlæt(ə)rəl mɪˈsteɪk/ *noun* a situation in which the legality of a contract is challenged, on the grounds that one party was mistaken about a fact or term of contract at the time of signing

unincorporated association /ˌʌnɪnkɔːpəreɪtɪd əˌsəʊsiˈeɪʃ(ə)n/ *noun* a body set up by means of a contractual association of its members, often used for non-profit purposes

uninsured /ˌʌnɪnˈʃʊəd/ *adjective* with no valid insurance ○ *The driver of the car was uninsured.*

United Kingdom /juːˌnaɪtɪd ˈkɪŋdəm/ *noun* an independent country, formed of England, Wales, Scotland and Northern Ireland ○ *He came to the UK to study.* ○ *Does she have a UK passport?* ○ *Is he a UK citizen?* Abbreviation **UK**

United Nations /juːˌnaɪtɪd ˈneɪʃ(ə)nz/ *noun* an international organisation including almost all sovereign states in the world, where member states are represented at meetings. Abbreviation **UNO**

United States Code /juːˌnaɪtɪd steɪts ˈkəʊd/ *noun* a book containing all the permanent laws of the USA, arranged in sections according to subject, and revised from time to time

United States of America /juːˌnaɪtɪd steɪts əv əˈmerɪkə/ *noun* an independent country, a federation of 50 states in North America. Abbreviation **USA**

COMMENT: The federal government (based in Washington D.C.) is formed of a legislature (the Congress) with two chambers (the Senate and House of Representatives), an executive (the President) and a judiciary (the Supreme Court). Each of the fifty states making up the USA has its own legislature and executive (the Governor) as well as its own legal system and constitution.

Universal Copyright Convention /ˌjuːnɪvɜːs(ə)l ˈkɒpiraɪt kənˌvenʃ(ə)n/ *noun* an international agreement on copyright set up by the United Nations in Geneva in 1952. Abbreviation **UCC**

COMMENT: Both the Berne Convention of 1886 and the UCC were drawn up to try to protect copyright from pirates; under the Berne Convention, published material remains in copyright until 50 years after the death of the author and for 25 years after publication under the UCC. In both cases, a work which is copyrighted in one country is automatically covered by the copyright legislation of all countries signing the convention.

universal franchise /ˌjuːnɪvɜːs(ə)l ˈfræntʃaɪz/ *noun* the right to vote which is given to all adult members of the population

universal suffrage /ˌjuːnɪvɜːs(ə)l ˈsʌfrɪdʒ/ *noun* same as **universal franchise**

unjust /ʌnˈdʒʌst/ *adjective* not according to legal or reasonable moral standards

unlawful /ʌnˈlɔːf(ə)l/ *adjective* against the law □ **unlawful sexual intercourse** sexual intercourse with someone who is under the age of consent, etc. □ **verdict of unlawful killing** (*in a coroner's court*) a verdict that a person's death was murder or manslaughter

unlawful assembly /ʌnˌlɔːf(ə)l əˈsembli/ *noun* a notifiable offence when a number of people come together to commit a breach of the peace or any other crime

unless order /ənˌles ˈɔːdə/ *noun* an order that a statement of claim will be struck out if a party does not comply with the order

unlimited company /ʌnˌlɪmɪtɪd ˈkʌmp(ə)ni/ *noun* a company where the shareholders have no limit as regards liability

unlimited liability /ʌnˌlɪmɪtɪd ˌlaɪəˈbɪlɪti/ *noun* a situation where a sole trader or each single partner is responsible for all the firm's debts with no limit to the amount each may have to pay

unliquidated claim /ˌʌnlɪkwɪdeɪtd ˈkleɪm/ *noun* a claim for unliquidated damages

unliquidated damages /ˌʌnlɪkwɪdeɪtd ˈdæmɪdʒɪz/ *plural noun* damages which are not for a fixed amount of money but are awarded by a court as a matter of discretion depending on the case

COMMENT: Torts give rise to claims for unliquidated damages.

unmarried /ʌnˈmærid/ *adjective* not legally married

unofficial /ˌʌnəˈfɪʃ(ə)l/ *adjective* not official

unofficially /ˌʌnəˈfɪʃəli/ *adverb* not officially ○ *The tax office told the company, unofficially, that it would be prosecuted.*

unopposed /ˌʌnəˈpəʊzd/ *adjective* (motion) with no one voting against

unprecedented /ʌnˈpresɪdentɪd/ *adjective* having not happened before, or having no legal precedent ○ *In an unprecedented move, the tribunal asked the witness to sing a song.*

unprofessional conduct /ʌnprəˌfeʃ(ə)l ˈkɒndʌkt/ *noun* a way of behaving which is not suitable for a professional person and goes against the code of practice of a profession

unquantifiable /ʌnˌkwɒntɪˈfaɪəb(ə)l/ *adjective* unable to be stated exactly

unreasonable /ʌnˈriːz(ə)nəb(ə)l/ *adjective* not fair or acceptable according to what might be usually expected

unreasonable conduct /ʌnˌriːz(ə)nəb(ə)l kənˈdʌkt/ *noun* behaviour by a spouse which is not reasonable and which shows that a marriage has broken down

unreasonably /ʌnˈriːz(ə)nəbli/ *adverb* in a way which is not reasonable or which cannot be explained ○ *Approval of any loan will not be unreasonably withheld.*

unredeemed pledge /ˌʌnrɪdiːmd ˈpledʒ/ *noun* a pledge which the borrower has not claimed back by paying back his or her loan

unregistered /ʌnˈredʒɪstəd/ *adjective* referring to land which has not been registered

unreliable /ˌʌnrɪˈlaɪəb(ə)l/ *adjective* being impossible to rely on ○ *The prosecution tried to show that the driver's evidence*

was unreliable. ○ *The defence called two witnesses and both were unreliable.*

unreported /ˌʌnrɪˈpɔːtɪd/ *adjective* **1.** not reported to the police ○ *There are thousands of unreported cases of theft.* **2.** not reported in the Law Reports ○ *Counsel referred the judge to a number of relevant unreported cases.*

unsafe /ʌnˈseɪf/ *adjective* referring to a judgment which is not acceptable in law and may be quashed on appeal

unsecured creditor /ˌʌnsɪkjʊəd ˈkredɪtə/ *noun* a creditor who is owed money, but has no mortgage or charge over the debtor's property as security

unsecured debt /ˌʌnsɪkjʊəd ˈdet/ *noun* a debt which is not guaranteed by assets

unsecured loan /ˌʌnsɪkjʊəd ˈləʊn/ *noun* a loan made with no security

unsolicited /ʌnsəˈlɪsɪtɪd/ *adjective* having not been asked for or explicitly agreed to ○ *unsolicited mail*

unsolicited goods /ʌnsəˈlɪsɪtɪd ˈɡʊdz/ *plural noun* goods which are sent to someone who has not asked for them, suggesting that he or she might like to buy them

unsolved /ʌnˈsɒlvd/ *adjective* not solved ○ *an unsolved crime*

unsound /ʌnˈsaʊnd/ *adjective* not reliable, effective or thorough ○ *The house is structurally unsound.* ○ *The statistics used to back up the investigation are unsound.* □ **persons of unsound mind** people who are not sane

unsworn /ʌnˈswɔːn/ *adjective* having not been made on oath ○ *an unsworn statement*

unwritten agreement /ʌnˌrɪt(ə)n əˈɡriːmənt/ *noun* an agreement which has been reached orally but has not been written down

unwritten law /ʌnˌrɪt(ə)n ˈlɔː/ *noun* a rule which is established by precedent

uphold /ʌpˈhəʊld/ *verb* to keep in good order □ **to uphold the law** to make sure that laws are obeyed □ **to uphold a sentence** to reject an appeal against a sentence ○ *The Appeal Court upheld the sentence.*

uplift /ˈʌplɪft/ *noun* in a conditional fee agreement, an extra fee paid by a client to a lawyer if the case is won

upper house /ˈʌpə haʊz/, **upper chamber** /ˈʌpə ˈtʃeɪmbə/ *noun* the more important of the two houses or chambers in a bicameral system ○ *After being passed by the legislative assembly, a bill goes to the* *upper house for further discussion.* Opposite **lower house**

urine sample /ˌjʊərɪn ˈsɑːmpəl/ *noun* a small amount of urine taken from someone to be tested

urine test /ˈjʊərɪn test/ *noun* a test of a sample of a person's urine to see if it contains drugs or alcohol

use /juːs/ *noun* **1.** land held by the legal owner on trust for a beneficiary **2.** □ **land zoned for industrial use** land where planning permission has been given to build factories

user's guide /ˈjuːzəz ɡaɪd/ *noun* a book showing someone how to use something

usher /ˈʌʃə/ *noun* somebody who guards the door leading into a courtroom and maintains order in court

usufruct /ˈjuːsjufrʌkt/ *noun* the right to enjoy the use or the profit of the property or land of another person

usurp /juːˈzɜːp/ *verb* to take and use someone's else role, position or right when you do not have the authority to do it

usurpation /ˌjuːzɜːˈpeɪʃ(ə)n/ *noun* the activity of taking and using a right which is not yours

usurper /juːˈzɜːpə/ *noun* somebody who usurps power ○ *The army killed the usurper and placed the king back on his throne again.*

usury /ˈjuːʒəri/ *noun* the practice of lending money at very high interest

utter /ˈʌtə/ *verb* to put a forged document or counterfeit money into circulation

V

v. against. Abbreviation of **versus** (NOTE: Titles of cases are quoted as *Hills v. The Amalgamated Company Ltd; R. v. Smith*.)

vacant /'veɪkənt/ *adjective* not occupied

vacantia ♦ bona vacantia

vacant possession /ˌveɪkənt pə'zeʃ(ə)n/ *noun* the right to occupy a property immediately after buying it because it is empty ○ *The property is to be sold with vacant possession.*

vacate /və'keɪt/ *verb* □ **to vacate the premises** to leave premises

vacation /və'keɪʃ(ə)n/ *noun* **1.** a period when the courts are closed between sittings **2.** *US* a period when people are not working

vagrancy /'veɪgrənsi/ *noun* the state of being a vagrant ○ *He was charged with vagrancy.*

vagrant /'veɪgrənt/ *noun* somebody who goes about with no work and no place to live

valid /'vælɪd/ *adjective* **1.** being acceptable because it is true ○ *That is not a valid argument.* **2.** being able to be used lawfully ○ *The contract is not valid if it has not been witnessed.* ○ *Ticket which is valid for three months.* ○ *He was carrying a valid passport.*

validate /'vælɪdeɪt/ *verb* **1.** to check to see if something is correct ○ *The document was validated by the bank.* **2.** to make something valid ○ *The import documents have to be validated by the customs officials.*

validation /ˌvælɪ'deɪʃ(ə)n/ *noun* the act of making something valid

validity /və'lɪdɪti/ *noun* the state of being valid ○ *He asked the jury to consider the validity of the witness's claims.*

valorem /və'lɔːrəm/ ♦ **ad valorem**

valuable /'væljʊəb(ə)l/ *adjective* being worth a lot of money

valuable consideration /ˌvæljʊəb(ə)l kənˌsɪdə'reɪʃ(ə)n/ *noun* something of value which is passed from one party (the promisee) to another (the promisor) as payment for what is promised

valuable property /ˌvæljʊb(ə)l 'prɒpəti/ *noun* personal items which are worth a lot of money

valuation /ˌvæljʊ'eɪʃ(ə)n/ *noun* an estimate of how much something is worth ○ *We had a valuation done on our house before making an offer for it.*

value /'væljuː/ *noun* the amount of money which something is worth ○ *the fall in the value of the dollar* ○ *He imported goods to the value of £250.* ○ *The valuer put the value of the stock at £25,000.* ■ *verb* to estimate how much money something is worth ○ *We are having the jewellery valued for insurance.*

Value Added Tax /ˌvæljuː ædɪd 'tæks/ *noun* a tax imposed as a percentage of the invoice value of goods and services. Abbreviation **VAT**

valued policy /ˌvæljuːd 'pɒlɪsi/ *noun* a marine insurance policy where the value of what is insured is stated

valuer /'væljʊə/ *noun* somebody who values property for insurance purposes

vandal /'vænd(ə)l/ *noun* somebody who destroys property, especially public property, wilfully ○ *Vandals have smashed the hanging baskets outside the community centre.*

vandalise /'vændəlaɪz/, **vandalize** *verb* to destroy property wilfully ○ *None of the phone boxes work because they have all been vandalised.*

vandalism /'vændəˌlɪz(ə)m/ *noun* the wilful destruction of property

variable /'veəriəb(ə)l/ *adjective* changing

variable costs /ˌveəriəb(ə)l 'kɒsts/ *plural noun* costs of producing a product or service which change according to the amount produced

variation /ˌveəri'eɪʃ(ə)n/ *noun* **1.** the amount by which something changes □ **seasonal variations** changes which take place because of the seasons **2.** a change in conditions ○ *The petitioner asked for a variation in her maintenance order.*

vary /ˈveəri/ *verb* **1.** to change ○ *Demand for social services varies according to the weather.* **2.** to cause something to change ○ *The court has been asked to vary the conditions of the order.*

VAT /ˌvi: eɪ ˈti:, væt/ *abbreviation* Value Added Tax

VAT declaration /ˈvæt dekləˌreɪʃ(ə)n/ *noun* a statement declaring VAT income to the VAT office

vault /vɔːlt/ *noun* an underground strong-room usually built under a bank

VC *abbreviation* Vice Chancellor

vehicle crime /ˈviːɪk(ə)l kraɪm/ *noun* offences involving vehicles, such as vehicle theft, joyriding and dangerous driving

vendee /venˈdiː/ *noun* a person who buys something, especially land and buildings

vendible /ˈvendɪb(ə)l/ *adjective* able to be sold ○ *For a patent application to succeed, the product being patented must be vendible.*

vendor /ˈvendə/ *noun* somebody who sells ○ *the solicitor acting on behalf of the vendor*

venue /ˈvenjuː/ *noun* a place where a meeting or hearing is held

verbal /ˈvɜːb(ə)l/ *adjective* **1.** using spoken words, not writing **2.** referring to spoken or written evidence ■ *verb* to use threatening words when interviewing a suspect

verbal agreement /ˌvɜːb(ə)l əˈɡriːmənt/ *noun* an agreement which is spoken and not written down

verbal evidence /ˌvɜːb(ə)l ˈevɪd(ə)ns/ *noun* written or spoken evidence. Compare **non-verbal evidence** (NOTE: British lawyers refer specifically to spoken evidence as **oral evidence**.)

verbally /ˈvɜːbəli/ *adverb* using spoken words, not writing ○ *They agreed to the terms verbally, and then started to draft the contract.*

verbals /ˈvɜːb(ə)lz/ *plural noun* words spoken to a police officer by a suspect (*informal*)

verbal warning /ˌvɜːb(ə)l ˈwɔːnɪŋ/ *noun* a stage in warning an employee that his or her work is not satisfactory, followed by a written warning if performance does not improve

verbatim /vɜːˈbeɪtɪm/ *adjective, adverb* in the exact words that were spoken ○ *Han-sard provides a verbatim account of the proceedings of the House of Commons.*

verdict /ˈvɜːdɪkt/ *noun* **1.** the decision of a jury or magistrate □ **to return a verdict** to state a verdict at the end of a trial ○ *The jury returned a verdict of not guilty.* □ **to come to a verdict, to reach a verdict** to decide whether the accused is guilty or not ○ *The jury took two hours to reach their verdict.* **2.** the decision reached by a coroner's court ○ *The court returned a verdict of death by misadventure.*

versa ♦ vice versa

versus /ˈvɜːsəs/ *preposition* against (NOTE: Usually abbreviated to **v.** as in *the case of Smith v. Williams*)

vest /vest/ *verb* to transfer to someone the legal ownership and possession of land or of a right ○ *The property was vested in the trustees.* (NOTE: You vest something **in** or **on** someone.)

vested interest /ˌvestɪd ˈɪntrəst/ *noun* **1.** a special reason for wanting things to go a particular way because you stand to benefit (NOTE: For example, a director holding shares in a company may be said to have a vested interest when voting on issues that affect share prices.) **2.** an interest in a property which will come into a person's possession when the interest of another person ends

vested remainder /ˌvestɪd rɪˈmeɪndə/ *noun* a remainder which is absolutely vested in a person

vesting assent /ˌvestɪŋ əˈsent/ *noun* a document which vests settled land on a tenant for life

vesting order /ˌvestɪŋ ˈɔːdə/ *noun* a court order which transfers property

vet /vet/ *verb* to examine someone or a document carefully to see if there is any breach of security ○ *All applications are vetted by the Home Office.*

veto /ˈviːtəʊ/ *noun* a ban or order not to allow something to become law, even if it has been passed by a parliament ○ *The President has the power of veto over Bills passed by Congress.* ○ *The UK used its veto in the Security Council.* ■ *verb* to refuse to allow something, especially to use an official power to do so ○ *The resolution was vetoed by the president.* ○ *The council has vetoed all plans to hold protest marches in the centre of town.*

COMMENT: In the United Nations Security Council, each of the five permanent members has a veto. In the USA, the President may veto a bill sent to him by Congress, provided he does so within ten days of receiving it. The bill then returns to Congress for further discussion, and the President's veto can be overridden by a two-thirds majority in both House of Representatives and Senate.

vexatious action /vek₁seɪʃəs 'ækʃən/ *noun* a case brought without proper grounds, the true purpose of which is to cause annoyance to the defendant (NOTE: A vexation action is most likely to be dismissed, with costs paid by the plaintiff.)

vexatious litigant /vek₁seɪʃəs 'lɪtɪgənt/ *noun* somebody who frequently starts legal actions to annoy people and who is barred from bringing actions without leave of the court

viable /'vaɪəb(ə)l/ *adjective* **1.** possible, likely to work □ **not commercially viable** not likely to make a profit □ **viable alternative** a different proposal which may work **2.** of an unborn child, capable of being born live and surviving

> COMMENT: A foetus is usually considered viable at 28 weeks. At this stage, it is considered a legal **person** and may not be aborted for whatever reason. Criminally liability also applies after this time for destroying the life of the child through negligence or a violent act (e.g. by attacking the mother).

vicarious liability /vɪ₁keəriəs ₁laɪə'bɪlɪti/ *noun* the liability of one person for torts committed by another, especially the liability of an employer for acts committed by an employee in the course of work. ◊ **frolic**

vicarious performance /vɪ₁keəriəs pə 'fɔːməns/ *noun* the performance of a contract where the work has been done by a third party

vice /vaɪs/ *adjective* a Latin word meaning 'in the place of' ○ *was present: Councillor Smith (vice Councillor Brown)*

Vice Chancellor /₁vaɪs 'tʃɑːnsələ/ *noun* a senior judge in charge of the Chancery Division of the High Court. Abbreviation **VC**

vice-consul /₁vaɪs 'kɒnsəl/ *noun* a diplomat with a rank below consul

Vice-President /₁vaɪs 'prezɪdənt/ *noun* the deputy to a president

> COMMENT: In the USA, the Vice-President is the president (i.e. the chairman) of the Senate. He also succeeds a president if the president dies in office (as Vice-President Johnson succeeded President Kennedy).

vice versa /₁vaɪsi 'vɜːsə/ *phrase* a Latin phrase meaning 'reverse position': in the opposite way ○ *the responsibilities of the employer towards the employee and vice versa*

victim /'vɪktɪm/ *noun* somebody who suffers a crime or a wrong ○ *The mugger left his victim lying in the road.* ○ *He was the victim of a con trick.* ○ *The accident victims* or *victims of the accident were taken to hospital.*

victimless crime /₁vɪktɪmləs 'kraɪm/ *noun* a crime where there is no obvious victim, e.g. shoplifting, prostitution

Victim Support /₁vɪktɪm sə'pɔːt/ *noun* a charitable organisation which supports people who have suffered the effects of crime

vide /'vɪdi/ *verb* a Latin word meaning 'see': used in written texts to refer to another reference

videlicet /'vɪdiːliset/ *noun* a Latin word meaning 'that is' (NOTE: usually abbreviated to **viz**)

video conferencing /'vɪdiəʊ ₁kɒnf(ə)rənsɪŋ/ *noun* a system of conducting a hearing using closed-circuit television and recording the events on tape

Vienna Conventions /vi₁enə kən 'venʃ(ə)nz/ *noun* conventions signed in Austria, generally relating to international treaties and the rights of diplomats

villain /'vɪlən/ *noun* a criminal (*informal*) ○ *The job of the policeman is to catch villains.*

villainy /'vɪləni/ *noun* a wilful illegal act

violate /'vaɪəleɪt/ *verb* to break a rule or a law ○ *The council has violated the planning regulations.* ○ *The action of the government violates the international treaty on commercial shipping.* ○ *The legislation was inapplicable in this case, and the country had not violated the Treaty.*

violation /₁vaɪə'leɪʃ(ə)n/ *noun* the act of breaking a rule ○ *The number of traffic violations has increased.* ○ *The court criticised the violations of the treaty on human rights.* □ **in violation of a rule** breaking a rule

violence /'vaɪələns/ *noun* an action using force □ **violence against the person** one of the types of notifiable offences against the person, e.g. murder, assault

violent /'vaɪələnt/ *adjective* using force ○ *a violent attack on the police* □ **to become violent** to start to attack

virement /'vaɪəmənt/ *noun* the transfer of money from one account to another, or from one section of a budget to another ○

Virement policy allows us to spend more in one area using the budget from another.

vires ♦ intra vires, ultra vires

virtue /ˈvɜːtʃuː/ *noun* good quality

virtute officii /vɜːˌtuːti ɒˈfɪsii/ *phrase* a Latin phrase meaning 'because of his or her office': by virtue of holding a particular role

visa /ˈviːzə/ *noun* a special document or special stamp in a passport which allows someone to enter a country ○ *You will need a visa before you go to the USA.* ○ *She filled in her visa application form.*

vis major /ˌvɪs ˈmeɪdʒə/ *phrase* a Latin phrase meaning 'superior force': a force of people or of nature such as a revolution or an earthquake which cannot be stopped

vital statistics /ˌvaɪt(ə)l stəˈtɪstɪks/ *noun* statistics dealing with births, marriages and deaths in a town or district

viva voce /ˌvaɪvə ˈvəʊtʃi/ *phrase* a Latin phrase meaning 'orally', 'by speaking'

vivos /ˈvaɪvəʊs/ *plural noun* a Latin word meaning 'living people.' ♦ inter vivos

viz ♦ videlicet

void /vɔɪd/ *adjective* not having any legal effect □ **to declare a contract null and void** to say that a contract is no longer valid ■ *verb* □ **to void a contract** to make a contract invalid

voidable /ˈvɔɪdəb(ə)l/ *adjective* being able to be made void

COMMENT: A contract is void where it never had legal effect, but is voidable if it is apparently of legal effect and remains of legal effect until one or both parties take steps to rescind it.

voided /ˈvɔɪdɪd/ *adjective* deprived of legal force

void marriage /ˌvɔɪd ˈmærɪdʒ/ *noun* a marriage which is declared not to have had any legal existence

volenti non fit injuria /vəʊˌlenti nəʊn fɪt ɪnˈdʒʊəriə/ *phrase* a Latin phrase meaning 'there can be no injury to a person who is willing': a rule that if someone has agreed to take the risk of an injury he or she cannot sue for it, as in the case of someone injured in a boxing match

volition /vəˈlɪʃ(ə)n/ *noun* the will to do something □ **of your own volition** because you decide to do something yourself ○ *She gave up her job of her own volition.*

voluntary /ˈvɒlənt(ə)ri/ *adjective* **1.** done without being forced or without being paid **2.** without being paid a salary

voluntary confession /ˌvɒlənt(ə)ri kənˈfeʃ(ə)n/ *noun* a confession made by an accused person without being threatened or paid

voluntary disposition /ˌvɒlənt(ə)ri ˌdɪspəˈzɪʃ(ə)n/ *noun* the transfer of property without any valuable consideration

voluntary liquidation /ˌvɒlənt(ə)ri ˌlɪkwɪˈdeɪʃ(ə)n/ *noun* a situation where a company itself decides it must close and sell its assets

voluntary manslaughter /ˌvɒlənt(ə)ri ˈmænslɔːtə/ *noun* the offence of killing someone intentionally, but under mitigating circumstances such as provocation or diminished responsibility. ♦ involuntary manslaughter

voluntary organisation /ˈvɒlənt(ə)ri ˌɔːgənaɪzeɪʃ(ə)n/ *noun* an organisation which has no paid staff

voluntary redundancy /ˌvɒlənt(ə)ri rɪˈdʌndənsi/ *noun* a situation where the employee asks to be made redundant, usually in return for a payment

voluntary unemployment /ˌvɒlənt(ə)ri ʌnɪmˈplɔɪmənt/ *noun* a situation where an employee resigns from a job of his or her own free will and does not look for another (NOTE: In this situation the person may not be entitled to claim unemployment benefits, or may have payments reduced.)

volunteer /ˌvɒlənˈtɪə/ *noun* **1.** somebody who gives or receives property without consideration **2.** somebody who offers to do something without being forced ■ *verb* **1.** to offer information without being asked ○ *He volunteered the information that the defendant was not in fact a British subject.* **2.** to offer to do something without being forced ○ *Six men volunteered to go into the burning house.*

vote down /ˌvəʊt ˈdaʊn/ *verb* □ **to vote down** to defeat a motion ○ *The proposal was voted down.*

vote in /ˌvəʊt ˈɪn/ *verb* □ **to vote someone in** to elect someone ○ *The Liberal Democrat candidate was voted in.*

vote out /ˌvəʊt ˈaʊt/ *verb* □ **to vote someone out** to make someone lose an election ○ *The government was voted out of office within a year.*

voter /ˈvəʊtə/ *noun* somebody who votes

voting /ˈvəʊtɪŋ/ *noun* the act of making a vote

voting paper /ˈvəʊtɪŋ ˌpeɪpə/ *noun* a piece of paper on which the voter puts a cross to show for whom he or she wants to vote

vouch for /ˈvaʊtʃ fɔː/ *verb* **1.** to state that you believe something is correct ○ *I cannot vouch for the correctness of the transcript of proceedings.* **2.** to say that you take responsibility for something ○ *I can personally vouch for the quality of our products.*

W

waive /weɪv/ *verb* to give up a right ○ *He waived his claim to the estate.* □ **to waive a payment** to say that payment is not necessary

waiver /ˈweɪvə/ *noun* an act of voluntarily giving up a right, or removing the conditions of a rule ○ *If you want to work without a permit, you will have to apply for a waiver.*

waiver clause /ˈweɪvə klɔːz/ *noun* a clause in a contract giving the conditions under which the rights in the contract can be given up

Wales and Chester Circuit /ˌweɪlz ən ˈtʃestə ˌsɜːkɪt/ *noun* one of the six circuits of the Crown Court to which barristers belong, with its centre in Cardiff

walking possession /ˌwɔːkɪŋ pə ˈzeʃ(ə)n/ *noun* temporary possession of a debtor's goods taken by a bailiff or sheriff until they can be sold to satisfy execution

wall safe /ˈwɔːl seɪf/ *noun* a safe fixed in a wall

wanted /ˈwɒntɪd/ *adjective* required for questioning as a suspect in a crime

war crimes /ˈwɔː kraɪmz/ *plural noun* criminal acts committed by a country, or by people in positions of power during time of war

ward /wɔːd/ *noun* **1.** a division of a town or city for administrative purposes □ **an electoral ward** an area of a town represented by a councillor on a local council **2.** a minor protected by a guardian ○ *Mr Jones acting on behalf of his ward, Miss Smith* **3.** a minor protected by a court ■ *verb* to make a child a ward ○ *The court warded the girl.*

warden /ˈwɔːd(ə)n/ *noun* **1.** somebody who is in charge of an institution **2.** *US* the head of a prison (NOTE: The British equivalent is **prison governor**.) **3.** somebody who sees that rules are obeyed

warder /ˈwɔːdə/ *noun* a guard in a prison

ward of court /ˌwɔːd əv ˈkɔːt/ *noun* a minor under the protection of the High Court ○ *The High Court made the girl a ward of court after her mother was declared unfit.*

wardship /ˈwɔːdʃɪp/ *noun* **1.** the role of being in charge of a ward ○ *The judge has discretion to exercise the wardship jurisdiction.* **2.** the power of a court to take on itself the rights and responsibilities of parents in the interests of a child

wardship order /ˈwɔːdʃɪp ˌɔːdə/ *noun* an order made by the courts that a child should be made a ward of court, because their parents are unfit or absent

warehousing /ˈweəhaʊzɪŋ/ *noun* the act of storing goods ○ *Warehousing costs are rising rapidly.* □ **warehousing in bond** keeping imported goods in a warehouse without payment of duty, either to be exported again or for sale into the country when the duty has been paid

warrant /ˈwɒrənt/ *noun* **1.** an official document from a court which allows someone to do something □ **to issue a warrant for the arrest of someone, to issue an arrest warrant for someone** to make out and sign an official document which authorises the police to arrest someone **2.** an official document authorising the payment of money ○ *a dividend warrant*

warrantee /ˌwɒrənˈtiː/ *noun* somebody who is given a warranty

warrant of attachment /ˌwɒrənt əv ə ˈtætʃmənt/ *noun* a warrant which authorises the bailiff to arrest a person in contempt of court

warrant of committal /ˌwɒrənt əv kə ˈmɪt(ə)l/ *noun* same as **committal warrant**

warrant of execution /ˌwɒrənt əv ˌeksɪˈkjuːʃ(ə)n/ *noun* a warrant issued by a court which gives the bailiffs or sheriffs the power to seize goods from a debtor in order to pay his or her debts

warrantor /ˌwɒrən'tɔː/ *noun* somebody who gives a warranty

warranty /'wɒrənti/ *noun* **1.** a guarantee ○ *The car is sold with a twelve-month warranty.* ○ *The warranty covers spare parts but not labour costs.* **2.** a contractual term which is secondary to the main purpose of the contract **3.** a statement made by an insured person which declares that the facts stated by them are true

wash sale /'wɒʃ seɪl/ *noun* the activity of buying stock and selling it almost immediately, to give the impression that business is good

wasted costs order /ˌweɪstɪd kɒsts 'ɔːdə/ *noun* an order by a court that a party has to pay the costs involved in a case which has to be postponed because the party's representative is badly prepared or incompetent

watch /wɒtʃ/ *noun* a group of people who patrol the streets to maintain law and order

watch committee /'wɒtʃ kəˌmɪti/ *noun* a committee of a local authority which supervises the policing of an area

watchdog /'wɒtʃdɒg/, **watchdog body** /'wɒtʃdɒg ˌbɒdi/ *noun* **1.** a body which sees that the law is obeyed ○ *The Commission acts as the watchdog for competition law.* **2.** a body which takes note of what official bodies such as government departments or commercial firms are doing to see that regulations are not being abused

water cannon /'wɔːtə ˌkænən/ *noun* a device which shoots a large volume of water at high pressure (NOTE: Used by police for riot control purposes.)

water pollution /'wɔːtə pəˌluːʃ(ə)n/ *noun* the polluting of the sea, rivers, lakes or canals

weapon /'wepən/ *noun* □ **offensive weapon** an item which can be used to harm someone physically, e.g. a gun, a knife □ **carrying offensive weapons** the offence of holding a weapon or something such as a bottle which could be used as a weapon

Weekly Law Reports /ˌwiːkli 'lɔː rɪ ˌpɔːts/ *plural noun* regular reports of cases published by the Council of Law Reporting. Abbreviation **WLR**

weight /weɪt/ *noun* **1.** the mass of an object **2.** the quality of a piece of evidence ○ *The eye-witness account of what happened carried a lot of weight.*

welfare /'welfeə/ *noun* the state of being well cared for ○ *It is the duty of the juvenile court to see to the welfare of children in care.*

Wells notice /'welz ˌnəʊtɪs/ *noun* a notice from the US Securities and Exchange Commission informing the recipient that a lawsuit will be filed against him or her and outlining the charges and evidence supporting them

Welsh Assembly /ˌwelʃ ə'sembli/ *noun* the centre of devolved Government for Wales, made up of elected members

Western Circuit /ˌwestən 'sɜːkɪt/ *noun* one of the six circuits of the Crown Court to which barristers belong, with its centre in Bristol

whatsoever /ˌwɒtsəʊ'evə/ *adjective* of any sort ○ *There is no substance whatsoever in the report.* ○ *The police found no suspicious documents whatsoever.*

whereas /weər'æz/ *conjunction* as the situation is stated, taking the following fact into consideration ○ *whereas the property is held in trust for the appellant* ○ *whereas the contract between the two parties stipulated that either party may withdraw at six months' notice*

whereby /weə'baɪ/ *adverb* by which ○ *a deed whereby ownership of the property is transferred*

wherein /weər'ɪn/ *adverb* in which ○ *a document wherein the regulations are listed*

whereof /weər'ɒv/ *adverb* of which □ **in witness whereof I sign my hand** I sign as a witness that this is correct

whereon /weər'ɒn/ *adverb* on which ○ *land whereon a dwelling is constructed*

wheresoever /ˌweəsəʊ'evə/ *adverb* in any place where ○ *the insurance covering jewels wheresoever they may be kept*

White Book /'waɪt bʊk/ *noun* a book containing the Rules of the Supreme Court and a commentary on them

white collar crime /ˌwaɪt ˌkɒlə 'kraɪm/ *noun* crime committed by business people or office workers, e.g. embezzlement, computer fraud or insider dealings

White Paper /ˌwaɪt 'peɪpə/ *noun* a report issued by the government as a statement of government policy on a particular problem, often setting out proposals for changes to legislation for discussion before a Bill is drafted. Compare **Green Paper**

whole-life insurance /ˌhəʊl 'laɪf ɪn ˌʃʊərəns/ *noun* an insurance policy for which the insured person pays premiums for an entire lifetime and the insurance company pays a sum when he or she dies (NOTE: For life insurance, British English prefers to use **assurance**.)

whole life tariff /ˌhəʊl ˈlaɪf ˌtærɪf/ *noun* a recommendation from the judge that a prisoner receiving a life sentence should never be released from prison

COMMENT: A whole life tariff can only be recommended for the most serious crimes, usually multiple murders involving pre-planning, abduction or terrorism.

wholly-owned subsidiary /ˌhəʊlli əʊnd səbˈsɪdjəri/ *noun* a company which is owned completely by another company

wilful /ˈwɪlf(ə)l/ *adjective* **1.** of a person, determined to do what he or she wants ○ *He was described as a wilful child.* **2.** done because someone wants to do it, regardless of the effect it may have on others ○ *the deliberate and wilful misuse of personal data*

wilfully /ˈwɪlfʊli/ *adverb* done because someone wants to do it, regardless of the effect on others ○ *He wilfully set fire to the building.*

wilful misconduct /ˌwɪlf(ə)l mɪsˈkɒndʌkt/ *noun* an act of doing something which harms someone while knowing it is wrong

wilful murder /ˌwɪlf(ə)l ˈmɜːdə/ *noun* murder which is premeditated

wilful neglect /ˌwɪlf(ə)l nɪˈɡlekt/ *noun* intentionally not doing something which it is your duty to do

will /wɪl/ *noun* a document by which a person says what they want to happen to their property when they die. Also called **last will and testament**

COMMENT: To make a valid will, a person must be of age and of sound mind; normally a will must be signed and witnessed in the presence of two witnesses who have no interest in the will. In English law there is complete freedom to dispose of one's property after death as one wishes. However, any dependant may apply for provision to be made out of the estate of a deceased under the Inheritance (Provision for Family and Dependants) Act. Writing a will does not bind you to do what you say you are going to do in it. If in your will you leave your car to your son, and then sell the car before you die, your son has no claim on the will for the value of the car.

winding up /ˌwaɪndɪŋ ˈʌp/ *noun* liquidation, the closing of a company and selling its assets

winding up petition /ˌwaɪndɪŋ ˈʌp pəˌtɪʃ(ə)n/ *noun* an application to a court for an order that a company be put into liquidation

window /ˈwɪndəʊ/ *noun* □ **window of opportunity** a short moment when the conditions for something are especially favourable

wind up /ˌwaɪnd ˈʌp/ *verb* **1.** to end something such as a meeting ○ *He wound up the meeting with a vote of thanks to the committee.* **2.** □ **to wind up a company** to put a company into liquidation ○ *The court ordered the company to be wound up.*

winter fuel allowance /ˌwɪntə ˈfjuːəl əˌlaʊəns/ *noun* financial help towards heating bills given by the Government to someone who is over 60 years old (NOTE: This is made out of the Government's **Social Fund**.)

wire fraud /ˈwaɪə frɔːd/ *noun* in the USA, the crime of using interstate telecommunications systems to obtain money or some other benefit by deception

wiretapping /ˈwaɪətæpɪŋ/ *noun* the action of secretly listening in on a telephone line

with costs /ˌwɪð ˈkɒsts/ *adverb* □ **judgment for someone with costs** a judgment that the party's plea was correct and that all the costs of the case should be paid by the other party

withdraw /wɪðˈdrɔː/ *verb* **1.** to say that a charge, accusation or statement is no longer valid ○ *The prosecution has withdrawn the charges against him.* ○ *He was forced to withdraw his statement.* **2.** to take money out of an account ○ *to withdraw money from the bank* or *from your account* ○ *You can withdraw up to £50 from any bank on presentation of a banker's card.* **3.** to take back an offer

withhold /wɪðˈhəʊld/ *verb* not to give something such as information which should be given ○ *She was charged with withholding information from the police.* ○ *Approval of any loan will not be unreasonably withheld.*

without prejudice /wɪðˌaʊt ˈpredʒʊdɪs/ *preposition* a phrase spoken or written in letters when attempting to negotiate a settlement, meaning that the negotiations cannot be referred to in court or relied upon by the other party if the discussions fail

witness /ˈwɪtnəs/ *noun* **1.** somebody who sees something happen or who is present when something happens □ **to act as a witness to a signature** to sign a document to show that you have watched the main signatory sign it □ **in witness whereof** the first words of the testimonium clause, where the signatory of the will or contract signs **2.** somebody who appears in court to give evidence ■ *verb* to sign a document to show that you guarantee that the other signatures on it are genuine ○ *to witness an agreement* or *a signature* □ **'now this deed witnesseth'** words indicating that the details of the agreement follow

witness box /'wɪtnəs ˌbɒks/ *noun* a place in a courtroom where the witnesses give evidence

witness of fact /ˌwɪtnəs əv 'fækt/ *noun* somebody who gives evidence to say that facts in a claim are true

witness protection /'wɪtnɪs prəˌtekʃən/ *noun* an official scheme for making sure that a person giving evidence in a trial is not threatened or harassed for doing so

witness statement /ˌwɪtnəs 'steɪtmənt/ *noun* a written statement made by a witness and signed, containing evidence which he or she will make orally in court

witness summary /ˌwɪtnəs 'sʌməri/ *noun* a short document which summarises the evidence which will be in a witness statement, or which lists points on which a witness will be questioned in court

witness summons /'wɪtnəs ˌsʌmənz/ *noun* a court order requiring someone to appear as a witness and if necessary produce documents relevant to the case (NOTE: Since the introduction of the Civil Procedure Rules, this term has replaced **subpoena ad testificandum** and **subpoena duces tecum.**)

WLR *abbreviation* Weekly Law Reports

woman police constable /ˌwʊmən pəˌliːs 'kʌnstəb(ə)l/ *noun* a female police officer ○ *Woman Police Constable MacIntosh was at the scene of the accident.* (NOTE: It is usually abbreviated to **WPC.**)

Woolf Reforms /'wʊlf rɪˌfɔːmz/ *plural noun* reforms to the legal system instituted by Lord Woolf in 1999 with the aim of making civil litigation more accessible and less costly (NOTE: The Woolf Reforms resulted in the introduction of the Civil Procedure Rules.)

Woolsack /'wʊlsæk/ *noun* the seat of the Lord Chancellor in the House of Lords

word /wɜːd/ *noun* □ **to give one's word** to promise ○ *He gave his word that the matter would remain confidential.*

wording /'wɜːdɪŋ/ *noun* **1.** the way that something is expressed in words ○ *Did you understand the wording of the contract?* **2.** the full text of an insurance policy (NOTE: An insurance policy is usually evidenced by a slip, a wording and a cover note.)

words of art /ˌwɜːdz əv 'ɑːt/ *noun* words that have a special meaning in law

working party /'wɜːkɪŋ ˌpɑːti/ *noun* a group of experts who study a problem ○ *The government has set up a working party to study the problems of industrial waste.* ○ *Professor Smith is the chairman of the working party on drug abuse.*

Working Tax Credit /ˌwɜːkɪŋ 'tæks ˌkredɪt/ *noun* a tax credit given to a person who is working on a low income

work in hand /ˌwɜːk ɪn 'hænd/ *noun* work which is in progress but not finished

work permit /'wɜːk ˌpɜːmɪt/ *noun* an official document which allows someone who is not a citizen to work in a country

wound /wuːnd/ *noun* a cut done to the skin of a person ○ *She has a knife wound in her leg.* ■ *verb* to injure or to hurt someone in such a way that his or her skin is cut ○ *He was wounded in the fight.*

wounding with intent /ˌwuːndɪŋ wɪð ɪn'tent/ *noun* the offence of injuring someone, especially when trying to resist arrest

WPC *abbreviation* woman police constable

wreck /rek/ *noun* **1.** the action of sinking or badly damaging a ship **2.** a ship which has sunk or which has been badly damaged and cannot float ○ *Oil poured out of the wreck of the ship.* ○ *They saved the cargo from the wreck.* **3.** a company which has become insolvent ○ *He managed to save some of his investment from the wreck of the company.* ■ *verb* to damage badly or to ruin ○ *They are trying to salvage the wrecked ship.* ○ *The defence case was wrecked by the defendant's behaviour in court.*

writ /rɪt/ *noun* a legal document which begins an action in the High Court □ **to serve someone with a writ** to give someone a writ officially, so that he or she has to defend it or allow judgment to be taken in their absence

writ of fieri facias /ˌrɪt əv ˌfaɪraɪ 'feɪʃiæs/ *noun* a court order to a sheriff telling them to seize the goods of a debtor against whom judgment has been made (NOTE: often abbreviated to **fi. fa.**)

writ of habeas corpus /ˌrɪt əv ˌheɪbiəs ˈkɔːpəs/ *noun* a writ to obtain the release of someone who has been unlawfully held in prison or in police custody, or to make the person holding them bring them to court to explain why they are being held

writ of summons /ˌrɪt əv ˈsʌmənz/ *noun* ♦ **claim form**

written application /ˌrɪt(ə)n ˌæplɪ ˈkeɪʃ(ə)n/ *noun* the first part of proceedings in the European Court of Justice, where an applicant makes a written application against which the defendant may reply in writing (NOTE: The papers will then be examined by the judge rapporteur and one of the Advocates General, before moving on to oral hearings.)

wrong /rɒŋ/ *noun* an act against natural justice or which infringes someone else's right (NOTE: Civil wrongs against persons or property are called 'torts'.)

wrongdoer /ˈrɒŋduːə/ *noun* somebody who commits an offence

wrongdoing /ˈrɒŋduːɪŋ/ *noun* activity which is against the law

wrongful /ˈrɒŋf(ə)l/ *adjective* unlawful

wrongful arrest /ˌrɒŋf(ə)l əˈrest/ *noun* the act of arresting a person for a crime they did not commit

wrongful dismissal /ˌrɒŋf(ə)l dɪsˈmɪs(ə)l/ *noun* the removal of someone from a job for a reason which does not justify dismissal and is in breach of the contract of employment

COMMENT: An employee can complain of wrongful dismissal to a county court or, where the compensation claimed is less than £25,000, to an employment tribunal.

wrongfully /ˈrɒŋf(ə)li/ *adverb* in an unlawful way ○ *He claimed he was wrongfully dismissed.* ○ *She was accused of wrongfully holding her clients' money.*

wrongful trading /ˌrɒŋf(ə)l ˈtreɪdɪŋ/ *noun* a situation in which a company continues to trade even though its directors should have concluded that it had no reasonable prospect of remaining solvent

wrongly /ˈrɒŋli/ *adverb* not correctly ○ *He wrongly invoiced Smith Ltd for £250, when he should have credited them with the same amount.*

YZ

yardie /ˈjɑːdi/ *noun* a member of a Jamaican gang engaged in drug-related organised crime (*slang*)

year and a day rule /ˌjɪə ənd ə ˈdeɪ ˌruːl/ *noun* an ancient rule that a person could not be convicted of murder if the victim died more than 366 days after the attack

COMMENT: The rule was abolished in 1996, as it had come to be used as a defence in cases of work-related deaths, such as from asbestosis or radiation, which may occur many years after the first contamination.

year end /ˌjɪər ˈend/ *noun* the end of the financial year, when a company's accounts are prepared ○ *The accounts department has started work on the year-end accounts.*

yellow dog contract /ˌjeləʊ ˈdɒg ˌkɒntrækt/ *noun US* a contract of employment where the employee is forbidden to join a trade union

young offender /jʌŋ əˈfendə/, **youthful offender** *US* /ˌjuːθf(ə)l əˈfendə/ *noun* a person aged between seventeen and twenty years of age who has committed an offence

Young Offender Institution /ˌjʌŋ ə ˈfendə ˌɪnstɪtjuːʃ(ə)n/, **young offenders institution** *noun* a centre where young offenders are sent for training if they have committed crimes which would usually be punishable by a prison sentence

young person /ˌjʌŋ ˈpɜːs(ə)n/ *noun* somebody over fourteen years of age, but less than eighteen

youth /juːθ/ *noun* a young person

Youth Court /ˈjuːθ kɔːt/ *noun* a court which tries offenders between the ages of 10 and 18. Former name **Juvenile Court**

youth custody order /juːθ ˌkʌstədi ˈɔːdə/ *noun* a sentence sending a young person to detention in a special centre

zipper clause /ˈzɪpə klɔːz/ *noun US* a standard clause in a contract of employment, which tries to prevent any discussion of employment conditions during the life of the agreement

zone /zəʊn/ *verb* to order that land in a district shall be used only for one type of building ○ *The land is zoned for industrial use.*

zoning /ˈzəʊnɪŋ/ *noun* an order by a local council that land shall be used only for one type of building

SUPPLEMENTS

Legislative procedure

UK Parliament
Devolved governments
European Union
United States

Court Systems

England and Wales
Scotland
Northern Ireland
United States

Jury Service

Types of Sentence

Resources on the Internet

Legislative bodies
Resources for lawyers
Professional bodies
Legal resources for laypersons

Legislative procedure in the UK Parliament

Green Paper Stage — a paper discussing the issues surrounding the proposed bill (optional)

White Paper Stage — a paper stating current policy on the issues surrounding the proposed bill (optional)

Draft Bill Stage — the wording of the Bill is drafted

First Reading — the Bill is presented formally in Parliament as a reading with no debate or decision

Second Reading — the Bill is read again to the House and a debate takes place

Committee Stage — a *standing committee* (a committee of about 18 house members, more for long or complicated bills) debates whether each clause and schedule of the Bill should be kept or dropped

Report Stage — the whole house looks at the amendments proposed by the standing committee and propose and debate any of their own

Third Reading Stage — the whole redrafted Bill is read once more in the House and briefly discussed

Lords Approval Stage — the House of Lords takes the Bill and goes through the same procedure from First to Third Reading, debating any amendments. The Lords and Commons agree on a final text

Royal Assent Stage — royal approval is given and the Bill becomes a statute (Act of Parliament)

Legislative procedure in the UK Parliament *cont.*

Important Note: The Parliament Act

The entire process of passing a Bill into law must take place in a single Session of Parliament. This means that the House of Lords are able to 'kill' a Bill they don't wish to pass by delaying until the end of Session, forcing it to be dropped. This is known as a *suspensory veto*.

If this happens, the *Parliament Act 1949* provides for the Bill to be re-introduced and passed in the following Session without the approval of the Lords, under the following conditions:

1. The Lords had sufficient time to debate it before the end of the session (at least one month).
2. The wording of the Bill hasn't changed since the last presentation.
3. One year has passed since the Bill was given its Second Reading in the Commons.

Private Members' Bills go through the same procedure from First Reading. However, there is intense competition for the little Parliamentary time available for considering these. Unless the Bill is completely uncontroversial it is likely to be formally objected to at some stage, and therefore dropped.

Otherwise, it is more or less 'nodded through' without much scrutiny or debate.

Legislative powers in devolved Parliaments

Scotland: Since the *Scotland Act 1998*, which established the country's devolved government, Scotland may pass its own primary legislation in areas of national concern such as health, education, tourism, culture and local government. Certain *reserved matters* such as international policy, defence and drugs law, however, must still be dealt with by the UK Parliament.

Stage 1	the draft Bill is submitted to Parliament with its Explanatory Notes (the purpose of the Bill explained in layman's terms), its Policy Memorandum (a description of how the Bill affects current policy) and its Financial Memorandum (the Bill's financial implications)
Stage 2	the relevant Parliamentary committee considers the Bill and suggests amendments
Stage 3	the Bill is considered at a meeting of the whole Parliament and amendments are debated. A vote is then taken to pass the law
Royal Assent Stage	royal approval is given and the Bill becomes a statute (Act of the Scottish Parliament)

Northern Ireland: In the same way as Scotland, Northern Ireland has the power to pass primary legislation on certain matters such as health, education, agriculture and transport. It may not pass laws relating to criminal law or civil defence.

Wales: The Welsh Assembly currently only has the power to pass secondary legislation which modifies statutes passed by the UK Parliament. However, when the *Government of Wales Act 2006* comes into force it will provide for a referendum to be held, in which Wales may be granted further legislative powers.

Legislative procedure in the European Union

Proposal	the European Commission drafts the text of a Bill
First Reading	the European Parliament submits the Bill to a committee reading and a report is prepared with suggested amendments
Common Position	the European Council either accepts the amended Bill or suggests its own amendments (NB this is the first point at which the Bill can be passed)
Recommendation	a further committee assessment is undertaken of the Council's proposed amendments at Parliament and a recommendation given
Second Reading	Parliament debates the committee's report and vote by absolute majority whether to accept the Council's amendments and on further amendments of their own
Amended Proposal	the Commission looks at Parliament's second reading decisions and drafts an amended proposal for the Council, who vote whether to accept or modify it (this is the second point at which the Bill can be passed)
Conciliation Committee	a committee of members from both the Council and Parliament meet to agree on a joint text
Third Reading	Parliament meets to finally discuss whether to adopt the Bill as law. If no mutual agreement can be reached the Bill will lapse

Legislative procedure in the US

Introduction   the draft Bill is submitted to the House without reading or debate (at any time while the House is in session)

Referral to Committee   the Bill is published and assigned an identification number, then sent to the appropriate committee (of 19) according to its subject

Committee Action 1   relevant offices and departments give their input, reports are prepared on the validity of the Bill and committee meetings are held

Committee Action 2   a public hearing may be held before a sub-committee with the questioning of witnesses and the attendance of interested parties

Markup   the subcommittee prepares a report on the hearing with any relevant amendments to the Bill

Final Committee Action   the full committee reads and amends the Bill and either reports it back favourably to the House, tables it or discharges it (thereby preventing it from progressing any further), or reports it back without recommendation (rare)

House Floor Consideration   the committee report is debated in the House and any further amendments voted on

Resolving Differences   the Bill is sent to the Senate for house floor consideration and an identical version is agreed on by both bodies, possibly with the help of a mediating committee

Final Step   the Bill is approved (signed) by the President and becomes a Law

Jury Service

Under the *Juries Act 1974*, some categories of people could claim exemption if called for jury service. This included doctors, members of the clergy, politicians, police officers, judges and lawyers. However, these exemptions were abolished by the *Criminal Justice Act 2003* with the aim of widening participation and making juries more representative of the larger community. It made provision for almost every UK citizen to serve on a jury.

You are *eligible* for jury service if:

- you will be at least 18 years old, and under 70 years old, on the day that you start your jury service;
- you are registered on the electoral roll;
- you have lived in the United Kingdom, the Channel Islands or the Isle of Man for any period of at least 5 years since you were 13 years old

You *do not* qualify if:

- you are under 18 or over 69 years of age on the date you would start your jury service;
- you are currently on bail in criminal proceedings;
- you have served time in prison in the United Kingdom, the Channel Islands or the Isle of Man within the last 10 years:
- you have received a community order or a suspended sentence in the United Kingdom, the Channel Islands or the Isle of Man within the last 10 years;
- you suffer from a mental disorder for which you are receiving residential or regular out-patient treatment

Any person summoned for jury service may apply for discretionary excusal or deferral if they wish. A decision will be made at the Jury Central Summoning Bureau based on the details given. Jury service may only be deferred once, for up to 12 months after the original date of summons.

Types of Sentence

Discharge

A convicted offender may be given a discharge for a lesser offence if they show remorse, or if the trial process and criminal record is considered to be enough of a punishment or deterrent to reoffending.

A discharge can be conditional or absolute. After a conditional discharge, if the offender commits another crime within a period of time (usually 2 or 3 years), they may be re-sentenced for the original offence.

Under an absolute discharge, no penalty is imposed.

Fine

Most convictions in the UK are punished by a fine, often in combination with another measure such as a community order. The maximum amount allowed for the fine is determined by the *standard scale*, from level 1 (currently denoting a maximum fine of £200) to level 5 (currently £5,000).

The amount of the fine is influenced not just by the nature of the crime, but also by the offender's ability to pay.

Community Order (non-custodial sentence)

These are handed down when the offender is unlikely to pose a risk to the public. There are various types of community order, including:

• Unpaid work for the community, e.g. cleaning up graffiti or collecting litter;

• Reparation, putting right the specific harm caused by their crime, such as by paying a fine to the victim or replacing stolen / damaged possessions;

• Surveillance (in which the offender is obliged to observe a curfew or to report to officials at regular intervals);

• Compulsory drug rehabilitation

There are also specific orders aimed at young offenders, which concentrate largely on supervised community rehabilitation and providing opportunities for training and education.

Imprisonment (custodial sentence)

Sentencing an offender to imprisonment is considered to be disruptive to rehabilitation and so should be avoided for all but the most serious of offences .

However, the judge's priority must be the protection of the public. A serious offence will usually lead to an automatic prison sentence of some length.

Types of Sentence _cont._

Restrictions on sentencing for serious offences:

Murder	Mandatory life imprisonment
Serious sexual and violent offences* (including manslaughter, rape, grievous bodily harm, wounding with intent, aggravated burglary, robbery and some firearms offences); trafficking class-A drugs	Discretionary, although a life sentence, or 'imprisonment for public protection' must be passed if the offence committed was grave, if there is a serious risk of reoffending and if this risk presents a significant danger to the public. All also carry a discretionary maximum sentence of life imprisonment.
Other sexual and violent offences* (including ABH, affray, arson, criminal damage, incest, indecent assault and sexual abuse)	Discretionary, although an 'extended sentence of fixed term' (a longer than usual sentence) must be passed if the there is a serious risk of reoffending and if this risk presents a significant danger to the public.
All other offences (such as theft, fraud, embezzlement, harassment and nuisance)	Discretionary sentence of fixed length. Guidelines issued by the Sentencing Guidance Council must be considered where applicable.

* these offences, also known as 'specified offences', are listed in Schedule 15 to the _Criminal Justice Act 2003_.

NOTE: The actual length of custodial sentence to be served is one half of the sentence imposed. It may be reduced further by mitigating factors such as entering a guilty plea, and will usually be discounted by the number of days the offender has spent in custody awaiting trial.

At this point the offender:

a) becomes eligible for parole (if serving a mandatory or discretionary life sentence or if they have been imprisoned for public protection)

b) will be released (for all other fixed-length sentences). They will remain on license for the rest of the duration of their sentence.

A 'whole life tariff' (a recommendation that the offender should spend the rest of their life in prison) is available to judges as a sentencing option for only the most serious crimes, usually multiple murders involving pre-planning, abduction or terrorism.

The Court System of England and Wales

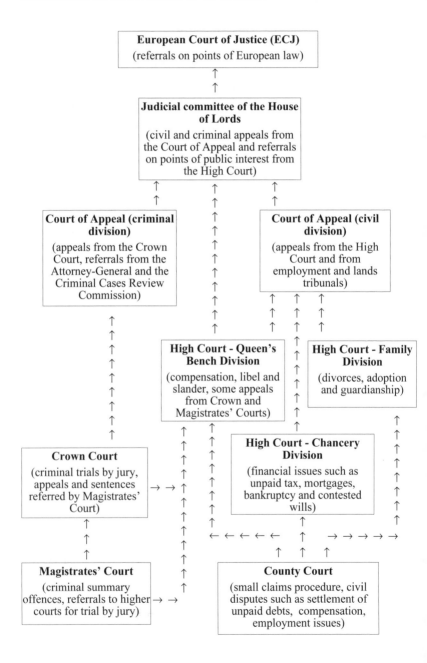

European Court of Justice (ECJ)

(referrals on points of European law)

Judicial committee of the House of Lords

(civil and criminal appeals from the Court of Appeal and referrals on points of public interest from the High Court)

Court of Appeal (criminal division)

(appeals from the Crown Court, referrals from the Attorney-General and the Criminal Cases Review Commission)

Court of Appeal (civil division)

(appeals from the High Court and from employment and lands tribunals)

High Court - Queen's Bench Division

(compensation, libel and slander, some appeals from Crown and Magistrates' Courts)

High Court - Family Division

(divorces, adoption and guardianship)

Crown Court

(criminal trials by jury, appeals and sentences referred by Magistrates' Court)

High Court - Chancery Division

(financial issues such as unpaid tax, mortgages, bankruptcy and contested wills)

Magistrates' Court

(criminal summary offences, referrals to higher courts for trial by jury)

County Court

(small claims procedure, civil disputes such as settlement of unpaid debts, compensation, employment issues)

The Court System of Scotland

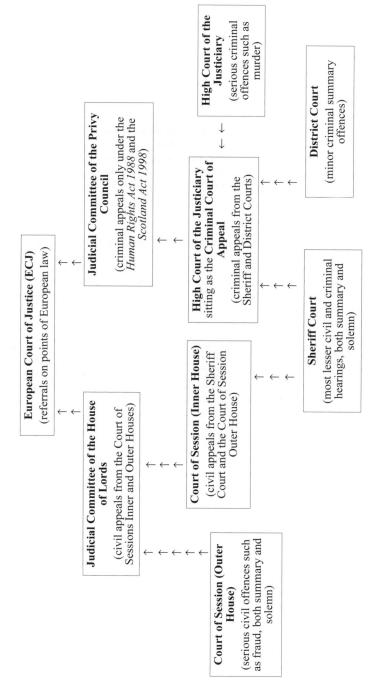

European Court of Justice (ECJ)
(referrals on points of European law)

Judicial Committee of the Privy Council
(criminal appeals only under the *Human Rights Act 1988* and the *Scotland Act 1998*)

High Court of the Justiciary
(serious criminal offences such as murder)

Judicial Committee of the House of Lords
(civil appeals from the Court of Sessions Inner and Outer Houses)

High Court of the Justiciary sitting as the **Criminal Court of Appeal**
(criminal appeals from the Sheriff and District Courts)

District Court
(minor criminal summary offences)

Court of Session (Inner House)
(civil appeals from the Sheriff Court and the Court of Session Outer House)

Sheriff Court
(most lesser civil and criminal hearings, both summary and solemn)

Court of Session (Outer House)
(serious civil offences such as fraud, both summary and solemn)

The Court System of Northern Ireland

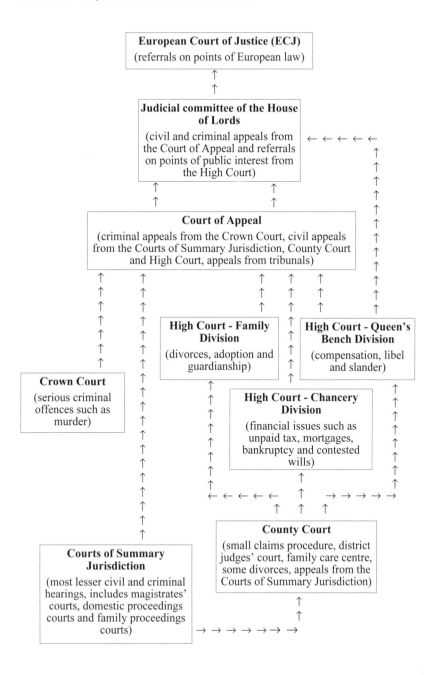

European Court of Justice (ECJ)
(referrals on points of European law)

Judicial committee of the House of Lords
(civil and criminal appeals from the Court of Appeal and referrals on points of public interest from the High Court)

Court of Appeal
(criminal appeals from the Crown Court, civil appeals from the Courts of Summary Jurisdiction, County Court and High Court, appeals from tribunals)

High Court - Family Division
(divorces, adoption and guardianship)

High Court - Queen's Bench Division
(compensation, libel and slander)

Crown Court
(serious criminal offences such as murder)

High Court - Chancery Division
(financial issues such as unpaid tax, mortgages, bankruptcy and contested wills)

County Court
(small claims procedure, district judges' court, family care centre, some divorces, appeals from the Courts of Summary Jurisdiction)

Courts of Summary Jurisdiction
(most lesser civil and criminal hearings, includes magistrates' courts, domestic proceedings courts and family proceedings courts)

The Court System of the United States

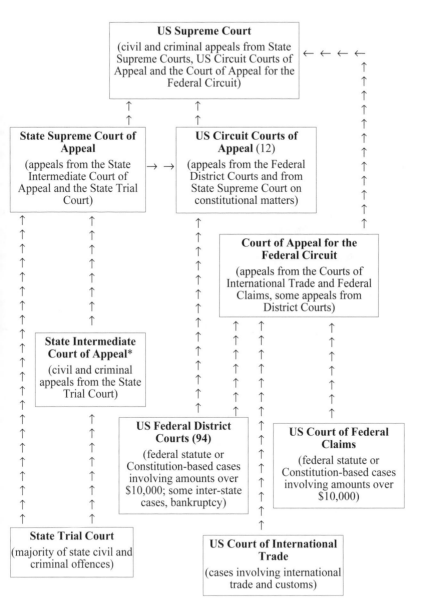

US Supreme Court

(civil and criminal appeals from State Supreme Courts, US Circuit Courts of Appeal and the Court of Appeal for the Federal Circuit)

State Supreme Court of Appeal

(appeals from the State Intermediate Court of Appeal and the State Trial Court)

US Circuit Courts of Appeal (12)

(appeals from the Federal District Courts and from State Supreme Court on constitutional matters)

Court of Appeal for the Federal Circuit

(appeals from the Courts of International Trade and Federal Claims, some appeals from District Courts)

State Intermediate Court of Appeal*

(civil and criminal appeals from the State Trial Court)

US Federal District Courts (94)

(federal statute or Constitution-based cases involving amounts over $10,000; some inter-state cases, bankruptcy)

US Court of Federal Claims

(federal statute or Constitution-based cases involving amounts over $10,000)

State Trial Court

(majority of state civil and criminal offences)

US Court of International Trade

(cases involving international trade and customs)

* present in 40 US states. In states where there is none, appeals from the State Trial Courts go directly to the State Supreme Court.

Legal Resources on the Internet

Legislative bodies:

Council of the European Union
www.consilium.europa.eu

European Parliament
www.europarl.europa.eu

National Assembly for Wales
www.wales.gov.uk

Northern Ireland Assembly
www.niassembly.gov.uk

Scottish Parliament
www.scottish.parliament.uk

United Kingdom Parliament
www.parliament.uk

United States House of Representatives
www.house.gov

United States Senate
www.senate.gov

Resources for lawyers:

British and Irish Legal Information Institute
Searchable databases of legislation and case law from the UK and Republic
of Ireland and from the European Court of Justice.
www.bailii.org

Casetrack
Full-text transcripts of legal judgements (subscription service).
www.casetrack.com

Chambers and Partners
Legal publishers with a comprehensive resource centre for students.
www.chambersandpartners.com

Eur-LEX
Guides and free access to European Union legislation.
http://eur-lex.europa.eu

Legal Resources on the Internet *cont.*

European Journal of International Law
All aspects of international and European law, published 5 times annually.
www.ejil.com

Infolaw
A legal web portal, including an RSS feed for legal news.
www.infolaw.co.uk

Law Brief Update
Free e-mail newsletters on recent UK case law developments.
www.lawbriefpublishing.com

Law.com (US law)
A complete online resource for legal news and publications.
www.law.com

Law Gazette Online
The leading legal weekly in the UK, focusing on the solicitors' profession.
www.lawgazette.co.uk

Legal Week
A weekly trade magazine for people in the legal profession, with job listings.
www.legalweek.com

Lexis Nexis Butterworths
Useful links to legal news, events and job listings.
www.lexisnexis.butterworths.co.uk/law

National Archives
The official archive for the UK Government.
www.nationalarchives.gov.uk

New Law Journal
Subscription details for the legal journal, issued weekly.
www.new-law-journal.co.uk

Office of the Law Revision Council (US law)
A complete guide to the US code by its official publishing body.
http://uscode.house.gov

Office of Public Sector Information:
UK legislation including statutory instruments of Wales, Scotland and
Northern Ireland, available online.
www.opsi.gov.uk/legislation/

Solicitors' Journal
Distinguished weekly journal with coverage of most areas of legal practice.
www.solicitorsjournal.com

Legal Resources on the Internet *cont.*

The Lawyer
News, jobs and training for professionals in commercial law.
www.thelawyer.com

THOMAS (US law)
Searchable legal databases from the Library of Congress.
http://thomas.loc.gov/

Waterlow Legal
A range of legal information including professional directories.
www.waterlowlegal.com

Web Journal of Current Legal Issues
The first UK legal journal to be available only online, published bimonthly.
http://webjcli.ncl.ac.uk/

Professional bodies:

Assets Recovery Agency
An organisation which seizes profits made from criminal activity.
www.assetsrecovery.gov.uk

Bar Council
The professional body representing barristers in England and Wales.
www.barcouncil.org.uk

Bar Library
A resource for barristers at the Bar of Northern Ireland.
www.barlibrary.com

Child Exploitation and Online Protection Centre
A government agency which investigates child sex abuse on the Internet.
www.ceop.gov.uk

Council for the Registration of Forensic Professionals
A professional body for forensic practitioners in the UK.
www.crfp.org.uk

Criminal Cases Review Commission
An independent public body which assesses whether criminal convictions
should be sent to appeal.
www.ccrc.gov.uk

Crown Office and Procurator Fiscal Service
The body responsible for prosecuting criminal cases in Scotland.
www.crownoffice.gov.uk

<u>Legal Resources on the Internet</u> *cont.*

Crown Prosecution Service
The body responsible for prosecuting criminal cases in England and Wales.
www.cps.gov.uk

European Law Students' Association
An independent membership body for law students across Europe.
www.elsa.org

Expert Witness Institute
An organisation promoting and training expert witnesses as a legal resource.
www.ewi.org.uk

Faculty of Advocates
The professional body representing the Scottish Bar.
www.advocates.org.uk

Faculty of Forensic and Legal Medicine
An organisation promoting excellence in forensic training.
www.fflm.ac.uk

Forensic Science Service
Provides forensic science technology and services to UK police forces.
www.forensic.gov.uk

Her Majesty's Court Service
The body responsible for managing the court system in England and Wales.
www.hmcourts-service.gov.uk

Home Office
A UK Government department responsible for police and the justice system.
www.homeoffice.gov.uk

Incorporated Council of Law Reporting for England & Wales
Free case summaries and daily reports of court proceedings.
www.lawreports.co.uk

Independent Police Complaints Commission
An organisation which oversees how complaints against the police are
handled.
www.ipcc.gov.uk

Institute of Legal Executives
The representative body for legal executives in the UK.
www.ilex.co.uk

Law Commission
An independent statutory body which monitors and reviews UK legislation.
www.lawcom.gov.uk

Legal Resources on the Internet *cont.*

Law Society
The representative body for solicitors in England and Wales.
www.lawsoc.org.uk

Law Society of Northern Ireland
The representative body for solicitors in Northern Ireland.
www.lawsoc-ni.org

Law Society of Scotland
The representative body for solicitors in Scotland.
www.lawscot.org.uk

Legal Services Commission
The organisation which administers legal aid in the UK.
www.legalservices.gov.uk

Ministry of Justice
The UK government department responsible for the justice system and the prison and probationary service.
www.justice.gov,uk

National Policing Improvement Agency
An organisation which investigates possible police reform in the UK.
www.npia.police.uk

Northern Ireland Court Service
The body responsible for managing the court system in Northern Ireland.
www.courtsni.cov.uk

Police - Could You?
Information on recruitment into the UK police force.
www.policecouldyou.co.uk

Public Prosecution Service
The body responsible for prosecuting criminal cases in Northern Ireland.
www.ppsni.gov.uk

Scottish Court Service
The body responsible for managing the court system in Scotland.
www.scotcourts.gov.uk

Serious Fraud Office
A UK Government department which prosecutes serious fraud cases.
www.sfo.gov.uk

Solicitors Regulation Authority
The body responsible for regulating solicitors in England and Wales.
www.sra.org.uk

Legal Resources on the Internet *cont.*

UK Centre for Legal Education
An organisation promoting high standards in legal education.
www.ukcle.ac.uk

Legal resources for laypersons:

British Employment Law
Specialised advice for employers, employees and legal professionals.
www.emplaw.co.uk

Citizens Advice Bureau Online:
A guide to finding your local CAB and the services they offer.
www.citizensadvice.org.uk

Community Legal Service Direct:
Free advice on legal issues including legal aid.
www.clsdirect.org.uk

Consumer Direct
Practical advice for consumers, an initiative of the Office of Fair Trading.
www.consumerdirect.gov.uk

Crimestoppers
A UK charity providing an phone service which can be used by members of
the public to give anonymous information to the police.
www.crimestoppers-uk.org

Directgov
Advice on crime prevention and victim support.
www.direct.gov.uk

Law Centre Federation
Free legal representation for the most disadvantaged members of society.
www.lawcentres.org.uk

Rape Crisis
Advice, support and a guide to resources for victims of rape.
www.rapecrisis.org.uk

Survivors' Trust
An umbrella organisation for voluntary groups helping survivors of rape and
sexual abuse.
www.thesurvivorstrust.org

Victim Support
A charitable organisation offering support to witnesses and victims of crime.
www.victimsupport.org.uk